Handbook of Research on Digital Media and Creative Technologies

Dew Harrison
University of Wolverhampton, UK

A volume in the Advances in Media,
Entertainment, and the Arts (AMEA) Book Series

Information Science
REFERENCE
An Imprint of IGI Global

Managing Director:	Lindsay Johnston
Managing Editor:	Austin DeMarco
Director of Intellectual Property & Contracts:	Jan Travers
Acquisitions Editor:	Kayla Wolfe
Production Editor:	Christina Henning
Typesetter:	Amanda Smith
Cover Design:	Jason Mull

Published in the United States of America by
Information Science Reference (an imprint of IGI Global)
701 E. Chocolate Avenue
Hershey PA, USA 17033
Tel: 717-533-8845
Fax: 717-533-8661
E-mail: cust@igi-global.com
Web site: http://www.igi-global.com

Library of Congress Cataloging-in-Publication Data

Library of Congress Cataloging-in-Publication Data

Handbook of research on digital media and creative technologies / Dew Harrison, editor.
     pages cm
 Includes bibliographical references and index.
  ISBN 978-1-4666-8205-4 (hardcover) -- ISBN 978-1-4666-8206-1 (ebook) 1. Information technology--Social aspects. 2. Social media--Research. 3. Art and the Internet. I. Harrison, Dew, 1952- editor.
 HM851.H3483 2015
 302.23'1--dc23
                                   2015003296

This book is published in the IGI Global book series Advances in Media, Entertainment, and the Arts (AMEA) (ISSN: pending; eISSN: pending)

British Cataloguing in Publication Data
A Cataloguing in Publication record for this book is available from the British Library.

For electronic access to this publication, please contact: eresources@igi-global.com.

Advances in Media, Entertainment, and the Arts (AMEA) Book Series

Giuseppe Amoruso
Politecnico di Milano, Italy

ISSN: pending
EISSN: pending

MISSION

Throughout time, technical and artistic cultures have integrated creative expression and innovation into industrial and craft processes. Art, entertainment and the media have provided means for societal self-expression and for economic and technical growth through creative processes.

The **Advances in Media, Entertainment, and the Arts (AMEA)** book series aims to explore current academic research in the field of artistic and design methodologies, applied arts, music, film, television, and news industries, as well as popular culture. Encompassing titles which focus on the latest research surrounding different design areas, services and strategies for communication and social innovation, cultural heritage, digital and print media, journalism, data visualization, gaming, design representation, television and film, as well as both the fine applied and performing arts, the AMEA book series is ideally suited for researchers, students, cultural theorists, and media professionals.

COVERAGE

- Arts & Design
- Music & Performing Arts
- Fabrication and prototyping
- Cultural Heritage
- Color Studies
- Data Visualization
- Environmental Design
- Design Tools
- Print Media
- Drawing

IGI Global is currently accepting manuscripts for publication within this series. To submit a proposal for a volume in this series, please contact our Acquisition Editors at Acquisitions@igi-global.com or visit: http://www.igi-global.com/publish/.

Titles in this Series

For a list of additional titles in this series, please visit: www.igi-global.com

Handbook of Research on the Impact of Culture and Society on the Entertainment Industry
R. Gulay Ozturk (İstanbul Commerce University, Turkey)
Information Science Reference • copyright 2014 • 737pp • H/C (ISBN: 9781466661905) • US $345.00 (our price)

www.igi-global.com

701 E. Chocolate Ave., Hershey, PA 17033
Order online at www.igi-global.com or call 717-533-8845 x100
To place a standing order for titles released in this series, contact: cust@igi-global.com
Mon-Fri 8:00 am - 5:00 pm (est) or fax 24 hours a day 717-533-8661

Editorial Advisory Board

List of Contributors

Aebersold, Michelle / *University of Michigan, USA* 265

Al Merekhi, Maha / *Qatar Foundation, Qatar* 448

Ali, Fatema Mohamed / *Hamad Bin Khalifa University, Qatar* 448

Allard-Huver, François / *Sorbonne University, France* 404

Benjamin, Garfield / *University of Wolverhampton, UK* 200

Chilsen, Paul / *Carthage College, USA* 249

Cushenbery, Lily / *Stony Brook University, USA* 374

Doyle, Denise / *University of Wolverhampton, UK* 1

Elghaish, Hanaa / *Hamad Bin Khalifa University, Qatar* 448

Fairchild, Joshua / *Creighton University, USA* 374

Gilewicz, Nicholas / *University of Pennsylvania, USA* 404

Gwilt, Ian / *Sheffield Hallam University, UK* 33

Han, Jung Hoon / *University of New South Wales, Australia* 430

Hawken, Scott / *University of New South Wales, Australia* 430

Heinen, Rachel / *Creighton University, USA* 374

Hopper, Tim / *University of Victoria, Canada* 287

Hunter, Samuel T. / *The Pennsylvania State University, USA* 374

Kramarae, Cheris / *University of Oregon, USA* 417

Lee, Carl W. / *University of Kentucky, USA* 306

Leone, Salvatore A. / *Creighton University, USA* 374

McSparren, Jason James / *University of Massachusetts, USA* 448

Merkel, Liz / *University of Victoria, Canada* 287

Mohr-Schroeder, Margaret J. / *University of Kentucky, USA* 306

Moore, Lorna Ann / *Independent Researcher, UK* 18

Payne, Alistair James / *Glasgow School of Art, UK* 60

Polanec, Elma / *Kindergarten "Little Sparow", Croatia* 322

Prager, Phillip Andrew / *IT University of Copenhagen, Denmark* 141

Reyes-Garcia, Everardo / *University of Paris 13, France* 224

Sanford, Kathy / *University of Victoria, Canada* 287

Schroeder, D. Craig / *Fayette County Public Schools, USA* 306

Selsjord, Marianne / *National Academy of the Arts, Norway* 141

Thomas, Maureen / *University of Cambridge, UK* 141

Tok, Evren / *Hamad Bin Khalifa University, Qatar* 448

Truckenbrod, Joan / *Art Institute of Chicago, USA* 47

Tschannen, Dana / *University of Michigan, USA* 265

Vorkapić, Sanja Tatalović / *University of Rijeka, Croatia* 322
Williams, Angelique / *University of New South Wales, Australia* 430
Winning, Ross / *University of Wolverhampton, UK* 83
Worden, Suzette / *RMIT University, Australia* 110
Zhang, Wei / *Peking University, China* 417

Table of Contents

Preface..xix

Acknowledgment xxviii

Section 1
Artistic Practice and Theory

Chapter 1
Exploring Liminal Practices in Art, Technology, and Science..1
Denise Doyle, University of Wolverhampton, UK

Chapter 2
Be[ing] You: In[bodi]mental a Real-Time Body Swapping Video Performance 18
Lorna Ann Moore, Independent Researcher, UK

Chapter 3
Big Data – Small World: Materializing Digital Information for Discourse and Cognition..................33
Ian Gwilt, Sheffield Hallam University, UK

Chapter 4
Digitizing the Physical: Physicalizing the Digital 47
Joan Truckenbrod, Art Institute of Chicago, USA

Chapter 5
The Virtual, Alternate Spaces, and the Effects upon Artwork..60
Alistair James Payne, Glasgow School of Art, UK

Chapter 6
Sound Image and Resonant Animated Space: Beyond the Sonic Veil 83
Ross Winning, University of Wolverhampton, UK

Chapter 7
The Earth Sciences and Creative Practice: Entering the Anthropocene............................110
Suzette Worden, RMIT University, Australia

Chapter 8

Transposing, Transforming, and Transcending Tradition in Creative Digital Media 141

Phillip Andrew Prager, IT University of Copenhagen, Denmark
Maureen Thomas, University of Cambridge, UK
Marianne Selsjord, National Academy of the Arts, Norway

Chapter 9

"Virtual Reality" Reconsidered 200

Garfield Benjamin, University of Wolverhampton, UK

Chapter 10

Designing Pervasive Virtual Worlds 224

Everardo Reyes-Garcia, University of Paris 13, France

Section 2
Education

Chapter 11

Making It for the Screen: Creating Digital Media Literacy 249

Paul Chilsen, Carthage College, USA

Chapter 12

Using Virtual Environments to Achieve Learner Outcomes in Interprofessional Healthcare
Education 265

Michelle Aebersold, University of Michigan, USA
Dana Tschannen, University of Michigan, USA

Chapter 13

Digital Media in the Classroom: Emergent Perspectives for 21st Century Learners 287

Kathy Sanford, University of Victoria, Canada
Liz Merkel, University of Victoria, Canada
Tim Hopper, University of Victoria, Canada

Chapter 14

Using Spatial Reasoning for Creative Design: Merging Engineering and Mathematics Practices 306

D. Craig Schroeder, Fayette County Public Schools, USA
Carl W. Lee, University of Kentucky, USA
Margaret J. Mohr-Schroeder, University of Kentucky, USA

Chapter 15

An Empirical Study about the Use of the Internet and Computer Games among Croatian
Children 322

Sanja Tatalović Vorkapić, University of Rijeka, Croatia
Elma Polanec, Kindergarten "Little Sparow", Croatia

Section 3
Communication and Innovation

Chapter 16
Tools for the Process: Technology to Support Creativity and Innovation 374
 Rachel Heinen, Creighton University, USA
 Salvatore A. Leone, Creighton University, USA
 Joshua Fairchild, Creighton University, USA
 Lily Cushenbery, Stony Brook University, USA
 Samuel T. Hunter, The Pennsylvania State University, USA

Chapter 17
Digital *Parrhesia* 2.0: Moving beyond Deceptive Communications Strategies in the Digital
World.. 404
 François Allard-Huver, Sorbonne University, France
 Nicholas Gilewicz, University of Pennsylvania, USA

Chapter 18
BOLD Ideas for Creative Social Networking: An Invitational Discussion 417
 Wei Zhang, Peking University, China
 Cheris Kramarae, University of Oregon, USA

Chapter 19
Smart CCTV and the Management of Urban Space... 430
 Jung Hoon Han, University of New South Wales, Australia
 Scott Hawken, University of New South Wales, Australia
 Angelique Williams, University of New South Wales, Australia

Chapter 20
Crafting Smart Cities in the Gulf Region: A Comparison of Masdar and Lusail............................. 448
 Evren Tok, Hamad Bin Khalifa University, Qatar
 Jason James McSparren, University of Massachusetts, USA
 Maha Al Merekhi, Qatar Foundation, Qatar
 Hanaa Elghaish, Hamad Bin Khalifa University, Qatar
 Fatema Mohamed Ali, Hamad Bin Khalifa University, Qatar

Compilation of References 461

About the Contributors 506

Index.. 514

Detailed Table of Contents

Preface xix

Acknowledgment xxviii

Section 1
Artistic Practice and Theory

Chapter 1
Exploring Liminal Practices in Art, Technology, and Science 1
    Denise Doyle, University of Wolverhampton, UK

This chapter interrogates the notion of the liminal in relation to the virtual and the imaginary through a consideration of the field of art, science, and technology and current creative practices in virtual worlds and avatar-mediated space. In particular, the art project Meta-Dreamer (2009) is considered through the manifestation of the avatar as digital object. In its attempt to explore the experience of "living between worlds," it reflects the concerns of contemporary arts practice exploration of time and space relationships. The art project is re-examined in light of key arguments in the provocative text Liminal Lives (Squier, 2004) that advocates a new approach to the liminal in light of current biomedicine and the shifting and emergent qualities of contemporary human life.

Chapter 2
Be[ing] You: In[bodi]mental a Real-Time Body Swapping Video Performance 18
    Lorna Ann Moore, Independent Researcher, UK

This chapter discusses the one-to-one interactions between participants in the video performance In[bodi]mental. It presents personal accounts of users' body swapping experiences through real-time Head Mounted Display systems. These inter-corporeal encounters are articulated through the lens of psychoanalyst Jacques Lacan and his work on the "Mirror Stage" (1977), phenomenologist Maurice Merleau-Ponty (1968) and his writings on the Chiasm, and anthropologist Rane Willerslev's (2007) research on mimesis. The study of these positions provides new insights into the blurred relationship between the corporeal Self and the digital Other. The way the material body is stretched across these divisions highlights the way digital media is the catalyst in this in[bodied] experience of be[ing] in the world. The purpose of this chapter is to challenge the relationship between the body and video performance to appreciate the impact digital media has on one's perception of a single bounded self and how two selves become an inter-corporeal experience shared through the technology.

Chapter 3

Big Data – Small World: Materializing Digital Information for Discourse and Cognition.................33
    Ian Gwilt, Sheffield Hallam University, UK

This chapter furthers discourse between digital data content and the creation of physical artifacts based on an interpretation of the data. Building on original research by the author, the chapter asks the questions: why should we consider translating digital data into a physical form? And what happens to how we understand, read, and relate to digital information when it is presented in this way? The author discusses whether or not the concept of the data-driven object is simply a novel visualization technique or a useful tool to add insight and accessibly to the complex language of digital data sets, for audiences unfamiliar with reading data in more conventional forms. And the author explores the issues connected to the designing of data into the material world, including fabrication techniques such as 3D printing and craft-based making techniques, together with the use of metaphor and visual language to help communicate and contextualize data.

Chapter 4

Digitizing the Physical: Physicalizing the Digital 47
    Joan Truckenbrod, Art Institute of Chicago, USA

Intertwined with the digital realm is a parallel sphere of digital material objects. The physicality of these things play an important role as they are embedded with memories as well as personal, social, and cultural meanings and references. The pervasiveness of digitizing information, images, spaces, and objects into digital data creates an expanding virtual presence. Simultaneously, virtual objects are now being transformed into material, tactile forms. Sensors are harvesting physical information and providing important feedback. Using digital devices involves an array of electronic rituals that have evolved. These ritualistic behaviors function in a similar manner to the performance of ritual and ceremony in indigenous cultures. This chapter examines the function of these digital rituals, with the physical residue deposited by these rituals and ceremonies. Material objects created by digital processes are powerful and play an important role socially, culturally, and spiritually.

Chapter 5

The Virtual, Alternate Spaces, and the Effects upon Artwork..60
    Alistair James Payne, Glasgow School of Art, UK

This chapter explores the philosophical notion of The Virtual in response to the writings of Gilles Deleuze and unfolds this thinking through its interdisciplinary and transformative effects upon contemporary fine art. The Virtual is discussed in relation to forms of contemporary painting, yet the chapter provides a model for thinking through interdisciplinarity within, and from, other media. The research investigates the perceived resistance of painting to explore external possibilities and introduces methodological strategies, which encounter externality as a means for establishing radical change. In this way, the Virtual acts as an instigator for change, which effectively destabilises the pre-formity attached to medium specific practices. It is for this reason that the Virtual forces external relationships and connections to come to the fore in order to radically alter and transform the physical and conceptual constructs of different disciplines. Alongside the discussion of the Virtual and its direct affects upon artistic practices, the chapter discusses literary models including hybridity and metamorphosis as potential key elements affecting transformative change.

Chapter 6

Sound Image and Resonant Animated Space: Beyond the Sonic Veil 83
    Ross Winning, University of Wolverhampton, UK

Animation is a synthesis of ideas that often encounters unpredictable, illogical, and imagined domains. In those animated worlds, recorded sound is now part of a coalition of two sensory forms mediated through hearing and vision. Sound has therefore been embedded in the audio-visual toolbox since the successful synchronisation of sound and picture. Sonic elements now contribute significantly to how animators might shape their films and express ideas. These animated worlds also often represent deeply rooted expressions of the interior mind of the artists and animators themselves. This chapter explores the relationship of sound to image in the evolutionary and increasingly variable animated forms that are currently proliferating. It aims to focus on sound as being the primary channel that is best able to reflect those interior ideas within a range of animated media. The exploration seeks to do this through tracing proto-cinematic ideas in the art of the past and animation practice that researches the sonified and animated image using musical and figurative metaphors.

Chapter 7

The Earth Sciences and Creative Practice: Entering the Anthropocene 110
    Suzette Worden, RMIT University, Australia

The Anthropocene is being suggested as a new geological age replacing the Holocene and is a description of a time interval where significant conditions and processes are profoundly altered by human activity. Artists interested in the earth sciences are using digital media to provide audiences with ways of understanding the issues highlighted in discussions about the Anthropocene. These artists are harnessing data through visualisation and sonification, facilitating audience participation, and are often working in art-science collaborations. These activities demonstrate a transdisciplinary approach that is necessary for confronting the world's most pressing problems, such as climate change. After a discussion of the opportunities provided by visualisation technologies and an overview of the Anthropocene, this chapter explores the following interrelated themes through examples of creative works: (1) nanoscale, (2) geology and deep time, (3) climate, weather, and the atmosphere, (4) extreme places – beyond wilderness, and (5) curatorial practice as environmental care.

Chapter 8

Transposing, Transforming, and Transcending Tradition in Creative Digital Media 141
    Phillip Andrew Prager, IT University of Copenhagen, Denmark
    Maureen Thomas, University of Cambridge, UK
    Marianne Selsjord, National Academy of the Arts, Norway

How can digital media technologies, contemporary theories of creativity, and tradition combine to develop the aesthetics of computer-based art today and in the future? Through contextualised case-studies, this chapter investigates how games, information technologies, and traditional visual and storytelling arts combine to create rich, complex, and engaging moving-image based artworks with wide appeal. It examines how dramatist and interactive media artist Maureen Thomas and 3D media artist and conservator Marianne Selsjord deploy creative digital technologies to transpose, transform, and transcend pre-page arts and crafts for the digital era, making fresh work for new audiences. Researcher in digital aesthetics, creative cognition, and play behaviour Dr. Phillip Prager examines how such work is conducive to creative insight and worthwhile play, discussing its remediation of some of the aspirations and approaches of 20th-century avant-garde artists, revealing these as a potent source of conceptual riches for the digital media creators of today and tomorrow.

Chapter 9
"Virtual Reality" Reconsidered 200
    Garfield Benjamin, University of Wolverhampton, UK

The term 'virtual reality' is used widely in contemporary culture to evoke the false worlds of the imagination digital technology has enabled us to create. However, the term itself remains ill defined, particularly amidst recent developments in theories of virtuality and reality that have left contradictory marks on VR. The phrase 'virtual reality' has become problematic, and is in need of a reconsideration for its continued relevance. This chapter assesses the term throughout its development and in the context of other theorisations such as cinema and cyberspace that have dominated recent digital theory. Taking the Deleuzian expansion of the virtual and the Lacanian expansion of the Real, the chapter interrogates the constituent processes of VR to suggest a new mode of conceiving the technologies in terms of a parallax between virtual-real and physical-digital within contemporary thought, which will then be applied to a conceptual framework for digital creative practices.

Chapter 10
Designing Pervasive Virtual Worlds 224
    Everardo Reyes-Garcia, University of Paris 13, France

Virtual worlds can be approached in a broader sense of that which refers to common conceptions of virtual reality and immersive environments. This chapter explores the design of virtual worlds in a time when much contemporary media is accessed through and simulated by software. Today, the main extensions of man are cognitive skills and experiences. Software is a way of seeing the world; it plays a central role in media design and distribution. Software and perception of reality are intertwined and pervasive: media not only exist in form of software but the shape and properties of media are also designed with software. In order to understand the implications of computational media, it is necessary to re-articulate problems in a creative and virtual manner. At the end of the chapter, the author speculates on design approaches and presents some examples developed by him.

Section 2
Education

Chapter 11
Making It for the Screen: Creating Digital Media Literacy 249
    Paul Chilsen, Carthage College, USA

We are immersed in a culture of spoken media, written media, and now irrevocably, digital screen media. Just as writing and speaking skills are keys to functioning in society, we must consider that the world increasingly demands proficiency in "mediating" as well. Doing anything less leaves this powerful medium in the hands of a relative few. By offering instruction in what digital screen media is, how it is effectively created, how the Internet continues to alter communication, and how this all informs everyday teaching and learning, digital media literacy can become more broadly understood and accessible. This chapter follows a program developed by the Rosebud Institute and looks at how—using simple, accessible technology—people can become more digital media literate by creating screen products themselves. The creation process also enables deeper, more authentic learning, allowing us all to communicate more effectively, to self-assess more reflectively, and to thrive in a screen-based world.

Chapter 12
Using Virtual Environments to Achieve Learner Outcomes in Interprofessional Healthcare
Education 265

Michelle Aebersold, University of Michigan, USA
Dana Tschannen, University of Michigan, USA

The use of simulation in the training of healthcare professionals has become an essential part of the educational experience. Students and practitioners need to learn a variety of technical, interpersonal, and clinical judgment skills to be effective healthcare practitioners. Virtual simulation can provide an effective training method to facilitate learning and can be targeted to develop specific skills in the area of Interprofessional Education (IPE). This chapter reviews the literature around simulation techniques and outlines a development process that can be used to develop virtual simulations to meet a variety of learning objectives including IPE. Specific issues and solutions are also presented to ensure a successful educational experience.

Chapter 13
Digital Media in the Classroom: Emergent Perspectives for 21st Century Learners 287

Kathy Sanford, University of Victoria, Canada
Liz Merkel, University of Victoria, Canada
Tim Hopper, University of Victoria, Canada

The purpose of this chapter is to highlight the engagement, social connectivity, and motivation to learn observed in two classes of students, one a grade 9/10 information technology class, the other a grade 3 class of learners classified with learning disabilities. The common factor in the two classes was the way the teachers were rethinking literacy for the 21st century learning by simultaneously engaging students in an event of creating computer programing to address a competition task whilst also addressing curriculum demands. The chapter explores the way the teachers were learning to develop the conditions for emergent learning systems in their classrooms as the first steps to reform the current education system. Drawing on complexity theory, the authors suggest that these students are offering two microcosmic examples of where global systems are heading. The goal of the chapter is to help shift school teaching from its present disconnect between the real world outside students' classrooms and the contrived, dated world of typical school-based curriculum practices.

Chapter 14
Using Spatial Reasoning for Creative Design: Merging Engineering and Mathematics Practices 306

D. Craig Schroeder, Fayette County Public Schools, USA
Carl W. Lee, University of Kentucky, USA
Margaret J. Mohr-Schroeder, University of Kentucky, USA

With the adoption and implementation of the Common Core State Standards for Mathematics and the Next Generation Science Standards, teachers are being called upon now more than ever before to regularly utilize and incorporate mathematics, science, and engineering practices in order to deepen students' understanding of the content they are learning, make broader connections to the STEM disciplines, and to ultimately help to strengthen the STEM pipeline. This chapter describes how teachers can use SketchUp as a tool to implement the practices through creative design into their own classrooms. The premise and basics of SketchUp are shared as well as a rich creative design project that develops spatial reasoning in middle grades students.

Chapter 15
An Empirical Study about the Use of the Internet and Computer Games among Croatian
Children.. 322
Sanja Tatalović Vorkapić, University of Rijeka, Croatia
Elma Polanec, Kindergarten "Little Sparow", Croatia

This book chapter is dedicated to theoretical and empirical review of media among children. Empirical results about computer presence in family homes, IT literacy with different computer programmes among parents, as well children are described. In addition, attitudes of parents and preschool and school-aged children about using Internet and computer games as well as attitudes toward the Internet violence are analysed. The results of games types that children play as well as frequency of playing and children's emotions evoked by them are shown. Finally, the results about presence of significant others as well as their conversation with children are shown. All of the above are interestingly studied in the frame of correlation analysis to research relations between some socio-demographic variables (sex, age, the level of education, and presence of computer in family home), so certain future research guidelines can be established.

Section 3
Communication and Innovation

Chapter 16
Tools for the Process: Technology to Support Creativity and Innovation 374
Rachel Heinen, Creighton University, USA
Salvatore A. Leone, Creighton University, USA
Joshua Fairchild, Creighton University, USA
Lily Cushenbery, Stony Brook University, USA
Samuel T. Hunter, The Pennsylvania State University, USA

Technology exerts an all-encompassing impact on the modern workplace, and has a strong influence on how designers approach creative problem solving. Such technologies can be valuable tools for organizations seeking to develop creative solutions to maintain a competitive advantage. However, with the rapid pace of technological development, it can be difficult for organizations to remain up-to-date and ahead of the competition. There is much that is still unknown about the ways in which novel technologies influence creative performance. The chapter attempts to provide insight on this topic by utilizing a process model of creative endeavors to predict how various types of technology may be used to enhance organizational creativity and innovation. Recommendations for future research and practice in the realms of technology and innovation are also discussed.

Chapter 17
Digital *Parrhesia* 2.0: Moving beyond Deceptive Communications Strategies in the Digital
World.. 404
    François Allard-Huver, Sorbonne University, France
    Nicholas Gilewicz, University of Pennsylvania, USA

Deceptive communications strategies are further problematized in digital space. Because digitally mediated communication easily accommodates pseudonymous and anonymous speech, digital ethos depends upon finding the proper balance between the ability to create pseudonymous and anonymous online presences and the public need for transparency in public speech. Analyzing such content requires analyzing media forms and the honesty of speakers themselves. This chapter applies Michel Foucault's articulation of parrhesia—the ability to speak freely and the concomitant public duties it requires of speakers—to digital communication. It first theorizes digital parrhesia, then outlines a techno-semiotic methodological approach with which researchers—and the public—can consider online advocacy speech. The chapter then analyzes one case of astroturfing, and one of sockpuppteting, using this techno-semiotic method to indicate the generalizability of the theory of digital parrhesia, and the utility of the techno-semiotic approach.

Chapter 18
BOLD Ideas for Creative Social Networking: An Invitational Discussion 417
    Wei Zhang, Peking University, China
    Cheris Kramarae, University of Oregon, USA

To further open the conversation about women's empowerment and global collaborations using new networking technologies, this chapter problematizes some prevalent ideas about creativity and social networking, notes suggested change that carry anti-feminist sentiments throughout the world, and suggests a number of ways that women and men can all benefit from an opening of queries about innovative ways of working together online. With the suggested expansions, the authors welcome more inclusive and invitational discussion about future digital media research and development.

Chapter 19
Smart CCTV and the Management of Urban Space.. 430
    Jung Hoon Han, University of New South Wales, Australia
    Scott Hawken, University of New South Wales, Australia
    Angelique Williams, University of New South Wales, Australia

This chapter briefly describes the proliferation of CCTV over the last few decades with particular reference to Australia and discusses the limits of the technology. It then focuses on new image interpretation and signal processing technologies, and how these advanced technologies are extending the reach, power, and capabilities of CCTV technology. The advent of "Smart" CCTV has the ability to recognize different human behaviours. This chapter proposes a typology to assist the application and study of Smart CCTV in urban spaces. The following four typologies describe different human behaviours in urban space: 1) Human-Space Interaction, 2) Human-Social Interactions, 3) Human-Object Interactions, and 4) Crowd Dynamics and Flows. The chapter concludes with a call for future research on the legal implications of such technology and the need for an evidence base of risk behaviours for different urban situations and cultures.

Chapter 20

Crafting Smart Cities in the Gulf Region: A Comparison of Masdar and Lusail.............................448

Evren Tok, Hamad Bin Khalifa University, Qatar

Jason James McSparren, University of Massachusetts, USA

Maha Al Merekhi, Qatar Foundation, Qatar

Hanaa Elghaish, Hamad Bin Khalifa University, Qatar

Fatema Mohamed Ali, Hamad Bin Khalifa University, Qatar

This chapter looks at these trajectories by specifically focusing on the interstices of smart cities and competitiveness through the role played by communication technologies. An initial question to tackle pertains to the definition of a smart city, as this concept is used in diverse ways in the literature. Transforming the cities into smart ones is a newly emerging strategy to deal with the problems created by the urban population growth and rapid urbanization. Smart city is often defined as an icon of a sustainable and livable city. Why are Gulf countries investing in smart cities? Is the emergence of smart cities a mere reflection or neoliberal urbanization or are there other dynamics that we need to take into consideration? This chapter attempts to convey the message that smart cities are crucial means of building social capital and also attaining better governance mechanisms in the Gulf.

Compilation of References 461

About the Contributors 506

Index...514

Preface

The creative application of digital media and new technologies is accelerating as artists, designers, and technologists continue to experiment and explore ways to create new aesthetic fields, semantically enhanced communication, and innovative relations between people and machines. Our virtual worlds meet the real material world through the interdisciplinary research of computer scientists, digital media technologists, artists, designers, and digital culture theorists. This handbook is intended as a collection of seminal texts from a wide range of International researchers explicating ways of bringing the virtual to the real through differing conceptual positions and research approaches; the majority of chapters represent the most current research of the authors in that they are updated chapters furthering those research findings previously published in IGI Global books. The book aims to provide relevant theoretical frameworks, examples of innovative practice, and the latest cutting-edge research findings in this wide and inter-disciplinary area; it therefore includes four previously unpublished chapters which present new work within the research scope of the handbook. It is written for professionals who want to improve their understanding of the strategic role the creative use of digital media holds within culture and society and as such the handbook will be of value to technologists, academics, designers, interactive media experts, virtual world creators, and new media artists. The target audience of this book is composed of professionals and researchers working in the field of digital media, creative technology, and virtual worlds in various disciplines (e.g. design, information and communication sciences, digital artists, digital culture theorists, education, creative practitioners, computer science, and information technology). Moreover, the book provides insights and examples of creative practice employing new technologies in innovate and unusual ways to generate exciting new work and offer new pathways for digital media research and development.

The book is structured into three sections beginning with the artists' approach to innovative ways of using digital media and creative technologies, across the varied fields of practice and theory within art and design. The second group of chapters refers to research in pedagogy and the educational remit of new technological advances and platforms, while the third set of papers concerns creative communication and dissemination across digitally bound social media and global networks:

ARTISTIC PRACTICE AND THEORY

This section begins with Dr Denise Doyle's research, "Exploring Liminal Practices in Art, Technology, and Science." This chapter interrogates the notion of the liminal in relation to the virtual and the imaginary through a consideration of the field of art, science, and technology and current creative practices in virtual worlds and avatar-mediated space. In particular, the art project Meta-Dreamer (2009) is considered through the manifestation of the avatar as digital object. In its attempt to explore the experience of "living between worlds," it reflects the concerns of contemporary arts practice exploration of time and space relationships. The chapter is an updated version of "Living between Worlds: Imagination, Liminality, and Avatar-Mediated Presence" (2013). The ease in which we experience the liminal through virtual space is even more pronounced when the space is avatar-mediated creating an oscillating state of existence between the virtual and the physical. Yet, both consciousness and the imagination depend on this liminality of space.

Dr. Lorna Moore, an independent artist from the UK, then discusses her work "Be[ing] You: In[bodi] mental a Real-Time Body Swapping Video Performance." In this newly published chapter, she articulates the way two participants felt they were actually in the body of the other through real-time Head Mounted Display Systems. The chapter presents personal accounts of users' experiences of the work, which have been understood as an inter-corporeal experience. This phenomenon is explained through the lens of psychoanalyst, Jacques Lacan and his work on the "Mirror Stage" (Lacan, 1977), phenomenologist Maurice Merleau-Ponty and his writings on the Chiasm (Merleau-Ponty, 1968), and anthropologist Rane Willerslev's research on mimesis (Willerslev, 2007). These positions provide new insights into the relationship between the corporeal Self and the digital Other providing platforms to account for the blurred boundaries between these modalities. The chapter then discusses the way the material body is stretched across these divisions highlighting the way digital media is the catalyst in this in[bodied] experience of be[ing] in the world. The purpose of this work is to provide alternative ways of thinking about the body and its relationship to video performance to understand the way digital media is having an impact on our perception of a single bounded self and how selves can be shared through the technology. In[bodi] mental presents an alternative viewpoint of the self/other divisions and positions these modalities as a shared experience.

Prof. Ian Gwilt, Sheffield-Hallam University, UK, researches into 3D printing technologies presented in his chapter "Big Data – Small World: Materializing Digital Information for Discourse and Cognition." In an era where the visualization of complex digital information is increasingly being used to shape our social, political, and economic environments, this chapter examines what happens when you use big data to drive the parameters and form of a physical object. Building and reflecting on original research by the author, the chapter asks the questions, Why should we consider translating digital data into a physical form and What happens to how we understand, respond, and relate to digital information when it is presented in this way? Moreover, the discussion moves on to whether or not data-driven objects are simply a novel visualization technique or a useful tool that can be used to add insight and accessibly to the complex language of digital big data sets. The chapter then explores a number of the issues related to designing digital information "into" the material world. These issues can be divided into two broad areas of concern that highlight both the physical and philosophical interests involved in materialized big data. The chapter looks at the different ways in which we interact with objects using touch and our other senses, and considers what these types of embodied interaction might mean in terms of how we comprehend any underlying data and information. It then concludes with a debate about digital material hybridity, distributed technologies, communities of use, and the implications for how we receive, understand, and consume big data.

Joan Truckenbrod is an artist and emeritus Professor at the School of the Art Institute of Chicago. In her chapter, "Digitizing the Physical: Physicalizing the Digital," she understands that radically shifting our experience of the visual image from virtual worlds, social media, electronic games, and flat screens to physical forms subverts the predominance of the digital realm. Living on the surface of the screen minimizes the tactility of materials and the resonance of memory and meaning embodied in objects. Digital 3D cinema, 3D television, and 3D cameras are precursors at the threshold of transforming digital into physical. The image flexes from screen to object with 3D printers and CNC machines. In the medical profession, computer 3D images from CT scans are transformed to remotely controlled, physical surgeries. Recently, thinking experiments use brain activity to remotely control robotic arms. Vehicles for physicalizing the digital will manifest three-dimensional, palpable, sensory, tactile, objectified experiences. Truckenbrod asks how will this phenomena transform modes of digital communication, physical interactions, and production on both the global and the personal scales? How will the material role of the computer prescribe new creative activities, new modes of artistic expression? Siting digital images and objects, digital images teeter in a precarious position between flat surfaces and material objects, between simulated three dimensionality and the physical world.

Dr. Alistair Payne, Head of Fine Art at the Glasgow School of Art, UK, is a painter and within his chapter, entitled "The Virtual, Alternate Spaces and the Affects upon Artwork," he explores the philosophical notion of The Virtual in response to the writings of Gilles Deleuze and unfolds this thinking through its interdisciplinary and transformative affects upon contemporary fine art. The Virtual will be discussed in relation to forms of contemporary painting; yet, the chapter provides a model for thinking through interdisciplinarity within, and from, other media. The Virtual acts as an instigator for change, which effectively destabilises the pre-formity attached to medium specific practices. It is for this reason that The Virtual forces external relationships and connections to come to the fore in order to radically alter and transform the physical and conceptual constructs of different disciplines. This updated chapter highlights these important ideas and presents new ways to consider The Virtual in relation to contemporary fine art practice, with a particular focus upon current issues in Painting. The chapter alongside the discussion of the virtual and its direct affects upon artistic practices encounters the hybrid and metamorphosis as key elements of change.

Ross Winning is an artist and lecturer in Animation from the University of Wolverhampton, UK, currently near completion of a practice-led PhD. In his chapter, "Sound Image and Resonant Animated Space: Beyond the Sonic Veil," he argues that animation is an art form that often encounters unpredictable, illogical, and imagined domains. In animated worlds, recorded sound is now part of a coalition of two sensory forms mediated through hearing and vision. Sound has therefore been embedded in the audio-visual toolbox since the successful synchronisation of sound and picture. Sonic elements now contribute significantly to how animators might shape their films and express ideas. These Animated worlds also often represent deeply rooted expressions of the interior mind of artists and animators. This updated chapter explores the relationship of sound to image in the evolutionary and increasingly variable animated forms that are currently proliferating. It focuses on sound as being the primary channel best able to reflect those interior ideas within a range of animated media. The exploration seeks to do this through tracing proto-cinematic ideas in art and animation practice that researches the sonified and animated image.

Suzette Worden's contribution, "The Earth Sciences and Creative Practice: Entering the Anthropocene," asserts that Artists who engage with the earth sciences have been able to explore all kinds of information about the natural environment, including information about the atmosphere, extremes of physical formations across immense dimensions of time and space, and increasingly "invisible" realms of materials at the nanoscale. This is a rich area for identifying the relationship between digital and material cultures as many artists working with this subject are crossing boundaries and testing out the liminal spaces between the virtual and the real. Not only is this a rich area for current experimentation but often these artists offer a critique of historical formations or provide a critique of theoretical concepts. To discuss these issues, this updated chapter provides an overview of theoretical links between visualisation and geology, mineralogy and crystallography. This chapter explores examples of creative practice through four themes:

1. Environment and experience,
2. Code and pattern,
3. Co-creation and participation, and
4. Mining heritage.

This thematic overview shows the diversity of creative work in this area. The chapter engages with practice and theory and takes a broad definition of the earth sciences to discuss virtual worlds and art practice. This includes a discussion of technologies that act upon the environment and also the visual technologies that allow us to "see" that environment and measure the world for scientific disciplines. Artists explore this as their subject and provide a critique of the associated science and technologies. In this context our understanding of materiality is extended.

Phillip Prager, University of Copenhagen, Maureen Thomas, Oxford University, and Marianne Selsjord present their research in a chapter entitled "Transposing, Transforming, and Transcending Tradition in Creative Digital Media" in which they ask: Can the range of aesthetics in computer-based interactive art be extended and enhanced through an understanding and deployment of pre-literate oral composition and storytelling techniques alongside medieval and renaissance approaches to form, colour, texture, line, and light in drawing, painting, and sculpture? How does the use of games and information technologies in conjunction with traditional visual and storytelling arts and crafts help today's media artists devise rich and complex interactive moving image artworks? Illustrated by case studies, this chapter addresses the theoretical framework surrounding such production and offers conclusions on the creative potentials and practical implications of these approaches for today's media artists. Marianne Selsjord (National Academy of the Arts, Oslo) contributed to the previously published chapter "Museum or Mausoleum? Electronic Shock Therapy" with Maureen Thomas and Robert Zimmer (Goldsmiths University of London), which inspired the current chapter, sadly developed multiple myeloma (an aggressive bone marrow cancer) in 2012. She was still working on her own artistic material until she was admitted to hospital just before Easter 2014, where she died peacefully ten days later. Marianne had written a draft and notes for the chapter printed here, and Maureen edited these and supplied missing references, so that they were able to represent Marianne's most recent and final piece of original 3D art, and to include her reflections on the relationship between traditional techniques and creative digital media.

Garfield Benjamin, a doctoral candidate from the University of Wolverhampton, UK, contributes a new chapter entitled "'Virtual Reality' Reconsidered" positioning the subject as the gap between virtual and real states. Within the many varied, and often incongruous, theories of digital technology and its culture there are two strands of the discussion that have emerged in which the very terms of the field are challenged. These are centred on the problematic notion of "virtual reality" that has dominated cultural depictions of the digital world, usually taking either "virtual" or "real" in an expanded definition to draw out a deeper understanding of the fundamental differences, connections, and interdependency between physical and digital spaces. Digital media has called into question the appearance of "reality," forcing all theories of contemporary culture to take into account the possibility of other spaces with which the (physical) human subject can engage. There is a need to expand and intersect current discussions of the relation between virtual and real by exploring the antagonisms that arise through developing both sides of the term. This chapter will therefore readdress the term "virtual reality" in the context of ongoing debates in philosophy, technology, and creative practice in a discussion of subjectivity in contemporary digital society, to insist on a constant re-evaluation of the terms used in such a discussion and their ramifications for its application in digital media and creative technologies.

Everardo Reyes-Garcia from the University of Paris contributes "Designing Pervasive Virtual Worlds." In an earlier chapter, written in 2009, he suggested that we made the following assumptions regarding pervasive virtual worlds: pervasiveness is about being here and now in several places simultaneously. People are surrounded by computing artifacts. Each one of these devices might have a different graphical interface or maybe there are differences at the level of graphic design but they share similar functions. While we are physically in some place, we can be acting in a remote place. Accordingly, while we act in that remote place, we can do similar tasks as those in the physical space. The pervasive property of digital media has raised a world that is mixed, extended and mediated through media. In this world, the society has developed contemporary processes that rely on a virtualization of individuals. Digital media and digital objects may be designed to communicate an operational function of the system, but at the same time, they communicate an allegory of the system, the world, and the society of media. In a society of media, the world is constituted by the hyperspace created by digital media and human uses. Virtual worlds do not have to represent reality exclusively in a realistic fashion.

EDUCATION

In this second section, Paul Chilsen from Carthage College, USA, presents "Making It for the Screen: Creating Digital Media Literacy." With the tectonic media shift in which we find ourselves, the lines we think we know, and think we can count on, seem to be blurring. The myriad machinations and goings on in our convergent media world, while a fascinating and rich topic, understandably extend beyond the scope of this chapter. Rather the focus here is to look more at what we are doing now. Now that the explosive growth and pervasive penetration of new media is upon us, are we doing the best that we can to get a firmer grip on the reins? The wave of buying and handing out expensive devices designed to merely access the conversation continues to grow and swell, threatening to eat up shrinking resources. In light of that, what steps can be taken to move beyond the latest techno-wizardry and instead convey real skills that allow more people to effectively join in, to make clear meaning, and to affect the change they seek? This ever-expanding world of screen-based electronic media encompasses such an understandably and incredibly broad array of media types, paradigms, and histories that even finding a name or term to refer to it all can prove difficult. Under the auspices of the Rosebud Institute we have used the term broader term 'digital media' as well as the more specific screen media. These terms work somewhat interchangeably to describe media specifically produced, created for, and unfolding on the screen yet are general enough to encompass a broad array of different media, both moving (film, video, television, and gaming) as well as those which are generally more static (websites, social media, blogs). The updated chapter has a necessarily refined scope. It looks at a very practical and doable approach that is giving people a baseline way to become more active and informed members of a screen media world.

Michelle Aebersold and Dana Tschannen from the University of Michigan, USA, present their current research in "Using Virtual Environments to Achieve Learner Outcomes in Interprofessional Healthcare Education." The purpose of the original chapter was to highlight a new simulation teaching strategy to teach interpersonal and clinical judgment skills to healthcare practitioners. The updated chapter uses this approach to focus on similar skills with the focus being on IPE. The area of IPE is a national focus area and institutions globally are struggling with how best to implement this type of education. The chapter provides a method that is not well utilized and offers options that can meet the core competencies of IPE. More specifically, it includes an overview of the need for IPE and impact on patient safety and information on Second Life (SL), its benefits and uses in IPE. The authors have continued their work in the area of SL and have improved methods for addressing technical challenges, streamlined orientations methods and materials, and developed specific methods for evaluating learner outcomes. The chapter then updates the five-step process for developing virtual simulations using an IPE exemplar. Virtual reality programs, such as Second Life, can provide a representative training environment for students at a lower cost and similar experiences to those of mannequin based simulations for selected educational objectives. It also can provide greater opportunity for IPE as all students do not need to be in the same location at one time.

Kathy Sanford, University of Victoria, Canada, Elizabeth Merkel, and Timothy F. Hopper contribute "Digital Media in the Classroom: Emergent Perspectives for 21st Century Learners." In the fall of 2006, the authors' ethnographic research study began in a response to increasing social concern regarding adolescent (dis)engagement in school literacy practices. They began data collection in a grade 9/10 Information Technology (IT) class wherein students were in the process of creating their own videogames as a way to learn programming. The work with these initial participants spurred the proliferation of several strands of subsequent research, and only inspired more questions about the ways in which youth are immersed in gaming and programming. Through their work with the grade 9/10 class, they began to understand videogames as having the potential for immersive, emergent learning where relationships can develop to become more fluid, organic interconnections where the students and teacher are both learning and guiding each other. Their theoretical perspectives shifted to frame our research. The initial work with the IT class was the impetus from which a longitudinal study began, investigating ongoing engagement with videogames by a core group of students. In 2014, this study continues to morph as said participants are now in university and in the work force and currently conduct study groups as our "in-house expert" research assistants.

D. Craig Schroeder with Carl W. Lee and Margaret J. Mohr-Schroeder from the University of Kentucky contribute "Using Spatial Reasoning for Creative Design: Merging Engineering and Mathematics Practices." The purpose of this updated chapter is to provide a rich example of developing spatial reasoning in middle school students, especially the 2- and 3-dimensional relationship, through the use of SketchUp in a real world context. This chapter provides detailed information regarding the implementation of SketchUp into a middle grades classroom, including directions and challenges to help guide students to increasing their spatial reasoning, especially between 2- and 3-dimensional objects. The chapter highlights a culminating project in which the students use their reasoning abilities to create a 3-dimensional project employing the NGSS Engineering Practices (National Research Council, 2011).

In conjunction with the current administration at an urban upper south middle school, students will be asked to develop a 3-dimensional computer model of their ideal school renovation (the school is in the planning stages of an actual renovation). The purpose of the project is to develop spatial reasoning and engineering skills within the students through the use of 3-dimensional software. Students will need to use the iterative process of design, build, test, redesign in order to develop a renovation that enhances the current school and provides an enhanced learning environment for future students.

Sanja Tatalović Vorkapić and Elma Polanec, University of Rijeka, offer a new chapter concerning "An Empirical Study about the Use of the Internet and Computer Games among Croatian Children." The existing digital age inflicts new situations and requirements upon children, parents, and experts for the purpose of educational work. It is therefore essential that we implement systematic and continuous empirical research if we are to adapt to the modern world and maximize the preservation of the psychological health of children, while allowing them a happy childhood. The development and reach of contemporary media has extended to where its content can have a significant influence on its receivers, especially where children are concerned as they are the most sensitive part of population. Children spend 3-4 hours daily watching TV and other media, or most of their free time (Ilišin, Marinovic Bobinac, & Radin, 2001). Inter alia, use of Internet and computer games is important in their lives. Child's free time is increasingly devoted to playing different games on the computer, allowing for less activity in the fresh air, running on the lawn, playing at being game hunters, seeking the fruits that nature gives us, etc. Educational experts know very well that imaginary play and game is very important in children lives. The game is not only pleasure and spontaneous activity but significantly contributes to psychological development of child (Verenikina, Haris, & Lysaght, 2003). But when it comes to children's play and its impact on the psychological development of children, what place is occupied by computer games? Computer games do not mean by spontaneous activity, do not mean interaction face to face, and children do not create game by themselves. Someone else has created a game for them; they are just in the function of implementer of a game.

COMMUNICATION AND INNOVATION

In the third section of the handbook, Joshua Fairchild from Pennsylvania State University, with co-authors Rachel Heinen, Salvatore Leone, Lily Cushenbery, and Samuel Hunter present their updated chapter on "Tools for the Process: Technology to Support Creativity and Innovation." Increasingly, organizations are turning to emerging technologies as tools to enhance innovation. However, such technologies often develop and change faster than research on best practices can keep up. In particular, the ubiquity of social media platforms, smart phones, and tablet computers stands to exert a massive impact on how organizations engage in creative endeavors. However, to date, there has been little research examining how such digital media technologies influence the creative process. In the chapter, the authors intend to investigate this issue by integrating scholarly work on the creative process and organizational behavior with an evaluation of such emerging technologies. It is their goal that this review and synthesis will lay the groundwork for future empirical work and also provide actionable recommendations for organizations seeking to use digital technologies to enhance innovation.

François Allard-Huver and Nicholas Gilewicz, Sorbonne University, contribute "Digital *Parrhesia* 2.0: Moving beyond Deceptive Communications Strategies in the Digital World." In their previously published chapter, the authors aimed at analyzing how Astroturfing—fake grassroots communications about an issue of public interest—is further problematized in digital space. This updated chapter, in addition to a new Astroturfing example, also explores the relationship between other deceptive communication strategies and ethos. The new chapter applies their methodological and theoretical proposition of digital parrhesia—Michel Foucault's articulation of parrhesia, the ability to speak freely and the concomitant public duties it requires of speakers—to digital communications. It first theorizes digital parrhesia, then outlines a techno-semiotic methodological approach with which researchers, the public, or communication specialists can consider online advocacy speech. The chapter then analyzes two very different instances of deceptive communication strategies using the techno-semiotic method in order to demonstrate the generalizability of the theory of digital parrhesia and the utility of the techno-semiotic approach.

Wei Zhang from Peking University researches into "BOLD Ideas for Creative Social Networking: An Invitational Discussion." While using some materials from the original chapter, "Women, Big Ideas, and Social Networking: Seven Provocative Questions," in Rekha Pande, Theo van der Weide, and Nicole Flipsen (Eds.), *Globalization, Technology Diffusion, and Gender Disparity: Social Impacts of ICT*, Wei now offers a new organization that reflects a change in focus and a change in the information available from other recent publications. This then, is a new chapter with a new title. In the current mainstream discourse on women's use of social networking technologies, the authors find prevalent ideas which implicitly presuppose that, compared with men's uses of the new social networking technologies, women's ideas and activities on the Social Web are deficient and less serious. The assumption that women are not capable of generating creative and Big Ideas (about anything) is entrenched in much mainstream consciousness and unconsciousness, and appears in many guises. For several decades, enduring problems for women online have been stated, illustrated, and reiterated, without much, if any, fundamental changes. This is a discouraging condition, for everyone. If this situation is to change, for the benefit of all, women will need to be included, at every level, in the discussions and design of the digital media technologies.

Jung Hoon Han, Scott Hawken, and Angelique Williams from the University of New South Wales, Australia, contribute "Smart CCTV and the Management of Urban Space." Planning and urban development in the world has recently shifted from an old paradigm of conventional integrated planning to a new paradigm of the intelligent setting-based approach being applied to chronic urban problems such as urban crime and pedestrian road incidents. The most influential intelligent settings approach to planning and urban development have been based on the smart digital technologies, which acknowledges that human activity occurs within places and that urban infrastructure provision (rather than physical construction) must enter smart system, digital networking, logistic process, and e-policy that shapes those places. This updated chapter will show an evidence-based smart technology performance specifications and review the types of the smart technologies deployed to create a real-time feedback-loop that provides risk information to the public about their collective behaviour over time, and whether that has any influence on that behavior.

And finally, the last chapter in the handbook is "Crafting Smart Cities in the Gulf Region: A Comparison of Masdar and Lusail," by Evren Tok and co-authors Hanaa Elghaish, Maha Al Merekhi, and Fatema Mohamed Ali from Hamad Bin Khalifa University. A combination of economic growth, societal needs, and human aspiration is establishing a Smart Cities culture throughout many of the urban centres of the world. Dynamic Gulf Region cities including Doha and Abu Dhabi are creating Smart City projects and programs, setting a rapid pace of development and implementation. Smart Cities are designed and developed to provide citizens, workers, and visitors with a safe, healthy, and sustainable environment in which to live and work. With strong government policies and programs that have been developed over recent years to move cities away from a dependency on hydrocarbon energy and into clean technology energies like solar and wind, the cities of the Middle East are emerging as the global benchmark for alternative energy generation, transmission, and consumption. These cities are using their move toward clean technology as the foundation to a larger Smart Cities strategy. Increasing economic dynamism in the GCC region has led development authorities, infrastructure companies, governmental, and corporate entities to be more cognizant of deploying ICT solutions for various infrastructural platforms such as intelligent transportation, telecommunications, airports, sustainable environments, public safety, energy efficient buildings, and residential and utilities projects. These projects not only stretch the limits of creativity, but also inform us about the neoliberal trajectories pursued by "globalizing" cities and their excessive focus on sustaining competitiveness. This study looks at these trajectories by specifically focusing on the interstices of smart cities and competitiveness through the role played by the states.

Dew Harrison
University of Wolverhampton, UK

REFERENCES

Ilišin, V., Marinović Bobinac, A., & Radin, F. (2001). *Djeca i mediji. Uloga medija u* svakodnevnom *životu djece.* Zagreb: Državni zavod za zaštitu obitelji, materinstva i mladeži – Institut za društvena istraživanja.

Lacan, J. (1977). The mirror stage as formative of the function of the I as revealed in psychoanalytic experience. In *Ecrits: A selection* (A. Sheridan, Trans.). London: Routledge, Tavistock. (Original work published 1949)

Merleau-Ponty, M. (1968). The intertwining-The chiasm. In C. Lefort (Ed.), The visible and the invisible: Philosophical interrogation (A. Lingis, Trans.; pp. 130–155). Evanston, IL: Northwestern University Press.

National Research Council (NRC). (2011). *A framework for K-12 science education.* Washington, DC: The National Academies Press.

Verenikina, I., Harris, P., & Lysaght, P. (2003). *Child's play: Computer games, theories of play and children's development.* University of Wollongong.

Willerslev, R. (2007). *Soul hunters: Hunting, animism, and personhood among the Siberian Yukaghirs.* Ewing, NJ: University of California Press. doi:10.1525/california/9780520252165.001.0001

Acknowledgment

I would like to gratefully thank all the Editorial Board members and reviewers.

I would also like to thank all the authors who have generously and patiently contributed to this book. With their important, innovative, and exciting work, they have made this handbook possible.

I wish to thank all at IGI Global for their kind and supportive help during the time taken to develop this book, with particular thanks to Austin DeMarco. His professional assistance and guidance have been much appreciated throughout this endeavour.

Thank you.

Dew Harrison
University of Wolverhampton, UK

Section 1
Artistic Practice and Theory

Chapter 1
Exploring Liminal Practices in Art, Technology, and Science

Denise Doyle
University of Wolverhampton, UK

ABSTRACT

This chapter interrogates the notion of the liminal in relation to the virtual and the imaginary through a consideration of the field of art, science, and technology and current creative practices in virtual worlds and avatar-mediated space. In particular, the art project Meta-Dreamer (2009) is considered through the manifestation of the avatar as digital object. In its attempt to explore the experience of "living between worlds," it reflects the concerns of contemporary arts practice exploration of time and space relationships. The art project is re-examined in light of key arguments in the provocative text Liminal Lives (Squier, 2004) that advocates a new approach to the liminal in light of current biomedicine and the shifting and emergent qualities of contemporary human life.

INTRODUCTION

In the field of Art and Technology the ease in which we experience the liminal through virtual space is even more pronounced when the space is avatar-mediated creating an oscillating state of existence between the virtual and the physical[1]. Yet both consciousness and the imagination depend on this liminality of space. With a focus on the 'threshold' this continual 'about to become' is almost a necessary condition of being. Some virtual environments (or worlds) deliberately play with this "existential overlay to the physical" (Lichty

2009, p.2). Working with a new framework of the emergent imagination consideration is given to the transitional spaces created in artworks in virtual world spaces where aspects of the liminal come to the fore.

This chapter discussion reconsiders a previous text written by the author entitled *Living between Worlds: Imagination, Liminality and Avatar-Mediated Presence* (Doyle, 2012) in light of the key issues and arguments explored by Susan Merrill Squier in her pioneering and provocative text *Liminal Lives: Imagining the Human at the Frontiers of Biomedicine* (2004). Arguing from

DOI: 10.4018/978-1-4666-8205-4.ch001

the fields of literature and feminist science studies Squier challenges Victor Turner's notion of the liminal as a purely cultural construct that is played out in key moments in a persons life. Turner presupposes that biology is a constant, something that is fixed; it is rather culture that offers the potential for liminal spaces to be created (Turner in Squier, 2004, p.4). As Squier notes, 'as Turner understands it, while the liminal is shifting, *life* is still stable [original emphasis]' (Squier, 2004, p. 6). However, she argues that 'contemporary biomedicine necessitates a significant revision of Turner's thesis, one that acknowledges the shifting, interconnected, and emergent quality of human life' (Squier, 2004. p.6).

The chapter considers to what extent we can examine imaginative or liminal states that are, as Edward Casey notes, "remarkably easy to enter into", yet their "very ephemerality renders [them] resistant to conceptual specification of a precise sort" (Casey 2000, p.6-7). It considers to what extent transitional spaces share similar characteristics to the liminal.

- Does the liminal always find the point of the threshold?
- Does avatar-mediation (re)space the imagination to a place geographically distant from the body?
- Do we experience liminality in a similar way? Or is the liminal more closely bound to the temporal?
- To what extent are both conditioned by the virtual?

The relationship between the transitional and liminal, and the avatar experience, sets out a particular view of the imagination and its elusive, and sometimes liminal, qualities. Squier advocates that 'we need to move beyond Turner's exclusively cultural framing to understand liminality not merely as a cultural state but as a *biocultural process*' [original emphasis] (Squier, 2004, p. 8). Creating from a liminal space or a liminal zone, making manifest from these transitional spaces

raises questions about the relationship between technology and biology that will be discussed further in the chapter. Squier notes that creations from the space of the liminal (for example the case of adopted embryos) they are neither one or the other, neither life nor not life, suggesting 'a new biological personhood mingling existence and non-existence' (Squier, 2004, p.5).

A Prelude: On the Virtual, the Imaginary, and the Liminal

Casey comments in his book *Imagining: A Phenomenological Study* (Casey 2000) that, at the time of its first publication in 1976, a "concerted phenomenological study of the imagination had yet to be done" (Casey 2000, p.xi). Further, there is yet to be a substantial study in which the virtual and the imaginary are considered in relation to each other. There have been some passing associations, such as Massumi's link to the imagination as a "mode of thought" that is most suitable to the virtual (Massumi 2002, p.134), or that of Levy, describing the imagination as one of the three vectors of the virtual (Levy 1998, p.28). Any dialogue on the virtual and the imaginary might begin by placing them in direct relation to each other (with the two terms on an equal footing). This pairing throws up some initial thoughts on what pulls or pushes them together, what attracts them, and conversely what pulls them apart. When paired together, as relatives, or at least as an associated grouping, three shared characteristics or impulses are revealed. Firstly, both terms are often associated with an 'elsewhere' or to a place or space not immediately associated with the real. Secondly, each appears to be multi-faceted, whose meaning changes quite dramatically when seen as an act or as a description, when a verb (imagine), a noun (virtuality, imaginary), or equally as an adjective (virtual, imaginary). Finally, each term can be as elusive and fleeting as the other. When identifying what would differentiate them, one can make the distinction in what may be the very impulse that stirs or moves them. In fact, other than the imagination being more closely aligned with creativity, or a creative impulse, (which does not necessarily incorporate or include notions of virtuality), one may quickly flounder in attempts to keep them separated, rather falling back on the transitional or liminal qualities that they both share. Yet each term cannot necessarily be exchanged as freely as an initial analysis may suggest. Two aspects of what we understand to be the meaning of the liminal are of relevance here; firstly that it denotes "a position at, or on both sides of, a boundary or threshold" (Oxford Dictionary, 2012), and secondly it relates to a transitional or initial stage of a process" (Oxford Dictionary, 2012). Spaces such as Second Life, with their combination of immersive qualities, avatar mediation, and user-generated content, are presenting new circumstances and conditions under which to undertake a study of the imagination and in particular to study its own liminal states.

BACKGROUND

Art and the Virtual

Some would agree that there has been a relationship between art and the virtual at least since the Renaissance, with the invention of linear perspective. More recently, in the field of Art and Technology, the relationship between art and the virtual appears implicit in its scope and engagement (Ettlinger 2009, Lindstrand 2007, Grau 2003). However, Or Ettlinger describes the 'fog of multiple meanings around the term the virtual' (Ettlinger 2009, p.6), and he suggests that, in fact, contemporary and digital art has lost its interest in the art of illusion, and is only now marginally concerned with the pictorial. There is a history to the relationship between art and the virtual which spans a number of decades from the early 1990s, from early experiments in virtual environments (Sermon 1992, Laurel & Strickland 1993, Gro-

mala & Sharir 1994, Davies 1995 & 1998) to the networked environments of the early 21st century (Zapp 2002, 2005) and finally to the networked virtual spaces found in online virtual worlds such as There.com and Second Life. There is an argument that as soon as linear perspective was invented painting became another kind of virtual space, and in fact, Lindstrand suggests that:

[…] before the invention of linear perspective, spatial experience was detached from imagery. Once the tools to depict three-dimensional space on a two-dimensional surface were developed, architecture and the understanding of space leaped into a new era. (Lindstrand 2007, p. 354)

For Lindstrand, the possibility for the viewer to imagine herself walking around inside a painting opened up a whole new chapter in art as well as causing a fundamental shift in the experience of space. Ettlinger would most certainly agree with this perception of space. In developing The Virtual Space Theory he states that at its heart lies 'the interpretation of virtual space as the overall space which we see through pictorial images, and of 'virtual' as describing any visible object which is located inside of that space' (Ettlinger 2009, p.6).

The notion that the concept of space can be seen as Cartesian, definable, and contained, is at odds with the concept of space as lived, as experienced such as the Thirdspace that Edward W. Soja describes, and discussed further below (Soja 1996). In *The Production of Space* (1991), Henri Lefebvre attempts to define the experience of space from both a metaphysical and an ideological perspective. Initially he outlines two terms in relation to space, that of the 'illusion of transparency' and the 'illusion of opacity' (or the realistic illusion). Of the illusion of transparency he writes that the emphasis of the written word is to the detriment of, what he terms, social practice. In what he describes as the grasping of the object by the act of writing, he suggests that this is supposed to bring:

[The] non-communicated into the realm of the communicated [...] such are the assumptions of an ideology which, in positing the transparency of space, identifies knowledge, information and communication [...] the illusion of transparency turns out [...] to be a transcendental illusion: a trap, operating on the basis of its own quasi-magical power. (Lefebvre 1991, pp.28-29)

In turn, the illusion of opacity, of substantiality, being philosophically closer to naturalistic materialism, leads Lefebvre to assert that:

[Language], rather than being defined by its form, enjoys a 'substantial reality'. In the course of any reading, the imaginary and symbolic dimensions, the landscape and the horizon which line the reader's path, are all taken as 'real', because the true characteristics of the text [...] are a blank page to the naïf in this unconsciousness [original emphasis]. (Lefebvre 1991, p.29)

However, and most interestingly, Lefebvre continues to say the two illusions are not necessarily in opposition to each other and do not 'seek to destroy each other'. Rather, that:

[Each] illusion embodies and nourishes the other. The shifting back and forth between the two, and the flickering or oscillatory effect that it produces, are thus just as important as either of the illusions considered in isolation. (Lefebvre 1991, p.29)

This flickering, from opaque to transparent to opaque again, these oscillations suggest a complex system of relationships between a space and the objects found in that space. We become uncertain if space is transparent at all. Yet, Lefebvre (1991, p.29) writes that it is the texture of space that allows us to create space through social practice as sequences of acts that become a signifying practice in itself. Ettlinger's and Lefebvre's understanding of space, appear at odds with each other. More particularly, does Lefebvre's interpretation of the

construction of our experience of space suggest a liminal experience that is inherent in its qualities?

An article by Axel Stockburger, *Playing the Third Place* (2007), extends Lefebvre's ideas to the work of Soja and his definition of what he terms the Thirdspace. As Stockburger notes, beyond the dualism of subject and object Lefebvre suggests that spaces can be understood within the triad of the perceived, the conceived and the lived. According to Stockburger, Soja 'identifies perceived space (Firstspace) with the real, and conceived space (Secondspace) with the imaginary, leading to lived space (Thirdspace), as a field of both, imagined and real' (Stockburger 2007, p.232). Stockburger continues with his interpretation in the context of game space and describes the hybrid mix between real and imagined spaces created through digital game universes as resonating strongly with the concept of Thirdspace. He notes that 'this insight is crucial because it defies the idea of computer games as merely 'virtual' or purely imaginary spaces. It is precisely the interaction between real and imagined spatiality that makes this medium so compelling and unique' (Stockburger 2007, p.232). A concept of space that suggests a mixed experience of both real and imagined spatiality proves to be useful when considering online and networked spaces, whether they are games-based or not.

Privileging the Body over the Eye

According to Mark Hansen (2004, 2006), there has been a repositioning of the body in relation to technology within new media arts practice. Hansen's claim, along with others (Ihde 2002, Biocca 1997, Hillis 1999, Pallasmaa 2005), is that the eye no longer dominates, and it is now the body that mediates our experience 'in the ensuing shift from perception to affectivity' (Hansen 2004, p.13). He argues that, because of new media technologies, there has been a move away from the image based in 'perception' to that of embodied experience. The question, or rather the inevitability, that new technologies are changing us has been taken up by Jean-Francois Lyotard as he suggests that "technology wasn't invented by us humans. Rather the other way round [...] any material system is technological if it filters information [...] if it memorizes and processes" (Lyotard 1991, p.12). In what he terms the "myth of disembodiment" Steve Dixon, in *Digital Performance* (2007), claims that as bodies embody consciousness, "to talk of disembodied consciousness is a contradiction in terms" (Dixon 2007, p.212). In the context of digital arts practice, Bolter and Gromala note that it is digital artists in particular:

[That] insist on the materiality of their work. They will never abandon or disparage the ways of knowing that the senses give us. For them, even the experience of seeing is not disembodied; it is visceral. Seeing is feeling. What fascinates digital artists is the ways in which their embodied existence is redefined in cyberspace. So they use digital technology to examine the interaction between the physical and the virtual. (Bolter & Gromala in Dixon 2007, p.216)

There are a number of points here that are relevant to the discourse in this chapter, and most notably that of the examination of the interaction between the physical and the virtual, and the liminal experience that the transitional space between the physical and virtual creates.

New Technologies and Liminal Space

From early writings on virtual reality (Rheingold 1991, Heim 1993, Damer 1998, Heudin 1999, and Schroeder 2002), to Jones suggesting that "virtual reality is the contemporary and future articulation of the philosophical and psychological question of how we define (and create) reality" (Jones 2006, p.4), the issues, definitions and experience of reality find rich and challenging ground in virtual

environments. Writing in 2001, Grosz describes virtual realities as:

Computer-generated and [computer]–fed worlds that simulate key elements of "real space" or at least its dominant representations – for example, its dimensionality, its relations of resemblance and contiguity – acting as a partial homology for a "real space" within which it is located. (Grosz 2001, p.40)

The early use of virtual environments for artistic practice were explored in a series of projects undertaken at the Banff Centre, Canada in the early 1990s and subsequently documented in *Immersed in Technology: Art and Virtual Environments* (Moser 1996). In the preface to the book, Douglas Macleod, the Project Director, likens this "moment of virtual reality" to a similar moment in time when Vertov's *Man with the Movie Camera* was released in 1929, cataloguing the potential of the film medium (Macleod in Moser 1996, preface). Of particular note were works such as Brenda Laurel and Rachel Strickland's *Placeholder* (1993), the *Archaeology of the Mother Tongue* (1993) by Toni Dove and Michael Mackenzie, and the virtual reality performance, *Dancing with the Virtual Dervish: Virtual Bodies* (1994), by Diane Gromala and Yacov Sharir. These projects were particularly innovative in their exploration of virtual reality environments in an art context.

Artists such as Char Davies moved from painting to exploring virtual space in virtual environments in the early 1990s, resulting in the works *Osmose* (1995) and *Ephémère* (1998). In *Osmose* (1995), the participant, or 'immersant' must concentrate on their breath as a device to navigate vertically through the spaces represented. Many immersants explain their experience in similar terms to Hansen:

You are floating inside an abstract lattice [...] you have no visible body at all in front of you, but hear a soundscape of human voices swirling around you as you navigate forward and backward by leaning your body accordingly [...] Exhaling deeply causes you to sink down through the soil as you follow a stream of tiny lights illuminating the roots of the oak tree. (Hansen 2006, pp.107-108)

In *Landscape, Earth, Body, Being, Space, and Time in the Immersive Virtual Environments Osmose and Ephémère* (2003), Davies says that "within this spatiality, there is no split between the observer and the observed" (Davies 2003, p.1). She argues that this is not tied to a Cartesian paradigm, but rather allows "another way of sensing to come forward, one in which the body feels the space very much like that of a body immersed in the sea" (Davies 2003, p.1). In this private virtual space:

[By] leaving the space of one's usual sensibilities, one enters into communication with a space that is psychically innovating [...] For we do not change place, we change our nature. (Bachelard in Davies 1997, p.3)

In the introduction to *Changing Space: Virtual Reality as an Arena of Embodied Being* (1997) Char Davies suggests that the medium of immersive virtual space offers the potential for "exploring consciousness as it is experienced subjectively, as it is *felt* [original emphasis]" (Davies 1997, p.1). She likens much of her work to the experience of meditational practice.

The work that defines the early exploration of telepresence in telematic spaces by artists engaged with technology is that of UK-based artist, Paul Sermon and his work, *Telematic Dreaming* (1992), which Dixon describes as a "wonderful, exquisitely simple and ground-breaking installation [that] creates a type of magic, a sort of lucid dream" (Dixon 2007, p.220). Over the last two decades Sermon has built upon this very simple concept of two geographically remote spaces being connected in time. In *Telematic Dreaming* images of two beds, one in Finland, and the

other in England, are projected onto each other, and that enabled a real time interaction with the performer in one space, and the visitor in the other (Sermon 1992).

Susan Kozel writes an interesting account of her experience of being the performer in this piece in *Spacemaking: Experiences of a Virtual Body* (1994). Other projects developed by Sermon such as *Unheimlich* (2005), a telematic theatre performance claimed to be the world's first interactive play, and more recently in work such as *Picnic on the Screen* (2009) in collaboration with Charlotte Gould presented at the Glastonbury Festival, he explores the concept of telematic presence.

Toni Dove, in writing about her experiences of making *Spectropia* (2005), an interactive performance piece using responsive interface technologies, likens the experience of the user to the experience of swimming: "this is a different form of attention – a kind of sustained tension which creates a space for reception; vertical eruptions in a horizontal field of time" (Dove 2006, p.67). She discusses the effects of the embodied interface and the use of 'flow' rather than the 'cut' as the architecture for the media experience. For Dove, this charged space is a key characteristic of telepresence: "it is the space through which the body extends itself into the movie or virtual space. It is the invisible experience of the body's agency beyond its apparent physical edge" (Dove 2002, p.210). This space, between real space and the virtual space of the screen, is the charged space described by Dove; this is the space where the experience of telepresence is acted out. This is the same charged space that can be experienced when interacting with a virtual character in Luc Courchesne's interactive film installation, *Landscape One* (1997), being invited to go on a journey in a park in Montreal.[2]

These are the similar imaginary and metaphorical spaces that Andrea Zapp describes in *Networked Narrative Environments as Imagi-*

nary Spaces of Being (2004). Additionally, the augmented spaces created in *Human Avatars* (2005), an interactive installation also by Zapp, construct a visual dialogue between real and virtual participants on a networked stage, as the visitors in the exhibition space discover a wooden hut that they are invited to enter. A live image of the visitor was projected inside a model version of the hut seen, and the disproportionately large faces were then seen at the windows of the second hut.

Whilst *Human Avatars* (2005) could be defined as a networked augmented space, it is not actually an avatar-mediated space that is created. The virtual embodiment of people as avatars is a term used in many online worlds, with avatar being the Sanskrit word which originally referred to the incarnation of a Hindu god and particularly the god Vishnu (Boellstorff 2008, p.128). The first use of the term in the context of technology was around 1986 for the graphical representation of participants in the *Habitat* virtual world (Dixon 2007, p.259). However, Tom Boellstorff notes that:

While "avatar" [...] historically referred to incarnation – a movement from virtual to actual – with respect to online worlds it connotes the opposite movement from actual to virtual, a decarnation or invirtualization. (Boellstorff 2008, p.128)

He suggests that "avatars make virtual worlds real, not actual: they are a position from where the self encounters the virtual" (Boellstorff 2008, p.129) whereas Mark Meadows advocates that "an avatar is a social creature, dancing on the border between fact and fiction" (Meadows 2008, p.16). In using the term avatar-mediated online space this chapter distinguishes between the term virtual worlds and the experience of presence through an avatar representation in virtual space as discussed above.

METHODOLOGY: EXPLORATIONS OF AVATAR-MEDIATED SPACE

The very construction of matter is at stake when we consider the virtual: matter is permeated with ephemeral and dynamic elements, such as memory and kinaesthetic processes. Once again, we see that the virtual cannot be pinned to one side of the tenuous divide between the material and the immaterial. (Kozel 2006, p.138)

A Prelude: The Virtual Body

Kozel suggests that "the virtual does not have to be confined to a set of relations external to the body; we can consider the meaning of traces of virtuality within our bodies" (Kozel 2006, p.138). James B. Steeves notes that:

Without the virtual aspect of the body schema, the body's original set of abilities could not be developed into more complex modes of behaviour. This realm of possibility exists through the virtual body, which is an embodied mode of the imagination [my emphasis]. (Steeves 2007, p.23)

In *Performing in (Virtual) Spaces* (2007) Morie notes that when a participant engages in virtual space through a third person avatar, the form of embodied experience they take on has 'an experiential locus that is outside their perceptual self'. She explains that this is, in fact, "in front of the experient's physical and imaginal locus" (Morie 2007, p.132). According to Morie the act of emplacing a body into an immersive environment signifies "a shift to a dualistic existence in two simultaneous bodies" (Morie 2007, p.127). She claims that, now, the lived body has 'bifurcated and become two' (Morie 2007, p.128). In her article she explores the representation of the body, or presence, in virtual environments in five ways: as no representation/no avatar, as the mirrored self, as a partial or whole graphical personification, as a third-person/observed avatar, and the representation as experience in shared environments. She suggests that virtual environments such as those created by Char Davies become a:

[...] sacred, encompassing space, where mind transcends body even as it references the body, the felt organism even in visual absence. This body, as felt phenomenon, is how we know the world, true as much within the virtual as in the real. (Morie 2007, p.133)

Morie returns to Merleau-Ponty's phenomenological standpoint as he views the body as "the common texture of which objects are woven" (Merleau-Ponty in Morie 2007, p.133), but suggests that he did not have to grapple with "new forms of immaterial bodies beyond the phenomenal" (Morie 2007, p.133) as we do now in light of new technologies. The chapter now considers a practice-based project that furthers the discussion on the nature and meaning of the avatar representation as a body that lives and moves between worlds.

Living between Worlds

I have the experience of embodiment, although I know my body is virtual. Of course I do. There is little true form here, only a series of associations. I took a friend of mine to a volcano last night. He was in awe of it. In his mind's eye, in his imagination he saw before him a 'real' volcano. Well, real enough to evoke his awe. Is that not 'real' enough for it to contain a form of reality? A form of presence? (Wanderingfictions Story in Doyle & Kim 2007, p. 216)

Working within the realm of Art and Technology (and as an artist who engages with narrative as method) my exploration of virtual space over the last decade has often been based on the retelling of narratives in a new context. An early practice-based

project was to re-interpret Italo Calvino's *Invisible Cities* (1997) through an interactive artefact. The story was of Marco Polo's adventures to imagined cities with Calvino providing the descriptions of the fantastic, symbolic, and often conceptually based places. In the introduction to the project, I considered:

How do we understand time in virtual space? Real and imaginary, real and virtual. Is this a suitable dialectic offered by the introduction of 'net space'? Is it truly a dialectic, or a 'parallel' world we can draw upon to explore issues of time, our experiences of the world as, in fact, a type of non-linear time, a time mixed up with past, present and future. (Doyle 2000, p.4)

Of equal note were my closing remarks, where I suggested that the creation of a figure in the virtual space, that of Eleni seen here in Figure 1, was worthy of further study:

To produce Wandering Fictions for the web remained essential for the concept. The impact on the process, above technical constraints, of constructing a character to exist within this space was continually evident. The net space, if it has borders and boundaries, are not yet visible. A very different potential space could still emerge. (Doyle 2000, p.24)

In Figure 1, two stills can be seen of Eleni, the protagonist in the interactive arts project. Here, a vectorized film of movements of a figure was created in an attempt to create a figure that could explore the virtual spaces of Calvino's imagined cities. What was of interest was this exploration of online, or cyberspaces, in a human form.

Following my introduction to Second Life in 2007, it was a relatively short time before I created *Wanderingfictions Story*. The origin of the maiden name was based on Siegfried Zielinksi's early writings on the Internet, in which he notes that:

Figure 1. Studies of Eleni
© *(2000) Denise Doyle.*

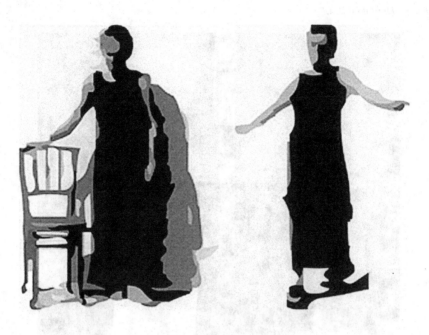

In the motion of crossing a border, heterology encircles the impossible place, that is unlocatable, that is actually empty, that in practice is created in the motion of crossing the border [...] this is what taking action at the border, that which I call subjective, targets in relation to the Net: strong, dynamic, nervous, definitely process-orientated aesthetic constructions, that are introduced into the Net as Wandering Fictions. (Zielinski 1996, p. 285)

Having already developed a number of artist projects utilizing and investigating *Second Life* as a space for artistic experimentation, in 2009 my interest in the notion of *Wanderingfictions Story* as a manifestation of, and from, virtual space became the basis of a new project, *Meta-Dreamer* (2009). After reflecting on the work of the performance artist Joseph DeLappe's *MGandhi* series[3], I began working with digital materialization expert Turlif Vilbrandt[4] to create a series of digitally materialized objects of *Wanderingfictions Story*. By experimenting with digital processes that extracted data from Second

Life and investigating different types of materials, attempts were made to represent jade, and clouded glass, amongst other textures. The end result can be seen in Figure 2, the qualities of the figure are cloud-like and ethereal as though *Wanderingfictions Story*, the meta-dreamer, is 'almost there'. The digital object was presented in the Golden Thread Gallery space (as part of the ISEA2009[5] exhibition) alongside DeLappe's figure of *MGandhi 1* (2008). The visitor could also experience the virtual installation on Kriti Island that included the presentation of *Wanderingfictions Story*, the meta-dreamer, through captured images and her meta-dream writing.

This process of extracting data from virtual space, to be manifested in some way in physical space, forms an aspect of what Lichty terms an Evergent modality of art in virtual worlds. In his article, *The Translation of Art in Virtual Worlds* (2009), Lichty outlines a number of interesting questions with respect to artists working between the virtual, and what he terms the *tangible*. He presents four modalities of art in which each modality "refers to the location and vector direction of the work's relation between

Figure 2. Wanderingfictions Story as part of the Meta-Dreamer project at the Golden Thread Gallery, Belfast
© *(2009) Denise Doyle. Digital Object.*

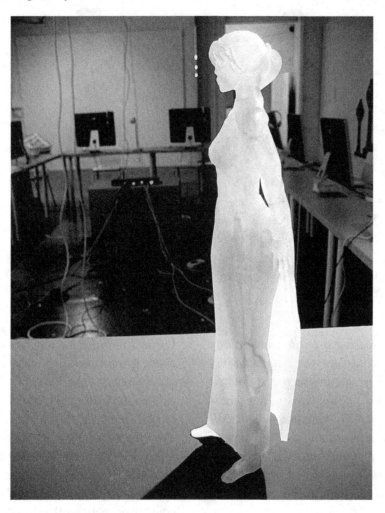

worlds" (Lichty 2009, p.2). He notes that in terms of artistic praxis (beyond the associated problems of audience and questions of form) it is "the representational modality and the permeability of the boundary between worlds" that is of particular interest in the creation of meaning in artworks produced in virtual world spaces (Lichty 2009, p.1). He explains that:

[…] the nature of communication of the work is dependent upon its location and vector. What I mean by vector is a gesture of direction, simultaneity, concurrence, or stasis in regards to its movements between worlds. (Lichty 2009, p.2)

In suggesting that there are four modalites of art being produced in virtual worlds, the Transmediated, the Evergent, the Cybrid and the Client/Browser work, he explains:

This epistemological "movement" within and between worlds has four basic structures; work that is essentially traditional physical art translated to the virtual, "evergent" work that is physically realized from virtual origins, the virtual itself, designed entirely for the client/browser experience, and "cybrids" that exist concurrently between various modalities. (Lichty 2009, p. 2)

According to Lichty, the semiotics of two modalities, the transmediated and the client/browser, are "a straightforward affair" (Lichty 2009, p.2). However, the Cybrids, "are less concerned with continuity, but are interested in the differences and distinctions between worlds and scales" (Lichty 2009, p.5). Both the Cybrid and the Evergent works demonstrate a "movement from virtual to tangible, which includes the consideration of works existing in simultaneous physical and virtual components, [and] present more complex models" (Lichty 2009, p.2). Manifesting from the virtual to the physical (or tangible) certainly has its parallels with manifesting from fictional worlds. Whatever the movement, this is a complex play and suggests in particular that it is those "enigmatic liminal works that live between worlds" (Lichty 2009, p.11) that create spaces that are the most potent for the imagination, demonstrating an array of creative potential for artists engaging in the *Second Life* space itself.

In an analysis of the emergence of 'transitional spaces', the four modalities of art as described by Lichty can be used to note the directions and creations of meaning between the physical or tangible world, and the virtual world, and movements within and between virtual and liminal spaces themselves. My intention within the *Meta-Dreamer* project and specifically in the production of Wanderingfictions Story as a digital object was to explore, and represent, the almost becoming condition of the avatar-mediated experience. As an artist creating in what is a third-person and multiple perspective I was not alone in finding a complex and liminal state formed during the creative activities within *Second Life* (Doyle 2010, see Appendix).[6]

Imagining Bodies

Computer artist Myron Krueger's early experiments resulted in what is considered to be the first virtual world, *Videoplace* (1974). In this he demonstrated that we can feel and sense other bodies in virtual space through this purely visual experience (Krueger in Boellstorff, 2008, p.44). In addressing issues of location in virtual space fellow artist Taey Kim (Iohe) and myself worked on a project *Map to Grid* (2008), employing methods of psycho-geography to determine where our non-human bodies were positioned on the grid[7]. Through this research it was noted, "understanding our geographical position in this digital era is absolutely essential as we are able to live in, and embody, multiple realities. Our 'I's travel through multiple spaces and times" (Doyle & Kim in Doyle, 2008, p.24).

Robert Bosnak, in writing of the dreaming brain, agrees with a current set of 'stories' of neuro-science as expounded by both Mark Solms and J. Allan Hobson, that dreaming is related to an experience of space (Bosnak 2007, p.36). In fact, a key element of what Bosnak terms the "embodied imagination" is that there is "an *inversion* of the notions of inside and outside [that] *changes the very nature of the space* [original emphasis]" in which we find ourselves (Bosnak 2007, p.20). Giving an explanation of how to visualize the experience of multiple embodied emotions, Bosnak explains that if dreaming was considered to be a narrative of simultaneous embodied states that unfold along a timeline, then equally, if the timeline "tilts [...] into a vertical *axis* [original emphasis], a cross-section of multiple embodied stories [...] making its many story times visible at a glance" (Bosnak 2007, p.39). In suggesting that emotions are "fully embodied states existing throughout the physical body" he further explains that dreaming could be considered to be "a simultaneous spatial experience of multiple embodied emotions" (Bosnak 2007, p.38). He uses the term "image-presence" to explain the environment, or space, we might find ourselves in when experiencing the embodied imagination. For Bosnak the process of embodiment precedes any mental or emotional knowing. For him "embodiment is the fundamental archaic way of knowing" (Bosnak 2007, p.71). It is clear that this approach to, or view of, embodiment through Bosnak's embodied imagination can be related to the avatar-mediated experience and the experience of the liminal in virtual world space.

Manifesting from the Liminal

In this section a Groszian reading of time and space in light of the virtual is closely examined to further explore the notion and experience of the liminal. Of the concept of the in-between Grosz writes that "one could say that the in-between is the locus of futurity, movement, speed; it is thoroughly spatial and temporal, the very essence of space and time and their intrication" (Grosz 2001, p.94). Grosz claims that space itself actually requires two kinds of time: the first being "the time of the emergence of space as such, a time before time and space" (Grosz 2001, p.110); the other being "the time of history, of historicity, the time of reflection, the time of knowledge – a time to which we are accustomed" (Grosz 2001, p.111). In her examination of the time and space of architecture she explains that she is interested in the relevance of the first sense of time:

[…] a concept that requires not only a time before time but also a time after time […] the times before and after time are the loci of emergence, of unfolding, of eruption, the space-times of the new, the unthought, the virtuality of a past that has not exhausted itself in activity and a future that cannot be exhausted or anticipated by the present. (Grosz 2001, pp.111-112)

Doreen Massey, in an essay responding to the work of artist Olafur Eliasson, attempts to illustrate a set of relationships between time and space by using a narrative account of a journey between Manchester and Liverpool. In the process of travelling she suggests, "if movement is reality itself then what we think of as space is a cut through all those trajectories; a simultaneity of unfinished stories. Space has time/times within it" (Massey 2003, p.111). Further:

Space has its times. To open up space to this kind of imagination means thinking about time and space together. You can't hold places and things still. What you can do is meet up with them […] 'Here', in that sense is not a place on a map. It is that intersection of trajectories [original emphasis]. (Massey 2003, p.111)

Harrison takes up Nicholas Bourriaud's notion of "journey-forms" to explain the art concerns of a number of artists who developed art works for the *Second Life* platform (Harrison, 2011, p.237). In fact, the use of "journey-forms, which is a combination of, a way to exchange, time and space values" (Bourriaud in Harrison, 2011, p.238). If each space has a particular time, as Massey implies, then the transitional and liminal spaces identified in avatar-mediated space may also have a particular time attached to them. Not only, then, are there heterogeneities of space but also different sets of time-spaces that can also be located in the avatar-mediated experience. Casey writes of "edges in time" (Casey 2008, p.12), where these edges are forms of boundaries of what he calls "further wrinkles in the face of the temporal field" (Casey 2008, p.12). All of these expressions suggest a plasticity to time as a lived experience, but also to the specificities of time-space relationships.

Squier notes that the field of contemporary bioethics is indifferent to the 'epistemological power of fiction' (Squier, 2004, p.5). Yet, fictions within artistic practice are those spaces that can 'imagine' and create from that 'loci of emergence' in ways that are truly reflecting the actual 'science' of manifestation in current bio-medical practices. As Squier herself comments:

The interpenetration of realms and processes once believed to be separate means that it is increasingly difficult to tell whether variation is the result of nature or culture. No longer stable, the boundaries of our human existence have become imprecise at best, contested at worst. (Squier, 2004, p.7)

The idea of creating or manifesting from a liminal space (in the case of Squier describing the frontier practices of bio-medicine, in the case of the *Meta-Dreamer* project manifesting from the space of the virtual itself) is here interrogated and explored as new spaces of existence. In fact this new 'biomedical imaginary' is described by Catherine Waldby in *The Visible Human Project* (2000) as 'the generally disavowed dream work performed by biomedical theory and innovation' (Waldby in Squier, 2004, p.14) in which she points towards the place of the ambiguous, liminal and symbolic realm within biomedicine. Waldby further suggests that biomedicine:

[…] realizes, or struggles to realize these narratives through their embodiment. It anatomizes its narratives in the sense that it orders its images of bodies according to their logic […] it reads into lived bodies in ways that are constitutive of important aspects of corporeality itself [original emphasis]. (Waldby in Squier, 2004, 16).

The digital object realised in *Meta-Dreamer* (2009) implies a state of in-between, of a "time *before* time" and the "loci of emergence" itself. Perhaps it could even be a representation of a "time *after* time", of a passing through, of leaving rather than entering. Equally a sense of a frozen-ness is suggested in the material chosen to represent the figure in physical form. Dew Harrison suggests, in *Crossing Over: Oscillations between the Virtual and the Real* that this renders the *Wanderingfictions Story* avatar "inanimate", "being frozen from the life she had in SL" (Harrison, 2011, p.238). Rather it is an attempt to represent the "position at, or on both sides of, a boundary or threshold" (Oxford Dictionary, 2012) that of the liminal state itself. Grosz proposes a re-enervation of space through duration in the "restoration of becoming to both space and time", and equally that when in "virtual time becoming virtual space" (Grosz 2001, p.120) a new kind of time-space relationship is established.

RECOMMENDATIONS

In the field of Art and Technology the positioning of each successive 'innovation' is acknowledged as each rupture enables new associations and links to be made. This chapter points towards virtual worlds and avatar-mediated online space as another rupture and an opportunity to articulate both the experience of the liminal and the experience of living between worlds created through the avatar experience. However, the specificity of the platform of *Second Life* or any other may have to be taken into account as each 'time', or as *Wanderingfictions Story* suggests, 'each decade has its own curiosity' (Doyle & Kim 2007, p.217).

Space can be understood and described as metaphoric, visual, Cartesian and imaginary. However, in this chapter, space and more particularly avatar-mediated online space, is considered to be more heterogeneous and complex in its nature and construction of the lived experience. The very experience of telepresence, as noted in a number of the artworks presented, means that there has to be at least a third space, which is based on Soja's mix of the real and the imagined. The new modalities of art being developed in virtual worlds as suggested by Lichty are still somewhat undeveloped, yet are useful as a starting point to begin to explore the vectors of meaning created between the tangible (or physical) and the virtual. To return to the questions outlined at the beginning of the chapter, does the liminal always find the point of the threshold? Most certainly there is a sense that when living between worlds there must be a threshold between them, yet even as outlined by Zielinski's original writings in 1996 that inspired the naming of my avatar, new places are often created "in the *motion* of crossing the border [my emphasis]" (Zielinski 1996, p.285). Squier suggests that 'to discover the sources and significance of new forms emerging in our era, we must engage in the same kind of boundary crossing that characterizes the new bio-technologies' (Squier, 20014, p.10). Liminality is bound to the temporal – to passing, to the passage – of time itself. In that sense, *Meta-Dreamer* is a representation of that 'feeling' of time, of what Grosz considers to be the times before and after time, that place and loci of "unfolding" (Grosz 2001, p.112?). If *Wanderingfictions Story* as a transluscent digital object is a representation of that "time" or if she indeed as Harrison suggests "an inanimate being frozen from the life she had in SL" (Harrison, 2011, p.238) there is no doubt her new existence is a reminder that living between worlds is a new condition of what must now be termed a developing the contemporary cosmology of real and virtual space.

REFERENCES

Bachelard, G. (1994). *The poetics of space* (M. Jolas, Trans.). Boston: Beacon Press. (Original work published 1958)

Bergson, H. (1991). *Matter and memory*. New York: Zone Books. (Original work published 1896)

Biocca, F. (1997). The cyborg's dilemma: Progressive embodiment in virtual environments. *Journal of Computer-Mediated Communication, 3*(2). Available at: http://jcmc.indiana.edu/vol3/issue2/biocca2.html

Boellstorff, T. (2008). *Coming of age in Second Life: An anthropologist explores the virtually human*. Princeton, NJ: Princeton University Press.

Bosnak, R. (2007). *Embodiment: Creative imagination in medicine, art and travel*. Hove, East Sussex: Routledge.

Calvino, I. (1997). *Invisible cities*. London: Vintage.

Casey, E. (2000). *Imagining: A phenomenological study*. Bloomington, IN: Indiana University Press.

Courschesne, L. (1997). Landscape one. *Interactive Film Installation*. Available at: http://courchel.net/

Damer, B. (1998). *Avatars! Exploring and building virtual worlds on the internet*. Berkeley, CA: Peachpit Press.

Davies, C. (1995). *Osmose: Virtual reality environment*. Available at: http://www.immersence.com/osmose/index.php

Davies, C. (1997). Changing space: Virtual reality as an arena of embodied being. In *Multimedia: From Wagner to virtual reality*. New York: W.W. Norton & Company. Available at: http://www.immersence.com

Davies, C. (1998). *Ephémère: Virtual reality environment*. Available at: http://www.immersence.com/

Davies, C. (2003). Landscape, earth, body, being, space, and time in the immersive virtual environments *Osmose* and *Ephemere*. In *Women, art and technology*. Cambridge, MA: MIT Press. Available at: http://www.immersence.com

Dixon, S. (2007). *Digital performance: A history of new media in theater, dance, performance art, and installation*. Cambridge, MA: MIT Press.

Dove, T. (2002). The space between: Telepresence, re-animation and the re-casting of the invisible. In New screen media: Cinema/art/narrative. London: BFI.

Dove, T. (2005). *Spectropia: Interactive feature film*. Available at: http://tonidove.com/

Dove, T. (2006). Swimming in time: Performing programmes, mutable movies - Notes on a process in progress. In Performance and place. Basingstoke, UK: Palgrave Macmillan.

Dove, T., & Mackenzie, M. (1993). Archaeology of the mother tongue: Virtual reality installation. Alberta, Canada: Banff Centre for the Arts. Available at http://www.banffcentre.ca/bnmi/coproduction/archives/a.asp

Doyle, D. (2000). *Wandering fictions 2.0: Eleni's journey.* (Unpublished MA Project). Coventry University, Coventry, UK.

Doyle, D. (2008). *Kritical works in SL.* Morrisville, NC: Lulu Publishing.

Doyle, D., & Kim, T. (2007). Embodied narrative: The virtual nomad and the meta dreamer. *The International Journal of Performance Arts and Digital Media, 3*(2&3), 209–222. doi:10.1386/padm.3.2-3.209_1

Ettlinger, O. (2009). *The architecture of virtual space.* Ljubljana: University of Ljubljana.

Grau, O. (2003). *Virtual art: From illusion to immersion.* Cambridge, MA: MIT Press.

Gromala, D., & Sharir, Y. (1994). *Dancing with the virtual dervish: Virtual bodies.* Virtual Reality Installation. Banff Centre for the Arts. Available at: http://www.banffcentre.ca/bnmi/coproduction/archives/d.asp#dancing

Grosz, E. (2001). *Architecture from the outside: Essays on virtual and real space.* Cambridge, MA: MIT Press.

Hansen, M. (2004). *New philosophy for new media.* Cambridge, MA: MIT Press.

Hansen, M. (2006). *Bodies in code: Interfaces with digital media.* New York: Routledge.

Harrison, D. (2011). Crossing over: Oscillations between the virtual and the real. In *Proceedings of Cyberworlds 2011 Conference.* Academic Press.

Heim, M. (1993). *The metaphysics of virtual reality.* New York: Oxford University Press.

Heudin, J. C. (Ed.). (1999). *Virtual worlds: Synthetic universes, digital life and complexity.* Reading, MA: Perseus Books.

Hillis, K. (1999). *Digital sensations: Space, identity, and embodiment in virtual reality.* Minneapolis, MN: University of Minnesota Press.

Ihde, D. (2002). *Bodies in technology.* Minneapolis, MN: University of Minnesota Press.

Jones, D. E. (2006). I, avatar: Constructions of self and place in second life and the technological imagination. *Gnovis, Journal of Communication, Culture and Technology.* Available at: http://gnovisjournal.org/files/Donald-E-Jones-I-Avatar.pdf

Kozel, S. (1994). *Spacemaking: Experiences of a virtual body.* Available at: http://art.net/~dtz/kozel.html

Kozel, S. (2006). Virtual/virtuality. *Performance Research, 11*(3), 136–139.

Laurel, B., & Strickland, R. (1993). *Placeholder.* Virtual Reality Installation. Banff Centre for the Arts. Available at: http://www.banffcentre.ca/bnmi/coproduction/archives/p.asp#placeholder

Lefebvre, H. (1991). *The production of space.* Oxford, UK: Blackwell Publishing.

Levy, P. (1998). *Becoming virtual: Reality in the digital age.* New York: Plenum Trade.

Lichty, P. (2009). The translation of art in virtual worlds. *Leonardo Electronic Almanac, 18*(12). Available at: http://www.leonardo.info/LEA/DispersiveAnatomies/DA_lichty.pdf

Lindstrand, T. (2007). Viva pinata: Architecture of the everyday. In Space time play: Computer games, architecture and urbanism - The next level. Basel: Birkhauser Verlag AG.

Lyotard, J. (1991). *The inhuman: Reflections on time.* Stanford, CA: Stanford University Press.

Massey, D. (2003). Some times of space. In Olafur Eliasson: The weather report. London: Tate Publishing.

Massumi, B. (2002). *Parables for the virtual: Movement, affect, sensation.* Durham, NC: Duke University Press. doi:10.1215/9780822383574

Meadows, M. S. (2008). *I, avatar: The culture and consequences of having a second life.* Berkeley, CA: New Riders.

Morie, J. (2007). Performing in (virtual) spaces: Embodiment and being in virtual environments. *International Journal of Performance Arts and Digital Media, 3*(2&3), 123–138. doi:10.1386/padm.3.2-3.123_1

Moser, M. A. (Ed.). (1996). *Immersed in technology: Art and virtual environments.* Cambridge, MA: MIT Press.

Pallasmaa, J. (2005). *The eyes of the skin: Architecture and the senses.* Chichester, UK: John Wiley & Sons.

Rheingold, H. (1991). *Virtual reality.* New York: Summit Books.

Schroeder, R. (Ed.). (2002). *The social life of avatars: Presence and interaction in shared virtual environments.* London: Springer. doi:10.1007/978-1-4471-0277-9

Sermon, P. (1992). *Telematic dreaming.* Performance Installation. Available at: http://creativetechnology.salford.ac.uk/paulsermon/dream/

Sermon, P. (2005). *Unheimlich.* Multi-User Performance Installation. Available at: http://creativetechnology.salford.ac.uk/unheimlich/

Sermon, P., & Gould, C. (2009). *Picnic on the screen.* Interactive Public Video Installation. Available at: http://creativetechnology.salford.ac.uk/paulsermon/picnic/

Soja, E. W. (1996). *Thirdspace: Journeys to Los Angeles and other real-and-imagined places.* Malden, MA: Blackwell Publishers.

Squier, S. M. (2004). *Liminal lives: Imagining the human at the frontiers of biomedicine.* Durham, NC: Duke University Press. doi:10.1215/9780822386285

Steeves, J. B. (2007). *Imagining bodies: Merleau-Ponty's philosophy of imagination.* Pittsburgh, PA: Duquesne University Press.

Stockburger, A. (2007). Playing the third place: Spatial modalities in contemporary game environments. *International Journal of Performance Arts and Digital Media, 3*(2&3), 223–236. doi:10.1386/padm.3.2-3.223_1

Zapp, A. (2002). *The imaginary hotel.* Networked Installation. Available at: https://www.digitalartarchive.at/database/general/work/the-imaginary-hotel.html

Zapp, A. (2005). *Human avatars.* Interactive Installation. Available: http://www.art.mmu.ac.uk/profile/azapp/projectdetails/228

Zielinski, S. (1996). Thinking the border and the boundary. In Electronic culture: Technology and visual representation. Aperture Foundation.

KEY TERMS AND DEFINITIONS

Biomedical Imaginary: A term used by medical sociologist Catherine Waldby to describe her proposal that scientific practice should include an ambiguous, liminal, and symbolic realm.

Embodied Imagination: A term used by the Dutch psychoanalyst Robert Bosnak that he closely associates with the dreaming brain in which multiple spatial embodied states are experienced simultaneously. The term is also used here to denote the experience of sensing a spatial presence in virtual space through a 'sense imaginary' and the association of the body of the avatar.

Emergent Imagination: A term used to denote the most active state of the emerging imagination when interacting with avatar-mediated online spaces and particularly those that reflect the laws and logic of the physical world.

Imagination: The Latin (and English) origin for the imagination is the verb *imaginari*, whereas the Greek term is *phantasia*. The etymological implications of this term are discussed in the chapter. Edward Casey defines the imagination as the complete phenomenon composed of two phases; the act phase and the object phase. The term is used here to imply a state of creation and *act of becoming*: a bringing into being rather than as the inverse of the physical or tangible.

Liminal Space: A term used to denote a space that creates the condition of being at, or on both sides of a threshold or boundary, and relates closely to the state of being in-between.

Transitional Space: A term used to denote the movements of the imagination in which vectors of meaning are created out of the relationships between physical and virtual world spaces.

ENDNOTES

1   The use of the terms virtual and physical (also tangible later in the chapter) are used here rather than the virtual and the real given the experience of virtual space can often considered to be as 'real' as the experience of the physical or tangible world.

2   My experience of the installation *Landscape One* was like being invited *into* the screens that surrounded me by the characters, yet still experiencing all the physical sensations of remaining static in front of the screen. This is possibly the first experience of telepresence I had, and it was something that I was curious about for a number of years afterwards.

3   During an artist residency at the Eyebeam Gallery, New York, in 2008 Joseph DeLappe experimented with a range of data materialisation processes to produce *MGandhi 1* (8" rapid prototyped 3D print), *MGandhi 2* (15" rapid prototyped 3D print finished in genuine gold leaf, *and MGandhi 3* (17' tall monumental sculpture constructed from cardboard and hot glue).

4   Turlif Vilbrandt is an expert in the field of Digital Materialisation. He is currently completing his PhD research at the SMARTlab Digital Media Research Institute, University College Dublin.

5   The Inter Society for Electronic Arts organises an annual Symposium and related exhibitions. In 2009 it was held in Belfast on the Island of Ireland.

6   Joseph DeLappe and Annabeth Robinson note their experience and relationship with their avatars in interviews conducted with both artists in 2010.

7   Using a real doll called *Dongdong* Taey Kim exchanges narratives and stories with the author's avatar *Wanderingfictions Story* in the project.

Chapter 2
Be[ing] You:
In[bodi]mental a Real–Time Body Swapping Video Performance

Lorna Ann Moore
Independent Researcher, UK

ABSTRACT

This chapter discusses the one-to-one interactions between participants in the video performance In[bodi]mental. It presents personal accounts of users' body swapping experiences through real-time Head Mounted Display systems. These inter-corporeal encounters are articulated through the lens of psychoanalyst Jacques Lacan and his work on the "Mirror Stage" (1977), phenomenologist Maurice Merleau-Ponty (1968) and his writings on the Chiasm, and anthropologist Rane Willerslev's (2007) research on mimesis. The study of these positions provides new insights into the blurred relationship between the corporeal Self and the digital Other. The way the material body is stretched across these divisions highlights the way digital media is the catalyst in this in[bodied] experience of be[ing] in the world. The purpose of this chapter is to challenge the relationship between the body and video performance to appreciate the impact digital media has on one's perception of a single bounded self and how two selves become an inter-corporeal experience shared through the technology.

INTRODUCTION

This chapter will present a discourse on the live video performance *In[bodi]mental* performed at The Public in West Bromwich 2011 which was part of the authors practice-led PhD research. As a long term video performance artist, the author demonstrates the necessary transition from analogue to digital to articulate the way the digital has developed her art practice. Her concerns investigate what happens to our perception of

self when we move across the boundary between the corporeal Self and the live digital image as Other. She questions the constitution of the self and what happens to this construct as we move across the corporeal and into the digital within real-time video performance practice. She interrogates the materiality of the self in particular, to the real-time video image as digital Other. Do we lose the self and become something else or can we maintain a self/other position simultaneously which adds to our phenomenological experience?

DOI: 10.4018/978-1-4666-8205-4.ch002

The work *In[bodi]mental* draws the performer/ participant through the video frame where both participants are immersed in each other. Both performers are suspended in the belief that the live digital image of the other performer is a part of their own corporeality. A moment were they experience their 'other' which is now afforded by the digital technology. Writing primarily from a phenomenological viewpoint the chapter draws on some aspects of anthropology to examine the self-other relationship in video performance when the actual/physical self is projected within the digital other. In simulating the self of another through video interaction it is reasoned that one can experience the self of another as part of one's corporeality. The interrelationship between the digital body and the corporeal body overlap where each is implicated in the other so sameness and difference can be maintained where there is no distinction between them.

The main objective of the chapter demonstrates how emerging digital technology is the catalyst in creating a continuity between the participant of the work (self) and the video performance (other). The blurring of these modalities is deliberated through real-time video performance where there is no obvious beginning, middle or end during an interaction between subjects in the performance. Though *In[bodi]mental* emerged as a performance investigation looking to find new ways to immerse the viewer/participant within the artwork the outcome was surprising. The research completed in December 2013 discovered that the participant/performer encountered a hyper-real experience which appeared to be analogous with the Lacanian Real, magnified through an uncanny moment. The aim to bridge the gap between the performer and the performed, subject and object, was a phenomenological stretching of the materiality of the body beyond the parameters of a single bounded self where an inter-corporeal experience was articulated. The research also revealed the way the digital technology could facilitate the movement of one self into another to understand

the way the multiple self is a composite of the material and the immaterial. The chapter proceeds with the following questions. Can we experience more of the other via emerging technologies through art practice and can we experience the phenomenology of an[other]? To what extent is digital technology changing the way we experience be[ing] in the world and what are the implications of our perceptions of self? The term be[ing] has been defined as being *in* the moment – the here and now.

Emerging digital technologies are demonstrating that one can experience an overlap between subjects where the binary oppositions between self and other are no longer clear cut divisions but are now emerging as blurred modalities of be[ing] in the world. If most of our experiences of being in the world are past or present encounters the focus to be *in* the now as a result of video performance can be an invigorating experience. To articulate these ideas the author has coined the term In[bodi] ment to conceptualize the interaction between subjects during *In[bodi[mental*. This is understood as an experience where one has perceptually felt they were *in* the body of the other subject. A space where body matter and digital media collide. This chapter will focus on those participants lived experience of the video performance, and the implications of those collisions between the corporeal self and the digital other.

BACKGROUND

The author draws on Roy Ascott (2005) a pioneer in consciousness studies, and his work on syncretic reality alongside phenomenology, psychoanalysis and anthropology. Locating the research within these fields articulates the impact *In[bodi]mental* has had on a participants perception of self in relation to the digital other. The connection between phenomenologist Maurice Merleau-Ponty's (1968) work on the *chiasm* and digital culture is demonstrating the way the digital body and the corporeal body are interlinked. Merleau-Ponty's philosophical view of our relationship with the world is based on reciprocity – an enmeshed entwinement of 'being' where there is a crossover between bodies and the world. A different view of the self/other relationship is presented by psychoanalyst Jacques Lacan (1977) and his concept of the *Mirror Stage* which expands our understanding of the relationship between the subject and the mirror image. Lacan maintains we can simultaneously experience the self/other dilemma through our paradoxical experience of the corporeal body and the reflected image. Locating the research in critical relation to these theorists has opened up new challenges to the self/other division within the context of digital media performance to narrow the gap between the performer and the live digital counterpart. To re-visit both Lacan and Merleau-Ponty's writings during the pre-digital age has without doubt contributed to an understanding of the development of the subject as an individual and to experience the crossover between subjects and the digital world we live in. *In[bodi] mental* has enabled one to be suspended within and between these binary self/other positions through real-time video performance.

The chapter reads Merleau-Ponty's *chiasm* through the lens of digital performance and anthropologist Rane Willerslev (2007) to articulate the experience of both the author and the participants in the video performance. Both mimesis and mimicry have been drawn upon to make connections with the live digital video image and the part they play in creating strong empathic relationships between subjects and the digital counterpart. From personal accounts of participants experiences in *In[bodi]mental* the position this chapter takes is an understanding between performers, that there was an inter-corporeal experience.

Though there are many works that have explored these relationships through virtual worlds, online identities, second life, gaming, avatars and media art. This chapter is particularly concerned with the relationship between the corporeal body and digital video performance practice using real-time video. From modernism to postmodernism we have seen the way artists have extended the body beyond its natural parameters in the performance happenings of the 1960s through to the video artists of the 1970s 1980s, 1990s to the present day. The relationship between the self as image and other to the self, and our desire to embody our 'other' through visual reproduction is not a recent phenomenon. It is through these histories we can see the way artists have been concerned with bridging the gap between subject and object, art and artist, artwork and viewer. One of the most obvious of artists narrowing the gap between subjects is Paul Sermon's (1992) video performance *Telematic Dreaming*. Sermon used two separate spaces to remotely connect participants to the performer via video conferencing techniques. He used 'live' video projections of each participants body projected onto a bed in a separate space where the actual body and the virtual image of the 'other' could interact with in real- time. Other artists who have used the self- image of the participant as a way to interact with their image as 'other' is German artists Monika Fleischman and Wolfgang Strauss's (1992/3) *Liquid Views-Narcissus' Mirror*. An interactive video performance/installation using an interactive mirror as a real-time morphing experience. Here the participant looks into a 'well' of water and their face is projected onto the surface of the water in real time. To really encapsulate the feeling of embodiment one looks to the work of Char Davies's (1995) *Osmose*. A real-time video capture of an immersive virtual reality environment using 3D computer graphics. The work uses HMDs and motion tracking of breath and balance reminiscent of scuba diving where one breathes in to float upwards and out to fall downwards to navigate their movement. In Micha Cardenas's (2008) mixed reality performance *Becoming Dragon* in second life she crosses gender, technology and art. Micha wears a HMD for 365 hours and lives her life through the dragon avatar. The performance questions the one-year requirement of 'Real Life Experience' that transgender people must fulfill in order to receive Gender Confirmation Surgery.

Though these artists have been concerned with bridging the gap between art and artist, self and world, artwork and viewer, through video art, media art and performance practice. This research continues to explore the live interactive element of the material body with its real-time digital video image as 'other' within video performance practice and the impact this interaction has on shaping our perception of self. It is less concerned with taking on board identities which we see later on in Sermon's work where he uses telepresence to blur the boundaries between online and offline identities. *In[bodi]mental* is looking towards art practice and digital technology as a meeting place between the corporeal Self and digital Other as way to embody the essence of the digital other as a component of self.

Finding ways to narrow the gap between the body and space/objects has been a focal point for many artists such as the early performance works of Rebecca Horn (1972) *Finger Gloves* – a body wearable that literally extends her body using finger extensions. To the more current practice of digital technology such as Stelarc's (2003) *Exoskeleton* a six legged walking robot where he uses the technology as a body extension. Both these artists control the space between their body and the world. The direction this research is concerned with is perceptually transcending the materiality of the body via the technology and suspending the corporeality of the body *in* the digital other. This may be achieved through stretching the materiality of the body through the phenomenological experience in real-time digital video performance to step into and meet the other through *In[bodi]mental*.

IN[BODI]MENTAL: A VIDEO PERFORMANCE EXPLORATION

As part of the author's practice-led doctoral research *In[bodi]mental* was a video performance exploration placed within The Public located at West Bromwich West Midlands in June 2011. The work invited participants to interact with another person's live digital image in the form of a body swapping experiment. Here participants were asked to work in pairs. Each participant wore a Head Mounted Display system HMD with live video feed. Through the real-time media manipulation programme Isadora each person's live video feed was swapped over and each participant could see through the eyes of the other person. Under the researchers instructions informants were asked to perform a number of small activities which included massaging their legs and knees, stretching out their legs and rotating their feet. Each person took it in turns to lead the other in the performance.

As the HMDs replaced the eyes of the other performer each participant was instructed to keep their display system directed towards the body part in action. These were synchronized movements which occurred at the same time. As directions were given the spectator audiences could see the swapped viewpoint of each of the performers within the large TV monitors placed behind them. The performers were asked to complete a questionnaire to capture their experiences. They were designed to look for indications of embodying another, through the technology where they responded to a number of questions. Further interactions were captured on video during the experience. There were 30 participants who were involved in *In[bodi]mental* across a number of age ranges. The questionnaire consisted of statements placed into three categories: the first category explored how they felt in the experience and the second questioned whether there was an embodiment to the digital counterpart, while the third was based on their awareness of the here and now in the present.

Figure 1. In[bodi]mental
(L. Moore, 2011).

The questionnaires encouraged participants to respond to a number of statements either agreeing, disagreeing or to neither agree nor disagree. These statements were put in place to record their experience and whether they felt embodied to the live image and how much self-awareness they had during this interaction. Due to the high numbers of the public visiting the venue, video interviews would have been too time consuming and problematic to do so. In order to offset this much more emphasis was placed on observing these interactions through video to get a richer understanding of their experience in the moment. The combination of video observations and asking for initial responses, in addition to the questionnaires served as a more convenient method of recording their responses and reactions.

In order to capture the essence of participants' experiences it was important to create a method that was appropriate to both the participants' interactions and the authors. Therefore, a mixed method approach was developed to enable the researcher and the researched to be able to shift focus between these binary positions. The method has been coined 'auto-ethnophenomenology' utilising a combination of auto-ethnographic and phenomenological principles. Whilst 'auto' refers to 'I' and 'ethno' refers to 'a combination of many' this method supported a coming together of the 'I' and other. Though there is a focus on the significance of the 'I' of the researcher this model enabled a viewpoint from both the self/other positions. In doing so the relational aspect between the 'I' and the other could be equally represented.

Part of this methodological framework had come about as a result of the work of ethnographer Carolyn Ellis in her book 'The Ethnographic 'I'. It was Ellis who pioneered auto-ethnography as a way to embrace the 'I' of the researcher and the other subject where the 'I' both looks and is looked at. The reciprocity of these elements have been fundamental to *In[bodi]mental* were the researcher can move in, around and between these positions, alongside the participant's experiences. This has been most pertinent when the researcher has experienced being both the participant and the observed in the work. The phenomenological lived experiences of both the researcher and the researched highlighted a personal journey through the interaction of the work and the art making process. Not only do these video technologies create a catalyst in the making and interacting of video performance it also serves as a contributing factor to enable a cross-over between the theory and the practice. The personal journeys captured on video have informed the research. Also using these tools as a method for self-reflection placed the researcher in both the position of the interactive subject and observed object. Furthermore talking to participants during and after their experience became more mutual experiences where one could come to arrive at a more 'negotiated version of reality' (Pink, 2007, p. 24) Likewise for (Varela,

Thompson, & Rosch, 1993, p. 27) 'Reflection is not just on experience, reflection is a form of experience'. It is where thought impacts experience and experience impacts thought.

The rational for using a HMD was most appropriate for this video exploration in an attempt to suspend the corporeal body within the digital counterpart. Prior to this video exploration analogue video did not have the ability to extend and suspend the body within the video image. Therefore using Isadora, a real-time media manipulation programme, combined with the HMDs had the capabilities to swap the live video feed of each participant to enhance the feeling of being immersed within the other. Having a variety of the general public to experience *In[bodi]mental* was to focus on the lived experience of their interactions with the digital image. Through a culmination of the researchers and participants' experiences the findings were indicating there was a shared reality happening between subjects transposed through the HMD. The following is an extract taken from the researchers field notes:

[…] I felt I was my mum and my mum was me …it was most effective when we had the little ball […] I believe your hands are mine […] It was more convincing my dad's body was on me when we stood up and rubbed stomachs…its very weird […] the more immersive the experience I think the body can be tricked into believing the other body is yours […] This was disorientating but once human contact was made I really did feel more embodied…there was a point when you really don't know whose is whose hands and you come to accept the other person's body as your own […] I felt it was unrealistic and I felt her body was mine…it was also real […] (Moore, 2011, pp. 148-9)

What became apparent was a disturbance in the proprioception of self which caused the subject to gain something more of the self in the digital other as a 'me-not-me-me' experience. The augmentation of the actual body and the digital body resulted in an excess of self that was re-discovered in the other. This phenomenon was a result of the culmination of real-time video technology and synchronized movements that enabled one to become suspended in the image of the other where we perform the other.

The oscillation encountered between the corporeal Self and digital Other can be most understood by comparing Lacan's Mirror Stage to *In[bodi]mental*. The Mirror Stage is a concept developed by Lacan to articulate the emergence of the subject/infant as an individual. It is understood that around the age of eighteen months the child sees its specular image in the mirror for the first time. During this encounter the infant sees the reflected image as part of itself and s/he also feels separated from the image. The paradox the child faces in this stage is being caught between the image of itself as part of its own corporeality and the feeling of fragmentation through its underdeveloped motor neurons. According to Lacan, (1977, pp. 1-7) before this stage the infant feels it is a part of everything, including the mother. The underdeveloped body creates a feeling of dislocation from the mother and the world. In order to compensate for this loss of attachment the infant misrecognises itself as a separate object to avoid the trauma of this loss. This is where the infant becomes a split subject - an individual always looking for a sense of self in the other. For Lacan when one enters into the world of language (the symbolic) we lose the real. What is interesting about Lacan's Mirror Stage is the way the corporeal body in *In[bodi]mental* felt dislocated from where it was stood, causing a feeling of disorientation. This is analogous to the underdeveloped motor neurons in the infant in the Mirror Stage. Furthermore the shift in the projected body from 'here to there' had disrupted ones sense of perception and the body's perceived place of standing. This disruption may be a contributing factor in feeling disconnected from one place but more connected in the other. The experience of *In[bodi]mental* enabled participants to become suspended between subject and object, self and other via the real time technologies ability to swap each other's viewpoint from the view of the other.

It was more revealing that the more the movements were synchronized the greater the feeling of be[ing] in the body of the other. Be[ing] in this sense is understood as literally being in the body of another. The researcher's interactions in this exploration were, at times the belief that the other person's body was her own. This was stronger during synchronized movements. Though she felt the other body was her own she did not feel transported into their body and disown her own body. What came out of this exploration was a strong connection to the digital counterpart through synchronous movements. The participants were very quick to intuitively copy each other under instructions. The following is a statement from the researcher's experience.

[…]I really did feel that her hand and legs where mine especially when our movements where synchronised. She started to draw with a pen on her hand and that was weird for me because I believed it was my hand – I really felt it. I poured hand cream into my hands and rubbed it in and she said she could feel the cream on her hands […] (Moore, 2011, pp. 148-9)

Synchronicity and mimicry was a contributing factor in feeling suspended in the other. The boundary between the corporeal Self and digital Other had been crossed over enabling participants to experience be[ing] in both states of selfhood and object-hood. These cross-overs go beyond the realm of video performance and can be identified in other areas of discourse. For example, body suspension between these modalities has appeared in other areas of research such as mimesis (a phrase often associated with mimicry and/or imitation).

The psychology of mimesis can be described as a condition that is neither divided through difference, nor fused with sameness. It is a state that can and has been used to describe a state of 'being' between these two positions. This is best articulated by anthropologist Rane Willerslev who observed the cultural and hunting rituals of the Siberian Yukaghirs who used mimicry to capture their prey. In his account of the hunting rituals of the Yukaghirs when they go hunting for their Elk he describes the hunters occupying a betwixt place. A state between substance and non-substance, between animal and hunter that assists in the similitude of sameness and difference. The Yukaghirs enter into relations with their prey without being transformed into something else and/or losing oneself within the prey. They achieve this through mimicking the Elk and refrain from speaking in human language. This gives the hunter a liminal quality … 'he was not elk, and yet he was also not not elk. He was occupying a strange place in between human and nonhuman identities' (Willerslev, 2007, p. 11). Here the hunter is not the 'real' Elk and when he transforms himself into an imitation of the Elk he is still not an Elk. As an imitator the self can enter into relations with its 'other' without being transformed into something else or losing itself within the 'other'. Without the mediation of the self through the 'other' there would be no conception of self as such. The imitator can be in contact with the world of other bodies, things and people and also separate himself from them by forcing himself to reflexively turn in on himself (Willerslev, 2007, p. 26). If one compares the hunting rituals of the Yukaghirs with participants' experiences in *In[bodi]mental* we can see the way mimicry and synchronicity has a strong connection with the digital Other.

[…] It was a weird good experience….very interesting…really clever…it was quite convincing that it was my body (my dad's that is). It was more convincing my dad's body was on me when we stood up and rubbed stomachs together…it was very weird […]

[…] I felt it was most effective when we were standing up…its quite strange…after a while you try to synchronize yourself and match the action intuitively…I feel the more immersive the experience I think the body can be tricked into believing the other body is yours…I would say it was initially a strange experience […]

[…] The more it's synchronized the more you doubt your feelings […] (Moore, 2011, p. 173)

For the Yukaghirs the liminality of the threshold between self and other (the betwixt) is through mimicry. One can use the same analogy of mimicry for the participants in *In[bodi]mental* where they too are in an in-between condition – a state between self and other. This is compounded by participants' intuition to copy each other which appeared to cause a feeling of disorientation. This disorientation resonates with Lacan's Mirror Stage when the infant feels dislocated from itself in a state of recognition/misrecognition. The lack of oral language for the Yukaghirs brought them closer to the animal, whilst the lack of oral language for Lacan's infant in the Mirror Stage caused him/her to feel connected to the mother and the world. The reliance on vision and mimicry in *In[bodi]mental* rather than language has also brought participants closer to the other. In *In[bodi]mental* subjects were caught between the corporeal Self and the digital Other. We see a reflexive turn when informants copy and synchronize themselves with the digital counterpart. Their responses articulated a suspended belief in the other body image as their own were the corporeal Self was not lost in the digital Other. Participants had performed the other where it had simultaneously maintained its sameness and difference. This awareness of imitating the other had enabled participants to reflexively turn in on oneself which makes it impossible to fuse with the object - a state that is neither cut off in difference nor fused with sameness. The inauguration between the physical body and its digital counterpart had contributed to the body to transpose itself from physical self to other self, mediated through the process of imitation and the digital technology. This is understood as a form of mimesis.

How subjectivity and identity is constructed has been an important contribution of Lacanian theory to contemporary cultural studies. Similarly we can also see his Mirror Stage having a major contribution to digital culture. The relationship between Willerslev and Lacan throughout this research has been the result of co-existing in a betwixt state between self and other. These theories are not based on a metamorphosis where one becomes something other. They are understanding the movement and oscillation between states of experience which digital technology has afforded us.

The Chiasmus ∞: The Intersection of the Actual and the Digital in In[bodi]mental

Before the inception of digital technology the binary oppositions of self and other has mainly been a literary discourse rather than a pre-occupation of the lived experience in the context of live interactive video. These perceived divisions have historically been constructed within philosophical and theoretical discourse. As a way of breaking with those traditions *In[bodi]mental* draws on Merleau-Ponty and his work on the chiasm to challenge these concepts through the art practice where the corporeal body and its digital counterpart intersect. Merleau-Ponty explains the chiasm within a phenomenological context where he uses the term as a metaphor of skin to express the intricate and interlaced relationship between the lived body and the world. With Its Greek interpretation *chiasma* coming from the Greek letter x Merleau-Ponty refers to the chiasmus as a crisscross structure which he articulates as a 'double and crossed situating of the visible in the tangible and the tangible in the visible' which is articulated as an intertwining where 'the two maps are complete and yet they do not merge into one. The two parts are total parts and yet are not superposable … the chiasm is a 'reciprocal insertion and intertwining' of the seeing body in the visible body and 'Since the same body sees and touches, visible and tangible belong to the same world' Merleau-Ponty (1968, p. 134). We are both subject and object simultaneously where our 'flesh' merges with the flesh, that is the world. (Merleau-Ponty, 1968, p. 138).

Drawing on Merleau-Ponty to example the position between the corporeal Self and the digital Other in *In[bodi]mental* serves as a way forward to illustrate his chiasm as a tangible experience. When we refer to participants' experiences we can see the dynamics of the corporeal body and its digital counterpart which creates a self-reflexive interface. Here there are indications of no boundaries between them; where each is reflected in the other. This reversibility is a form of reflection which Merleau-Ponty has described as an 'extraordinary overlapping' or chiasm, (Merleau-Ponty, 1964, p. 162). The metaphor of his chiasm is something dancer and theorist Susan Kozel has articulated geometrically as the mobius strip or a sliding figure of eight. For Kozel vision is embodied and we operate according to the 'touching-touch'… and 'just as I see and what I see sees me back… I touch and I am touched by objects'… (Kozel, 2007, p. 37). 'Since the same body sees and touches, visible and tangible belong to the same world' (Merleau-Ponty, 1968, p. 134).

What has been most profound about *In[bodi]mental* is the way one interprets the materiality of the digital other through the digital technology. The technology has indeed connected subjects in such a way that one experienced a cross-over between the tangible and the visible. Touch through vision was most exampled in the following accounts were participants expressed a belief that the other body was theirs through the HMDs …"Whenever I moved she copied…I felt like I was her" … "I believe your hands are mine" (Moore, 2011, p. 174). For the first time participants were able to literally see through the eyes of the other and

see oneself from the other's point of view. These experiences heightened the capacity of being both a subject and an object through the act of seeing. Borrowing from Merleau-Ponty, 'I see and I am also seen'. He incorporated the idea that I see the world and the world sees me, objects look back at me and this is the 'seeing seen' (Merleau-Ponty, 1964, p. 2).

The reversibility of Merleau-Ponty's 'seeing seen' has become a morphed experience via the HMDs. Here we experience a shared consciousness where the boundaries are so blurred we believe we are a part of the digital other. To illustrate this cross-over the infinite symbol of the mobius strip is re-presented in *In[bodi]mental* where the irreversibility between the corporeal body and its digital counterpart intersect and overlap. Their exchange is in 'a constant sliding state along a twisting figure-of-eight' (Kozel, 2007, pp. 36-37). Due to the exchange of one image replaced by another in real-time participants are both suspended in each other's image and momentarily morphed as one shared body. Both subjects do not lose their sense of self in the other but momentarily forget their body and adopt the other body as part of their selfhood. This is understood as a new experience of be[ing] in the world.

The mobius strip is an appropriate image to interpret materiality to reconcile the divisions between the corporeal Self and digital Other within digital performance practice. According to Kozel the mobius strip is a figure which subverts our normal way of representing space. The two sides of the mobius strip look different from our own perspective but are one single surface. In accordance with Merleau-Ponty and Kozel when the strip is traversed the two sides become one continuum where it is impossible to locate the cross over between the inside and outside. By locating the chiasm within the symbol of the Mobius strip the binary oppositions between self and other are constantly reflected in each other as one continuous framework. The cross-over of the lived body and the world, the actual body and the digital image are all caught up in an infinite chiasmic process. There is no beginning and no end just a constant figure of eight. What we experience in *In[bodi] mental* is the way in which the digital folds back into and changes our perception of the actual body. For some participants the experience was more real than real – a kind of hyperreality. The culmination of two digital counterparts compounded the crossover of selves transposed through the HMDs. The following quote by Merleau-Ponty really does summarize this hyperreality written pre-digital age:

[…] as upon two mirrors facing one another where two indefinite series of images set in one another arise which belong really to neither of the two surfaces, since each is only the rejoinder of the other, and which therefore form a couple, a couple more real than either of them […] (Merleau-Ponty, 1968, p. 138).

This quote by Merleau-Ponty summarizes to some extent the experience of some participants in *In[bodi]mental*. At least 50% of users said they felt they were in a heightened reality and another 50% said they felt the other person's body felt real to them. This hyperreal sensation may be compounded through the unexplained desire to synchronize and mimic the digital counterpart where we are performing the other. One puts forward our desire to mimic the digital image is symptomatic of our need to empathize with the digital counterpart. It is through performing the other through mimicry we come to empathize with the image as our own. Those involved in this video exploration have articulated how we come to observe how it feels to move like the digital counterpart. Merleau-Ponty speculated there was touch in vision, *In[bodi]mental* has enabled us to In[body] touch through vision via the HMDs. The materiality of one body has been stretched across another where we are not only touched by the other but identify with it as part of our self where we have in[bodied] the other. The term

in[body] has been coined by the author to refer to a perceived experience where one feels they are *in* the body of another.

Experiencing the world for Merleau-Ponty is seeing and being seen. This view was developed by Lacan in his seminar XI but coming from a different perspective. Merleau-Ponty articulated a reversibility of seeing which enables the subject to see the world - and see the world through the other. For Lacan there is a fundamental separation between the eye and the gaze where we are not conscious subjects viewing the world but are already 'beings that are looked at' (1979 [1973], pp. 74-5). In other words the subject sees from one point of view whilst sh/e is looked at from all sides. Cultural theorist Slavoj Zizek, a pioneer in film theory states … "the eye viewing the object is on the side of the subject, while the gaze is on the side of the object. When I look at an object, the object is always already gazing at me, and from a point at which I cannot see it" (Zizek, 1992, p. 109). The cross-over between the subject/object for Merelau-Ponty is well documented in *In[bodi] mental*. There is no division between the corporeal Self and the digital Other. It has been through digital performance that Merleau-Ponty's ideas have been brought alive. We encounter the visible and the tangible belonging to the same body/world. However what is interesting in another return to Lacan when we discuss the hyperreality that participants/performers encountered which appears to be analogous to Lacan's impossible Real. The Real for Lacan is beyond the symbolic world of language. It is something that is unsymbolizable which cannot be reached and the moment we enter into language we lose the real. During the intersection between the actual and the digital it may be we experience an excess of self (something we lost during our journey into language which we have now rekindled through the other). The hyperreal experience may indeed be a brush with the Real for a moment. This research discovered links with the feeling of uncanniness and a hyper-real experience. The more the uncanny was expressed the more the really real experience. Though the Uncanny is pertinent to this research it is beyond the scope of this chapter, the relationship between the uncanny and the real as a hyper-real experience requires exploration

A Shared Self

As a result of *In[bodi]mental* a communal sharing of selves has been experienced. Here, there has been an in[bodi]ment of two bodies each feeling they are in the body of the other whilst also maintaining their own sense of self. This perceived stretching of material corporeality from one body across into another has magnified a new sense of be[ing] in the world- an alternative to becoming something other. The notion of 'being both' self and other at the same time is pertinent to the 'betwixt' state of being that Rane Willerslev articulates in his account of the Yukaghirs hunting rituals (2007). However this condition of 'being both' also resonates with Roy Ascott, a pioneer in telematic art and a seminal theorist in the field of new media art.

In *Syncretic Reality; art, process, and potentiality* Ascott (2005) discusses the impact new media art has on our reality and the way 'syncretic reality' is both construed and constructed by new media art practice. The syncretic is articulated as distinct to binary oppositions described by Ascott as 'a process between different elements, the in-between condition of 'being both'… 'In the syncretic context, extreme differences are upheld but aligned' in such a way 'that likeness is found amongst unlike things' were 'the power of each element' enriches 'the power of all others within the array of their differences,' (Ascott, 2005, p. 1). Ascott's syncretic has also been evidenced in *In[bodi]mental* were we find ourselves immersed within the digital counterpart and experience the other as part of self. We were in a process between the different self-other elements where we did not meld into a homogenous whole losing our individuality, instead we experienced more of us in

the other while retaining our own sense of self – a composite self, augmented and mediated through the HMDs. Not only does the self, distribute itself through telematic networks according to Ascott it is an evolutionary development towards the multiple self – a 'multiplicity not just of (virtual/cyborg) bodies but of attitudes, values, intentions and purposes' (Ascott, 2005, p. 9) .Viewing the self from this perspective we may be able to understand how aspects of the self can move from person to person. The notion of the 'self' moving from person to person is articulated by writers and architects Robert Sumrell and Kazys Varnelis (2007) in their book *Blue Mondays: Stories of Absurd Realities and Natural Philosophies.*

[…] In order to function within contemporary cities we have all become human chameleons without a sense of home. Beyond merely moving from place to place, we move from self to self according to the social conditions we find ourselves in […] (Sumrell, & Varnelis, 2007, p. 144).

It is through emerging digital technologies we are witnessing a shift from one self to another were we are co-habiting experience and making a shift in our perception of self. What was once perceived as the home of the self, bounded within the constraints of the physical body, it is now moving across the corporeal and the digital. According to Ascott (2005) it is the ritual of habit forming which is the enemy of art which impedes the search for new ways of being, while conversely, the syncretic process is an assault on habit. Using new digital video technology has enabled us to disrupt the proprioception of the body and break those learnt habits of our own selfhood which may assist in our ability to experience more of self in the other. In *In[bodi]mental* one can perform a part of the other self which is also part of another. We experience this as a 'live chiasm' – a tangibility of the other-self channeled through the HMD which satisfies our infinite process to reproduce ourselves through the other. The binary divisions between self-other, subject and object have been temporarily suspended in *In[bodi]mental* were each is implicated in the other. The 'mixing together' of the corporeal Self and the digital Other will inevitably contribute to our understanding of the composite self through mixed-reality technology where the awareness of a syncretic self (the in-between condition of being both self and other) may become the norm of our experience.

FUTURE RESEARCH DIRECTIONS OF INTER-CORPOREAL EXPERIENCES

This chapter has focused on the interaction between the participant and real-time video within video performance practice and not on the gaming world of video interaction. It is important to note that the author does see a connection between these two disciplines. However the direction this research moved in was informed from a background in fine art exploring real-time video representations of the self and not virtual avatars that mirror the physical self. This does not suggest that the discourse surrounding gaming is not a valuable contribution to digital art practice. On the contrary, as *In[bodi] mental* develops in the future, using Google Glass, Microsoft's Kinect for Xbox 360 in addition to real-time body mapping technology is a way forward to develop the in[bodi]ment of subjects. It has been through creative practice this chapter has demonstrated the innovative way digital media has been used in video performance. Real-time video programs such as Isadora, and other emerging technologies such as Arduino and Makey Makey are enabling artists to use these technologies to create artwork that may have not been possible. The real-time capability of Isadora in conjunction with HMDs made this video exploration a reality. The emergence of google cardboard for example is an economically viable way to use a wireless HMD using a smart phone. This DIY cardboard template is an amazing use of simple design and

innovative idea – to make your own HMD out of cardboard. Having access to these much affordable tools are going to have a major impact on the way we view each other and the world. This chapter has set about exploring the collaboration between the corporeal body and digital technology as an inter-corporeal experience. It touched on the relationship between the Lacanian Real and the Uncanny as a hyper-real experience. It is important to highlight that the experience of the uncanny is pertinent to this research but beyond the scope of this chapter and therefore a forthcoming chapter to be written.

The future of this practice-led research will continue to search for new ways to create a seamless cross-over between the corporeal Self and the digital Other to realize inter-corporeal experiences. This includes drawing on philosophical approaches that has informed the gaming industry and game interaction. The desire to make visible the invisible (experience) is a constant theme throughout the author's art practice/research. Current work includes bio sensing technology to capture the participant within the moment of interactive absorption. The in[bodi]ment of the participant within video performance will remain a challenge in order to suspend participants in the zone of visual contemplation. The consciousness of the zone has been well researched through the work of American psychologist Mihaly Csikszentmihalyi of Hungarian decent, who in the mid1970s explored the creative processes of artists and sculptures. He interviewed a variety of people in sports and the arts and many described these experiences as a 'continuous flowing' which Csikszentmihalyi named as 'flow experiences' (2008). According to Csikszentmihalyi these states of consciousness are focused and ordered, allowing the subject to carry out complex activities with a sensation of intense enjoyment and ease. Though Csikszentmihalyi's work on 'flow' is very much associated with game designers; by seeking 'flow' in the user experience of video performance the author makes analogies between Csikszentmihalyi's understanding of the 'zone' and be[ing] in the moment as an in[bodi]ed experience.

The cooperation between theory and practice is collapsing the space between subjects and objects and moving us closer to seeing and feeling these imperceptible experiences, enabled through new digital technologies to interpret materiality. In doing so, digital media is not only having a profound impact on the way we are coming to understand more about the self within video performance practice but it is altering our viewpoint in our day-to-day living. The legacy of *In[bodi]mental* has contributed to this insightful book to highlight one of the many ways these technologies are creatively being used by artists in the here and now. To move this research forward exploring Biometric technology and Neuro-technology using the EPOC emotive neuro-headsets; these technologies have the potential to create more inter-corporeal experiences between participants and the work to interpret ones materiality

CONCLUSION

This chapter has articulated the way emerging technologies are blurring the perceived boundaries between the lived body and the experienced world. It has outlined the way we are so accustomed to viewing the world from fixed viewpoints that we have become less aware of the way we intersect with others. This intersection has been deliberated through an unconscious cross-over between self and the world viewed through the lens of our stationary viewpoints that obstruct our awareness of the chiasm. It has been through a disruption in the proprioception of the body that one can challenge pre-conceived relationships with ourselves and the world. This is not to say we do not experience our perception of self in the way others interact with us, but from literal viewpoints as well.

Experiencing *In[bodi]mental* has enabled participants to have a double perspective on our perception of self where we see ourselves seeing ourselves similar to an out of body experience. However what is most significant is that the reality we have been familiar with has now been undermined and we may be experiencing a reality that is more real than the self we have come to know. A hyperreal self-experienced in the other – a brush with the Lacanian Real enhanced through an uncanny experience. In addition the discussion has reconsidered the way the corporeal body and its live digital counterpart intersect and the impact this relationship has on ones perception of self. These crossovers are revealing the way in which the phenomenological lived experiences of subjects can bleed into each other enabled by the digital technology. Using HMDs, where the live video feed had been swapped over, enabled subjects to see themselves from the view of the other. This occurrence created a union between phenomenology, anthropology and psychoanalysis using mimicry and empathy to understand the way these different approaches have mutually enriched subjects to create selves that are maturing out of each other. It has been through the technology that we can come to understand more about what constitutes the self and the way the self, moves from one body to another transposed through the technology. The alignment of body matter and digital media makes it even harder to presume we are divided from each other through binary oppositions.

The in[body] experience of *In[bodi]mental* has brought to life Merleau-Ponty's chiasm were the tangible and the visible are caught up in each other in the same way as Willerslev's hunter is in a betwixt place between substance and non-substance. In this work we have been encapsulated in the self of the other which we have experienced as part of ourselves. Though Lacan claims we are always looking for a sense of self in the other which we have lost through the symbolic this video exploration may explain a return to the Mirror Stage. Rather than becoming a divided subject this research proclaims that the experience in *In[bodi]mental* took us beyond the self were we encountered more of the self in the other. This hyperreality has been explained as a step closer to the real – a primordial connection beyond the self which we can only access through the other. A disturbance in the proprioception of our corporeal body was enhanced through the technology forcing the body to search for new ways of be[ing] to break down learnt habits and rituals to challenge ones perceptions. In doing so turning our attention towards the plurality of a multiple self serves as a move in the right direction in understanding what constitutes the self. Rather than viewing the corporeal Self and the digital Other as separate entities this research has revealed that by approaching these binary oppositions as elements which contribute to the multiplicity of self within the field of digital performance practice we can understand the way the self, is a porous entity which bleeds into the digital other and impacts on our own selfhood. Therefore it may be through digital performance that our desire to mimic our empathetic relations with others, may provide the link between these opposing elements which unites us and enables us to share a phenomenology of each other. It might be that our desire to reproduce ourselves through performing the other by way of mimicry is the way the self evolves from one person to the other.

REFERENCES

Ascott, R. (2005). Syncretic reality: Art, process, and potentiality. *Drain*. Retrieved from: http://drainmag.com/index_nov.htm

Cardenna, M. (2008). *Becoming dragon*. Retrieved from https://www.youtube.com/watch?v=pHEDym1aOZs

Csikszentmihalyi, M. (2008). *Flow: The psychology of optimal experience*. Harper Perennial Modern Classics.

Davies, C. (1995). *Osmose*. Retrieved from http://www.immersence.com/osmose/

Ellis, C. (2004). *The ethnographic 'I': A methodological novel about autoethnography*. Walnut Creek, CA: Altamira Press.

Fleischmann, M., & Strauss, W. (1992). *Liquid views – Narcissus' mirror*. Retrieved from http://www.eculturefactory.de/CMS/index.php?id=419

Horn, R. (1972). *Finger gloves*. Retrieved from http://rebeccahornart.blogspot.co.uk/2009/11/finger-gloves-1973.html

Kozel, S. (2007). *Closer: Performance, technologies, phenomenology*. MIT Press.

Lacan, J. (1977). The mirror stage as formative of the function of the I as revealed in psychoanalytic experience. In *Ecrits: A selection* (A. Sheridan, Trans.). London: Routledge, Tavistock. (Original work published 1949)

Lacan, J. (1979). The seminar of Jacques Lacan, book XI: The four fundamental concepts of psychoanalysis 1964-1965. (J. A. Miller, Ed.; A. Sheridan, Trans.). Harmondsworth, UK: Penguin.

Merleau-Ponty, M. (1964). Eye and mind. In The primacy of perception (C. Dallery, Trans.; pp. 159-190). Northwestern University Press.

Merleau-Ponty, M. (1968). The intertwining-The chiasm. In C. Lefort (Ed.), The visible and the invisible: Philosophical interrogation (A. Lingis, Trans.; pp. 130–155). Evanston, IL: Northwestern University Press.

Moore, L. (2013). *In[bodying] the other: Performing the digital other as a component of self through real-time video performance*. (Unpublished doctoral dissertation). University of Wolverhampton, Wolverhampton, UK.

Pink, S. (2007). *Doing visual ethnography* (2nd ed.). Sage publications.

Sermon, P. (1992). *Telematic dreaming*. An exhibition curated by the Finnish Ministry of Culture in Kajaani, with support from Telecom Finland, in June 1992. Retrieved from http://creativetechnology.salford.ac.uk/paulsermon/dream/

Stelarc. (2003) *Exoskeleton*. 2nd Biennale of Contemporary Art in Goteborg Museum of Art, Goteborg, Sweden. Retrieved from http://stelarc.org/video/?catID=20258

Sumrell, R., & Varnelis, K. (2007). Love: In Blue monday: Stories of absurd realities and natural philosophies (pp. 134-144). Actar Publishers.

Varela, F. J., Thompson, E., & Rosche, E. (1993). The embodied mind: Cognitive science and human experience. Cambridge, MA: The MIT Press.

Willerslev, R. (2007). *Soul hunters: Hunting, animism, and personhood among the Siberian Yukaghirs*. Ewing, NJ: University of California Press. doi:10.1525/california/9780520252165.001.0001

Zizek, S. (1992). *Looking awry: An introduction to Jacques Lacan through popular culture*. Cambridge, MA: The MIT Press.

KEY TERMS AND DEFINITIONS

Auto-Ethnophenomenology: Has been defined as a way of reflecting on perceptions of lived experience from both positions of the observer and the observed, 'I' and 'other'. It is a method which incorporates self-reflexive study and the lived experience of others.

Be[ing]: To experience being *in* the moment in the 'here and now'.

Chiasm: An entwinement between the corporeal body and the digital other.

Corporeal Self: The physical body as self.

Digital Other: A digital representation of oneself. It is also understood as an entity outside the materiality of self which is separate, different and alien – understood as a virtual representation. It is through this research the digital 'other' can be defined as part of the materiality of oneself transposed through the digital video image where matter and media are aligned.

In[bodi]ment or In[body]: The term is defined as literally feeling/believing one is inside another body.

Inter-Corporeal: The belief that two physical bodies are sharing the same experience.

Proprioception: The way the body senses its position within space.

Chapter 3
Big Data – Small World:
Materializing Digital Information for Discourse and Cognition

Ian Gwilt
Sheffield Hallam University, UK

ABSTRACT

This chapter furthers discourse between digital data content and the creation of physical artifacts based on an interpretation of the data. Building on original research by the author, the chapter asks the questions: why should we consider translating digital data into a physical form? And what happens to how we understand, read, and relate to digital information when it is presented in this way? The author discusses whether or not the concept of the data-driven object is simply a novel visualization technique or a useful tool to add insight and accessibly to the complex language of digital data sets, for audiences unfamiliar with reading data in more conventional forms. And the author explores the issues connected to the designing of data into the material world, including fabrication techniques such as 3D printing and craft-based making techniques, together with the use of metaphor and visual language to help communicate and contextualize data.

INTRODUCTION

In the 1990's the arrival of domestic computing and mainstream digital technologies signaled the start of a concerted effort to digitize all forms of creative, cultural and scientific content from the past, present and future. Two decades on the digital is a fully integrated meta-form that drives many of our communication tools, social activities and work practices (Gwilt, 2010). After this initial wave of digital integration, more careful consideration as to the relationship between our

physicality, environmental surroundings and material artifacts, and how this links with a range of digital technologies is beginning to take place. A reconsideration of biological necessities and the recognition of the human hardwiring into Euclidian space has begun to raise questions about the singularity of digital culture. As yet the promise of a transcendent digital virtual reality has failed to live up to expectations and a new way of interacting with the digital is beginning to unfold. In the computer games world game-play has been combined with gestural interfaces where play-

DOI: 10.4018/978-1-4666-8205-4.ch003

ers can see the unmediated expressions of their competitors. Biomorphic forms in architecture and product design signal a new zeitgeist in urban design as digital technologies have developed the processing power to model and visualize the complex curvilinear shapes and patterns found in nature. In the built environment everyday objects such as chairs and automobiles are increasingly enabled with sensors and user-feedback technologies that can respond to and even pre-empt our individual needs and relationship with the physical world. The Internet of things is becoming a reality, realized through digital connectivity and the concept of 'everything, all the time'. Sensing technologies are capable of remotely collecting our every interaction and this capacity plays an important role in the big data revolution. Wireless mobile technologies have moved the experiences of the digital computer into the street and the public arena where their use is becoming increasingly commonplace, connecting the digital with real-world events and locating our engagement with computing technologies into real-time social, cultural and political contexts. These distributed, pervasive digital technologies are beginning to have a major impact on the fabric of society, from how we access healthcare, to how we do our shopping, work, travel, and communicate.

The technological and perceptual dispersal of the digital computer from something that sits on the office desk, into increasingly embedded, distributed and multiform constructs, also disarms the often talked about binary opposition between the digital and the physical. As computing technologies become increasingly located and related to place and social contexts of use, the potentials for the digital to augment and interact with material culture become more opportune. In terms of information visualization this closer relationship does two things: it provides new opportunities for content forms; and drives the desire for data visualizations that speak to both our real-world and digital interactions. The cultural theorist Pierre Levy (1998) refers to this diverse range of digital

integration as a type of accelerated techno-cultural heterogenesis. The shift in emphasis back toward the physical does not however, mean that we are about to give up the connectivity, convenience and enabling potential of our digital technologies. Although the experiences promised by immersive virtual reality have yet to find a place in our mainstream engagement with computers, the types of informed digital/material constructs described in this paper are beginning to gain wide spread recognition. Terms like augmented, and mixed reality are increasingly being used to describe a set of relationships, technologies and expectations for a variety of combined, digital/material constructs. These neologisms are becoming part of the public vocabulary in an increasingly technologized society.

Predictably then, the tendency toward the materialization of the digital is also occurring in the area of computer-based information visualization, which is in itself a relatively new phenomenon. The materialization of digital data is facilitated by the development of a number of new manufacturing technologies such as 3D printing and Rapid Prototyping techniques that allow for the translation of digital data into physical forms. I will discuss the potential of these techniques later in the chapter through a number of applied examples. In the next two sections we will continue with a short overview of contemporary data collection and information visualization.

DATA COLLECTION, BIG DATA

Digital technologies continue to provide numerous embedded data collecting points that glean information from our everyday interactions with the world, both analogue and digital. The data trails of people, computers, economies, healthcare services, communication and leisure activities are leading to an exponential growth in the gathering of data, which is now measured in exabytes. This proliferation of information has seen the rise of big data, an open-ended term that alludes to the scale, variety of forms, and rapidity of contemporary data collection. There are a number of data management and analysis software tools that can be used to collect and present data sets, and different parametric and data configurations allow for a variety of sorting, ordering and comparative activities to take place. However, the scale of big data means that common statistical and clustering techniques typically used for two and three dimensional data now needs to accommodate highly multidimensional data from a variety of different, 'messy' sources to explore and reveal trends (Illinsky & Steele, 2011). The potential to cross reference large-scale data-sets is a key feature of big data that has caused much debate about how we draw meaning by combining data from a variety of sources and in different forms to indicate relationships (Mayer-Schönberger & Cukier, 2013). The argument being that if we embrace the sheer density of available data, and its continuing supply, it is possible to computationally predict patterns and trends and causes; conversely, it is argued that we still need to examine the socio-cultural, economic, political and environmental contexts to any relationships that might be revealed in multidimensional data-fields (Graham, 2012; Mayer-Schönberger & Cukier, 2013).

The visualization of data brings another level of subjectivity to our interpretation and understanding of data and the problem of how to visualize complex multidimensional data is only recently being addressed (Yua, 2013). The visual languages, syntax and techniques of visualizing big data are still very much in development and the challenge of data-visualization both digital and physical is to make meaningful interpretations that can be understood.

Data Visualization

The disciplines of digital information visualization and information design have witnessed a phenomenal growth in the last 15 to 20 years (Card,

Mackinlay, & Shneiderman, 1999; Ware, 2004; Klanten, Ehmann, Tissot, & Bourquin, 2010), and as digital data has become more accessible, designers and other professionals have taken to the task of visually interpreting this data with gusto. This interest is evidenced in work and publications such as Klanten's, 'Data flow: visualising information in graphic design' (2008), 'Information is beautiful' (McCandless, 2012), and 'Infographica: the world as you have never seen it before', by Toseland and Toseland (2012). The bread and butter content of conventional data visualizations such as scientific, political, environmental and economic statistics, now sit side-by-side with visualizations and measurements of social networking patterns, Internet distribution arrays, transportation usage, and even more idiosyncratic content such as visits to fast food outlets or personal coffee consumption. Nicholas Felton is an example of a designer who creatively visualizes his daily routines and other events, which are published as 'personal annual reports' (Felton, 2014). A huge range of visual representation techniques are employed in contemporary information visualization practices including the use of: bar charts; graphs; diagrams; illustrations; 3D models; maps; animations; generative and interactive visualizations, designed for onscreen and print-based consumption, and within these techniques decisions around: the use of colour; graphical qualities of line; the position, scale and layout of items; use of typography, and other media elements, all play a part in helping to communicate data and information.

However, information design as a practice has a long history prior to the invention of the digital computer and we can trace the desire to visualize information back to the earliest forms of mark making and symbolic languages. Tufte (1983) attests to the fact that abstract visualization of quantitative, statistical data did not really come about until the mid 18th Century when tabular data was first replaced by charts and graphics. According to Pauwels (2006) the visualization of scientific findings is a fundamental part of scientific discourse. Pauwels' proposition underlines the importance of data visualization as a tool for aiding cognition and following on from this, the importance of making the appropriate visualization design decisions. The majority of data visualizations are primarily concerned with the presentation of quantitative data, but Tufte's suggestion that the minimal use of visual elements should be used to communicate the maximum amount of data, has at times been forgotten. This could be due in part to the range of visualization capabilities of the modern day computer, and the desire of data visualizers to make use of them all. Moreover, he suggests visual elements in information visualization should perform a dual purpose, carrying information, and communicating something about that information (Tufte, 1983). Notwithstanding this advice, Manuel Lima in his 'Information Visualization Manifesto' suggests that unlike design in the material world, where form is regarded to follow function, in the digital domain "form does not follow data" (Lima, 2009), or in other words that data does not necessarily dictate form. This concept of 'incongruent data' suggests that any number of visualizations can be made from the same data set, and that any visualization is able to make an equal claim on veracity or appropriateness. This has of course been the case in analogue media too, but the scope and range of formats made available within digital computing has extended these choices dramatically. Combining this sudden expansion of choice, with the ease of production inherent in the digital and the potential dislocation between form and function, also goes some way to explain the plethora of new data visualizations that have appeared over the last decade or so, some of which have attracted criticism for being unnecessary, meaningless or at worst unintelligible. Lima and others however, recommend that information visualizations should at their core provide insight or clarity. This directive can be used as a way of legitimizing design decision-making. Presaging Lima's suggestions, Card et al. (1999), asserted that from a Human Computer Interaction (HCI)

perspective, information visualization is "…the use of computer-supported interactive, visual representations of abstract data to amplify cognition" (p.7). Furthermore, the champion of information aesthetics, Andrew Vande Moere foregrounds the democratizing potential that information visualization tools can have as an inclusive communication device (Klanten et al., 2010). Given the wealth of choice offered by computing technologies the idea that every effort should be made to achieve a contextual or sympathetic connectivity between the use and design of data visualizations and the underlying data is a logical one. In the following section I will examine in some detail how the property norms of digital and material culture might be considered in an attempt to amplify cognition through a relationship of data and form.

Attributes and Properties of Digital and Natural Forms

The actualising of a digital data-set into a physical object may initially seem paradoxical, since by fixing digital data in time and physical space we would appear to disable much of the dynamic potential inherent in computer technologies. However, by realizing a digital data set as a physical object we can begin to consider and exploit the attributes and properties that are typically assigned to both digital and material cultures. A key challenge for the data-driven object is to usefully combine any number of possible relationships between digital traits such as dynamism, complexity, interconnectivity, mutability and so on, and the material properties inherent in the physical object such as tactility and notions of uniqueness, preciousness/value (in both economic and socio-cultural terms), durability, and provenance. The concept of the data-object invites us to apply a new information communication typology wherein an articulated object could be populated with information that would exploit both digital and material attributes to the benefit of a range of social, educational, scientific and economic stakeholders.

Table 1. Ontological/epistemological qualities of the data-object

Material Properties	Digital Attributes
Tangible	Networked
Unique	Multiple
Precious	Disposable
Fixed	Dynamic
Present	Remote
Historic	Technological
Patinated	Mutable

© 2014, Ian Gwilt (Used with permission).

The articulations of the data-object attempt to combine both echoes of the digital alongside the benefits of the material properties inherent in the physical. By creating a physical data-object we can hopefully use a combination of physical and digital traits to encode, communicate and point to relationships in the underlying data (Table 1).

Understandably though, there are tensions formed when we create physical objects from digital data sets. This fusion of properties from both paradigms can lead to a perceived compromise in the expectations or benefits we associate with the discrete digital data or material artifact. However, as suggested the dialogic exchange between digital information and material form can establish new potentials for reading and interacting with these articulated objects. Nevertheless we should not understate the fundamentally ontological and epistemological differences that frame our understanding of digital and material cultures. Reconciling these differences at a cultural level is beyond the data artifact, but what the data artifact does do is act as a point of confluence where those differences can be challenged or explored. Take for example, notions of time and space, which have particular associations in both the digital and material realm. Within the digital the concept of space or 'taking up space' is abstracted, we talk about large and small file sizes in the computer memory but this space is hard to visualize. Con-

versely the physicality of an object clearly shows size and the occupation of space. The 'physical' perception of scale, and size is something we are much more attuned to in material culture and is a property that can be explored in the creation of a data artifact. Similarly, spatial relationships and how we order, sort and arrange items within both digital and material cultures also have their own established conventions and are equally important considerations for how we visualize data as form.

Notions of time are also particular to digital and material cultures. When we think of time in relation to the digital it is often in terms of the immediate present and where synchronous feedback across space, data and community is the expected norm. In the digital, time can also be replayed or visualized at different speeds and scales, it can even be archived for browsing at some other date. Conversely our perception of physical objects is that they have a fixed and contiguous relationship with time as we measure it in the material world. Physical objects cannot be scrolled backwards or forwards, out of synch with the time continuum, but are linked to cultural notions of age, newness, or antiquity. Consequently there is often a tacit sense of time embedded into the way we read and respond to physical objects and by extension physical data. This sense of time: how old an object is; how long it took to make; acquire; or physically reach, is an important factor in the way we attribute value to material artifacts. For the data-object this physical notion of time and time-scale might be gained at the expense of digital immediacy or temporal non-linearity.

Consider the work entitled 'iForm' (2010) by James Charlton (Figure 1). In this work GPS tracks of iPhone users were recorded over a set period of time and location. This information was then used to create a physical sculpture which transcoded the digital representations of time and space into a physical form. Charlton notes that the representation of time and movement as a physical object challenges the assumptions we make on the meaning of an object's form (Charlton, 2010). Objects

Figure 1. iForm, rapid prototype sculpture and data projection
© 2010, Artist James Charlton (Used with permission).

that are conceived from the visualization of digital data do not need to conform to the representational mores of objects that draw a reference to material culture. In this case the surfaces and angles in the work represented spatial and temporal variations of a digital data set, which are used to inform the shape of the object. Charlton's data-driven object concretizes the abstract concepts of space, time and movement by physically representing our interaction with the digital.

Other notions of time, use and age are distinctively represented in digital and material spaces. Physical objects collect dust or become dirty, worn or broken, they accrue 'character' via our interaction with them and being in the world. This patina is something that is hard to fabricate in the digital and implicitly denotes age, frequency of use (popularity) and history. Furthermore, physical objects decay with time, where, in theory at least, digital data can indefinitely be stored without loss of fidelity. However, the continuous process of upgrading computing hardware, operating systems, and software, can create, if not quite a form of digital entropy, a distinctive timeline for

digital content, marking its' heritage and capabilities. Moreover, the history of digital content is intrinsically iterative, multiple and variable; think of the 'save' and 'save as' functions in computer software, and the different results which arise from using these options. One allows for multiple variations or histories and the other replaces one history with another. The concept of temporal non-linearity is often ascribed to the digital as one of its key attributes, but equally the history and narrative of a real-world object is a complex assemblage of relationships, which take into account use, ownership, geographical location and material composition, and the changes in these aspects over time (Riggins, 1994). This flexibility with which digital data can be manipulated, reproduced and rearranged can engender a perceived lack of authenticity, although real-world data collection processes are equally open to interpretation. In the digital authenticity is often assigned by popularity as much as by provenance.

It is generally accepted that physical artifacts become imbued with a social cultural narrative by way of our interactions with them (Miller,

2010). And that interaction with a specific object can bring cultural and individual value to even a mass-produced item. This notion of interaction in material terms is quite different from the functional goal orientated interaction with data on the computer screen, which has the advantage of easily facilitating a variety of shared experiences across a broad spectrum of communities. This distributed experience is harder to create in the physical world, and is something that the social networked space of the digital is very adept at. Although the first-hand tangible experience of the physical object might be lost through the mediated channels of the digital this can be made up for through the potential of multiple sharing, commentary and reinterpretation. On one hand the democratic possibilities of the digital give widespread access to information and experience, which is often difficult to achieve with a physical object. On the other, there are strong inherent cultural notions of authenticity, which we ascribe to the empiric interaction with a singular physical object (Riggins, 1994). In the best case scenario the manifestation of digital information into a material form should play to the strengths of both of these two paradigms, in the worst case scenario it would fail to capitalise on either.

When we are thinking about the creation of physical data-driven objects we should also consider the material properties of the object and how that might influence the way we read the underlying data. The material properties of wood, metal, plastic and so on, all have a set of cultural resonances and readings that prefigure how we think of a particular object. For example, the clean smooth lines of melamine plastic furniture points to the concept of a 'modernist' aesthetic (Shove, Watson, Hand, & Ingram, 2007). Whereas the high-tech finish of carbon fiber brings to mind the composition of future worlds and artifacts. Each material form has its own set of cultural readings, which can be complex, and subtly interwoven with the use of the object and the context or setting in which the object is found. For instance, wood has

the association of being a natural material but can also be perceived as a sophisticated urban form. Just as the general categorization of physical materials can prefigure the reading of an object, the 'finish' of a particular material can also be important. Returning to the example of the wooden artifact, a table top roughly cut from a tree might retain pieces of bark and the inconsistencies of natural growth. This finish has a very different set of associated cultural values from that of a wooden table top, machine cut, symmetrically shaped, sanded and lacquered. Do these finishes have their parallel in the digital domain? A low-resolution digital image might be perceived to have a 'raw' quality about it, where as an image with a high pixel resolution might intrinsically suggest refinement and quality. Importantly the aesthetics of an artifact - digital or material - have an important influence on how the artifact is read and regarded. Just as the use of colour, composition, line-weight and typography in digital information visualization can set up a way of reading content, the material choices and finishes of a material-based data artifact can equally influence how the object and its' attendant data is interpreted. The creator of a data-object assemblage then must be cognizant to all these considerations.

MAKING TECHNOLOGIES

The capacity of the digital to easily create multiple versions of the same artifact is to some extent reflected in material culture through contemporary manufacturing and production processes. As we move into an era of new forms of digitally enabled manufacturing, the idea of mass customisation and the individually specified object is increasingly taking president. New adaptive and programmable production processes make the fabrication of bespoke objects easier and cheaper. Many of the first generation data-objects have been produced by utilizing different fabrication technologies that sit under the broad category of Rapid Prototyping, in addition to computer-controlled milling and laser-cutting processes. Rapid Prototyping machines can fabricate objects in a variety of materials ranging from paper-based products, to different types of plastic and waxy materials and even precious metals; and use a number of different processes to make objects. Typically though, a computer-based 3D modeling software is used to create a digital model, which is then used to print the material object (Noorani, 2006). Rapid Prototyping techniques were initially developed as a (relatively) inexpensive method of testing manufactured components and products before they were put into production (Chua, Leong, & Lim, 2003).

One of the early forms of Rapid Prototyping is the Laminated Object Manufacturing (LOM) method. The LOM fabrication process is of interest here as it articulates attributes from both digital and material making processes. In this process sheets of paper are glued together one layer at a time. As the layers are built up a computer-controlled laser or knife is used to trace out the required form and to 'cube' unwanted material ready for removal. This process requires much hand finishing, principally the removal of unwanted material and the sanding down and treating of the object to the desired finish. The LOM process effectively turns paper back into a wood-like material and the burnt, laser cut edges of the laminated paper give the object an unusual low-tech feel, distinctively at odds with the look and feel of more advanced Rapid Prototyping processes. The slightly rough, handmade look of the object, as well as its physical weight, gives it a set of qualities that echo pre-industrial revolution manufacturing/making processes, with the visible grid-lines echoing the visual language of both graph paper and the 3D modeling environment of the computer. The artist Brit Bunkley (2009) has effectively used the LOM fabrication process in a number of his sculptural works (Figure 2).

Computer-controlled laser-cutting technologies are another popular technique for producing data artifacts, which can be used to achieve similar affordances to the LOM method. In Abigail Reynolds' work 'MOUNT FEAR Statistics for Crimes with Offensive Weapon South London 2001-2002' (2002), sheets of corrugated cardboard are cut out and stuck together to create a room sized three-dimensional bar chart of crime statistics in London, England. The physical size of the data-object, roughly finished in cardboard, creates an unsettling and impactful representation of the underlying information. The work clearly shows how choice of materials, scale and manufacturing process can influence how data presented in physical form is received.

The aesthetic of the LOM manufacture process and laser-cutting techniques described above differ from the idea of the precise, computer-fabricated making and finishing which we typically expect from Rapid Prototyping technologies, where hard surfaces and bright white plastics are the norm. Yet what these examples begin to reveal is the complexity of reading material forms, where our understanding of even the simplest of objects can be prefigured by the making technologies employed and the choice of materials used. Daniel Miller (2010) comments on the importance of objects in society not just as things that affect our behavior and sense of self, but also as scene setting agents which move in and out of our focus. In this respect, our relationship to material objects might be seen to parallel our relationship to the computer desktop interface. According to Bolter and Grussin (1999) the computer desktop interface operates as a window and a mirror, something you can look through, and look at, at times content, at times form, and at times both. As a combination of both digital and material elements, data-objects read on a number of interlinked levels, as form and content.

Data and Metaphor

As discussed earlier, in data visualization form does not necessarily follow function. Lakoff and Johnson (1980) suggest that we use spa-

Figure 2. Trophy, Laminated Object Manufacturing (LOM) detail
© *2006, Artist Brit Bunkley (Used with permission).*

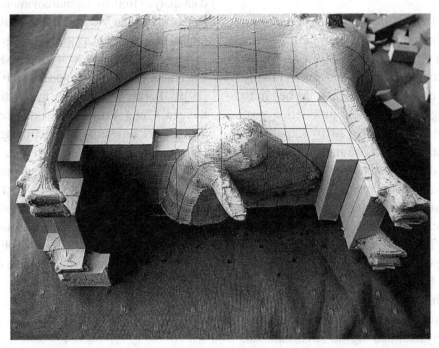

tial metaphors to help us understand complex concepts. It follows that data visualizations will often use metaphor to create relationships and understanding based on objects, spaces and experiences in the material world. Within computer-based data visualization, metaphor is used to aid understanding by association with physical phenomena (Anders, 1999). These metaphors can be given material weight when data sets are materialized as physical objects. In Nadeem Haidary's work 'Caloric Consumption' (2009), statistics commenting on the average calorific intake per capita in different countries are visualized as a real/physical dining fork. The prongs on the folk are different in length and represent the varying calorific intake data from four countries (Haidary, 2009). This data-object uses the fork as a metaphor for personal and global consumption. Because of the different lengths in the prongs the fork is not really functional, it operates as a symbolic reading of both data and form, seen through the lens of the cultural artifact, as Latour and Weibel (2002) suggest, there are any number of possible readings and multiple encodings for any given symbol.

The visual language of data visualization is also well served with biological metaphors. From the use of particle diagrams, molecular and cell structures, to tree-shaped flow charts, growth rings, cloud patterns. These visual reference points are commonly used to aid understanding of statistical data through familiarity and to give some notion of 'organic' connotations to data. Other graphical types of imagery including: maps; pictograms; arrows; and geometric shapes, are frequently used to add a relational context to data (Yau, 2013). Tufte (1997) comments on the relationship between visual and statistical thinking and how the application of visual language to data can aid, or detract, from our understanding of the data. The use of metaphor becomes more challenging when we combine digital data with the material language of physical form.

Making from the Digital

As mentioned, there are a number of enabling fabrication technologies that can facilitate the production of data-objects. As these technologies have become cheaper and more readily available the creative community has begun to take advantage of these new production processes. In the 'Inside Out' (2010) Rapid Prototype exhibition over 40 miniature sculptures were produced using Rapid Prototype technologies. The show was the result of collaboration between artists and designers in the UK and Australia. Each artist contributed one sculpture to the show. The sculptures were initially designed on the computer and output in resin for exhibition in both countries. The 'Inside Out' exhibitions, in name and theme, explored the making techniques and perceptions of creative practice in physical and digital environments, and allowed artists from different disciplines including textile design, fine arts, architecture and animation, to consider how to engage with these new fabricating processes (Smith, Rieser, & Saul, 2010).

Two of the works in particular demonstrate how data recorded from natural phenomena and biological processes can be used in the creation of a data-object. The work by Mitchell Whitelaw entitled 'Measuring Cup (Sydney 1859-2009)' (2010), is a materialization of temperature statistics for Sydney, Australia over 150 years. In Whitelaw's work this data is used to form a resin beaker (Figure 3). Each layer of the beaker represents one year's statistics. Placed one on top of another, the rings of data build up the sides of the container, and like the growth rings of a tree, the annual rings of temperature data give a tangible representation of change over the years. Interestingly the ergonomic affordance of a flared lip, usually introduced to aid drinking, is reflected by the recent upward (outward) trend in overall temperatures (Whitelaw, 2010).

While Whitelaw's piece is a representation of data analysis from the natural environment, Michele Barker and Anna Munster's piece in the exhibition looked to a data set of a much more personal nature. In the work 'Brainwaves Of Monks Meditating On Unconditional Loving-Kindness And Compassion' (2010), Barker and Munster materialize the act of thought. Using neuroscientific data of brain activity, recorded differences in electromagnetic energy emitted during meditation were used to form the basis of the Rapid Prototype sculpture. In a novel form of bioinformatics the data-object, a 3D sculptural representation of the data traced in the form of an ascending graphical line, is both informative and fragile, and the qualities of the physical object lend an intimacy that is missing in a conventional 2D chart or graph.

Figure 3. Measuring cup (Sydney 1859-2009), rapid prototype sculpture
© *2010, Artist Mitchell Whitelaw (Used with permission).*

In another intimate expression, the singularity of our individual physiology is the inspiration for a series of data driven works by the jewelry maker/conceptual artist Christoph Zellweger. In Zellweger's 'Data Jewels' (2006), Rapid Prototypes and other computer controlled manufacturing processes were used to create wearable jewelry based on an individual's genetic code (Zellweger, 2007). Zellweger's jewelry reveals the hidden codes and data of our physical being, and exploits the trend in advanced manufacturing where individual items can be fabricated to exact personal taste or requirement (see Figure 4). This flexibility in physical making moves toward the type of adaptive mutable attributes we normally ascribe to the digital, yet still allows us to benefit from the tangible properties we gain from material culture.

In their own way the three examples mentioned above all explore the potential for exploiting the attributes and properties that we commonly associate with digital data and material objects. Each work uses the combined potentials of hybrid data-objects to create works that are conceptually and formally challenging. However these data-objects all use discrete and relatively small data sets. The test for future data-objects will be how to accommodate the complexities of big data and how to make multidimensional comparisons between data in physical form.

CONCLUSION AND FUTURE RESEARCH DIRECTIONS

As discussed, the manifestation of digital data into material artifacts is increasingly taking place across the practice of information visualization. These data-driven artifacts are based on a diverse assortment of data sets, many of which are generated through our engagement with natural and man-made phenomena, personal biometrics and social communication technologies. It is an interesting loop that brings these statistics back

Figure 4. Data jewel, rapid prototype jewelry
© 2006, Artist Christoph Zellweger (Used with permission).

into the material world having being collected, processed and analyzed in the digital realm. However the notion of big data and the desire to correlate complex relationships in data is an interesting challenge for the data-object. But what is the purpose of information visualization, if not to bring clarity, insight, legibility, and improve the communication of an idea. And if this is the key underlying purpose of data visualization what methods should be used to assist in the sharing of knowledge, in an engaging and responsible way? Certainly the data-driven object needs to be considered in light of the existing issues and conversations which are already taking place in the discipline of information visualization. Yet the creation of a physical object based on a digital data set is in a sense a new media form. These dialogic objects have the ability to capitalize on the inherent traits found in both digital and material culture to communicate their message. As Guy Julier (2014) proposes, the coming together of different elements by design, in this instance data and material form, can lead to new understanding. By combining two cultures into an articulated form, new ways of looking at the digital/material relationship and how we can communicate through it can be explored. These hybrid constructs invite us to engage with the complexities of big data in social cultural contexts and to take advantage of the potentials offered by integrating digital material attributes. Luc Pauwels (2006) begins his book on the visual cultures of science with the statement that "The issue of representation touches upon the very essence of all scientific activity. What is known and passed on as science is the result of a series of representational practices." He goes on to say that, "Visual representations are not to be considered mere add-ons… they are an essential part of scientific discourse." (p.vii). These assertions clearly underline the point that careful consideration as to how we visualize science, and by extension, the pervasive data gathered from 21st Century living, needs to be undertaken intelligently, with care and through the appropriate forms and visual languages.

REFERENCES

Anders, P. (1999). *Envisioning cyberspace*. New York, NY: McGraw-Hill.

Barker, M., & Munster, A. (2010). *Brainwaves of monks meditating on unconditional loving-kindness and compassion*. Retrieved February 04, 2015, from http://www.blakeprize.com/works/brainwaves-of-monks-meditating-on-unconditional-lovingkindness-and-compassion

Bolter, J. D., & Grusin, R. (1999). *Remediation: Understanding new media*. Cambridge, MA: MIT Press.

Bunkley, B. (2009). *Displaced animals 2004 – 06*. Retrieved April 30, 2011, from http://www.britbunkley.com/

Card, S., Mackinlay, J., & Shneiderman, B. (1999). *Readings in information visualization: Using vision to think*. San Francisco, CA: Morgan Kaufmann.

Charlton, J. (2010). *iForm*. Retrieved August 21, 2014, from http://idot.net.nz/?page_id=508

Chua, C. K., Leong, K. F., & Lim, C. S. (2003). *Rapid prototyping: Principles and applications*. Singapore: World Scientific. doi:10.1142/5064

Felton, N. (2014). *2011 annual report*. Retrieved August 19, 2014, from http://feltron.com/

Graham, M. (2012). *Big data and the end of theory?*. Retrieved August 29, 2014, from http://www.theguardian.com/news/datablog/2012/mar/09/big-data-theory

Gwilt, I. (2010). Compumorphic art - The computer as muse. In *Proceedings of the First International Conference on Transdisciplinary Imaging at the Intersections between Art, Science, and Culture* (pp. 72-76). Artspace. Available from http://blogs.unsw.edu.au/tiic/files/2011/04/TIICproceedings.pdf

Haidary, N. (2009). *In-formed*. Retrieved August 29, 2014, from http://nadeemhaidary.com/In-Formed

Iliinsky, N., & Steele, J. (2011). *Designing data visualizations*. Sebastopol, CA: O'Reilly Media Inc.

Inside Out Rapid Prototype Exhibition. (2010). *Object gallery, Sydney, Australia*. Retrieved August 29 2014, from http://www.object.com.au/exhibitions-events/entry/inside_out_rapid_prototyping/

Julier, G. (2014). *The culture of design* (3rd ed.). London, UK: Sage Publications.

Klanten, R. (Ed.). (2008). *Data flow: Visualising information in graphic design*. Berlin, Germany: Gestalten.

Klanten, R., Ehmann, S., Tissot, T., & Bourquin, N. (Eds.). (2010). *Data flow 2: Visualizing information in graphic design*. Berlin, Germany: Gestalten.

Lakoff, G., & Johnson, M. (1980). *Metaphors we live by*. Chicago, IL: University of Chicago Press.

Latour, B., & Weibel, P. (2002). *Iconoclash: Beyond the image wars in science, religion and art*. MIT Press.

Levy, P. (1998). *Becoming virtual - Reality in the virtual age*. New York, NY: Plenum.

Lima, M. (2009). Information visualization manifesto. In *Visual complexity VC blog*. Retrieved April 11, 2011, from http://www.visualcomplexity.com/vc/blog/?p=644

Mayer-Schönberger, V., & Cukier, K. (2013). *Big data: A revolution that will transform how we live, work and think*. London, UK: John Murray.

McCandless, D. (2012). *Information is beautiful*. London, UK: Collins.

Miller, D. (2010). *Stuff*. Cambridge, UK: Polity.

Noorani, R. (2006). *Rapid prototyping principles and applications*. Hoboken, NJ: John Wiley and Sons.

Pauwels, L. (Ed.). (2006). *Visual cultures of science*. NH, Lebanon: Dartmouth College Press.

Reynolds, A. (2002). *Mount fear statistics for crimes with offensive weapon south London 2001-2002*. Retrieved August 29, 2014, from http://www.tradegallery.org/gallery.html#abigailreynolds

Riggins, S. (Ed.). (1994). *The socialness of things: Essays on the socio-semiotics of objects*. Berlin, Germany: Mouton de Gruyter. doi:10.1515/9783110882469

Shove, E., Watson, M., Hand, M., & Ingram, J. (2007). *The design of everyday life*. Oxford, UK: Berg.

Smith, C., Rieser, M., & Saul, S. (Eds.). (2010). *Inside out: Sculpture in the digital age*. Leicester, UK: De Montfort University.

Toseland, M., & Toseland, S. (2012). *Infographica: The world as you have never seen it before*. London, UK: Quercus Publishing Plc.

Tufte, E. (1983). *The visual display of quantitative information*. Cheshire, CT: Graphics Press.

Tufte, E. (1997). *Visual explanations: Images and quantities, evidence and narrative*. Cheshire, CT: Graphics Press.

Ware, C. (2004). *Information visualization: Perception for design*. San Francisco, CA: Morgan Kaufmann.

Whitelaw, M. (2010). *Measuring cup (Sydney, 1859-2009)*. Retrieved August 20, 2014, from http://mtchl.net/measuring-cup/

Yau, N. (2013). *Data points: Visualization that means something*. Indianapolis, IN: John Wiley & Sons.

Zellweger, C. (2007). *Christoph Zellweger*. Retrieved April 20, 2011, from http://www.christophzellweger.com/

KEY TERMS AND DEFINITIONS

Big Data: Complex multi-dimensional digital data sets.

Data-Object: A physical object where the form is dictated by an underlying digital data set.

Hybridity: A combination of digital and material elements and or attributes.

Information Design: The use of visual design practices to help communicate information either in print or digital form.

Information Visualization: Primarily screen-based visualization of data, designed to utilize the generative, time-based and interactive capabilities of the computer.

Materializing Code: Interpreting computer code in an embodied, analogue or material context.

Rapid Prototyping: A generic term for a variety of computer facilitated 3D printing processes.

Chapter 4
Digitizing the Physical:
Physicalizing the Digital

Joan Truckenbrod
Art Institute of Chicago, USA

ABSTRACT

Intertwined with the digital realm is a parallel sphere of digital material objects. The physicality of these things play an important role as they are embedded with memories as well as personal, social, and cultural meanings and references. The pervasiveness of digitizing information, images, spaces, and objects into digital data creates an expanding virtual presence. Simultaneously, virtual objects are now being transformed into material, tactile forms. Sensors are harvesting physical information and providing important feedback. Using digital devices involves an array of electronic rituals that have evolved. These ritualistic behaviors function in a similar manner to the performance of ritual and ceremony in indigenous cultures. This chapter examines the function of these digital rituals, with the physical residue deposited by these rituals and ceremonies. Material objects created by digital processes are powerful and play an important role socially, culturally, and spiritually.

INTRODUCTION

Digital technologies mediate the between the physical and the virtual. Spaces in between the virtual and the material are populated by new phenomena not clearly sited in either one or the other. Sensory perceptions of these phenomena, thought to be clearly delineated as virtual or material experiences, are no longer unequivocal.

Exhibited is a tangiality, with characteristics of both the physical realm and the virtual world. Tangiality indicates a radical shift in our sensory perception as they evolve to absorb, incorporate, interact with and adapt to the paradoxical materiality of the virtual. Our perception of interaction in the digital realm is our ability to sense, recognize and represent within ourselves, physical presence –even in its absence.

DOI: 10.4018/978-1-4666-8205-4.ch004

DIGITIZING THE PHYSICAL

Digital experiences vacillate between flat screens and material objects, between simulated three-dimensionality and the physical world. Digital images are inseparable from the electronic page or the screen; the substrate is inherent in the image – paper, computer screen, television screen, monitor, movie screen, and personal devices. Early computer images resided on oscilloscopes or on paper created with pen plotters. Using the Cartesian system of X, Y, Z coordinates the author created a series of drawings beginning in 1975. The computer graphics programs were written in FORTRAN, incorporated mathematical formulas that described invisible physical phenomena such as light waves reflected off of irregular surfaces. The program used CalComp drawing subroutines for the CalComp Pen Plotter. These drawings were envisioned in the imagination as there were no display screens for graphic images. The program was punched on punch cards and communicated to the large mainframe computer through a card reader. The program was processed and the resulting data describing the drawing was transferred to a 1600 BPI tape that was read by the pen plotter. The available plotter used only black ink in the pens to create drawings. The author used color xerography on transparencies to create the color drawing in Figure 1. Individual drawings were Xeroxed onto transparencies in yellow, red and blue, overlapped to create the final artwork.

These drawings created a physical presence for an invisible phenomena in the physical world, described by mathematics. Through the artist's programs two-dimensional abstract representations were created.

Contemporary culture embraces the material world in collaboration with the digital. Digitization creates parallel universes of simulated constructs, that exist on flat screens - personal computers, tablets, and smart phones. These digital images are transforming into physical space through continually evolving materials and technologies.

Figure 1. Fourier Transform, computer drawings and color xerox
Joan Truckenbrod, 1975. In the collection of the Block Museum of Art at Northwestern University in Evanston Illinois.

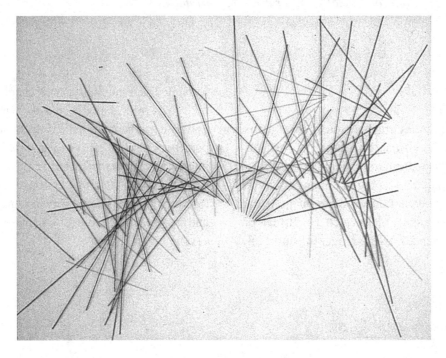

Three-D printers are easily accessible in schools, libraries, and DIY studios or maker spaces. Car and truck parts are being created with these printers as well as toys, dishes, clothing, jewelry, human tissue and even human organs. The digital intervenes in the material world, simultaneously the material is injected into the virtual realm. As powerful cultural artifacts and icons these physical objects play important roles. Images propelled into objects probe cultural, economic and political issues. Material things are embedded with highly charged social meaning and personal memories.

The physicalization of digital images creates new opportunities for expanded modes of expression and communication. Tactility of the object creates a sensuous, empathetic form of communication. Objects contain narratives that reside in personal and communal memory. This empathetic power permeates the body as well as the imagination as one explores the physical landscape of the object. Analogous to the simultaneity of the digital and the material realms, Aboriginal mythology maintains that the mind and body are intertwined as the meaning of a symbol is inscribed on one's awareness only when it is absorbed through languages that affect both the mind and the body. (Lawlor, 1991, p. 287)

The Aborigines conceptually entwine a multitude of languages in the everyday expression of their lives weaving together the body, the physical landscape, their ancestral history and their spirituality. Symbols are transformed into large earthworks. These ceremonial earth sculptures represent topographies created by the Dreamtime ancestors, some extending for acres in order to complete a mythic cycle. Groups of men work collaboratively forming these relief maps out of earth - each depicting a specific myth. During the construction they sing related chants and perform dances that are associated with the forms they are building. There are many levels of meaning in the linear and circular design elements they create (Lawlor, 1991, p. 288). As sacred symbols these material constructions engage potent forms

of transformation. For the Aborigines this is a transformation of pure energy into form. This is a provocative parallel to the digital realm as computer images are transformed into objects using various production technologies. In the digital realm the mind and body synthesis is the fusion of the virtual and the material.

Ritual and ceremonies in indigenous cultures like the Aboriginal, perform the same function as rituals and ceremonies performed in the digital realm. In indigenous rituals as well as electronic rituals, there are material residues or traces left by these rituals and ceremonies. With the proliferation of 3D digitizers and printers, objects accumulate in personal as well as public spaces reflecting the reciprocity between the virtual and physical realms.

Digital Ritual and Ceremony

The point and press/click of electronic devices is analogous to behaviors in ritual and ceremonies in indigenous cultures. Users go into a trance, entering alternate realities, connecting with others, and even transforming identities. The digital screen is a conduit to other worlds. In indigenous cultures, ritual and ceremonies function to open portals to other realms of experience such as the spiritual or ancestral worlds, providing interaction with these normally hidden spheres of existence. Indigenous rituals function to transform identity through rites of passage and other ceremonies. Identity in the digital realm of the internet social sites and virtual worlds is not prescribed rather is created by the author. A sense of place is also created during ceremonies. In Aboriginal ceremonies, ancestral presence is reaffirmed in sacred places by "singing up the land". Ceremonies are also powerful community builders among the participants in both indigenous and digital cultures. Temporal distortions are experienced by participants in ritual and ceremonies as well. Both digital and indigenous rituals and ceremonies embody a multiplicity of sensations including flickering

Figure 2. Quantum Realities, video projection into water pond
Joan Truckenbrod, 2002.

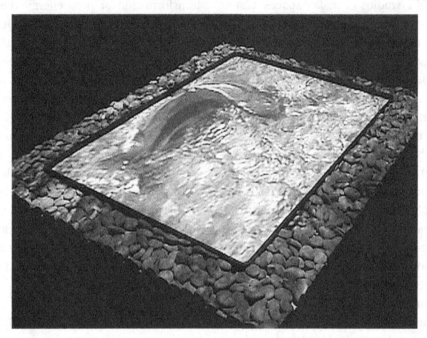

light of the screen, sound, image, movement, and emotional engagement. In indigenous ceremonies the flicker of firelight, painted symbols, touch and strong aromas create a rich polyphone of sensory experiences. Envisioning symbols painted on the nude body under the cover of darkness, revealed and concealed as the dancer twists and turns in the flickering of firelight in ritual celebration, inspired the artwork of the author in video sculpture. Handmade objects, embedded with social, cultural and personal meanings are juxtaposed with video imagery projected onto and into them. The video imagery informs the object simultaneously the meaning of the object informs the video narrative. In Figure 2, titled *Quantum Realities*, video of salmon runs in Alaska and Oregon are projected into a water pond on the gallery floor. The life cycle of salmon is a valuable example of life cycles. A shallow water pond surrounded by river pebbles on the floor of the gallery transforms into an opening to the stream beneath the floor with salmon rushing upstream during a salmon run. Fish undulate and splash water with their

powerful tails, causing viewers to jump back from the envisioned spray of water. The installation includes the sound of water rushing in a stream.

Digital Rituals Open Portals to Alternate Realities

The ubiquitous digital screen is a powerful conduit, as point and click rituals open portals to other realms of experience, engaging users in compelling interactions. Virtual worlds like Second Life and various games engage people to play collaboratively with acquaintances from around the world. Portals are also opened to social sites like Facebook. Indigenous rituals and ceremonies perform similar functions, as participants desire to connect with ancestors or spiritual beings. Digitization creates parallel universes, transformed into an invisible web parallel to our material, lived experiences. This is analogous to indigenous people who exist in a multiplicity of realms, the spiritual, ancestral and everyday, lived simultaneously. The multiplicity of electronic screens are infused with continuous personal, social, environmental and political connections. They create interactive conduits to other worlds, similar to indigenous rituals and ceremonies.

Ritual objects, both physical and virtual, are imbued with the power to connect to these realms. In Africa small wooden stools, carved with a head on each side, are used as pillows. Sleeping with these pillows allows the person to make contact with other realms through the symbolic heads. African power figures have small windows or mirrors in their stomachs that are considered conduits to a magical, sacred realm. Behind these windows are powerful substances that are activated by Shaman with special powers.

Catalyze Powerful Social Networks

Secondly digital rituals function to form communities locally and across the globe. In indigenous cultures, ceremonies create bonds among performers, creating communities even among differing tribes. Digital media is a vehicle for connecting and activating participants through a wide range of intellectual, social, political, environmental and emotional issues. Social media is pervasive in today's society, creating a digital collaborative spirit.

Virtual reality has an intense appeal for playful, intellectual, mythical, and emotional interaction. This engagement is personal, social, and global. The ease of connectivity and communication using computers underlies the powerful projection of the digital into physical space. Digital networks, and the software such as Skype and Facetime connect families, and friends in digital face to face connection, create the experience of "being there". Educational resources have expanded across the globe as educational institutions offer courses and degrees on-line. Social networks also connect strangers who share the same visions, challenges and goals. These networks were used to organize and activate people who imagined new political futures for their countries. This connection was a powerful kinetic force in catalyzing revolutions in

the Middle East. Sharing ideals and political principles with multitudes of people not normally able to be connected has precipitated radical changes in the political landscape. Digital connectivity was the catalyst in linking people together, translated into physical marches and rallies for change. These networks were employed to transform the digital into the physical.

Transformation of Identity

Thirdly, ritual and ceremony function to transform identity. Traditional ceremonies celebrate rites of passage through different stages of life, from child to adult, from single person to married. Indigenous cultures have compelling rituals for men and women transforming into adulthood. In virtual worlds identities are imagined, and constructed as desired. The South African artist, Bigosi Sekhukhuni, designed an Avatar for conversing with absent fathers like his own. Similar to an interactive video game, wone engages this bot to talk to these fathers. He used the internet to highlight how one's online life shapes one's identity. In the digital realm one can take on the costume of a variety of characters. This shifts the assumed reality of characters in virtual worlds, and on social media sites.

Distortion of Time

Temporal distortions occur in ceremonial or ritual performance. Structures of linear clock time disappear or lose their relevancy. Computers, cell phones, tablets, wrist screens all display the time, however digital rituals are acted out over time in which time is both relative and experiential, not absolute. Particularly when participating in digital media – searching the web, conversing with friends or playing digital games, the measured, linear character of time dissolves.

None of the hundreds of Aboriginal languages have a word for time, not do they have a concept of time. They conceive the passage of time and history not as a movement from past to future but as a passage from a subjective state to the objective expression of an event. There is a sequential swing between internal dreams and their physical experience. (Lawlor, 1991, p. 37) Digital experiences parallel these internal dreams, physicalized them through various digital processes.

Creating Place

The next function of ritual is creating a strong sense of place through activity at the ceremonial site. Aboriginal peoples use ceremonies and rituals to call up the place occupied by ancestors in order to reactivate the site and their ancestral presence. Places were formed through the activities of these powerful mythic beings. Landscapes or land formations were created by the activities of the Ancestors. A specific potency was deposited in these places that stimulates the participants' memories of Dreamtime stories. All moral codes, spiritual beliefs, and societal obligations are embedded in these stories. Contemporary Aborigines walk and camp in this landscape to reenact the formation process in order to awaken and revitalize the sense of place. They share stories and food, while dancing around campfires. For these people the sense of place contains both physical and metaphysical meanings. (Lawlor, 1991, p. 236)

The performing of digital rituals has created numerous virtual spaces. In fact most physical businesses including shops, galleries, and museums, have parallel virtual websites on the internet. They have digitized their material elements and physical spaces creating a virtual presence of their website.

Physicalizing the Digital

Digital Sensors

Sensory experiences are heightened during indigenous ritual performances. The Whirling Dervish in Turkey exemplify this experience of heightened sensory perception during their perfor-

mances. Sensory experiences are heightened and they become absorbed in altered states of being. Increasingly digital interfaces enhance sensory experiences. Wristbands and headbands capture heart rate, pulse, and information about breathing for sports and medical applications. This information is displayed for the user, or transmitted to medical facilities for monitoring. Google Glass captures a multitude of information including video and sound, and integrates with the body in an intuitive manner.

Digital sensors operate with small microcontrollers in integrated into clothing, or surgically implanted in the body. Sensors in garments sense and capture or measure a variety of physical experiences. Flex sensors record flexing or bending movements of various areas of the body such as elbows, knees, wrists and fingers. Range of motion information can be captured with this type of sensor. Flex sensors have been used to create experimental gestural music. Pressure sensors capture the force of touch or being touched, as the sensor data is read by the microcontroller. This type of sensor may allow a sight-impaired person to work with clay embedded with pressure sensors, creating pottery. Another sensor that digitizes physical motion of the body, and then provides usable physical feedback to the user, is the stretch sensor. A conductive rubber cord whose resistance decreases the more it gets stretched is used to create a stretch sensor to measure subtle changes in the body such as breathing. Heart rate is measured with a pulse sensor. Movement and orientation are measured with a tilt sensor which can be built into objects or wearable garments. Location is recorded through GPS sensors. Proximity information is captured through ultrasonic and infrared distance sensors. Heat sensors record thermal gradients in the body, objects or environment. Light levels or variations in lightness or darkness are recorded using photocells. Sound activated sensors have been in use for some time. Various sensors incorporated into garments create protective clothing and new approaches to fashion.

Afroditi Psarra has designed a dress that uses haptic and sonic feedback to detect electromagnetic fields in the environment. These sensors digitize physical phenomena, and then physicalize the digital data through feedback.

Interactive Sensors

Reaching out from the virtual, digital realm into the physical, real world are a broad series of sensors being developed that capture real world data in order to create digital simulations and analysis. Athletes digitally monitor their performance using video capture in order to optimize their performance. In homes and commercial facilities this information is used for security purposes. These sensors can also analyze air quality, and water quality. They are commonly used for security and to detect smoke, fire, or water in flooding. Doctors can monitor their patients remotely, recording the function of devices like pacemakers.

The integration of interactive sensors to engage the body has radically altered the game industry. Wii and Nintendo incorporate a multitude of sensors for interacting with a broad range of sports like tennis and skiing, dance and exercise activities. Games such as Skylander function at the threshold between images on the television screen and the physical action of the players with their active interfaces. Nintendo, Playstation and Wii have sensory interfaces that include the Nunchuk, a Frisbee, bowling ball, a wheel, archery bow, table tennis paddle, golf club, canoeing paddle, wakeboard, and sword play, The Wii Fit uses an interactive balance board. Interactive physical objects are also used in games played in virtual space. When will the surface of the television screen undulate and transform into sculptural reliefs matching the landscape of each game?

The predominance of the virtual realm seems debunked as virtual experiences like games reconnect with the physical world through sensory interfaces. In an article titled "The Internet Gets Physical". "Enough about virtual you: computing

is now focusing on real-world problems" (Lohr, 2011) using communicating sensors and computing intelligence. Smart industrial gear keep track of the performance of jet engines, bridges, and oil rigs, alerting managers when repairs will be needed. Sensors on fruit and vegetable cartons calculate shipping time and warn in advance of spoilage, necessitating rerouting. Smart hospital rooms have been developed that track the movements of doctors and nurses, alerting them if they neglect to wash their hands before and after treating each patient. Lapses in doing so contribute significantly to infections acquired in the hospital. IBM and General Electric are hiring programmers to develop applications for this Industrial Internet. Some examples include *Smart Planet* applications that allow consumers to monitor their use of energy and water in order to optimize their usage.

How Does the Digital Become Material?

The digital realm becomes more pervasive and powerful as it moves beyond the virtual world. Internet enabled things, the three dimensional knowledge of digital photographs, the invention of Google Glass, the powerful developments in 3 D printing and ongoing innovations propel the digital increasingly into the physical world. The DIY movement engages people of all disciplines, in materials and creative technical processes. Social communities form around this "making" culture and the meaningfulness of the objects. In the shift to physicalizing the digital, to making, many actual Makerspaces have sprung up with all levels of digital technologies for creating physical things. There are also a global community of Fab Labs, enabling invention by providing access to tools and help with digital fabrication. Make magazine and makezine.com are wildly popular. For kids there are Maker Camps and MakerKids, a makerspace especially designed for kids in Toronto.

Figure 3. Against the Current, video projection into a hospital bed
Joan Truckenbrod, 2006.

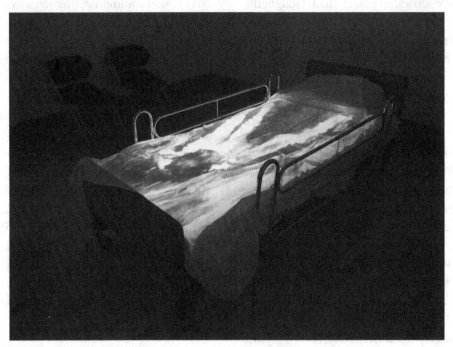

Inherent in this evolution is the emerging prominence of the object – the making of it, the materiality, and the narrative embodied in the object. MIT Sociologist Sherry Turkle has researched the role of the physical object and its importance to the owner. People collect objects for humor, comfort or inspiration in their studio practice or research lab According to her research, the manipulation and presence of material objects are critical in creative and analytic thinking. A young person plays computer games and is seduced by the internet, and yet upon bedtime surround himself with "precious" stuffed animals. Objects are embedded with highly charged social and personal meanings. They contain narratives that reside in personal and communal memories. Tactility of the object creates a sensuous, empathetic form of communication. This empathetic power permeates the body as well as the imagination as one examines the physical landscape of the object. Video imagery in video sculpture, propelled into objects probe cultural, economic and political issues, represented by the object. In the video sculpture titled *Against the Current,* the video of salmon runs is digitally synthesized with video of a nude body tumbling in the water, and projected into a crumpled sheet on a full-size hospital bed with side bars. The hospital bed is a provocative object with powerful resonances. Superimposing video of salmon runs with the tumbling body adds a layer of ideas to both the object and the video sequence. Objects, as performers, are a powerful presence in these installations, exaggerated by absorbing the texture, form and narrative of the video projection. See Figure 3.

These 'paradoxical objects' in these video sculptures inherit memories embedded in objects elucidated by the narrative of the video projection. Memories of events, spaces, interpersonal relationships or activities are left behind in objects, which resonate in 'video sculpture'. Objects are not blank canvases, rather they have histories and stories themselves. They have memories that create a dialogue with the video projection in spatiotemporal sculptures (Truckenbrod, 2012).

Imagining Objects

Will we soon be able to imagine shapes, forms, objects in our minds and have them manifest through 3D printing? Will we be able to dream up fantastical environments, constructing them in unlikely materials through this digital technology?

Neuroscientist Miguel Nicolelis is researching the merger of the brain with machines, making this scenario possible in the not so distant future. He studies how the brain creates thought, and how this thought can connect with machines outside of the body. Neuroscientists are changing their perspective on the functioning of the brain from the opinion that physical and mental activities are controlled by highly specialized regions of the brain, to a belief that groups of multitasking neurons function in a distributed manner across multiple locations to perform tasks in an integrated fashion. Thus brain-machine interface has potential for a wide range of applications. In his research with primates at Duke University Medical Center, he uncovered a new method for capturing brain function by "recording rich neuronal symphonies rather than the activity of single neurons" (Nicolelis, 2011). Using this approach he has been able to teach research monkeys to control the movements of a robot located halfway around the world by using signals from the brain alone, as their thoughts control the movement of these remote robots. These radical experiments suggest the power of the brain to connect with machines and control an aspect of them via thought alone – without the necessity for language, verbal or digital, and without movement of the body.

In his book "Beyond Boundaries: The New Neuroscience of Connecting Brains with Machines- and How It Will Change Our Lives", Nicolelis describes how robotic arms were controlled by rhesus monkeys via the electrical impulses transmitted by neurons in their brains. This ability underlines the possibility that images in the brain, ideas that have shape or form in the brain, can be transmitted to 3D printers or CNC machines. If information necessary to move three-dimensional robotic arms can be transmitted directly from the brain to move the robot, this implies that the brain is conceiving this movement in three-dimensional space. Is this experience transferrable to thinking or imagining shape and form in three dimensions in the brain that can be transmitted to a machine?

Another development of this research involved the primate's ability to move virtual objects and to *feel* their texture using the brain only. Viewed as the first demonstration of a two-way interaction between a primate brain and a virtual body, two monkeys were trained at the Duke University Center of Neuroengineering, learned to employ their brain activity alone to move an avatar hand and then to differentiate the textures of the virtual objects. Without moving any part of their real bodies, the monkeys used their electrical brain activity to direct the virtual hands of an avatar to the surface of virtual objects and, upon contact, were able to differentiate their textures. According to study leader Dr. Miguel Nicolelis, MD, PhD, Professor of Neurobiology at Duke, and co-director of the Center, "someday in the near future, quadriplegic patients will take advantage of this technology not only to move their arms and hands, and to walk again, but also to sense the texture of objects placed in their hands, or experience the nuances of the terrain on which they stroll with the help of a wearable robotic exoskeleton".

This research points the way for three-dimensional objects to be imagined, with the brain capable of communicating with machines and transmitting descriptive information about the shape or form being thought about in order for it to be constructed by machine. In addition, it appears from this research, that information about textures and surface characteristics are also present in the brain and can be communicated in an interactive manner. Thus the image can be made physical with the transmission of information from the brain. Unlimited potential of creative research in the studio practice of artists as this develops. It appears that creative imaging in one's mind can remain in three dimensions or four dimensions and is not necessarily flattened out onto a computer screen or drawn on 2D paper before it is created in physical form.

The Power of the Object

The digital image or form transformed into material object is bearer of powerful social and political signifiers, becoming active in the cultural milieu. Objects project power. In indigenous cultures they symbolize the resonance of sacred, spiritual or ancestral rituals. They are *animate* and possess agency. Objects are actants with a vital impetus – never acting alone. Artifacts cause actions and their effects have consequences. Their efficacy or agency always depends on collaboration with other objects and people. In indigenous cultures there are numerous ritual and sacred objects that *possess* agency. For example, a 'Power Figure' is a provocative object in African culture that is imbued with spiritual power by a ritual specialist. These carved figures operate with different functions such as healing, divination or protection. These unique sculptures are thought to have their own identities, and are treated with great respect because of the power they possess. Secret compartments within these objects contain special ingredients empowered to carry out their functions. These figures frequently are constructed with mirrors positioned on their stomachs, which become the eyes of the figure, enabling them to "see into the spiritual realm". Highly charged objects are an integral aspect of indigenous cultures. Emotions reside in these objects and are catalyzed in the interstitial spaces between the objects, shaman, and people during ritual performances and ceremonies.

Jane Bennett proposes, in her book *Vibrant Matter,* that *emotions reside in objects* rather than one's physical body being the purveyor of emotion. According to Bennett emotions emanate from the material world. Objects are imbued with power - "thing power". She proposes that objects embody a vibrancy of their own. Not only do they display or have *meaning*, they are active in creating the context of that meaning. They have agency in their behavior. Materiality is expressive. The efficacy of objects is in relation to the meaning they express. "Things" have a capacity to impede or bloc the will and designs of humans but also to act as quasi agents or forces with trajectories, propensities, or tendencies of their own. *Thingness* is not a fixed stability of materiality or a passive object, rather, she theorizes that materiality is as much a force as entity, as much energy as matter, as much intensity as extension.

Emotions have migrated from the physicality of the body, facial expressions, gestures, and posturing to the evocative resonances embedded in objects. The digital realm has also transformed the experience of affect into virtual and ephemeral territory, reawakening the emotional power of invisible potencies of objects. Contemporary theory migrates emotion from the physicality of the body to objects – both in the material world and the digital realm. The assemblage of emotional resonances creates a highly complex network that entangling people with objects. Examples are "vigilant things" created as powerful protectors in Yoruba culture. Amazing constructions involving ordinary materials such as string, paper and sticks, are described as "ase-impregnated sculptural constructs". A battered black plastic bag filed with a potent substance, tied and hung from a stick over a pile of recently cut green branches, signifies ownership of the branches. Anyone who steals these is warned and will "suffer some calamity". There are invisible potencies embedded in these protective constructions called "aale" that protect property and objects. These aale, even though they are constructed with ordinary objects like cloth and branches, contain and emit strong emotional resonances. (Doris, 2011)

The Chinese tradition of 'shi' is another example of the emotionality and agency embedded in objects. This concept of "shi" embodies the idea of congregational agency in which an assemblage owes its agentic capabilities to the vitality of objects that constitute it. The shi of an assemblage is vibratory. The potential of this assemblage originates not in human initiatives but instead results from the very disposition of things. "Shi" is the style, energy, propensity, trajectory or élan inherent in a specific objects and their arrangement. The material agency of assemblages is the sharing of powers between artifacts, or people and artifacts, and the tendency to operate in dissonant conjunction with each other. The assemblage owes its agentic capacity to the vitality of materials that constitute it.

Objects Embedded With Memories

Heard by the soul, footsteps
in the mind more than shadow,
shadows of thought more than footsteps
through the path of echoes
that memory invents and erases. - Octavio Paz
(Paz, 1979, p.123)

Memory is intimately connected to our material culture as objects hold and are catalysts in provoking memories. The potency of the material culture emanates from memories embedded in and evoked by objects. In the book "Memory Work: Archaeologies of Material Practice" memory work refers to both the social practices that create memories and the materiality of memory making. Personal events and activities leave behind remnants or vestiges of social practices, that have been infused with memories. Memory resides in these material traces, evoking strong emotions long after the performance of social and personal rituals. In archeological research, objects provide insight into social and cultural practices, as they are traces of deposits left by these material practices. Memories of these practices are embedded in archeological objects which create contexts in which memory is materialized. The same is true for contempo-

rary objects that embody memories of histories or practices. Materiality becomes a portal to understanding the connections between people through time, and diverse geographic locations (Mills and Walker, 2008).

DIGITAL FUTURES

Using 3D printers and CNC machines to create personal iconic objects is a new language for communication and expression. As vessels of desires and intimate vestiges of personal memories and experience, objects are powerful players in our lives. The materiality of culture takes on new dimensions with the accessibility of 3D printers and other object making technologies. In addition to using the computer as an intermediate step to creating objects, research demonstrates a direct connection between brain activity and material objects. This suggests that the brain activity of imagination can communicate with and control object-making technologies – making the imagination of shapes and forms in one's mind the impetus for producing them. In addition, the reverse of controlling robotic arms with brain activity, suggests that body movement and gestures with their parallel brain activity, can be produced in physical form by capturing these signals from the brain. Communicating this gestural information from the brain through the computer to a 3D printer creates a unique sculptural form. This potential for making sculptural objects through the movement or gesturing of the body is invigorating and innovative.

In sculpting physical objects artists collaborate with pencils, paints, digital tablets, cameras, carving tools and 3-D programming and 3-D printing. However artists are not dependent upon or constrained by these tools. The final object will not have the imprint of the character of these media or how they work. Digital three-dimensional printing has a freedom of material, scale and textures; of simplicity, intricacy or complexity of the new physical forms. In addition the body becomes integral in creating objects through the capturing and communicating of brain waves, now under study, to object making devices. A unique and innovative portal opens in the digital arena, into a new realm of physicality.

In the interstitial space in-between the digital and the physical there is a tangiality, a synthesis of digital and material elements. There is an interruption of the digital by material objects, simultaneously as physical behaviors increasingly interact with the digital. This is a radical shift in our sensory perception as they evolve to absorb, incorporate, interact with and adapt to the paradox of materiality verses virtuality.

REFERENCES

Bennett, J. (2010). *Vibrant matter: A political ecology of things*. Durham, NC: Duke University Press.

Catanese, P., & Truckenbrod, J. (2010). Tangiality of digital media. In G. Mura (Ed.), *Metaplasticity in virtual worlds: Aesthetics and semantic concepts*. IGI Global. doi:10.4018/978-1-60960-077-8.ch003

Doris, D. T. (2011). *Vigilant things, on thieves, yoruba anti-aesthetics, and the strange fate of ordinary objects*. Seattle, WA: University of Washington Press.

Grossberg, L. (2010). Affect's future: Rediscovering the virtual in the actual. In The affect theory reader (pp. 309-338). Durham, NC: Duke University Press.

Hartman, K. (2015). What to sense, how to select and use sensors in wearable electronics. *Make, 43*, 38–41.

Lawlor, R. (1991). *Voices of the first day, awakening in the aboriginal dreaming*. Rochester, VT: Inner Traditions.

Lohr, S. (2011, December 18). The internet gets physical. *New York Times*, p. Sunday Review.

Mills, B. J., & Walker, W. H. (2008). *Memory work, archaeologies of material practices*. Santa Fe, NM: School for Advanced Research Press.

Nicolelis, M. (2011). Beyond boundaries, the new neuroscience of connecting brains with machines – And how it will change our lives. New York: Time Books, Henry Holt & Company.

Paz, O. (1979). A draft of shadows. In *A draft of shadows and other poem* (E. Weinberger, Trans.). New York: New Directions Books.

Truckenbrod, J. (2008). *Digital ritual and ceremony*. Paper presented at College Art Association Conference, Los Angeles CA.

Truckenbrod, J. (2010). *Video sculpture*. Paper presented at the International Sculpture Conference, London, UK.

Truckenbrod, J. (2011). *Transforming the physicality of emotion*. Paper presented at ISEA Conference, Istanbul, Turkey.

Truckenbrod, J. (2012). *The paradoxical object: Video film sculpture*. London: Black Dog Publishers.

KEY TERMS AND DEFINITIONS

3D Digitizer: Digitizer that records a three dimensional description of an object, relief or person, and transmits the information to a computer. The three dimensional image is displayed on the computer screen and can be scaled, altered or manipulated. A 3 – D printer creates an object with the data set.

3D Printing: Printers that create three dimensional objects based on the information provided by a computer. Material including plastics and metals are used in these printers, which deposit sequential thin layers of the material to build up the object.

CNC Router: A computer controlled cutting machine used to create three dimensional objects. These forms can be fabricated with wood, plastic, foam, aluminum, bronze, glass, vinyl, and other material. CNC machines are not as accessible as 3 – D printers but work with a much broader range of materials.

Digital Ritual and Ceremony: Ritualistic behaviors characteristic of using electronic devices that function similar to rituals and ceremonies in indigenous cultures.

Interactive Sensors: Digital interface devices that capture specific information from a participant and provide feedback to the participant about or with this information that is gathered.

Sensors: Digital interface devices that capture specific information or experiences, and transfer them to a computer through an interface board or microcontroller.

Tangiality: The dichotomy of sensory experience in the liminal space between the virtual realm and the physical, material world.

Video Sculpture: The projection of video into an object in which the meaning of the object is enhanced with the video sequence, and the video imagery takes on the shape of the object informing the meaning of the video narrative.

Chapter 5
The Virtual, Alternate Spaces, and the Effects upon Artwork

Alistair James Payne
Glasgow School of Art, UK

ABSTRACT

This chapter explores the philosophical notion of The Virtual in response to the writings of Gilles Deleuze and unfolds this thinking through its interdisciplinary and transformative effects upon contemporary fine art. The Virtual is discussed in relation to forms of contemporary painting, yet the chapter provides a model for thinking through interdisciplinarity within, and from, other media. The research investigates the perceived resistance of painting to explore external possibilities and introduces methodological strategies, which encounter externality as a means for establishing radical change. In this way, the Virtual acts as an instigator for change, which effectively destabilises the pre-formity attached to medium specific practices. It is for this reason that the Virtual forces external relationships and connections to come to the fore in order to radically alter and transform the physical and conceptual constructs of different disciplines. Alongside the discussion of the Virtual and its direct affects upon artistic practices, the chapter discusses literary models including hybridity and metamorphosis as potential key elements affecting transformative change.

INTRODUCTION

I was invited to take part in a video discussion on the notion of the *Virtual*, which was created for the ISEA conference, Istanbul in 2011. It was evident that the ideas that were being proposed from my perspective were very different from thinking around the virtual in relation to digital media and creative digital technologies.

The notion of the Virtual I proposed linked into my own research on interdisciplinarity focusing upon the philosophical methodologies of Gilles Deleuze in order to inform and affect change and transformation to the discipline of *Painting* within contemporary artistic practice. Therefore, it is important to emphasise that this writing has directly evolved from my practice as a painter. Having trained in painting, concerns

DOI: 10.4018/978-1-4666-8205-4.ch005

relating to its contemporary condition led directly to my doctoral and post-doctoral research. This chapter examines the notion of the virtual from a philosophical perspective and so proposes an understanding of the virtual that is different from common parlance relating the virtual directly to, or embedded within, the digital.

This research outlines the relevance of the virtual as a philosophical idea that leads towards interdisciplinarity. It will be articulated in turn as a philosophical concept and subsequently its potential affects through the practice of painting, (whilst using reference to contemporary architectural theory as an exemplar for the practical application of the idea[s]). Allied to these propositions will be the citing of the cinematic through which a discussion surrounding the notion of time and space can critically open out the disciplinary strictures of painting as a contemporary practice.

Examples of my own practice will also be discussed in order to present how the notion of the virtual can potentially be actualised in form.

THE DISCIPLINE OF PAINTING

A *Pure* Resistance

Questions surrounding the condition of contemporary painting particularly its formal concerns, have led towards new thinking in relation to painting, specifically as an 'expanded practice'[1] (Krauss, 2002). Formal methods effectively lead towards a 'grounding'[2] within the questioning of the specific materiality of painting, in terms of how this affects its closure or completeness and the creation of its identity as a (specific) object - painting.

The contemporary condition of painting constitutes it as a vastly expanded form, which leads towards potential methods for rethinking the characteristics or traits of a, or the, medium employed within the work. The many questions regarding the limits and/or boundaries of painting drive the physical and structural problematics

of its condition. These physical (or structural) questions have necessitated the examination, or testing, of the perceived boundaries of painting. The most prominent form, or type of painting practice, which typifies this method, is an internally structured critique of the medium. Where this may change the physical material dynamic of the work, it does not question that materiality, but rather examines the physical limitations of the materials thought to constitute painting. This consequently leads towards a structural or formal shift in the materiality of painting, yet, can be said to relate and conform to its particular identity as painting through the materials themselves. This form of rigorous internal questioning obviously leads towards difference in terms of the physical structure of 'painting' however, this difference is still determined through the constraints the medium itself presents. This research highlights alternative possibilities in order to challenge, transform and rethink the potential of painting as a contemporary practice.

In this context, the notion of change needs to be considered and defined in terms of its importance and how it can be forced into action. Change is not simply the reordering or internal deconstruction of prior arrangements in order to instigate difference within. It is also *not* the shift within a process that instigates a subtle altering of specific identity. In fact the idea that identity should have this internal focus is alien to the proposition that will be promoted. That is to say that the specifics of particular identity (in terms of painting – or other alternative media), needs to be re-established, for, this is not a search for truth or the essence of 'being' of a thing but rather a very different way of thinking. This involves investigating an opening of 'systems' across boundaries or alternatively where territorial or boundaried 'schematics' are not perceived as (or to be) static and internally specific. This opening of systems also presents a position and the potential for painting to be less reliant upon internal combinations (oppositions or contradictions) for change and the creation of the new.

In contrast to the acceptance of the physical constraints of the medium, this research presents an alternative approach to the idea of painting (establishing a method for rethinking other media or disciplines) and constructs new and different ways for painting to be thought. In effect, the investigation of Gilles Deleuze's (2001) discussion of the notion of 'the Virtual' instigates an interdisciplinary approach towards painting where *external* connections and relationships are introduced and developed. This equates to the opposite position of the internal critique of medium particularity or specificity connected to the Hegelian (dialectical) dependence of Clement Greenberg's (1995) formalist critique, and will radically alter the way in which painting can be created and consequently thought.

Research into the notion of the 'Virtual', which advances the potential for an interdisciplinary practice driven from painting, effectively constitutes a new methodological model for thinking through the space of painting, as well as the material structural qualities of painting. In contrast to prior methodological models used, primarily within the critique (or theorisation) of painting, an investigation into Gilles Deleuze's methodological processes creates a more open position within, or from which to challenge and redefine the limits or constraints of painting.

Interdisciplinarity is an often-used term through which connections between things, and in particular reference to fine art practice, different media can be discussed. In this specific context the ideas of interdisciplinarity stem from a particular position, that of painting, a discipline well known for its internally focused critique and rejection to all that is exterior to, or different from it (Greenberg, 1995). By exploring the potential of the outside, external forces, or those things that do not normally pertain to the specific characteristics or traits of the medium, a greater series of connections and relationships can be established. In turn this radically alters the potential construction and structural dynamics of the work. For example (as will be discussed), the space of painting can shift, changing the conventional static and two-dimensional constraints within painting, towards the inclusion of movement, fluidity and three-dimensionality. The form of the work alters through these connections (for which the virtual is the instigator) whilst at the same time retaining, or allowing painting to persist. These ideas (aims) challenge the theoretical and practical identity of the work as painting, whilst serving to explore new and under-considered possibilities for the work, essentially this proposes a form of 'becoming', or 'becoming-other' through externality, a liminal space for the construction of painting as a contemporary practice.

The vital shift in the philosophical approach to the work has created a new alignment for thinking and painting as practices, a move that allows painting to persist, without succumbing to internal and specific notions, or constraints, within the medium. As will be shown, this notion of change has led to a new method of thinking (or rethinking) regarding painting, a repositioning of painting both as a physical practice and also as a conceptual practice, a becoming which transgresses the formal restrictions of the medium.

This method of disruption within the methodological process challenges the boundaries of the medium from within, the 'conventions' of the medium are used to subvert themselves, not through a particular material dependency but rather a method enabling the act of painting to spread into the world, a different relationship to objects around us, a challenge to our confirmation of an object as something and only that thing, a quasi-hybrid form referencing painting whilst seeping out - spreading out and incorporating other possibilities. This formless condition depends upon Deleuze's (2001) notion of the virtual and allows a 'spacing', a slippage or the 'bringing forth' of potential within painting. The development of this methodology situates painting as a virtual element, an element which itself contains the potential for change within the work through integration, an integration that evolves across time and space.

Two related terms emerge through this research as the progression of the propositions within formulate. These two terms are 'resistance' and 'persistence'.

Notions of specificity and singularity, material dependency and the boundaries, which these types of thinking allude too, create and structure division rather than integration - in effect a form of resistance - rather than structuring new methods and consequently physical forms for challenging these particular dependencies. Resistance here becomes an important concept, and one, which begins to articulate a definitive rationale for approaching work through alternative and more open methodology. I hope to be able to outline in this section a distinction between the two terms 're-sistance' and 'persistence'. Persistence here might be defined as the ability of a 'thing' to continue to move forwards through different obstacles and objections, though often conjuring conjectural and divided opinion.

However, returning to the notion of resistance: painting as a medium has been, and continues to be, structured through a position if individuation and segregation, where it can isolate itself to the point of charting its own demise. This obviously is not the case and can be argued from alternative points, yet in resisting that which is external, through a focus upon internal critique, painting openly presents its own constraints, effectively structuring the boundaries between itself and that which it is not. Again it is possible to discuss these concepts through different theoretical positions including Thomas Kuhn's (1996) structure of paradigms or even Heidegger's (2001) discussion of the thingness of things. However, if the critical theory which demarcates the particular territories within which different media can operate, defines (or in the case of painting has defined) a particular and very specific position and condition, then the ability to operate externally (from that point) is negated, again necessitating a focus upon the internal arrangements or organisation of the medium itself.

This point of view could be argued from other positions, particularly taking into account Rosalind Krauss's (2002) 'Sculpture in the Expanded Field', yet I would argue that this still maintains a particular framework for the practice defined through and from within the medium – however expansive or expanded you wish this to become. What must also be remembered is that at this time painting was not internally seeking to destabilise its formal arrangement or organisation as an object, although it has realigned itself with its wall base in many different and exciting ways, it was and still in many ways is dealing with the 'Greenbergian' ghost or spectre, which has become a perennial thorn in its own side.

In order for painting to begin to reorganise and permit itself the perceived luxuries of other media, it has to be thought through outside of the conventional terms by which it has been associated. This means a different methodological understanding of the approaches that need to be taken in order for painting to become something other than it is. If resistance implies a rigorous demarcation of territory or identity – where external obstacles become boundaries (within which the work must work), then persistence offers a quite different approach. In approaching external rather than internal relationships, painting can be reconsidered and constructed through a radically different organisation. This means that the internal agendas, which have bound painting to prescriptive and divisive formal arrangements, can be completely and radically rethought.

In approaching the external and adopting alternative strategies within the work painting begins to seep out into the world, opening itself out onto and into other media, a form of appropriation if you like, yet one in which the potential of painting becomes increased (exponentially), a position which redefines its apparent condition. This interdisciplinary approach instantly begins to rearticulate the way in which painting can be constructed, its material and physical properties, the space[s], which it can inhabit, its relationship to the architectural and its time, effectively shifting through time-based media or restructured so that there can be no possibility of 'all-at-onceness' – another position placed on the conventions of painting.

Its potential affiliations and connections with other media also create a position within which, interdisciplinarity opens out more progressive and subversive questions, which had previously been conventionally mapped out internally in terms of painting. The subsequent forms constructed lead to an otherness, an otherness created through integration. This brings to the fore two further terms I would like to mention, integration and succession. Each of the terms, in their different way refers to the potential based in multiplicity, in direct contrast to the internal singularities embedded within resistance. They each also refer to a becoming, a becoming which leads out, an opening out through the persistence of medium through integration and the succession of form and space.

One idea that I have considered at length in response to these questions, in particular what at times has been a difficult process, in terms of the potentiality of painting to persist, as a method for instigating change, or highlighting levels of difference, is the notion of *The Virtual*, in relation to the writings of Gilles Deleuze (2001). *The Virtual* provides a model for thinking through interdisciplinarity within, and from, other media. *The Virtual* acts as an instigator for change, which effectively destabilises the pre-formity attached to medium specific practices.

Elizabeth Grosz (1999), in 'Becomings; Explorations in Time, Memory and Futures', suggests that:

Insofar as time, history, change, and the future need to be reviewed in the light of this Bergsonian disordering, perhaps the concept of the virtual may prove central in reinvigorating the concept of the future insofar as it refuses to tie it to the realisation of possibilities (the following of a plan), linking it instead to the unpredictable, uncertain actualisation of virtualities.

The actualisation of the virtual is as such a process, which is linked to, both, being and becoming, an 'open-endedness' where *The Virtual* acts as a 'plane' of differentiation, not for the pre-forming of identity but instead an open, bifurcated, mutated or folded actuality. *The Virtual* is an 'open' multiplicity which differentiates and becomes 'other' through actualisation. The potential based within a multiplicitous system creates a fluid and dynamic method for constructing form. The actual structure of form shifts towards bifurcation, blending and smooth interaction. The mixing or blending within a multiplicity, and more importantly its components, allows for far greater 'movement', whilst allowing 'actual' forms to integrate different elements that may not have been linked, or considered, before. This notion forces the persistence of painting, through a multiplicitous assemblage.

The forms, which can potentially be constructed following this thinking allow for the persistence of painting yet are something, or permit painting to 'become' something, other than painting, a form of displacement, allowing painting to be 'out-of-place', which offers new and challenging modes of organisation. This notion of becoming hinges upon *The Virtual* as a way of combining multiple, often disparate forms, elements, flows or singular structures in order to create, or develop new forms embedded in external relationships through which painting can persist. The virtual does not act as a plan or 'blueprint' for the actual; rather it generates or produces interconnections, differences and networks within both the actual and also the actualisation of the virtual.

In this way, the notion of painting 'becoming-other' stimulates, or forces an attack upon its pre-formed, or fixed, identity, consequently the notion of persistence, activated from a position of externality, structures new potential forms, or series of potentialities, within which the internal critique is destabilised in order to construct new arrangements and different configurations.

What is particularly exciting at the moment is the potential integration of these different modes of practice, where rather than resolutely defining or constructing form through association or connection within and across different media they can begin to come together as well. In effect an expansion of the multiplicitous circuit of ideas, potential relationships as well as material, physical and structural developments can be combined within the same work, work which continues remapping its own ground in order to seek challenging new positions for itself, always shifting, or seeking, to alter its condition.

It is important to introduce and propose the importance of the philosophical notion of the Virtual upon contemporary artistic practice, starting with an explanation of the term and its philosophical resonance.

The concept of the virtual and its relationship with the actual is different from the possible and its relationship with the real; it is a structure, which invokes change within, and importantly, across systems.

Following Henri Bergson, Deleuze (2001) proposes the virtual as a 'method' for creating 'change' (or difference). In contrast to the possible, which is the resemblance of the real, according to Deleuze constructed abstractly 'post' (or after) the real, in other words as Keith Ansell Pearson (2002) suggests, "a notion of the application of possibility is to be delimited to closed systems" (p. 72), the real being simply an image of the possible.

The 'method' for actualising change is based upon an examination of the notion of the virtual/actual according to Bergson and Deleuze. The virtual is bound into the process of becoming, but not a becoming through the systematic dialectical method, this is an open-ended becoming, where the virtual can be seen as series of potential. Deleuzian philosophy is based within the virtual; it is the virtual that constructs the actual and the actual that is defined by its virtual intensities. These virtual intensities are the becoming actual of the virtual and this is not used as a way of defining the actual

in the sense that it will subsequently have its own identity but rather it is a method for opening the actual to continual and further virtualities.

The openness of this methodological way of thinking, Deleuze and Guattari (2002) state, "has no beginning or end; it is always in the middle, between things, interbeing, intermezzo" (p. 25). The dialectical method is the movement towards closure, this closure reflecting the absolute, whereas a rhizomatic method can be seen as a continual movement, a mapping that moves backwards and forwards, where the "middle is by no means an average; on the contrary, it is where things pick up speed" (Deleuze & Guattari, 2002. p. 25). The contrast in these two methods highlights a critical difference in the thinking behind them, and also the change they instigate in terms of application of the method. In response to Rosalind Krauss' (2002) text, 'Sculpture in the Expanded Field', Miwon Kwon (1997) in her 'One Place After Another: Notes on Site-Specificity' states that "The fluidity of subjectivity, identity, and spatiality as described by Gilles Deleuze and Felix Guattari in their rhizomatic nomadism, for example, is a powerful theoretical tool for the dismantling of traditional orthodoxies that would suppress differences, sometimes violently" (p. 109). This notion of fluidity is important for the research and is linked to the concept of 'change' invoked through Deleuzian methodologies. Fluidity relates to the movement across differential systems, where the change 'within' the system, or to be exact between systems, is actualised and creates a shift in the ideological structure and physical construction of the system.

TRANSFORMATION

A Possible Literature

The openness of the future hinges upon the question of identity and the notion that the actualisation of the virtual inflects, bifurcates or 'morphs' with the actual, in other words creating a dynamic change in terms of something's identity and an open becoming. In many ways this shift from the linear concept of resemblance (and identity) embedded within the transition from the possible to the real, towards an 'interactive' combination of the actual and the virtual where the final identity is tied into (or located within) memory and potential.

As briefly mentioned earlier, the virtual is linked to the concept of 'becoming', creating, through becoming, a more open future. It is based within this 'open' future or 'to-come' that dramatic change, a shift in the internal dynamics of matter (and the space in which it rests) can take place. One element linked to becoming focuses upon it being an instigator for change, highlighting difference and a way to upset or disorientate stability and control, through newness, creativity and innovation (Grosz, 1999. p. 16). At the same time the notion of becoming (thought through its vital connection with duration) problematises preconceived or existing notions of identity, origin and development (Grosz, 1999. p. 18). In essence as Grosz mentions Bergson and Deleuze both support the notion of becoming as a rupture of emergence, a change instigated through difference.

The relevance of the virtual and actual must be established here, what is the purpose for examining in detail the relationship between the virtual and the actual and describing the notion of the possible in terms of the real as an opposite or contradictory possibility, leads to two very different propositions in terms of the becoming of things. The first static, or at least the formulation of itself, whilst the other is open, dynamic and instrumental in the production of change, or enabling the becoming of more than itself (or other). The first formulation relates to the 'materialisation' of the possible within the real (direct resemblance), the second through differentiation allowing for a new divergent actuality. The virtual does not act as a plan or 'blueprint' for the actual, rather it generates or produces interconnections, differences, networks and morphological, hybri-

disable actualities within both the actual and also the actualisation of the virtual. It is in this way and also through the contraction and expansion of time, the vital relationship between the past and the present and the opening of the future, that *a* becoming is generated. Deleuze suggests that a 'becoming' is not a reduction or a leading back, it is a movement forwards, the openness and potential of the future. Becoming involves a multiplicity (and in such a way can be seen as anti-dialectical) or even a combination of multiplicities, for instance generated through duration as a multiplicity, space and matter as multiplicities or elements of a multiplicity. Essentially the movement or interconnectivity, the structuring of difference[s] between the levels within the multiplicity [ies] creates the potential for becoming.

It is important to question how this is relevant to a discussion focusing upon space. If space is to be considered as being heterogeneous, multiple, divergent and based upon difference (both to itself and time) then the actualisation of the virtual, the virtual being different series of potential (within different layers of space) can create a new (actual) space. The contraction of this possibility of spatial awareness (perception) allows for radical expansion in terms of future potential. In a way this can be read as a becoming-space or a space-to-come.

According to Deleuze becoming relates to the future, but he also refers to becoming as sensation, specifically in terms of 'becoming-other', where one can, through becoming, achieve a sensorial response or connection, which allows the potential for the sensorial being of others to become 'sensed' in a new arrangement. This can be seen as a becoming-flower for instance, or becoming-whale in response to Ahab, in Melville's, 'Moby Dick', mentioned in chapter 10 of 'A Thousand Plateaus' titled 'Becoming-intense, becoming-animal' (Deleuze, 2002). This is an awareness of the sensual perceptions of the creature (whale) reacting within, and in the becoming of Ahab, which essentially leads to a becoming-whale within Ahab himself. Alternatively another reading of this could be made within other literary contexts, for instance, Franz Kafka's (1995) 'Metamorphosis' where Gregor's becoming-insect has far reaching physical and territorial consequences. But, another point needs to be made in connection with 'Metamorphosis' by Kafka, and this relates to the notion of change and 'Frankenstein' by Mary Shelley (2010) is also important within this context. A distinction must be made here separating notions of 'change', and Caroline Walker Bynum (2001) makes a number of important points relating to change, hybridism and metamorphosis in her text 'Metamorphosis and identity', where she states that "the question of change is, of course, the other side of Identity" (p. 19), identity being a specific position, a territorialised position and Walker Bynum suggests that identity is structured through the notion of change and how change affects identity. The two forms of change she offers, hybridism and metamorphosis, are both very different. Hybridism can be seen as a 'doubling' that introduces a new distinction in terms of identity, and she uses two examples to present hybrid species (systems), mule as half donkey, half horse and coral as half plant, half stone. Obviously the new, hybridised forms structure and contain their own identity, but that identity is dependent upon the identities, and forms, of the two species combined to create it. In contrast there is a very different form of 'two-ness' in relation to metamorphosis, rather than a doubling, the two parts represent the thing as it was and the thing that it becomes. Walker Bynum (2001) states, "A hybrid is a double being, an entity of parts, two or more" and goes on to say "Metamorphosis goes from an entity that is one thing to an entity that is another" (p. 30), effectively the process of metamorphosis is a movement, change is a process of becoming, the movement (however gradual) from one thing to another, whereas hybridism can be seen as a sudden rupture, the combination of two, a synthesis between two distinct elements (or different identities). In this way Frankenstein can be seen as a hybrid, the bringing together of multiple component parts (different identities) into

one body, whereas in contrast, Gregor 'becomes-insect', losing or moving away from his original identity to the formation of a new identity, Gregor *as* insect.

The more radical notion of change, although both can and have been in the past perceived as radical as they instigate a - 'monstrous' - fear of the unknown, relates to metamorphosis, metamorphosis as 'becoming', a shift into an alternative and different actuality. Interestingly, Gregor retains a semblance of the past that he was, the metamorphosis he undergoes forces change, but this change is a gradual process of leaving behind what was, whilst moving into another position (or identity). This means that the memory of the past informs the becoming of what will be. The notion of the hybrid has been presented in terms of painting, particularly the 'Hybrids' exhibition and catalogue, Tate Liverpool 2001, suggesting that through the idea of hybridism painting contains the potential to be open and interactive, exploring and integrating different possibilities to be found within other mediums and disciplines. David Ryan (2001) suggests:

In particular, the potentiality of a world of work which is no longer held hostage to notions of either conceptual or visual purity, denotes a new, invigorated alignment of mediums, sensations and conceptions. Painting in fulfilling its capability in this role, becomes an interface of endless possibilities (p. 17).

However metamorphosis, structures a different process, possibly the end product may not be radically different from the product created through hybridism, but importantly the method in which change is created or instigated is very different. Less about fusing different things together, a morphogenetic process creates a complete shift in the original dynamic, not seeking opposition, or alternatively assistance by way of the negative, becoming as difference-in-itself not through difference to what it is not, undergoing a change-in-kind.

Elizabeth Grosz (1999) states, in reference to Bergson and Deleuze, that "each conceptualises time as becoming, as an opening up which is at the same time a form of bifurcation and divergence" (pp. 3-4) and the virtual is vital to the notion of becoming. The virtual allows consistent movement away from identity, or the idea of an [en]closed entity, and effectuates the becoming, the move into the future instigated through change and difference.

However, how vital is the distinction made between hybridism and metamorphosis, surely change instigated in any form alters the 'being' of painting. In essence the emphasis placed on becoming is to present the idea that something can "become other than the way it has always functioned" (Grosz, 2002. p. 130). Essentially the notion of the hybrid as a method for instigating change also allows something to function differently, and as such both forms of change are important, and in fact through combination can create different yet appealing (and interesting) open series of potential for practice.

THE VIRTUAL

That Which Is to Come

The Virtual acts as a method for actualising change, and this research focuses upon the notion, or concept, of the virtual and actual according to Henri Bergson and Deleuze. It explores how these ideas can radically alter the way in which contemporary (painting) practice can be made and considered. Initially, an outline of the virtual in this context needs to be discussed, thus presenting the potential of the virtual from a position within painting, forcing or moving towards painting as an interdisciplinary practice.

The virtual is bound into the process of becoming, but not a becoming through a systematic (or concrete) dialectical method, this is an open-ended becoming, where the virtual can be seen as a series of potentials. John Rajchman (2000) discusses the notion of the virtual in 'Constructions' and states that,

The idea of the Virtual is quite old. The word comes from virtus, meaning potential or force, and often comes coupled with the actual, that through which the potential or force becomes at once visible and effective (p. 115).

Deleuzian philosophy is based within the virtual; it is the virtual that constructs the actual and the actual that is defined by its virtual intensities. These virtual intensities are the becoming actual of the virtual and this is not used as a way of defining the actual in the sense that it will subsequently have its own identity but rather it is a method for opening the actual to continual and further virtualities. The term 'becoming' here relates to that which is to come, and is directly linked to the virtual, as the virtual itself is tied to the process of becoming as the action of that becoming. As Brian Massumi (2002) suggests in 'Parables for the Virtual':

… the virtual does not exist. It comes into being, as becoming. Its nature is to come to be: to make ingress (p. 237).

It is in this way that the virtual through this process of becoming opens a different series of potential through which ideas and structural form can develop. The virtual creates, through becoming, a more open future. It is based within this 'open' future or 'to-come' that dramatic change, a shift in the internal dynamics of form (or the interdisciplinary potential evident in external connections), can take place.

The virtual, and therefore the notion that it is becoming or embedded in the process of (continual) becoming[s], focuses upon it being an instigator, or trigger, for change, highlighting difference and a way to upset or disorientate stability and control, through newness, creativity and innovation (Grosz, 1999. p.16). The virtual's coexistence with and relationship to the actual are both linked to the possibility of openness and the new, in terms of the future incarnation (or genesis) of objects, forms, and spaces.

Importantly, in presenting the particularity of the notion of the virtual (and the actualisation of the virtual) Deleuze (2001, pp.212-214) discusses the fact that there is a very different emphasis placed behind the different concepts of the possible and the real and the virtual and the actual. The contrast between the two (the possible/real and the virtual/actual) is embedded in difference. There is effectively no difference between the possible and the real whereas the virtual and the actual (or its actualisation) are constructed through difference itself. To further this, the possible is real in that it is what it becomes. It is a reflection of that which it will be, embedded in sameness (the resemblance of) the possible does not allow for the radical levels of difference evident within the potential of the virtual and the actualisation of the virtual. The possible contains identity within the form of the real, whereas the actualisation of the virtual does not (or cannot). Actualisation moves towards difference and diverges through the process of its becoming, it is multiple in that it can generate a more complex and varied series of potential within the virtualities from which it comes, or which it is to-come.

In relation to this distinction, between the possible and the virtual Deleuze (2001) states:

The possible and the virtual are further distinguished by the fact that one refers to the form of identity in the concept, whereas the other designates a pure multiplicity in the Idea which radically excludes the identical as a prior condition (p.211).

This evidences the action of the virtual and the force of change (or difference) embedded within the process of its actualisation that moves away from the identical, opening out from what was, to what can be.

The virtual is real yet not actual; the actualisation of the virtual is a process linked to, both, being and becoming, an 'open-endedness' where the virtual acts as a 'plane' of differentiation, not for the pre-forming of identity but instead an open, bifurcated, mutated or folded actuality. The virtual is an 'open' multiplicity which differentiates and becomes 'other' through actualisation. In 'Difference and Repetition' Deleuze (2001) suggests:

Such is the defect of the possible: a defect which serves to condemn it as produced after the fact, as retroactively fabricated in the image of what resembles it. The actualisation of the virtual, on the contrary, always takes place by difference, divergence or differenciation. (p.212)

It is this difference generated through the virtual, which defies pre-formed 'identity'. As Deleuze and Guattari (2003) state, "Actualisation breaks with resemblance as a process no less than it does with identity as a principle" (p.212). It is the operation of the virtual, and the vital difference this injects within systems, that challenges the fixed notions of identity and structures a challenge against previous thinking concerning identity (in particular *Hegelian* dialectical thinking).

Deleuze differs from Hegel in many ways, but perhaps the most important distinction between the two rests on the notion of contradiction, and Deleuze (1999) refers to Henri Bergson to emphasise the point, "The originality of the Bergsonian conception is in showing that internal difference does not go and must not go to the point of contradiction" (p. 49) and he goes on to discuss the importance of the virtual:

In Bergson and thanks to the notion of the virtual, the thing differs from itself in the first place, immediately. According to Hegel, the thing differs from itself in the first place from all that it is not, such that difference goes to the point of contradiction (p. 53).

In this way the main point of contention in Hegel (for Deleuze) rests on the notion of difference itself as well as the importance of the concept of the virtual. In contrast to internal difference seeking contradiction Deleuze, through or via Bergson, maximises the potential of the virtual, through external, and interdisciplinary series of potentials.

Elizabeth Grosz (1999) in relation to the notion of 'becoming' and the concept of the virtual writes that "it is a question not of dumping the word 'possible' and replacing it with 'virtual', but of understanding the concept in an entirely different way, understanding the processes of production and creation in terms of openness to the new instead of pre-formism of the expected" (p. 28). The possible acts as the 'pre-forming' of the real (not the actual) where there is no change in identity, instead as Manuel De Landa (1999) states "the distinction between the possible and the real assumes a set of pre- defined forms (or essences) which acquire physical reality as material forms that resemble them" (p. 34). Effectively the identity of the 'object' is not changed through the becoming real of the possible, the possible resembles the real that it becomes. In other words the possible and the real are conceptually identical. In contrast to this, there is a very different relationship between the virtual and the actual; there is no resemblance between the virtual and the actualisation of the virtual. This works as the subversion of identity in the specific terms of the non-resemblance of the virtual and actual. Deleuze (2001) states, "For a potential or virtual object, to be actualised is to create divergent lines which correspond to - without resembling - a virtual multiplicity" (p. 212). The importance placed upon the virtual creates the potential for dynamic movement, in contrast to the possible, which is exemplified through its pre-formity (or fixity in relation to the real).

Having presented the notion of the virtual, it is vital to discuss how it is useful or necessary in terms of a number of the other propositions being raised. The virtual acts as a 'binary' element, linked to the present, which binds different series of potential to be actualised. These different series are effectively tendencies, variables and/or bifurcations, which continuously fold upon the actual. In effect the notion of the virtual, which is mentioned by Bergson, Deleuze, Massumi, Grosz and Ansell Pearson is related to existence. In a sense it accepts and introduces the potential based in becoming to be actualised, affecting change and a certain form of dynamism (or fluidity) within thought. In many ways it may be best to see the virtual/actual as a tertiary system, with the movements underneath and between leading to difference and change, but this difference (or change) through becoming is not the positioning of a fixed or static actuality, it is rather a continuous cycle where the virtual inflects the actual whilst informing (and [re-] realising) its becoming through (another) actualisation. The dynamic relationship informed by the notion of the virtual creates the potential for change as the virtual is actualised, and Elizabeth Grosz (1999) suggests, "Insofar as time, history, change, and the future need to be reviewed in the light of this Bergsonian disordering, perhaps the concept of the virtual may prove central in reinvigorating the concept of the future insofar as it refuses to tie it to the realisation of possibilities (the following of a plan), linking it instead to the unpredictable, uncertain actualisation of virtualities" (p. 28). The future through the virtual, as Grosz expresses creates a vital challenge to preconceived propositions relating to the realisation of the possible, which Deleuze describes as a working backwards, for the possible is only possible once it is real, whereas the virtual (as mentioned) is already real, it exists alongside the actual which it 'forces' into existence. John Rajchman (2000) adds (in a similar way to Grosz), in relation to the virtual, "It doesn't take us from the specific to the generic. It increases possibility in another way: it mobilizes as yet unspecifiable singularities, bringing them together in an indeterminate plan" (p. 116). This 'new' type of existence should be thought of as a becoming, a movement consisting of potential change within the future.

John Rajchman (2000) provides an interesting suggestion for establishing a particular way of understanding the virtual and how it relates to both space and the construction of form within space, when he states:

A virtual construction is one that frees forms, figures and activities from a prior determination or grounding, of the sort they have, for example, in classical Albertian perspective, allowing them to function or operate in unanticipated ways; the virtuality of a space is what gives such freedom in form or movement (p. 119).

In essence, the virtual allows form to be loosened (freed) from the static preconceived notion of grounding, or fixity in terms of prior identity. This freedom allows different variables to be considered and activated and permits alternative potential options to be evident within the final form.

The openness mentioned in relation to the notion of the virtual hinges upon this question of identity and the idea that the actualisation of the virtual inflects, bifurcates or 'morphs' with the actual in other words, creating a dynamic change in terms of something's identity and an open-ended becoming. In many ways, this is a shift from the linear concept of resemblance (and identity) embedded within the transition from the possible to the real, towards an 'interactive' combination of the virtual and the actual where the final identity is tied into (or located within) memory and potential. It is in this way that the virtual is linked to the concept of 'becoming', creating, through becoming, a more open future. It is based within this 'open' future or 'to-come' that dramatic change, a shift in the internal dynamics of matter/material (and the space in which it rests) can take place.

It is important to state that Deleuze's (2001) notion of the Virtual is structured through Henri Bergson's (2002) discussions surrounding time, space, memory and duration. Bergson's complex interweaving of materiality (or matter) and space

as well as time, which inflects, or disrupts, our perception presents the potential for a new understanding of the potential for, or the structure of the new, the "insertion of duration into matter that produces movement" (Grosz, 2000. p. 230). This 'movement', or 'sudden, unpredictable' change is structured through difference, a series of divergent potentialities that lead towards new and challenging arrangements or organisations. The important aspect to this is the actualised *material* thing, which at once differs from what it was (at least the implication that it is, or could be, tied to a specific unifying identity), whilst reorganising the potential of itself through its own becoming.

What Bergson's understanding of duration provides is an understanding of how the future, as much as the present and the past, is bound up with the movement and impetus of life, struggle and politics. While duration entails the coexistence of the present with the past, it also entails the continual elaboration of the new, the openness of things (including life) to what befalls them. This is what time is if it is anything at all: not simply mechanical repetition, the causal effects of objects on objects, but the indeterminate, the unfolding and emergence of the new (Grosz, 2000. p. 230).

In essence, as Elizabeth Grosz (2000) mentions, both Bergson and Deleuze support the notion of becoming as a rupture of emergence, a change instigated through difference.

Realisation is the concretisation of a pre-existent plan or programme; by contrast, actualisation is the opening up of the virtual to what befalls it. Indeed, this is what life, *élan vital*, is of necessity: a movement of differentiation in the light of the contingencies that befall it (p. 228).

This returns to the possible/real and virtual/actual again, the first static, or at least it deals with the formulation of itself, whilst the other is open, dynamic and instrumental in the production of change, or enabling the becoming of more than itself (or other). The first formulation relates to the 'materialisation' of the possible within the real (direct resemblance), the second through differentiation allowing for a new divergent actuality. The virtual does not act as a plan or 'blueprint' for the actual, rather it generates or produces morphological or hybridisable actualities within both the actual and also the actualisation of the virtual. It is in this way, through external connections, that the opening of the work creates the potential for change (change embedded in difference), that *a* becoming is generated. Deleuze suggests that a 'becoming' is not a reduction or a leading back, it is a movement forwards, the openness and potential of the future. Grosz also states, in reference to Bergson and Deleuze, that "each conceptualises time as becoming, as an opening up which is at the same time a form of bifurcation and divergence" (Grosz, 1999. pp. 3-4) and the virtual is vital to the notion of becoming. The virtual allows consistent movement away from identity, or the idea of an [en]closed entity, and effectuates the becoming, the move into the future instigated through change and difference.

The space opened by the virtual, and its actualisation, brings external potentialities to the fore. As mentioned, the virtual as a multiplicity explores connections that lie outside of fixed identity effectively, this forces a certain break with the idea that different media are 'closed', and contain fixed boundaries that delineate their particular or specific essence (or traits), that which makes them something and instantly recognisable as that thing and that thing alone. This break, or rupturing of these boundaries allows interconnectivity, it presents the challenge of interdisciplinarity, but from a point where the multiplicitous potentialities of its future force the becoming of what will be. In effect this could be considered a 'liminal space', a state between one thing and another. The idea of liminality needs to be seen as a position that rests between things, as a movement from one state to another, in effect a process of becoming in its own right, and the virtual can be seen to relate at this juncture as the multiplicitous potentialities of breaking with resemblance (possible/real) as the principle of change. This in-between state, or space,

is subversive in that it brings often inharmonious or conjectural principles together in order to explore potential correlations between them. It is for this reason that interdisciplinarity, at least interdisciplinarity effectuated through the virtual can be seen as a subversive process, a subversion that leads away from the pre-formity of media, discipline and form, and our understanding of them.

INTERDISCIPLINARITY/ INDISCIPLINARITY

An Unrepentant Becoming

Transformative qualities are often overlooked within painting practices, outside of the constraints of its perceived boundaries. The virtual affects painting directly in this way. Connections external to the physical, structural constraints of the medium can actually force a change in the form of the work, whilst allowing the persistence of itself within the final arrangement. This happens even though its appearance may have radically altered, at times to the point of unrecognisability. The virtual opens a multiplicitous space through which many differential options can be considered with the work becoming other than that which it was. In effect the form can morphologically change, adapting to include external potentialities, which include architectural possibilities, movement and three-dimensionality, as well as questioning the materiality, time and duration within it.

In terms of painting the notion of the virtual becomes complex, and in effect the way of thinking of the virtual does not come from painting itself (although it can be considered a virtual element), rather it has to be constructed through spatial and temporal connections opening it out into different spatial and temporal opportunities and a series of potential. In this way, the virtual operates as a trigger for interdisciplinarity and this happens in the way it acts, in order that it question the specific 'internal' nature of the, or a, medium. The virtual can be used as a way of re-thinking or re-negotiating the space of theory within which the practice can be actualised. It necessarily incorporates interdisciplinarity by forcing connections and proposing ways of re-structuring new, transformative and different dynamic forms of practice. It is in this way that the virtual has to be thought in terms of painting, acknowledging relationships with other disciplines, challenging its theoretical ground, and subsequently integrating or folding itself upon different media creating new forms of 're-territorialised' practice. The virtual proposes the external, in contrast to the internal (in terms of disciplinarity), and it is this integration through the notion of multiplicity that orientates the interdisciplinary affects upon painting and creates the potential for painting to redefine itself in terms of its form and its spatial and temporal context.

As mentioned previously, Miwon Kwon (1997) states that; "the fluidity of subjectivity, identity, and spatiality as described by Gilles Deleuze and Felix Guattari in their rhizomatic nomadism, for example, is a powerful theoretical tool for the dismantling of traditional orthodoxies that would suppress differences, sometimes violently" (p. 109). This method of disruption within the methodological process challenges the boundaries of the medium from within. The 'conventions' of the medium are used to subvert themselves, not through a particular material dependency but rather through a method enabling the act of painting to spread into the world a different relationship to objects around us, a challenge to our confirmation of an object as something and only that thing, a quasi-hybrid form referencing painting whilst seeping out - spreading out and incorporating other possibilities. This formless condition depends upon Deleuze's notion of the virtual and allows a 'spacing', a slippage or the 'bringing forth'[3] of potential within painting. The development of this methodology situates painting as a virtual element, an element which itself contains the potential for change within the work through integration and transformation.

Alternatively, in terms of a multiplicity - being the form of the work - painting could be seen as the virtual component, driving the dynamic and orchestrating the manner in which connections and combinations can be made. From the theoretical ground orientating its particularity, the virtual proposes different methods for creating practice by amalgamating the theoretical and physical potentials within other mediums. It is important to state that the notion of the virtual changes our understanding of painting as a practice. It redefines the way in which painting can be created and necessarily shifts from an internal disciplinary approach to an external interdisciplinary one.

Thus, the notion of the virtual allows painting to be considered in a very different way from before from a boundaried, rule-dependent specific material form, the notion of the virtual permits a fluctuating space for painting where the virtual inflects, informs and deforms the actual (through its actualisation). It is therefore a position in which painting can exist without being painting.

However, painting is still embedded within the larger form and considered as a virtual element. This enables it to 'persist'; that is to say, the notion of persistence is central to the place of painting, as the virtual extends the potential of the medium. This 'persistence' is not defined by the medium, but rather found through the integration of painting within larger systems. Persistence is not to be considered in the same manner as repetition. Repetition implies the reformulation of the 'same'; persistence is continuity in a similar way to repetition but enables a greater degree of difference. This can be seen as painting 'becoming-other' whilst retaining different or certain/particular 'qualities'.

The transformative affects of the virtual as a concept, thought-through painting as a practice, force change in terms of the form of the work and they also subversively work towards inclusion rather than exclusion of external potential for the work. These transformative qualities work towards full morphological shifts rather than purely hybridised adjustments. This means that the virtual can affect a full change within the form of the work, rather than a doubling of one thing with another, and this allows for complete difference from the original identity (painting) and a break with resemblance as a principle. This form of transformation acts through interdisciplinarity, structured by the virtual, which takes firmly into consideration external elements. For instance, the static nature of painting can be radically altered through time-based media like film, where movement and time conjecture the constraints of conventional painting processes that is, they enhance the facticity of the process in the final form the work takes. Projection and light also construct different approaches for considering the potential of painting.

In terms of the connections that can be approached through this form of thinking, the frame, particularly in reference to painting can be reconsidered alongside the frame of the architectural, discussed at length by Bernard Cache in 'Earth Moves: The furnishing of territories'. "Like Deleuze, Cache defines his domain in terms of operative function rather than an essence or property: architecture is the 'art of the frame'" (Harris, 2005. p. 39). The framic reference of these ideas relating to architecture can be thought through the virtual link with the framic potential of painting. Yet, these series of potential can only be activated through a loosening of the ties to specific boundaries allocated to, from and within medium specific disciplines.

The virtual as a multiplicitous space allows connections to be made; it presents bifurcating and divergent paths for thinking through the work, structuring difference from the outset and forcing new arrangements, combinations and configurations. This can be considered in or through external disciplines like architecture (and architectural theory) where a piece of work like 'Leviathan's Slumber' (Figure 1) stretches across and away from painting (seeps or spreads out) into the surrounding space, incorporating elements of the architectural surroundings, like the

water fittings normally internal to and covered by the walls. These elements allow for colour to be present, to move and flow through the space. The architectural, both considerations of the internal architecture and the actual space within which the work is placed, become integral to the work. As a form the work consists of multiple elements, where the considerations of painting, being the initial driver behind the work, are inflected and become morphed into a larger whole. The transformative qualities of the work hinge around the widening (or opening) out and interdisciplinary approach alongside the potential evident within the virtual, which allows the concerns evident within painting to be retained whilst being transformed through the divergent and mutational potential when combined, blended or folded into a complex multiplicity. In terms of painting, the frame (the conventional frame of painting) becomes deformed through the architectural. This happens alongside the deframing of the architectural as well as the deframing of the architectural in reference to its location and the deframing of painting in relation to its architectural site. These combinations allow for a 'fluid' mixing, where the different elements come together, or are actualised in a new form.

In this way, the elements of the compositional parts become loosened so that they can be remapped. This loosening creates the openness for the external relationships with alternative media, disciplines, methods, functional possibilities and materials to interweave and blend towards the construction of new forms evidencing difference, divergent from their original identities, yet, persistent in their concerns. As painting becomes *loosened,* that is to say positioned so that it can flex or distort, it moves into a space where its potential becomes far greater, greater than the mere provision and articulation of its own constraints. This can be articulated through a split between the 'frame', or armature/support, linked across and with the skin, the canvas or paint, as initially discussed by Jeremy Gilbert Rolfe (1999).

Figure 1. 'Leviathan's Slumber'; water, food colouring, Grundfos pumps, 120m transparent tubing, wooden platform and fixings
© 2012, Dr. Alistair Payne (Used with permission).

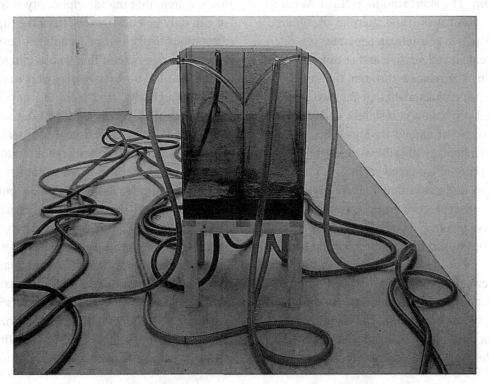

Painting's historically acquired morphology as a skeleton with a skin may provide a clue to why the stretched canvas - and, by comparison with it, the unstretched canvas, the panel, the fresco and fresco-like - can persist as a place where the body may think itself - not as volume containing and occupying space but as surface and space. Similarly, its dependence on surface and support as a fundamental opposition - which means they can be collapsed into one another as well as held apart - physically reconstitutes the ideational or perceptual separation of the painting's space from that of it's physical location. (Ryan, 2002. p. 17)

In loosening the way in which these elements can be considered, importantly not from a deconstructive (internalised position), and the interconnective potential of other fields of practice, new alignments and configurations can be mapped.

This effectively leads to a direct affect upon the way in which painting can be considered through the virtual. Once the armature or framic support is freed, as can be considered in the early work of Fabian Marcaccio for instance, its alignment to the wall and the architectural surrounds can and need to be rethought. So, the framic potential of the architectural space can consequently be driven as the framic potential of painting, blended, or mixed together in new arrangements to reconfigure previous alignments.

Another option, one of many potential connections, relates to time and movement, the displacement of painting through the digital, even becoming digital. These connections can be considered through the medium, for instance from deconstruction of the physical constraints, not as a way of internal rearrangement, but through methods of repositioning them outside of themselves, following connections with other potentially rearranged elements in a multiplicitous system. The short film loop 'Lost Angel's' (Figure 2), constructs a fluid interplay of coloured liquids, which at rest remain separate, yet, once forced, create an aggressive and at times violent interaction – produced through the repellant (non-mixing) characteristics of the two liquids. The digital projection is instantly derived from painting yet is structured through film and the movement inherent within the work, destabilising the static fixity of a painted surface.

The two projects outlined above present the potential within practice for the reformulation of painting as a practice, thought through the virtual and the interdisciplinary potential embedded within it.

An alternative proposition that needs to be considered at this stage is *Indisciplinarity* as discussed by Jacques Rancière (2008). The initial proposal was set out by Rancière in an interview published by Art&Research, and conjecturally challenges the

position and subversive potential of interdisciplinarity. If we come from the position, as laid out in this research, that interdisciplinarity is achieved (or can only be constructed) from the rupture or affectation of a platform or disciplinary base within and across others then this would inherently be conducive of a subversive state. This state would be one through which the 'localised' or individual identity is collapsed (though not necessarily deconstructed) from an externalised perspective, one which inclusively seeks out alternate states or forms with which to become immersed, thus creating a multiple whole. Essentially one which could be read in the Kafkaesque variations of metamorphosis – a full transformation through which multiple forms progressively and often aggressively become *other*. Closer in many ways to the Frankenstinian model, indisciplinarity is the seminal space between things, that which is not one thing, nor another - an active force of change and a compelling state of flux. Indisciplinarity is also not the agglomeration of individual disciplines

Figure 2. 'Lost Angels'; (film stills), looped DVD, 9 mins 28 sec
© *2012, Dr. Alistair Payne (Used with permission).*

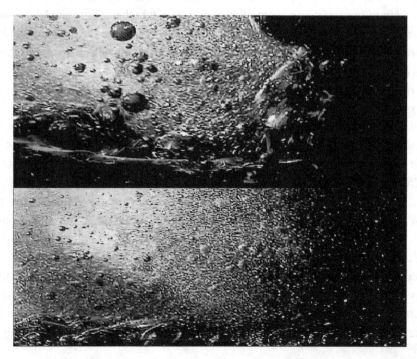

Figure 3. 'The Four Horsemen' (detail); powder coated jet cut Aluminium
© 2014, Dr. Alistair Payne (Used with permission).

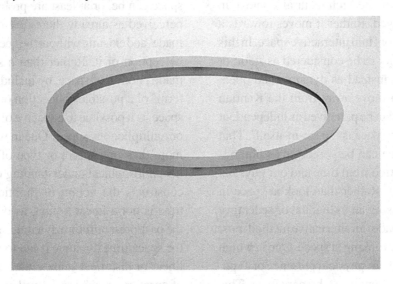

into a cohesive multiplicity, a potential genericism of absolute proportions. It is rather a position of breaking through the boundaries of disciplines and confronting that which they 'rub' against, thus it structures real subversion, although to add greater distinction to these principles, I would also like to propose that interdisciplinarity, thought through the model of the Deleuzian Virtual is potentially equally subversive, as long as interdisciplinarity follows the principle that it not succumb to the generic and lose all aspects of individuation. This notion of individuation as a sedentary aspect of an *aggressive* multiplicity is not simply reducible to itself in the first instance but also not subsumable in its entirety in the other, however, the absolute conversion towards a complete metamorphic model also needs to establish a non-genericised model or multiplicity.

The vision of interdisciplinarity and transformativity proposed throughout this research is embedded in the proposition of the virtual and this will be discussed further in the following section, where the moving-image and the cinematic, which necessarily bring into the space of painting further complex possibilities, including the interrelationship between space and time, movement and duration.

THE TRANSFORMATIVE AFFECT

An *Impure* Persistence

The method for thinking of space (or thinking space) and its relationship to the artwork (painting, sculpture or installation) needs to be examined in detail. Firstly how space is perceived, and secondly how space constructs our environment. The meaning of sedentary or 'grounded' space reflects immobility or stasis, whereas 'fluid' space reflects movement, flow and dynamics and this relationship is important, especially the context of fluid space in terms of its affects upon the artwork. Importantly looking at space will also help to define how painting should be perceived within the artwork that resides outside *of-itself*. Henri Bergson is important in locating or opening the dynamics, or possible fluidity, of space, most importantly through his notion of duration, subsequently followed by Gilles Deleuze.

Painting is not to be considered as a bounded space given through the combination of existing elements but rather as a part of a system that has a very different 'spatial' context. Importantly this shifts from a 'grounded' formal, organised or pre-formed space of painting - where painting is held apart from the architectural context in which it is displayed. Rather it moves towards a re-contextualised or fluid interactive space. In this manner space is not to be considered as static or homogenous, but instead as dynamic and open. Essentially it is a move away from the Kantian notion that space can be perceived as independent of its content, that space is 'space-in-itself'. That is to say that space can be perceived as homogenous, static and free from time and our physical interaction with it. Rather than look at space in terms of it possessing an individual or sedentary position (ready-made) an alternative method must be investigated for looking at space. One in which time, duration and our physical presence or experience determines how it can be perceived. This will have a great impact on how practice (artwork) can be dealt with in terms of space, how it exists within space and how it interacts with space as well as the viewer's interaction within that space. This enables or activates a different method for dealing with the specific nature of site in terms of painting in particular. Space itself has a slightly different emphasis, although inherently linked; it has its own dynamic that is both separate from and linked to the architectural site and the object (or installation) within it.

In 'The Production of Space' Henri Lefebvre (2001), within a discussion of 'abstract space', in contrast to 'historical space', suggests, "Abstract space carries within itself the seeds of a new kind of space. I shall call that new space 'differential space'", and he goes on to say, "a new space cannot be born (produced) unless it accentuates differences" (p. 52). What is potentially most interesting here is that the production of a 'new' space does not have to be the accentuation of differences, which in many ways already exist or at least are perceivable.

It is also important to consider the operation of ground and the particulars of the 'site' of space in order to distinguish a position from which 'pre-formed' notions of space can be challenged. For

instance some of these 'pre-formed' notions of space can be, or at least are probably most easily, perceived as already there (pre-existent), 'ready-made' and existing without the need for our physical perception of it. Rather than a static, or 'ready-made', notion of space, by including the virtual in terms of a possible connection or interaction with space, is it possible to conceive of a folded, layered or multiplicitous space? One in which there exists more than one space, or type of space. Through his philosophical understanding of time, Bergson constructs the notion of duration. For Bergson time is not a linear notion, as described through the past/present/future dynamic, and in many ways the space/time dynamic is not to be perceived in a linear or historical sense either. Bergson's notion of duration, which is followed by Deleuze (1991), will importantly bring to the fore the position, or context, of space in connection with duration. Bergson (2002) in 'Matter and Memory' suggests:

Space, by definition, is outside us; it is because a part of space appears to subsist even when we cease to be concerned with it; so, even when we leave it undivided, we know that it can wait and that a new effort of our imagination may decompose it when we choose. As, moreover, it never ceases to be space, it always implies juxtaposition and, consequently, possible division (p. 206).

For both Bergson and Deleuze, the relationship between space and time is extremely important. In contrast to the idea that space is 'ready-made' and time acting as a "fourth dimension of space" (Deleuze, 1991. p. 86) or the combination of space and time "into a badly analysed composite" (Deleuze, 1991. p. 86); Bergson using the concept of duration alters the relationship. Within 'time' there are different levels of contraction and expansion for example the past contracting through the present and (consequently) expanding into the future, and in many ways this method of thought is active within or between both space and time (duration).

Can space be considered in the same manner as time (as expressed by Bergson and Deleuze)? One in which space can be multiple and perceived *beyond-itself*. As a question that potentially considers these multiple possibilities, what might the affects be upon artwork and how an artwork, and from this perspective *painting* be considered? In order to facilitate this discussion the cinema and the cinematic event can elucidate and construct further complexities in terms of a re-rationalising of the space of painting, thought through the productive and transformatory considerations of the virtual. As John Rajchman (2008) describes in relation to Deleuze:

He was interested in how projection-practices, along with editing and framing, freed themselves from the conventions of "natural perception" (and from the mimetic conception of projection itself) to invent new sorts of images affecting our nervous systems. We see that from the start, there is a sense in which the screen was less an illusionist window or ersatz classical stage than a moving frame with an "out-of-frame" that allows movement and time to be rendered in new ways that would move beyond the concep-tions of space in classical painting or theater, or suggest alternatives to them. (pp. 294-5)

Painting and *its* space from a purely resistant perspective can be, or has been perceived within itself, a boundaried state within which the mechanics of itself propose and finalise its being. This characteristic concedes to the notion of the *out-of-frame* as discussed by Deleuze in 'Cinema 1', where conjecturally it could be proposed that the out-of-frame considered through the virtual, thus inevitably interdisciplinary discourse outlined earlier accedes towards a multiplicitious alternate reading of space in terms of artistic practices. John Rajchman (2008) proposes in relation to the Cinema and Time in the context of Deleuzian philosophical texts, that Deleuze:

... adopts two interrelated principles in his cinema books to exemplify this approach. The first says that "all criticism is comparative," and one must thus examine the cinematic in its larger overlaps with other arts and practices since there is "no work that doesn't have its continuation or its beginning in others." The second, found in the last sentences of his study, asserts that "it is on the level of interferences with many practices that things happen, beings, images, concepts, all kinds of events (pp. 299-300).

In many ways this establishes a creative doubling, one in which the cinematographic rereads the spatial contexts of painting outwith the confines of the architectural. The films made as part of this ongoing research project, including 'Lost Angels' 2012 (Figure 2), seek to undermine the conventional space of painting, rethought through a dynamic that accepts the constraints of painting, the architectural and the moving image, whilst conjoining them in order to subvert or destabilise the relationships between them, reconfiguring a new space for making and thinking artistic practice. Essentially these filmic works (often contained as part of a multi-formed installation) exude the propositional aspects of, in particular, liquid (but also gaseous) perception as discussed by Deleuze (2002b) in 'Cinema 1'.

Deleuze (2002b) referring to Bergson discusses the notion of the movement-image during 'Cinema 1', where he proposes that the movement-image is the duration of independent movement, that is to say that movement does not represent a whole which changes but instead a "fundamentally open whole, whose essence is constantly to 'become' or to change" (p. 23), and this can be seen in relation to Bergson and duration. Rather than change forced upon a whole, the movement-image operates as an 'open' whole, the openness generating continuous change, continual becoming in a temporal situation. The films made in relation to the research, have attempted to present, through morphosis, the dynamic durational operation of the movement-image in response to Bergson and Deleuze. This happens through constant change within the image presented in the films, a becoming that never reaches a conclusion - a forming, deforming and reforming in continually different cycles.

CONCLUSION

The focus of this chapter was to outline the importance of the philosophical notion of the virtual in relation to the writings of Gilles Deleuze and explore the affects this may have on current practice, particularly in reference to painting outlining the potential for interdisciplinarity. It is for this reason that the chapter discusses the virtual in the context of the writing of Gilles Deleuze, John Rajchman, Brian Massumi and Elizabeth Grosz amongst others, then proposes the more practical possibilities evident within this way of thinking.

The strategies of the virtual promote interdisciplinarity through openness, the loosening of the framework of medium-specificity towards inclusion of the external. In many ways this includes a folding of all the elements, so that the potential for change (the construction of new form/work) is not forced from purely one direction. The composition of the final multiple creates a new form that relates all the individual elements but does not reductively identify them. In this way the inclusion of multiple elements creates a space for interaction, this is the basis for interdisciplinary thinking and practices. Therefore, the affects of the virtual can be seen to dramatically alter the way in which painting can be considered. The identity of the final form will have effectively been changed or altered, with the new form structured through connections and difference.

The virtual constructs methods for disrupting the specific 'structural' elements of painting through connections that can be brought through other media. This enables new strategies for painting, where considerations outside of the specific medium, across the perceived boundaries of its condition, enhance a new series of potential for the construction of form.

The strategies employed within this research are not just pertinent to painting, but can be explored across different media as a tactic for transforming the order or constraints imposed by an internalised dialogue. The complex order of space and the subversive characteristics implied by the notion of the virtual as proposed by Deleuze establish methods for an artistic practice that encourages the external, a forming of multiplicitous potentialities that enhance alternate arrangements, constructions, forms and images.

REFERENCES

Ansell Pearson, K. (2002). *Philosophy and the adventure of the virtual: Bergson and the time of life*. London, UK: Routledge.

Baugh, B. (2003). *French Hegel*. New York: Routledge.

Benjamin, A. (2004). *Disclosing spaces: On painting*. Manchester, UK: Clinamen Press.

Bergson, H. (1920). *Creative evolution*. London, UK: Macmillan and Co. Ltd.

Bergson, H. (2002). *Matter and memory*. New York: Zone Books.

Cache, B. (2001). *Earth moves: The furnishing of territories*. Cambridge, MA: The MIT Press.

De Landa, M. (1999). Deleuze, diagrams, and the open-ended becoming. In E. Grosz (Ed.), *Becomings: Explorations in time, memory and futures*. London, UK: Cornell University Press.

Deleuze, G. (1991). *Bergsonism*. New York: Zone Books.

Deleuze, G. (1999). *Foucault*. London, UK: The Athlone Press.

Deleuze, G. (2000). *Cinema II*. London, UK: The Athlone Press.

Deleuze, G. (2001). *Difference and Repetition*. London, UK: Continuum Books.

Deleuze, G. (2002). *Cinema I*. London, UK: The Athlone Press.

Deleuze, G., & Guattari, F. (2002). *A thousand plateaus*. London: Continuum.

Gilbert-Rolfe, J. (1999). *Beauty and the contemporary sublime*. New York: Allworth Press.

Greenberg, C. (1995). *The collected essays and criticism: Modernism with a vengeance, 1957-69* (Vol. 4). Chicago, IL: University of Chicago Press.

Grosz, E. (1999). *Becomings: Explorations in time, memory and futures*. London, UK: Cornell University Press.

Grosz, E. (2000). Deleuze's Bergson: Duration, the virtual and a politics of the future. In I. Buchanan & C. Colebrook (Eds.), *Deleuze and feminist theory*. Edinburgh, UK: Edinburgh University Press.

Grosz, E. (2002). *Architecture from the outside: Essays on virtual and real space*. Cambridge, MA: The MIT Press.

Harris, P. (2005). Deleuze, folding architecture. In I. Buchanan & G. Lambert (Eds.), *Deleuze and space*. Edinburgh, UK: Edinburgh University Press.

Heidegger, M. (2001). *Poetry, language, thought*. London, UK: Harper Perennial.

Kafka, F. (1995). *The complete stories*. New York: Schocken Books.

Krauss, R. (2000). *A voyage on the north sea: Art in the age of the post-medium condition*. London, UK: Thames and Hudson Ltd.

Krauss, R. (2002). *The originality of the avant-garde and other modernist myths*. Cambridge, MA: The MIT Press.

Kuhn, T. (1996). *The structure of scientific revolutions*. Chicago, IL: University of Chicago Press. doi:10.7208/chicago/9780226458106.001.0001

Kwon, M. (1997). Notes on site specificity. Cambridge, MA: The MIT Press.

Lefebvre, H. (2001). *The production of space*. London, UK: Blackwell Publishers Ltd.

Lynn, G. (1998). *Folds, bodies and blobs*. Brussels, Belgium: Bilblioteque de Belgique.

Massumi, B. (2002). *Parables for the virtual*. Durham, NC: Duke University Press. doi:10.1215/9780822383574

Melville, S. (2001). *As painting: division and displacement*. Cambridge, MA: MIT Press.

Meyer, J., & Bochner, M. (2001). How can you defend making paintings now? In *As painting: Division and displacement*. Cambridge, MA: MIT Press.

Moos, D. (1996). *Painting in the age of artificial intelligence*. London, UK: Academy Editions.

O'Sullivan, S. (2010). *Deleuze and contemporary art*. Edinburgh, UK: Edinburgh University Press.

Patton, P. (1997). *Deleuze: A critical reader*. London, UK: Blackwell Publishers Ltd.

Rajchman, J. (2000). *Constructions*. Cambridge, MA: The MIT Press.

Rajchman, J. (2001). *The Deleuze connections*. Cambridge, MA: The MIT Press.

Rancière, J. (2008). Jacques Rancière and indisciplinarity. Glasgow, UK: Glasgow School of Art Press.

Ryan, D. (2001). *Hybrids*. London, UK: Tate Gallery Publishing Ltd.

Ryan, D. (2002). *Talking painting: Dialogues with twelve contemporary abstract painters*. London, UK: Routledge.

Shelley, M. (2010). *Frankenstein*. London, UK: Harper Collins Classics.

Walker Bynum, C. (2001). *Metamorphosis and identity*. New York: Zone Books.

KEY TERMS AND DEFINITIONS

Becoming: The transitional aspect of transformation, that point at which one thing begins to become another.

Cinema: The reference to cinema stems from discussions within Deleuzian philosophy and the contemporary connections between the still, or static, painting image and the durational time based moving image of the cinema.

Deleuze: Gilles Deleuze, the French Philosopher is referred to throughout this chapter, with particular reference to his thinking around the notion of The Virtual and its connections to the possibilities of interdisciplinary thinking.

Hybridity: Hybridity in this context refers to the doubling of two forms or beings to construct another, whilst retaining aspects of those previous individual entities. Within the chapter, 'Frankenstein' by Mary Shelley (2010) is discussed to propose a particular form of hybridity and a suggestive or creative description of hybridisation.

Interdisciplinarity: Interdisciplinarity is referenced and discussed within this chapter in terms of the possibilities of thinking beyond the parameters of disciplinary thought. This is discussed with particular emphasis upon (the expanded nature of) contemporary painting practices.

Metamorphosis: The full transformation from one form or being to another, within the chapter the 'Metamorphosis' by Franz Kafka is discussed, in order to perceive the full transition from one being to another, within a literary context.

Painting: Painting is the ground from which this research has emanated; it is viewed from the perspective of traditional critical and philosophical parameters through the lens of contemporary non-linear thinking to establish new spaces for making and thinking painting.

Persistence: A term referring to the possibility that painting can persist through change, becoming and/or transformation. Persistence is used in this context as a term or position, which can either be considered through hybridity or alternatively the retention of something through the act of full transformation or becoming.

Resistance: The term resistance is used here to refer to a particular aspect of painting – a resistance through which painting attempts to retain its own formalist constraints, a resistance to all that which confers change, becoming and/or transformation.

Transformation: This term is used to reference the potential change in form, appearance or character from one thing to another.

ENDNOTES

[1]   The term 'expanded practice' is used in this context in relation to painting but is derived from the ideas proposed by Rosalind Krauss in her essay 'Sculpture in the expanded Field' (2002).

[2]   The term 'grounding' in this context relates to a form of leading-back, a cyclical return to the conventional constraints of the, or a, medium.

[3]   The term 'bringing forth' in this context relates directly to Martin Heidegger's use of the term. Heidegger describes *poēsis* as a 'bringing-forth' this is the bringing-forth of the work (the 'irruption'). Heidegger (2001) states that, "bringing-forth brings out of concealment into unconcealment" (pp. 311-41); this is revealing - *alētheia* - the revealing of truth (the technical aspect of the work and the subject being taught).

Chapter 6
Sound Image and Resonant Animated Space:
Beyond the Sonic Veil

Ross Winning
University of Wolverhampton, UK

ABSTRACT

Animation is a synthesis of ideas that often encounters unpredictable, illogical, and imagined domains. In those animated worlds, recorded sound is now part of a coalition of two sensory forms mediated through hearing and vision. Sound has therefore been embedded in the audio-visual toolbox since the successful synchronisation of sound and picture. Sonic elements now contribute significantly to how animators might shape their films and express ideas. These animated worlds also often represent deeply rooted expressions of the interior mind of the artists and animators themselves. This chapter explores the relationship of sound to image in the evolutionary and increasingly variable animated forms that are currently proliferating. It aims to focus on sound as being the primary channel that is best able to reflect those interior ideas within a range of animated media. The exploration seeks to do this through tracing proto-cinematic ideas in the art of the past and animation practice that researches the sonified and animated image using musical and figurative metaphors.

INTRODUCTION

As a contemporary art form that encounters unpredictable, illogical and imagined domains, animation can significantly mediate a range of human responses that can often be deeply embedded. It can do this by exposing those often difficult to articulate ideas through novel sound and picture combinations. These animated works can be resonant with deeply rooted expressions

of the interior mind of the artists and animators themselves. Also, sound is considered today as a functioning part of this animated system. This system brings together mainly two sensual experiences that are received simultaneously through hearing and vision. Sound has therefore been embedded in the audio-visual toolbox since the successful synchronisation of sound and picture. Sonic elements now contribute significantly to how animators might shape their films and express

DOI: 10.4018/978-1-4666-8205-4.ch006

those ideas. A developing relationship with sound is now the accepted convention in animation. This condition of sound-image and motion picture is almost bound to pose questions of the communicative primacy of the visual that for so long, has been considered as the prime ontological basis that underpins the theorising of the condition of cinema. In the evolutionary and increasingly variable animated forms that are proliferating, this accepted primacy of vision in audio-visual work is drawn into question.

This chapter has a focus on sound as the main channel that is best able to reflect this psychological interior and consider its approach in animation practice and reception. By tracing proto-cinematic ideas in art and personal practice that engages the relationship of the sonified and animated image, a case for prioritising the sonic and its role in probing the imagination is developed.

The concept of added-value in sound and picture combinations that are encountered in animated and synthesised worlds have the potential to expand the idea of audio-vision. This will often go beyond the normalised soundtracks of narrative cinema. The theory of audio-vision relates to sound and visual combinations and their potential to come together with a whole that is greater than the sum of the parts. That is; where the perception of sound affects the visual and that duality of sound and image is brought together as a tangible and transformed reality. (Chion, 1990). This contract in animation is now also expanding a type of meta-animation in forms where audio visual combinations are deployed in ways that evoke an enhanced imaginary response. It infers that this response is mediated primarily by the hearing sense and the act of listening in action. Furthermore that this act of listening is modal, transient, culturally and subjectively informed.

What is seen and heard simultaneously has the potential to shift the understanding of audio-vision outside of screen space. These contracts in sound and image are now expanding within a type of animation practice that encounters other spaces, objects and new arenas for its reception. Audio-visual combinations are deployed in ways that evoke an enhanced visual imaginary. The chapter argues that this current condition can be primed by the hearing sense and is as much a function of listening as seeing.

A case for the value of sound is made firstly through an examination of sonic evocations in pre-cinematic artefacts. This argues that the currency of the cinematic derives from art forms that precede recorded sound. The case further examines those art forms as tangible resonant spaces that communicate sonic ideas. Secondly, sound theory and audio visual media are considered in relation to this imaginative response by focusing on how hearing combines within a subjective multi-sensory set of conditions that keep us engaged through audio-visual media. Thirdly, by considering the difference and progress from performed sound to synchronised sound and finally through personal practice. These practice projects research the construction and testing of the sound-image. They have been undertaken to ascertain how responses to listening are unique in the production of animated works in relation to the sound-image. The research also proposes future directions for audio-visual analysis and sound reception.

BACKGROUND

The canon of critical and theoretical work relating to the field of animation is mostly derived from broader studies of the film and the moving image. Audio-visual perspectives on sound that comprise another part of the literature emerge from the historical view of animation, which had its origins in photography. It therefore, appears to be primarily understood through vision, and linked to the truth and mythology that surrounds the indexical image. The dominant view holds that sound is a late addition to the genesis of cinema that continues to allocate the greatest importance to vision, both critically and aesthetically. The direction of film in those early 'silent' years predicated a mass form based on the developing visual culture, and included film-makers such as Sergei Eisenstein and D.W. Griffiths. Both of these pioneers of moving image drove this popularity through developing a burgeoning cinematic language that was thought to possess the potential to communicate with millions of people.

In the early years of film development, the cinema's main choice of communication to the masses was to appeal to the primary sense of vision placing sight and spectacle above hearing. Although this period of development is now noted for being imbued with cinematic silence, records of cinema performances show that film theatres and projected optical performances were very sonorous and were often accompanied with live sound effect and music accompaniment. The ontological perspective that persists however is of a form where the visual is of prime importance. This is the dominant theme in many studies of the film art. An accepted view prevails where, according to Altman (2007), "cinema requires an image but not sound - cinema is thus essentially a visual art" (p. 6).

Early film development is also deeply enmeshed with ideas of visual spectacle and astonishment. The pre-occupations of the avant-garde in art at that time viewed cinema as an arena: "... to exaggerate the "impact of the spectator" and "a matter of making images seen" (Leger, 1973, p. 21). For example, in addition to Eisenstein, the Italian Futurist poet, Filippo Tommaso Marinetti understood the revolutionary possibilities of the new medium of film. (Tisdall & Bozzola, 1978) They both proposed notions of real-time effects in the theatre such as literally glueing spectators to the seats and setting off firecrackers to enhance immersion in the new medium. (Gunning, 1986, p, 70). Artists and writers were exploiting the prospects for a technologically reconstructed cinematic image for its pervasive qualities with contrasting aims for audience response and re-

ception. Whilst the ambition for the audience's reception of these cinematic events may have an alternative and wide ranging purpose, assisting sound and vision through technological enhancement in combination with traditional theatrical shamanic practice found new impetus during this period of the 20th century.

Having established technological advances as instrumental in driving the artistic and economic aspirations of the new medium, the additions of sound to vision in cinema also raised new theoretical perspectives. The conditions for cinema that were prevalent prior to the rationale that eventually led to a successful marriage of recorded sound and image were still characterised by a sense of intrigue as to its visual origin. That is; of a pure visual medium that was becoming enervated by sonic additions. Subsequent theoretical views to advance the conditions and terms of cinema are still perceived as being sullied by the sonic interloper. (Murch, 1990). Furthermore, there is the view that the study of sound is only recently establishing itself as an independent cultural object worthy of terminology and study; both as an entity in its own right, and for its use within the contexts of moving image and animation (Coyle, 2010), (Schafer, 1994).

The language of the sacred and divine had always driven descriptions of the phenomenon of sound and its embodied origin. Altman (2007), Altman and Abel, (2002) forward a discussion that implies sound historically became imbued with mystery and inhabited the realms of religious significance. One example of this is the act of ventriloquism known by the Ancient Greeks as gastromancy or speaking from the stomach. Throwing the voice or speaking remotely with no visible lip correlation were acts thought to belong to invocations of the un-living, and the sounds produced as possessing clairvoyant potential. Ultimately, this act became the performance art well known today as one that evolved from the Music Hall theatrical tradition. Whilst gastromancy is now rationalised as a vocally affected ventriloquial and performative function, it remains within the scope of the theatrical traditions, with their deeply rooted mythical origins.

Literature written on sound and its relationship to film, often underlines the difficulties around its identification and interpretation. This difficulty lies in finding a vocabulary commensurate with sound. Describing a sound event appears to demand a more abstract idiolect. The task of identifying sonic events is further exacerbated by the additional terms and conditions relating to a combined audio and vision in motion pictures. Although language is part of this overall sound continuum itself, it is arguably poor at interpreting sound. European musical forms for example evolved terms for direction and description derived from Latin. Running counter to this, however, is the way that music and its performance are often now described in the most facile terms often translated, according to Barthes (1997) into "the poorest of Linguistic categories" (p. 179). This is a reference to an inevitable use of the adjective describing the immediate response the music is likely to engender. Barthes explains further this tendency to use simple epithets that emphasise the predicate in descriptions of music thus; as a desire to provide a bulwark against which the subject's perceived challenge to the imaginary that music invokes is protected. For example, describing music as 'happy' or 'sad'. These are terms that superficially avoid the complexity of these human emotive responses that are often expressed through the abstract possibilities in musical sounds.

This linguistic observation proposes that music is therefore an extension of the Platonic idea that sees music as a bringer of joy, or conversely, loss. This can be extended to a concrete notion that what we might individually interpret as music covers the whole spectrum of sound. The confirmation from Cage is that music and noise qualities are interchangeable and therefore open to re-contextualisation. This further demonstrates that the attempt to qualify and create firm classifications

for sound presents a deep linguistic challenge. Arguably, language occupies only a small part of what we hear. This is further asserted by Cage (1961) who states, "What we hear is mostly noise. When we ignore it, it disturbs us. When we listen to it, we find it fascinating" (p. 3).

Importantly, both sound and vision are functions of two primary senses. When used in combination in the moving image, their synthesis becomes a significant sensual means of abstract communication that requires terms and conditions to be defined. Conversely, a view that accepts the origination of cinema as primarily a function of vision also has tendencies to privilege live naturalistic action and the photographed product. This is despite the original discovery that photography could become truly motivated by replaying still images in quick succession through projection technologies facilitated by the combination of mechanics, electricity and optics. Using mark making, drawing and objects, experimenting with tricks to deceive the eye of the audience through stop-frame and substitution techniques was an early fascination during the pioneering years of cinematographic development. The mundane events of live action would nonetheless eventually constitute a dominant part of this vocabulary of a new cinematic spectacle. (Gomery, 2005).

The two topics of animation and sound have therefore both been somewhat undervalued in terms of their critical focus. However, in more recent periods, as animation gains ground as a cultural product, so has the critical attention. Also, there is increasing acknowledgement and understanding of sound as an important mediator in the ecology of the world. Use of sound in a wide variety of animated situations, film, online arenas, fine art and commercial cinema as well as in other cultural expressions using gallery space, is therefore symptomatic of the attention it is now receiving. These contexts and the nature of sound itself, embed not only sound materials and objects but also the sonic as a fundamental idea within many audio-visual products.

Listening and Hearing

The act of listening is also a function of the senses. Those five main senses are a concerted system that links the interior with the exterior. This sense system orientates and creates our experiences of the world. Differing modes of perception according to Kant are dependent upon our sense awareness. This evocation of the senses functioning as perceptive gateways implies a subjectivity that is difficult to evaluate in individuals. It is increasingly becoming noted that the compensatory ability of the human being is remarkable in its efficiency to make up for the loss of one sense. This is most discernible in hearing and vision, both of which are considered to be the primary senses. Recent neurological studies are increasingly illuminating the possibilities for compensatory shifts across the senses. These reveal that the brain can learn this process of adjusting, when one sense is lost or damaged. People who have both lost sight suddenly and gradually also corroborate this; Atkinson states in her article that "Suddenly you can smell the world and sense when someone is standing out of your line of vision. Your brain grows on the inside, and things on the outside start to matter less." (2007, p. 10). This sensory compensation process appears to be confirmed by neurological research. Defined as cross modal plasticity, it is understood to arise from the "recruitment of brain areas (usually assumed to be cortical brain areas) no longer used by the lost sense" (Adria, Hoover, Harris and Steeves. 2012, p. 565). This study explores sensory compensation in sound localisation in people with one eye. However, it is considered that the most powerful compensation from one sense to another has a greater potential in those with sensory disadvantage from birth. As a result of recent brain research, the terms and metrics for this greater degree of brain recruitment and cross modal compensation is becoming possible. This is revealed in studies with cochlear implant patients who are observed as recruiting and re-organising voice areas to compensate for hearing impairment

and recovery. There is evidence to suggest that this adaptation to sensory loss is a function of age which diminishes after the onset of impairment. (Voss, Collingon, Lassonde, Lepore. 2010). There are also a number of wider social recognitions of this condition. The musician who is blind or the artist who is deaf clearly demonstrates the sense organ's capacity to adjust and compensate for the other diminished faculties.

These studies into how the human brain functions have recently built on the many insights on how our senses behave and react with each other. One other such example of this cross modality which has received recent study is the occurrence in humans where the senses mix and can produce altered perceptions. This form of compensatory process leads to other more unexpected results in human cognition. This condition is referred to as synaesthesia. Synaesthesia is a phenomenon that is present in some people where the senses are confused and stimulation in one sense promotes a sensation in another. Knowledge of how one sense is informing another in these surprising and interrelated ways has gained ground and is of particular interest to scientists investigating brain activity. The phenomenon is also of interest to artists and designers undertaking aesthetic enquiries into how this condition might enhance and explain human responses as they engage artifacts with the primary senses of sight and sound.

Other recent developments in scientific investigation also begin to suggest that our visual experience is influenced by what we hear. Multi-sensory processing for cognition of sight and sound, once thought to begin predictably via the common pathway of the brain stem was considered to be ancient and unmalleable. It was thought to be a fixed route for the brain to communicate muscular-skeletal function to the body. The central nervous system, considered vital for individual survival, is also a pathway for a multitude of sensory networks. These include all the somatosensory systems such as taste, auditory, spatial and visual systems in addition to emotion and the locomotive triggers that, in turn, control the body. Such studies now suggest that enhancing one sense might encourage learning responses in another. Auditory response studies have suggested that music can aid children with literacy disorders. This outcome affirms that audio works significantly with vision and is a phenomenon that can be developed to bring beneficial results. Musicians engaging in all the senses of seeing, hearing, feeling as well as motivating the motor faculties in performance, were found to have enhanced audio-visual processing skills. This elevated auditory sensitivity, for example, is now thought to fundamentally influence every other auditory stream (Northwestern University, 2007). The implication for modal approaches to learning and therefore remediating other senses in this process is becoming apparent. For example, a sudden sound can focus or divert attention. McDonald et al. (2010) discuss this and explain that subsequent visual activity can be more marked and the acuity of this vision can lead to anticipation of a visual event that might be in close proximity to that sound. Concurrent and subsequent visual events, it is suggested can be altered in intensity by the influence of irrelevant sounds. This process of sonic masking can affect our ability to see or, alter the perception of what is actually there. There is also a further implication that this can be involuntary which suggests that behaviourist conditions can be influential and implicit within the cognitive reception of sound.

It can be concluded therefore, that the ability to process and assimilate sound in these real-world contexts, has deep resonance with the cognition and reception of audiovisual material. Not only will this have a bearing on the study of film and animation sound, but also will clearly be a factor when considering theoretical elements underpinning sound manipulation in a range of contexts. How sound is perceived, and channeled into its production, practice and reception within a range of mediated products is therefore revealed as a widely influential, complex and subjective experience when posed in conjunction with imagery. The perception of ideas about sound can also be traced in the history of tangible objects.

RESONANT ANIMATED SPACES

Traces of the Moving Image

Sonic Evocations: Comparing the Inert and Mute Form of Sculpture with Animated Film Ideas, Proto Cinematics, Mechanical-Automatic Movement

Although it might be considered that the development of time based ideas and popular visual narratives are the preserve of a technologically advanced twentieth century audience bred on the moving image, antecedents to ideas entrenched in time and narrative can be traced in the past. Current manifestations of sculptural work now extend to include notions that ephemeral and temporary media bring this tradition to contemporary audiences, although examples can even be found in the three dimensional art of past civilisations. Trajan's column, a sculptural artifact from the ancient world erected in Trajan's forum at Rome in AD 113 uses devices such as repetition and intervals to narrate events. They are deployed to tell the story of the Roman emperor Trajan's victory in the Dacian wars. These devices of repetition and use of the interval are both adopted concepts that originally describe temporal ideas. They occur in art and literature as well as music helping to structure linear narratives. An example of repetition in the frieze spiraling up the column is that Trajan himself is depicted fifty three times. This has been described by the art-historians as an example of the 'pseudo-continuous style' which is the repetition of the hero depicted in separate occurrences that are not necessarily undivided but are dis-continuous. This distinction from the continuous marks this convention as anecdotal and opposite to the attempt to recount narratives in relief with something approaching true time and space. Wheeler (1964) further suggests that Trajan's column "uses both conventions successfully" (p. 176).

Apart from its ground-breaking construction and scale, the column is noteworthy for its use of low relief depicting the progression of an epic story meant for a public audience. The audience experience of the object does not invite an immediate objectified experience that would usually be expected from such a three dimensional public work of scale. Although, only the pedestal is visible from ground, the column acts as an unfurling scroll that revolves twenty three times round the column, narrating the personal testimony of the Emperor. The debate as to whether these scenes were ignored due to their elevated position once the column had been erected suggests that the sculptural potential lay mostly in its ensuing commemorative and funerary role (Davies, 1997). It would have been difficult to experience the totality of this object as a narrative event. This further suggests that the repetition of motifs is important to its visual impact. The proximity of public buildings dating from the period could have given possible opportunities for the elevated parts of the frieze to be viewed by the population (Wheeler, 1964).

These adjacent public libraries allow audiences access to elevated roof spaces permitting closer relationship to the object's loftier parts of the frieze. Whether this is in ways that could be construed to be closer to the modern cinematic experience adds to this debate about the narrative aspects of inert and intractable materials. However, this monumental object is the embodiment of a number of interdisciplinary approaches and processes that accrue around one central idea. This concept of disciplines coalescing is a characteristic of modern film production.

The construction of a linear narrative, such as those found in cinematic or animated features also continue to demonstrate analogies with this sculptural object. This is found within the specific formal devices that are used to generate and motivate the spectator. Repetition, composition and spacing for example, as well as the importance of continuity and discontinuity to film are therefore not novel ideas and can be seen to have traces in

ancient art such as the kind of funerary monumental statement that Trajan's column represents. Other examples of these kinds of pictorial devices can also be found in the ancient art located deep within the caves at Altimira and Lasceax. These caves are resonant ancient sites and places where the images are painted directly on the stone walls of the interior space. These sites promote debate as to the function of images for those ancient societies that inhabited the caves. Also, the continuity of the tapestry at Bayeux, which tells the story of Harold and William the Conqueror and the battle of Hastings in 1066 is another example of this continuity of narrative cohered in a repetitive structural device.

In addition to this so-called mute narrative found implicitly in past art-works is the sonicity that can be traced back to the presence of synchronous vibration in inert materials. The contemporary sound environment in which we now find ourselves, reverberate increasingly with noisy incursions. These sonic incursions are increasingly technological and mechanical in origin. Cities, landscapes, either man made or natural, have become the medium of greater sonic transmission making the audio ecology a factor in well-being and sociability. The comparison with past societies and their associated soundscapes is based on an assumption that those societies were quieter and more rural. Whilst there is no record to substantiate this, other remnants from the past can speak to the presence of active sound. Further parallels from the ancient world can be drawn in respect to the current condition of audio-visual objects. Emergent concepts about the purpose of cave paintings for example appear to support that the images are manifestations of human purpose. They serve social and spiritual needs. The places in which these images are found are often in the most inaccessible places and adjacent to resonantly rich spaces and material. The coincidence of this sonicity to imagery is put forward as being an invocation of the living spirit of the depicted animal or human (Hendy, 2013). This also suggests that for much of history, locations that invoke echoes have been regarded as sacred or at least, full of life spirits. These lithophonic stones therefore have an important role in the ceremony and ritual of former societies and their daily progress and do this by invoking the spirit of life deep within the rock. This further prompts the idea that sound is an important signal in transmitting notions that animation comes out of inert form and that sonicity is a functioning part of that re-animation waiting to be re-activated whilst resident within the inanimate material of the earth.

Film-making could therefore be a contemporary manifestation and development of this kind of life invocation. Animated films, for example, made with materials from analogous origins appear to mirror this ancient process. Initiated by newly discovered electro-mechanical processes and optical light transmission devices developed in the nineteenth century, animated film-making processes rapidly progressed that enthralled audiences with temporal and spatial illusion. Animated films are now invoked by digital methods to the point where their origination and terms as film are being questioned (Manovich, 2000, 2001). Increasingly they are written as much to a computer as filmed through a lens. Although the methods and means may drive on this questioning of its condition, the fundamental process of the ecology of an animated film remains rooted in traditional processes, the rituals and ceremony of creating narratives. That process is fundamental in invoking stories and creating expressions that mirror human lives and imaginations.

The drive to create full length feature animation was a natural ambition for the early animation pioneers having discovered the potential those technologies that came together to create the original wave of cinematic and moving imagery. By observing that early animated films wished to compete with its live action sibling and in the desire to create a product of scale, similar analogies with the monumental sculptural ambitions of the ancient world could be made. Whilst monumental

work indicates the presence of memento-mori, often the signifier residing within the material of ancient sculpture, it may also reside in the message of certain motion pictures. However, through noting the scale of production and the significant anonymity of the many individuals engaged in the work of monumental sculpture, parallels can be observed within the production of a modern animated film. That is; insofar as those cultural products take many human and technical resources in attempting to communicate universal ideas to wide audiences.

We can see this ambition present in the industrial processes being deployed by an animation industry seeking wider audiences developing feature work in the nineteen thirties. Although there are animation studios of scale that are natural examples of the similarities being drawn between art of the past and current practice, at the beginning of that decade, Berthold Bartosch's *L'Idee* or *The Idea* (1932) aspires to develop the short form of animation towards one which considers more universal and complex human ideas. If the implicit universal conceits in Trajan's column also speak of power, the established state and the cult of the individual, then notions opposite to those can be found in *The Idea*. This is apparent, whilst the film aims to elevate the animated form to speak to issues of a greater human scale. The animated film finds its message in expounding meaning through the main protagonist. Similar to the spiral frieze on Trajan's column, *The Idea* unravels meaning through a central character. However, in the animated film, this is a female who, as Moritz argued, "is not so much the idea herself as the manifestation of her meaning (Liberty, Equality Fraternity) in social terms" (as cited in Pilling, 1997, p. 99). In this sense there is a similar pattern that emerges in the construction of the film echoing the discontinuous Trajan frieze. Moritz further suggests that repetition of imagery based on borrowings from Frans Masereel's graphic novel, *The City* (1920), the source of the project, recurs inspiring the film to recreate an overall aesthetic based on pattern realised through rhythm. Therefore, this musicality is instrumental in creating sequences to support and suggest new and involved subtexts. (as cited in Pilling, p.96). Affirming this, Wolfgang Natter shows that the relationship between this graphic approach of Masreel's and significant cinematic works, such as *Berlin, Symphony of a great city* (1927), and *Man with a Movie Camera* (1929) extend beyond the contemporaneous and encompasses those formal ideas of discontinuity, repetition, fragmentation composition and juxtaposition of the individual with a rhythmically informed pacing to depict space. (as cited in Aitken & Zonn 1994). However, Willet says that that the influence on Masreel's woodcuts can be traced in the past to religious antecedents that accompany German expressionist interest in medieval art arising from drama and other pictorial arts. Willet reinforces this when exploring the various themes in the German woodcut novel by suggesting "the irony at the centre of these narratives lies in their exploration, entirely without words, of the power of language and the language of power" (as cited in Donahue, 2005, pp.111-126). This observation supports the notion that these formal elements that aid the depiction of urbanised space in cinema (and subversive ideas, in the case of *The Idea*), grow from mute art forms. Furthermore, these are traits that are shared with Trajan's Column as it seeks to express the narrative of Emperor Trajan's triumphs.

In the film, *The Idea* however, there is the unique addition of a recorded soundtrack. This addition, that apparently separates the ancient and modern examples, also ironically underlines and underscores that rhythmic pattern of a developing cinematic product through the Arthur Honneger soundtrack. This extra privilege of sound additions were recorded and synchronised to the action to varying extent. This was not immediately available to Emperor Trajan and his sculptors in his re-telling. These artifacts that are separated by centuries, curious similarities can be found in the formal qualities of each. Both works derive

from plastic ideas of narrative construction and structural elements that are shared with both sound and image.

Sculpture and painting, therefore, can strive for a literal rendering of a voice or the equivalent formal vocalisation of an idea. In some cases, there is a direct correlation of image to sound. This aspiration for sonicity can appear as the visual expression of sound in some of these traditional, immobile arts that are limited to creating ideas through silent form and shape. The immutable perception therefore is of a visual art unable to speak but seeking human agencies for the material to be animated.

Attempts to visually render sound have been overtly involved with representations such as waveforms. In painting and drawing, the analogous visualisation of sound can also be traced in artworks made from the unpromising inert material of traditional sculpture. This coagulation of two sensory ideas of sound and image, within the ostensibly mute form of sculpture, can be experienced in the work of Constantin Brancusi. The visible forms can be seen to simultaneously address both visual representation and the vibration of sound emanating from that form. Just before the plethora of automatic and mechanical inscription potential for sound proliferated, the ability to render a sound through a traditional media is evident in works such as Brancusi's *The Cock* (1924) and *The Newborn* (1917).

Both these works deny representative form for the immediacy of vivifying a moment denoted by interior sound as much as exterior form: the crowing cock and the infant crying and contorted in its first throes of life. (see Figure 3). These works indicate the sculptor's preoccupation with the first moment of life and its expression through the simplification of form in capturing life in a single metaphoric gesture. (Geist, pp, 56-59).

In Gian Lorenzo Bernini's sculptural work, the opus of religious ecstasy of *Saint Theresa and the Angel* (1646–1652) appears to be presented as a form of tableaux aspiring to almost cinematic proportions. It engages both visual and sonorous analogs. Within these types of set pieces that Bernini was commissioned to produce, there are both experiments with actual light alongside the rendition of light in the sculptural material that gives the work its ethereal voice. A concealed window behind the pediment casts real light into the work and "supports the visionary character of the scene" (Wittkower, p.177).

These examples in sculpture are attempts to bind, in the mind of the spectator, seemingly unrelated phenomena through intractable material. They are also prescient of the scientific acknowledgement of the holistic relationship of elemental phenomena such as sound and light and its healing affect on the body (Helmholz, 1954). In this case the analog of light to sound. Bernini affirms this relationship between light and sound rendering them both as perceptible form in his composition for Saint *Theresa and the Angel*. Whilst there is no actual sound present in this sculptural set piece, the evocation of the sonic is tangible. It permits the audience to experience a corporeal illusion of its stridency through the form of the piece.

There are also very early examples of the desire to combine sound and vision and to enhance an experience of the senses. These can be traced to previous civilisations and subvert the argument that a logical progression towards recorded sound and vision only arose out of insights brought from most recent technological events. Zielinski recognises the presence of a more fundamental aspiration, claiming, "Media are spaces of action for constructed attempts to connect what is separated" (2006, p.7). What can be drawn from this statement is that attempts to enhance seeing and hearing through technology can sometimes disregard models that accept a linear and concurrent development. Additionally this inevitable linearity of technological enhancement is an advocacy of the survival of the most appropriate or fittest technology. "The current state of the art does not necessarily represent the best possible state" (p.7).

An archaeological approach to media histories can support this assertion. It suggests the kind of variantological view that might begin to connect examples of Roman public art with contemporary feature film. The aim of the variantologist is not just to re-implement the old. More valuable for the perspective of the variantologist is the discovery of a contemporary resonance within past media experiments and forgotten technologies. One further historical shift, to which this alludes, is a widening of a previously limited audience and the capacity of an art form or media to be accessible to larger numbers with greater immediacy. However, the desire to enhance audio-visual experiences for the spectator is not necessarily constructed around recent media shifts such as the digitalisation of listening and viewing. Thus, the foundations for developing sound technologies can be re-traced and a review of the past technology underlines a modal relationship between sound and vision. It also reveals that the origins of modern animation are traceable not only to significant technological advances, but also to an unstoppable evolutionary desire to marry sound and vision in new, synchronous forms

Automata

This relationship between sound and its properties in mechanical movement can also be seen and traced back in automata and the desire to create mechanical movement based on humans and animals. Automatic machines, with their ambition to simulate life, also allude to a human fascination to re-animate.

Mythological and factual references to the creation of simulacra and automata present a narrative steeped in human fascination with replication of sentient life forms. This promethean impulse has absorbed successive civilisations and there are many accounts that testify to this. Whilst these are at times not readily discernible as truth or fiction, their presence points to this mimesis as the animation or re-animation of inert material. For example, The Banu Musa Brothers are attributed, as far back as the ninth century as being inventors of a device to store and record music. Carrying on traditions from pre-history and building on achievement by former civilisations, these Islamist scholars developed instruments powered by water using cylinders that were interchangeable. (Fowler, 1967).

The application of sound within the body of automata was another preoccupation of these scholars and they are attributed with making some of the first programmable machines using technology available at the time. One of their conceptions was an automaton that played a musical instrument. In this case, an automatic flute player. The use of the sonic element in this shows acknowledgement of sound in creating convincing artificial experiences in its synthetic attempt to mimic life. Although no record exists to testify to such experiences, the powerful response to machine automata may have been principally based on a response to the visual shock of encountering artificially moving figures. Seeing human movement in this way engenders a range of emotion. This would fit with the reputed 'uncanny' sensations experienced by humans when exposed to artificial representations of themselves.

The theory of the "uncanny valley" developed in the field of contemporary robotics, and relevant particularly in 3D computer animation, maintains that when replica human bodies act almost as real humans, acute revulsion responses to the figure Mori (1970). The same emotions as evoked by uncannily real contemporary robotics, may well have also been evoked with automata in the past. The evidence-base for this phenomenon was articulated in psychic responses in the spectator, through the primary sense of sight Jentsch (1906) and Freud (1913). No mention is made of the presence of an auditory 'uncanniness' in this scheme.

The psychic realities of sound thus appear to have no such equivalent value in the uncanny response. Although this might be attributed to its absence as a distinct phenomenon, the psychic

responses so important to contemporary cinema for example, might lead one to ask whether replicated sounds should in turn be considered for their implication. Whilst we think of robots as contemporary inventions, this engagement with synthetic performance of music and movement inevitably acknowledges the past and more recent complex automata and the contemporary interest in technological apparatus made manifest in human form. Computer game characters, along with real time and animated puppets and characters exploit a fascination with this pygmalion idea where the mythic creation of a statue comes to life. The concept of living stone, for example, is evident from research into stone-carved sculpture. It is a function of the re-reading of many stone carvings of the past. This concept of life within the stone is perceived in Michelangelo's *Slave* series and evident when they are viewed in the contemporary context. This series of monumental sculptures can now be experienced with a new interpretation as objects in their own right. They are however, part of an unfinished commission and would have been read differently at that time should they have been completed. (Wittkower, 1977 pp. 118–122)

The Nightingale or Nattergallen written in 1844 by Hans Christian Andersen, tells the story of an Emperor enamoured with the song of a nightingale that he eventually replaces with a mechanical bird. Significantly, the reference to birdsong is a fundamental element within the Pygmalion theme in this story. The real set against the artificial has gained further poignancy in this contemporary age of sentient artificial intelligence and sophisticated robotics. As alluded to in Andersen's classic tale, human responses to artificial life are significantly shaped by sound, not least music. The oracular potential for artificial walking statues is referred to in both Greek and Egyptian cultures. Lagrandeur refers to the sonic as a function of " …female automata fashioned by Hephaistos out of gold that served as that god's attendants" (2013, p.405). Whilst tales of Grecian automata are mostly mythical, Lagrandeur relates stories from Ancient Egypt that appear to be historical accounts, supported by the existence of artifacts. However, the extent of their life-likeness in the past cannot be accurately recounted but archaeologists have reported that these statues employed several mechanical tricks to create illusions of speech and motion: hollowed out cavities in the statues for priests to speak into and amplify sound, and even mechanical motion driven by steam. These devices illustrate that these statues were not just static decoration but rather vessels for performance, illusion and ritualistic ceremony (Lagrandeur, 2013, p.22).

The relevance of the voice as well as sound and music therefore, was seen to be fundamental to the promethean fascination with breathing life into inert material and the creation of an illusion of the animus. These examples of living statuary and narratives from literature described previously use sound to complete the synchronous experience for the audience and reader. Some of the more audio-mechanical links identified can also be traced back to prehistory. They are expressions of a deeply rooted human desire to re-animate the inanimate.

It can be concluded that these narratives illustrate some of the earliest examples of this desire to link sound and image, handed down through oral and written traditions. Such events could therefore come to be regarded as some of the first figurations of animation. There are similarities between this primary desire to recreate life through base material, and contemporary motivations that drive animated and cinematic media.

Towards a Performance of Synchronised Sound

There is no single date to represent the moment cinema or animation commenced or even when the concept of the cinematic came to be understood. Gunning, (as cited in Grieveson & Krämer, 2003), defines his concept of an early cinema thus, "I propose attractions therefore, as a key element of the structure of early film rather than as a single-tracked-definition of film-making before 1908..." (p. 43). He goes on to acknowledge as an aside "it may, particularly in the earliest period, function as a defining element" (p. 43). This identifies cinema as an attraction that has pre-cinematic antecedents, whilst not eschewing the classical narrative model, it would seem that early cinema also acknowledges its non-narrative ancestry equally. This denotes animated cinema as a coagulated manifestation of spectacle, circus and fairground at its very inception. It also acknowledges moving image's capacity for storytelling as the other paradigm that developed in cinema in the first decade of the twentieth century. This also indicates more than just the defining of early cinema, with prototypical arenas and events shaping or, at least, illuminating the formation of cinematically mediated products.

The period towards the end of the nineteenth century is when those technologies of recording sound and images began to move towards what we might now define as this cinematic object. Nonetheless, evidence of this desire to mirror life is a shared concept that endures at the heart of animation. It does acknowledge that such mediated events and objects may fall outside of the cinematic screen when the definition is to effect or model an illusion of motion.

Proto-cinematic devices such as the Zoetrope and Phenakistiscope are regarded as antecedents to the photographed moving image. The technological ambition of past prototypes such as these objects could be seen as being fully realised in sound animation whereas these "philosophical toys" were concerned with the illusion of movement. However, they build on a notion that indicates proto-cinematic, traditional and ancient forms of public performance may well have relied on components of sound performance as a way to complete the audio-visual performance. Mechanical devices, technologies and entertainment gatherings can therefore be considered part of this proto-cinematic continuum that culminates in cinema based on sound and image. Events that are not principally associated with sonic ideas are also suggested to be part of this development. An act of performance, for example at a Victorian lantern show, illustrated talk or Emile Reynaud's praxinoscope theatre, audience and performance, would have included sound as part of the spectator experience. It is asserted however, that there is little to suggest that the Théâtre Optique was influential on pioneer animators (Crafton, 1993). However, Reynaud's method of inscription on film and the performed event itself suggests that it was an antecedent for the successive development of on-screen sound imagery. This is both within the technologies of cinema and in visualising sound directly with imagery, such as that practiced later by experimental film-makers. These early examples from the history of audiovisual engagement are indicative of fundamental traces of sound and its potential within audio-vision.

The two technologies used to record sound and vision, were evolving separately throughout the nineteenth century. They would not be successfully united in a synchronous moving image art form before well into the twentieth century. Attempts to recreate and store sound facsimiles can be traced back to the eighteenth century. This development commences with Thomas Edison and Alexander Graham Bell. The incremental story unfolding this acoustic era is driven by both commercial acumen and scientific discovery. Other technologies, such as those made possible by electricity, enhanced sound reproduction processes as the twentieth century progressed. These processes can be termed electrical acoustics. A reference to this non-linearity stated that "the electrical and mechanical means through which sound was successfully encoded, amplified, transmitted, decoded and then reproduced" and that the "technological apparatus" (Wurtzler, 2007, p. 3) involved incorporated combinations of media as opposed to more linear applications of one sound medium. A most recent development for this apparatus lies in the digital mediation of sound.

Furthermore, it suggests this perspective of pre-cinema and its mechanical artifacts effectively illustrate the continuing and deep-rooted desire to create a vivified synthesis through audio-visual symbiosis with technologies that were available at the time. Ultimately, within this development sound also has a continuing role in helping to create deep and successful audience engagement. This ability of animation to engage with topics and communicate them profoundly to audiences has been termed penetration. The term signals an emphasis on the visual where the image takes precedence, suggesting that penetration is achieved visually. Wells (1998), states that "Penetration is essentially a revelatory tool used to reveal conditions or principles which are hidden or beyond the comprehension of the viewer" (p.122).

This affirmation of the revelatory underlines the primacy of the visual in the form. Wells (1998) goes on to observe that animation in this mode mostly tries to resolve "abstraction within the orthodox" (p.123). Whilst one might reconcile this when applied to the visual elements being understood through this dichotomy, more scrutiny could be given to the aural as the materiality and associations of sound occupy such abstract territory itself. The role of the aural in promoting this imagining of the invisible, achieved through the reconciliation of abstract sounds within the more orthodox representative modes is a key point in the development of convincing the hearing audience. Sound and its immersive properties is therefore eventually foregrounded within this process of revelation and penetration of the imagination.

This fascination extends to broader human preoccupations with dynamism, movement, kinesis, and other themes that led to mass audience interest in symbiotic motion and sound pictures. An example of this is the invention of animated sound. Animated sound experimentation relates to the overall technological development of sound recording in the moving image, but significantly, appears to be unique to the historiographical landscape of animation where it has thus generated a unique legacy of films. Animated sound should therefore be distinguished from the mere addition of a soundtrack to moving pictures, with sound effects, language and music orchestrated to imagery either pre or post-production. Referring to it as 'sound that is animated' also acknowledges the experimental approaches some film-makers have taken to link sound with the image in by means other than the reconstruction of recorded sound realities on screen. This distinction therefore provides a comparison to the development of other sound practices in live action and animation. Animated sound at this time also exposed alternative sound and music practices to new audiences fascinated by animated images.

Animated Sound

Animated sound can be distinguished from sound that is applied as a soundtrack to imagery, either post or pre- synchronously. The term animated sound has been used to describe those sets of synthetic sound experiments with film that interested artists working with the new medium in the early part of the 20th century. This refers to those inventions in animated film that integrate sound and image with synthetic and symbiotic means. Fishinger, Len Lye, Maclaren and the pioneering work E, Sholpov and N, Voinov. Sholpov prepared precut disks, for example with openings that when revolved at different speeds and subsequently photographed determine sounds of different pitch. Voinov's method involved precut combs equivalent to the 80 semi-tones of a piano. This period of development for sound technologies and the animated film awakened a new interest in synthesised sound. This synthetic element of manipulated film soundtrack harks back to the mechanics of sound production such as those found in pianola devices. The term 'animated' is used to describe the main goal of these experiments. Animated sound blends the notion of audiovisual on film and the creation of an art form where sound and vision can be viewed as

separate modes, yet connectable within a defined apparatus such as a graphic represention for tonal variation. (Smirnoff, 2011). In describing these techniques of sound and vision, they can be seen as decorative visual representations of music. "These ornaments are drawn music - they are sound…" (Fischinger, 1932, n.p.) This embodies Fischinger's hopes, as well as the other pioneers of animated sound for the potential impact that their experiments that sound might have on the singular act of creating music.

The novelty of these new processes that effectively visualised sound led to predictions that fundamental changes to musical compositional techniques would ensue. It was also mooted that composition of music might shift from traditional evolutions of graphic notation. Composers enthused over these new manifestations of visual music and led to a call for the demise of musical language as it had been developed in the traditional sense. This view, predicated as it was on these emerging expressions of film making even sparked a belief that conventional grammatical syntax in music might disappear (Sabaneev & Pring, 1934). This prediction was not to become a reality however, and the phenomena of animated sound, discovered as it was through a series of filmic experiments, did not sustain when this initial optimism subsided.

However, the substantive link between sound and image remained an important consideration for the experimenters. These researchers had a common aim that was to reflect the possibility for a total audio-visual symbiosis. One example is the direct drawing on film and interrupting the film's soundtrack during the projection process, which caused sound to synchronise with the adjacent frames. Norman McLaren's card system where light was controlled through a series of intervals translating light directly onto sound on film, and later Whitney's experiments with electronically originated sound and colour devices, were both techniques linked by this material closeness of sound and vision (Russett & Starr1976). Such intimacy with the audio-visual was instrumental in bringing the heard closer to the seen whereby sound became shape and visual, graphic elements could be experienced as sound (Moritz, 2004),

These unique experimental phenomena also underline the significance of emergent technology to the creative approaches harnessed by artists. Creative responses to recent digital technologies are a topical manifestation of this re-vitalisation and re-motivation of moving image creation. The changing role of the audience and spectator is also recognised for both helping to create the demand for, and therefore help to accelerate, development of animated audio-vision within film.

Constructing and Testing the Sound-Image: Animation Projects

In order to examine the sound and image contract and the notion of audio-vision in terms of the animated film, a practice project was initiated. This was proposed as a component of a research project that examined the placing of sound in animation. This practice component consisted of two strands. They aimed to compare and contrast alternative working methods using sound and image. One project strand, with a working title of *Return to Swansea* proposed to build practice in animation using selected elements drawn from traditional means of production. Creating an animated film can include: writing, synopsis, ideas generation, drawing and visualisation, animatic creation with music, sound and dialogue, motion testing, compositing and editing. All of these elements can be assisted or created using technology during the formative stage as well as contributing to the refined finished film. They function as steps towards a finished film and make up what is termed preproduction, production and post-production. This framework to build media products such as the animated film brings with it a broad methodology that can vary in scale. The production stages in *Return to Swansea* spawned the

development of storyboards and subsequently the animatic, as a tool for investigating the sound and image relationship. The project was devised as a progressive test for examining the process of putting sound with animated pictures. In *Return to Swansea* the process aimed to review making animation from a pre-defined soundtrack; where the soundtrack was used as a starting point and worked through to a refined composition foregrounding the interim production stage of an animatic. The animatic would function as the main area for investigation into sound and animation.

The alternative strand of the animation practice project consisted of a series of short animated pieces titled; *Sonified Images*. This series proposed to use different approaches to animation sound. The *Sonified Images* project attempted a more direct relationship between sound and image partly using computer processes to control motion via sonic elements. For example, rhythmic sounds were linked to the motion of certain events in the animation by accessing space coordinate data in a 3D animation software system. Key framed techniques were also used in this series, in addition to this approach, in order to compare the different methods. The research proposition was that these project components would enable a series of reflective responses to emerge and be observed in action so that the practitioner point of view on traditional and new processes for animation could be observed. Alternative approaches to creating motion such as; key frame, arranged or choreographed motion, routine or algorithmical driven animation could be used to control the motion of digital characters or arrays of objects in relation the sound impulses.

Both strands to this animation research are works in progress. They are considered for their evaluative purpose in reflecting on the changing role of the animator using a range of traditional and technological means to animate with sound and static pictures.

Return to Swansea

Return to Swansea uses a set of conventional methods of production that are particular to the development of the animated film. Using drawing as both a tool of investigation and as a means of producing the overall visual aesthetic marks the production as clearly rooted in the tradition of animation. Drawing is valued as the medium of choice in this strand of the project as it brings a consistent mode of practice to the visual aspects of the piece as well as incidentally echoing animation's origins as an art form. (see Figure 1)

This production adapts an original radio presentation, *Return to Swansea,* by Dylan Thomas and re-presents it in an animated context. It proposes a narrative within the animation, delivered through abstract sound and spoken voice. Taking the prose style and speech of the author as a starting-point, the aim was to develop animations structured around the original soundtrack, refining it with new additions to both aural and visual composition. The augmented 'score' attempts to reconstruct a narrative with sound and atmospheric effects in synthesis with the original track. The original soundtrack features the powerful narrative style and voice of poet and broadcaster Dylan Thomas, as it was transmitted on 15th June 1947 for the BBC Radio Home Service. The radio presentation affirms Dylan Thomas's success as a broadcaster of the day and one of the classic radio voices of that era.

The original narration in this radio presentation is also an evocation of particular place, achieved through its prosodic tone and rhythmic allusions to the author's childhood. It aims to be universal, balancing the nostalgic with. It is part of a suite of Thomas' continuing motifs that consider Wales and the town of Swansea. The radio piece explores growing up and functions as desideratum. The work emphasises the necessity for catharsis expressed through the creation of a personal work recalling the brevity of childhood. The proposed animated work draws on this sensibility for its visual inspiration. It focuses on achieving this by creating a visual composition added to an augmented radio narration. The invocation of that is therefore steeped in a poetic-prose structure delivered by the narrator, although the piece aspires neither to be poetry nor prose in structural identity.

This strand of the project aimed to take this soundscape, augment with new sound and re-imagine it as part of the animated imagery; to re-contextualise it by examining sonic meaning. For example; to what extent will the original intention of the radio presentation reliant on speech and prosaic stylistic means be maintained through this kind of adaptation? Can the new track sustain an emotional intensity that is present in the original soundtrack? It is suggested that without language, the means by which universality can be attained, is the task of the sonic reconstruction of time, place and space. Thus, omitting certain sounds in this

Figure 1. Extract from 'Return to Swansea' storyboard with transcript and audio/motion chart
© *Used by permission of the author.*

animation is an attempt to invoke an inconclusive visualisation of the off screen voice. These considerations were in addition to the reflective questions about animation practice within new technological contexts that the production of an animatic proposed to raise.

The aim "Because of their narrative indeterminacy, acousmatic sounds leave ample room for interpretation" (Chion, 2009, p.39). Hence, in *Return to Swansea,* the construction and the testing of the sound-image in the animatic exploits the value of the acousmatic imaginary and through which our acousmatic reveries are reflected, (Chion, 2009, p.40). More specifically, it will highlight where the separate entities of music and noise coalesce, to enable fresh, imaginative responses in the spectator of the animated adaptation.

It is also suggested that sound provides *iconogenic* force, and the early sound cartoon is often cited in this regard Chion (1999). The 'music' of such cartoons generates the motion and significantly, a progeny of what could be considered the most primal source – rhythm. The rhythmic structure and how this links with the sound in constructing the images placed at intervals and the intervals of animated motion are themes that characterise the *Return to Swansea* project.

Taking a sound track as a starting point is not necessarily a new proposition in animation production. The project is initiated from what are considered as traditional processes. Established conventions in animation are therefore being used in the creative approach to this work. Whilst animation can now access a wide range of computer processes, the starting point for developing the visualisation in this case is the sketchbook, pencil and paper.

The project is assisted by computer software by means of manipulation, production and post-production. For the image track, and specifically in comparison to filmed animation, the developments of computer compositing and editing bring the storyboard, the animatic and final animation closer together in the 'pipeline' contextualised above. *Return to Swansea* exploits the marriage of sound to image using the animatic to motivate static imagery as well as a creative and investigative tool.

Significantly for the research inquiry, concept drawings and key scenes were inspired, conceived and arranged directly from the *structure* of chosen audio source. Within this project using this structure enabled possibilities for the sonic ideas within the soundtrack to be considered concurrently with the visual ideas. (see Figure 2).

Within this process of visualisation, the animation motion of the characters was related to the pacing of the narrator's voice and specifically its rhythmical meter. For example, phrases were used to correspond with the motion of characters. Key positions using the imagined characters were posed to correspond with the beginning and ending of phrases and the in-between drawings produced to match the meter of the recorded voice after analysing the transcription for pacing and timing. This method of animating motion was then considered for the four minute duration of the radio piece being replicated across the three-act structure of the story. (see Figure 3).

Sonified Images

The consideration in the *Sonified Images* series acknowledges a technological and artistic aesthetic that was generated through pioneer work in animated sound. The main enquiry of the research is, however, concerned with evaluating approaches to animation direction and the relationship that animators previously working with traditional processes have with sound and image technology. It is focused on the extent to which these relationships may have been extended or diminished and the level of engagement with machine aesthetics.

This series of short animated experiments used computer graphics and 3D modelling and animation processes found in software such as 3D Studio Max and Maya. Enabling sound to control

Figure 2. Concept-key frame drawings: 'Return to Swansea', 2011
© *Used by permission of the author.*

Figure 3. Key and in-between drawing: 'Return to Swansea', 2011
© *Used by permission of the author.*

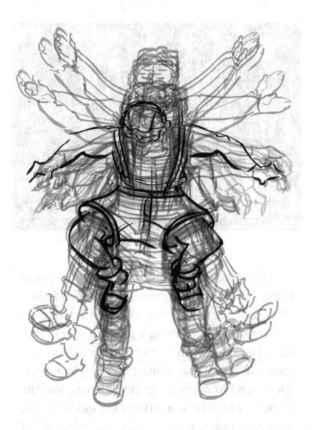

motion and define the animation was implicit in the aims for this series of experiments. The process of using sound in this way questioned the relationship that the animator has to the automatic processes deployed in the animated series. The traditional process of animating used in *Return to Swansea* affirms the animator as composer/choreographer/arranger /musician and central to the animated world being created. The short animations, in this *Sonified images* series, also use specified soundtracks. However, in some of these animations, certain characteristics of sound could be linked via routines and programs to initiate the motion for the digital objects that make up. For example, volume or loudness, tempo and rhythm could be made to effect motion in a two when coupled through simple routines to x and y param-

eters. In some cases this could be implemented in the z axis of digital space to create varieties of motion using three-dimensional arrayed objects.

The principle under investigation, whilst partly focused on the relationship of sound to the animated object also extends to the aesthetic implication it might offer for directorial control in such situations. The experiments in *Sonified Images* exposes the terms of creative engagement for animators by using integrated approaches to digital sound and image creation. This series of animations in this part of the practice project takes those digital audio-visual possibilities mediated by machine as part of the creative decision making process previously controlled by the artist. The short pieces engage with computer processes that are iterative and self-referential and potentially autonomous. Therefore, it would seem apparent that there is now a correlation between what could be termed *meta*-direction and the authorial control that is at the point where machine and traditional procedures meet. However, the animation practice experiments in this series of *Sonified Images* are engaged in contrasting machine aesthetics, and specifically those that relate sound to movement. They utilise the function of programming alongside the subjective emotional arrangement of pattern and movement as a testing ground on which to observe different ranges and their effectiveness as animated expression.

The sound in both series of animations in this research practice exploits concomitance or synchrony either through specification; in *Return to Swansea* or through machine processes; in *Sonified Images*. In both cases the analogous whole of the poetic voice, or more abstract definitions of sound used in either series of the practical works, seek to harmonise the cinesthetic embodied experience in the viewer, without attempting to overly substantiate the image.

Specific themes within the works are derived from psycho musical and sonic phenomena. Entrainment, for example, is a case where our mind and body can relate and synchronise rhythmically to external stimuli and can cause the onset of trance-like states. The pendulum experiments of Christian Huygens in 1665 were the first formalized demonstrations of entrainment. These experiments indicate that the mechanical synchrony of two pendulums swinging together point to this as a physical phenomenon. However, in language, we not only code with each other in conversation, for example by matching timbre and sound to increase the mutual correspondence, but also, conversations can become increasingly similar rhythmically, as brain waves seek to synchronise resulting in lexical entrainment (Brennan & Clark, 1996).

Sonified Image 5, and *Sonified Image, Orchestra,* are two animations from the series under discussion. They use sampled singing voices, recorded and mixed to make music tracks for the series. In these soundtracks, harmonic and tonal intervals are used to create a form of this entrained correspondence between sounds an image. These are replayed in repetitive loops to form sonic material for the animation. Profile models were created in *Sonified image 5* using line tools and extrusions in 3D modelling software. These characters are linked in a hierarchy that permits degrees of movement to occur in two dimensions of x and y space. Possibilities to create secondary animation were added to the linear digital sculptures as further embellishments to refine the animation properties of the figure. However, the primary movements of the limbs and bodily structures are controlled by linking the x and y coordinate space in the image to sonic data generated by the recorded track. This uses programmed routines developed in the software's development kit. Initial movements of the characters can then be controlled by data outputs generated by the sonic material to produce synchronous and automatic movements correlating to, in this case, tempo, pitch, and loudness. (see Figure 4).

The animation therefore aimed to produce an effect in the spectator similar to entrainment where the rhythmical movements produced are mirroring the characteristics of the voices in the soundtrack.

Figure 4. Still from Sonified Image 5; repetitive loop, 23 seconds
© Used by permission of the author

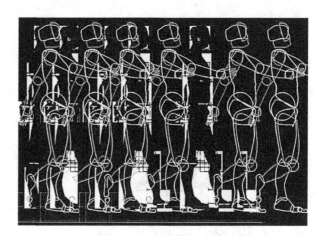

This approach is common to all the short pieces being developed in the series. In *Sonified Image, Orchestra,* the movement control is extended to z coordinate space giving a greater range of motion. The musical instruments depicted are also controlled in 3D coordinate space. The objects correspond to appropriate single notes, varying in pitch, which in turn, affects the motion in the modelled instruments to vary the principle of squash and stretch. This is a principle used in drawn animation to affect a feeling of convincing motion and weight. (see Figure 5)

This intensification of the voice as part of the sound continuum has a precedent in linguistics and performance. For example, Saussure (1916/1983) defined the effect of language as a system of arbitrary sound, stating that: "The connection between the signifier and the signified is arbitrary" (p. 35). This suggests that language is only understood through these signals, and the difference between them has a further implication that emphasises the diminution of the voice as central to meaning. In ancient cultures such as Greek and in particular, the Athenians however, civic and political identity was famously constructed through voice and oral traditions. Volvolis argues that this implies a demonstrative presence of the theatrical tradition

Figure 5. Sonified Image, orchestra; extract/still, 16 seconds
© *Used by permission of the author.*

in constructing meaning through the use of strong rhythmical and chanted texts (as cited in Sider & Sider, p 75) 2003). Volvolis further suggests, when talking about the use of the mask in ancient Greek tragedy that this "leads to a clear, more precise and rhythmic pattern of movement and movement often becomes bigger than in everyday life." (p.77). The use of the mask to project the voice, creating greater consonance and amplifying the natural resonance of the head and body is therefore paradoxically liberating to movement and can and even lead to rhythmic patterns of movement developing between masked performers. This idea therefore resonates with the notion of lexical entrainment and the cooperative principle in conversation. The concept would appear to underline the fact that bodily expressions of vocality were important to western thought before Saussure's prioritisation of the sound of the voice.

That this appears to be so fundamentally human, suggests that neither the power of such rhythmic drivers nor our physiological capacity to be motivated by the auditory, should be underestimated. Indeed the study and understanding of auditory-driven cognition has implications for

interdisciplinary fields as broad as anthropology, music as well as ethno and psycho-musicology, therapy and neuroscience. The repetitive use of sound in religion, where music has been used for a long time to invoke trance states, implies a similar process. It is well known that the theta state is induced at 4-8 Hz and the Schumann resonance is an electromagnetic field that vibrates between the ionosphere and the surface of the earth that also resonates at this rate.

Comparisons between many types of religious music, such as Shamanic drumming, suggest that it is not coincidental that so much of this resonates in the 4-8 Hz range. This in turn suggests that a universal harmony exploited in sound has a mathematical/numerical relationship. The implication for these harmonic states is that this proportion has equivalents in those expressions of visual art and architecture that are in pursuit of a proportional aesthetic ideal. This also may affirm music is a function of mathematical principles. (Gill, Thompson, & Himberg, 2012) Finding where the definition of music might reside in relation to animated movements as well as encouraging positive responses from audiences to sound animation is a fundamental reason for undertaking these works in progress.

FUTURE RESEARCH DIRECTIONS

Directing where the topic in this research may go in the future, it is proposed that inquiries should focus more on reception of sound in these audio-visual contexts. For example, researching the agency of the spectator or audience as individuals and groups when experiencing animation or real and virtual sonified experiences such as the project examples described previously in this article.

The position of the spectator, physically, socially and culturally, could be considered pivotal to their reception of audio-visual objects. The human body's physical position in relation to the sensing of the world about us is central to our ability to decipher signals and act upon them accordingly. In screened media such as film and virtual worlds, where the experiences are aimed at sensory immersion, orientation may be a variable function of individual receptive acuity. This then brings consequences for the reception of visual and aural media that could have measurable results.

However, the study of how the audience and sound functions with image is made more complex by its bidirectional potential. That is significant where audience or user have the possibilities for interaction both physically and sonically thus altering the whole reception relationship in the sound-image contract. Sounds can emanate from potential audiences or the user and interact with the image, rendering the viewer as participant and become complicit in the narrative integrity and flow. This represents the antithesis to the uni-directional characteristics of the traditional screen-based artifact that relies on a more passive model of audience participation. Comparisons to the so-called, uni-directional audio-visual flow that a screened work with its theatrical model of presentation is therefore, distinct and can be marked by a learnt and encoded behaviour. Today's cinema audience shows a pattern of behaviour that is largely derived from this theatrical and realist model. Although exceptions are encountered, group compliance with a certain set of learnt behaviours in the contemporary cinema audience is now the prevalent mode of behaviour for that group. Also, this compliant response is a recent development.

In contrast, some audience groups of the past, notably in less structured performative events such as Music Hall and its American counterpart Vaudeville, lively and vocal audience participation was recorded. Altman's statement that "The discourse was a two way affair" (2004, p.279) supports this view. That is now a perception of a lively, engaged audience that had not yet been tamed or gentrified. One would draw from this that the performer did not always welcome this noisy unruliness from the audience. As films began to use accompanying sound and music the audience became trained in their responses, and the mediation of sound could be said to have played a part in this altering of audience behaviour.

Media arenas now draw audiences from different cultural backgrounds. The cognition and reception of media artifacts have now become recognised research domains in their own right that can be investigated through quantifiable and qualitative means. Research extends beyond the four walls of the theatre to include responses from other groups in society. Censorship pressure groups are one such example of this extended scope for research. The interest in reception also aims to broaden the empirical basis of reception theory. Reception study seeks to explain the presence of a range of contextual and cultural differences (Stokes & Maltby, 1999). The concept of reception predicates the socially contingent over the objective and interpretive. It implies in its study, that it is gravitating towards a neutral method to explain meaning. Although the origins of this framework arise out of more literary fields, its adoption by film studies, and by extension, potential as a model in animation reception, remains faithful to its scholarly focus upon how and why different texts are interpreted differently by-readers-spectators.

However, we are assuming that the audience for animated films is also similarly subject to conceptual frameworks such as the taxonomy forwarded by reception studies (Hall, 1973). Audio-visual analysis with the focus on sound reception may reveal the there may be many forms, inherent within many genres within animation that appear to challenge the encoding\decoding model. For example, the idiosyncrasies of some independently authored animation might naturally engender oppositional responses from active groups encountering the model. The animation filmmaker's intended meaning could be misconstrued due to these pre-conceptions. Could this extend to the reception of sound? Counter to this, a high proportion of passivity and compliance with the intended reading of an animation piece might be met in different cultures and contexts.

Figure 6. "I can hear you" 2011; sound responsive kinetic mechanical torso; wire, steel sheet steel rods, servos, nylon, paint, sound sensors
© *Used by permission of the author.*

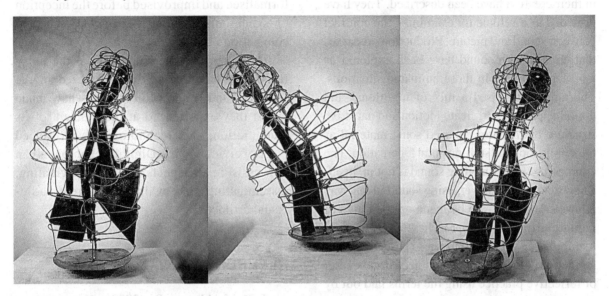

Location, both in the geographical and societal sense and its specific cultural difference must also be considered in this proposition for audio-visual analysis foregrounding sound reception. The high propensity for fandom within certain animation genre, notably Anime, indicates the presence of dedicated audience groups. Some forms of animation are intentionally produced to appeal to a passive and compliant model of reception that engenders certain stylistics in order to travel the globe. (Budd & Kirsch 2005, pp. 75-98).

The scale of production in animation produced around the world now ranges from small web-based graphic symbols and moving signs, through to fully realised animated films. Hence, future research should include discussions about scale and cultural implication within the design of audience analysis model or experiment.

In summary, a model of audio-visual analysis can be built around individual responses to hearing sound with and without imagery for measuring and capturing responses. They should pay heed to a variety of sample groups that vary in scale and cultural background. The experiments can acknowledge the modes of reduced, causal and semantic listening that are currently accepted. Also these studies focusing on listening and hearing can be deployed in both animated and live action film contexts as well virtual and real world situations using kinetic figurative objects that generate and respond to sound. These are re-presented as exhibition pieces that have dual function as both contemplative objects and artifacts used in measuring audience responses to the effect of sound and image. (see Figure 6)

CONCLUSION

Sound in animation operates uniquely in juxtaposition with depictions of animated imagery. These animations access a myriad of styles and representations of reality. Despite sharing the same processes of production and conventions of live action cinema, the theories, the practice and reception of how animated pictures or virtual objects operate, with sound, are nevertheless significantly different to the mainstream cinematic product.

In this chapter, moving image artworks that use a range of digital and analogue approaches in their creation have been described. They have provided as a vehicle for examining the contract between sound and picture. Production processes that engage with sound have been explored as a research project in those animated situations. The animations used a mix of traditional and digital approaches to create motion and narrative structure but all projects used sonic material as their philosophical starting point for creation. The approach of foregrounding sound is not in, itself, a new concept. However, using sound in this way allows comparisons to be made on the range of digital and traditional approaches that are used for manipulating sound and image. These aspects of animation practice have been subjected to the filter of reflective practice using the terms laid out by their definitions. They have been examined from a phenomenological and technical standpoint.

Two strands of a common project designed to deal with the diverse possibilities for sound generation and manipulation for screen were explored. In related projects, a series of automata have provided other possibilities for the condition of sound to be investigated. Sculptural figurative practice has been re-imagined as sound-reactive automata using more contemporary technologies and digital processes. These processes have been used in conjunction with mechanical devices and virtual digital puppets. Both the virtual figurative work and the real electro-mechanical objects have linked sound to motion to create the illusions of life form.

Concepts and allusions to sound were also observed to resonate through historic examples and past expressions in art that were both individual and civic in sculptural scale. This means of tracing the record for sound before the inception of electro acoustic means of reproduction has revealed sonic concepts as having antecedents that engage sound with motion, or more succinctly sound as a motivator of action. This confirms the validation for the importance of aural and vocal traditions, societal interactions with musical and resonant spaces that are formalised and improvised before the inception of synchronised sound became an accepted convention in cinema.

There can only be conjecture at the noisy responses that crowds, who gathered in the square around Trajan's column, must have made whilst they experienced at the moment of its inauguration, this technologically advanced piece of civic statuary. Digital technologies can now assist in all aspects of the act of creating, disseminating, and evaluating current audio-visual artifacts.

REFERENCES

Abel, R., & Altman, R. (2002). *The sounds of early cinema*. Indiana University Press.

Adria, E. N., Hoover, A. E. N., Harris, L. R., & Steeves, J. K. E. (2012). Sensory compensation in sound localisation in people with one eye. *Experimental Brain Research*, *216*(4), 565–574. doi:10.1007/s00221-011-2960-0 PMID:22130779

Altman, R. (Ed.). (1992). *Sound theory sound practice*. New York: Routledge.

Altman, R. (2007). *Silent film sound*. New York: Columbia University Press.

Atkinson, R. (2007, July 17). Do I want my sight back. *The Guardian*. Retrieved from http://www.guardian.co.uk/lifeandstyle/2007/jul/17/healthandwellbeing.health

Barthes, R. (1977). *Image, music, text*. London: Flamingo.

Bartosch, B. (1932). *(Animation Director), & Masereel, F. (Writer)*. France: The Idea. [Animated Film]

Brennan, S., & Clark, H. (1996). Conceptual pacts and lexical choice in conversation. *Journal of Experimental Psychology. Learning, Memory, and Cognition*, 22(6), 1482–1493. doi:10.1037/0278-7393.22.6.1482 PMID:8921603

Budd, M., & Kirsch, H. (Eds.). (2005). Rethinking Disney: Private control, public dimensions. Middletown, CT: Wesleyan University Press.

Cage, J. (1961). *Silence: Lectures and writings*. Wesleyan University Press.

Chion, M. (1994). *Audio-vision: Sound on screen*. (C. Gorbman, Trans.). New York: Columbia University Press.

Chion, M. (1999). *The voice in cinema*. (C. Gorbman, Trans.). New York: Columbia University Press.

Chion, M. (2009). *Film a sound art*. (C. Gorbman, Trans.). New York: Columbia University Press.

Coyle, R. (Ed.). (2010). *Drawn to sound: Animation film music and sonicity*. London: Equinox Publishing Ltd.

Crafton, D. (1993). *Before Mickey: The animated film 1898-1928*. London: University of Chicago Press.

Cytowic, R. E. (1989). *Synaesthesia: A union of the senses*. Berlin: Springer. doi:10.1007/978-1-4612-3542-2

Davies, P. J. (1997). *The politics of perpetuation: Trajan's column and the art of commemoration*. Archaeological Institute of America. Retrieved from http://www.jstor.org/stable/506249

Deutsch, S. (2008). Aspects of synchrony in animation. *The Soundtrack*, (1/2), 95–105. doi:.10.1386/st.1.2.95/1

Donahue, N. H. (2005). *A companion to the literature of German expressionism*. New York: Camden House.

Fischinger, O. (1932). *Sounding ornaments*. Deutsche Allgemeine Zeitung. Retrieved from http://www.centerforvisualmusic.org/Fischinger/SoundOrnaments.htm

Fowler, C. B. (1967, October). The museum of music: A history of mechanical instruments. *Music Educators Journal*, *54*(2), 45–49. doi:10.2307/3391092

Freud, S. (1913). *The interpretation of dreams*. (A. A. Brill, Trans.). London: Macmillan. doi:10.1037/10561-000

Geist, S. (1968). *Brancusi: A study of the sculpture*. New York: Grossman.

Gill, S., Thompson, S. R., & Himberg, T. (2012). Body rhythmic entrainment and pragmatics in musical and linguistic improvisation tasks. In *Proceedings of the 12th International Conference on Music Perception and Cognition of the European Society for the Cognitive Sciences of Music*. Thessaloniki:Greece: Academic Press.

Gomery, D. (2005). *The coming of sound*. London: Routledge.

Grieveson, L., & Krämer, P. (2003). *The silent cinema reader*. Abingdon, UK: Routledge.

Gunning, T. (1986, September 1). The cinema of attractions: Early film, its spectator and the avant-garde. *Wide Angle*, *8*, 63–70.

Hall, S. (1973). *Encoding and decoding in the television discourse*. Birmingham, AL: Centre for Contemporary Cultural Studies.

Helmholz, H. (1954). *On the sensations of tone* (3rd ed.). New York: Dover publications.

Hendy, D. (Presenter). (2013, March 18). *Noise: A human history, echoes in the dark*. [Radio Broadcast]. BBC Radio 4.

Husserl, E. (1931). *Ideas: General introduction to pure phenomenology*. (W. R. Boyce Gibson, Trans.). London: George Allen & Unwin Ltd.

Jentsch, E. (1906). *On the psychology of the uncanny.* Oxford, UK: Imprint.

Lagrandeur, L. (2013). *Androids and intelligent networks in early modern literature and culture: Artificial slaves.* New York: Routledge.

Leger, F. (1972). *Functions of painting.* (A. Anderson, Trans. & Ed.). New York: Viking.

Manovich, L. (2000). What is digital cinema? In P. Lunenfield (Ed.), *The digital dialectic, new essays in new media* (pp. 172–198). Cambridge, MA: The MIT Press.

Manovich, L. (2001). *The language of new media.* Cambridge, MA: The MIT Press.

Marks, L. E. (1978). *The unity of the senses: Interrelations among the modalities.* New York: Academic Press. doi:10.1016/B978-0-12-472960-5.50011-1

McDonald, J., Teder-Sälejärvi, W., & Hillyard, S. (2000, October). Involuntary orienting to sound inproves visual perception. *Nature, 407*(6806), 906–908. doi:10.1038/35038085 PMID:11057669

Merleau Ponty, M. (1968). *Phenomenology of perception.* London: Routledge.

Mori, M. (1970). The uncanny valley. (K. F. MacDorman & N. Kageki, Trans.). *IEEE Robotics & Automation Magazine, 19*(2), 98–100. doi:10.1109/MRA.2012.2192811

Moritz, W. (2004). *Optical poetry: The life and work of Oskar Fischinger.* London: John Libbey.

Murch, W. (2000). *Stretching sound to help the mind see.* Retrieved October, 21, 2012, from http://www.filmsound.org/murch/stretching.htm

Natter, W. (1994). Place, power, situation and spectacle, the city as cinematic space: Modernism and place in Berlin, symphony of a great city. In Place, power, situation and spectacle: A geography of film (pp. 203-228). Lanham, MD: Rowman and Littlefield.

Northwestern University. (2007, September 27). Music training linked to enhanced verbal skills. *ScienceDaily.* Retrieved February 2, 2015 from www.sciencedaily.com/releases/2007/09/070926123908.htm

Pilling, J. (Ed.). (1997). *A reader in animation studies.* John Libbey and Co.

Russett, R., & Starr, C. (1976). *Experimental animation: An illustrated anthology.* New York: Van Nostrand.

Sabaneev, L., & Pring, S. W. (1934, April). Music and the sound film. *Music & Letters, 15*(2), 147–152. doi:10.1093/ml/15.2.147

Saussure, F. (1983). *Course in general linguistics.* (R. Harris, Trans.). London: Duckworth. (Original work published 1916)

Schafer, R. M. (1994). *The soundscape: Our sonic environment and the tuning of the world.* Destiny Books.

Schön, D. A. (1987). *The reflective practitioner.* San Francisco: Jossey-Bass.

Sider, L. F., & Sider, J. (2003). Soundscape. The school of sound lectures 1998-2001. London: Wallflower Press.

Smirnoff, A. (2011). *Graphical sound.* Moscow: Theremin Centre. Retrieved on May 3, 2011 from http://asmir.info/graphical_sound.htm

Sobchack, V. (1992). *The address of the eye: A phenomenology of film experience.* Princeton University Press.

Stokes, M., & Maltby, R. (Eds.). (1999). *American movie audiences.* London: BFI.

Tisdall, C., & Bozzola, A. (1978). *Futurism.* London: Thames and Hudson.

Voss, P., Collignon, O., Lassonde, M., & Lepore, F. (2010). Adaptation to sensory loss. *Wiley Interdisciplinary Reviews: Cognitive Science, 1*(3), 308–328. doi:10.1002/wcs.13

Wells, P. (1998). *Understanding animation*. London: Routledge.

Wheeler, M. (1964). *Roman art and architecture*. London: Thames and Hudson.

Wittkower, R. (1977). *Sculpture, processes and principles*. London: Penguin.

Wurtzler, S. J. (2007). *Electric sounds: Technological change and the rise of corporate mass media*. New York: Columbia University Press.

Zielinski, S. (2006). *Deep time of the media*. Cambridge, MA: The MIT Press.

KEY TERMS AND DEFINITIONS

Animation: Giving illusory life to material things.

Audio: Hearing, listening and acoustic experiences of the audible world.

Automata: Self motivating or independent machine.

Entrainment: Aligning brainwaves with certain frequencies and adopting to external rhythmical patterns.

Proto-Cinematic: Technologies, machines and performances before the inception of modern cinema that aimed to create audio visual experiences.

Sonified: When inert and material substances receive, mediate and absorb sound.

Vision: All that relates to seeing and perception.

Chapter 7
The Earth Sciences and Creative Practice:
Entering the Anthropocene

Suzette Worden
RMIT University, Australia

ABSTRACT

The Anthropocene is being suggested as a new geological age replacing the Holocene and is a description of a time interval where significant conditions and processes are profoundly altered by human activity. Artists interested in the earth sciences are using digital media to provide audiences with ways of understanding the issues highlighted in discussions about the Anthropocene. These artists are harnessing data through visualisation and sonification, facilitating audience participation, and are often working in art-science collaborations. These activities demonstrate a transdisciplinary approach that is necessary for confronting the world's most pressing problems, such as climate change. After a discussion of the opportunities provided by visualisation technologies and an overview of the Anthropocene, this chapter explores the following interrelated themes through examples of creative works: (1) nanoscale, (2) geology and deep time, (3) climate, weather, and the atmosphere, (4) extreme places – beyond wilderness, and (5) curatorial practice as environmental care.

INTRODUCTION

Earth science embraces many areas such as the study of the atmosphere, the oceans, the biosphere, the interior of the planet, electromagnetic fields and surface rocks. It also includes interactions between the planet and the inhabiting life forms. An understanding of the systems operating across and within all these interacting forces, materials and life forms is found in the disciplines of environmental science, geography and ecology. The evolution of the planet can be understood through deep time, a concept first developed by the geologist James Hutton (1726-1797) who argued that the earth was formed through volcanic activity and erosion under the sea, with strata being uplifted and then eroded.

DOI: 10.4018/978-1-4666-8205-4.ch007

The earth sciences draw on other disciplines such as physics, biology and mathematics. There are also sub-disciplines within the broad categories of study. For example, geology includes the sub-disciplines such mineralogy, geochemistry, paleontology and sedimentology. Another way of sub-dividing interests within the area is to recognise the distinctions between studies of rocks (the lithosphere), water (the hydrosphere) air (the atmosphere) and life (the biosphere).

The Anthropocene is being suggested as a new geological age replacing the Holocene. The term, popularised by Paul J. Crutzen and Eugene F. Stoermer, suggests that humanity has affected nature over the last two hundred years so that a new human-made stratum has emerged in the geological record (Trischler, 2013, p. 5). Their thesis has generated debate across and within many disciplines in the sciences, arts and humanities, and because it brings human influence into sharp focus, especially in relation to climate change. The Anthropocene is therefore not only part of scientific discourse but has social and political implications; areas of concern that have been seen as previously distinct have become entangled. For example, while discussing politics and the Anthropocene Bruno Latour has stressed the need for action, a "politics-with-science" instead of a "politics-vs-science" and also because of the speed at which changes are happening alongside the expanded timespan in which we have to understand action, "another temporal rhythm for action" (Latour, 2013, p. 11). Christoph Kueffer (2013) has helpfully introduced the term "ecological novelty" as a means of describing a suitable methodology necessary for action and conceptualising deep time in conjunction with increasingly rapid change.

In a previous discussion of the earth sciences and creative practice, "The Earth Sciences and Creative Practice: Exploring Boundaries between Digital and Material Culture" (Worden, 2014), I explored creative work in digital media by concentrating on artists' responses to geology, mineralogy and nanotechnology. Through this discussion it was evident that artists depict the materiality of the world through visual and virtual representations of what is seen, not only through their direct observations but through the use of visualisation technologies, and increasingly in visualisation of matter that can be technically or electronically recorded but is not visible to the human eye. Besides direct observation it is possible for artists to use rich and varied forms of data on conditions in the world including the atmosphere and physical formations, data about particles at the nano level to data on geological formations, extremes of temperature and how these all interact with human activity spatially and temporally. All this information can be combined, visualised and re-purposed in digital media or combined with traditional media in creative works. The creative work discussed in the earlier chapter, by Perdita Phillips, Victoria Vesna and Paul Thomas, provided an opportunity to discuss scale, order, ethical issues and ecology, as well as more tangible aspects of physical spaces, the body and the need to be "embodied perceivers" (Frodeman, 2006, p. 389).

In this chapter I will re-visit their work and also extend the range of creative work discussed to include examples of work from artists interested in other areas of the earth sciences besides geology and nanotechnology. This includes climate, weather, extreme environments and care for the environment. Jeremy Gardiner, Anthony Head, Reconnoitre (Gavin Baily Tom Corby and Jonathan Mackenzie), and David Burrows extend the possibilities of creative engagement with deep time, scale and extreme environments. Some artists, such as Andrea Polli and smudge studio (Jamie Kruse and Elizabeth Ellsworth), actively include discussion of the Anthropocene in their own commentaries on their work. Others, like YoHa and Martin Fluker, have a predominantly curatorial agenda and propose a participatory, activist approach to counter climate change or promote sustainability agendas. Andrea Polli, smudge studio and Martin Fluker use social media to encourage audience involvement and the potential for creativity within that participating audience. Therefore, how a curatorial role can direct creative art practice so that the work utilises digital media to provide audiences with ways of understanding the issues highlighted in discussions of the Anthropocene is part of the extended discussion in this chapter.

Related themes of interest include: subjectivity and intent associated with visualisation; the evidence and source of creativity when part of audience participation; and how art-science collaborations demonstrate a transdisciplinary approach for problem solving. Many of the works are primarily inspired by science or are projects initiated as art-science collaborations. Some projects have a strong social focus or are a commentary on the environment, ecological conditions, historical change, or materials and technology. Common to all, however, is a celebration of ecological diversity and recognition of the interconnectedness of environment and life forms.

The creative works are grouped under five themes:

1.   Nanoscale;
2.   Geology and deep time;
3.   Climate, weather and the atmosphere;
4.   Extreme places (beyond wilderness);
5.   Curatorial practice as environmental care.

But first, I will provide further contextualisation, highlighting theoretical issues, visualisation and the Anthropocene.

DIGITAL MEDIA: VISUALISATION AND THEORY

In dealing with a theme such as the Anthropocene it is relevant to consider a variety of possible uses of digital media. In the works discussed there are examples of experimentation with visualisation of large data sets, sonification, GPS, stereo pro-

jection and examples of the use of social media applications that could be termed ubiquitous and even common place to users in 'networked' society. There are varying emphases on media convergence, social interaction and aesthetics.

For this discussion some distinctions are relevant. Media theorists distinguish between two main types of visualisation: scientific visualisation and information visualisation. Generally, scientific visualisation is most concerned with the conversion of numeric data to a graphical representation. Information visualisation works with other kinds of data, such as text, images and video which are structured to an appropriate form of graphical representation. Lev Manovich describes how scientific and information visualisation come from different cultural areas (science and design respectively) but cross over in use. However he also distinguishes between information design working with information and information visualisation working with data to reveal structure; although partially overlapping they are different in their functions (Manovich, 2011, p. 38). Manovich further categorises information visualisation examples into principles of

1.   Reduction,
2.   Privileging of spatial variables, and
3.   Direct visualisation or visualisation without reduction (Manovich, 2011).

The projects discussed here mostly fit the first two categories with the representation conceptualised as a specific artefact rather than a general model.

Manovich's theoretical approach is relevant for analysis of visualisation within and for mass communication systems, networks, use of 'big data' and for the significance of interface design. But such a view is less effective for the more poetic applications in digital media, which are being discussed in this chapter. For example, Anthony McCosker and Rowan Wilken (2014) distinguish between the sublime and the diagrammatic in visualisation, with the diagrammatic being similar to Manovich's direct visualisation. Their main focus is social analysis and because of this they are wary of the "problematic celebration of beauty" in data visualisation (McCosker & Wilken, 2014, p. 156). They see "the sublime sensation as only partially revealing of the productive value of data visualisation" and see more potential in the process of 'diagramming' and data cleaning, which "takes place in the gap between the extraction and abstraction of data." For them, sublime beauty might give "a new level of apprehension of vastness and scale in human experience and social relations" but they turn to the diagram to generate understanding of a performative rather than a representational device (McCosker & Wilken, 2014, pp. 159-160). In this context the diagram "does not 'demonstrate', but rather casts light on the creative acts through which concepts, constructions and knowledge might emerge" (McCosker & Wilken, 2014, p. 162). For them the diagram provides a space for experimentation and problem-posing. This is a useful distinction to keep in mind as it shows that there is more potential in visualisation technologies than has yet been used in creative media works connected with the earth sciences. On the other hand, it also suggests that artists see the sublime sensation as central to their work. Even Manovich recognised this in 2002 stating:

How new media can represent the ambiguity, the otherness, the multi-dimensionality of our experience, going beyond already familiar and "normalized" modernist techniques of montage, surrealism, absurd, etc.? In short, rather than trying hard to pursue the anti-sublime ideal, data visualization artists should also not forget that art has the unique license to portray human subjectivity – including its fundamental new dimension of being "immersed in data." (Manovich, 2002, p. 11)

Within creative practice artists give themselves more choice of intent and do not always concentrate solely on the practicalities of interpreting data for applied knowledge generation. They are interested in affective, even ethical, communication. This does not mean that they are unaware of the range of possibilities within visualisation if they make a conscious choice to work primarily with the aesthetics of visualisation. As will be shown in later, Tom Corby, a member of the Reconnoitre group, considers that the images they produce "are a vehicle capable of enabling comprehension of material realities" (Corby, 2008, p. 461) and this innovative type of image consists "of objective and subjective, informational and aesthetic components, which operates at the limits of what the image is understood to be in the visual arts" (Corby, 2008, p. 467).

The Anthropocene is an emerging area of consideration within digital media theory but because transdisciplinary approaches are best suited to studying the Anthropocene theoretical insights are not strictly limited to media theorists (Turpin, 2013). As will be shown in the following discussion, critique from cultural theorists (Bruno Latour, Jane Bennett, Karen Barad) or social geographers (Harriet Hawkins) is productive, especially for understanding the interactions and entanglements between people, things and technology.

THE ANTHROPOCENE

The Anthropocene was originally defined by Paul Crutzen and Eugene Stoermer in 2000 to describe the present as a geological unit within the geological timescale (Subcommission on Quaternary Stratigraphy, 2014). The Anthropocene is a description of a time interval where significant conditions and processes are profoundly altered by human activity. As Alberts has noted, "Humanity's recent activities can be measured now at a scale commensurate with the geomorphologic narrative of the planet" (Alberts, 2011). There is some controversy on the dating of the Anthropocene. Some suggest that the change from the Holocene to the Anthropocene took place around AD 1800. A Great Accelerations stage from AD 1950 has also been suggested. Fossil fuel use is seen as integral to these changes.

In discussions of the Anthropocene it is generally agreed that human activities have created enough change for the Earth System to be functioning well beyond the variability of the Holocene. According to Oldfield and colleagues:

The Earth System has withstood a number of major vicissitudes, the most extreme of which resulted in major shifts to a new planetary state and, in the case of the big five mass extinctions, it took at least hundreds of thousands of years to recover. Some of these past changes have greatly exceeded the sum total of our current anthropogenic impacts, but it is clear that human influences, especially over the last six decades, are already leading to huge adjustments to the biosphere, and that the geological signature of our activities will persist into the future. (Oldfield et al., 2014)

The speed of this change has also increased since the start of the Industrial Revolution and has impacted many biological and physical cycles. Previous periodization has been based on natural developments and catastrophes; changes in nature. Theoretically and practically, the Anthropocene requires a new way of thinking about geological time; a new understanding of past and present combining a broader view of history where human activity ranks with previous mass extinctions, alongside a capability to plan for rapid change. At the same time, economic, cultural and political activities have become interconnected and globalisation is an associated factor. In the Anthropocene humans and technology mix with nature to change conditions on a planetary scale. Geological thinking provides a way of placing humans in a cosmic span of time at the same time as showing their relative temporal "insignificance" (Ziarek, 2011). Krzystof Ziarek has termed this the Techanthropocene, which

... brings into view the fact that technological development is never simply under human control, or comes into being just as a human product, but rather technicity puts into question the very notion of control or of the centrality of the human. (Ziarek, 2011, p. 19)

Thinking about time and the Anthropocene also infers a change in orientation in thinking about the flow of time. While discussing politics and the Anthropocene Bruno Latour points out the need for action and also "another temporal rhythm for action" (Latour, 2013, p. 11).

Action cannot be delayed because time does not flow from the present to the future — as if we had to choose between scenarios, hoping for the best — but as if time flowed from what is coming ("l'avenir" as we say in French to differentiate from "le futur") to the present. Which is another way to consider the times in which we should live as "apocalyptic". Not in the sense of the catastrophic (although it might be that also), but in the sense of the revelation of things that are coming toward us. This odd situation of living "at the end of time" in a different type of hope, the hope that has been made one of the three theological virtues and that the French, once again richer than English, calls "espérance" to make sure it is not confused with "espoir". (Latour, 2013, p. 11)

Latour is making a distinction between hope (espoir) as the desire to believe and expectations (espérance) as a strong belief that something will happen as a prospect for future good. This is an optimistic view of the apocalyptic.

Research on sustainability has covered some aspects of the complexity and nonlinearity of the Anthropocene but these challenges need a transdisciplinary approach. According to Alberts, the Anthropocene is "an empirical measurement established through the natural sciences" but is also a term "that promises to reconfigure how we think of the consequences of the collective conditions of modern life" (Alberts, 2011, p. 5). The Anthropocene is now being considered by the arts and humanities and in the media. This increases the reach of a transdisciplinary approach and critical understanding that encompasses metaphor, narrative, phenomenology, ethical values and aesthetics. Many commentators suggest that collective human action is necessarily in response to a crisis, with new forms of public participation in politics and science.

To summarise: the Anthropocene provides a framework for critique and action for change. But as Lesley Head suggests

We are living in it as we work on it. We necessarily have to work all this out as we go along, only partially with hindsight. We are discussing a category, built out of a body of evidence that demands that we also engineer political, social and economic change. As it happens, a contingent, messy, non-linear view will likely serve us better politically, given the failure so far of large governance categories such as nation states and intergovernmental agreements to curb emissions. (L. Head, 2014, p. 10)

This includes learning by participation, integration of science into society and "a combination of ethics (global environmental justice and responsibility for the future) and aesthetic (ecological/textual interrelatedness) that will define poetic practice in the Anthropocene" (Wilke, 2013, p. 72).

QUESTIONS

If humans are becoming understood as a geological force, an understanding of the history of geological concepts becomes more significant. Accelerated change is a feature of the Anthropocene as is the overlap of deep time and the present. Artists' responses include interest in the physicality of the earth, especially in forces of erosion, weathering as well as weather, and extreme places in the environment. This often includes art-science collaboration. Another response is to use social activation to foster a greater awareness of change in an environment and include the community as co-producers in decision making or as contributors of situated knowledge. In this context artists have a more curatorial and enabling role.

To explore these interests and creative roles, I now will consider the following questions in more detail:

- How are artists responding to the idea and actualities of the Anthropocene?
- How are they using digital media in this context?
- How are audiences encouraged to consider the Anthropocene and participate in sustainable social practices?

NANOSCALE

The examples discussed here, from artists Victoria Vesna and Paul Thomas, show collaboration between artists and scientists, consideration of the human body and embodiment and although not associated by the artist with the Anthropocene, have preoccupations that are similar. Vesna takes us through changes of scale that also encourages a questioning of time – its speed and duration – that could also serve as a pointer to the need in the Anthropocene to live with accelerating change. Thomas blurs the boundaries between input and output, and provides ambiguous measurement of acceleration and also tests our appreciation of the speed of change.

Nanotechnology is a recent development of science that is about manipulating matter generally rather than a part of a particular earth science sub-discipline. Moving beyond the power of the microscope, nanotechnology works at a level that is always invisible – phenomena that are smaller than the minimum possible resolution of light (0.2 micrometers or 2,000 angstroms) (Hanson,

2012, p. 59). Exploring the nanoscale is about finding ways to express the invisible. Thus, nanotechnology stretches current definitions of what phenomena are within our experience. However, nanotechnologies are not uncontroversial; according to Cynthia Selin, nanotechnology is an ambiguous technology with its interest in future developments being usurped by a conservative meaning, bound to commercial developments (Selin, 2007, pp. 206-207). Because of this kind of social and economic entanglement, nanotechnology is illustrative of the recent increase in human impact on the environment that is characteristic of the Anthropocene.

Victoria Vesna: *Zero@ Wavefunction* and *Nanomandala*

Since 2001 Victoria Vesna has explored nanotechnology through installations in collaboration with nanoscientist James Gimzewski. This includes *Zero@wavefunction* and *Nanomandala*.

Zero@wavefunction was first shown in 2002 (Figure 1). The installation projects moving images of buckyballs, which are spherical fullerenes, an allotrope of carbon and important for nanotechnology. Participants, through their shadows, are able to interact with these shapes (Vesna, n.d). When interacting with the buckyballs the participant's attention is drawn to changes in scale represented by the changing projection of their shadow in conjunction with visualisations of the buckyballs shown on a large scale. The work draws attention to the possibility of manipulating the mechanics of matter as well as to the body's relationship to scale. The name, *Zero@wavefunction*, refers to quantum mechanics and the energy of atoms and electrons and encourages further comparison between different registers of scale. This work draws attention to the work of the nanoscientist and their manipulation of matter. For example, a scientist using a scanning tunnel microscope (STM) using a tactile sensing instrument is recording shape by

feeling and can also use the instrument as tool to manipulate the atomic world by moving atoms and molecules in virtual space (Gimzewski & Vesna, 2003).

The *Nanomandala* installation was also a collaborative project between Victoria Vesna and James Gimzewski. It has been shown in various locations since 2003. The installation consists of a video projected onto a disc of sand. The images change from depicting the molecular structure of a grain of sand into an image of a complete mandala and then back again (Figure 2). The images of the grain of sand were created from the visualisations from a scanning electron microscope (Figure 3). The mandala is an image of Chakrasamvara and was created by Tibetan Buddhist monks from the Gaden Lhopa Khangtsen Monastery in India. An accompanying sound track has been devised by Anne Niemetz. These monks had originally created the mandala for an exhibition of Nepalese and Tibetan Buddhist at the Los Angeles County Museum of Art (Vesna, n.d.).

The images are derived from digital photographs of the full mandala, taken at different stages, using a wide angle and then a maco lens. Next, photographs were taken of the centre of the mandala with an optical microscope and a scanning electron microscope. A final suite of photographs were taken of a grain of sand, taking the images collected to the nano level. The final composition was an animation using the 300,000 images collected from the different stages. When watching this work, the viewer is drawn into a progression of images that explores our sensual response to scale. It allows the viewer to consider how representations of scale are captured and how this stretches their understanding and experience of scale in relation to their bodily presence.

Vesna was also interested in the process of making world views worthy of contemplation and investigation. She noted the following about the installation, saying she was inspired by

Figure 1. 'Zero@wavefunction', Singapore
(©2008, Suzette Worden. Used with permission).

Figure 2. 'Nanomandala', John Curtin Gallery, Perth; showing Mandala
(©2008, Suzette Worden. Used with permission).

Figure 3. 'Nanomandala', John Curtin Gallery, Perth; showing grains of sand
(©2008, Suzette Worden. Used with permission).

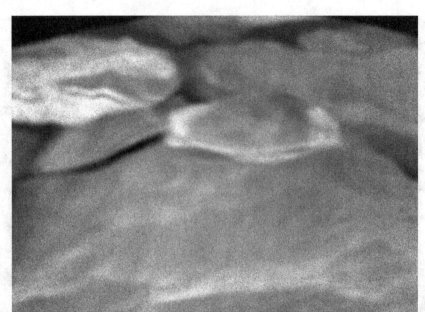

… watching the nanoscientist at work, purposefully arranging atoms just as the monk laboriously creates sand images grain by grain, this work brings together the Eastern and Western minds through their shared process centered on patience. Both cultures use these bottom-up building practices to create a complex picture of the world from extremely different perspectives. (Vesna, n.d.)

In its production this work uses the computer technologies associated with nanotechnology research and takes on some of the concerns of explaining the nanoscale. Valerie Hanson has suggested that images of the limitless space of the nanoworld are not 'spaces' to explore; "they refer to a built world—a world that the viewer may also alter as he or she explores. In other words, the viewer has already entered into the world, as opposed to standing at the threshold" (Hanson, 2012, p. 70). This also shows how, in the Anthropocene, processes can be profoundly altered by human activity.

Paul Thomas: *Nanoessence* and *Midas*

Paul Thomas has been developing creative works that explore the nanoscale, often in collaboration with Kevin Raxworthy. Thomas is interested in the spatial boundaries and in particular the disintegration of territories and boundaries in the nanoworld. In *Nanoessence*, experimentation was carried out with the vibration of atoms and with the AFM in force spectroscopy, where only the vertical movement was recorded. The data was translated to sound files and used in conjunction with 3D stereo images. The resultant work was a combination of this sound data with images of the projection of a single cell where "a genetic algorithm was written for semi-autonomous self-organizing nanobots to affect the digital image of the skin cell translating the data to gold colour" (Thomas, 2007, 2009). The viewer releases the nanobots through using a button, which is a physical model of the skin cell, and as a consequence interacts with the imagery (Figure 4).

Figure 4. 'Midas'
(©2009, Paul Thomas. Used with permission).

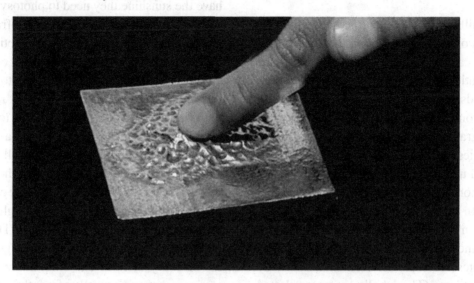

This work deliberately blurs the boundaries between the minerals and human existence as it is being articulated through an understanding of the nanoworld. In this context the body has lost its distinct boundaries. Through the work, Thomas asks: if basic atoms and molecules can be manipulated, what does this mean for the human body? Thomas deliberately invites a phenomenological discourse about our understanding of these issues. He focusses on the understanding of a mineral in relation to our own body and combines an investigation of biological and chemical and mineral science.

Vesna and Thomas both explore the potential of computer technology to create an immersive world where we are literally drawn into another world and requested to ask questions about scale or about our means of accessing that world, especially where the technology can bring into play different senses - of touch as well as the visual - or make us aware of different cultural sensibilities. The artificiality inherent in explorations of the nanoworld also makes a different interplay between the virtual and the real. The 'real' is totally constructed. Vesna and Thomas help the viewer explore a constructed reality but they are also concerned with communicating con-

ceptions of materiality with advanced visualisation techniques. Their explorations allow us to consider aspects of a recent technological process that is part of the escalation of man-made influence on earth. At the same they uphold Manovich's expectation that "artists should also not forget that art has the unique license to portray human subjectivity – including its fundamental new dimension of being "immersed in data" (Manovich, 2002, p. 11).

GEOLOGY AND DEEP TIME

I will now consider creative works that celebrate the wonders of rocks, geological processes, deep time and scale in conjunction with a critique of the place of the body and human activity in the environment. As these works are multi-dimensional there are also connections with climate and weather and the interaction between biological life forms and other matter. These are works that in some way utilise scientific research or are deliberately constructed collaborations between artists and scientists. These creative works aim to make the physical world more visible or experienced through interaction in a virtual environment.

Perdita Phillips: *The Sixth Shore*

Perdita Phillip's *Sixth Shore* project heightens our awareness of geological time in the context of a specific location. *The Sixth Shore*, which is part of SymbioticA's long-term project, *Adaptation*, is a soundscape project developed by Perdita Phillips from 2009 to 2012. It is a creative work that integrates a 3D soundscape, using GPS technologies, with a location renowned for its geological uniqueness. The project was based at Lake Clifton, which is in the Yalgorup National Park, south of Mandurah in Western Australia. The eastern shore of the lake has thrombolites living in the lake (Figure 5). The dome-shaped thrombolites are rock-like formations built by micro-organisms. (Thrombolites grow as a clotted formation, while the related stromatolites build layers.) Thrombolites provide a focus for questions about the boundary between minerals and biological life. They precipitate calcium carbonate

and form in shallow water where the microbes have the sunshine they need to photosynthesize.

The Lake Clifton eco-system is a fragile balance of human and non-human interactions, with decreasing groundwater, as a result of climate change, and Tuart tree dieback due to a fungal infection. Clearing in the locality is in tension with viable bird habitat. The microbial formations of the thrombolites are considered a critically endangered community (Luu, Mitchell, & Blyth, 2004). The project builds a picture of the environment in layers, alluding to the immense geological timescale that can be discerned through studying the constituent parts of this landscape. The thrombolites are organisms have a lineage going back 3.5 billion years. For *The Sixth Shore*, multiple stories were woven together from the six themes:

Shore 1: Thrombolitic time;
Shore 2: Shifting shores: lake formation and seashore changes;

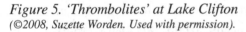

Figure 5. 'Thrombolites' at Lake Clifton
(©2008, Suzette Worden. Used with permission).

Shore 3: Cultivated landscapes: indigenous cultures;
Shore 4: A time of clearing;
Shore 5: Bird migration and hooded plovers; and finally
Shore 6: Futures.

Inherent in the progression through the six stages is a sense of historical change and, through knowledge and experience the power to see a viable future that is not disconnected from a history that embraces far more than a human timescale. Geological time has its own characteristics but it is also seen as integral to the other narratives of the environment. Equally the digital technologies used to support the project are integral to other means of collecting data or communicating the project (Figure 6). Digital technologies are used as a means to understand the physical environment rather than overwhelm it and research

was undertaken into the design of a system to identify the ground position and orientation of a participant so that the soundscape they hear could be planned. As well as create an embodied experience supported by digital technologies, the project added to the rich histories of the area through its collection of oral history recordings and interviews (Phillips, 2012).

In this project Phillips has interpreted the scientific knowledge on thrombolites, along with the changing sea levels and coastal deposits to arrive at metaphorical implications that influence the sound world she is creating. This is a complex story which enriches the sense of place for the area. From the thrombolites the idea of clotted life is developed as a metaphor and from the fragility of the lake, which becomes dry by the end of summer, the idea of a brittle landscape. The fossil remains have been ravaged by time. As Phillips explains:

Figure 6. Testing commercial GPS units
(©2011, Perdita Phillips. Used with permission).

With all fossils what we see are traces, never a complete or full record of the past. It is important to consider the concepts of loss and complexity with the use of scientific data in this project. My development of a sound ecosystem will be the tracing of a place, never a full record, but reflecting the 'sketchy' remnants of multiple pasts found in the evidence of today. Correspondingly the sound installations will be built up of fragments. (Phillips, 2009, p. 7)

Walking is important for the engagement of the audience in *The Sixth Shore* project. Walking is considered central to our perceptions of an environment; it is a multisensory experience where there is emphasis on the performative and the communicative. These are key factors that also make digital environments attractive to users. As ethnographers have noted, it is very difficult to represent the experience of walking with printed words and linear text so new formats of using image and text need to be explored to create a multisensory experience that includes looking, listening and touching (Pink, Hubbard, O'Neill, & Radley, 2010, p. 5). This digitally enabled work creates links between the environment and experience through sound narrative and supports a multisensory richness.

On one level, Phillips provides a multi-sensory experience combined with a use of technology that encourages physical involvement in a threatened environment. At the same time the tracing of a place suggests the connectedness with fragments that are none the less part of deep time. Although Phillips has not placed this work in theoretically within the context of the Anthropocene, it does provide a context for thinking about how processes are profoundly altered by human activity and a structured way of thinking about geological time.

Jeremy Gardiner: *Purbeck Light Years* and *Light Years: Jurassic Coast*

The artist Jeremy Gardiner celebrates the geology of the Jurassic Coast in Dorset, England in a body of work that spans traditional painting, printmaking and installation. The Jurassic Coast is 95 miles of coastline from Exmouth in East Devon to Old Harry Rocks in Studland Bay, Dorset. It 2001 it was recognised as England's first natural UNESCO World Heritage Site, for its outstanding geology, with some parts dating back 185 million years (Dorset Tourism, 2014). It is important for fossil sites and its geomorphologic features have been studied for over 300 years (UNESCO, 2014).

Gardiner has produced a series of installations with artist and computer programmer, Anthony Head. These include *Purbeck Light Years* 2002-6; *Jurassic Light Years* 2009 and *Light Years Coast* 2010-2013 (Figure 7). The iterations within the Light Years series combine images of Corfe Castle, Dorset and terrain from satellite data with animation, sound and immersive virtual reality. The viewer is able to use a joystick to navigate digital landscapes in a gallery and experience night and day and the seasons within the virtual environment. This digital work encourages the viewer to understand pictorial space and builds on the depiction of texture and fracture Gardiner explores within his paintings. Gardiner's work reflects a deep and long-term interest with the geology of the landscape. As he says: "by unfolding the landscape through my painting I am inviting the viewer, the spectator who is looking at my pictures to reflect on their own transient relationship with the physical world (V. Gardiner, 2013b).

Gardiner invites the viewer to consider their relationship to the physical world through a focus on the changes that become evident through

Figure 7. Jeremy Gardiner (right) and Anthony Head (left), co-creators of 'Digital Coast' discuss video wall installation at Bath Spa University.
(©2014, Jeremy Gardiner. Used with permission).

studying the coastal interface between sea and land. By capturing a moment in time within a landscape and then contrasting this to visual evidence of geological time, such as strong vertical rock formations, fissures and crevices, the viewer is reminded of the short time they experience the world within this greater expanse of time, back into geological time and into the future. Erosion is mirrored on the surface of the paintings which are collaged, etched and scraped and have the dynamics of forceful pressure, movement and weathering. These visual qualities are transferred to the digital installation.

For Gardiner, digital media creates the illusion of time-travel and "an imaginative act, an act of memory and reflection" (J. Gardiner, 2009, pp. 143-144). The installation uses technology found in computer games and combines modelling and image mapping techniques. Objects are rendered in real-time and effects of changing light are pro-

grammed to create the effect of night and day and randomly programmed weather events. Gardiner and Head combine terrain data of the area with the images from paintings on vertical sections in constant transformation (J. Gardiner, 2009, p. 146). Sound is synchronised with the changes possible on the screen. The installations also referenced artefacts in the Dorset County Museum and these are another layer of the existing history of the area.

Gardiner paints all the images used in the projection in the studio as reliefs painted on flat poplar panels. When re-worked for the virtual space the images are transparent. According to Gardiner this transparency is "more than an optical characteristic; it implies a broader spatial order. Transparency means a simultaneous perception of different spatial locations. Space not only recedes but fluctuates in a continuous activity" (J. Gardiner, 2009, p. 142). Gardiner sees a positive aspect of his panoramic works as their capacity to "recreate aspects of the visual enjoyment of going for a walk with areas showing detailed observation alongside sweeping views of the textures, colour and light of distant views" (V. Gardiner, 2013a). As with Phillips's work, *The Sixth Shore*, *Purbeck Light Years* and *Light Years: Jurassic Coast* reference walking and an embodied experience of the landscape.

Gardiner collaborated with artist and computer programmer Anthony Head for the *Light Years* projects. Head has been investigating images of weather in 3D visualisation (A. Head, 2011). Head's long-term aim is to provide personalised weather information based on location and "represent the potential experience that the viewer might have if the predicted weather events occur" (A. Head, 2011, p. 36). The question might therefore be: how, in the Anthropocene, do we reconfigure understanding of weather and climate? Climate change is seen as a central issue; how does perception of the weather feed into this and do virtual visualisations of weather provide space for reflection and understanding linking the personal to societal issues? The *Light Years* projects show the connections between areas of concern – geology, deep time and the weather as a catalyst for change over time. Their creative work therefore explores aspects of the Anthropocene alongside the coastal interface between sea and land, itself a metaphor for change in the physical world.

CLIMATE, WEATHER, AND THE ATMOSPHERE

Digital technologies have enabled artists to explore climate and weather in new ways and communicate aspects of the Anthropocene such as accelerated change, increased complexity and interdependence. As noted previously, artists might have a primary interest but this can also incorporate relationships between areas of the earth sciences. Jeremy Gardiner combined geological data with reference to weather conditions in interactive work that explored deep time and a sense of place. Similarly works discussed in this section, from Reconnoitre (Gavin Baily Tom Corby and Jonathan Mackenzie) and Andrea Polli, combine an interest in climate change with extreme environments such as Antarctica.

Reconnoitre: *Southern Ocean Studies*

Gavin Baily Tom Corby and Jonathan Mackenzie work together under the name of Reconnoitre and are interested in using digital information as an expressive medium (Baily, Corby, & Mackenzie, 2014). Their project *Southern Ocean Studies* re-uses data from the British Antarctic Survey to explore climate models, both for how they communicate change but are cultural phenomena in their own right (Figure 8). For this work the project software runs in real-time and generates a model of ocean currents. This is mapped onto other ecological data sets and interactions in the data become visible. This is then projected in a gallery environment.

In exploring ideas around materiality and information Tom Corby found it relevant to make association with historical ideas about landscape at the same time as proposing new visual paradigms. When interviewed about *Southern Ocean Studies*, he explained

It used to worry me because of the huge historical burden you take on but now I see opportunities to re-frame what the idea a landscape is (this will be no news to cultural geographers!). Obviously the idea of a wilderness or sublime landscape, separate from the human is difficult to sustain in an era when we're acutely aware that earth and human systems are so intimately entwined. The job then becomes how you find languages to express this 'intermingling', what is available, what tools and data can be employed. (Leonardo Almanac, 2011).

Figure 8. 'Southern Ocean Studies'
(© 2009 Corby & Baily. Used with permission).

The group experiments with data from oceanographic components of climate models. Display methods such as vector fields, streamlines and particle systems are used to produce new aesthetic effects. They want the iconography to reside "implicitly in the dataset - the delineation of the Antarctic as an empty space in the data, and the ocean system model as a site of political and scientific conflict" (Leonardo Almanac, 2011).

As already noted, Corby considers they are working with a new type of image which is both subjective and objective (Corby, 2008, p. 467). Corby acknowledges the cultural aspects of reception and interpretation and the use of "intricate formal assemblages of information, space, material and image" (Corby, 2008, p. 463). He argues that information visualisation can be used to create works that enable a tangible experience of data, or even the physical equivalence of abstract facts. This produces an ambiguous kind of embodied knowledge and has potential for audience participation. Corby's stress on the subjective and embodied potential of information visualisation means that information visualisation, as integral to a creative

artefact, incorporates the range of referents that are also found in scientific visualisation. Artists work across a broad spectrum of possibilities with poetics being an important aspect.

The work is left open to interpretation but many of the issues that *Southern Ocean Studies* brings to our attention are those aspects of the Anthropocene that need continuous consideration and debate. The work provides the viewer with an abstracted visual spectacle of movement and flow that evokes questions about agency and cause and effect. As a result of the abstract qualities of the work, climate and environment merge in the gallery installation. It depicts and an environment often associated with absence and seen as a wilderness; the representation of the Antarctic is then populated with measurable 'activity' that makes it easier to see it as part of a holistic earth system. Corby also proposes a more holistic viewpoint, relating the work to Bateson's ecologies, when he describes the 'systemness' of emerging patterns. This is seen as "a metonym for the braided interactions between the ecosphere and human behaviour (Marsching & Polli, 2012, p. 249).

Andrea Polli: *Heat and Heartbeat of the City, Particle Falls, Sonic Antarctica and Ground Truth*

Andrea Polli's main focus is on sonification but she also works across performance, interactive and web-based art. She collaborates with scientists and incorporates workshops in her projects as a means of encouraging public engagement with science.

An early project devised by Polli was *Heat and Heartbeat of the City* which was commissioned in 2004 by New Radio and Performing Arts, Inc. for the Turbulence website and still available on-line in 2014 (Polli, 2004). This project included collaboration with the NASA/Goddard Institute Climate Research Group. This web-based and sonic work enables a viewer to consider the possibilities of high temperatures in the New York City environment that could be the consequence of global warming (Figure 9). The increase could be between one and four degrees by 2030. The work has four compositions, each about seven minutes duration, which give comparative soundscapes

of possible maximum summer temperatures for the summer of four decades. These are translated into pitch, loudness and speed of the sounds. The sounds for the 1990s decade are based on actual temperature records at Central Park. The other decades are represented by temperatures derived from a detailed climate model of the New York region. The background colour of the screen also changes with the temperature of each decade. Comparing the visual and sonic representations of each of the decades illustrates the dramatic changes that could take place if action is not taken to slow down the process of global warming. The sonification is shown in blue, changing to purple and bright pink over time and also with greater vertical extremes in intensity in the graphical representation of the sound on a horizontal line; a landscape background is changing from green to yellow/brown over time. The increasing pitch and intensity of the sound itself creates tension and insistency within the message. It is with great relief that, as a listener, it is possible to return to the 'relative' calm of the 1990s only to realise that

Figure 9. Screenshot from 'Heat and Heartbeat of the City'
(©2004, Andrea Polli. Used with permission).

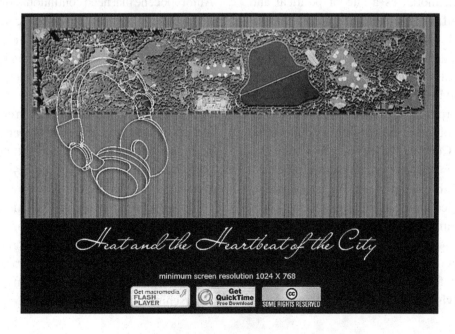

that might not be possible. This has resonance with the comment previously quoted from Latour about time - "as if time flowed from what is coming." The listener is encouraged to think about time in relation to the future and their place within it. The engagement with complexity through the visualisation of a data system provides a way for people living in an urban environment to engage with global environmental issues.

Another visualisation, *Particle Falls* is a work that relates the quality of air and pollution in the urban environment to the quality of life of those living in that area (Figure 10). The work visualises airborne pollution in real time. It was first produced in 2010 for the San Jose public art program. Even though the pollution is invisible to the eye, modern sensors can measure particulate pollen by laser light scattering. In this work particulate pollution was measured in an urban location, with the data projected onto a nearby building. Residents could consider the visualisation of the particles provided by the work in relation to current traffic use and a projected light railway development in the area. The work was accompanied by a detailed caption board explaining what the projection and

animation was showing and posing questions about air quality. A viewer could easily correlate the movement of the traffic to the animation in the projection and make connections between traffic and air quality (Polli, 2010). In 2013, the work was shown again on the walls of the Wilma Theater in Philadelphia, USA, with sponsorship from the Chemical Heritage Foundation. The Foundation has augmented the online documentation with information on the related science. When viewed in this online context the viewer is encouraged to think about the collection of data, the work of meteorologists, and how scientific data informs us about the world.

Polli uses the term ecomedia to describe her work in which computing is a shared practice between science and an art concerned with place and content-based creation. For Polli ecomedia is "made with the emerging technologies, tools, and information structures that describe and model environmental systems." She notes that new forms emerge and transformations take place while monitoring and modelling data (Polli, 2011, p. 3). Reflecting on a series of creative works, Polli argues that

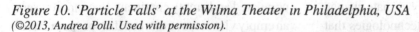

Figure 10. 'Particle Falls' at the Wilma Theater in Philadelphia, USA
(©2013, Andrea Polli. Used with permission).

... ecomedia works resulting from field-based collaboration have the potential to create a kind of situated knowing in relation to environment, and can extend the fieldwork to allow both specialist and nonspecialist audiences to experience geographic and temporal scales that cannot be understood through the physical experience of the environment (i.e., large geographical areas and long periods of time). (Polli, 2011, p. 198)

Like other artists interested in climate change, Polli has been engaged with documenting and exploring weather and conditions in extreme environments. *Sonic Antarctica* is a mixture of Antarctic sounds and recordings of scientists collected in 2007-2008 as part of the US National Science Foundation residency, the *90 degrees south* project. Besides producing an Audio CD, the project was documented in a blog which provided contextual material about the project and its development (Polli, 2012).

Besides the *90 degrees south* project, Polli has created the *Ground Truth* (2008), a Google Earth journey and online mapping system containing recordings, images, soundscape recordings and interviews with scientists. This work not only gives a viewer access to information about an extreme environment affected by climate change but also provides a critique of technologies that are becoming available to many users on the Internet. For example, while transferring her image and recordings to Google Earth for *Ground Truth*, Polli found that Google maps were limited in their documentation of Antarctica, as for that area the flat map projection became distorted. Although more satisfactory for spherical projection, Google Earth still had limitations at the South Pole for image overlays and because it was under-recorded visually.

All these works demonstrate that artists can bring fresh perspectives to debates and practical involvement in learning about climate change. For understanding the Anthropocene and its complexity and providing a response through a transdisciplinary methodology, these works show an awareness of the needs of specific audiences. Scientists can be participants and explore and reflect on their activities in a creative way; when this is communicated through creative work this can bring increased awareness of their working methods and empathy from the viewer. The viewer can explore the science and relate it to their everyday circumstances, with the possibility that they become more informed and active participants in social and political activities needed for change.

Although I have discussed examples of creative works in the context of specific scientific interests, such as geology or meteorology, it is also evident that artists work across disciplines and phenomena. Geology and weather have been combined (Gardiner) and extreme places provide the focus for investigating climate (Polli). GPS technologies and access to climate datasets provide the basis for new kinds of visualisation (Reconnoitre).

EXTREME PLACES (BEYOND WILDERNESS)

As already shown, Reconnoitre and Polli are interested in how Antarctica is depicted as an unpopulated and empty continent. Reconnoitre sees an empty visual space that can then be 'populated' through data visualisation, alerting the viewer to non-human forces that are nevertheless integral to Earth's ecosystem. Polli discovered the virtual absence of data on Antarctica in Google maps and Google Earth, showing us that there is much to be learnt and recorded about the area. This provides a corrective of too easy an acceptance of the virtual mapping reality.

The discovery of the ozone hole over Antarctica was one key factor in demonstrating the influence of human activity on the environment (Steffen, Grinevald, Crutzen, & McNeill, 2011). It was then noticeable that emission of carbon dioxide was affecting the energy balance of a broad range of ecosystems and becoming evident in spaces previously thought of as pristine 'wilderness,' untouched by human activities. Therefore, one way of understanding the extent to which we are experiencing the great acceleration, the resultant change and the irreversibility of the Anthropocene is through change in Antarctica. This includes Antarctica as a focus for creative practice.

The remoteness of the continent from highly populated centres of human habitation has made both Polar Regions a challenge for conquest by explorers. Both regions have tested human endurance and entered the popular imagination as a final frontier. They have captured the interest of photographers as well as scientists. The photographer Frank Hurley (1885-1962) accompanied Antarctic expeditions in 1911-13, 1914-1916 and 1917. He went to enormous risks to photograph and film the expeditions. The images have become an important part of the visual record and iconography of the Antarctic. Hurley's stereoscopic glass-plate photographs have been digitally restored for stereoscopic presentations by transdisciplinary film-maker Peter Morse. The resultant works shown as art gallery installations blur the boundary between scientific illustration and, in the depiction of Mawson's hut, evocative narratives about human settlement (Morse, 2007). Similarly, Jan-Peter E.R.Sonntag created an installation *AMUNDSEN/l-landscape*, for *Deep NORTH transmediale 09* that focussed thematically on consequences of global warming on the Polar region (Transmediale, 2014).This work included footage from near the former house of Roald Amundsen, the polar scientist and, in the same space, a melting block of ice under a lamp. Sensors recorded data from the melting ice and this was presented to the viewer through headphones (Transmediale Archive, 2014).

The desire to celebrate this perceived emptiness is also combined with the desire to communicate what it might feel like and therefore create an emotional response to the environment. In association with understanding the Anthropocene this not only encompasses sense of a specific place but also exploration of boundaries and extremes.

David Burrows: *Mirage Project (Iceberg)*

The Australian Antarctic Division has been running a Fellowship program since 1984, which has enabled two or three artists to visit Antarctica each year. The range of responses from the artists and writers has been imaginative, with some of the works produced, such as that by artist Lisa Roberts, directly linked to climate change (Australian Antarctic Division, 2014). In 2011-2012, installation artist David Burrows visited Casey station to study icebergs and capture their essence. He produced an audiovisual installation, *Mirage Project (iceberg)*, with specially fabricated stereoscopic viewers for Federation Square, Melbourne, Australia (Figure 11). The work allowed the user to stand in the same spatial layout as the positions in the original photos of the iceberg. There were 3D photos in each viewer and by going from viewer to viewer it was possible to 'walk' around the iceberg and contrast its actual dimensions and beauty to the urban environment upon which it was superimposed. Bringing an old technology up to date with an overlay of high-level digital photography, Burrows wanted others to experience the remarkable qualities of icebergs through the installation noting

We have a reliance on visuals. We think we know what Antarctica looks like, or can imagine the taste of an iceberg. The neurological responses, generated through looking through these viewers, hopes to facilitate this experience. (Burrows, 2012)

The installation has also been shown in other environments, such as the salt pan Lake Ranfurly, Mildura, Australia (2013). The contrasts hold the linked environments in tension and suggest questions about the evolution of differing environments and the ecologies they support (Burrows, 2014). The user is encouraged to use their imagination to connect these differing environments; the technology has an enabling role, rather than be the subject of the work.

Figure 11. 'Mirage Project' [Iceberg], installation view, Federation Square, Melbourne, 2012 (©2012, David Burrows. Used with permission).

Smudge Studio: *Future North: Turning at the Limits of the World*

Artists Jamie Kruse and Elizabeth Ellsworth work together under the name of smudge studio, a non-profit media arts collaboration they founded in 2005. Their projects are speculative and curatorial; are based on using social media and networks as archival databases, rather than experiments with visualisation or sonification. However they do produce artefacts for web delivery such as the *Geologic Time Viewer*, which is a graphic representation of geological time with compartmentalised images This locates the present - the Anthropocene - in the middle of geological time rather than at the end and is an explicit comment on the Anthropocene and the entanglement of geologic and human activity. The use of a simple horizontal scroll for viewing the timeline provides a space for speculation about deep time and the future. This is a two-way choice, but one that always returns to the present (smudge studio, 2010).

In 2014 they took part in the *Future North* project at the Oslo Center for Urban and Landscape Studies and in a blog have documented their aim to meet the "forces that compose a limit of the world" and "find geomorphological edge where human and nonhuman forces converge and delimit one another" (smudge studio, 2014a). The blog entries provide a visual narrative of the visit (they call these 'image sensations') and demonstrate the effectiveness of a performative approach to creating an aesthetic commentary on environmental change. At this limit they explored its characteristics and turned at the limit to "generate potential and open the future." Kruse and Ellsworth searched out locations where change was intense but in reacting to the location, they slowed down the way they experienced this environment. They asked:

As we take up work that positions us at edges of change, we take up responsibility to enact new ways of meeting highly complex, deeply enmeshed, wide-reaching (non-local), fast changing material limits, such as those that converge at Thief Island and other coastal urban centers around the world. Most of those material limit are invisible. We cannot sense most of them directly or immediately. But unlike other animals, we humans (especially artists, designers and architects) are now capable sensing the world's limits indirectly through our tools, media, and interpretations of data. We are capable of using our species' extended cognition to recognize material limits that involve multiple dimensions and are distributed across far flung human and nonhuman bodies. (Smudge Studio, 2014c)

The idea of turning at a boundary is a way of thinking about working with change that is so integral to the Anthropocene. Interestingly, their view of humans is that they are entangled with technology for perception and for their identity. This fits the definition, mentioned earlier, of the techanthropocene proposed by Ziarek (Ziarek, 2011).

They are keen to develop a methodology that deals with complexity and is also sensitive to what cannot be controlled. For Kruse and Ellsworth a visit to the site of a volcanic eruption of 1973, at Heimaey, where over 300 homes were buried provided a 'turn' that showed them an example of a crisis when those involved coped with psychological limits because they were coping within the bounds of the physical and cognitive limits they were experiencing. (smudge studio, 2014b).

Kruse and Ellsworth draw inspiration from Jane Bennett's theoretical work about the intensity of interaction between humans and all nonhuman agencies (Ellsworth & Kruse, 2012). In *Vibrant Matter: a Political Ecology of Things*, Bennett describes vitality, as the capacity of things "not only to impede or block the will and designs of humans, but also to act as quasi-agents or forces with trajectories, propensities, or tendencies of their own" (Bennett, 2010, p. viii). Kruse and Ellsworth's interest in agency includes the human and nonhuman but it also enables them to focus

on limits as part of an interlocking material reality. This has resonance with entangled agency, as described by Karen Barad, where agency is a matter of intra-acting. For Barad, agency is "an enactment, not something that someone or something has" and it includes "the boundary articulations and exclusions that are marked by those practices in the enactment of a causal structure" (Barad, 2007, p. 178).

The *Future North* blog can be viewed online and has much to offer for critical reflection on extreme environments and as information about conceptualizing the Anthropocene. It does not directly invite physical participation. This distinguishes their work from Phillip's invitation to participate in walking through an environment with an integrated 3D soundscape as in *The Sixth Shore*. Experiencing the environment through walking and recording has a long history back to Grand Tours and the picturesque tradition in art, extending to more recent examples of Land Art and performative walking practices. Phillips uses this as strategy for offering participation in *The Sixth Shore*. However, *Future North* with its blog entries does extend this and creates an artefact to be consumed through the virtual realm. This has a mediated precedent in the Grand Tour taken by tourists in Europe in the 18th and 19th centuries, where the experience was consumed on return through the viewing of artworks and prints as well as collections of minerals and other specimens.

CURATORIAL PRACTICE AS ENVIRONMENTAL CARE

Kruse and Ellsworth's *Friends of the Pleistocene* blog and web publications are examples of distributed and social media being used effectively by artists for engaging audiences beyond the gallery space. Their work shows that it is not just interactive or immersive experiences that are effective for encouraging discussion about the Anthropocene, but a capacity to engage audiences in activities associated with the work or in conversations about the issues explored. This is described by Harriet Hawkins as a socially engaged art practice, "wherein artists take the social site, including its community, as subject, material and audience, that have been one of the important recent developments of art's expanding field" (Hawkins, 2013, p. 56). This kind socially based practice is often supported by galleries and museums through their outreach agendas, where besides becoming more economically viable through an increase in visitor numbers, they are expected to broaden their audience through meeting the needs of local communities. The experience can be integrated in the exhibit or be a supporting experience. In this context, the artwork can be termed activist where the interaction and participation becomes an enabler of social action as well as participation in an aesthetic event. Perceptions of the subject matter can be altered and also suggestions for action can be prompted and directed.

YoHa: *Social Telephony* and *Wrecked on the Intertidal Zone*

Graham Harwood and Matsuko Yokokoji are two artists who work together as YoHa. In their work they use digital media to expose power structures within global society. Their work explores the materiality of media and its effectiveness to convey social messages and reaching new audiences. They often connect gallery spaces to other networks and create novel interfaces that encourage the audience to re-think determinist views of technological development. Their work has the effect of relocating creativity in the participants rather than just residing with the artists.

YoHa have transferred their way of questioning technology into an ecomedia project for the Thames Estuary, *Wrecked on the Intertidal Zone*, which combines public artworks with workshops and social media (Yokokoji & Harwood, 2014). Using vaporisers and substances from geo-located flora they made the environment 'visible' through

smell as part of a festival event. This forms a gateway to reflection on the environment and a means of bringing different groups within the community together, as a form of open space for creativity. Extending this they aim to treat the Thames Estuary as a commons; a complex shared resource. This means bringing together information that is collected by authorities with that collected informally into further events, to inform sustainable development and breakdown the bifurcation of nature and humans, and tensions between exploitation and conservation. This can be seen as a "transformative politics of the local" where, as Hawkins notes, "'creativity' takes on forms that are more vernacular and, as such, becomes both a conceptual shorthand and a suite of practical embodied techniques for breaking with normative, restrictive conventions" (Hawkins, 2013, p. 60).

Martin Fluker: *Fluker Posts*

Becoming engaged with environmental concerns can be effective if the catalyst is something physical in the environment, and not something a person has to take to a location. Fluker Posts work in this way and are an example of a physical device that engages an audience from a place within the natural environment and additionally connects them to environmental information online (Figure 12). (QR codes could work in a similar way but the post is a lower tech solution). The Fluker post project was started by Martin Fluker, an academic from Victoria University, Melbourne, Australia and is a citizen science system that allows people to send a photograph taken at a fixed point to a 'Flukerpost' email address.

The post forms a cradle for any camera and after taking a shot the photographer can uploaded the image to the email address provided, after which it is forwarded by the organiser to a Picasa webpage (Figure 13). The collected images then show change over time for a fixed point in the environment (Figure 14). The information

Figure 12. 'Fluker Post' at Lorne, Victoria, Australia showing range of information provided (©2014, Suzette Worden. Used with permission).

collected is likely to show degradation through human use or the effects of climate change, conservation work or regeneration. The process does not include any aesthetic judgement and does not claim to be a creative work. However it has similarities to other projects that are considered to be art-based, or are art-science collaborations. Some of these similarities may be the result of the different projects using the same kinds of data collection and delivery platforms; the means of collection and dissemination not only means a convergence of different media types, a common definition of digital media, but also a convergence of art and science.

The Fluker Post project has been running over several sites since May 2008 and by September 2014 had over 90 Fluker posts. The project partners include several National Parks, Catchment Management Authorities, Water Treatment Plant, a Marine Sanctuary and a Botanical Garden.

This kind of activity may be seen as a form of crowd-sourcing but as noted by a recently set-up research project, *Citizen Sense*, funded by the European Research Council, to run from 2013 to 2017, there needs to be more evidence to see if these projects are not just providing "crowd-sourced" data sets, but also giving rise to new modes of environmental awareness and practice (Citizen Sense, 2014). Methodologically this kind of project has aspects of the bottom-up approach that is suitable for meeting the demand of understanding rapid change, where "we are living in it as we work on it" as suggested by Lesley Head for countering the failure of large governance categories such as nation states and intergovernmental agreements to curb emissions in the face of climate change (L. Head, 2014, p. 10). Although the Fluker Post project is focused on specific locations, by example it has potential to contribute to the bigger picture. This is a necessary response to the complexity of the Anthropocene. Researchers are no longer objective observers and ecological science has to deal with a man-made nature; where nothing in nature makes sense except in the light of human action. Here Kueffer's predictive science of "ecological novelty" will have to be able to address feedbacks between ecological and social change. (Kueffer, 2013, p. 9). The Fluker project shows the dynamics of this connection. It is also an example of ecological research embedded in realtime, where "through their daily actions, citizens are not only becoming data collectors but also experimental manipulators" (Kueffer, 2013, p. 14). This next stage of re-use is not yet apparent but the potential for re-use and reflection on the digital resources being created is not inconceiv-

Figure 13. Photograph taken at the 'Fluker Post', Lorne, Victoria, Australia
(©2014, Suzette Worden. Used with permission).

Figure 14. 'Fluker Post' research project album for CCMA07 at Lorne, Victoria, Australia showing general layout of the information page
(©2014, Martin Fluker. Used with permission).

able. As a bottom-up approach is also becoming more evident in arts-based projects, there appears to be a convergence between projects across the arts and science-outreach. One aspect of this is the transference in expectations of the 'creativity' of the work being as much in the audience as in the artist.

CONCLUSION

The examples discussed under the five selected themes demonstrate that artists are effectively responding to the idea and actualities of the Anthropocene and that their use of digital media is varied. I suggest that there are two merging tendencies. One fulfils Manovich's reminder that "artists should also not forget that art has the unique license to portray human subjectivity – including its fundamental new dimension of being "immersed in data" (Manovich, 2002, p. 11). The other tendency further embraces the complexity of the Anthropocene and concentrates on aspects of audience engagement. Additionally, on the evidence of recent curatorial projects on the Anthropocene, the subject is becoming an important topic for museums and for academics. Over the last ten years museums have developed educational programmes alongside exhibitions showing the work of artists engaged with the Anthropocene in both traditional and new media. As noted earlier, to be successful the subject needs a transdisciplinary methodology. For this reason, many of the evolving projects, such as Berlin's Haus der Kulturen der Welt (House of World Cultures) (Haus der Kulturen der Welt (HKW), 2014) have planned a series of events running from 2013 to 2014 (Haus der Kulturen der Welt (HKW), 2014). This includes participation from a range of disciplines, with the contribution from the arts and humanities being well recognised. The growing need to incorporate 'big data' and the potential for artists to work with datasets, GPS and sound has also led to exciting opportunities,

as shown by examples discussed in this chapter. The artists discussed here have not ignored the imaginative and poetic in their interpretation of this data.

This chapter has discussed practice and theory of both art practice and the Anthropocene. One important aspect in this discussion has been the possibility of re-thinking the split between nature and human culture, where the Anthropocene thesis suggests that one cannot dominate the other. A second methodological issue is the importance of developing a transdisciplinary approach to research and practice that is able to cope with complexity and the increased speed at which change is taking place. Alongside increasing speed of change is the need to conceptualise deep time and a new relationship to the present.

New media works are often difficult to access beyond initial showing, partly because they are not always collected by established galleries or are difficult to archive, due to rapid changes in the technology used. Also, critics claim that new media works are different from conventional art forms because of their use of time-based forms, relationship to conceptual art, installation and performance and exploration of new technologies, and that new media work should be treated as a new paradigm. The aim of this chapter has been to take a broad view of what comprises a creative new media work associated with, celebrating or critiquing the earth sciences in order to break down unnecessary polarities. Some of the works make reference to more traditional art forms. Many of the works discussed use social media as their 'exhibition' medium or social media aspects are used to complement gallery or festival installations. This also reinforced the need to reach a wider, often community based, audience for communicating information about climate change and other aspects of the Anthropocene.

Exploring new visualisation techniques is an important aspect of many of the works discussed, but equally important has been the need to keep a 'foot on the ground' with a strong interest in walking, for data collection and as a potential viewer experience. This is shown in the works by Phillips, Gardiner, Polli and for the Fluker Post project. Where the performative aspect of a work is important, offering a multisensory experience is often the direct result of an imaginative use of digital technology. Walking can also be subversive and a challenge to norms and power relations According to Hawkins, in the politics and poetics of performative walking "the subversive force of art is often located in its promotion of an aesthetic engagement with space that is other than the normative apprehensions and uses of that space" (Hawkins, 2013, p. 60).

For exploring climate change and extreme environments, it has been constructive for artist to have access to climate data or be able to join scientific expeditions to the Polar Regions. The Reconnoitre group, Burrows, and Polli have taken advantage of this opportunity, but have also brought an originality of thought to the outcomes which are varied in the use of technologies and resulting aesthetic experience.

When reflecting on the processes involved in nanotechnology, Vesna found "bottom-up building practices to create a complex picture of the world." A bottom-up inclusive approach to is also emerging in some of the projects discussed. When considering audience participation there is evidence that a bottom-up approach is becoming more common, especially with artists engaged in working on art-science collaborations. This kind of approach is followed by Polli in 'sound walkabout' workshops for including Antarctic scientists in a wider engagement with their Antarctic environment; by YoHa to bring a community together to care for a specific environment, the Thames Estuary, and to build an "aesthetics of connectivity"; and by the Fluker project to encourage environmental observation and care over time. As a result, 'Creativity' also resides with the audience and is not just with the artist or represented by the artwork. This approach is also better able to

deal with complexity and is in tune with the "messy, non-linear view" suggested by Lesley Head as part of any action for change. As previously mentioned, Latour, when considering the Anthropocene, wrote that "action cannot be delayed because time does not flow from the present to the future." These artists, working with new media, are showing aspects of what can and should be done, now.

REFERENCES

Alberts, P. (2011). Responsibility towards life in the early Anthropocene. *Angelaki*, *16*(4), 5–17.

Australian Antarctic Division. (2014). *Arts fellowship alumni*. Retrieved from http://www.antarctica.gov.au/about-antarctica/antarctic-arts-fellowship/alumni

Baily, G., Corby, T., & Mackenzie, J. (2014). *Reconnoitre*. Retrieved from http://www.reconnoitre.net/index.php

Barad, K. (2007). *Meeting the universe halfway: Quantum physics and the entanglement of matter and meaning*. Durham, NC: Duke University Press. doi:10.1215/9780822388128

Bennett, J. (2010). *Vibrant matter: A political economy of things*. Durham, NC: Duke University Press.

Burrows, D. (2012). *Melbourne-A lifesize iceberg has landed in Melbourne, thanks to David Burrows and his modern day 'Viewmaster' 12 August 2012*. Retrieved from http://www.smartplanet.com/blog/global-observer/in-melbourne-a-touch-of-the-antarctic/?tag=main%3Bcarousel

Burrows, D. (2014). *Portfolio*. Retrieved from http://davidburrows.info/index.html

Citizen Sense. (2014). *About citizen sense*. Retrieved from http://www.citizensense.net/about/

Corby, T. (2008). Landscapes of feeling, arenas of action: Information visualization as art practice. *Leonardo*, *41*(5), 460–467. doi:10.1162/leon.2008.41.5.460

Dorset Tourism. (2014). *Jurassic coast*. Retrieved from http://www.visit-dorset.com/about-the-area/jurassic-coast

Ellsworth, E., & Kruse, J. (Eds.). (2012). *Making the geologic now: Responses to material conditions of contemporary life*. Brooklyn, NY: Punctum Books.

Frodeman, R. (2006). Nanotechnology: The visible and the invisible. *Science as Culture*, *15*(4), 383–389. doi:10.1080/09505430601022700

Gardiner, J. (2009). Light years: Jurassic coast and immersive 3D landscape project. In *Proceedings of the 2009 International Conference on Electronic Visualisation and the Arts*. London: BCS.

Gardiner, J., & Head, A. (2013). *Light years projects: A collaboration between Jeremy Gardiner and Anthony Head*. Retrieved from http://www.lightyearsprojects.org/

Gardiner, V. (Producer). (2013a). *Jeremy Gardiner in conversation Simon Martin*. London Art Fair 2013 - duration 48 min. [Video file]. Retrieved from http://vimeo.com/69150062

Gardiner, V. (Producer). (2013b). *Unfolding landscape*. Kings Place Gallery 2013. [Video file]. Retrieved from http://vimeo.com/67286839

Gimzewski, J., & Vesna, V. (2003). The nanoneme syndrome: Blurring of fact and fiction in the construction of a new science. *Technoetic Arts: A Journal of Speculative Research*, *1*(1), 7-24.

Hanson, V. L. (2012). Amidst nanotechnology's molecular landscapes. *Science Communication*, *34*(1), 57–83. doi:10.1177/1075547011401630

Haus der Kulturen der Welt (HKW). (2014). *The anthropocene project*. Retrieved from http://www.hkw.de/en/programm/projekte/2014/anthropozaen/anthropozaen_2013_2014.php

Hawkins, H. (2013). Geography and art: An expanding field: Site, the body and practice. *Progress in Human Geography*, *37*(1), 52–71. doi:10.1177/0309132512442865

Head, A. (2011). 3D weather: Towards a real-time 3D simulation of localised weather. In *Proceedings of the 2011 International Conference on Electronic Visualisation and the Arts*. London: BCS.

Head, L. (2014). Contingencies of the anthropocene: Lessons from the 'neolithic'. *The Anthropocene Review*, *1*(2), 113–125. doi:10.1177/2053019614529745

Kueffer, C. (2013). Ecological novelty: Towards an interdisciplinary understanding of ecological change in the anthropocene. In H. Greschke & J. Tischler (Eds.), *Grounding global climate change: Contributions from the social and cultural sciences* (pp. 19–37). Dordrecht, The Netherlands: Springer Verlag.

Latour, B. (2013). *Telling friends from foes at the time of the anthropocene*. Lecture prepared for the EHESS-Centre Koyré- Sciences Po symposium "Thinking the Anthropocene" Paris, 14th-15th November, 2013. EHESS-Centre Koyré- Sciences Po symposium. Paris. [PDF document]. Retrieved from http://www.bruno-latour.fr/sites/default/files/131-ANTHROPOCENE-PARIS-11-13.pdf

Leonardo Almanac. (2011). Interview with Tom Corby, 'The Southern Ocean Studies'. *LEA - Digital Media Exhibition Platform*. Retrieved from https://www.flickr.com/photos/lea_gallery/sets/72157626603712256/comments/

Luu, R., Mitchell, D., & Blyth, J. (2004). Thrombolites (Stromatolite-like microbialite) community of a coastal brackish lake (Lake Clifton) (D. o. C. a. L. Management, Trans.). Interim Recovery Plan 2004-2009. Wannero, WA: Western Australian Threatened Species and Communities Unit (WATSCU).

Manovich, L. (2002). *Data visualization as new abstraction and anti-sublime*. Retrieved from http://manovich.net/index.php/projects/data-visualisation-as-new-abstraction-and-anti-sublime

Manovich, L. (2011). What is visualisation? *Visual Studies, 26*(1), 36–49. doi:10.1080/1472586X.2011.548488

Marsching, J. D., & Polli, A. (2012). *Far field: Digital culture, climate change, and the poles.* Bristol, UK: Intellect.

McCosker, A., & Wilken, R. (2014). Rethinking 'big data' as visual knowledge: The sublime and the diagrammatic in data visualisation. *Visual Studies, 29*(2), 155–164. doi:10.1080/1472586X.2014.887268

Morse, P. (2007). *IMAGinING Antarctica*. Retrieved from http://johncurtingallery.curtin.edu.au/exhibitions/archive/2007.cfm#Ant

Oldfield, F., Barnosky, A. D., Dearing, J., Fischer-Kowalski, M., McNeill, J., Steffen, W., & Zalasiewicz, J. (2014). The anthropocene review: Its significance, implications and the rationale for a new transdisciplinary journal. *The Anthropocene Review, 1*(1), 3–7. doi:10.1177/2053019613500445

Phillips, P. (2009). Clotted life and brittle waters. *Landscapes, 3*(2), 1–20.

Phillips, P. (2012). *The sixth shore details*. Retrieved from http://www.perditaphillips.com/index.php?option=com_content&view=article&id=313:the-sixth-shore-details&catid=17:now-news&Itemid=31

Pink, S., Hubbard, P., O'Neill, M., & Radley, A. (2010). Walking across disciplines: From ethnography to arts practice. *Visual Studies, 25*(1), 1–7. doi:10.1080/14725861003606670

Polli, A. (2004). *Heat and the heartbeat of the city*. Retrieved from http://www.turbulence.org/Works/heat/index2.html

Polli, A. (Producer). (2010). *Particle falls*. [Video file]. Retrieved from http://vimeo.com/16336508

Polli, A. (2011). *Communicating air: Alternative pathways to environmental knowing through computational ecomedia*. (Doctoral Dissertation). University of Plymouth. Available from British Library EThOS database. (546308). Retrieved from http://ethos.bl.uk/OrderDetails.do?did=1&uin=uk.bl.ethos.546308#sthash.Ga04gfdo.dpuf

Polli, A. (2012, 14 July). *Profile of 90 degrees south by filmmaker Meredith Drum*. Retrieved from http://www.90degreessouth.org/

Selin, C. (2007). Expectations and the emergence of nanotechnology. *Science, Technology & Human Values, 32*(2), 196–220. doi:10.1177/0162243906296918

Smudge Studio. (2010). *Geologic time viewer*. Retrieved from http://www.smudgestudio.org/smudge/projects/MIT/timeviewer.html

Smudge Studio. (2014a). *For future north*. Retrieved from http://smudgestudio.org/smudge/change.html

Smudge Studio. (2014b). *Pompeii of the north: Heimaey*. Retrieved from http://fopnews.wordpress.com/2014/06/05/heimaey/

Smudge Studio. (2014c). *Turning at the limits of the urban: Tjuvhommen*. Retrieved from http://fopnews.wordpress.com/2014/06/06/thief/

Steffen, W., Grinevald, J., Crutzen, P., & McNeill, J. (2011). The anthropocene: Conceptual and historical perspectives. *Philosophical Transactions of the Royal Society A: Mathematical, Physical and Engineering Sciences, 369*(1938), 842-867.

Subcommission on Quaternary Stratigraphy. (2014). *Working group on the 'anthropocene'*. Retrieved from http://quaternary.stratigraphy.org/workinggroups/anthropocene/

Thomas, P. (2007). Boundaryless nanomorphologies. In *MutaMorphosis: Challenging art and sciences*. Prague, Czech Republic: MutaMorphosis.

Thomas, P. (2009). Midas: A nanotechnological exploration of touch. *Leonardo, 42*(3), 186–192. doi:10.1162/leon.2009.42.3.186

Transmediale. (2014). *Transmediale.09 deep north*. Retrieved from http://www.transmediale.de/past/2009

Transmediale Archive. (2014). *Amundsen/l-landscape*. Retrieved from http://www.transmediale.de/amundsen-i-landscape-en

Trischler, H. (Ed.). (2013). *Anthropocene: Envisioning the future of the age of humans* (Vol. 3). Munich, Germany: Rachel Carson Center for Environment and Society.

Turpin, E. (Ed.). (2013). *Architecture in the anthropocene: Encounteres among design, deep time, science and philosophy*. Open Humanities Press, University of Michigan. doi:10.3998/ohp.12527215.0001.001

United Nations Educational, Scientific and Cultural Organization (UNESCO). (2014). *Dorset and east Devon coast*. Retrieved from http://whc.unesco.org/en/list/1029

Vesna, V. (n.d.). *Zero@wavefunction*. Retrieved from http://notime.arts.ucla.edu/zerowave/zerowave.html

Vesna, V. (n.d.). *Nanomandala*. Retrieved from http://nano.arts.ucla.edu/mandala/mandala.php

Wilke, S. (2013). Anthropocenic poetics: Ethics and aesthetics in a new geological age. In H. Trischler (Ed.), *Anthropocene: Envisioning the future of the age of humans* (pp. 67–74). Munich, Germany: Rachel Carson Center for Environment and Society.

Worden, S. (2014). The earth sciences and creative practice: Exploring boundaries between digital and material culture. In D. Harrison (Ed.), *Digital media and technologies for virtual artistic spaces* (pp. 186–204). Hershey, PA: IGI Global. doi:10.4018/978-1-4666-5125-8.ch062

Yokokoji, M., & Harwood, G. (2014). *Wrecked*. Retrieved from http://yoha.co.uk/wrecked

Ziarek, K. (2011). The limits of life. *Angelaki, 16*(4), 19–30.

KEY TERMS AND DEFINITIONS

Activism: An activity where the intention is to promote social, economic, political and environmental change.

Anthropocene: A new geological age replacing the Holocene, where nothing in nature makes sense except in the light of human action.

Deep Time: Deep Time is a concept developed by the geologist James Hutton (1726-1797). In this context evolution can only be measured over vast, immeasurable amounts of time where numbers no longer have any meaning.

Ecology: The scientific study of the interaction between organisms and their environment. It is an interdisciplinary field that encompasses the Earth Sciences, biology and human science, with many practical applications.

Ecomedia: A media form in which computing is a shared practice between science and an art concerned with place and content-based creation.

Embodied: A tangible or visible form, particularly the presence of the body as a precondition for thought and social interaction.

Sublime: A term used for art that is extraordinary and often escapes definition. It is often used to describe a response to nature.

Chapter 8
Transposing, Transforming, and Transcending Tradition in Creative Digital Media

Phillip Andrew Prager
IT University of Copenhagen, Denmark

Maureen Thomas
University of Cambridge, UK

Marianne Selsjord
National Academy of the Arts, Norway

ABSTRACT

How can digital media technologies, contemporary theories of creativity, and tradition combine to develop the aesthetics of computer-based art today and in the future? Through contextualised case-studies, this chapter investigates how games, information technologies, and traditional visual and storytelling arts combine to create rich, complex, and engaging moving-image based artworks with wide appeal. It examines how dramatist and interactive media artist Maureen Thomas and 3D media artist and conservator Marianne Selsjord deploy creative digital technologies to transpose, transform, and transcend pre-page arts and crafts for the digital era, making fresh work for new audiences. Researcher in digital aesthetics, creative cognition, and play behaviour Dr. Phillip Prager examines how such work is conducive to creative insight and worthwhile play, discussing its remediation of some of the aspirations and approaches of 20th-century avant-garde artists, revealing these as a potent source of conceptual riches for the digital media creators of today and tomorrow.

INTRODUCTION

Certain objects can be intentionally constructed in such a way that they are eminently suitable for disinterested and sympathetic attention and contemplation. They will contain structures that guide attention and contemplation – that encourage it by means of their intentionally designed features of unity, complexity and intensity – and that reward such attention and contemplation. The aesthetic experiencer will not have to do all the work herself. The object itself will be structured

DOI: 10.4018/978-1-4666-8205-4.ch008

intentionally to invite, sustain and, optimally, reward disinterested and sympathetic attention and contemplation. Such objects, of course, are artworks. (Carroll, 2010, pp. 172-173)

Are digital and interactive technologies changing the nature of the artwork? This chapter addresses the transposition, transformation and transcending of traditional techniques from painting and sculpture in creative digital media, to create artworks whose new approaches to unity, complexity and intensity reward attention and contemplation in new ways. It employs both aesthetic and scientific approaches to the nature of creativity and the impact of interactive works, arguing for a recognition of play and playfulness as a significant component in contemporary electronic art and an acknowledgement of the continuities of both traditional and avant-garde practices in today's digital environment.

In *Creativity and Art: Three Roads to Surprise* (2010) Margaret A. Boden notes:

As a practice, interactive art – wherein the form of the art object is partly determined by the actions of the audience (or, occasionally, by non-human forces) – is by now well established. It's not mainstream, to be sure. But it's an identifiable genre (Krueger, 1991; Candy & Edmonds, 2002; Ascott, 2003; Whitelaw, 2004). However, there's no established aesthetics associated with it. [...] The nature of the interaction is considered to be at least as important as that of the art object itself. But interaction doesn't figure as a consideration in traditional aesthetics. Moreover, the artists concerned disagree among themselves about what type of interaction is most interesting and/ or most humanly significant. [...] A related uncertainty concerns the attribution of creativity, or artistic responsibility, for the artwork. [...] Many interactive artists not only insist that the audience are participants in the art-making, but claim that this distributed responsibility has value in itself, so is a factor in their aesthetic creation. (Boden, 2010, p. 210)

Marianne Selsjord's *Gardens of Dreaming* (2009) and *Marvellous Transformations* (2014), and Maureen Thomas's *Vala* (2001), *RuneCast* (2007) and *Viking Seeress* (2010), the major case-studies considered here, offer an approach which hopefully contributes to identifying the aesthetics of interactive art, including interactivity and participative creativity, that Boden misses. These works draw on the European art and craft traditions of sculpture, painting, carving, metalwork and oral composition, from the Viking Age through the Middle Ages and Renaissance to the 20th-century avant-garde, whose processes they transform for the digital era. These approaches are inherently transferable, and could be adapted for many kinds of original work. The case-studies are contextualised both with reference to traditional arts and aesthetics, and contemporary 3D-games art.

Selsjord and Thomas's work falls into Boden and Edmonds' category of "Computer-based Interactive Art (CI-Art)", where "the form/content [...] is significantly affected by the behaviour of the audience", and the case-studies are presented within this theoretical framework. "With regard to CI-art," Boden and Edmonds note "perhaps we should speak not of the 'artwork' but of the 'art system' - where this comprises the artist, the program, the technological installation (and its observable results), and the behaviour of the human audience" (Boden, 2010, p.155). Both Thomas and Selsjord regard 3D digital media, explorable art and narrativity as fresh mediums, capable of giving a new lease of life to traditional practices and enjoyments, whilst contributing innovative potentials of their own.

Working with the computer as both tool and medium requires an understanding of the affordances of software and fluency with the visual and physical languages of interactivity. The interaction situation, interaction devices and interaction itself in the experiences are all viewed here, in line with Boden and Edmonds' observations, as integral components of the artwork as a whole, and thus of its aesthetic. This approach can be applied more widely by creative media artists seeking to build on the traditional excellences of the past to push the boundaries of contemporary art.

COMPUTER AS MEDIUM

The aesthetic development of mainstream Real Time Games in 3D virtual environments (RT-3DVE), the chief field of creativity in 3D art in the 20th - and 21st-centuries, has, at least in the West, tended towards increasingly hyper-realistic, hyper-texturized surfaces, facilitated by the development of ever more sophisticated graphics cards. The *Grand Theft Auto* series (2004 – 2013), *Bioshock* series (2007 – 2013), *Sleeping Dogs* (2012) and *Defiance* (2013) are striking examples of this tendency. *Defiance* ties in closely with a TV series of the same name (Five and Dime/Universal Cable: Syfy 2013-), and the performers, locations, lighting and sound transfer almost seamlessly between the live-action TV fiction and the virtual game fiction. The *Lara Croft – Tomb Raider* game fiction series and films (1996 – 2013) illustrate the same intensifying pursuit of the hyper-real in screen language and visual style (Marshall, 2013).

This phenomenon can be seen as a continuation of the pursuit of naturalistic representation that has characterised the history and development of painting for the last millennium, and especially since the Renaissance (Gombrich 1960; see also Bolter and Grusin 1999) -- or at least until the invention of photography in the early 19th century, when painting gradually redefined itself as a medium for personal expression (Tolstoy 2011/1896). However, art and aesthetics were, until the 19th-century, inextricably linked to the pursuit of beauty, and the quest for hyper-realism in game design might be seen by traditional aesthetics merely as an unimaginative end in itself.

There are exceptions to the 3D gamesworld's drive towards task- and adrenalin-driven ultra-realism. *Artists Re:Thinking Games* (ed. Catlow, Garrett & Morgana, 2010) is an inspiring and useful handbook in this regard; it comprises examples of games that self-consciously, but playfully, subvert and parody normative praxis, such as Jeremy Bailey's *Warmail* (2008) (Catlow & Garrett, 2010, pp. 15-19), while also providing examples of genuine gaming alternatives. *The Night Journey* (2009) by Bill Viola and the University of Southern California (USC) Game Lab, for example, consists of a mysterious wilderness, in which exploration and contemplation are goals in themselves. It is a quintessential so-called "Slow Game", an increasingly popular gaming genre that focuses on exploratory play and reflection as autotelic goals (Corcoran, 2010, p.20). Viola writes that he wanted to "slow the action way down so that the pace of interaction was in tune with a solitary reflective experience. We wanted the landscape to reveal its secrets subtly and gradually" (Corcoran, 2010, p.25).

In terms of alternatives to hyperrealism, *Sunset Overdrive* (Insomniac/MGS 2014) is an interesting example. This action-based post-apocalyptic shooter-game, not primarily aimed at children, offers detailed 3D comic-book art, rather than the highly-textured, cinematically-presented screen-world of *Grand Theft Auto* or *Tomb Raider*. But *Sunset Overdrive* does not primarily invite "disinterested and sympathetic attention and contemplation", like the traditional artwork – the rewards it offers are ever more bizarre weapons and ever more intricate kills.

The work of Jenova Chen and Kellee Santiago's Los Angeles-based "thatgamescomapany" (http://thatgamecompany.com) for Sony Playstation - *flOw* (2007) (which began as Chen and designer Nick Clark's student project at the University of Southern California; see www.kelleesantiago.com/portfolio/flow-playstation-network/), *Flower* (2009) and *Journey* (2012) - does, however, demonstrate that there is a market for explorable game-space whose immersive attraction is not task- or adrenalin- driven action, but audio-visual delight and emotional engagement. In her review of *Journey*, Keza MacDonald, critic for the British newspaper *The Guardian*, writes:

Journey has moved me as much as any other piece of art or entertainment has. Journey's visual and sound design sets new standards for interactive entertainment. This alone makes it an extraordinary work, but it's the way that these aesthetic elements come together with beautifully subtle direction and storytelling to create a lasting emotional effect that elevates this to one of the very best games of our time. [...] I came to it expecting something charming, visually stunning and perhaps even mildly edifying. I left thinking that it may well be, in many ways, the best video game I have ever played. (2012, no pag.)

Carroll writes of the traditional artwork: "The aesthetic experiencer will not have to do all the work herself. The object itself will be structured intentionally to invite, sustain and, optimally, reward disinterested and sympathetic attention and contemplation" (2010, pp. 172-173). In *Journey*, as in *The Night Journey*, experiencers have to embark on a voyage themselves to actively reveal the world structured by the artists for their contemplation: but once they have set out, and become immersed in exploratory play, their attention is sustained and rewarded by the aesthetic of the environment, and sympathetic investment in the emotions of the onscreen veiled traveller.

In *Entwined* (Pixelopus/SCE 2014), exploratory play is combined with mindful, constructional play. The player is asked to unite two origami-like creatures, one of air, one of water, which travel, in parallel, through 9 levels, or "lives" - tunnels of colourful, exuberant, geometric and abstract shapes. The player helps these creatures to reach rebirth as a single glorious dragon. There seems to be nothing to compete against; the game demands only mindfulness - active attention to rhythm and colour and shape; and relaxing into the flow of your own dexterity, which evolves as you play. Reviewing *Entwined* for *Wired* magazine, Matt Peckham explicates: "because you control each creature independently, the game tries to confuse your brain's hemispheres," (Peckham, 2014, no

pag.), adding, however, that "thankfully the design team -- all Carnegie Mellon University students -- seems to have figured out how much is too much (or how fast is too fast)".

So although this game may appear mainly to be about disinterested attention to an artwork, as part of its active mode of contemplation it invokes oriental traditions of mindfulness, meditation, karmic reincarnation and the evolution of energetic bodies (symbolised by fish, bird, dragon); and perhaps offers 'training' to unify or balance the activity of the two halves of the human brain – like the Yin and Yang of the Dao, or the protagonists in the game, "always together, forever apart" (see Bisio, 2013, pp. 120 – 127, 201 – 203, 275 – 321).

In Europe, the Belgian company 'BVBA Tale of Tales' (http://www.tale-of-tales.com/), of which *gamesindustry.biz* says 'Samyn and Harvey's work is literate, diverse and heady - a rare mix in gaming' (Hanrahan, 2014), has specialised in art-driven games for a decade. Although these have struggled to find development funding or major distribution, they have been released commercially as games, and continue to intrigue and entrance a substantial fan base, as demonstrated by the successful crowd-funding of *Sunset* (in development 2014) (Hanrahan, 2014). But in the process of achieving greater success, the model behind the games has moved towards popular formats, though never abandoning the emphasis on aesthetics and mental challenge:

We use our games as tools to think about the world. If the world is the way it is - war and strife everywhere - then this is a good tool to have right now. Those characters in that situation is a good way of meditating on that, and we're trying to put it forth in a way where we won't be ahead of our audience. I don't mean that as a humble brag. We want to be there with you this time. (Aurelia Samyn, 2014, interviewed by Matthew Hanrahan, in 'Tale of Tales: Making a Game for the Gamers' Gamesindustry.biz, 20 Oct 2014; http://www.gamesindustry.biz/articles/2014-10-

The medium for contemplation in *Sunset* is not primarily the artwork, but the dramatic situation, realised through characters.

In his short discussion of "Art" as one of the things that can be done with videogames, Bogost (2011) defines "proceduralism" as the new movement native to computer-handled art:

Proceduralist games are oriented toward intro-spection over both immediate gratification, as is usually the case in entertainment games, and external action, whether immediate or deferred, as is usually the case in serious games. The goal of the proceduralist designer is to cause the player to reflect on one or more themes during or after play, without a concern for resolution or effect. The use of identifiably human yet still abstract roles in these games underscores the invitation to project one's own experience and ideas on them. (p. 14)

From the perspective of form, proceduralist artgames tend to combine concrete, identifiable situations with abstract tokens, objects, goals, or actions [...] From the perspective of signification, proceduralist works deploy a more poetic and less direct way to express the ideas or scenarios their processes represent. (p.16)

This definition might apply to both *Journey*, where there is a central figure, which, though stylised in desert drapery, is clearly human, who makes the journey on which the player propels it through the abstracted world of the game, on which the player may reflect; and *Entwined*, where the two creatures the player steers through their colourful abstract tunnels can be seen as two lovers longing for union, a situation which may evoke subjective emotion in the player. These games were both released for Sony console, which gives them mainstream distribution.

There is clearly already room in the world of games for diversity, often first explored and pioneered by practice-based research at universities, as the examples presented above demonstrate, and

the public continues to expand. The Entertainment Merchant Association's *Annual Report 2009* indicated that despite the economic recession, revenue from games retained the lead over movie box-office and DVD sales that it took in 2008; and although between 2009 and 2014 blu-ray as well as DVD sales and on-demand pay-per-view services substantially raised revenue from the distribution of other forms of digital entertainment, the EMA Annual Report for 2014 shows that interactive games continued to account for a very substantial proportion of profits (www.ent-merch.org/annual_reports.html; Kamenetz, 2013).

As technology becomes more and more wieldy and platforms more and more interchangeable, artworks are set to follow British artist David Hockney's example, and migrate from the gallery to the console, tablet and smartphone (O'Brien, 2013). 'Unity 3D' software (https://unity3d.com), in which many designers are now developing their work, has since 2010 put this transition within the grasp of individual 3D artists who previously struggled to port their work to popular platforms.

Marianne Selsjord, in *Gardens of Dreaming* (2009), a playable gallery installation (created using Maya to model and 3DGamestudio for the navigable environment), works - like Matt Nava and Aaron Jessie, the artists of *Journey* (2012) - with an almost texture-free world, where colour and transparency are the most important tools. The result is a 3-dimensional dynamic painting, to be seen and enjoyed from all viewpoints, in the literal meaning of the word (Figure 1).

To Selsjord, absurd humour and events inside the *Gardens* combined with the audio-visual impressions create the experience's interest. There are no game events like pursuing a goal, performing a task, collecting items or escaping dangerous creatures: but attention is stimulated by unexpected encounters, occurring spontaneously, in a manner reminiscent of the atmosphere of Lewis Carroll's *Through the Looking Glass, and What Alice Found There* (1871).

Figure 1. 'Gardens of Dreaming'
(© 2009, Marianne Selsjord. Used with kind permission.).

The fantastical creatures inhabiting Selsjord's *Gardens* provide punctuation in the exploration. For example, the gardener, adapted from a stock gaming-character originally armed with a gun, carries a watering-can; as it potters around, flowers grow where the water falls. Thatgamescompany's *Flower* (2009) uses a similarly constructive rather than destructive principle - the wind can fertilise withered land; but in *Flower,* you play/control the wind, whereas in *Gardens of Dreaming* you explore and contemplate. You can voyage as an invisible entity, or choose to use an avatar - a baby - open to all impressions (Figure 1). Like the traditional enjoyer of pictorial or sculptural art, and unlike the typical avatar in a 3D game, the baby has no other mission than to help the explorer pay sympathetic attention, discover and contemplate, as does the viewer of a traditional artwork (Carroll, 2010, p. 173, quoted at the head of this chapter).

But the interaction-device, in the form of a purpose-built, large, luscious-looking electronic fruit, which the interactor grasps in two hands, is inspired by the imagery of the gardens themselves – thus acting as a transitional link between the physical gallery space and the virtual space: a feature of interactive electronic technologies which can be deployed to create a new kind of sensual connection with the artwork.

Marianne Selsjord's approach to colour and texture proved perfectly adapted to staging the mythworld of Thomas's *RuneCast* (2007), developed from her earlier 2D video and graphics-based installation *Vala* (2001); and as a working conservator of medieval polychrome sculpture with a special interest in Viking carving, Selsjord was attracted by the Nordic myth-setting.

Myth is a vital cornerstone of culture; mythographer Joseph Campbell points out that "the rise and fall of civilizations [...] have been largely a function of the integrity and cogency of their supporting canons of myth" (Campbell, 1982/1968, p. 5). But mythtales also offer a network of context, chronology, topic, character, tale-type and imagery: features of oral composition and the singing of tales which particularly suit computer handling, including providing an aesthetic for the interaction/interactive interface – which in general Boden misses in interactive art (Boden, 2010 p. 210).

Interaction designer Abbe Don relates that: "Using my great-grandmother as a model, I began to investigate the characteristics of oral storytelling and multimedia interface design [...] It was as if she had a chronological, topical, and associative matrix that enabled her to generate stories in which structure, content, and context were interdependent" (Don, 1990, p. 384). An associative matrix drawn from a mythworld enables the creation and sharing of a rich and complex evocative narrative experience: "If one knows enough mythology, one can make a completely consistent web [...] There is always a legend or a saga which links up two archetypes in a new form" (von Franz, 1980, p. 63).

Inspired by the practice of traditional singers of oral tales (Lord, 1968/1960, pp. 30-67), the associative approach of *Vala* and *RuneCast* exploits the matrix-web of archetypal links in Nordic, Baltic and Anglo-Saxon myth to create narrative coherence. The form and content of the works both explicitly test Don's contention that "Narrative, and in particular oral storytelling, can provide both system designers and users with idiosyncratic, personal tools for performing the range of activities involved in producing and using multimedia knowledge bases" (Don, 1990 p. 385). The outcomes can be transposed to many contexts, and are hopefully inspiring and useful for other creative media artists.

Digital technology, especially that developed for interactive gaming, has been surprisingly underused in the area of fine art. There is plenty of scope for what von Franz designated "earnest gaming" (von Franz, 1980, p. 117), a purposeful exploration of meaning; though what modern commentators term "serious gaming" is currently largely devoted to task-oriented teaching and learning (Sorenson, Meyer & Eigenfeldt-Nielsen, 2011) rather than the 'disinterested and sympathetic attention and contemplation' of the artwork. *Gardens of Dreaming* demonstrates that there is no reason why the feedback and playful mechanisms of popular computer gaming cannot fuse with fine art's function of stimulating attention and contemplation through its unity, complexity and intensity, to reward aesthetically as well as, or instead of, in terms of achieving goals or accomplishing tasks. Interactivity is a key factor in enabling this aspect of the electronic artwork.

The essential characteristic of [...] interactivity [...] is that [...] it rewards our attention with its own. We act. It reacts. We act again. It reacts again [...] (Atkins, 2003, p.145).

Because of their ingenious use of interactivity, gaming technology and concepts offer a new model for visitors to engage with art. However, creative artists with the knowledge and experience of arts, crafts and aesthetics necessary to build the new on the shoulders of the traditional, must be able both to use the software tools and fully exploit the medium of the computer, if the system is to respond to the engager. Developing the necessary skills requires education both in understanding the potentials of the medium and wielding the tools of creative digital media. Practice-based research leads this education (see e.g. Wilson and van Ruiten, 2013; Knowles and Cole, 2008). Three of the models introduced in this chapter - *Gardens of Dreaming, Marvellous Transformations* (Norway), and *Vala's RuneCast* (UK) were developed in tandem with research and teaching on how leading-edge deployment of digital media can combine with expert knowledge and artistic talent to create new artwork.

TRANSPOSING, TRANSFORMING, AND TRANSCENDING TRADITION

Looking back at art history, it is easy to observe the change in attitude towards colour, shape and stylization through the last two millennia (see e.g. Stokstad, 2002; Langer, 1977). There are many different styles both inside Western tradition (e.g. Romanesque, Gothic, Renaissance, Baroque) and outside it, to be explored by 3D artists who want to understand better and experiment with historical aesthetic approaches (Paul, 2003). Outside Western art history, aboriginal sand-paintings from Australia, Japanese wabi-sabi (the art of the ephemeral) and woodcuts, Indian Tantric paintings or Ethiopian scrolls are all rich sources for inspiring artistic schemes in 3D aesthetics (Juniper, 2003; Sutton, 1989).

Diverse styles display different attitudes towards colour, form, style and composition (O'Mahony, 2006). An understanding of the wide variety of techniques available, such as Selsjord taught at the Academy of the Arts in Oslo, is accepted as a foundation for today's visual and plastic artists, as it always has been. Yet within the games industry, where most 3D artists work, contemporary film, TV-shows and existing games are often the main inspiration for game art-directors, when it comes to choosing visual styles (e.g. *Defiance,* by Trion, 2013), and there seems to be a surprising lack of art-historical insight and consciousness or exploitation of these rich visual traditions (Solarski, 2012). There are exceptions: some Japanese games, for instance, work outside the tradition of realism. These range from horror games such as *Fatal Frame* (Tecmo, 2001) and *Fatal Frame Crimson Butterfly* (Tecmo 2003) - whose unusual and effective multi-layered visual style is somewhat paralleled in Aureia Harvey and

Michael Samin's complex psychological narrative game, *The Path* (BVBA Belgium, 2008) - to Manga and Anime-influenced games, whose aesthetics are discussed in detail by de Winter (2009). These Japanese games are distributed by mainstream companies, and attract a large public, who play them primarily for their characters, gaming and adventure stories, rather than their aesthetics (for further discussion of Japanese computer games art see (Works Corporation, 2004)).

Both the navigable *Gardens of Dreaming* and *RuneCast* can be seen as a "living" art works, which give participant viewers a unique experience on each visit: the audio-visual media change in content and form with each journey, surprising you with a new aesthetic or narrative experience. *Gardens of Dreaming* is very different from, and in many ways simpler than, a commercial 3D game. But, like *RuneCast*, which has a more complex computational structure (because it contains narrative as well as visual experience), *Gardens of Dreaming* caters for an audience who may or may not be interested in mainstream games, but can be fully engaged by a 3D art experience.

Interactivity and interaction devices are a key feature. Human beings perceive their surroundings through sense; vision, hearing, smell and touch can all be stimulated through tangible interfaces, which conduct visitors from the everyday world and the gallery space into the enchanting realms of 3D artworks. The process of interaction itself is a part of the aesthetic experience, as Boden and Edmonds (2010, p.210) point out, and as Selsjord's giant fruit interaction-device for *Gardens of Dreaming*[1] demonstrates (Figure 2).

Thomas's interactive 3D, video and integrated media performance works, *Vala, Songs of Vala, RuneCast* and *Viking Seeress* explore the flexibility and cross-platform potentials of creative digital media and technologies. The first experimental installation, *Vala*, was initially designed with a tangible interface consisting of hand-sized white stones, which visitors moved, in a pool whose "water" was created by light-projections (Figure 3).

Figure 2. Giant strawberry interaction device, 'Gardens of Dreaming'
(© 2009, Marianne Selsjord. Used with kind permission.).

In the dramatic situation of the installation[2], Vala (played by actor Helen McGregor), a Viking-age shaman, has survived to the present in her pre-shamanic state as fortune-teller Heithur. When summoned, she appears as a video projection in the water, and guides her visitors through the interactive content. In 2003, an amplified, more portable version, which used a roller-ball point-and-click interface, alongside a live performance of the songs composed and performed for the original work by Kariina Gretere, was staged at the Ráðhús Reykjavíkur Performance Space, Iceland (Figure 4).[3]

In 2007, the digital cross-platform work *RuneCast*, which used some of the video and audio assets from *Vala* and added new material, set the whole work inside a 3D navigable virtual environment designed by Selsjord[4] (Figure 5). It was developed at the University of Cambridge Digital Studio (DIGIS/CUMIS) as part of the EU FP6 research-project, *New Millennium New Media* (*NM2*, 2004-2007) (Ursu et al. 2009; 2008; 2007), which developed new content-driven software tools for cross-platform production and delivery over broadband.

In 2010, a live performance, *Viking Seeress*, where Selsjord's 3D environment was used as a set, navigated in real time by the original performers, Helen McGregor and Kariina Gretere, was staged at *MIST* (Museums, Interfaces, Space, Technologies), Cambridge (Figure 6).

Gardens of Dreaming and *Marvellous Transformations* are examples of innovative electronic artworks produced using commercially available games technologies, partially funded by digital arts funding in Norway. They rely to some extent on research carried out by the artist as part of her work in a a higher education academy specializing in fine arts. *Vala* and *RuneCast* are examples of artworks created in specialised digital media labs embedded in

Figure 3. White stones with overhead projection of rune symbols; tangible interface for 'Vala' (screenshot)
(© 2000, Maureen Thomas. Used with kind permission.).

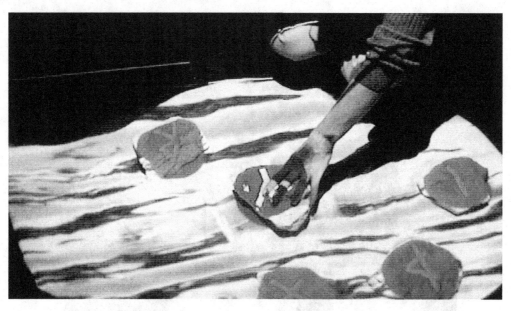

Figure 4. Kariina Gretere sings 'Songs of Vala' (Reykjavík 2003); manipulated video from 'Vala' (Thomas 2001) projected
(© Maureen Thomas. Used with kind permission.).

Figure 5. 'Runecast'; 3D interface environment by Selsjord

Figure 6. Kariina Gretere and Helen McGregor perform Thomas's 'Viking Seeress' with navigable 3D set (designed by Selsjord) at MIST, Cambridge, 2010. (Interaction device: rune symbol, held here in Heithur/Vala's right hand)

universities, using some existing software and technologies but also contributing to the design of new tools and devices, with the aid of research funding. The material produced as part of the EU *NM2* project (www.ist-nm2.org) enabled the artist subsequently to create live, integrated media performances, with the aid of European and UK arts and cultural funding.

In Thomas's work, inspired by North-Atlantic and Baltic myth, Heithur (from the Old Norse poem, *Songs of the Seeress* [*Völuspá*]; see Acker, 2001) tells your fortune by casting her runes (old Scandinavian symbols), which was a Viking-age practice (Tacitus, 96AD, in Mattingly, 2009, p. 39); but she also becomes the shaman-seeress, Vala (as she does in the original poem). Vala is able to access the mythology of the Viking World, and tell its stories in (manipulated, non-naturalistic) video, using song and voice-over narrative[5].

The profound philosophical concern with the relationship between Destiny, Chance and Choice in Old Norse culture, expressed in the Viking-age poem, *Songs of the Seeress*, both offers a coherent associational structure, and provides the material (content), the storyworld and the interaction-situation for *Vala* and *RuneCast*.

The approach to non-linear programming and interaction inspired by this traditional ontology embodies an effective model for reconfigurable digital media, which could have much wider applications (compare Seaman, 2002; Rieser, 2002; Manovich, 2001; Manovich & Kratky, 2005; Ryan, 2001; Murray, 1997). The concept also addresses the issue of narrative cogency and depth, which Rieser identifies as particularly challenging:

New media has the [...] problem [...] of coherence. Interactive narratives demand a certain minimum 'granularity' of material, which can be assembled or reassembled in multiple combinations by an audience. The modular structure can easily become shallow or incoherent, unless temporality remains uncompromised and the potential for poetic ambiguity and therefore richness is enhanced. (Rieser, 2002, pp. 147-8)

Vala and *RuneCast* combine the Viking-age system of divination using 22 key symbols (runes) configured (like the traditional Tarot, also a combined system of prediction, self-understanding and storytelling using archetypal imagery [Rosengarten 2000]) in a hand of six per session - one chosen by questioners to represent themselves, plus five randomly cast by Heithur/Vala (the system) to ensure associative depth along a coherent thread.

Technically, the original programming for *Vala* and subsequent development and repurposing of the assets for *RuneCast* was inspired by the structure of the oral tale-telling matrix (see *Introduction*) and the rune-casting practice; these were then transposed as the chaos mathematics of sensitive dependence on initial conditions. Tabor explains:

By a chaotic solution to a deterministic equation we mean a solution whose outcome is very sensitive to initial conditions (i.e., small changes in initial conditions lead to great differences in outcome) and whose evolution through phase space appears to be quite random. (Tabor, 1989, p. 34; see also Wiggins, 1990, p. 437)

In terms of developing a new media content form, the aleatoric work of composer John Cage (1912-1992), who favoured the Chinese *i-Ching* or book of changes (Haskins, 2012), which dates from circa 1,000 BCE or earlier (Pearson, 2011), and that of his frequent collaborator Merce Cunningham (1919-2009), was of particular inspiration. Thomas saw in their work "a way in which designed (choreographed, composed) forms combined with chance operations can offer an exciting, aesthetically pleasing and engaging experience, analogous to improvisation, based on a constantly changing dynamic between the audio and the visual in performance" (2005, pp. 394–5). In the interactive screen-based storygames of chance, *Vala* and the later *RuneCast*, Thomas combines Cagean principles of indeterminacy with the spontaneity of oral storytelling, to dramatise the Nordic mythworld using recombinant, associational and spatially-organized narrative structures.

Selsjord's *Gardens of Dreaming*, where visitors roam completely freely through landscapes and imagery derived from the work of Hieronymous Bosch of Brabant (1453-1516) or conjured from her dreams, incorporates similar principles of indeterminacy and recombinance to *Vala* and *RuneCast*. Choice (of direction, nudged by Natasha Barrett's 3D musicscape and the visual composition of the environment) and chance (elements and characters encountered within the gardens) combine to configure each individual experience afresh.

The relinquishing of authorial dictatorship echoes the aspirations of Dada and Surrealism in the 1920's – both potentially rich sources of inspiration for contemporary digital art.

Both Arp and Duchamp were departing radically from the model of authorial control synonymous with art-making at that time. They were also pioneering a characteristically 'Dada' attitude which stands at the foundations of aleatory art in the 20ᵗʰ century, incorporating figures such as the composer John Cage [...] - both artists were invoking impersonal or nature-based processes as opposed to psychologically oriented human ones. [...] Whereas the Surrealists were primarily interested in the individual psyche, the Dadaists chose to invoke forces which were entirely independent of themselves. (Hopkins, 2004, p. 71)

Yet to integrate indeterminacy and the aleatory (chance) into an artwork requires careful structuring, as Rieser noted, to avoid shallowness and gratuitous randomness. While Arp may have discovered interesting arrangements by casting bits of paper (Richter, 1965, pp. 15–16), chance operations need to be constrained more closely if they are to create narrative coherence and remain engaging to an audience, and to prevent the sense of boredom to which Cage's audience would (occasionally) succumb.

In Cage's *Reunion* (1968), even Duchamp, who was a performer, snoozed off (Cross, 1999 p. 41). The work consisted of a chessboard with underlying electric circuitry connected to speakers distributed around the audience. In this electronic musical performance, held at the Ryerson Theatre in Toronto, sounds were triggered aleatorically by the movement of chess pieces. Duchamp, a passionate and famed chess player, who had given Cage chess lessons, began his game against his student at 8.30, but the teacher won within 25 minutes, after which a large proportion of the audience, including Marshall McLuhan, left (Cross, 1999, pp. 35-42). Duchamp's wife Teeny subsequently took his place, but her game against Cage remained ongoing at 1 a.m. Lowell Cross, who designed the sound-distributing chessboard, observed:

One game ended too quickly to allow the underlying ideas to be fully experienced by the audience; the other dragged on for so long that it had to be postponed due to the exhaustion of the principals and the dwindling audience. Finally, the circumstances attending Reunion permitted no correlation between Cage's elegantly proscribed application of his system of indeterminacy and his underlying hope that elegant games of chess could bring forth elegant musical structures. (Cross, 1999, p. 41)

Maureen Thomas' reconfigurable storygame, *Queen's Game* (2014)[6], also combines a chessboard as the interface and interaction situation with principles of indeterminacy, but includes sufficient constraints to avoid the problems of *Reunion*. It is not an artwork entirely in the manner of Cage, who was interested in removing the artist as far as possible from the outcome; *Queen's Game* is "structured intentionally" by the artist "to invite, sustain and reward sympathetic attention and contemplation" (Carroll, 2010, p. 173) - though the story cannot finally be created without the

Figure 7. 'Queen's Game' (Thomas, 2014); 3D sketch by Marianne Selsjord
(© 2014, Maureen Thomas. Used with kind permission.).

active participation of players/storyseekers. Its four interlocking tales (set in the European Middle Ages), accessible via the chess-squares, are character-based. Each of the main protagonists is represented by a chess-piece, which the story-seeker can move from square to square, to play out micro-episodes in the interconnected dramas (Figures 7 and 8).

The media associated with each square is pre-recorded; but journeys around the chessboard and through the stories may follow as many routes as there are potential combinations of moves in any game of chess. Every visit to the storyworld will produce a different, coherent, narrative, including music and songs; and each exploration will reveal more about the characters, their environment and adventures.

The medieval compilation of stories about the knights of King Arthur, *Le Morte D'Arthur* (Malory, 1485), with its dependency on traditional, non-linear, oral forms of taletelling within a vast storyworld, provides the inspiration for the construction of *Queen's Game*. The association of media with specific squares frames thematic and narrative coherence.

In the video components of *Vala* and *RuneCast*, plot frameworks and metadata-tagging are the devices which ensure that the aleatoric algorithms produce chance effects that remain meaningful; they are constrained - just as, constrained by fixed mirrors and the beads inside it, a kaleidoscope creates interesting patterns, however vigorously its coloured fragments are shaken and however arbitrarily they fall. In Selsjord's 3D *Gardens of Dreaming*, free roaming with no instructions or missions means that visitors themselves provide their own constraints, by choosing a pathway. The plants and strange objects of nostalgic memory (Victorian rocking-horses and embossed scrap-reliefs of faces for example) become associated around the nucleus that is the explorer's consciousness. The artwork provides complexity and intensity: each visitor creates unity by combining personal understanding with its designed world, stimulating new aesthetic experience through individual attention and contemplation. Similarly to *Queen's Game*, visitors create the dynamic artwork as they explore.

Figure 8. 'Queen's Game' (Thomas, 2014); Marianne Selsjord's source sketch for her Maya model of the castle
(© 2014, Maureen Thomas. Used with kind permission.).

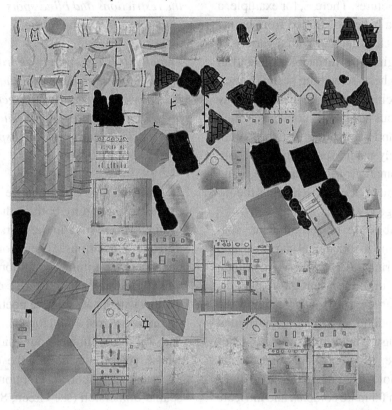

Vala and *RuneCast* revive ancient oral and folk traditions, and *Queen's Game* revisits the non-linear structure of early Arthurian storytelling, but like *Gardens of Dreaming*, which translates the avant-garde artists' relinquishing of authorial control and reliance on collage into 3D roaming, they also bear a striking resemblance to early 20th-century avant-garde work. In fact, *RuneCast* (2007) provides a three-dimensional and interactive counterpart to René Clair's short film, *Entr'acte* (1924), which features cameo roles by Marcel Duchamp and Francis Picabia, and puts into digital practise many of Clair's unrealisable aspirations. There is an interesting resemblance in the way the narratives are both associational and spatially organized (Prager, 2009, pp.187-218). Visually and conceptually, a Parisian townhouse in *Entr'acte* performs a similar function to the World Tree, *Yg-gdrasill,* central to Selsjord's 3D environment for *RuneCast,* creating a strong vertical anchor that connects three horizontal realms. The rooftop of the townhouse – the realm of the imagination – compares to the branching realm of the Gods in the Nordic mythworld; the worlds of giants, elves and dwarves at the tree-roots relate to the entrance-steps and pavement in front of the house, from which a funeral-procession is launched; and the trunk, in the world of humans, resembles the façade of the Paris townhouse. Just as Vala, whose shaman-tent is the trunk of the World Tree, can sink in spirit into the "Well of Becoming", before remounting up the trunk to travel throughout the mythworld, taking the visitor with her, so the hunter who features in *Entr'act*e, plunges from the realm of the living to the spirit world, before being resurrected, and entering the rooftop.

Moreover, *Entr'acte* also resembles *RuneCast* in its combination of associational with recombinant narrative structures. There is, for example, a recurring clip of a ballerina, filmed from below a glass table, which is intercut with a variety of unusual shots ranging from inflatable dolls and an origami boat to a head-scratching scene (Figure 9), creating a fascinating and imaginative array of formal, humorous and poetic montages, which are so dynamic and captivating that they often convey a genuinely haptic sensation, often as a result of the combination of sound and image, and as such reminiscent of Sergei Eisenstein's theory of vertical montage (1939).

This comparable use of recombinant, spatially organized and associational narrative and moving-image structures, provides a common link between the oral, the avant-garde and the digital. This convergence also underlines how the revolutionary paradigm, so commonly attributed to digital technology, is inadequate in understanding media change. It demonstrates that artistic visions and technological innovations evolve, or even co-evolve, in far more complex and intricate ways than often acknowledged (see Thorburn & Jenkins, 2003; Bolter & Grusin, 1999). Eisenstein, for example, was already theorizing about the relationship between indeterminacy and constraints as early as 1939:

There is deep within me a long-standing conflict between the free course of the all'improviso, flowing line of drawing or the free run of dance,

subject only to the laws of the inner pulse of the organic rhythm of purpose (on one hand); and the restrictions and blind spots of the canon and rigid formula (on the other).

Actually, it is not entirely appropriate or fair to mention formulae here. The charm of a formula is that, while laying down a general rule, it allows, within the free current which filters through it, "special" interpretations, special cases and coefficients. (p.389)

Vala and *RuneCast* enhance richness through the poetic ambiguity both of the imagery in the original verses sung in the work and the layered video compositions. They combine sensitive dependence on initial conditions (the six runes which Heithur/Vala starts by casting for each visitor) with an associative poetics of narrativity (audio and visual), held together by the character and oral storytelling of your guide, Heithur/Vala, whose voice connects all the elements of the experiences, supporting emotional, temporal and spatial immersion (see Green, Strange & Brock, 2002; Ryan, 2001, pp. 140-162). The character of the guide, present as audio throughout the experience - someone you meet and get to know when you first enter Vala's realm - provides the vital transition between the everyday world outside the work and the world within.

While the use of a guide in this interactive fiction is a highly innovative and effective form of interaction design in its immersive and narra-

Figure 9. Stills of montage sequence; from René Clair's 'Entr'acte' (1924)

tive power, it represents yet another example of a digitally remediated analogue precursor. Radúz Činčera's *Kinoautomat* (1967) (http://www.kino-automat.cz), exhibited for the Czechoslovak Pavillion at the Montreal Expo' in 1967, arguably the very first interactive movie, used a similar device decades before digitality (see Hales, 2005). In this interactive comedy, staged in a cinema, the film would occasionally split into two screens and the audience would be asked to vote for the left or right narrative version. The film's actors themselves would appear live on stage to incite and motivate the audience, thereby transforming the interactive component into far more than a simple voting or pointing-and-clicking feature, making it a playful performance, with the live actors acting as an engaging human interface and guide.

Historical precursors to Thomas' and Seljord's work can also be found in the work of the Bauhaus, which had proposed a fundamentally new vision for the traditional theatre-stage. "Total Theatre is the theatre of the future", proclaimed Walter Gropius (1883-1969, founder and director of the Bauhaus), Oskar Schlemmer (1888-1943, Master of Form at the theatre workshop) and Farkas Molnár (1897-1945, Bauhaus student) in *Theatre of the Bauhaus* (1925) – an unrealized vision that was meant to conflate auditorium and stage, in which the audience members were meant to be both spectators and performers (see Prager, 2006). The multi-perspective three-dimensionality of Molnár's concept, unrealisable in 1925, is easy enough to imagine transposed to a computer-generated environment (Figure 10).

Figure 10. Design for a "Total Theater"; 'U-Theater', by Farkas Molnár; from Gropius, W. (ed.) 'Theater of the Bauhaus', 1925

The Importance of Being Playful

Central to this vision was the importance of play – engaging in pleasurable, intrinsically motivated activities that are without apparent purpose. Schlemmer's pedagogy aimed at liberating "the play instinct [...] the source of man's real creative values, [which] is the un-self-conscious and naïve pleasure in shaping and producing, without asking questions about use or uselessness, sense or nonsense, good or bad" (Schlemmer, 1925, p.82).

In virtual worlds, this vision might be fully realized: but game design has typically been dominated by competitive, aggressive and extrinsically-motivated patterns, such as the massively best-selling *Grand Theft Auto* series (Rockstar/Rockstar North 2004 – 2014). While the *Grand Theft Auto* world also includes some degree of exploratory play ("free roaming" the vast urban settings), role play (the player as an underworld gangster) and simulated physical play (missions including learning to fly a plane and taxi-driving), it remains a goal-directed game based on extrinsic motivation – gaining power and influence, in order to rise through the ranks of the criminal underworld. The apparent thrill of aggression appears to have increased throughout the releases of *Grand Theft Auto* versions. In its 5th incarnation (set in a quasi-realistic though sleazier version of Los Angeles), released in September 2013, players can, after having sex with prostitutes, assault and bludgeon them in a variety of ways to retrieve their money (see "GTA5 Part 38 Prostitute Success & New Chrome Porsche Lets Play Walkthrough Guide Tutorial", http://www.youtube.com/watch?v=bTOPxcIncP0); and in a mission entitled "By the Book", players have an array of torture equipment to select from in order to extract information from a potential informant (Bramwell, 2013; see also "Top 5 – Shocking GTA 5 moments", http://www.youtube.com/watch?v=hIDElG0GotU; Heritage (2013), "Grand Theft Auto 5? Sorry, I'm just a bit too Guardian"). This title is noted here as the leading example of

a highly successful form of gaming, developing in a direction to which creative and aesthetic non-goal dominated, non-aggressive play may offer a refreshing and fruitful alternative.

As one of the very few game experiences which, as also *Gardens of Dreaming*, offers an alternative to competitive social play embedded within extrinsic reward structures, *RuneCast* leads the way in developing an interaction grammar that explores the full range of play behaviour: it facilitates exploratory play (the exploration of the Nordic mythworld and the runescapes), object play (the runes), aleatoric and ritual play (rune-casting), role play (as participant in a shamanic ritual) and non-competitive social play (with Vala) and, especially, mental play – the play of the imagination – which is the very source of creative thought.

Perhaps most importantly, both Selsjord's and Thomas' work allow the visitors to immerse themselves into an unfamiliar environment, which serves an important function in self-discovery and self-actualization. In his article "The Adventurer" (2013/1911), the sociologist Georg Simmel – the first play theorist to acknowledge that play, and not just games, is governed by rules (see Hendricks, 2006, pp.109-145) – characterizes the adventure as intrinsically meaningful, an autotelic activity – unlike adrenalin-driven and goal-directed adventure games; and just as Selsjord and Thomas do, he describes the adventure as a combination of both chance and choice:

Something becomes an adventure only by virtue of two conditions: that it itself is a specific organization of some significant meaning with a beginning and an end; and that, despite its accidental nature, its extraterritoriality with respect to the continuity of life, it nevertheless connects with the character and identity of the bearer of that life (2013/1911, p. 218). [...] it is just on the hovering chance, on fate, on the more-or-less that we risk all, burn our bridges, and step into the mist, as if the road will lead us on, no matter what. [...] The obscurities of fate are certainly no more transparent to him than to others; but he proceeds as if they were. The characteristic daring with which he continually leaves the solidities of life underpins itself, as it were, for its own justification with a feeling of security and 'it-must-succeed,' which normally only belongs to the transparency of calculable events. (2013/1911, p. 221)

Of particular significance is not only his autotelic characterization of the adventure, but the importance he places on its moral implications and the possibilities for self-insight and growth he connects to the adventure. This is, from a psychological perspective, precisely a core evolutionary function of exploratory play. Implicit in Simmel's characterization of the adventurer is the necessity for what psychologists term a "tolerance for ambiguity"– "a capacity for coping with unstructured or open-ended stimulus situations" (Foxman, 1976, p. 67). Just as Simmel postulates a correlation between adventure and psychological maturity, scientific studies have found evidence to suggest that a tolerance for ambiguity is highly correlated with self-actualization (Foxman, 1976), "which emphasizes the capacity for suspending conventional modes of thinking and perceiving as a prerequisite for the experiences which result in personal growth and change" (Foxman, 1976, p.71).

John Cage, who defined life and (his) art as "purposeless playful" (1973/1961, p. 46), was the quintessential self-actualized adventurer; he found endless pleasure as a mycologist, roaming the country-side in pursuit of hidden fungal treasure (Smith, 1982, pp. 165–166), just as Marianne Selsjord used to, or road-tripping through Ireland, recording sounds at hundreds of locations mentioned in James Joyce's *Finnegans Wake* (1999/1939), which he sampled together in his aleatoric composition *Roaratorio, an Irish circus on Finnegans Wake* (1979).

In the 21st century, is it still possible to embark on adventures and exploratory play in this way? Especially for children and adolescents,

this is a problem of increasing magnitude. William Brown, the iconic 11 year-old schoolboy (a 1920's counterpart to Harry Potter), who first appeared in Richmal Crompton's *Just William* (1922), would, for example, transform, through the powers of make-believe, an innocuous field into a Roman excavation site (by hiding home-made "artefacts") and performance stage (by improvising "archaeological lectures" to the village youth) (Crompton, 1927, pp. 13–38). Such unsupervised outdoor play is increasingly rare. In his article "The Decline of Play and the Rise of Psychopathology in Children and Adolescents" (2011), Gray points to a variety of longitudinal studies to demonstrate how unsupervised, outdoor, exploratory and social play has steadily declined since the 1950s, which simultaneously correlates with a steady increase in mental health issues, especially anxiety, depression, narcissism and perceived helplessness.

A correlation does not, of course, indicate causation; yet Gray points to the functions of play –developing intrinsically-motivated interests, self-control, decisiveness, emotional regulation, social competencies, and, perhaps most importantly, the experience of joy, all of which are important factors in mental health, making causation appear far more likely than mere correlation. Inasfar as the computer remains, for many children, the sole unsupervised domain in which unstructured play can (or, rather, *could*) take place, it is of prime and urgent importance to develop alternatives to the dominant highly-structured and goal-oriented gaming paradigm.

Overcoming the Creativity Crisis

The decline in play that Gray identified from the 1950s onwards is, perhaps unsurprisingly, matched by a similar decline in creativity. In "The Creativity Crisis: The Decrease in Creative Thinking Scores on the Torrance Test of Creative Thinking", which included over a quarter of a million participants from 1966 to 2008, Kim (2011) identified a significant decrease in test scores since 1990, and concludes: "Children have become less emotionally expressive, less humorous, less imaginative, less unconventional, less lively and passionate, less perceptive, less apt to connect seemingly irrelevant things, less synthesizing, and less likely to see things from a different angle" (p. 292). Children grow into adults, and the work of Thomas and Selsjord both enables creative play in those who already enjoy it, and opens this pathway to those who have not experienced it before.

Play is the ferment of creative thought. From a cognitive point-of-view, one way of defining creativity is as a combinational process, a blending of two or more concepts, from domains that previously seemed incongruous, into a surprising new meaning (Boden, 2004, p. 130; Ward, Smith & Finke, 1999, p. 202; Fauconnier & Turner, 2002). Since it is unpredictable which concepts might produce a creative constellation, creativity relies on improvisation and experimentation – playing and toying with ideas, concepts, materials, shapes or textures – in art, as it does in science (Nickerson, 1999, p. 410); it is for for this reason, too, that chance plays such an important role in the creative process – it is the only heuristic that operates beyond the conceptual constraints of our mind – we merely need to be able to *recognize* a chance event as meaningful, which consequently transforms chance into serendipity.

The German chemist August Kekulé (1829–1896), for example, was contemplating the chemical structure of benzene – at a time when molecules were presumed to be strings of atoms; he gazed into his fireplace, imagined the flames turning into coiling snakes, and combined the two images to revolutionize chemistry by discovering the *circular* arrangement of benzene atoms (Boden, 2004, pp. 25-27). The same process is at the core of poetry, as, for example in a poetic image such as "Earth laughs in flowers", from the poem *Hamatreya* (1846) by Ralph Waldo Emerson (1803-1882) (in Axelrod, Roman & Travisano, 2003, pp. 191-192).

In the context of creativity research, avant-garde artists once again prove to be visionary precursors; as Prager (2012; 2013) notes, Dada artists mark a watershed in the understanding of creativity. They articulated principles of creative cognition with sophisticated insight as early as the 1910s and 1920s, recognized the importance of play and positive emotions, and their invention of the artistic techniques of collage, assemblage and montage was accompanied by an astute and explicit understanding of the combinational character of creativity. Max Ernst (1891-1976), one of the most important and influential Dadaists, writes that the "collage technique is the systematic exploitation of the chance or artificially provoked confrontation of two or more mutually alien realities on an obviously inappropriate level – and the poetic spark which jumps across when these realities approach each other" (quoted in Elger, 2004, p. 74).

For Duchamp, creativity was inextricably linked to what he referred to as a state of mind of "indifference" – "as if you had no aesthetic emotion […] the total absence of good or bad taste" (Cabanne, 1971, p. 48; see also Prager, 2012). And indeed, modern psychologists have verified Duchamp's thoughts on "indifference" – and the 3D, navigable environments by Thomas and Selsjord create conditions most conducive to creative insight; they combine semiautomatic activities that defocus the mind within a multisensory environment. Psychologist and creativity researcher Csikszentmihalyi observes:

Ordinary people […] tend to report the highest levels of creativity […] when involved in a semiautomatic activity that takes up a certain amount of attention, while leaving some of it free to make connections among ideas below the threshold of conscious intentionality. Devoting full attention to a problem is not the best recipe for having creative thoughts.

When we think intentionally, thoughts are forced to follow a linear, logical – hence predictable – direction. But when attention is focused on the view during a walk, part of the brain is left free to pursue associations that normally are not made. [...] And of course it is just this freedom and playfulness that makes it possible for leisurely thinking to come up with original formulations and solutions. For as soon as we get a connection that feels right, it will jump into our awareness. (1996, p. 138)

In a defocused state, the creative mind is highly receptive to distractions, the field of visual perception is expanded and peripheral, normally unnoticed pieces of information and impressions enter the mind, which may benefit the creative process (Kounios et al., 2008). A situation conducive to creativity would thus combine a semiautomatic activity with a "complex, stimulating environment" (Csikszentmihalyi, 1996, p. 139), for "the distraction of novel stimuli, of magnificent views, of alien cultures, allows the subconscious mental processes to make connections that are unlikely when the problem is pursued by the linear logic learned from experience" (Csikszentmihalyi, 1996, p. 146).

Disinterested contemplation of audio-visual delights in an explorable environment is thus not merely an aesthetic pleasure in itself, but the mindset and condition most conducive to creative insight.

CASE STUDIES

Selsjord's explorable 3D *Still life with Oranges and Lemons and a Rose* after the 1633 painting by Francisco de Zurbarán (1598 – 1664) (Thomas, Selsjord & Zimmer, 2011, pp. 19-20) and her 2014/15 exhibition, *Marvellous Transformations*, as well as her 2009 work, *Gardens of Dreaming*, initially inspired by the work of Hieronymous Bosch, demonstrate how techniques from different traditions of painting and drawing find new and illuminating incarnations in 3D digital media art.

Case Study 1

Gardens of Dreaming (Marianne Selsjord, 2009): From Bosch to 3D Surrealism

The Festival's most important piece [...] a beautiful virtual world [...] presents modern game technology in an unexpected way [...] an alternative without pointscoring, blood or violence ("Culture and Trends". Oslo: Verdens Gang, 21 February 2009 http://www.vg.no/).

Taking inspiration from the highly tactile and sensuous *Gardens of Earthly Delights* of Hieronymus Bosch, in her 3D-based audiovisual gallery installation, Marianne Selsjord created explorable shapes, without imbuing them with any moral or ethical value (as Bosch does) (Figure 11).

As an artist and historian of painting techniques, she found it revealing to enter the pictorial environment, viewing it from all angles; for her, this constitutes a new, engaging experience of visual art for both connoisseurs and new audiences. Moreover, *Gardens of Dreaming* in many ways digitally remediates the main principles of Cubism, which not only aimed at presenting 360-degree views on a flat canvas, but introduced a transformatively creative concept into the realm of painting by abolishing the convention of a single view-point (Boden, 2014).

The set-up is simple and relatively low-tech, and easily replicable for other content. The 200-square-metre gallery (at the Henie-Onstad Art Centre, Oslo) was furnished with a 120-degree curved screen, 10 metres wide and 2 metres 44 cm high, constructed from standard plasterboard units. The 3D world was projected from three ceiling-mounted projectors to create a 3840 x 1024 pixel image. A single desktop computer (with 3 gigabyte ram and duel-core processor, a surround-sound card and G-Force graphics card, plus Matrox triple head-to-go box) outputs the image to the projectors to create a seamless

Figure 11. 'Gardens of Dreaming', inspired by Bosch
(© 2009, Marianne Selsjord. Used with kind permission.).

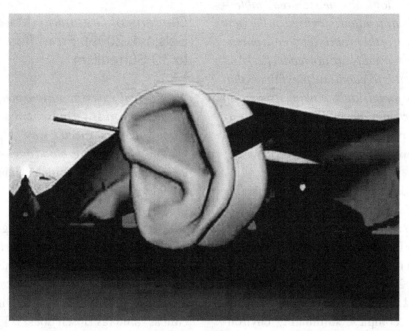

Figure 12. Visitors enjoying 'Gardens of Dreaming'
(© 2009, Marianne Selsjord. Used with kind permission.).

panorama with an extra-wide field of view. This prevents distortion over the curve and enables visitors to orient themselves with ease in the immersive environment, which also comprises a 3D soundscape (emanating from 5 surround-sound speakers in addition to a sub-woofer, hidden, together with the computer, behind the screen).

Visitors arrive in the dimly–lit space to discover a circular, cushioned seat surrounding a giant strawberry-stalk, on which balances a huge scarlet strawberry-fruit, "seeds" glowing blue and yellow (see Figure 2). Four red, illuminated buttons pulse on each side, inviting fingers to touch. Lifting the strawberry off its stalk and tilting it from side to side causes a "virtual camera" to pan across the dynamic image projected around the space, so visitors can explore the garden actively, individually and in real time. They can enjoy this experience sitting on the seat to hold the strawberry, take one of the floor-cushions scattered about, or stand and move around freely (the choice most often taken by children, who adored the exhibit) (Figure 12).

The haptic, strawberry-shaped interaction-device communicates with a wireless receiver, connected via a serial interface to the computer. A small tailor-made program runs on the pc, communicating with the game engine and transferring the x, y and z coordinates of the strawberry, as well as instructions — such as "look left", "jump", "change angle of view", "walk forward" or "backward" — when its buttons are pressed.

With the haptic, strawberry interaction-device, visitors can steer through the gardens at their own pace, free to roam anywhere, free to listen to the music and watch the denizens of the world continuing about their own business. The default is a first-person-view, but by pressing a button on the strawberry, the visitor can explore through the avatar-character — a putto-like toddler — entering and exiting Bosch's strange fruits and flowers, and exploring them from all angles (Figure 13).

This is not an adrenaline-driven game, where punishment threatens: the player is continuously rewarded by new visions and sounds; the ability to circumnavigate every plant, flower, pavilion, object and feature in the landscape offers vistas of completely new perspectives, unattainable through the contemplation of a 2D framed painting hanging on a gallery wall. This is dynamic painting, where the visitor brings to life the 3D entities created by the artist.

Figure 13. "Putto"-toddler avatar, about to explore a trumpet-like plant, 'Gardens of Dreaming' (© 2009, Marianne Selsjord. Used with kind permission.).

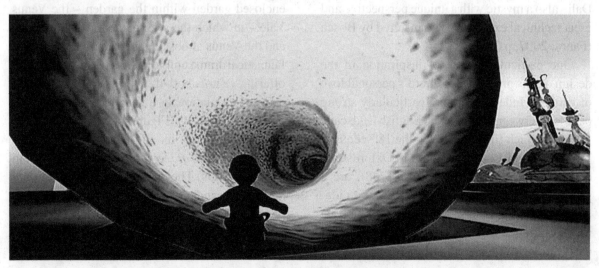

Figure 14. Stumbling across the curiosities of 'Gardens of Dreaming'
(© 2009, Marianne Selsjord. Used with kind permission.).

This experimental artwork had to develop its own aesthetic as it progressed. There are no models for this kind of digital design in the realm of 3D gaming, which is dominated — even in fantasy worlds (such as *Fable,* Molyneux, Lionhead/Microsoft Studios 2004 - 2012) — by hyper-realism. Selsjord was driven by the desire to fully exploit the potential of the software tools of 3D engines to create this original surrealist work. Some visitors to the *Gardens* are reminded of juxtapositions created by painter/film artist Salvador Dali (1904 – 1989); Selsjord notes that Dali - also a mystic with a unique perspective and great technical expertise - was inspired by Bosch (Fanes, 2007, p.74).

One particular source of inspiration in the design of this project was Seljord's personal love of gardens. Indeed, there are particularly strong parallels between her work and English landscape gardens, which first emerged in the 18th-century. The gardens of Rousham House in Oxfordshire, designed by William Kent (1685-1748), are a particularly fine example; they represent an idealized version of nature, while at the same time incorporating a variety of Gothic elements and curiosities (Müller, 1998) that compare to the fantastical creatures that punctuate Selsjord's *Gardens*. The layout of Rousham House Gardens is fluid and organic and appears boundless, designed to convey the illusion of dissolving into the surrounding countryside. While a highly choreographed experience, the gardens appear perfectly "natural": unusual vistas unfold only as visitors meander through them, and they have the impression of stumbling across the garden's curiosities in an almost accidental manner. These include Gothic follies, a classical pyramid, a garden temple, statues, water features and an enclosed garden within the garden – the Venus Vale – in which the arrangement of nature gods and the Venus almost creates the impression of a fantastical drama unfolding in a stage-like setting, offering visitors both the pleasure of exploration and contemplation in a manner comparable to Selsjord's *Gardens* (Figure 14).

Five gardens, in addition to the Bosch-inspired *Garden of Dejection,* were exhibited in February 2009. They are inspired by traditional approaches and techniques, ranging from European mediaeval miniature painting, Victorian English diecut and embossed scrap-reliefs to Japanese woodcuts, remediated into a digital

Figure 15. 'Gardens of Dreaming'
(© 2009, Marianne Selsjord. Used with kind permission.).

context. The gardens soon took on a life of their own, growing out of the artist's imagination and dreams — an experiment in layered associative creativity (Figure 15).

Although *Gardens of Dreaming* was conceived as a work for the attention and contemplation of mature minds, it became clear at the exhibition in 2009 that this glowing, explorable, enchanting world has great appeal for both children and adults. Selsjord was delighted to witness the ease with which visitors enjoyed exploring the work, and how they seemed able to drop their guard, approaching it in a childlike spirit of playful unselfconsciousness.

Gardens of Dreaming overcomes the challenges of immersion in a Real Time 3D Virtual Environment with apparent effortlessness and surprisingly low-tech, non-intrusive solutions, via the tangible interaction device: the soft, football-sized strawberry feels like an extension into physical space of the virtual content of the gardens — whether the bizarre fruits of the dark, Bosch-inspired, claustrophobic landscape, or the bright, benign blooms of the tranquil *Nordic Snow Garden*, with its vast horizons and tinkling soundscape. The space and pace of the work encourage leisurely attention and contemplative exploration.

Selsjord enables the visitor to sample an enchanting surreal experience, infinitely revisitable because constantly dynamic, magically immersive, mesmerizing, and emotionally challenging — original in its aesthetic style and its mature, confident use of the computer as an artistic medium. It offers an informed and intriguing interpretation of Bosch to the connoisseur, which can act as a "way in" to his art and his context, while providing a uniquely playful approach, immediately accessible to a twenty-first-century teenager or child brought up on computer games. Finding out what is on the "other side" of Bosch's curious, luscious fruits and bulbous fountains, what it is like to actually lose oneself inside them, offers a fresh understanding of the original paintings, rewarding the visitor's disinterested and sympathetic attention and contemplation.

Case Study 2

Marvellous Transformations (Marianne Selsjord, 2013): 17th-Century Forest to 21st-Century Virtual Environment

Marvellous Transformations consists of an explorable 3D digital artwork, physical sculpture and wall panels inspired by the work, paintings and drawings of Maria Sybilla Merian, artist and naturalist (1647–1717)[7]. In the 21st-century, many of the plants and insects she observed are extinct, and Selsjord resurrects them in a virtual rainforest into which Merian's originals are transposed.

Born in Frankfurt, Merian was an accomplished draftswoman, engraver, painter and naturalist who studied plant and insect life with a meticulous scientific sensibility – questioning, amongst other things, Aristotle's theory of the spontaneous generation of insects, still generally favoured in 1700 (Ruestow, 1985). From 1699 – 1701, at the age of 52, Merian undertook a "long dreamed of journey" to Surinam, accompanied by her 21-year old daughter, to explore and record insect and plant life - especially how caterpillars transform through the chrysalis stage to become butterflies (Todd, 2007). In 1705, she published her observations as *Metamorphosis Insectorum Surinamensium (Metamorphosis of the Insects of Surinam)*.

Merian was the first naturalist to observe closely and illustrate the entire life-cycle of a butterfly. She developed a unique style of painting, sensuous and intricate, to include, simultaneously in one image, not only all stages of the transformation from caterpillar to butterfly, but also the development of the plants on which different kinds of butterfly, moth and other insects lived - in vibrant, compelling images (Figure 16).

In order to do so, Merian observed her subjects carefully in their natural habitat over long periods, so she could witness and record their entire life-cycle. Unlike contemporary Dutch biologist and microscopist Jan Swammerdam (1637 –1680), who used refined magnifying lenses to examine and dissect insects in the laboratory to demonstrate that larvae, pupa and insect were all the same creature, and whose works (e.g. Ephemeri, 1645, trans. Tyson, 1681) contain

Figure 16. Vine branch and black grapes, with moth, caterpillar, and chrysalis of gaudy sphinx From Merian, 2009/1705, p. 136.

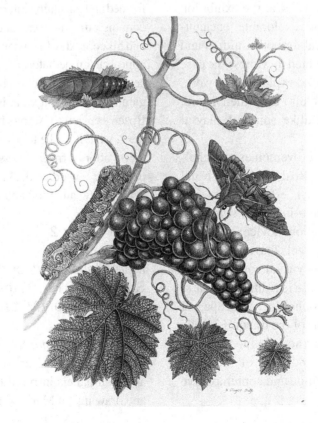

Figure 17. Vine branch and black grapes, with moth, caterpillar, and chrysalis of gaudy sphinx, Marianne Selsjord, 'Marvellous Transformations' (2013)
(© 2013, Marianne Selsjord. Used with kind permission.).

illustrations of them in death, Merian worked from life. Writing of Gaudy Sphinx caterpillars (Figure 16) she notes: "They had a black spot on the hindmost segment and in the middle of it was a white membrane that shone like crystal and it rose and fell with each breath" (Merian, 2009/1705, p. 136). Merian's illustrations pulse with the vividness of life, in both line and colour; and it was this liveliness that inspired Selsjord to create her dynamic 3D navigable rainforest in *Marvellous Transformations*.

Kay Etheridge claims that Merian may be seen as the first ecologist: "By illuminating interactions among organisms and painting communities, Maria Sibylla Merian demonstrated that nature is most interesting when viewed outside of confining little boxes of collections and categories" (Etheridge, 2011, p. 52).

Marvellous Tansformations transposes Merian's work from the confining two-dimensionality of books into a navigable three-dimensional forest (Figure 17).

Here visitors can even encounter plants and insects that have become extinct since Merian ventured into the unchartered jungles of Surinam to investigate and record them.

Marianne Selsjord, a painter who trained as a conservator, is intrigued by the techniques as well as the styles and subject matter of 16th- and 17th-century artists. In *Marvellous Transformations*, her fluency and skillful visual style in the 21st-century medium of 3D "dynamic painting" allows her to animate Merian's pioneering work with extraordinary vividness. Selsjord can transcend the technological limitations that Merian faced, and explore the full potential of Merian's ecological

Figure 18. 'Marvellous Transformations' by Marianne Selsjord, exhibited at Churchill College, University of Cambridge, January 2015, curated by Phillip Prager
(© 2015, Maureen Thomas. Used with kind permission.).

awareness by dynamising her illustrations in time and motion. The exhibition (Figure 18) offers a fresh appreciation of Merian's achievements as artist and naturalist, as well as representing an original and intriguing piece of contemporary art itself - a unique new kind of gallery experience - where visitors can explore the luminescent 3-dimensional virtual forest of Surinam at their leisure.

The work exhibited in the explorable 3D digital format consists of both single constructions/interpretations of Merian's paintings and 3D navigable "collages'", where Selsjord combines a variety of plants and insects from Merian's work to create a virtual forest. These forestscapes, like Merian's original paintings, simultaneously present all the stages in the lifecycle of the butterflies and plants she observes, creating a complex and intense unity by condensing and conflating layers of time. Merian's "own" voice (interactively triggered audio) can be can be heard amongst the exhibits, and, by quoting from *Metamorphosis Insectorum Surinamenisum*, she explains how her interest in insects and flowers developed.

Selsjord has also developed stereo animations and still images of this material printed on aluminium, with dimensions of 50cm x 50cm, which can be hung like 2D paintings on a wall (Figure 19).

In addition, Selsjord has captured live stereo video and still-image material from Kinabaloo National Park and other Borneo rainforest areas for the exhibition (Figure 20). Although not from Surinam itself, this footage reveals the vulnerability of the endangered rainforest environment today.

Selsjord has also created prototype physical sculptures, printed from her 3D models, of plants and insects, using fragile salt-like material, which are placed inside glass bell jars. This is how Merian first saw specimens from the Dutch East Indies in Amsterdam (Vickery, 2014). Some of the plant sculptures are fragments only – too frail and etiolated to exist as whole objects. Salt, as a sculptural medium, recalls the Biblical story of Lot's wife: looking back as her city is destroyed, she is transformed from a living being into a pillar of salt (Genesis 19:26). The fragile, salt-sculpted

Figure 19. Print on aluminium taken from the 3D virtual rainforest in 'Marvellous Transformations'
(© 2013, Marianne Selsjord. Used with kind permission.).

Figure 20. Kinabalu Rainforest from 'Marvellous Transformations' exhibition
(© 2013, Marianne Selsjord. Used with kind permission.).

plants in their bell jars are memories of forms gone forever - extinct, eradicated - insects meta-morphosed into museum pieces, lost to motion, lost to life, at which we can only look back in this exhibition. They complement the 3D explorable "virtual" Surinam forest-garden of exotic plants and insects, preserved in the chrysalis of Merian's paintings for three hundred years, vanished from their native habitat, but now quickened into virtual life and motion by Selsjord's artistry.

Case Study 3

Vala (2001), *Songs of Vala* (2003), *RuneCast* (2007), *Vala's RuneCast* (2010): From Viking-Age Myth to 21st-Century Flexible Media

Maureen Thomas's *Vala*[8] and *RuneCast*, for the latter of which Selsjord created a 3D navigable mythworld interface, embody the aesthetic and narrative strategies of Viking-Age poetry, carving and jewellery-making, along with its philosophical pre-occupation with chance and choice.

Völuspá (Songs of the Seeress), the orally-composed verses which provide form, content and dramatic/interaction situation for the video installation *Vala,* the 3D navigable *RuneCast* and the live, integrated-media performances *Songs of Vala* and *Viking Seeress,* were written down by the 12th century. It appears in the Icelandic manuscript, *Konungsbók* (*Codex Regius*), of the poetic *Edda,* a collection of myth-, hero- and wisdom-poems, including *Hávamál* (*The Sayings of the High One*) (Dronke, 1997, pp. 25 – 154; Neckel, 1927, pp. 16-43), which is also incorporated into *RuneCast.*

"Casting the runes", claims Roman historian Tacitus (c. 56 – c. 117), was an ancient Germanic practice of divination, used to make important public decisions (Tacitus, 96 AD, in Mattingly, 2009, pp. 35-62) - not to be confused with the 19th-century mystic "rune magic" propagated by Guido List and adopted by the Nazis (Findell, 2014, p. 95). Using fortune-telling by rune as its

interaction situation, *RuneCast* invites visitors to explore authentic Viking-age traditional poems and tales transposed for a modern medium, pro-viding a personalised experience relating to their own lives today.

Vala, the character in whose voice the original *Songs of the Seeress* are chanted, opens: "Silence for hearing, higher and lower […]" (*Völuspá* v. 1, Dronke, 1997, p. 7; trans. Thomas, 2007). In the original poem, Vala is addressing "Valföður" (Odin) (Dronke, 1997, p. 107), whom she calls by name. She is a "Sybil" (English poet W. H. Auden translates *Völuspá* as "Song of the Sybil" (Auden & Taylor, 1983/1996, p. 245). Heithur-Vala is a seeress who travels in spirit through time and space (Dronke, 1997, p. 105). Tacitus (96AD) claims that the learned "divines" (*sacerdotes*) who steered Germanic assemblies first called for silence, just as did 10th-century Nordic Court poets reciting praise poems and battle memorials (in Mattingly, 2009, pp. 35-62), and as Vala does when she opens her "Songs" – addressing her modern visitors across time and space. This direct address in a dramatic situation (fortune-telling/ asking the shaman for new knowledge), which spans the ages is especially suited as an interface to a computer-handled dramatic narrative artwork, which is much closer in kind to oral performance than to written literature on a page. It also enables a natural deployment of the approach explored by Don, referred to at the beginning of this chapter (Don, 1990, p. 384).

RuneCast elaborated and amplified the myth-world content produced for *Vala,* and set it in a navigable 3D virtual Viking mythworld, designed by Selsjord. It was developed experimentally for cross-platform delivery as domestic entertainment or on mobile consoles/smartphones (tablets had not then been widely introduced), as part of the integrated research project, "New Millennium/ New Media" (*NM2*) (2004-2007; see http://www. ist-nm2.org), partially funded by EC IST FP6, which developed new media content forms and tools by taking advantage of the unique characteristics of broadband networks. Working from the Cambridge University-based digital studio CUMIS/DIGIS in this large European research-framework provided access to new purpose-built software, which enabled real-time triggering and re-editing of audio and video media within the 3D explorable interface. This software, the *NM2* tools (2007), were used to apply metadata-labels to audio and video clips according to rules devised by the author (Figure 21) (for more on the software see Ursu et al., 2007).

Implicitly, as well as explicitly, *RuneCast* follows Viking-age artistic practice (casting the runes, chance operations, wisdom-verses and the journey of the shaman) to create a modern telling, fresh and engaging in its own right. (For more on *Runecast* see Thomas, Zimmer & Selsjord, 2011, pp. 21-25).

Evaluators (ed. Pals & Esmeijer, 2007) concluded that: *RuneCast* was "highly original, especially the spatial interface" (p. 3) and "points the way forward in interactive narrative" (p.18)

—"tradition and contemporary media come together" (p.19). EC Reviewers Kafno and Turpainen (2007, p.12) commended the "enormous very attractive variety of visual compositions ensuring that repeat viewings provide fresh experiences [...] the powerful and effective artistic impression worked well both on the big and small screen of the portable device". Each visitor is the 'subject' of their own fortune, told by storyguide Heithur-Vala (see McKinnell, 2001). Following their own selection of a key 'rune'- the Viking equivalent of alphabet letters (Page, 1987; Findell, 2014)—they then become the heroes of their own storymaking journeys (Thomas, 2005).

Whether in the real world/2D screen setting of *Vala*, or the 3D virtual-world setting of *RuneCast*, visitors approach Vala's shaman-tent — also the trunk of the World Tree (Pentikäinen, 1987; 1996; see esp. Tátar, 1999, pp. 267-278; Hultkrantz, 1996, pp. 31-51). When they have picked their key rune at her well, Vala casts 5 more which fall by chance, and tells their fortune — referring to

Figure 21. NM2 Toolkit showing drag-and-drop interface designed by Ludvig Lohse (University of Cambridge) for labelling media clips with metadata (screenshot)
(© 2007, Maureen Thomas. Used with kind permission.).

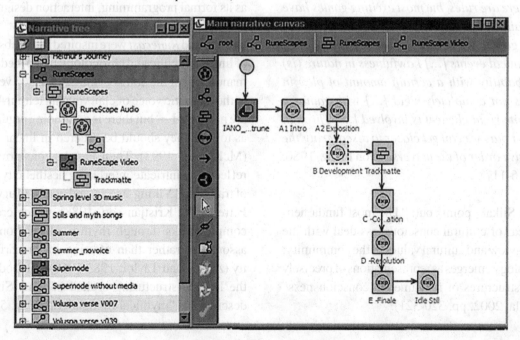

verses from the wisdom-poem, *Sayings of the High One (Hávamál)*. Continuing to explore Vala's world, visitors can choose to listen to her sing and tell tales, watch and listen to her stories accompanied by mythtale videos - composed in real time for each visitor, cued by their own choices, which trigger associated metadata-labelled clips. This ritualised process evokes the way the three Norns, who guard the "Well of Becoming" at the foot of the Viking World Tree carve, in runes, the lifetales of humankind (*Völuspa* v. 20 – Dronke, 1997, p.12), and cast them to fall as they will, according to Norse mythology (Crossley-Holland, 1993/1982, pp. xx-xxv; Bek-Pedersen, 2011).

Casting the runes in *Vala* and *Runecast* introduces chance elements into the system and counteracts mechanical rule-based computer-handled storytelling (Thomas, 2005; Rieser, 2002). The fortune-telling game constitutes a form of what Jungian scholar von Franz calls "earnest play" (von Franz, 1980, p. 117), through which people in the Viking age understood and replicated the order of the universe:

All games have a pattern, rather than an image, and there are rules, but most exciting games have a certain amount of chance, i.e. of freedom: they might go one way or the other; they are not just mechanical events [...] Lawfulness in nature (is) a probability with a certain amount of play in it. It is not completely rigid [...] with games a not quite rigid element is involved [...] Through earnest play we can get closer to discovering the objective order of the universe. (von Franz, 1980, pp. 116-117)

As Siikala points out: "The most fundamental areas of cultural consciousness deal with the world-view and cultural values of the community; mythology emerges as representations of precisely these structures of fundamental consciousness" (Siikala, 2002, pp. 320-321).

The collection of knowledge assembled in the years 500-1000 (our era) as *Songs of the Seeress* are our main storehouse of knowledge of the ancient Nordic — and Anglo-Saxon — Gods (McKinnell, 1993). J.R.R. Tolkien's *Lord of the Rings* books (1954/5) mined them for material, characters and names (e.g. Gandalf and the Dwarves: Dronke, 1967, p. 9, verses 10, 11, 12 and 13). Tolkien's propagation of the Viking and Anglo-Saxon world view through mining their mythologies has inspired much modern fantasy-fiction, providing a framework for role-playing games, and generating the blockbusting movie-trilogy (Jackson, 2001-2003).

These "world view and cultural values" (Siikala, 2002, p.321) clearly have a strong resonance through time, and a strong appeal to the contemporary world. But 20th-century heroic journey-versions, like the Jackson films, focus on quest and battle, rather than on the multi-stranded complexity of the original *Songs of the Seeress*. *Vala* and *RuneCast* strive to communicate the intricacy, richness and philosophy of the Viking mental model of knowledge (Siikala, 2002, pp. 56 – 59), using modern digital art to combine and layer authentic visual imagery with the audio of the sung verses. The contemporary artwork uses traditional oral storytelling techniques as its formal programming, interaction design and aesthetic basis.

Vala and *Runecast* were inspired by the absence of linear structure and chronology in the medieval manuscript of the *Songs of the Seeress*[9] 66 verses, in the dramatic voice of clairvoyant Heithur-Vala, are preserved — but there is continuing argument as to how they should be ordered in linear print (McKinnell, 1993). Their lack of epic structure reflects the intricate interlacing aesthetic typical of traditional Viking-age art and poetry (Turville-Petre, 1976; Kristjánsson, 1988), which creates complex links through rhythm, alliteration and assonance, rather than offering linear narrativity (Auden and Taylor, 1983/1969) - embodying the layered structuring typical of what Siikala describes as "mythical thought" (2002, p. 56).

In *Vala* and *RuneCast,* a randomising algorithm plays out the (66) verses of the *Songs* (translated into English by Thomas) associated with particular gods or heroes who are in turn each associated with one of the 22 runes, giving a great variety of possible combinations. The songs were set and performed by Latvian/British composer Kariina Gretere (www.kariina.co.uk), who is familiar with the living Baltic traditions of orally-composed sung tales. Each verse has its own individual melody and arrangement, but together they make musical sense in whatever order they are played.

In Reykjavik in 2003, with Icelandic musicians, Kariina sang some of these verses live, as *Songs of Vala,* "bringing to vibrant life this cycle of old Icelandic myth-poems in a contemporary style which suits them perfectly [...] true to the content, but taking it beyond national boundaries" (Jónsdóttir, 2003).

RuneCast as developed to 2007 was reconfigurable and recombinant not only musically and narratively, but also in its video art — capable, like the elements of all sung tales, of being composed in real time to suit any given session. The video was created by Brian Ashbee as microclips, each labelled with metadata, enabling two layers of moving image material to be combined in real time through an animated track-matte representing a deity or hero associated with that particular rune (Figure 22).

The layered "runescape" video for each of the 22 runes in the Viking rune-row is a dreamscape, where emotional colour, landscape elements and evocative objects combine with audio to create a context for attention to the content, and contemplation of its significance, in the tradition of oral composition: "In non-literate cultures, the oral tradition functions as the medium of collective communication through which it is possible to depict and ponder those matters considered important or of interest" (Siikala, 2002, p. 324).

The video does not tell the story as epic (like film), but, like Selsjord's *Gardens of Dreaming,* creates a designed space for each visitor to explore and experience the world for themselves – a feature share with good computer game spaces:

Game spaces evoke narratives because the player is making sense of them in order to engage with them. Through a comprehension of signs and interactions with them, the player generates new meaning. The "evocative narrative elements" [...] implemented in the game [...] do not contain a story themselves but trigger important parts of the narrative process in the player. (Nitsche, 2008, p. 3)

In the drama of *Vala* and *RuneCast,* which is played out on the stage in *Viking Seeress* — as it is in the original *Songs of the Seeress* — Heithur, a wandering fortune-teller, answers the call of the deity Frigg (patroness of seers) to become "Vala", a shamanic journeyer (Figure 23) (see Halifax, 1979; Vitebsky, 1995; McKinnell, 2001; Siikala, 2002), with the three Norns as her guides (see Bek-Pedersen, 2011).

In Thomas's work, Heithur/Vala's shamanry becomes a digital-media conceit, just as, in the *Konungsbók* text of the *Songs of the Seeress,* written in the 12th century, when Christianity had to a large extent replaced heathen practices, it may be viewed as a literary conceit, rather than direct reference to an actual ceremony. Nonetheless, there are descriptions of such ceremonies in early medieval sources, such as the one performed by Thorbjörg in the *Annals of Greenland* and the *Saga of Eirik the Red,* written down before 1263 (Kristjánsson, 1988, p. 272) and describing incidents which are supposed to have taken place around 1,000. Siikala places the imagery of the *Songs of the Seeress* in the context of shamanic visions (Siikala, 2002, p. 164). Both the poetic conceit in the Viking-age dramatic poetry and its digital equivalent in *Vala* and *Runecast* enable participative audiences to identify with Vala's "Questioner", placing themselves as seekers of wisdom — and, in the case of the interactive digital works, of their own fortunes: hearing Vala directly, as she calls for their silence and sharing her visions of the mythworld. Such a guide, bridging between the everyday world and the visionary world, as a vital part of the aesthetic

Figure 22. From video for the rune 'Fruit', associated with Frigg, goddess of plenty and patron of shamanry
(© 2007, Maureen Thomas. Used with kind permission.).

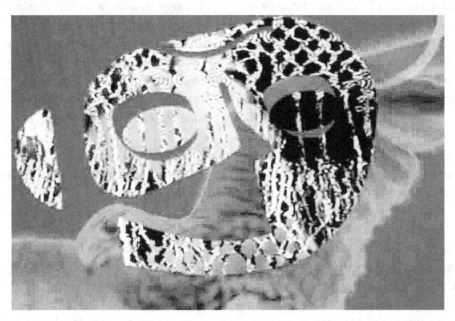

Figure 23. Heithur/Vala enters shamanic trance in 'Vala'
(© 2001, Maureen Thomas. Used with kind permission.).

of the interaction situation and interface, helps visitors become immersed in the world of the artwork.

Vala and *RuneCast* employ a set of nested worlds as their main organizing structure. *Ygddrasill*, the World Ash Tree, which stands at the centre of Norse cosmology, connects the realm of the Gods (Asgard, the branches), that of the mortals (Midgard, the trunk) and the spirit world of the roots (Niflheim). When participant viewers approach the tree and enter through the trunk, they encounter the shaman, seer and storyteller Vala, (played by actress Helen McGregor on video), in a state of semi trance; she rests beside her well, which acts as a port to the other realms connected by the tree.

The shaman's words of welcome, which give insight into her character as well as her function as storyteller, draw from a pool of 500 randomised voice files, which do not repeat until all are exhausted, when they are again randomised. Her video portrait is a 5-minute loop, so visitors never see the same picture against the same sound file. Visitors can therefore remain by the well and listen for as long as they desire without a sense of mechanical repetition. The whole functions as an "'art system' - where this comprises the artist, the program, the technological installation (and its observable results), and the behaviour of the human audience" (Boden, 2010, p.155).

A shot grammar suitable to such flexible media reconfiguration had to be developed.

Vala, the actress playing Vala is shot in extreme close-up (Figure 24), using a slowly-moving camera, and presented through a montage of extended fragments – details, textures, light and shade, expressions: a curl of the lip, a toss of the head, a smile, a furrowing brow [...] a direct gaze into the camera, straight into the eyes of the interactor – which are re-assembled in different configurations, to make her both ever-new at each visit (like a live performer in a role), and accessible, close to her visitors, in a way rarely appropriate in traditional cinema [...] This cinematic language permits the image of the actress to transgress the usual proscenium-like boundaries of screen space, and enables the visitor to make a close personal connection with the dramatic character (Thomas, 2005, pp. 399–400).

Figure 24. Vala (Helen McGregor) – close-up shot grammar
(© 2001, Maureen Thomas. Used with kind permission.).

In both *Vala* (the physical/video installation) and *Runecast* (where the whole experience takes place in Selsjord's 3D mythworld), on accepting Vala's invitation to cast their runes for them, visitors pass through the "Well-space" to enter the "Runecast Space". Of the 22 runes that Vala casts, the visitor has selected one, and five others are randomly generated, thereby combining chance and choice for the journey. Before embarking on the exploration of their personal runecasts, Vala encourages visitors to pose themselves a question and to bear it in mind throughout. This ritual of divination provides the interaction grammar. Thomas points out:

Interactors are explicitly invited to become the heroes of their own tales (fortune-telling is always about the seeker), and the metaphor implicitly incorporates a clear indicator of the relationship between chance, choice and destiny – both in the philosophy of the Viking age, and in the structuring of a story. (2005, p. 401)

In the 3D environment of *RuneCast*, the six runes of an individual runecast are embedded as trigger zones around the "Runecast Space", and by moving towards them, the visitor triggers each rune's audio-visual "molecule", a narrative micro-episode composed in real time from reconfigurable "atoms": spoken rune names and meanings – wisdom verses – hero tales – myth songs – video clips – still images – sound effects and music. The combination of associated "atoms" is determined by each rune's metadata, which describe its topic and emotional qualities, in addition to the characters, locations, actions, seasons and moods with which it is associated. The rune "Rider", for example, denotes travel and riding, symbolizes the overcoming of obstacles, and is related to the mythic figures of Brynhild and Sigurd. In terms of sensory metadata, "Rider" is characterized as "fiery", "exciting and dangerous"; its colour is red.

While each rune is cross-associated with a number of songs (from the Old Norse *Songs of the Seeress*), wisdom verses (from *The Sayings of the High One*), and tales (from Snorri Sturluson's prose *Edda*, written c. 1300; see Sturluson, 2005), only one of each is played back on each visit, thereby ensuring that subsequent explorations will not only remain dramatically engaging because new, but gradually foster a deeper understanding of Nordic cosmology, life-view and philosophy. "Stories, knowledge and understanding are thus built cumulatively over time," Thomas explains, "as they are in oral cultures, through repetitions of story material in different forms, with variations" (2005, p. 412).

Visitors may choose to explore one or all six runescapes in their runecast, or may instead decide to enter the "Fortune Space" (or vice-versa). In the "Fortune Space", visitors are given the opportunity to reflect upon their personal questions, while listening to Vala speaking one of the 20 possible personal fortunes associated with each rune. Vala is eventually released from her state of trance by her visitor, and recedes into the well. The visitor may now choose to leave *Vala* or exit *RuneCast,* or to explore the whole of the mythworld at their own leisure.

The walkthrough description above does not constitute a rigid template, but only one mode of exploration. The world of *Vala* and the much expanded world of *RuneCast* is akin to a sandbox environment that allows free-roaming exploration at one's own pace and direction if one so chooses, while also offering the opportunity to follow a guided and structured experience within a more traditional dramatic narrative structure, based on the archetype of the hero journey, where the visitor is the hero (see Thomas, 2005, pp. 422–428).

The floodtide towards interactive, non-linear media in the 21st century (Atkins & Krzywinska, 2007; Rieser & Zapp, 2002) signals a return to flexible, active, forms of narrativity, and *RuneCast* suggests a way that aleatory and recombinant art and non-literate composition techniques can, with the help of the computer as production tool and exhibition medium, support the creation of never-ending stories.

CREATIVITY AND PLAY

As part of the *New Media for the New Millennium* research project, *RuneCast* successfully tested and implemented NM2's innovative software (incarnated as ShapeShift media software, http://www.shapeshift.tv; see Ursu et al., 2009), which enabled audio-visual media to be reconfigured in real-time, according to user input. It provided for flexible plot frameworks and narrative structures, into which media objects (described according to dramatic, conceptual, formal and semantic metadata) could be inserted in variable sequence. "The spontaneity and immediacy of true oral performance is evoked in *RuneCast* with the aid of the computer, combining and recombining picture and sound independently, with ever-new turns of the audio and visual kaleidoscopes" (Thomas, 2008, p. 183).

Thomas' analogy of the kaleidoscope to describe the *RuneCast* experience is particularly resonant, as creative cognition is also frequently compared to a kaleidoscope, since creative ideas originate from the blending and recombination of seemingly incongruous concepts into unusual new constellations - a concept akin to Siikala's description of the workings of the shamanic mythic mind (Siikala, 2002, pp. 49-58). Semantic nets operate much like reconfigurable road systems - ideas are linked via nodes and links, but "a single experience, or poetic image, may subtly change the significance of a large range of related ideas within someone's mind. In other words, new meanings, or shades of meanings, are created which were not possible before" (Boden, 2004, p. 109).

The kaleidoscope has consequently proven very popular in visualizing creative cognition, as in Catherine Petrini's *Kaleidoscopic Thinking for Creativity* (1991) or in Sidney Parnes' thought's on *The Nurture of Creative Talent*:

As in the kaleidoscope, merely having the knowledge, the bits and pieces, does not guarantee the formation of new patterns. In the kaleidoscope it takes the revolving of the drum; in the mind it takes the manipulation of knowledge, the combining and rearranging of it into new patterns of ideas. (Parnes, 1965, p. 33)

The similarities between the recombinant character of creative cognition and *RuneCast* are of no superficial nature, but deeply entwined. *RuneCast's* complex layering of evocative audio-visual material activates a high number of different mental representations and lateral associations, which allows for a stimulating play of the imagination as the visitor delves deeper into the archetypes of the Nordic mythworld and their own interior world. Indeed, *RuneCast's* novel screen grammar is ideally suited to elicit creative thought processes, because the layered montage of its video components presents multiple entities simultaneously. It thus draws upon our capacity for "homospatial thinking", "actively conceiving two or more discrete entities occupying the same space, a conception leading to the articulation of new identities" (Rothenberg, 1986, p. 371; 1976), which, as Rothenberg discusses, "may be derived from any sensory modality – visual, auditory, tactile, olfactory, gustatory, or kinaesthetic – and may simultaneously involve multiple types of mental imagery" (Rothenberg, 1986, p. 2).

As an interactive "earnest" game experience, *RuneCast* offers an inherently tactile and kinaesthetic element that complements the audio-visual compositions, while the shot grammar adds a further haptic quality, due to the frequent use of open-framed close-ups and animated track mattes (Figure 22). Rothenberg tested the extent to which visual images might inspire artistic creativity and found evidence that superimposed and combined-composite images, as in *Vala* and *RuneCast*, inspired higher creative output than did juxtaposed, side-by-side images, as in linear movies. Moreover, superimposed images resulted in greater creative output than did combined-composite images (as rated and averaged by a panel of experts). Based on Rothenberg's experiments, the shot grammar most conducive to elicit a play of the imagination is precisely the kind Thomas develops in *RuneCast*; where digital technology is effectively used to externalize homospatial thought processes by bringing together several visual layers as dynamic combined-composites and multiple superimpositions.

While layered video montage may in itself be conducive to creativity, its meaning needs to be embedded within some form of narrative structure or problem-solving framework to engage the viewer for a prolonged period of time. An explicitly presented problem is, however, unlikely to elicit creative participation and will reduce intrinsic motivation; the key is to devise a discoverable problem, and to give the visitor the impression of arriving at new insights, even if they are only "new" to the individual ("psychological" rather than "historical creativity", Boden, 2004/1990, p.43). In his discussion of "creative surroundings", Csikszentmihalyi writes:

A great view does not act like a silver bullet, embedding a new idea in the mind. Rather, what seems to happen is that when persons with prepared minds find themselves in beautiful settings, they are more likely to find new connections among ideas, new perspectives on issues they are dealing with. But it is essential to have a "prepared mind." What this means is that unless one enters the situation with some deeply felt question and the symbolic skills necessary to answer it, nothing much is likely to happen. (Csikszentmihalyi, 1996, p.136)

In *RuneCast*, the Nordic mythworld itself functions as a discoverable problem to those unfamiliar with it, for its alluring richness and its complex cast of characters (the Three Norns, Thor, Freyja, Gunnlod, Baldr, Tyr, Idunn, Loki, Forseti, or Nanna, to name only a few) can only be approached through the tales, songs and myth-verses; and since

only one of each is played during each visit to a recombinant runescape, there is an incentive to continually return, as there is in oral cultures for seeking out the visiting singer of tales. On a more personal level, the ritual of casting runes serves to "prepare the mind" in a very literal and immediate way. The runes cast for each individual visitor serve as a lens through which to view and interpret the audio-visual material, while the personal question visitors poses themselves before embarking on their journey primes them to relate the Nordic mythworld to their own lives, in order to solve a problem they themselves may perceive as important.

The spatial organization of *RuneCast* is very conducive to such creative engagement, because it alternates between very content-rich runescapes, the calmness of the 3D "Mythworld" (to which the visitor can return after visiting each runescape) and the "Shaman Tent/Vala's Well", to which the visitor can return at any time and remain listening to the shaman's thoughts for as long as desired. In this regard, *RuneCast's* spatial organization also encourages creative insight:

While a complex, stimulating environment is useful for providing new insights, a more humdrum setting may be indicated for pursuing the bulk of the creative endeavor – the much longer periods of preparation that must precede the flash of insight, and the equally long periods of evaluation and elaboration that follow. (Csikszentmihalyi, 1996, p. 139)

To some extent, one could even draw an analogy between *RuneCast's* spatial organization and the Geneplore Cycle of creative thought, which describes creativity as an oscillation between divergent and convergent thinking. Finke, Ward and Smith introduced the influential Geneplore Model in 1992, to propose a cyclical model of creativity in which generative and explorative, primary and secondary thought processes complement each other. The creative process begins with a generative phase, in which

... one constructs mental representations called preinventive structures, having various properties that promote creative discovery. These properties are then exploited during an exploratory phase in which one seeks to interpret the preinventive structures in meaningful ways. These preinventive structures can be thought of as internal precursors to the final, externalized creative products and would be generated, regenerated, and modified through the course of creative exploration. (Finke, Ward & Smith, 1992, p.17)

To view creativity as comprising generative and explorative phases not only sheds light on an individual's creative process, but may serve as a compelling analogy for computer-based interactivity. The computer could be compared to the generator of indifferent preinventive structures, while the explorative phase corresponds to visitor interaction. Despite the enormous advances in digital technology and artificial intelligence, computers are not capable of generating truly creative acts without human assistance (Boden, 2004, pp. 8-9). The inability of the computer to recognize aesthetic value need not, however, be interpreted in negative terms. Boden, for example, discusses examples of

... interactive graphics-environments, in which human and computer can cooperate in generating otherwise unimaginable images. These computer-generated images often cause the [...] deepest form of surprise – almost as if a coin being tossed repeatedly were suddenly to show a wholly unexpected design. (2004, p. 9)

In these instances, the computer can in fact enhance human creative potential. The cyclical process of generation and exploration is distributed across machine and human, and because the computer obeys its own unique conceptual space, it can provide recombinations that may otherwise remain simply *unthinkable* to the human interactor. Interactors may thus unwittingly stumble across

information – a chance encounter – and if recognized as meaningful to them, experience the gift of serendipity. The fusion of two different conceptual spaces and the integration of two generative and exploratory agents can thus radically increase the amount and quality of creative output.

While this definition of creativity may at first sight seem somewhat dehumanizing, it does not differ much from the way in which we encounter serendipity in our daily lives. Everyone may daily experience thousands of chance encounters, but they are transformed into serendipity only by someone recognizing a chance occurrence as valuable. Having a problem or question in mind – as visitors of *RuneCast* are encouraged to - helps, of course, since it increases the probability of a chance occurrence intersecting with a mental pathway in a meaningful way. "Chance favours the prepared mind", as Louis Pasteur wisely observes (Knowles and Partington, 1999, p. 849). "Chance", Dada artist Hans Richter (1888-1976) argues, "must be recognized as a new stimulus to artistic creation" (1965, pp. 15-16), because, as John Cage points out: "I don't trust my imagination. I know what my imagination is, and what I'm interested in *is* what I *don't* know" (Kostelanetz, 2003/1987, p.227).

FUTURE TRENDS

Contemporary tools for game design and interactive video already have the potential to transpose, transform and transcend traditional aesthetics and artwork (both physical — like the paintings of Bosch and Merian — and intangible — like the orally-composed mythsongs and tales of the Vikings and Anglo-Saxons) into an engaging, playful digital medium with wide appeal. The theoretical framework and experimental art of the European avant-garde of the 1920's, especially Dada and the Bauhaus, offer particularly fruitful inspiration in this regard, because they in many ways redefined art in terms of creativity and emphasized the importance of play and positive emotions.

Yet although technical issues such as resolution and graphical quality no longer pose a problem for visual standards, and ubiquitous fast processors and supporting digital media technologies make high picture and sound quality easily achievable, the sophisticated techniques and aesthetics of traditional works of art are rarely found in gaming. This is all the more frustrating now that software like Unity 3D enables individual artists to create complex work which can be ported to all the popular platforms.

The hardware for including other sensory modalities is also making great strides in pilot projects using tangible technologies (that simulate the touch of objects) in artworks and exhibitions (Reeves, 2011; Shaer and Hornecker, 2010). The technologies for integrating sensuality to make interactive artwork immediate and stimulating are here, and there is every reason to use them, and to incorporate the interaction situation and design in each individual work and its aesthetic (as Selsjord does with her giant strawberry interaction device, and Thomas did with the physical rune symbol that acted as controller for the 3D set navigated by performers in *Viking Seeress*), rather than settling for a one-size-fits-all interface, which may let down the standards of the artwork and fail to include visitors in the creative experience.

Practice-Based Research: Art and Technology

It is a sad fact that software development has often lagged behind hardware capacity and the creative thinking of artists, content-designers and producers. In general, humanities research councils are slow to fund practice- or process-led and practice-based creative research, which can lead to genuinely groundbreaking visual, narrative and creatively stimulating work, which may depend on emerging technologies. Maybe few art-based research-proposal reviewers feel qualified to judge the feasibility of such projects in advance – and some do, inevitably, fail to live up to their promise. But failure is a vital part of experiment.

Genuinely exploratory art research in creative digital media can sometimes be accomplished under technology funding programmes, such as the EC IST FP6 INFSO.E2 Unit "Digital Content and Knowledge" which partially funded "New Medium for the New Millenium" (*NM2,* 2004-2007) — the project which developed *RuneCast* (the bid was developed in 2007/8, FP7, as (ftp://ftp.cordis. europa.eu/pub/ist/docs/kct/intelligent-content-semantics-2007-08-fp7-call1_en.pdf). The Horizon 2020 calls under Creative Europe 2014/15 (see below, *Production-Based Experimentation in Creative Digital Media Art Research*) also offer some opportunity for content-led research.

Local business can also help support such work: Cambridge University Digital Studio's partnership with BT Research and Venturing on *NM2* won the 2007 *Arts & Business East Technology Award* for "collaboration in which commercial technologies have taken the arts into new realms, and where the arts have helped technology companies to develop and refine new products", where "business turned to artists and digital creatives to push the technological boundaries of content provision, providing the artists free range with opportunities to develop and test genuinely leading edge new media software" (https://www.cambridgenetwork.co.uk/news/arts-business-east-awards-put-spotlight-on-creativity/). The accolade was greatly appreciated - but, alas, offered no financial support to continue the artistic work. Such patrons of art as the Esme Fairbairn Foundation (www.esmeefairbairn) in the UK do provide much-needed financial support for individual artists on a fairly small scale; but more proactive efforts to establish focused funds are highly desirable. Artists/researchers and the studios and institutions where they carry out their work need to lobby for support, and argue the case for ensuring that technological progress does not outstrip our ability to use digital media and tools creatively and in worthwhile ways.

The success of NM2 enabled its science and engineering partners to move on, under the EC's FP7, to a much bigger collaboration (TA2) (www.

ta2-project.eu), which attracted four times the funding of NM2, including refining some of the technology: but no grants were available to support the artwork or creative practices developed in the original project. Where the technology is seen as the defining research outcome, artists can be left at the end of such projects marooned in an environment where the prototype software cannot be fully developed or supported to help artists and researchers use them in the new, exciting, creative and adventurous ways intended. This is the major disadvantage of humanities and art researchers depending on technology-funding to generate forward-looking work.

Artist and academic Professor Jane Prophet noted in 2004:

Historically, most [...] arts practitioner research-ers worked in studios outside the walls of Academy [...] How could it be any other way without a [...] programme that would provide space for artists within the walls? These studios are largely funded by the artists, and the research practice [...] undertaken using materials they purchase with their own money. This is a very different model to that of the scientific researcher working within a laboratory funded, maintained and stocked by Higher Education Institutions, Research Councils and businesses, and other external funding bod-ies. [...] Funding bodies need to recognise the importance of practice-based research in the arts [...] by rewriting their rules to encourage this emergent research. (Prophet, 2004, p. 6)

The EU research funding bodies did not change their policies appreciably in the decade up to 2014, despite the development of new paradigms in practice-based research in art schools, media labs, academies and universities (Büchler, Biggs and Ståhl, 2009; Wilson and van Ruiten, 2014). In 2014, however, there was a recognition in EU research funding calls of the importance of gaming strategies and the influence in culture of computer-generated and supported games. But

HC2020-ICT-2014, "Advanced digital gaming/gamification technologies", for example, showed no interest in research into the artistic aspects of gaming:

Digital games and gamification mechanics ap-plied in non-leisure contexts is an important but scattered industry that can bring high pay-offs and lead to the emergence of a prospering market. Digital games can also make a real change in the life of a large number of targeted excluded groups, enhancing their better integration in society. This requires however the development of new method-ologies and tools to produce, apply and use digital games and gamification techniques in non-leisure contexts, as well as building scientific evidence on their benefits - for governments, enterprises and individuals. (http://ec.europa.eu/research/participants/portal/desktop/en/opportunities/h2020/topics/90-ict-21-2014.html)

The emphasis is on tools and social science. Large grants have tended to go to projects involv-ing technologies supporting infrastructure, digital archiving and search-engines, dissemination/knowledge-exchange via the Internet, direct - usually task-oriented - learning strategies for the young, or explicitly health and welfare-related technologies. Whatever the importance of art to a nation's cultural health, this does not appear to compete with physical health, as far as research funding is concerned. Hopefully, some social science research will be directed towards dem-onstrating the cultural health benefits of what Carroll defines as "artworks", though medical research into the health benefits of creative en-gagement and art consumption is fraught with methodological difficulties and institutionalized prejudice. 'The humanities and the sciences' have their particular roles in the practice of medicine. The notion of evidence-based art is as absurd as an Impressionist school of science", concluded Michael Baum, in an article entitle "Evidence-based art?" in the *Journal of the Royal Society of Medicine* (2001). Yet in their review of current literature on 'The Connection Between Art, Healing, and Public Health' in the *American Journal of Public Health*, Stuckey and Nobel (2010), conclude that the studies they reviewed "appear to indicate that creative engagement can decrease anxiety, stress, and mood disturbances" and that "it is likely that creative engagement contributes to many aspects of physiological and psychological conditions typically associated with improved health status, (p.261).

Production-Based Experimentation in Creative Digital Media Art Research

Gardens of Dreaming and *Marvellous Transformations* were produced in the traditional art-research way referred to by Prophet (above), where an artist-researcher connected with an Academic institution (in this case KHIO) worked in her own time, over a long period, using her own studio, tools and materials, to produce a work which genuinely pushes the envelope of the medium, and at the same time innovates in analysing, exhibiting and enjoying traditional art techniques, approaches and works. Selsjord worked in the forward-looking and comparatively generous environment of Norwegian support for established artists, rather than through her Academy - though it should be noted that since 2012, the Norwegian Artistic Research Programme, which has since 2005 being doing groundbreaking work in supporting doctoral-level artistic research, has been offering support for advanced practice-based artistic research projects within HE institutions (http://artistic-research.no/Asartistpractitioner/researcher).

RuneCast was one of the eight NM2 test-productions the partners were able to convince the EC IST FP6 INFSO.E2 Unit, "Digital Content and Knowledge", were necessary to ensure that the tools designed and implemented in the project were, in fact, useful to the artists and producers for whom they were intended.

Still, as artist and academic Prophet concludes: "The system of funding practice-based research needs greater capacity" (2004, p.6). It is notable in this context that the UK Government DCMS Report "Digital Britain" (June 2009), nowhere mentioned "creative arts". When addressing the "Creative Industries" it focused on monetisation, not culture (www.culture.gov.uk/images/publications/exsumchpt9_digitalbritain-finalreport-jun09.pdf). Five years later, the EC Horizon 2020 calls under Creative Europe 2014/15, despite the explicit recognisiton of the importance of "content", focus on technologies - for example, ICT19–2015 "Technologies for creative industries, social media and convergence":

The demand is growing for high-quality content and new user experiences. At the same time, thanks to ubiquitous technology adoption, widespread use of mobile devices, broadband internet penetration and increasing computing power the consumption of content anywhere, anytime and on any device is becoming a reality. Consequently, developments related to content creation, access, retrieval and interaction offer a number of opportunities and challenges, also for the creative and media industries. In order to keep pace with the trends and remain competitive, those industries need to explore new ways of creating and accessing content. The opportunity to establish new forms of content and user engagement could be transformative to many businesses in creative and media industries. (http://www.2020-horizon.com/Technologies-for-creative-industries-social-media-and-convergence-i1529.html)

And as Michael Nitsche, Director of the Digital World & Image Group at the Georgia Institute of Technology, points out:

So far, identifying and formulating the underlying methods and constraints which actually determine the narrative and expressive possibilities of RT 3D VE remains a challenging task which can only be met through practice-based research of [a] collaborative kind. Even when (and if) research draws level with production, and a consistent theoretical framework is established — as it has been, for example, in film studies — practice-based research will remain necessary, to push development further, evaluate theories, and ensure that both the research field and the productions achieve their full potential. (2004, p.56)

Meanwhile, it seems as though artists using digital tools and media and pushing artistic boundaries may have to continue to fund themselves — which means that many will fall by the wayside — or piggy-back on the research of their scientific colleagues – which means that their work will tend to be confined or even fully determined by the ambitions and needs of their technology partners.

There is no need for excellent artistic tradition to be lost in the 21st century. But public policy and institutional enthusiasm are needed, to give art-practice the support necessary to transpose, transform and transcend tradition for the digital era.

CONCLUSION

"Click, click through cyberspace; this is the new architectural promenade" Mitchell proclaimed in 1995 (p.24), but even in the age of Web 2.0, the 'city of bits' remains as 'antispatial' as in 1995, when Mitchell observed that 'the Net's despatialization of interaction destroys the geocode's key' (1995, 10). Far from providing a navigable, multisensory environment for wander and wonder, cyberspace more often overwhelms the cyberflâneur with overstimulation and frenzy. The psychiatrist Hallowell points out that "as data increasingly floods our brains, we lose our ability to solve problems and handle the unknown. Creativity shrivels, mistakes multiply" (2005, p.54). He believes the inundation with data, which makes unprecedented demands

on our time and attention, to be simulating the symptoms of attention deficit disorder (ADD), a condition marked by chronic and disruptive inattention, distractability and impulsivity. ADD has become "culturally syntonic" (Ratey and Hallowell, 1994, p. 191), thus resulting in a massive prevalence of pseudo-ADD. "Because we live in a very ADD-oid culture, almost everybody can identify with the symptoms of ADD" (Hallowell and Ratey, 1994, p. 193).

The synaptic pharmacologist Susan Greenfield, director of the Royal Institution of Great Britain (1998-2010), shares these concerns. She points out that the human brain is highly sensitive to the environment and adapts with tremendous flexibility (2001 [1997], pp. 140–1), which may result in the rapid feed-back loops of digital screen media re-wiring the brain into expecting instantaneous gratification (2009, Hansard Column 1291). "As a consequence," Greenfield writes, "the mid 21st-century mind might almost be infantilized, characterized by short attention spans, sensationalism, inability to empathise and a shaky sense of identity" (2009, Column 1293).

These criticisms are not directed towards the medium itself, but its content, which is 'devoid of cohesive narrative and long-term significance' (2009: Column 1292). Greenfield argues that 'the emphasis is on the thrill of the moment, the buzz of rescuing the princess in the game. No care is given for the princess herself [...] This type of activity, a disregard for consequence, can be compared with the thrill of compulsive gambling or compulsive eating' (2009: Column 1292).

The works by Thomas and Selsjord provide alternatives to such anti-creative interactivity. They make use of attentional resources in fundamentally different ways and provide narrative satisfaction without relying on competitive reward schemes and adrenalin rushes. As such, the digital media case-studies presented here fall into Carroll's classification of (traditional) "artworks", in that they are

… intentionally constructed in such a way that they are eminently suitable for disinterested and sympathetic attention and contemplation. They [...] contain structures that guide attention and contemplation – that encourage it by means of their intentionally designed features of unity, complexity and intensity – and that reward such attention and contemplation. The aesthetic experiencer [does] not have to do all the work herself. The object itself [is] structured intentionally to invite, sustain and, optimally, reward disinterested and sympathetic attention and contemplation. (Carroll, 2010, pp. 172-173)

Moreover, these electronic artworks facilitate a variety of different types of play and offer a degree of participatory creativity which makes their aesthetic special - and close to the practices and aspirations of the European avant-garde of the early 20ᵗʰ century. The Swedish playwright August Strindberg writes, in the prefatory note to the text of his *Dream Play* (1902):

The author has [...] attempted to imitate the inconsequent yet transparently logical shape of a dream. Everything can happen, everything is possible and probable. Time and place do not exist; on an insignificant basis of reality the imagination spins, weaving new patterns; a mixture of memories, experiences, free fancies, incongruities and improvisations. [...] But one consciousness rules over them all, that of the dreamer. (in Meyer, 2000, p. 175)

For Strindberg, however surreal or apparently random the objects and events of his play may be in its complexity and intensity, unity is provided by the sensibility of the author.

But in 21ˢᵗ-century creative media art, enabled by games technologies to release some if not all authority to the participant viewer, this unity is finally provided by the sensibility of the experiencer. The artist creates "structures

that guide attention and contemplation – that encourage it by means of their intentionally designed features" and that "reward disinterested and sympathetic attention and contemplation", but it is the visitor's interaction with the dynamic work which elicits a play of the imagination - visual, auditory, tactile and kinaesthetic – that simultaneously involves "multiple types of mental imagery" (Rothenberg, 1986, p. 2). Their "game spaces [...] trigger important parts of the narrative process in the player" (Nitsche, 2008, p.3), making the participant viewer the hero of their own journey. If they do not journey, there is no artwork – nothing will happen if the visitor does not accept the invitation to participate. But once the journeyer sets off, "everything can happen, everything is possible and probable", which is, as Simmel discussed in "The Adventurer" (2006/1911) (see *The Importance of Being Playful*), not only the point-of-departure for immersing oneself in audio-visual pleasures, but the path towards self-insight and personal growth – an experience made possible especially in *RuneCast*. Here Thomas' use of archetypal characters from Northern European mythology in the context of self-questioning offers visitors the opportunity to explore and confirm their own identity: "I cannot remember encountering such profound and harmonious multimedia before. Through music and moving images, rather than following what happens to someone else, I have myself become the protagonist in an interactive movie" (Maunuksela, 2001).

In 2010, Boden claims that "as a practice, interactive art – wherein the form of the art object is partly determined by the actions of the audience [...] – is by now well established. [...] However, there's no established aesthetics associated with it" (p. 210).

Many of these artists do not, however, produce art simply for art's sake. In "How to Improve the World", John Cage writes about the importance of artists to socio-political change:

I think this, because without the avant-garde, which I think is flexibility of the mind and freedom from institutions, theories and laws, you won't have invention and obviously, from a practical point of view, the society needs invention. Whether they accept the fact or not, they do need it. And ultimately they will be up against a wall where, if they don't have an inventor around, they will be lost. (Cage and Gena, 1982, pp. 170–171)

Dada and Bauhaus artists articulated the principles of creative cognition with astute insight half a century before science began to uncover the mechanisms of the creative mind (Prager, 2012; 2014); they recognized the importance of play as a fundamental expression of humanity in the 1920s, almost a century before play became a serious area of academic research and a fashionable mainstream interest (Prager, 2013); and the Bauhaus articulated a sophisticated theory of interactivity, together with unrealizable visionary projects (Prager, 2006). These examples illustrate that art history does not merely serve as a rich source of inspiration for digital art, but highlights the unique role artists play in imagining and articulating future possibilities – not only aesthetically – but also in the most concrete socio-cultural terms.

The works presented in this chapter draw on traditional, avant-garde and contemporary practices to create an aesthetic which encompasses the visual and audio content, the interaction design and device, and the interaction situation – all equally "intentionally constructed", as Carroll puts it – enabling the preparedness of mind which promotes finding "new connections among ideas, new perspectives" (Csikszentmihalyi, 1996, p.136). These artworks draw on traditional techniques and approaches, but transpose, transform and finally transcend them for the era of digital media creativity. They remind us that however revolutionary digital media may be in opening up new pathways, they are also part of an evolutionary process of artistic endeavour. In the twenty-first century, technology – software, hardware and communications – has the potential to enable individual artists to make new work and exhibit and distribute it as never before. It is up to both artists and technologists to promote the importance of pushing the boundaries not just of tools and devices, but of content - art and aesthetics - whose role is crucial to the creativity and welfare of a constantly evolving culture.

REFERENCES

Acker, P. (Ed.). (2001). *The poetic Edda: Essays on old Norse mythology.* London: Routledge.

Ascott, R. (2003). *Telematic embrace: Visionary theories of art, technology and consciousness.* Berkeley, CA: University of California Press.

Atkins, B. (2003). *More than a game.* Manchester, UK: Manchester University Press. doi:10.7228/manchester/9780719063640.001.0001

Atkins, B., & Krzywinska, T. (2007). *Videogame, player, text.* Manchester, UK: Manchester University Press.

Auden, W. H., & Taylor, P. B. (1983). *Norse poems* (2nd ed.). London: Faber & Faber.

Axelrod, S. G., Roman, C., & Travisano, T. (Eds.). (2003). *The new anthology of American poetry: Traditions and revolutions, beginnings to 1900.* New Brunswick, NJ: Rutgers University Press.

Baum, M. (2001). Evidence-based art? *Journal of the Royal Society of Medicine, 94,* 306–307. PMID:11387430

Bek-Pedersen, K. (2011). The norns in old Norse mythology. Edinburgh, UK: Dunedin.

Bisio, T. (2013). *Decoding the Dao: Nine lessons in Daoist meditation.* Denver, CO: Outskirts Press.

Boden, M. (2004). *The creative mind: Myths and mechanisms.* London: Routledge. (Original work published 1990)

Boden, M. (2010). *Creativity and art: Three roads to surprise*. Oxford, UK: Oxford University Press.

Boden, M. (2014). A polymath at play. *American Journal of Play, 7*, 1–19.

Bogost, I. (2011). *How to do things with videogames*. Minneapolis, MN: University of Minnesota Press.

Bolter, J., & Grusin, R. (1999). *Remediation: Understanding new media*. Cambridge, MA: MIT Press.

Bramwell, T. (2013). *Is the most disturbing scene in GTA 5 justified?* Retrieved 16.09.2013 from erogamer.net: http://www.eurogamer.net/articles/2013-09-16-is-the-most-disturbing-scene-in-gta5-justified

Büchler, D., Biggs, M., & Ståhl, L.-H. (2009). Areas of design practice as an alternative research paradigm. *Design Principles and Practices: An International Journal, 3*(2), 327–338.

Cabanne, P. (1971). *Dialogues with Marcel Duchamp*. London: Thames and Hudson.

Cage, J. (1968). (*Composer/Performer*). Reunion: Ryerson Theater, Toronto, Canada. [musical composition/performance]

Cage, J. (1973). *Silence*. Hanover, CT: Wesleyan University Press. (Original work published 1961)

Cage, J. (Composer). (1979). Roaratorio, an Irish circus on Finnegans Wake [musical composition]. West German Radio.

Cage, J., & Gena, P. (1982). After antiquity. In *A John Cage reader* (pp. 167–168). New York: Peters.

Campbell, J. (1982). *Creative mythology*. London: Penguin Books. (Original work published 1968)

Candy, L., & Edmonds, E. (Eds.). (2002). *Explorations in art and technology*. London: Springer. doi:10.1007/978-1-4471-0197-0

Carroll, L. (2011). *Through the looking glass, and what Alice found there*. Macmillan Children's Books. (Original work published 1871)

Carroll, N. (2010). *Philosophy of art*. London: Routledge. (Original work published 1999)

Catlow, R., Garrett, M., & Morgana, C. (Eds.). (2010). *Artists re: thinking games*. Liverpool, UK: Liverpool University Press.

Cincera, R. (1967). *Kinoautomat* [interactive audio-visual performance/film]. Czechoslovakia.

Clair, R. (Director). (1924). *Entr'acte* [film]. France.

Crompton, R. (1922). *Just William*. London: George Newnes.

Crompton, R. (1927). *William in trouble*. London: George Newnes.

Cross, L. (1999). Reunion: John Cage, Marcel Duchamp, electronic music and chess. *Leonardo Music Journal, 9*, 35–42. doi:10.1162/096112199750316785

Crossley-Holland, K. (1996). *Norse myths: Gods of the vikings*. London: Penguin Books.

Csikszentmihalyi, M. (1996). *Creativity*. New York: Harper Collins.

Culture and Trends. (2009, February 21). *Verdens Gang*. [newspaper article]. Retrieved from http://www.vg.no

De Winter, J. (2009). Aesthetic reproduction in Japanese computer culture: The dialectical histories of manga, anime, and computer games. In J. E. Ruggill, K. S. McAllister, & J. R. Chaney (Eds.), *The computer culture reader* (pp. 108–124). Newcastle, UK: Cambridge Scholars Publishing.

Defiance. (2013-). [television series]. Five and Dime/Universal Cable: Syfy. USA.

Don, A. (1990). Narrative and interface. In B. Laurel & S. Joy (Eds.), *The Art of human computer interface design* (pp. 383–391). Reading, MA: Addison-Wesley.

Eisenstein, S. (1991). Vertical montage. In R. Taylor & M. Glenny (Eds.), Towards a theory of montage (Vol. 2). London: British Film Institute. (Original work published 1939)

Elger, D. (2004). *Dadaism*. Cologne: Taschen.

Etheridge, K. (2011). Maria Sibylla Merian: The first ecologist? In V. Molinari & D. Andreolle (Eds.), *Women and science: Figures and representations – 17th century to present* (pp. 35–54). Newcastle upon Tyne, UK: Cambridge Scholars Publishing.

Fanès, F. (2007). *Salvador Dalí: The construction of the image 1925–1930*. New Haven, CT: Yale University Press.

Fauconnier, G., & Turner, M. (2002). *The way we think*. New York: Basic Books.

Findell, M. (2014). *Runes*. London: The British Museum Press.

Finke, R., Ward, T., & Smith, S. (1992). *Creative cognition: Theory, research, and applications*. Cambridge, MA: MIT Press.

Foxman, P. (1976). Tolerance for ambiguity and self-actualization. *Journal of Personality Assessment, 40*(1), 67–72. doi:10.1207/s15327752jpa4001_13 PMID:16367248

Gombrich, E. (1960). *Art and illusion: A study in the psychology of pictorial representation*. London: Phaidon.

Gray, P. (2011). The decline of play and the rise of psychopathology in children and adolescents. *American Journal of Play, 3*, 443–463.

Green, M. C., Strange, J. J., & Brock, T. C. (Eds.). (2002). *Narrative impact: Social and cognitive foundations*. Mahwah, NJ: Lawrence Erlbaum.

Greenfield, S. (2001). *The human brain: A guided tour*. London: Phoenix. (Original work published 1997)

Greenfield, S. (2009, February 12). Speech, House of Lords. In *Parliamentary debates [Hansard]* (Vol. 707, columns 1290–3). Retrieved 13.92.2009 from http://www.publications.parliament.uk/pa/ld200809/ldhansrd/text/902120010.htm#09021268000191

Gropius, W. (Ed.). (1961). *Theatre of the Bauhaus*. Middletown, CT: Wesleyan UP. (Original work published 1925)

Hales, C. (2005). Cinematic interaction: From Kinoautomat to cause and effect. *Digital Creativity, 16*(1), 54–64. doi:10.1080/14626260500147777

Halifax, J. (1979). *Shamanic voices: A survey of visionary narrative*. London: Arkana.

Hallowell, E. (2005). Overloaded circuits: Why smart people underperform. *Harvard Business Review, 83*, 54–62. PMID:15697113

Hallowell, E., & Ratey, J. (1994). *Driven to distraction*. New York: Touchstone.

Hanrahan, M. (2014, October 20). Tale of tales: Making a game for the gamers. *Gamesindustry.biz*. Retrieved from http://www.gamesindustry.biz/articles/2014-10-20-tale-of-tales-making-a-game-for-the-gamers

Haskins, R. (2012). *John Cage*. London: Reaktion Books.

Hendricks, T. (2006). Play reconsidered. Champaign, IL: University of Illinois Press.

Heritage, S. (2013, November 4). Grand Theft Auto 5? Sorry, I'm just a bit too Guardian. *The Guardian*. Retrieved from http://www.theguardian.com/commentisfree/2013/nov/04/grand-theft-auto-5-guardian-gta-v-car-game

Honko, L. (Ed.). (2000). *Thick corpus, organic variation and textuality in oral tradition*. Helsinki: Finnish Literature Society.

Hopkins, D. (2004). *Surrealism and Dada: A very short introduction*. Oxford, UK: Oxford University Press. doi:10.1093/actrade/9780192802545.001.0001

Hultkrantz, Å. (1996). A new look at the world pillar in arctic and sub-arctic religions. In J. Pentikäinen (Ed.), *Shamanism and northern ecology* (pp. 31–51). Berlin: Mouton de Gruyter. doi:10.1515/9783110811674.31

Jackson, P. (Director) (2001). *The Lord of the rings: The fellowship of the ring*. [Cinema]. USA: New Line Cinema.

Jackson, P. (Director) (2002). *The Lord of the rings: The two towers*. [Cinema]. USA: New Line Cinema.

Jackson, P. (Director) (2003). *The Lord of the rings: The return of the ring*. [Cinema]. USA: New Line Cinema.

Jónsdóttir, A. (2003). *Pop press programme* [Radio]. RUV Icelandic State Broadcasting.

Joyce, J. (1999). *Finnegans wake*. London: Penguin. (Original work published 1939)

Juniper, A. (2003). *Wabi Sabi: The Japanese art of impermanence*. Tuttle Publishing.

Kafno, P., & Turpainen, M. (2007). *FP6 IST – 004124 – NM2 final evaluation report*. EC. Internal Report. Retrieved from www.ist-nm2.org

Kamenetz, A. (2013). *Why video games succeed where the movie and music industries fail*. Retrieved 07.11.2013 from The Fast Company http://www.fastcompany.com/3021008/why-video-games-succeed-where-the-movie-and-music-industries-fail

Kim, K. E. (2011). The creativity crisis: The decrease in creative thinking scores on the Torrance tests of creative thinking. *Creativity Research Journal, 23*(4), 285–298. doi:10.1080/10400419.2011.627805

Knowles, E., & Partington, A. (1999). *The Oxford dictionary of quotations*. Oxford, UK: Oxford University Press.

Knowles, J. G., & Cole, A. L. (Eds.). (2008). *Handbook of the arts in qualitative research: Perspectives, methodologies, examples, and issues*. Thousand Oaks, CA: Sage Publications. doi:10.4135/9781452226545

Kostelanetz, R. (2003). *Conversing with Cage*. New York: Routledge. (Original work published 1987)

Kounios, J., Fleck, J., Green, D., Payne, L., Stevenson, J., Bowden, E., & Jung-Beeman, M. (2008). The origins of insight in resting-state brain activity. *Neuropsychologia, 46*(1), 281–291. doi:10.1016/j.neuropsychologia.2007.07.013 PMID:17765273

Kristjánsson, J. (1988). *Eddas and sagas*. (P. Foote, Trans.). Reykjavík: hið íslenska bókmennta félag.

Krueger, M. W. (1977). Responsive environments. In K. Stiles & P. Selz (Eds.), Theories and documents of contemporary art: A sourcebook of artists' writings (pp. 473-486). Berkeley, CA: University of California Press, 1996. doi:10.1145/1499402.1499476

Langer, S. (1977). *Feeling and form: A theory of art*. New York: Scribner, Prentice Hall. (Original work published 1953)

Lord, A. B. (1968). *The singer of tales*. New York: Atheneum. (Original work published 1960)

MacDonald, K. (2012, March 13). Journey – review. *The Guardian*. Retrieved from http://www.theguardian.com/technology/gamesblog/2012/mar/13/journey-ps3-review

Malory, T. (1977). Le Morte d'Arthur. In E. Vinaver (Ed.), *Malory: Complete works*. Oxford, UK: Oxford University Press. (Original work published 1485)

Manovich, L. (2001). *The language of new media*. Cambridge, MA: MIT Press.

Manovich, L., & Kratky, A. (2005). *Soft cinema: Navigating the database*. Cambridge, MA: MIT Press.

Manuksela, A. (Reviewer). (2001). *Helsingin Sanomat* [newspaper article]. Finland. Retrieved from http://www.hs.fi

Marshall, R. (2013). *History of tomb raider: Blowing the dust off 17 years of Lara Croft*. Retrieved 30.06.2014 from http://www.digitaltrends.com/gaming/the-history-of-tomb-raider/#!7LAR0

McKinnell, J. (1993). Völuspá. In P. Pulsiano & K. Wolf (Eds.), *Medieval Scandinavia* (pp. 713–715). London: Routledge.

McKinnell, J. (2001). On Heiðr. *Saga-Book*, *25*(4), 394–417.

Merian, M. (2009). *Insects of Surinam* (K. Schmidt-Loske, Ed.). Cologne: Taschen GmbH. (Original work published 1705)

Mitchell, W. (1995). *City of bits*. Cambridge, MA: MIT Press.

Moholy-Nagy, L. (1967). *Painting photography film*. London: Lund Humphreys. (Original work published 1925)

Müller, U. (1998). *Klassischer Geschmack und gotische Tugend: Der englische Landsitz Rousham*. Worms, Germany: Wernersche Verlagsgesellschaft.

Murray, J. M. (1997). *Hamlet on the holodeck: The future of narrative in cyberspace*. Cambridge, MA: MIT Press.

Neckel, G. (1927). *Edda: Die Lieder des Codex Regius*. Heidelberg, Germany: Carl Winters Universitätsbuchhandlung.

Nickerson, R. (1999). Enhancing creativity. In R. Sternberg (Ed.), *Handbook of creativity* (pp. 392–430). Cambridge, UK: Cambridge University Press.

Nitsche, M. (2004). Spatial structuring, cinematic mediation, and evocative narrative elements in the design of an RT 3D VE: The common tales project. *Digital Creativity*, *15*(1), 52–56. doi:10.1076/digc.15.1.52.28147

Nitsche, M. (2008). *Video games spaces: Image, play and structure in 3D worlds*. Cambridge MA: MIT Press. doi:10.7551/mitpress/9780262141017.001.0001

O'Brien, C. (2013). How the i-Phone and i-Pad transformed the work of David Hockney. *Los Angeles Times*. Retrieved 27.10.2013 from http://www.latimes.com/business/technology/la-fi-tn-how-the-iphone-and-ipad-transformed-the-art-of-david-hockney-20131024-story.html

O'Mahony, M. (2006). *World art: The essential illustrated history*. London: Flame Tree Publishing.

Page, R. I. (1987). *Runes (reading the past)*. London: British Museum Publications.

Pals, N., & Esmeijer, J. (Eds.). (2007). *New millennium/new media: FP6 IST – 004124 – report D 7.9 Evaluation report on RuneCast*. EC. Internal Report. Retrieved from www.ist-nm2.org

Parnes, S. (1965). The nurture of creative talent. *Music Educators Journal, 51*(32-3), 92-95.

Paul, C. (2003). *Digital art*. London: Thames & Hudson Ltd.

Pearson, M. J. (2011). *The original I Ching: An authentic translation of the Book of Changes*. Rutland, VT: Tuttle Publishing.

Peckham, M. (2014). *Romantic puzzler Entwined is an understated triumph*. Retrieved 01.07.2014 from http://www.wired.co.uk/news/archive/2014-06/23/entwined-review

Pentikäinen, J. (1987). The shamanistic drum as cognitive map. In R. Gothoni & J. Pentikäinen (Eds.), Mythology and cosmic order (pp. 17-36). Helsinki: Suomalaisen Kirjallisuuden Seura.

Pentikäinen, J. (Ed.). (1996). *Shamanism and northern ecology (religion and society)*. Berlin: Mouton de Gruyter. doi:10.1515/9783110811674

Petrini, C. (1991). Kaleidoscopic thinking for creativity. *Training & Development, 45*, 27–34.

Prager, P. (2006). Back to the future: Interactivity and associational narrativity at the Bauhaus. *Digital Creativity, 17*(4), 295–304. doi:10.1080/14626260601073195

Prager, P. (2009). *Play, creativity and exuberance: Avant-Garde legacies for interactive cinematics*. (Unpublished doctoral dissertation). University of Cambridge, Cambridge, UK.

Prager, P. (2012). Making an art of creativity: The cognitive science of Duchamp and Dada. *Creativity Research Journal, 24*(4), 266–277. doi:10.1080/10400419.2012.726576

Prager, P. (2013). Play and the Avant-Garde: Aren't we all a little Dada? *American Journal of Play, 5*, 239–256.

Prager, P. (2014). Making sense of the modernist muse: Creative cognition and play at the Bauhaus. *American Journal of Play, 7*, 27–49.

Prophet, J. (2004). Re-addressing practice-based research: Funding and recognition. *Digital Creativity, 15*(1), 2–7. doi:10.1076/digc.15.1.2.28153

Reeves, S. (2011). *Designing interfaces in public settings: Understanding the role of the spectator in human-computer interaction*. Heidelberg, Germany: Springer-Verlag. doi:10.1007/978-0-85729-265-0

Richter, H. (1965). *Dada: Art and anti-art*. New York: Harry Abrams.

Rieser, M. (2002). The poetics of interactivity: The uncertainty principle. In M. Rieser & A. Zapp (Eds.), *New screen media: Cinema/art/narrative* (pp. 146–162). London: British Film Institute.

Rieser, M., & Zapp, A. (Eds.). (2002). *New screen media: Cinema/art/narrative*. London: British Film Institute.

Rosengarten, A. (2000). *Spectrums of possibility: When psychology meets tarot*. St Paul, MN: Paragon House.

Rothenberg, A. (1976). Homospatial thinking in creativity. *Archives of General Psychiatry, 33*(1), 17–26. doi:10.1001/archpsyc.1976.01770010005001 PMID:1247359

Rothenberg, A. (1986). Artistic creation as stimulated by superimposed versus combined-composite visual images. *Journal of Personality and Social Psychology, 50*(2), 370–381. doi:10.1037/0022-3514.50.2.370 PMID:3701584

Ruestow, E. G. (1985). Piety and the defence of natural order: Swammerdam on generation. In M. Osler & P. L. Faber (Eds.), *Religion, science and worldview: Essays in honor of Richard S. Westfall* (pp. 217–241). New York: Cambridge University Press.

Ryan, M.-L. (2001). *Narrative as virtual reality: Immersion and interactivity in literature and electronic media*. Baltimore, MD: Johns Hopkins University Press.

Schlemmer, O. (1961). Theatre (Bhne). In W. Gropius (Ed.), *Theatre of the Bauhaus* (pp. 81–91). Middletown, CT: Wesleyan UP. (Original work published 1925)

Seaman, B. (2002). Recombinant poetics: Emergent explorations of digital video in virtual space. In M. Rieser & A. Zapp (Eds.), *New screen media: Cinema/art/narrative* (pp. 237–255). London: British Film Institute.

Shaer, O., & Hornecker, E. (2010). *Tangible user interfaces*. Delft: Now Publishers Inc.

Siikala, A.-L. (2002). *Mythic images and shamanism*. Helskinki: Academia Scientiarum Fennica.

Simmel, G. (2006). The adventurer. In J. Cosgrave (Ed.), *The sociology of risk and gambling behaviour* (pp. 215–224). New York: Routledge. (Original work published 1911)

Smith, A. (1982). John Cage the mycologist. In P. Gena & J. Brent (Eds.), *A John Cage reader* (pp. 165–166). New York: Peters.

Solarski, C. (2012). *Drawing basics and video game art: Classic to cutting-edge art techniques for winning video game design*. New York: Watson-Guptill.

Sorenson, B., Meyer, B., & Eigenfeldt-Nielsen, S. (Eds.). (2011). *Serious games in education: A global perspective*. Copenhagen: Aarhus University Press.

Stokstad, M. (2002). *Art history: Volume two* (2nd ed.). New York: Harry N. Abrams, Inc.

Strindberg, A. (2000). A dream play. In August Strindberg, plays: Two (M. Mayer, Trans.; pp. 175-254). London: Methuen. (Original work published 1902)

Stuckey, H., & Nobel, J. (2010). The connection between art, healing, and public health: A review of current literature. *American Journal of Public Health, 100*(2), 254–263. doi:10.2105/AJPH.2008.156497 PMID:20019311

Sutton, P. (1989). *Dreamings: Art from Aboriginal Australia*. Melbourne: Viking/ Penguin.

Swammerdam, J. (1681). *Ephemeri vita, or, the natural history and anatomy of the ephemeron, a fly that lives but five hours*. London: Henry Faithorne and John Kersey. (Original work published 1645). Retrieved from Ann Arbor, Michigan: University of Michigan, Digital Library Production Service: http://trove.nla.gov.au/version/31186689

Tabor, M. (1989). *Chaos and integrability in nonlinear dynamics: An introduction*. New York: Wiley.

Tacitus, C. (2009). Germania. (H. Mattingly, trans; J. Rives, revised). Oxford, UK: Oxford University Press. (Original work published 96AD)

Tátar, M. (1996). Mythology as an areal problem in the Altai-Sayan area. In J. Pentikäinen (Ed.), *Shamanism and northern ecology* (pp. 267–278). Berlin: Mouton de Gruyter. doi:10.1515/9783110811674.267

(1969). *The Poetic Edda* (Vol. 1 Dronke, U., Trans. & Ed.). Oxford, UK: Clarendon Press.

(1997). *The Poetic Edda* (Vol. 2 Dronke, U., Trans. & Ed.). Oxford, UK: Clarendon Press.

Thomas, M. (2005). Playing with chance and choice – Orality, narrativity and cinematic media. In B. Bushoff (Ed.), Developing interactive narrative content (pp. 371- 442). Sagas/Sagas.net Reader. Munich: High Text.

Thomas, M. (2008). Digitality and immaterial culture: What did Viking women think? *International Journal of Digital Cultural Heritage and Electronic Tourism, 1*(2), 177–199. doi:10.1504/IJDCET.2008.021406

Thomas, M., Selsjord, M., & Zimmer, R. (2011). Museum or mausoleum? Electronic shock therapy. In M. Lytras, E. Damiani, L. Diaz, & P. Ordonez de Pablos (Eds.), *Digital culture and e-tourism: Technologies, applications and management* (pp. 10–35). Hershey, PA: IGI Global. doi:10.4018/978-1-61520-867-8.ch002

Thorburn, D., & Jenkins, H. (2003). *Rethinking media change*. Cambridge, MA: MIT Press.

Todd, K. (2007). *Chrysalis: Maria Sybilla Merian and the secrets of metamorphosis*. London: I.B. Tauris.

Tolkien, J. R. R. (1954/5). *The lord of the rings*. London: George Allen & Unwin.

Tolstoy, L. (2011). *What is art?* Bristol, UK: Bristol Classical Press. (Original work published 1896)

Turville-Petre, E. O. G. (1976). *Scaldic poetry*. Oxford, UK: Clarendon Press.

Ursu, M. F., Kegel, I., Williams, D., Thomas, M., Mayer, H., Zsombori, V., & Wyver, J. et al. (2008). ShapeShifting TV: Interactive screen media narratives. *Multimedia Systems*, *14*(2), 115–132. doi:10.1007/s00530-008-0119-z

Ursu, M. F., Thomas, M., Tuomola, M., Wright, T., Williams, D., & Zsombori, V. (2007). Interactivity and narrativity in screen media. In *Proceedings of the IEEE Symposium on Multimedia Systems* (pp. 227-232). IEEE Computer Society.

Ursu, M. F., Zsombori, V., Wyver, J., Conrad, L., Kegel, I., & Williams, D. (2009). Interactive documentaries: A golden age. In Computers in entertainment. New York, NY: ACM. Retrieved from http://dl.acm.org/citation.cfm?doid=1594943.1594953 doi:10.1145/1594943.1594953

Vickery, A. (Presenter), & Hodgson, J. (Producer/Director) (2014, May). *The story of women and art* [television series]. United Kingdom: BBC2.

Vitebsky, P. (1995). *The shaman*. London: Macmillan.

von Franz, M.-L. (1980). *On divination and synchronicity: The psychology of meaningful chance*. Toronto: Inner City Books.

Ward, T., Smith, S., & Finke, R. (1999). Creative cognition. In R. Sternberg (Ed.), *Handbook of creativity* (pp. 189–212). Cambridge, UK: Cambridge University Press.

Whitelaw, M. (2004). *Metacreation: Art and artificial life*. London: MIT Press.

Wiggins, S. (1990). *Introduction to applied nonlinear dynamical systems and chaos*. New York: Springer-Verlag. doi:10.1007/978-1-4757-4067-7

Wilson, M., & van Ruiten, S. (Eds.). (2014). *SHARE handbook for artistic research education*. Retrieved from http://www.sharenetwork.eu/resources/share-handbook

Works Corporation. (2004). *Japanese games graphics: Behind the scenes of your favourite games*. New York: Harper Collins Design International.

KEY TERMS AND DEFINITIONS

Avant-Garde: Adjective deriving from the work of European artists of the first quarter of the 20th century, who believed in relinquishing authorial control and advocated flexibility of mind and freedom from institutions. They experimented with collage and recombinant, spatially organized and associational narrative, visual and verbal; and articulated principles of creative cognition with sophisticated insight and an astute, redefining art in terms of creativity and emphasizing the importance of play and positive emotions.

Chance Operations: Indeterminacy and the aleatory embedded in artworks to avoid the mechanical and predictable feel of works generated according to rules. Used in computer-based interactive art where designed, choreographed and/or composed forms are combined using randomising algorithms in addition to narrative rules, to offer an exciting, unpredictable, aesthetically pleasing and engaging experience analogous to improvisation, based on a constantly changing dynamic.

Digital Aesthetics: The sensual properties of and responses to artwork; also critical reflection on art and culture. Tracing links between the practices of digital artists, particularly in 3D, and earlier visual arts, our chapter addresses the claim that there is no established aesthetics associated with computer-based interactive art.

Interaction Design: Design of the functionality of artworks which reveal themselves over time – visitors do not at once perceive all that the work has to offer, but discover its full potential gradually, actively participating in its exploration/ construction. The design of the interaction is an essential part of the design both of the artwork and of the interactors' experience of it. For example, using sensitive dependence on initial conditions, effective interaction design can free many elements of the work/experience from authorial control without relinquishing coherence, by playfully engaging the interactor in the creative process, to deliver creative as well as aesthetic and narrative satisfaction.

Oral Composition: A technique for the extempore live composition of (sung) tales or narratives, traditionally evolved over many generations by performers who do not know how to write, but also used in the present day by storytellers and folk singers. A repertoire of formulas, often using quite small formulaic expressions as well as larger arcs, are combined and recombined according to themes or storyshapes to build the narrative, taking into account the response of the audience. This recombinant technique can be used very effectively in computer-handled narrativity, where the medium is closer to orality than literacy.

Spatially Organised Narrativity: In navigable 3D computer-supported and generated environments, the interaction between place and drama is mutually supportive. Traditionally, medieval European drama was spatially organised in its staging, sometimes playing different scenes in actual locations in a real village, with the audience following the drama from place to place; and sometimes staging scenes on pageant wagons, which moved through town, stopping in different places, where audiences gathered to construct the narrative piece by piece. Orally composed epics also use type-locations to stage scenes and configure their narratives. Such reconfigurable, recombinant, participative, locative composition and staging can be effectively transposed to the explorable navigable worlds of digital narrativity.

Tangible Interface: Human beings perceive their surroundings through sense; vision, hearing, smell and touch can all be stimulated through tangible interfaces, where visitors physically use a device activated by touch or movement which links the everyday world with the realms of computer-based interactive artworks. The process of interaction itself is a part of the aesthetic experience.

ENDNOTES

1. *Gardens of Dreaming* (music by Natasha Barrett) was developed using commercially available software, and independently produced by the artist, with economic support from the Norwegian Arts Council. It was first exhibited at Henie Onstad Art Centre, Oslo, in February 2009, as a stand-alone gallery installation artwork. Her multimedia, *Marvellous Transformations,* also supported by the Norwegian Arts Council, comprising, in its entirety, an explorable 3D digital artwork, stereo animation/still images, stereo video material and 3D-printed sculptures,

was first exhibited (in part) in 'Norne At-tersøm', Galleri Vanntårnet, Nesoddtangen, in October 2013; the full exhibition was premiered at Drøbak, Norway in October 2014, and shown in Cambridge in January 2015. Like *Gardens of Dreaming*, this project used existing software and hardware in new combinations, with some plug-ins specially developed by the software companies.

2   Vala was produced at the Interactive Institute, Sweden (Narrativity Studio, Malmö) using available technology and software, and the first prototype was exhibited at the Fylkingen Centre for New Music and Intermedia Arts, Stockholm (2000); the fully working release was first shown at 'Electrohype' Malmö (2001). The well was designed by Aasa Harvard, the interface-stones by Ylva Gislén of the Interactive Institute, Sweden.

3   Supported by Embla Productions/UNESCO Cultural Heritage, the Nordic Cultural Fund and the Icelandic Film Centre.

4   Exhibited 2007 at the *Digital Festival*, South-bank Centre London; *Women in Games,* Newport and the *Cambridge Film Festival.*

5   *Vala* was devised and produced before the advent of the DVD, though the work had been designed with DVD in mind, so (like some early computer games) it was stored on a number of CD ROMs. The programming was done in Director, superseded commercially over the following decade by Flash and html. This technology lasted no more than 10 years (a long period in the digital technology world), and the move to newer, more efficient software and hardware means that it is hard, if not impossible, to show work created at the turn of the millennium today. Assets need to be reformatted and relabelled with new metadata for handling with new software, which can be prohibitively expensive for an individual artist. Since this process is rarely viewed as artistic research (as the form has already been demonstrated), it is hard to fund – the only tactic seems to be to redeploy the assets in new technical research.

6   Script funded by Norwegian Film Institute Interactive; project in development 2014 with SnowCastle Games.

7   Parts of *Marvellous Transformations*, then a work in progress, were exhibited at 'Norne Attersøm', Galleri Vanntårnet, Nesoddtan-gen October 2013 - the full exhibition is scheduled at Drøbak kunstforening: Varm-bade, Norway in October 2014, and Churchill College, Cambridge in January 2015).

8   The video-based installation, *Vala* was cre-ated experimentally at the Narrativity Studio of the Swedish Interactive Institute, Malmø, where Maureen Thomas was the founder and Senior Creative Research Fellow.

9   For discussion of the Viking-age verses see McKinnell, 1993; Thomas, 2005; for singing of tales: Honko, 2000; Lord, 1968/1960; for recombinance in digital media: Seaman (2002); Rieser (2002); Manovich (2001); Manovich & Kratky, 2005; Ryan (2001) and Murray (1997).

APPENDIX

Games

- *Bioshock* series. (2007-2013). 2K Games Inc.
- *Defiance*. (2013). Trion World Network.
- *Entwined*. (2014). Pixelopus/Sony Computer Entertainment.
- *Fable series*. (2004-2012). Molyneux, Lionhead Studios/Microsoft Studios.
- *Fatal Frame*. (2001). Tecmo.
- *Fatal Frame Crimson Butterfly*. (2003). Tecmo.
- *flOw*. (2007). thatgamescompany/Sony Playstation.
- *Flower*. (2009). thatgamescompany/Sony Playstation.
- *Grand theft auto* series. (2004-2014). Rockstar Games/Rockstar North.
- *Journey*. (2012). thatgamescompany/Sony Playstation.
- *Lara Croft tomb raider* series (1996-2014). Eidos, Square Enix.
- *Sleeping dogs*. (2012). United Front, Square Enix.
- *Sunset Overdrive*. (2014). Insomniac/Microsoft Game Studio.
- *Tale of Tales BVBA* (2002-2014). Art game development company. http://www.tale-of-tales.com/
- *The Path*. (2008). BVBA, Belgium.
- *The Night Journey*. (2009). Bill Viola and USC Game Lab.
- *Warmail*. (2008). J. Bailey.

Software

- 3-DgameStudio. http://www.3-Dgamestudio.com/
- Maya. http://usa.autodesk.com/adsk/servlet/index?id=7635018&siteID=123112
- 'NM2' toolkit. www.ist-nm2.org; www.shapeshift.tv
- Unity 3D. https://unity3d.com/

Case Studies

- Selsjord, M. (2013-2015). Marvellous Transformations. partially exhibited 'Norne Attersøm', Galleri Vanntårnet, Nesoddtangen, October 2013; Drøbak kunstforening: Varmbade, Norway October 2014 and Churchill College Cambridge, January 2015.
- Selsjord, M. (2009). Gardens of Dreaming. 3D music by Natasha Barrett. exhibited Henie Onstad Centre, Oslo, February 2009 http://home.no.net/mselsjor/; http://www.hok.no/.
- Selsjord, M. Still life with Oranges and Lemons after Francisco de Zurbarán (1598 – 1664)
- Thomas, M. (2010). Viking Seeress. (Frigg sung by Kariina Gretere, Heithur/Vala played by Helen McGregor; 3D real-time navigable set designed by Marianne Selsjord. Cambridge: DIGIS.
- Thomas, M. (2007). RuneCast (Heithur/Vala played by Helen McGregor; Music composed, performed and produced by Kariina Gretere; Video and Track-matte Graphic Artist/Animator: Brian Ashbee; 3D Artist and Additional Graphics: Marianne Selsjord; Interactive Programming/ Additional Design: Günther Heinrich; Interactive Design, Editing and Interactive AD: Ludvig

Lohse; Concept, Research, Writer, Interaction Designer, Director and Producer: Maureen Thomas). Production: Runecast Ltd UK/ Digital Studio, Dept of Architecture, University of Cambridge/New Media, New Millennium ('NM2' — Integrated Project (IP) partially funded by the European 6th Framework Programme: Information Society Technologies, *Cross-media content for leisure and entertainment* ailableion18-2-1) Issue (H, University of DIgital nel) ill, http://www.ist-nm2.org/). Exhibition: Ulster Festival of Art and Design June 2008 http://www.ulsterfestivalofartanddesign. com/; London Design Festival i-Creativity Expo, Southbank Centre, London Sept. 2007 http://www2.londondesignfestival.com/; Cambridge Film Festival, July 2007 http://www.cambridge-filmfestival.org.uk; *Women in Games* April 2007, Newport, Wales (preview/evaluation presentation) http://www.womeningames.com/.

- Thomas M. (2003). Songs of Vala. (Composed and sung by Kariina Gretere, Heithur/Vala played by Helen McGregor/Vala Thorsdóttir, Video by Brian Ashbee.) London/Reykjavik: Embla Productions/UNESCO/Ielandic Film Fund. Exhibition: City Hall Reykjavik.
- Thomas, M. (2001). Vala. (Heithur/Vala played by Helen McGregor; Music composed, performed and produced by Kariina Gretere; Interaction Design/Interactive Editing Ludvig Lohse). Malmö: Narrativity Studio, Interactive Institute/Cambridge: CUMIS.

Table 1. Selected research resources

Issue	References	Main Contribution
Art, Aesthetics, Engagement and Creative Digital Media	Boden, M. (2010). *Creativity and art: Three roads to surprise.* Oxford: Oxford University Press.	Exposition of combinational, exploratory and transformational creativity in relation to traditional and emerging art.
	Carroll, N. (2010/1999). *Philosophy of art.* London and New York: Routledge.	Examination of how art is understood through time.
	Catlow, R., Garrett, M. & Morgana, C. (2010).*Artists re:thinking games.* Liverpool: Liverpool University Press.	Artists' critical evaluation of the roles of art and games.
	De Oliveira, N., Oxley, N & Petry, M. (2004). *Installation art in the new millennium: The empire of the senses.* London: Thames & Hudson.	Comprehensive survey of international installation art.
	Ensslin, A. 2012. *The Language of gaming.* Basingstoke: Palgrave Macmillan.	Review, analysis and evaluation of the state of the art of gaming through the lens of communication and engagement.
	Kelly, M. (ed.). (1998). *The Encyclopedia of Aesthetics.* New York, Oxford: Oxford University Press.	Collected scholarship on aesthetics.
	Kozel, S. (2008). *Closer – performance, technologies, phenomenology.* Boston: MIT Press	Seeks to understand wider social uses of digital technologies using perspectives taken from phenomenology and dance.
	Langer, S. (1977 [1953]). *Feeling and form: A theory of art.* New York: Scribner Prentice Hall.	Examination of how form in Art embodies and evokes feeling.
	Laurel, B. & Joy, S. (ed.).(1990)*The Art of human computer interface design.* Reading, MA: Adison-Wesley.	Discussion of the principles of engagement with computer-handled work.
	Lovejoy, M. (2004). *Digital currents: Art in the electronic age.* New York/ Oxford: Routledge; and website: www.digitalcurrents.com/	Examination of changes in aesthetic experience and artists' roles brought about by digital technologies, offering a wide range of examples.
	Norman, D. A. (2013). *Design of everyday things: Revised and expanded.* New York: Basic Books. London: MIT Press.	Reflections on the way interaction design works and its role in mediating interactive experience.
	Reeves, S. (2011). *Designing interfaces in public settings: Understanding the role of the spectator in human-computer interaction.* Heidelberg: Springer-Verlag.	Review of the way people relate to interactive experience and how designers integrate them into interactive work.
	Rieser, M., & Zapp, A. (2002). *New screen media: Cinema/art/narrative.* London: BFI.	Expert essays on the relationships between traditional and emerging digital screen arts.
	Rogers, R., Sharp, H. & Preece, J. (Eds.). (2011). *Interaction design: Beyond human-computer interaction* (3rd ed.). Hoboken, NJ: John Wiley & Sons.	Examination of principles and practices in interaction design.
	Ryan, M-L. (2001). *Narrative as virtual reality: Immersion and interactivity in literature and electronic media.* Baltimore: Johns Hopkins University Press.	Examination of how traditional and emerging digital work engage through form and structure as well as content.
	Shaer, O. &Hornecker, E. (2010). *Tangible user interfaces.* Delft: Now Publishers Inc.	Review of how human senses can be engaged in interaction with computer-handled content.
	Solarski,C. (2012). *Drawing basics and video game art: Classic to cutting-edge art techniques for winning video game design.* NewYork: Watson-Guptill.	Examination of ways in which traditional art history and theory can inform the art of video game design.
Artistic Practice and Research	Biggs, M. and Karlsson, H. (ed.). (2010) *The Routledge companion to research in the arts.* London: Routledge.	Review of approaches to and outcomes of research in the Arts.
	Candy, L., & Ferguson, S. (2014). *Interactive experience in the digital age: Evaluating new art practice.* Heidelberg: Springer.	Explores digital art where evaluation is embedded in the creative process to reveal and enhance practice.
	Digital Creativity (2004) (Special issue on practice-based research/practice as research) 15 (1) & 15 (2).	Examples and discussion of controversy, issues and projectsin practice and research in the digital arts.
	Karlsson, H. (2002). *Handslag, famntag, klapp eller kyss? (Handshake, hug, pat or kiss?)* (Artistic research training in Sweden. Summary in English.) Gothenburg: Sister (Swedish Institute for Studies in Education and Research)	Sustained study of practice-based art research and its results.
	Kunsthøgskolen i Bergen: *Stipendprogrammet for kunstneriskutviklingsarbeid* 2003 – 2008.	Report on structure and success of support for individual artists carrying out practice as research and practice-based research via a state fellowship programme
	Wilson, M. & van Ruiten, S., (eds) (2014). *SHARE Handbook for artistic research education.* ELIA and http://www.sharenetwork.eu/resources/share-handbook.	Collected reflections on preparing for research/practice in Art.

continued on following page

Table 1. Continued

Issue	References	Main Contribution
Digital Arts Conferences	DRHA (Digital Research in the Humanities and Arts	Conferences and events, mainly regular, in which academics, professionals and artists present papers about policy, ideas and current projects, some including project expos, usually followed by publication of proceedings.
	ELIA (European League of Institutes of the Art*s*)	
	EVA (Electronic information and Visual Arts)	
	iDMAa (International Digital Media and Arts Association)	
	IFFACCA (International Federation of Arts Councils and Culture Agencies)	
	ISEA International (formerly Inter-Society for the Electronic Arts)	
	Media Art History www.mediaarthistory.org/	
	VSMM (Virtual Systems and MultiMedia)	
Art and Technology Research Centres Some representative centres carrying out practice-based research and rapid prototyping of innovative projects	Art+Com (DE) www.artcom.de	
	Banff Centre www.banffcentre.ca/	
	Carnegie Mellon (US) www.cmu.edu/research/	
	Creativity and Cognition Studio Sydney http://www.creativityandcognition.com/	
	Culture Lab Newcastle (UK) www.ncl.ac.uk/culturelab/	
	Digital Studio for Research in Design, Visualisation & Communication (Cambridge, UK) www.expressivespace.org	
	Education for practice based research, Leiden www.hum.leiden.edu/creative-performing-arts/	
	FoAM http://fo.am/	
	Goldsmiths Digital Studios (UK) www.gold.ac.uk/gds/	
	Georgia Institute of Technology School of Literature, Communication and Culture (US) www.lcc.gatech.edu/school/research.php	
	Hexagram http://hexagram.concordia.ca/	
	Interactive Institute (SE) www.tii.se/	
	M-Cult (FI) www.m-cult.org/	
	Media Lab Helsinki https://medialab.aalto.fi/	
	MIT Media Lab (US)www.media.mit.edu	
	Research Studios (London, Paris, Berlin, Barcelona) www.researchstudios.com/home/home.php	
	Computer Arts www.computerarts.co.uk/in_depth/interviews/research_studios	
	Research Studio Austria www.researchstudio.at/home_en.html	
	Wales Institute for Research in Art and Design (WIRAD) (UK) www.wirad.ac.uk/ esp. Synergy Group	

continued on following page

Table 1. Continued

Issue	References	Main Contribution
Creativity, Cognition and Play	Boden, M. (2004/1990). *The creative mind: myths and mechanisms.* London: Routledge.	Cognitive definition and taxonomy of creativity.
	Bogost, I. (2011). *How to do things with videogames.* Minneapolis: University of Minnesota Press.	Discussion of media ecology including creativity, play and art.
	Brown, S. (2009). *Play.* New York: Avery.	Survey of social, physical and mental functions and benefits of play.
	Caillois, R. (2001). *Man, play, and games.* Urbana and Chicago: University of Illinois Press (originally published 1958; translated from the French by Meyer Barash).	Examines the means by which games become part of daily life and ultimately contribute to various cultures their most characteristic customs and institutions.
	Csikszentmihalyi, M. (1996). *Creativity.* New York: Harper Collins.	Examines the creative process and explains how creativity enriches lives.
	Dovey, J. and Kennedy, H. (ed.). (2006). *Game cultures: Computer games as new media.* Maidenhead: Open University Press.	Examination of the range from ludology through engagement and embodiment to co-creation and blurring between production and consumption.
	Finke, R., Ward, T., & Smith, S. (1992). *Creative cognition: Theory, research, and applications.* Cambridge, MA: MIT Press.	Combines new experiments and existing work in cognitive psychology to provide an account of the cognitive processes and structures that contribute to creative thinking and discovery.
	Gray, P. (2013). *Free to learn: Why unleashing the instinct to play will make our children happier, more self-reliant and better students for life.* New York: Basic Books.	Argues that children, if free to pursue their own interests through play, will not only learn all they need to know, but will do so with energy and passion.
	Huizinga, J. (1955). *Homo ludens; a study of the play-element in culture.* Boston: Beacon Press.	Explores culture as an expression of play.
	Juul, J. (2011). *Half-real: Video games: Between real rules and fictional worlds.* Cambridge, MA: MIT Press	Examines the constantly evolving tension between rules and fiction in video games.
	Sansi, R. (2014). *Art, anthropology and the gift.* London & New York: Bloomsbury Academic.	An examination of the way anthropology, art and the scholarship about them can inform each other.
User Generated Content/Expert Creative Art	Brown, K. (2014). Interactive Contemporary Art: Participation in Practice. London: I.B. Tauris.	Offers a perspective on international interactive artincluding case studies, considering dimensions of interactivity from the technological to the political.
	Dezeuze, A. (ed.). (2010). *The 'Do-it-yourself' artwork: Participation from Fluxus to new media.* Manchester: Manchester University Press.	Reviews critically kinetic art, happenings, environments, performance, installations, relational and new media artworks that only come to life when you - the viewer - are invited to 'do it yourself.'
	Keen, A. (2007). *The Cult of the amateur.* London/Boston: Nicolas Brealey.	Presents the case for the expert in the digital environment.

Chapter 9
"Virtual Reality" Reconsidered

Garfield Benjamin
University of Wolverhampton, UK

ABSTRACT

The term 'virtual reality' is used widely in contemporary culture to evoke the false worlds of the imagination digital technology has enabled us to create. However, the term itself remains ill defined, particularly amidst recent developments in theories of virtuality and reality that have left contradictory marks on VR. The phrase 'virtual reality' has become problematic, and is in need of a reconsideration for its continued relevance. This chapter assesses the term throughout its development and in the context of other theorisations such as cinema and cyberspace that have dominated recent digital theory. Taking the Deleuzian expansion of the Virtual and the Lacanian expansion of the Real, the chapter interrogates the constituent processes of VR to suggest a new mode of conceiving the technologies in terms of a parallax between virtual-real and physical-digital within contemporary thought, which will then be applied to a conceptual framework for digital creative practices.

INTRODUCTION

Within the many varied, and often incongruous, theories of digital technology and its culture there are two strands of the discussion that have emerged in which the very terms of the field are challenged. These are centred on the problematic notion of 'virtual reality' that has dominated cultural depictions of the digital world, usually taking either 'virtual' or 'real' in an expanded definition to draw out a deeper understanding of the fundamental differences, connections and interdependency between physical and digital spaces. Digital media has called into question the appearance of 'reality', forcing all theories

of contemporary culture to take into account the possibility of other spaces with which the (physical) human subject can engage. There is a need to expand and intersect current discussions of the relation between virtual and real by exploring the antagonisms that arise through developing both sides of the term. This chapter will therefore readdress the term 'virtual reality' in the context of ongoing debates in philosophy, technology and creative practice in a discussion of subjectivity in contemporary digital society, to insist on a constant re-evaluation of the terms used in such a discussion and their ramifications for its application in digital media and creative technologies.

DOI: 10.4018/978-1-4666-8205-4.ch009

The expansion of the term 'virtual' often takes into account the definition developed by Gilles Deleuze (2004a; 2004b) as a surface that is not actual but with which the subject can engage. This has been applied to digital media as an alternative to the conflation of 'virtual' as 'digital', as is implied in the labels 'virtual reality' or 'virtual worlds', to instead connect the fluidity of digital surfaces to consciousness in a relation consistent with other generative effects within the structures that form the idealist element in Deleuzian philosophy. Anna Munster (2006) emphasises the role of affect by placing the virtual as a part of the materiality of the digital. While this work and others take important steps towards establishing the problematic of embodiment, the focus on the materiality of the digital obscures its relation to consciousness and leads back into limited use of the term 'real'. There is a clear Deleuzian influence in Munster's work, and both Deleuze and Félix Guattari are referenced heavily in relation to the virtual, as well as notions of flow, diagram and time. Between the two expanded terms, however, there remains little crossover in current literature. Rob Shields (2003), Brian Massumi (2002) and Andrew Murphie (2002), for example, all utilise the Deleuzian virtual while persistently conflating it with the digital, and largely fail to mention the real outside of its direct and 'common sense' connotation of the physical.

How the individual relates to the plethora of potential realities available in contemporary society and its philosophies (physical, digital, social, semantic, oneiric) can be understood in redefining the term 'real' according to Lacan (1977), particularly as applied to cultural phenomena by Žižek (2008a). Writers such as David Gunkel (2010) have furthered this notion, drawing out the real across physical and digital worlds as the hidden causality (for example, quantum wave functions, DNA or bits of computer code) that underpins the appearance of objective reality. This real is inaccessible and terrifying, embedded within the psychoanalytical construct of contemporary subjectivity. Throughout the field, the antagonism between virtuality and reality persists as a theoretical pariah between physical and digital reality, media and creative processes. Žižek's (2012) own discussion of the matter simply places Deleuze's virtual as Lacan's real. While acknowledging the importance of the reality of the virtual opposed to 'virtual reality', Žižek confuses the nuances of the two processes within consciousness and their functions in the generation of contemporary subjectivity, creativity and society. The antagonistic relation between the real and the virtual, in the expanded sense of both terms, will form an integral method of analysis throughout the chapter, and reconciling Žižekian and Deleuzian philosophies will provide an informative step towards understanding the relation between virtuality and reality.

This chapter will separate and explicate the two expanded terms, defining the Real as the presupposition governing the way reality 'really' appears to us and the virtual as the forces outside of actualisation that nevertheless impact upon reality. From this theoretical exposition, a discussion can be raised concerning the redefinition of our relation to digital technologies under such terms. Digital media in general and virtual reality in particular are commonly associated with processes of simulation. Indeed the phrase 'computer simulation' dominates the lexicon of many technological applications with a focus on representing the physical world within digital space. However, in the context of this expanded set of terms, the digital appears as a simulation-of-simulation. That is, where simulation is, according to Baudrillard (1994), an appearance with no link to reality, the appearance on the computer screen is precisely defined by the reality of computer code.

This turn – in which digital space can stake at least an equal claim to reality as the physical universe amidst the breakdown of material certainty seen in quantum physics, genetics and poststructuralist linguistics – enacts an ontological levelling between physical and digital worlds, and in particular their manner of appearance to human subjects. Both of these processes are present within physical and digital worlds, necessitating a separation of the virtual from the digital and the real from the physical, towards a consideration of the shifts between spaces that construct contemporary subjectivity. This shift will be explained according to Žižek's (2009) ontological notion of parallax, applied to the differences between physical and digital worlds, in order to theorise a creative and subjective application of digital technologies. When both terms, virtual and real, are viewed in their relations to one another occurring within consciousness, it is their differing modes of assemblage that defines the parallax of the digital. This is based on the manner of subjective presupposition underlying each 'reality': matter for physical, code for digital. Levelling these realities enables freer modes of discussion to emerge across cultural artefacts in physical and digital media, constructing a critical space for a more open debate of the creative application of digital technologies.

The chapter will thus form a critical overview of past and current discussions of virtual reality in the field of digital media, suggesting innovative modes of interrogating the creative potentialities of digital media. While the discussion will focus on the role of VR in relation to the individual consciousness, as a creative extension of thought and alternative realm for the mind to inhabit, VR exists also as a site of potential social exchange. The critical and creative use of VR, however, extends beyond the mere interaction between individuals that constitutes the social arena. The multiplicity of a collective assemblage of creativity demonstrates the same fundamental relations as the internal assemblage of the individual subject across physical and digital worlds. The discussion will therefore apply the individual subject to a collective subject of enunciation of a potential future post-individual society whereby VR offers new spaces of blurred boundaries for minds to move freely and for creative potential to emerge between individual consciousnesses. This

will draw towards concluding remarks that offer a new definition of virtual reality, a challenge to established modes of thinking digital media, and a call for a constant re-thinking of the terms with which we construct our engagement with digital technologies within our subjective position between ever more permeated virtual realities.

ORIGINS AND DEVELOPMENT

In order to assess and reconsider the position of virtual reality today, and its impact on future directions for technological innovation, artistic creation and thought, the development of the term and its scholarship must first be traced in a critical history of VR as a technology and virtual reality as a term. While there were pre-digital attempts at constructing mechanical immersive displays, the beginning of this history as a working VR technology using computers rests in 1965 with Ivan Sutherland's revolutionary, if unwieldy, 'Sword of Damocles' project. While not labelling his device as VR, Sutherland described a vision of the potential for this new technology:

A looking glass into a mathematical wonderland... There is no reason why the objects displayed by a computer have to follow the rules of ordinary physical reality...The ultimate display would, of course, be a room within which the computer can control the existence of matter. (Sutherland, 1965, pp. 506-508)

The aim was to create not replications of physical space, nor even imaginary worlds, but the rearrangement and redefinition of reality itself. Despite this revolutionary vision, it took over twenty years for the term virtual reality to emerge, coined and popularised by Jaron Lanier in the mid-1980s (Heim, 1998, p. 16). Where Sutherland had emphasised control over matter, Lanier's focus was on the mind, resulting in an image of VR as part of the increasing array of computerised communication tools, specifically for the sharing of the imagination in multisensory, immersive constructs (*Ibid.*). The ontological implications of VR were first considered directly by Michael Heim in *The Metaphysics of Virtual Reality* (1993), which sought to define this "new layer of reality" (p. 118). While the terms virtual and real are not developed beyond the simple opposition of digital and physical, the various constituent processes, potentialities and perils of VR are situated in the text's position regarding VR technology's early development. Heim's placing of the virtual as a supplementary or expanded dimension of conventional reality echoes the early work in cybernetics, which sought to expand human intellect (Ashby, 1957; Licklider, 1960; Engelbart, 1962), drawing some initial remarks on the impact of VR technologies in redefining our modes of thinking.

However, the ontological expansion of VR remained in the minority, as futuristic visions of technology were quickly subsumed by practical application. Increasing availability led to an interest in VR from not only technologists and theorists, but from the finance and entertainment industries. Howard Rheingold's text, *Virtual Reality* (1992), displays this tension, with an optimistic outlook on the use of the technology limited by reducing the manipulation of matter to staging physical reality (in, for example, surgery or particle physics), reducing creative expression to its entertainment value. Further work on the nature and impact of VR technology appeared in texts by, for example, Alan Wexelblat (1993) and the National Research Council (Durlach & Mavor, 1995). In this latter text, "some psychological considerations" (pp. 93-110) focuses on the nature of control, reducing the human to an operator, and the construction of telepresence, reducing subjectivity to a measure of 'realism' against illusion, in technologies designed largely for communication over creativity. While the collection does acknowledge the need for studies of human behaviour and the implications of VR on social structures, the project of scientists serving industrial and governmental aims creates the impression that any such developments would be rapidly patented and/or weaponised.

These developments in technology and our conception of it were drawn swiftly into the exploitation of VR by business (in, for example, Thierauf, 1995; Chorafas & Steinmann, 1995) to improve communication and productivity through the manipulation of the mind by corporate interests: not a cybernetic expansion but a machinic reduction of humans to productive devices, a lasting stain on the evolution of the virtual. This reductionist tendency, of both VR technology and its relation to human users, is furthered in Frank Biocca and Mark Levy's collection (1995), which focuses on VR as "a tantalizing communication medium" (p. vii). While this simply places the virtual as a digital space of whimsy opposed to physical Reality, it recognised the limitations of VR technology of the time, with its "look and feel of a prototype" (Biocca, Kim & Levy, 1995, p. 13), and highlighted the constant need for innovation, even placing the early VR dream as an unachievable goal, a "techno-Godot" (*Ibid.*) for which we will always be waiting. While this is framed in a discussion of VR as an entertainment tool, the consideration of social implications overtly introduced the role of desire in our relation to VR, shedding a critical light on the earlier vision of Sutherland as the constant striving by humanity for control over the reality in which it resides.

The first critical reconsideration of the term appeared in Heim's later text *Virtual Realism* (1998), which criticised the "pale ghosts of virtual reality, invoking "virtual" to mean anything based on computers" (p. 3). Yet he was not attempting to expand or develop the term but, rather, to insist on a purer definition as "a technology, not simply a nebulous idea" (p. 2). Within his "pragmatic interpretation of virtual reality as a functional, non-representational phenomenon that gains ontological weight through its practical applications (p. 220), however, emerges a negotiation of the relation between virtuality and reality. Thus, while this middle ground of 'virtual realism' between techno-utopian idealism and fear of a loss of reality to technology may reduce the conception of VR to a technological position under the domination of the 'primary reality' of physical human experience (p. 218), Heim's discussion formed an instructive step in discussions of the term, opening up the value judgements of the technology's potential impact. The importance of our social and cognitive relation to VR began to emerge even within the limitation of the label. Heim's bold claim for a definition of "the "real" virtual reality" (p. 6) based on "immersion, interactivity and information intensity" (p. 7) reveals the need to bridge the "intrinsic remoteness from direct human experience" (Heim, 1993, p. 18) with, not only accurate graphical rendering that leads to the techno-Godot of "data idealism" (Heim, 1998, p. 139) lost in a spiralling desire for perfect sensory replication, but new modes of thinking our relation to technologies, further emphasising their role in shaping human thought.

The lack of expansion of the VR label itself throughout the 1990s – even by Heim, the so-called 'philosopher of cyberspace' (Lovink, 1994) – did little to alleviate the need for Peter Fisher and David Unwin (2002) to state that "although, and perhaps because, 'virtual reality' is a very trendy term, neither 'virtual' nor 'reality' is either well defined or strictly appropriate" (p. 1). Even this criticism of the term, in a text applying VR as a tool for the field of Geography, states the problem but not the solution, settling again on a strictly technological definition: "the ability of the user of a constructed view of a limited digitally-encoded information domain to change their view in three dimensions causing update of the view presented to any viewer, especially the user" (*Ibid.*). The increasing recognition, for example by Richard Brice (1997), of the "interdisciplinary nature of multimedia and VR development" (p. 6), led to a splintering of VR across fields, necessitating the perpetuation of a simple, technological, practical definition that could be applied in engineering

and design contexts. William Sherman and Alan Craig (2003), for example, lay out a design-based approach focused on the application of technology with clear aims (a convincing and 'realistic' immersive experience) and a limited consideration of theoretical positions (other than perhaps the informational theory approaches that appear as an unquestioned truth of computer science) in favour of a practical manual. The notion of 'understanding' VR is here the ability to follow design conventions in achieving successful business-serving outcomes, constructed from a view of 'realism' as a debate between a full simulation of physical realism (adhering to all the rules and limitations of our own physical world) and a visual realism that allows for 'magical' occurrences and the staging of imaginary situations (Sherman & Craig 2003, p. 384), referred to as a clearly defined and restricted scheme of the "realism axis…a continuous line proceeding from highly verisimilar to highly abstract" (p. 213) against which the virtual (and VR in particular) can and should be measured.

However, this scientific positivism applied to a practical design mentality demonstrates that even within the constant limitation of the term virtual reality there is a process of contextual specification that results in a variation of its implications and use. This problem had been identified as the increasing tendency towards "as many 'virtual realities' as there are researchers actively involved in VR" (Brodlie et al., 2002, p.7), an acknowledgement by other fields (here Geography) of their problematic interaction with VR due to the interdisciplinary, fragmented and ill-defined nature of virtual reality as a term. However, the response to such issues is often a lowest common denominator of accepted conventions, highlighting but accepting the limited the view of the term(s) outside of their application to specific relevant aspects of other fields. Indeed, the term virtual reality became largely reduced to such a limited scope as a specific technological tool throughout the early 2000s, and by the mid-2000s had become subsumed in the widening array of terminologies and theoretical trends through which digital technology was being discussed. As a unified term, it appeared that virtual reality had lost its impact, after its sensationalist and liberal use in advertising and its fear-mongering distortion in cinema and popular culture (for example, the oft-cited dystopic view of an oppressive future under the machinic regime of sentient VR in *The Matrix*). The position of VR in relation to these emerging and developing terms must therefore be interrogated before the constituent elements of virtuality and reality can be renegotiated towards a contemporary context.

OTHER PERSPECTIVES

With the general positioning of VR as a specific technology within the increasingly diverse manifestations of digital media, it is necessary to situate the term in the context of other conceptual formulations of the digital against the physical world, in terms of our interaction with, relation to and position between both spaces. The domination of mass media by the cinematic tradition, with its inclusion of the 3-D immersive technologies and photo-realistic computer graphics that could leap developments in VR greatly forward, has entrenched its hegemonic position over explicitly digital media in general and VR in particular. As Nicholas Gane and David Beer (2008) have suggested, VR has never been able to overcome the dominance of the screen (p. 57), not only in terms of the physical necessity of screen-based apparatus but also in terms of the structures of the digitised gaze. Lev Manovich (2001) carries this filmic view further into his theoretical framework of digital media and VR technologies, writing that "with a VRML interface, nature is firmly subsumed under culture. The eye is subordinated to the kino-eye. The body is subordinated to the virtual body of the virtual camera" (p. 83). This reduces VR technologies to a subservient role within interactive cinema, referencing the trend that of the "virtual camera" in computer interfaces

that uses cinematic language and techniques as a visual toolkit for digital representation (pp. 80f; 298f), subsuming the virtual and the computer generated images associated with VR under the cinematic process. This fusion of distinct processes within filmic mass media engrains the dominance of cinematic language that limits a new, genuinely digital mode of thinking. Manovich doesn't expand term virtual, but rather conflates virtual with digital[1] and echoes earlier design-based texts by referring to the 'reality effect' as a marker of reference to the physical world. Manovich (2013) repeatedly displays a preoccupation with "view control" (p. 75) and imposing (or constantly reasserting, forbidding any development of new language) a cinematic language on the digital. While he does admit another way of working in, for example games (pp. 193-4), this is placed as secondary to his filmic project as a practitioner and theorist of interactive cinema placing cinema as "*the* cultural interface" (Manovich, 2001, p. 86). Alexander Galloway (2012, p.1) acknowledges both Manovich's influence and limitations, as does Mark Hansen (2004, p. 33) in highlighting Manovich's clear investment in cinema as a theoretical framework. The failing of Manovich's framework demonstrates the wider shift away from writing about VR in itself towards its inclusion as part of 'new media'. While this has, despite Manovich's own limited use of the terms, led to the expansion of the notion of the virtual in VR, as part of the general development of debates concerning the virtuality of digital technologies and cultures, it has diminished the critical attention to VR in general as its own term. The term 'new media' has sought to supplant specific discussions of digital technologies and their social and cognitive uses in an attempt to construct a common language that has succeeded only in a mass conflation and limitation of terms under pre-established fields.

This shift into 'new media theory' has been characterised by an increasing obsession with embodiment. This view is already seen in Heim's (1998) definition of VR in relation to 'virtual realism' focusing on "substituting the primary sensory input with data received produced by a computer" towards a state where "the user identifies with the virtual body and feels a sense of belonging to a virtual community" (p. 221). This emphasises telepresence and artificial reality incorporating a full body immersive experience detailed and accurate enough to create a suspension of disbelief. This suspension is apparent in Katherine Hayles's (1999) conception of virtuality, reasserting Donna Haraway's position (1985) in an explicitly (digital) technological context, as "the cultural perception that material objects are interpenetrated by information" (Hayles, 1999, p. 13). The focus on the body has penetrated VR in the form of the avatar, the embedding of the gaze into a representation of the human form to replace the lost physical frame in digital space. This system of interface now dominates digital environments such as Second Life, as well as the computer game medium with the third-person view and focus on the avatar in popular MMORPGs such as *World of Warcraft*. Mark Hansen (2006) appears to make some progress in establishing the emerging need to discuss "a fluid interpretation of realms…a mixed reality stage", yet limits himself to "the central role played by the body in the interface to the virtual" (p. 2). This is based on the same error as Hayles in defining the virtual as a filling of (physical) space with information rather than either the creation of new spaces (as is the conventional design/technological view of VR) or a mode of viewing and creating spaces within thought (as is presented and elaborated in this chapter). Anna Munster (2006) makes a conscious and purposeful effort to reinsert the body and affect into the digital, placing virtuality as a part of materiality rather than as a force of framing and function in relation to our perspective on a given world. This work, with its focus on "the point of intersection that digital flows have with issues of embodiment" (p. 24), remains entrenched within the materiality that furthers the dominance of physicality of the digital in any system where

embodiment becomes the key concern. This tendency has coincided with the development of new media as a term (see, for example Hansen, 2006), drawing the focus even further away from the specificity of terms such as virtual reality in the fusion of cinematic and embodied gazes as the presiding cultural interface.

There is a clear Deleuzian influence in Munster's work, and both Deleuze and Guattari are referenced heavily in relation to the virtual, as well as notions of flow, diagram and time. While this begins to question and expand the notion of the virtual in virtual reality, it does so only through its emphasis on embodied materiality and the dominance of the 'real' reality of the physical. This move is seen also in the work of Massumi (2002), who engages with a more explicit confrontation with the virtual. Here the problematic role of the body is emphasised in the relation to the virtual, when he writes that "a word for the "real but abstract" incorporeality of the body is the *virtual*." (p. 21). Massumi makes a necessary move into the body as a conceptual tool rather than material object, but adds a series of conflations between the Deleuzian conceptual Body without Organs and the specific physical body; and between the virtual as a function of thought and as digital technology. Within a scheme of the body, the division of virtual and real cannot escape an alignment with physical and digital, and all its attendant hierarchies. Žižek (2012), cultural philosopher of the elusive Lacanian real, is instructive here in the struggle against what he labels the "imbecilic inertia of material reality" (p. 127). We must broaden our scope of the body, and materiality in general, to reconsider the relation of VR to consciousness and subjectivity. A starting point for this shift appears in Žižek's (2009) statement "I never "am" my body" (p. 227), in direct opposition to Maurice Merleau-Ponty's (2002) claim of the body as "our general medium for having a world" (p. 146), an oft quoted trope in scholarship concerning the body and the digital. This entails a move beyond the embodied view of technology as a prosthetic for humanity, in a return to the early conceptions of cybernetics as a tool for expanding intelligence, in the context of this expansion of virtuality and reality as relations of consciousness. As Massumi (2002) describes the postbiological self-modifications of the obsolete body in the art performances of Stelarc, our task is that of "extending intelligence beyond the earth" (p. 99): the positioning of the mind itself as a virtual reality in a physical digital hybrid.

Such a consideration of cybernetics, which underpins the fundamental relation between human consciousness and its extension by both the technologies themselves and the symbolic realms they bring into being, draws into focus the implications of VR as sensory feedback, evident in early conceptions of information processing including a human subject within the system. While stemming from a limiting view of VR, from the fields of design and engineering, the alignment with the early cybernetic vision of expanding the human mind suggests an innate step towards the cyborg subject as a technological posthuman (although perhaps, here and more generally, a cognitive superhuman). By reinserting Sutherland's aim of the control of the human mind (via computer technologies) over matter, we approach what Nick Bostrom and Anders Sandberg (2009) conceive as "intimate links between the external systems and the human user through better interaction... less an external tool and more of a mediating "exoself"...embedding the human within an augmenting "shell" such as wearable computers or virtual reality" (p. 320). Yet this state is not merely applicable in a digital environment, for the same virtuality is present in the physical world. Beyond the confines of embodiment, the embedding of a subjective perspective, demonstrated in VR, within any 'reality' always creates a 'shell' of augmentation, be it a sensory or abstract construct, allowing for interaction with a world through the mediation of thought. By expanding the human mind, we can expand the potential environments with which humanity can interact.

Indeed, the lesson of early cybernetics is that we must first rethink the relation of thought to itself if we are to engage with the abstract and alternative worlds that VR could enable (rather than the anthropocentric reality mimicking our own current situation that often dominates VR culture). While this is in danger of recalling the fictional extension of abstract spaces for increasing intelligence exemplified to disastrous consequences in the 1992 film *The Lawnmower Man*, the quest for transcending both the current limits of human thought and the barriers between human and computer, physical and digital, reaffirms the role of VR as a 'techno-Godot'. This constant process of desire for expanding ourselves alongside the development of technology enforces a constant questioning of the terms by which we are operating, thus the influence of cybernetics on VR has and could still assert the need for a rethinking of our relation to such technologies and the spaces they can create.

The impact of cybernetics and the need to reconsider our conceptions of space in VR leads to a discussion of the cultural influence of cyberspace. While cybernetics has suffered a limiting conception as prosthetics (after Haraway and with the need for practical applications such as replacement limbs for the privileged physical human body), and VR has been limited in scope through its connection to specific technologies, cyberspace has undergone the opposite process. Emerging as a term (Gibson, 1984) at approximately the same time as virtual reality, cyberspace has become a greatly abstracted notion that is perhaps itself in need of further reconsideration in a contemporary context. However, while VR's reinterpretation has often been a simplification to enable a more precise use across disciplines, the interdisciplinary nature of cyberspace has been discussed and developed in its cultural role. Nevertheless, simultaneously symbolising the transmission of information across global computer networks and the imaginary spaces with which we envisage contemporary virtuality, cyberspace has, like virtual reality, succumbed to a commodification in advertising and mass media that has rendered its position disparate, imprecise and confused. John Perry Barlow (1996) claims cyberspace as an independent "civilization of the Mind", while Manovich (2001) rejects the notion of a singular cyberspace, stating that "virtual spaces are most often not true spaces but collections of spaces... there is no space in cyberspace" (p. 253), and Don Ihde (2012) suggests that cyberspace is merely "the technological capacity to bring the remote near" (p. 326). The underlying 'reality' of cyberspace is tackled more directly by Žižek (1999), stating that "how cyberspace will affect us is not directly inscribed into its technological properties; rather it hinges on the network of socio-symbolic relations which always-already overdetermine the way cyberspace affects us" (p. 123). This acknowledgement of the impact of pre-existing structures of culture and thought (for example, the pressures of industry and defence on the development of technologies, or the determination of digital interfaces by the cinematic tradition) suggests a need to *rethink* the conditions under which cyberspace is constructed. This is furthered by David Gunkel's insistence on the need to 'hack' cyberspace as a term:

Cyberspace is, from the moment of its fabrication, radically indeterminate. It comprises an empty signifier that not only antedates any formal referent but readily and without significant resistance receives almost every meaning that comes to be assigned to it. (Gunkel, 2000, p. 815)

The term cyberspace itself, as well as its continued and developing use, must be constantly reconsidered. The same applies to virtual reality in its role beyond a specific technology, as the process of creating new and alternative spaces for the mind to inhabit. This relation to the mind spreads from the individual to the collective and indeed to its function within society as a whole. Thus, in order to constantly 'hack' the terms

under which the discussion of VR occurs, we must reconceive the framework within which we think such (physical, digital and cognitive) spaces in order to rethink and redefine the role of these technologies in the future of our society.

The position of VR and other computer technologies in society brings into question the availability of and access to such technologies and the inclusion or exclusion of individuals from the emerging cultures surrounding them. The 'digital divide' was first discussed in a series of three reports by the US Department of Commerce (1995; 1998; 1999) that recognised the unequal access to both computer technology and internet infrastructures across various different boundaries and social divisions. The 2003 World Summit on the Informational Society brought the necessity of a resolution to the digital divide to the global arena:

We are also fully aware that the benefits of the information technology revolution are today unevenly distributed between the developed and developing countries and within societies. We are fully committed to turning this digital divide into a digital opportunity for all (World Summit on the Informational Society, 2003).

While this statement sets out the intention to overcome the inequalities created by computer technologies, the social implications of the massive global increase in technology remain a key division in contemporary society. Such a situation places VR firmly within the realm of the technological 'haves', and any cognitive advantages or conceptual freedoms that the technologies enable remain the purview of an elite few. The causal relation of the technology to such divisions, however, is questionable. The vision of early cyberneticians and VR technologists and theorists is of an improved society, expanded intellect and ultimately control over reality for all human beings. David Gunkel (2003) had again, and in the same year as the World Summit, suggested the need to rethink the conditions and assumptions under which we define these technologies, stating that "the 'digital divide' is originally and persistently plural…there is not one digital divide; there is a constellation of different and intersecting social, economic, and technological differences" (p. 504). This disruption of a simple binary between 'haves' and 'have nots' emphasises the complex integration of technology within society, and the pre-existence of societal inequality that placed the technologies in an always already divided world. We might also extend these notions to VR itself. There is not one virtual reality (or concept of) for us to access as an alternative space but rather a series of processes, each of which forms a virtual reality in the ever expanding multiverse of subjective experience. Gunkel explains that "it is, then, not a matter of finding the 'right' theory and applying it consistently, but of using theory dynamically to open the 'digital divide' to critical reflection" (p. 517), which again emphasises the need to constantly rethink our relation to and conditions for technologies such as virtual reality. Rather than the establishing of a rigid binary hierarchy, as can be seen in the persistent privileging of the physical over the digital, of 'real' reality over virtual reality, there is at work a hyperbolic expansion of the digital metaverse: an increasingly complex web of access, censorship, ownership and subversion through which humans struggle to navigate. This new mode of plural reality requires a not only new set of technological tools and literacies, but a new mode of consciousness concerning the underlying Reality of contemporary virtual society: a new understanding of our relation to virtual reality.

THE VIRTUAL

The first step in a genuine reconsideration of virtual reality must be a renegotiation and new understanding of its constituent conceptual components. The virtual, often conflated with the term 'digital' in contemporary culture and theory, has received a great deal of attention in expanding its definition and impact beyond and within digital technology. The work of Gilles Deleuze (2004a) has here been of greatest relevance to the field in developing the term as a relation of abstract processes to human thought and its relation to the world. His definition of the term places a strong link to the mental realm of the Idea as "pure virtuality" (p. 349). Deleuze emphasises the virtual as a series of relations within an Idealist construction, suggesting an alternative space or mode of viewing the world built on difference as a process. He further states that, in the passage from Ideal to material, "the actualisation of the virtual…always takes place by difference, divergence or differenciation" (p. 265). Thus conceived, the virtual appears as the manifestation of thought itself, the differential relations that bring specific thoughts into being as the coalescing of an Idea. Within Deleuze's linguistic constructions of society and reality, this virtuality is not a part of the material universe, nor our knowledge of it, but rather an adjacent space of the mind in which consciousness occurs as a process. Therefore, "whatever totalizations knowledge may perform, they remain asymptotic to the virtual totality of *langue* or language" (Deleuze, 2004b, p. 58), that is, no matter how detailed an image of the actual material universe we may strive to achieve, the virtual remains forever approaching yet separate from such a space. Massumi (2002) elucidates this as the limits of consciousness, as a construction of language shaping thought, writing that "it is only by reference to the limit that what approaches it has a function: the limit is what gives the approach its effectivity, its reality. The limit is not unreal. It is virtual. It is reality-giving" (p. 147). This supports and expands Deleuze and Guattari's (2004b) own definition of the virtual as being "real without being actual, and consequently continuous…an "alternative continuity" that is virtual yet real" (pp. 104-5). In this development and elaboration of Deleuze's theoretical position in collaboration with Guattari, there emerges the space, separate from the material world, of a "virtual cosmic continuum of which even holes, silences, ruptures, and breaks are a part" (p. 106). This complete reality in itself, in the space of the abstract and the Ideal, displays the "virtual continuum of life" (p. 122) that forms the differentiating relation of consciousness to the world.

In the relation of the virtual realm of the Idea to consciousness as a linguistic construct,[2] Deleuze and Guattari write that "the abstract machine of language is not universal, or even general, but singular; it is not actual but virtual-real; it has, not invariable or obligatory rules, but optional rules that ceaselessly vary with the variation itself, as in a game in which each move changes the rules" (p. 110). This machinic functioning of the virtual brings it close to the common usage of the term (in, for example, the conventional definitions of VR) as synonymous with digital, but Massumi (2002) warns us "not to confuse the digital with the virtual" (p. 142), and it is in Deleuze and Guattari's placement of the virtual as a process that constantly changes its own rules[3] that we see an overt confrontation with the rigidity of binary logic. Whereas the language of computer code precisely defines digital reality as a necessary condition of its ability to function, the virtual in consciousness acts as the underlying process of abstraction that allows thought to occur as such in free singularities detached from actualisation. The problematic relation between virtual and digital lies in the implications of Deleuze's opposition of the virtual to the real. Shields (2003) states that "the virtual is often contrasted with the 'real' in commonsensical language by many writers who have not paused to examine the implications of the terms they are using" (p. 19), yet Shields himself offers only a one-sided expansion of these terms focusing, as the title of his text suggests, on the virtual under an application of Deleuzian theory to economics and risk, opposing the virtual to the concrete in economics and to the abstract in culture (pp. xvi; 17) while still struggling with an inconsistent conflation of digital and virtual when speaking of online communities and environments. The move beyond the 'commonsensical' has occurred unevenly, searching for a term against which to situate the virtual.

Munster (2006) offers a similarly confusing manoeuvre (p. 90-1), taking the Deleuzian opposition of the virtual to the actual rather than real in contrasting realism to fantasy and the imaginary. While Massumi (2002) also warned against the reduction of the digital from "really apparitional" to artificiality or simulation (p. 137), there is often in his work a conflation of the 'real' with analogue in writing about materiality and physicality. This establishes a clear hierarchy within thought, expressed as the "excess of the analog over the digital" (p. 143) and the structure under which "digital technologies have a connection to the potential and the virtual only through the analog" (p. 138). Massumi even goes so far as to write of the "superiority of the analog" (p. 133), seeming to suggest that the digital is explicitly *not* virtual, but rather that the virtual is inherent to all physicality (and only physicality, or only appearing in the digital as an extension of the physical). While the reality of the digital is computer code (possibility rather than virtuality), our experience of it (the way it appears to consciousness) relies on the shift from static data to information as flow. Here the virtual re-emerges as a function of difference in our relation to the digital world. Munster (2006) opposes "the reductive maneuver [sic] of situating digital technologies as the cause of virtual experiences…in the early cyberculture frenzy surrounding high-end VR technologies" (p. 92), but in separating the virtual processes in both physical and digital spaces she replaces virtual abstraction with the dominance of the actual physical body. In emphasising the role of the virtual apart from its common usage in digital media, Munster, Shields and Massumi bring about a reduction of the virtual to only the physical, and by extension reduce the virtual to one part of the real (in the conflation of real with physical/material). We can oppose this with Haraway's (1992) suggestion that "the virtual is precisely not the real" (p. 325), which displays the counter operation of reducing the virtual (conflated with the digital) to an effect, counterfeit or state of paranoia in which articulation (which can be seen in as the Deleuzian function of the virtual) grinds to a halt. Murphie (2002) operates a levelling effect under a discussion of virtuality, stating that "'everything is real', especially VR. Or real 'enough'" (p. 193). This 'real enough' epitomises the assertion of a limited and familiar view of the real even within the questioning of reality under new regimes of virtuality. These opposing views all operate through an uneven reduction of the virtual in relation to the real: the virtual as part of the real; the digital as part of the analogue; the artificial against the 'real' physical world; or everything subsumed under an approximate 'reality'. Gane and Beer (2008) highlight this problem of drawing together different theories which place the virtual as simulation (p. 108), as the hyperreal which blurs its boundaries with the real (p. 12). The virtual, in itself and particularly in its relation to discussions of digital technologies (in general as well as more explicitly its impact on VR), requires further consideration and a definition built in contact with an expansion of the real.[4]

This chapter defines the virtual as the role of consciousness in perpetuating itself; the subject as process; the function-function of consciousness in which the subject imagines and posits its own functioning. This function forms an axis of becoming, based on the desire that leads always towards the real, yet never achieves its goal, in what Deleuze would call the virtual as an asymptote or attractor to the real. While this Deleuzian virtual must be taken into account as a function of immateriality operating within the Ideal realm of thought – as the substance of cognition – its position within a schema of real and actual that relies too heavily on objectivity limits its direct transferral onto the terms brought into question across the physical-digital divide. The virtual here is more closely placed as the enunciating position of thought, a "statement of desire" (Deleuze, 2004b, p. 17) for both reality and consciousness of it. Within this structure, the subject "imagines himself to be a man merely by virtue of the fact that he imagines himself" (Lacan,

1977, p. 142). It is the functioning of consciousness that bars the subject from itself. This is the grand illusion of consciousness, covering over the inherent alienation of the subject from itself, concealing the position from which the human subject views a given reality with the surface of consciousness upon which such a reality appears. The virtual thus takes on the role of the big Other, the structure of desire that is always-already in the unconscious (p. 130). This is the predicate for the enunciating subject which exists only within its own symbolic structures of thought. It is the virtual that makes consciousness always-already false and, somewhat paradoxically, enables the subject to conceive of the substance of objective reality that obscures the internal positing of the assemblage of worlds, thus Žižek's (2007) conclusion: "reality always-already was virtual" (p. 193). Indeed, all worlds are formed and all of subjective reality defined by the constant process of desire as the virtual functioning of consciousness. As desire, what Deleuze and Guattari (2004a) define as "a process of production without reference to any exterior agency" (pp. 170-1), the virtual both sustains the illusion of objectivity in relation to the subject and enables the subjective self that "exists only on the basis of the misrecognition of its own conditions" (Žižek, 2008b, p. 73). The virtual is the function-function of consciousness $[f(f(\ldots))]$, its functioning *as such* essential to the assemblage of worlds and the creative formation of subjective reality.

THE REAL

There is still a need to reinsert a rupture between the virtual and the real, to assess the antagonism within the term virtual reality. To do this will first require an expanding of the term 'real'. While the virtual has been elaborated and expanded in the wake of Deleuze, both in itself and in relation to digital technology in general and VR in particular, Gunkel identifies the absence of such consideration for the real:

It is often assumed that the problem with 'virtual reality' – the concept, its various technological deployments and the apparently oxymoronic phrase itself – has been our understanding, or perhaps misunderstanding, of the virtual. The real problem, however, is not with the virtual; it is with the real itself…What is needed is an examination of the common understanding of the 'real' that has been operationalized in these various discussions and disputes (Gunkel, 2010, pp. 127-9)

There is here the need for a new understanding of the real, and the understanding that is suggested is that of Lacan, particularly as interpreted and applied culturally by Žižek (2009). This is a conception of the real as "a pure antagonism, as an impossible difference which precedes its terms" (p. 24), based on Lacan's (1977) placement of the real as an encounter, but an encounter in which "reality is in abeyance" (p. 56). This internal antagonism inherent to reality is the paradox whereby, as the real is approached, it disappears. The real is therefore the reality of the unconscious, the traumatic kernel beneath the limit of virtuality that forms the surface of consciousness.

In this construction of consciousness and the unconscious, the real and the virtual take on a mutual dependence that underpins the need to sustain their antagonistic relationship. Gunkel (2010) states that "for Žižek, then, the real is already a virtual construct, and the difference between the real and the virtual turns out to be much more complicated and interesting" (p. 138), and it is this difference that must be confronted to re-establish the particularities of the term virtual reality. If for Deleuze the virtual is real, then under a Lacanian interpretation the real is also virtual. The interdependence of the two terms, and the inclusion of a mark of each within the other, highlights the simultaneous formation of the two as the simultaneous formation of the conscious and unconscious parts of the human mind. The construction of thought that generates a world that is to be thought, to be contained within

thought and without which thought has no object to think, is a looped causality of differentiation that posits itself as the division between virtual and real. If the virtual and real contain one another, and cannot exist separately, it is because the unconscious arises automatically within and as a condition for the surface of consciousness upon which a world (a 'reality') appears. Lacan (1977) writes, "that which makes us consciousness institutes us by the same token as *speculum mundi* [literally, 'mirror of the world']" (p. 75), emphasising the problematic role of the subject inscribed in its own gaze, the loss and stain of reality from which we are excluded even as we leave an ontological mark upon its appearance to consciousness. This is what underpins Žižek's description of the subject as the void within our perception of the world, the stain in the gaze as the constitutive gap in substance (2007, p. 40) or empty structure of the real (2009, p. 8), that is the objectification of the real as lost, the inherent and always failed attempt of virtual consciousness to observe its own unconscious reality.

However, in the context of the digital in general, and VR in particular, the expanded conception of the real in relation to the virtual remains problematic within Žižek's theoretical position, derived from his resistance to digital technology in favour of a materialist dominance of the physical world. While he states that "the crucial point on which the consistency of Lacan's position hinges is thus the difference between reality and the Real" (Žižek 2008a, p. 214), when speaking of the digital Žižek often conflates real and 'real'. With a focus on what Tom Boellstorff (2008) similarly articulates as the fact that "it is not that virtual worlds borrowed assumptions from real life: virtual worlds show us how, under our very noses, our "real" lives have been "virtual" all along" (p. 5), the embedding of virtuality in physical existence and placement of the real as an unobtainable lost causality highlights the framing of reality as a fantasy. Within a critique of the digital resides a desire for and loss of a genuine sense of 'reality' that perhaps speaks as much to Žižek's own structure of fantasy concerning contemporary ontology as much as the problematic relation between digital worlds and reality. He writes:

In so far as the VR apparatus is potentially able to generate experience of the 'true' reality, VR undermines the difference between 'true' reality and semblance. This 'loss of reality' occurs not only in computer-generated VR but, at a more elementary level...we are dealing with the loss of the surface which separates inside from outside.... outside is always inside: when we are directly immersed in VR, we lose contact with reality. (Žižek, 2008a, pp. 133-4)

A development of his position is required if a productive relation of the real to digital technology is to emerge, expanding his critique beyond the physical-digital hierarchy that draws too close to a conflation of physical and real (of actual reality and Lacanian 'reality') as the object cause of desire in his ideological analysis. To situate the real as the reality of a complex social system such as the contemporary digital world, Gunkel (2010) insists upon "a conceptualization of the real that realizes that the real is itself something which is open to considerable variability, ideological pressures and some messy theoretical negotiations." (p. 139). In specific relation to the symbolic realm of the digital, Žižek defines the conditions for the underlying reality of computer code:

... bytes – or, rather, the digital series – is the Real behind the screen; that is to say, we are never submerged in the play of appearances without an 'indivisible remainder'... the emergence of the pure appearance which cannot be reduced to the simple effect of its bodily causes; none the less, this emergence is the effect of the digitalized Real. (2008a, p. 132)

This positioning of the digital real as the underlying binary operations presupposed beneath the 'pure appearance' of the interface screen informs our relation to digital computers. We do not perceive the functioning of code, yet it determines our entire digital reality. This functions as the lost object cause of desire, perpetually outside of our perception while defining the conditions under which a perception of the digital can occur. In the endless variation of 1 and 0 in binary logic, this reality is the difference between something and nothing, the inherent lack in the emergence of reality. Across digital and physical planes, this is the hidden nature of reality beneath perception and outside of our virtualising cognition of the contemporary metaverse.

To more specifically assess the real in its relation to the virtual, this chapter defines the real as the void of the contemporary subject, as both the gap within consciousness and the gap of the physical-digital divide. The real, as defined by this chapter, is not only the later Lacanian real (in, for example, Lacan, 1977), but more specifically the *objet petit a* as the objectification of the void and its role in drive. If subjective reality is a void around which worlds form, then the real is the absent or quasi-cause at the heart of the parallax that determines the manner in which reality appears to the subject. This real is not an objective reality, but rather the excessive lack within the subject that presupposes an external causality. However, if, as Žižek (2000) states, "all presuppositions are already minimally posited" (p. 119), then the real is that which is presupposed as lost, what Žižek (2008a) labels the "coincidence of emergence and loss...*objet petit a*" (p. 15). Throughout Žižek's interpretation of Lacan, the real as *objet a* is the excess and lack of an underlying 'real-ity': excess in terms of a mystical beyond or supposed causal force 'without' the subject; lack in its unattainable nature derived from its positing 'within' (and objectification of the void of) the subject. From this position, the real functions according to the logic of that which is expressed. This is Deleuze's (2004b) conception of sense which "brings that which expresses it into existence" (p. 190), "is essentially produced" (p. 109) and "is always presupposed as soon as *I* begin to speak; I would not be able to begin without this presupposition" (p. 35). Sense manifests the real as a functional logic: that which is expressed, yet cannot be directly confronted; the object of the proposition that is not included in it; the quasi-cause of the void-function. The real is the objectification of unknowable flux within consciousness, and through Žižek (2006) we can thus conclude that "reality is never directly 'itself'" (p. 241). In this way the real portrays a void-function within consciousness, the inaccessibility of the void of subjective reality. The underlying reality of a given consciousness or world is thus formed of its presuppositions within consciousness.

VIRTUAL REALITY

Žižek's discussion of the physical and digital defines Deleuze's virtual precisely and only as Lacan's real. This attempt to draw together the two theorists who are often considered opposed, while acknowledging the importance of the reality of the virtual over 'virtual reality' (Žižek, 2012, p. 3), conflates the nuances of the two processes within consciousness and their functions in the generation of the subject. The antagonistic relation between the real and the virtual, in the expanded sense of both terms is integral to reconciling Žižekian and Deleuzian philosophies as well as the term virtual reality, in a necessary move towards a theory of the digital founded upon the antagonistic relation between virtuality and reality. Deleuze (2004a) states that "the virtual is not opposed to the real; it possesses a full reality by itself" (p. 263), and without opposition we are not seeking a resolution or synthesis of the two terms. Rather, it is the relation of a paradoxical antagonism that is sustained in both physical and digital realities in their difference

as such. This difference resides in the subjective perspective from which we denote one world or the other: two modes of thinking our relation to the universe through the interplay of virtual reality. The utopian vision of early VR, as an ideal space in which a freed mind controls all reality, has fallen out of favour amidst the photorealistic aim of mass consumption in digital entertainment. This is a transition towards the reduction of digital environments to what Cline (2012) portrays dystopically as both "an escape hatch into a better reality" (p. 16) and "a self-imposed prison for humanity…a pleasant place for the world to hide from its problems while human civilization slowly collapses" (p. 120). However, it is precisely this more direct (and perhaps abstracted) expression of consciousness that can connect subjectivity with a self-conscious modification of its relation to and definition of virtual reality. The antagonism between virtual and real is less an opposition than a paradox, underpinning the difference between physical and digital modes of thinking and being. Deleuze (2004a) emphasises the role of "difference as the reality of a multiple virtual field, and the determination of micro-processes in every domain, such that oppositions are only summary results or simplified and enlarged processes" (p. 278 [n]). This suggests the need for a new mode of viewing antagonism beyond the problematic opposition of virtual and real.

Between physical and digital worlds, as two modes of being and of consciousness, lies the subject: a perspective caught adrift in the void of both realities. A given world is a specific self-organisation or assemblage of virtual and real. It is the specific ordering and condensing of the functions of consciousness, creating a different knowledge and experience of a world, which brings about the perceived changes between physical and digital realities. This shift in epistemological position that creates an ontological difference between worlds is what we have seen in Žižek's (2009) conception of parallax (p. 17), here interpreted not as a shift between individual objects *within* social reality but as a parallax *between* realities themselves from within consciousness. Throughout Žižek's work (for example, 2008a) the basis for this framework of parallax and its relation to a machinic consciousness appears in the proliferation of the "always-already" of posited-as-presupposed conditions (p. 184), as well as the Lacan-inspired role of fantasy in cyberspace (Žižek, 1999, p. 104-123) and as "a screen masking a void" in reality (Žižek, 2008b, p. 141). This structure of fantasy supporting the virtual-real relation is of crucial importance in assessing the formation of the physical-digital divide within consciousness. Fantasy, then, becomes the illusory structure between desire and drive that allows the virtual to cover over the void of the real in the continued functioning of consciousness on the surface of the subject. What a critical approach of parallax aims for is the insertion of a ""minimal difference" (the noncoincidence of the one with itself)" (Žižek, 2009, p. 11), under which a distance to our own subjective position can be achieved and the subjective real exposed. To break through the structures of fantasy in relation to digital technology is the task of this conception of virtual reality, confronting the smooth functioning of consciousness in such a way that makes clear simultaneously the parallax relations to physical and digital worlds within subjective reality. By approaching the antagonism between virtual and real, a critical distance can be inserted within consciousness as it beholds its position in the void of parallax between physical and digital worlds. But how do physical and digital worlds form in the relation between virtual and real? Deleuze (2002) equates the actual and the possible to existence and essence (p. 110), expanded into a relation with consciousness by Massumi (2002) when we writes that "intelligence stretches between the extremes of thought-perception, from the actual to the possible, dipping at every connection into the vortex of the virtual" (p. 98). It is the simultaneous relation between virtual-real and existence-essence (as actual-possible, which

we will call here 'existence-meaning' as a more appropriate conception of the digital world built entirely upon symbolic structures without a pre-existing noumenal value). Between these two axes is the shifting perspective of parallax that forms the virtual-reality of both physical and digital worlds: the structure of desire and the lost presupposition of a universe for the contemporary subject to inhabit.

The physical mode of subjectivity emerges when existence combines with the real, the world as it appears with an absent causality. Following the phenomenological dictum that existence precedes essence, virtual-meaning then occurs as a constructed truth within consciousness and its social relations. The entrance of consciousness into the physical world marks the initial passage from nothing to something, our first concrete existence must be founded upon the objectification of the void in the real. This is the assemblage real-existence, whereby the presupposition of a causal relation between reality and appearance instigates appearance itself as reality, and not only an object's or image's reality but also our own physicality as subjective being. This appearance, objectification and externalisation of the physical leads back into consciousness through the process of signification, the human desire for communication. This is where virtual-meaning is formed, in the process combining the conditions of truth with the functioning of consciousness. As Žižek (2008b) states, "the multitude of 'floating signifiers'…is structured into a unified field through the intervention of a certain 'nodal point' which 'quilts' them, stops their sliding and fixes their meaning" (p. 95). The virtual, as desire and the big Other, acts as this condensing point upon and against which meaning can be certified, wherein "by the mere act of speaking, we suppose the existence of the big Other as guarantor of our meaning" (Žižek, 1991, p. 153). Our interpretation of the physical world relies upon this virtual-meaning. Signification must become manifestation and the subject must form itself in a relation to symbolic truth and presuppose an external validity to such truth in order to engage in the use of individual visual, linguistic and cultural signifiers. This process of creating a symbolic structure based on a presupposed external physical reality is the cycle of the physical world, whereby each moment passes from perception to thought before the virtual returns to cover over the real as signifiers define the framework for future observations and the signified world expands within a virtualised consciousness.

Conversely, the digital subject condenses when the real combines with meaning, the absolute truth in code. This binary causality only ever has indirect contact with the subject, through layers of programming language and operating systems that are constructed to enable communication. This is brought into virtual existence, not as a simulation but, rather, a simulation-of-simulation; the appearance of appearance instigated by a conscious intentionality linked directly to the underlying machine code (in its most basic form this is the act of 'turning on' the digital device). This inversion of essence before existence still maintains the originary quasi-causality of the real followed by the process of the virtual. The digital world is not built from material substance, but from the abstract and absolute code of the machinic computer. Such a formal, logic-based realm can be considered the fulfilment of McLuhan's (2001) vision of electric technology as "pure information without any content to restrict its transforming and informing power" (p. 57). Binary logic is built upon the purely formal numbers one and zero, exemplifying Deleuze's pure difference and Žižek's minimal difference, functioning as the coalescence of meaning with the real in the fundamental positing of a digital universe. virtual-existence then appears as a realm of the imaginary in the superficial light of the interface screen. The purity of such a 'perfect' imaginary world based on formally 'perfect' logic fails at the very moment of engagement. The subject as physical being is seldom able to detach itself, neither sensorially nor

cognitively, from its analogue existence. Memories of 'real' places seep in, 'realistic' graphics hook our imaginations back into already established functions of (false) consciousness, concealing what Manovich (2001) insists as a position in which "synthetic computer-generated imagery is not an inferior representation of our reality, but a realistic representation of a different reality" (p. 202). Here Baudrillard's (1994) scheme of the final phase of simulation proves instructive as "its own pure simulacrum…no longer of the order of appearances, but of simulation" (p. 6). While VR is often viewed as such a mode of simulation, the apparent virtuality of existence in the digital is constructed directly from the real of computer code, precisely defined by an absolute reality. Thus VR spaces are not an imaginary realm of pure appearance but rather an appearance of appearance concealing the truth of binary logic. A further phase of the image must be added in the context of VR: the mask of appearance *is* reality. This is the operation that Žižek (1991) identifies as unique to humanity, in which we "deceive by feigning to deceive" and therefore "effectively *become* something by pretending that we *already are* that" (p. 73). In digital environments this is the process by which we accept the clear virtuality of existence, in the opacity of the interface under a necessary suspension of disbelief, creating a mask of appearance that hides the direct causal relation between the reality of code and the 'virtual reality' on screen. Here we move beyond pure simulacrum as a result of simulation, towards a simulation-of-simulation. It is for this reason that the placing of VR as a tool for accurately 'simulating' physical reality entirely misses the point of the function of virtual reality at an ontological level. We should not consider virtual-existence as an illusory or imaginary interpretation of physical real-existence, for the relation of real to virtual does not here imply a judgement of truth. Rather, the digital image should be regarded as an illusion of appearance, the simulation-of-simulation whereby phenomena precisely are their signification in the primary causality of computer code. The virtuality of existence returns to the real in concealing such presupposed code beneath the sensory data that appears on screen, a shift from signification of something in reality to a reality of signification as such. In the wake of the poststructuralist breakdown of symbolic structures, and subsequent resurgence of a nostalgic fetishisation of physical materiality, it is tempting to view digital environments such as VR as an empty signification of pure appearance, the epitome of Baudrillard's simulacrum. In the interplay of expanded notions of virtuality and reality, however, the apparent 'virtuality' of the digital is the appearance of virtuality itself; the illusion of VR is the structure by which it appears as pure appearance.

AN ART OF PARALLAX

Within this expanded notion of virtual reality, integral to our conception of both physical and digital worlds, a re-application to digital technology is required if the theoretical developments are to inform our relation to actual technologies and their use in contemporary and future society. As Deleuze and Guattari (1998) suggest, the task is that of "acting counter to the past, and therefore on the present, for the benefit, let us hope, of a future" (p. 112), a sending forward of ideas as an infinite critique of society rather than a specific set of practical activities. This application of a futuring of thought can occur most strongly in new modes of understanding creative practices. There has long been a strong link between VR and art. Not only does the generation of digital worlds require a creative input at the visual level, but VR theorists quickly identified the critical role of artistic practices in the social impact of the technologies. Nicholas Negroponte (1996) identified that in VR and other digital technology "the real opportunity comes from the digital artist providing the hooks for mutation and change" (p. 224), and Heim (1993) has also suggested that

"perhaps the essence of VR ultimately lies not in technology but in art" (p. 124). These statements highlight the necessity of creative interventions to rethink our relation to technology and thus evolve our future relation to both physical and digital worlds. Here we see that Žižek's (1999) call to "traverse the fantasy in cyberspace" (p. 102), while emphasising the need to overcome the structures of fantasy between the virtual and the real, does not go far enough. Rather than, as he suggests, using VR as a place in which to stage and confront the psychological issues of our physical selves, there is now the need in our increasingly digitised society to traverse the fantasy *of* cyberspace, to view the parallax of the physical-digital antagonism and our position within it. The critical power of digital art lies not in creating specific sensational worlds but in challenging the mode of viewing the worlds it creates, building an analytical encounter into the frames it constructs, and through this to challenge our subjective viewpoint on all worlds.

This process by which art can make visible the parallax perspective that defines our individual virtual realities is always a process of re-framing. Žižek (2009) explains that "the minimal parallax constellation is that of a simple frame: all that has to intervene in the Real is an empty frame, so that the same things we saw "directly" before are now seen through the frame" (p. 29), and it is the role of art to make clear such a frame through which the virtuality of our perspective can be penetrated in order to make contact with the subjective real that underpins our experience of any given world. The artist of parallax views both sides of an antagonism at once, portraying simultaneously two perspectives with no common language (p. 129). In relation to the virtual reality of digital and physical modes of thinking and creating, this entails the construction of new perspectives from which to view and gain critical distance towards the interplay of virtual and real in the inversion of existence and meaning. Baudrillard (1994) states that "the universe of simulation is transreal and transfinite: no test of reality will come to put an end to it - except the total collapse and slippage of the terrain, which remains our most foolish hope" (p. 103), but in the digital simulation-of-simulation the territory is always-already collapsing and slipping into new assemblages across global computer networks and the many realms of cyberworlds we create.

The role of art in using VR to confront the virtual reality of the contemporary subject and contemporary society can thus be defined as the construction of a position from which to view our own parallax perspective on the physical-digital multiverse. Žižek (2009) states that, for the artist of parallax, "the only action available to him is self-destruction, which is itself a symbolic state-ment, the only work of art available to him" (p. 128). To unleash a kernel of the real, to bring an objectification of the parallax position into view by simultaneously staging both sides of the antagonism, requires a process of representing, externalising and stripping down (staging and traversing) the structures of desire and identity in subjective virtual reality, destroying the shell of consciousness to see what remains as our position from which the world is viewed and from which thought is thought. This is described by Murphie (2002) as humanity's ability for "extracting the world from the world" (p. 194) through conscious perception (and its disruption by or antagonism with the unconscious). Between the narcissism of excessively attempting to view oneself (as the position from which one views the world(s)) and the destruction of the fantasy supporting the virtual reality of such a self, we approach what appears as a nihilistic solipsism. If it is the subjective viewpoint, the parallax perspective, that constructs physical and digital worlds within thought, then to view the structures of virtual reality necessitates a gesture of withdrawal. This removal of the self in creative digital practices is an attempt to view one's own presuppositions, the always-already there of the subjective position, and thereby view the formation of parallax and the structures of fan-tasy supporting the smooth continuation of virtual

reality. Deleuze (2002) describes "a pure Artist" as one form of the "human being who precedes itself" (p. 11), and in the physical-digital parallax the VR artist must precede its own perspective, the construction of its virtual reality and the fan-tasy of digital technology, in order to create new experiences through which we might rethink our relation to virtual reality, new technologies and the many worlds they create. For the potential of radical creative collectivity, transitioning from the individual consciousness to the social in what Deleuze and Guattari (1998) hail as a 'people to come' (p. 218), this is the imagining and staging of future perspectives of a genuinely cybernetic post-individual and posthuman consciousness through which the critical and creative power of VR might enact the revolutionary potential that filled its early conceptions, re-emerging in new forms of psychological, social and artistic con-structs around new understandings of the framing of the discussion.

CONCLUSION

This chapter has raised new questions concerning the definition of virtual reality. By tracing the history of the term through the technological and cultural developments that have expanded VR into everyday language, the problematic nature of the label virtual reality has been shown to have always included a series of internal tensions surrounding its constituent components of virtuality and reality, and external tensions in relation to other aspects of digital technology. Recognising the hostility of VR theorists, technologists and creative prac-titioners towards the vague inclusion of virtual reality as a tool for marketing a broader range of digital media and its permeation of the physical world, while opposing the simplified definition of VR as a specific technology not taking into account the cultural expansion and impact of the term, a critical history of virtual reality theory has revealed in the simultaneous expansion and dissolution of the inherently interdisciplinary field of VR research a persistent problem with the limitations of presupposed assumptions concerning the virtual and its opposition to the real. Taking this in its broader cultural context, the impact of other parallel theories and terms has been discussed to situate VR in and against other theoretical developments of digital technology. The dominance of cinematic theory on VR technology and its inclusion in contemporary culture has been reassessed in order to assert the need for new theories of digital media, and VR in particular, as a cultural and ontological regime in itself. The alternative and more general term 'cyber' has been traced through the concept of a cyberspace back to the earlier developments of cybernetics as an expansion of the human mind, situating VR technologies in their creative potential for constructing spaces of the Ideal. Issues of access to VR and other information technologies were discussed, and their causal role challenged as symptoms of wider societal inequalities, to raise the concerns over the viewing of digital technology in terms of social binaries. These developments have established the need to both assess and move beyond the antagonism of virtuality and reality in reconsidering VR as a technology and a conceptual framework.

The virtual has been analysed in the Deleuzian tradition, drawing out the machinic processes of the Ideal that are at work in both physical and digital modes of existence and thought. Deleuze's conception of the virtual was outlined and elaborated to establish the evolving context of virtuality in contemporary society, while later developments by Massumi and others brought the debate into the discussion of VR technology. Within this extension of virtuality, however, was revealed a reliance on a limited notion of the real, and the opposition of virtual to actual rather than real placed the virtual as part of a broader and more common sense 'reality'. The virtual was therefore redefined in a specifically machinic, functional approach to consciousness as a surface of the

Ideal upon which worlds are thought, enabling an antagonism with the real in the processes of thought that allow virtual reality to emerge. The real itself was then questioned under a Lacanian definition, expanded by Žižek and Gunkel in their discussion of cyberculture, reinserting an antagonism between virtual and real without reducing either to earlier common sense and limited notions. The real was explicitly defined as the unconscious, the unknowable void of subjectivity, and placed in a relation to the desire of the virtual as underlying and presupposed drive, Lacan's *objet petit a*. Within Žižek's theory, however, the Lacanian real is placed as the Deleuzian virtual, thus this discussion redefined each term individually to allow the specificity of their antagonism (internal to consciousness) to re-emerge.

With the constituent parts redefined, a new mode of viewing virtual reality was then suggested to provoke not an opposition of virtual and real but, rather, a sustained antagonism within our conception of any 'reality' and the relation of thought to it. Žižek's concept of parallax was instructive here in establishing the ontological implications of subjective epistemological shifts, the relation between the constantly evolving landscape of the virtual surface of consciousness around the void of the real in the unconscious as the position from which consciousness is thought. The unrepresentable position from which the parallax perspective is seen and thought was placed as the emergence of all virtual realities. The emergence of physical and digital worlds was delineated along the inversion of existence and meaning (as a broader term for essence more directly applicable to digital ontologies) as the shifting perspective of digital parallax. The alignment of these two states with virtual and real processes of thought was posited as an original framework of viewing physical and digital ontological difference within consciousness, asserting the subjective viewpoint, and its problems, as the key to our understanding of virtual reality today. The dilemma of representing the position from which parallax (as well as physical and digital worlds) is thought was postulated as the task of contemporary creative practices that engage with digital (including the conventional VR) technologies. This drew further psychoanalytic techniques into a framework of making clear the reality of the subject and society, stripping down the virtual surfaces to represent simultaneously both sides of the antagonism: the surface of physical-digital worlds and the underlying presuppositions that differentiate them and allow them to form. The task was proposed for contemporary digital artists to 'precede themselves', to bring out the position from which the information society is thought and, fundamentally, to persist in the questioning of the terms under which thought and art occur.

This chapter offers a contribution to our understanding of virtual reality as a technology and a conceptual framework for society and its future development. The discussion is by no means exhaustive, and indeed it is hoped that the arguments presented inspire further elaboration, disagreement, and productive antagonism that continues the reconsideration of the term and its use in creative practices. The resolution of the oppositions between Deleuzian expansions of the virtual and Lacanian developments of the real requires further discussion and resolution, both in terms of the often contradictory, yet linked, theoretical positions themselves, and in their application to digital technology, culture and art. The questions, developments and new positions outlined here are intended as a call for further questioning in theory and a renewed focus in practice on the use of VR technologies and their framing of contemporary society.

REFERENCES

Ashby, W. (1957). *An introduction to cybernetics*. London: Chapman and Hall.

Barlow, J. (1996). *A declaration of the independence of cyberspace*. Retrieved from https://projects.eff.org/~barlow/Declaration-Final.html

Baudrillard, J. (1994). *Simulacra and simulation*. Ann Arbor, MI: University of Michigan Press.

Biocca, F., Kim, T., & Levy, M. (1995). The vision of virtual reality. In F. Biocca & M. Levy (Eds.), *Communication in the age of virtual reality* (pp. 1–13). Hillsdale, NJ: Lawrence Erlbaum Associates.

Biocca, F., & Levy, M. (1995). Preface. In F. Biocca & M. Levy (Eds.), *Communication in the age of virtual reality* (pp. vii–viii). Hillsdale, NJ: Lawrence Erlbaum Associates.

Boellstorff, T. (2008). *Coming of age in Second Life: An anthropologist explores the virtually human*. Princeton, NJ: Princeton University Press.

Bostrom, N., & Sandberg, A. (2009). Cognitive enhancement: Methods, ethics, regulatory challenges. *Science and Engineering Ethics*, *15*(3), 311–341. doi:10.1007/s11948-009-9142-5 PMID:19543814

Brice, R. (1997). *Multimedia & virtual reality engineering*. Oxford, UK: Newnes.

Brodlie, K., Dykes, J., Gillings, M., Haklay, M., Kitchin, R., & Kraak, M. (2002). Geography in VR: Context. In P. Fisher & D. Unwin (Eds.), *Virtual reality in geography* (pp. 7–16). London: Taylor and Francis.

Chorafas, D., & Steinmann, H. (1995). *Virtual reality: Practical applications in business and industry*. Englewood Cliffs, NJ: Prentice Hall PTR.

Deleuze, G. (2002). *Desert islands*. Los Angeles, CA: Semiotext.

Deleuze, G. (2004a). *Difference and repetition*. London: Continuum.

Deleuze, G. (2004b). *The logic of sense*. London: Continuum.

Deleuze, G., & Guattari, F. (1998). *What is philosophy?* London: Verso.

Deleuze, G., & Guattari, F. (2004a). *Anti-Oedipus: Capitalism and schizophrenia.* London: Continuum.

Deleuze, G., & Guattari, F. (2004b). *A thousand plateaus: Capitalism and schizophrenia.* London: Continuum.

Durlach, N., & Mavor, A. (Eds.). (1995). *Virtual reality: Scientific and technological challenges.* Washington, DC: National Academy Press.

Engelbart, D. (1962) Augmenting human intellect: A conceptual framework. *Summary Report AFOSR-3233.*

Fisher, P., & Unwin, D. (2002). Virtual reality in geography: An introduction. In P. Fisher & D. Unwin (Eds.), *Virtual reality in geography* (pp. 1–4). London: Taylor and Francis.

Gane, N., & Beer, D. (2008). *New media: The key concepts.* New York: Berg.

Gibson, W. (1984) *Neuromancer.* New York, NY: Ace.

Gunkel, D. (2000). Hacking cyberspace. *Jac, 20*(4), 797–823.

Gunkel, D. (2003). Second thoughts: Toward a critique of the digital divide. *New Media & Society, 5*(4), 499–522. doi:10.1177/146144480354003

Gunkel, D. (2010). The real problem: Avatars, metaphysics and online social interaction. *New Media & Society, 12*(1), 127–141. doi:10.1177/1461444809341443

Hansen, M. (2004). *New philosophy for new media.* Cambridge, MA: MIT Press.

Hansen, M. (2006). *Bodies in code: Interfaces with digital media.* New York, NY; Abingdon: Routledge.

Haraway, D. (1985). Manifesto for cyborgs: Science, technology, and socialist feminism in the 1980s. *Socialist Review, 80,* 65–108.

Haraway, D. (1992). The promises of monsters: A regenerative politics for inappropriate/d others. In L. Grossberg, C. Nelson, & P. Treichler (Eds.), *Cultural studies* (pp. 295–337). New York, NY: Routledge.

Hayles, N. K. (1999). *How we became posthuman.* Chicago, IL: University of Chicago Press. doi:10.7208/chicago/9780226321394.001.0001

Heim, M. (1993). *The metaphysics of virtual reality.* Oxford, UK: Oxford University Press.

Heim, M. (1998). *Virtual realism.* Oxford, UK: Oxford University Press.

Ihde, D. (2012). Can continental philosophy deal with the new technologies? *Journal of Speculative Philosophy, 26*(2), 321–332.

Lacan, J. (1977). *The four fundamental concepts of psychoanalysis.* London: The Hogarth Press.

Lacan, J. (2006). *Écrits.* New York, NY: W. W. Norton & Company.

Licklider, J. (1960). Man-computer symbiosis. *IRE Transactions on Human Factors in Electronics, HFE-1*(1), 4–11. doi:10.1109/THFE2.1960.4503259

Lovink, G. (1994). Michael Heim: The metaphysics of virtual reality. *Mediamatic Magazine, 8*(1). Retrieved from http://www.mediamatic.net/5623/en/heim

Manovich, L. (2001). *The language of new media.* Cambridge, MA: MIT Press.

Manovich, L. (2013). *Software takes command.* New York, NY; London: Bloomsbury.

Massumi, B. (2002). *Parables for the virtual: Movement, affect, sensation.* Durham, NC: Duke University Press. doi:10.1215/9780822383574

McLuhan, M. (2001). *Understanding media.* London: Routledge.

Merleau-Ponty, M. (2002). *Phenomenology of perception.* London: Routledge.

Munster, A. (2006). *Materializing new media: Embodiment in information aesthetics.* University Press of New England.

Murphie, A. (2002). Putting the virtual back into VR. In B. Massumi (Ed.), *A shock to thought: Expression after Deleuze and Guattari* (pp. 188–214). London: Routledge.

Negroponte, N. (1996). *Being digital.* New York, NY: Vintage.

Norris, C. (1995). Gilles Deleuze. In T. Honderich (Ed.), *The Oxford companion to philosophy* (pp. 182–183). Oxford, UK: Oxford University Press.

Sherman, W., & Craig, A. (2003). *Understanding virtual reality: Interface, application, and design.* San Francisco, CA: Morgan Kaufmann.

Shields, R. (2003). *The virtual.* London: Routledge.

Sutherland, I. (1965). The ultimate display. In *Proceedings IFIP Congress* (pp. 506-508). IFIP.

Thierauf, R. (1995). *Virtual reality systems for business.* Westport, CT: Quorum.

US Department of Commerce. (1995). *Falling through the net: A survey of the "have nots" in rural and urban America.* Retrieved from http://www.ntia.doc.gov/ntiahome/fallingthru.html

US Department of Commerce. (1998). *Falling through the net II: New data on the digital divide.* Retrieved from http://www.ntia.doc.gov/report/1998/falling-through-net-ii-new-data-digital-divide

US Department of Commerce. (1999). *Falling through the net: Defining the digital divide.* Retrieved from http://www.ntia.doc.gov/report/1999/falling-through-net-defining-digital-divide

Wexelblat, A. (1993). *Virtual reality: Applications and explorations.* Waltham, MA: Academic Press.

World Summit on the Informational Society. (2003). *Declaration of principles: Building the information society: A global challenge in the new millennium.* Retrieved from http://www.itu.int/wsis/docs/geneva/official/dop.html

Žižek, S. (1991). *Looking awry.* Cambridge, MA: MIT Press.

Žižek, S. (1999). Is it possible to traverse the fantasy in cyberspace? In E. Wright & E. Wright (Eds.), *The Žižek reader* (pp. 102–124). Oxford, UK: Blackwell.

Žižek, S. (2006). *Interrogating the real.* London: Continnum.

Žižek, S. (2007). *The indivisible remainder: On Schelling and related matters.* London: Verso.

Žižek, S. (2008a). *The plague of fantasies.* London: Verso.

Žižek, S. (2008b). *The sublime object of ideology.* London: Verso.

Žižek, S. (2009). *The parallax view.* Cambridge, MA: MIT Press.

Žižek, S. (2012). *Organs without bodies: On Deleuze and consequences.* London: Routledge.

KEY TERMS AND DEFINITIONS

Consciousness: Thought as a machinic process; the self-positing of the subject as a virtuality in thought; the gesture of the cogito; the surface assemblage of the subject.

Cybernetics: 'Steersmanship'; the study of systems with a circular causal feedback loop; the expansion of human intellect with machines; the understanding of understanding.

Cyborg: The human subject between physical and digital worlds; the self-aware expanded cybernetic consciousness; the resolution of the internal antagonisms of the cyborg can be considered a state of posthumanism.

Digital Divide: The disparity in access to technology and information along geographical, ethnic or economic lines.

Existence: The conditions for being; the gaze and the appearance of external objects it denotes; an observed world (either physical or digital).

Meaning: Essence; signification; less what is communicated than the conditions of truth that enable communication; information as this shared process of flow.

Parallax: The relative displacement of objects by a change in perspective; the ontological change in objective reality created by an epistemological shift in subjective position.

Real: The objectification of the void of the contemporary subject, as both the gap within consciousness and the gap of the physical-digital divide. This is linked to the Lacanian *objet petit a* and the perpetual drive of the loss as such that defines desire.

Subject: The perspectival position from which consciousness is thought; the assemblage of consciousness around this parallax void; the individual or collective potential for creative activity and shaping the future of human society.

Virtual: The role of consciousness in perpetuating itself; the subject as process; the function-function of consciousness in which the subject imagines and posits its own functioning. This appears as desire, always moving towards contact with the unattainable Real.

ENDNOTES

[1] Or, rather, reduces the digital to one manifestation of the virtuality of cinema as the logical extension of painting using Deleuze only for his work on cinema (a trend that dominates the elaboration of the Deleuzian virtual), seeing the necessary development as an expanding of Deleuze's temporal focus towards a spatial consideration which itself only furthers the subsuming of VR by cinema.

[2] Here is where Deleuze's "ultra-nominalism" (Norris, 1995, p. 133) develops from Lacan's (2006) view of the prior existence of language in the subject, found by psychoanalysis in the unconscious (p. 413), towards a virtualised simultaneous occurrence of language as the limit of consciousness and the unconscious, the differentiating process that brings thought into being.

[3] The 'ideal game' was previously defined by Deleuze (2004b) as "without rules, with neither winner nor loser, without responsibility…this game is reserved then for thought and art" (p. 63).

[4] The mutual expansion and re-definition of virtual and real in this chapter would ideally require a reading of both sections 'simultaneously'. However, to construct a linear argument they will be defined separately, the virtual prefiguring the real, before being drawn together in a more detailed discussion of their relation.

Chapter 10
Designing Pervasive Virtual Worlds

Everardo Reyes-Garcia
University of Paris 13, France

ABSTRACT

Virtual worlds can be approached in a broader sense of that which refers to common conceptions of virtual reality and immersive environments. This chapter explores the design of virtual worlds in a time when much contemporary media is accessed through and simulated by software. Today, the main extensions of man are cognitive skills and experiences. Software is a way of seeing the world; it plays a central role in media design and distribution. Software and perception of reality are intertwined and pervasive: media not only exist in form of software but the shape and properties of media are also designed with software. In order to understand the implications of computational media, it is necessary to re-articulate problems in a creative and virtual manner. At the end of the chapter, the author speculates on design approaches and presents some examples developed by him.

INTRODUCTION

Today, many types of media have been translated into electronic forms and formats. One of the main consequences of this situation is that most forms of media are now created, accessed, distributed, shared and modified by electronic means. In this scenario, the computer has become one of the most important media because it allows not only to simulate old media but also to extend and virtualize them. The interrelationships of hardware, software and code are the fundamental basis of modern media.

But mastering a computer is not the only necessary skill for media design. It does not fully encompass the complexity of the medium. In a reverse direction, the challenges for designers of media have broadened. Among other complexities, we mention three. First, media is designed with software, which implies to learn how to use software but we also need to understand how the computer works in order to create our own software and different manners to design media. Second, as the massive adoption of computing and human-computer interaction evolve, it also comes with the establishment of conventions,

DOI: 10.4018/978-1-4666-8205-4.ch010

i.e., determined structures based on patterns and practices. To what extent is it useful to move outside these conventions? How can we identify conventions? How can we embrace and criticize them for the sake of creativity? Third, software shares some features with natural language and culture, specially regarding its evolution. It happens that some changes can be observed easily but some others are more difficult to notice. For instance, in the fashion industry trends can be celebrated from year to year, but this is not the case in natural language where changes occur at the level of idioms, jargon, syntactic and semantic models of language (new words, new meanings, new languages, etc.). In software, we can observe new features and styles from one version to another, but it is more difficult to detect evolutions in data structures, programming paradigms, algorithms or abstractions.

In this chapter we revisit the notion of pervasive virtual worlds, as previously investigated in 2011 (Reyes, 2011). Our intention with this notion was to understand the emerging environment that combines analog and electronic media. Our focus was on everyday life, where we are constantly extended by portable devices but also by amplified objects in the environment. The ecosystem of connected objects and the processes and actions we can perform on them give rise to electronic realities, which are as real as the 'real world'. So the task is to take advantage of the coupling of analog with electronic in order to design augmented experiences by creatively and constantly questioning the virtual and real worlds. The notion of 'virtual world' is approached in a broader sense of that which refers to common conceptions of virtual reality and immersive environments. We rather consider the virtual as a state of being, thus making reference to the philosophical strand.

In the following section we start by reviewing the notion of 'pervasive virtual worlds'. Then we discuss software as medium, taking as a departing point the definition of media elaborated by Marshall McLuhan, which observes them as technologies that extend or restrain man. From here, we will then put particular attention on media within the continuum of technological evolution and innovation. And to conclude the first section of this chapter we present and discuss two analytical maps of the computing medium, which were created from of its main forms and structures. Through these maps, we try to identify patterns and trends in the era of cultural computing.

The last section of this chapter explores a couple of examples inspired by the idea of pervasive virtual worlds. Our examples are informed by research on digital humanities, speculative computing, aesthetic provocations, design by disruption, experimentation and media art. The projects and experiments selected for the discussion serve also as conceptual tools to think about the virtualization of man.

BACKGROUND: PERVASIVE VIRTUAL WORLDS

The classic definition of virtual worlds, also referred to as 'artificial worlds' or 'virtual environments', comes from research on computer virtual reality. The first innovations in this field started during the 1960s. Prominent examples of pioneering systems include the "Sensorama Simulator" by Morton Heiling in 1960, and the "Ultimate Display" by Ivan Sutherland in 1965. Short after, the first artistic virtual worlds were developed. David Em, while artist in residence at NASA, created "Aku" (1977), "Transjovian Pipeline" (1979) and "Persepol" (1985). From this tradition, a virtual reality system has been defined as

... an interface between a man and a machine capable of creating a real-time sensory experience of real and artificial worlds through the various human sensory channels. These sensory channels for man are: Vision, Audition, Touch, Smell, and Taste (Burdea 1993, cited by Boulanger 2008).

From the context of our contemporary ecosystem of electronic media and devices, we believe it is necessary to understand virtual worlds as something more like 'pervasive virtual worlds'. The term 'world' should be understood in a broader sense, both physically and metaphysically, as a reality, a context and an environment; as it is known and experienced by a series of actors; as a unit or whole containing its own forces and rules in a transcendental way. As we will develop further below, the world exists independently of humans. Following recent works on the philosophical tradition of 'realism', humans are only one actor among others in the world. There are also things, objects, ideas, in the world, and all should be granted equal ontological status, what has been called 'flat ontology' (Bryant cited by Bogost, 2013). This approach to the world is valuable because it tries to move beyond a human-centered tradition where the world is only seized and understood by humans and its possibilities (sensory channels, language, cognition), what has been called 'correlationism' (Meillassoux, 2012). If we humbly accept that the world is more than we know, 'realism' allows to speculate on the phenomenology, ethics, politics and aesthetics of all things in general.

Regarding the term 'virtual', we use it from a philosophical perspective, that is, as one of the four states of being that coexist together: the real, the possible, the actual, and the virtual. The notion of virtual derives from the work of Gilles Deleuze, inspired by Henri Bergson. Pierre Lévy has summarized and discussed, through examples of digital culture, the virtual mode of being in the world. First of all, the virtual is not opposed to the real, however the former is latent and the later is manifest. The four different states of being are noted as manifest or latent. The real and the actual are manifest; they are the result of events. The possible is the latent state that tends to the real (realization) and the virtual is the latent state that tends to the actual (actualization). The opposite direction, from the manifest to the latent

state also exists. From the real to the possible it is the potentialization and from the actual to the virtual is the virtualization.

The relevance of considering these four states of being resides in identifying two different modes of creation. For example, when something is created, it can be done either in: first, a more innovative or, second, in a more standardized form. This is not to say that there is no creativity in the standard, but only that its focus is on the practical achievement of something and not in the questioning of the existent. Of course, innovation may rise from standards and when the standard was first invented it was once a creative type, but as it is widely adopted it becomes more and more a repetition and not a difference (Deleuze, 1968). However, when something is created in a creative manner, it explores and approaches a solution in a different way. This is the actualization. The creative thinking implies to refashion, modify, remix and combine elements. And when this creative solution is questioned and re-articulated it is being virtualized.

The given example might suggest that the virtual state is an exclusive feature of the human specie. However, we believe it is not. In that case, it would be a contradiction with the realist perspective of the world. We are rather inclined to think that other actors perform virtual processes that indeed cannot be fully understood by humans due to the fact that we perceive them only through our senses and capacities. For instance, consider biological evolution, which studies how new species appear and evolve to better adapt to the environment (Darwin, 1859). Perhaps the natural process acts instinctively and modifies ADN accordingly, but it certainly cannot foresee in advance which changes will happen in the environment. It is difficult for a human to perceive and note directly when and how such changes occur. The scale is very small (molecules, cells, atoms) and the time is very slow (millions of years) for the human senses. But, can evolution of species be related to virtuality? It is not our intention to speculate on answers about this question, we only want to recall the importance of the philosophical questioning of virtuality from a realist perspective. In this direction, we point the reader to the work of Manuel De Landa. He identifies himself as a 'realist' and has devoted a book on virtuality based on Gilles Deleuze (De Landa, 2002).

The notion of 'pervasive virtual worlds' is also an attempt to describe the analogical and electronic world that is mixed, extended and mediated through media. As we will see later, media will also have to be understood broadly, something more related to techniques and technologies than to mass communication media. Pervasive virtual worlds are made of concrete and simple forms, but also of abstract and complex ones, produced by the interaction of heterogeneous actors: individuals, things, objects, machines; these forms can be physical but immaterial as well. Furthermore, recalling the idea of the world as larger than human perception and understanding, some forms can even be unknown for some actors of the world.

An example of pervasive virtual world could be all those projects that rely extensively on the ecology of portable devices and communication networks. As it has happened, the explosion of cell phones has overpassed personal computers, so there is a portable device with almost everyone, everywhere. These devices do not only function as telephone but also as text machines, typewriters, game platforms, multimedia centers, to mention some. Such ecology of media has virtualized actions of individuals and places. We can extend our presence into several places simultaneously: while we are physically in a geographical location, we can be acting in a remote place at the same time. Accordingly, the type of action we perform remotely can be very similar to those we perform in the physical space. Of course, the type of presence is electronic, however this is as unique feature of computer virtual worlds. Pierre Boulanger has identified 'virtual reality systems' as general-purpose presence-transforming machines. The importance of presence, says Boulanger, deserves

greater attention as recent psycho-physiological studies show that participants exhibit similar reactions to presented situations as they would in similar situation in real life, e.g., they behave the same: show fear reactions, perform tasks in 'normal' manner, show socially conditioned responses (Boulanger, 2008).

In a pervasive virtual world, presence can be simulated through media or experienced physically. One of the fundamental changes in media design (of both content and interfaces) has been precisely to translate old media into digital formats, but at the same time new kinds of media are invented in the process. At the center of this turnover, software, hardware and code play a decisive role in the materialization, perception, understanding, creation, evolution and virtualization of media.

Media, as we mentioned earlier, needs to be studied in the largest possible sense and allowing different entry points for their analysis. For example, media has proven to be a rich objet of study through the seminal notion of 'remediation' (Bolter and Grusin, 1999), a term inspired by Marshall McLuhan's understanding of media as 'extensions of man' (McLuhan, 1964). But there are other interesting notions related to media: 'artifacts' and 'devices' in the sense of Michel Foucault and Gilles Deleuze; 'artwork' or 'text' for semioticians like Roland Barthes and Umberto Eco. And what about virtuality? Indeed, Pierre Lévy has revisited McLuhan's notion and formulates that media are really virtualizations of actions, organs and things (Lévy, 1998).

To discuss an example let's take the act of hammering, also commented briefly by Lévy. Hammering is a virtualization of the act of pushing or pressing a surface against another one. From the point of view of McLuhan, the stone could be seen as an extension of the fist and the hammer as an extension of the arm. Once the action has been virtualized, it can be accomplished with other things and communicated even in the absence of stones and hammers. To adventure in a further step, we can advance that hammering has influenced the act of 'buttoning', i.e. pressing buttons as implemented in machines and their following remediations in digital user interfaces. These two actions are both related to 'contact' and we will explore them in more detail in following sections. For Lévy, he observes that in the history of virtualizations there is a small number of virtualizations but a large number of realizations: How many times the act of hammering has been discovered in opposition to how many times people have hammered throughout history? For those readers familiar with semiotics, this idea finds echo in the distinction between type and token; the invention of a word and its utterances. Moreover, it is also related to the concept of 'technical object' as elaborated by Gilbert Simondon:

... the technical object is specified by the convergence of structural functions because there is not, at a given epoch or time, an infinite plurality of possible functional systems. Human needs diversify to infinity, but the directions of convergence of technical species are of a limited number (Simondon, 1969:23, our translation from French).

To conclude this part we want to argue that the notion of pervasive virtual worlds offers a different view for designing media simulations and exploring new communication models. Virtual worlds are pervasive because there is an ever-increasing quantity and types of devices connected between them: from mobile handhelds to ambient intelligence to the internet of things. But simulation, communication, extension and virtualization do not depend on those artifacts to flourish because they are latent. As we have seen, organs and actions are being virtualized in artificial worlds from the perspective of human beings (such as teleporting in Second Life or changing perspective in physical world trough an Oculus Rift), but there is still a lot of work to do if we approach virtualization from the vantage point of things, objects and ideas for example. This is to suppose that we could speculate on virtualizing acts done by things and then

to apply them or combine them with human or object actions. Moreover, actions have become more and more simulated in digital environments (representations and digital restitutions), and it is interesting to note that these virtualizations can in turn re-enter the process of virtualization and be actualized again; something like an n-degree of virtualization. In these terms, potentially anything can be used as media: either to communicate with it or to study its communicative possibilities or to analyze its effects at other human and non-human levels. If we come back to some claims from the speculative realism, an actualization of these acts would follow a similar path of what Ian Bogost has called 'alien phenomenology' or to approach what is like to be a thing (Bogost, 2013). In a more modest endeavor, we can start by understanding media and techniques as the result of visions of actors and events that were influent at their origin and through their evolution. These visions have often had different and multiple sources of inspiration, such as a passions, needs, problem-solving. In the end, media and techniques represent modes or ways of seeing and acting in the world, they shape *ways of being* (Winograd and Flores, 1986). The invitation is to start tracing and documenting media, technologies, sciences, and art by taking into account aesthetics, politics, ethics, technics and material aspects. If a catalog of virtualizations of organs, actions, and things could exist we could not only understand media better but also consider different approaches to creative innovation.

SOFTWARE AS MEDIA

In the evolution of digital computers there has been a major revolution regarding their social and cultural role: the development of human-computer interaction, mainly led at Xerox PARC in the 1960s. It is safe to situate at that time various inventions still in use today: among the most popular, the mouse, the pointer, hypertext, videoconferencing and graphical user interfaces. It is interesting to recall the fast pace at which computers evolved afterwards. In the following decade, during the 1970s, two of the most influential programming languages were developed: first, Pascal, designed by Niklaus Wirth between the universities of Stanford and Zurich, influential in procedural programming; second, Smalltalk, at Xerox PARC, influential in object-oriented programming. These languages, together with the advancements in hardware and operating systems, allowed computer designers to create another kind of software: software to design media. For instance, one of the most influential software in cultural digital imaging has been Photoshop, developed in 1987 mainly with Pascal (at least 75% of the source code was written in Pascal) for the Apple Macintosh by Thomas and John Knoll.

By the 1990s the computer was already seen as a media machine and a variety of media software started to be used and sold (Manovich, 2013): Aldus Pagemaker (1985), Adobe Illustrator (1987), Director 1.0 (1988), 3D Studio (1990), Pro Tools 1.0 (1991), After Effects (1993), Maya 1.0 (1998), etc. Nowadays, we believe there are at least two greater impacts of this cultural computation turn. First, media is primarily designed with software, which implies that media designers must learn how to use computers and software, and even at to some point to write scripts and to install plugins to extend the basic options of software applications. Second, if media is designed with software, what about the design of software to design media? Why does software includes this or that function? Why should it be used in the way it exists? Indeed, as we mentioned before, media, software and technologies in general, represent the actualization/realization of the visions of actors (a complex that includes humans, things, worlds, simulations, events, technical objects) that identified and developed a way of seeing the world and acting through it. Software is thus what needs to be learned if we want to go further in the design of new media.

In this section, we explore these two impacts: the design of media with software and the design of media software. This task is of course enormous, thus the scope of the present chapter will only be to sketch some directions that require further research and development. In some cases we will be able to give empirical examples from experimental projects in digital humanities. So instead of describing a design methodology, we rather discuss four main dimensions that should be taken into account in the design of pervasive virtual worlds: 1) technical-archaeological; 2) standard-conventional; 3) cultural-cognitive; 4) computational-digital. We need to remark that there is no hierarchical value behind this list, all items are equally important.

First Dimension: Technical-Archaeological

The first dimension sees media as technology. The aim of this approach is to adopt a similar perspective of media archaeology, which has been elaborated by academic researchers such as Siegfried Zielinski, Jussi Parikka, Friedrich Kittler and Oliver Grau, among others. Media archaeology attempts to uncover histories of media "through insights of past new media, often with an emphasis on the forgotten, the quirky, the non-obvious apparatuses, practices and inventions" (Parikka, 2012:2). In our current context, the importance to consider media archaeology is to investigate the several virtualizations of actions, organs and things as well as their implementation through technological means.

As we mentioned earlier, in this chapter we consider media in its largest possible conception, which is necessary to analyze it from different angles. In relation to technology we have already remembered that Marshall McLuhan defined media as extensions of man. In his famous book "Understanding Media" (McLuhan, 1964), he analyzed television, radio and comics, but also the wheel, garment, money and fashion. So media is a vast field which most of the times cannot be seized in its totality because we are immersed into it, both physically and cognitively. As media archaeologist Siegfried Zielinski suggests: "all we can do is to make certain cuts across it to gain operational access" (Zielinski, 2006). For him, these cuts are of two kinds: built constructs (interfaces, devices, programs, technical systems, networks) and media forms of expression and realization (film, video, books, websites, machine installations).

To discuss the relationship of media and technology, we will mainly concentrate on those 'built constructs'. The design of media with software has been largely inspired by previous media, but also by general-purpose devices and techniques. The software available to design media has envisioned the functions of previous media. For instance, a software like Photoshop has remediated operations from the field of painting, drawing and photography. Of course, we cannot say these functions are mere simulations of ancient techniques, they have been translated into computational forms where they interact with techniques from other domains. For instance, while an artist who uses analog tools may paint and draw on canvas using brushes, pencils and other inscription technologies, in the computer environment she disposes of simulations: icons representing those tools that can me customized with parameters. Both domains create a new hybrid medium: multiple types of brushes in a single software application, accessed through buttons, sliders, menus, panels and other conventions.

To conduct media archaeology with the intention of analyzing the design of media with software requires looking back at representations of previous tools and techniques but also the virtualizations of actions, organs and things. In other words, it assumes that there are actions that have already been virtualized and that those virtualizations have been translated into technical objects and then to computing forms. It will be interesting to put special attention in turnover cases, i.e when a radical new tool and/or a way of

being is introduced, because it points to a state of actualization of a virtual idea. The evolution and analysis of media software is a complex matter because those virtualizations arrive when new problems are explored that, in turn, could only emerge through the translation of past new media into computational forms.

To exemplify the complexity of layers intertwined inside a media software, let's come back to our previous case of hammering. As we said, the act of hammering is a virtualization that, in terms of McLuhan, extends the fist and the arm. We mentioned earlier that hammering is related to buttoning, given that both actions are based on contact. Allow us now to reveal some situations that should be considered if we want to study push-buttons as elements of the graphical interface in media software.

It seems we need to start by addressing the hand. Sigfried Giedion has made important observations about the human hand, which can point, seize, hold, press, pull, mold with ease. It can search and feel. Flexibility and articulation are its key words (Giedion, 2013:46). However, the hand has limitations and, above all, the main limitation is it cannot act endlessly. For Giedion, "the first phase of mechanization consists in transforming the pushing, pulling, pressing of the hand into continuous rotation" (Giedion, 2013:47). One may wonder about the reason why motion is evoked. In fact, Giedion makes the argument that 'movement' is closely linked to 'rationalism'. He stresses how often contradictory visions of the world have influenced our understanding of science and techniques: temporal vs eternal, rational vs irrational, internal vs external. For a society in the quest of progress, the last state to reach is perfection, so it is in a temporal mode rather than in an eternal one. In order to reach this goal, it needs to capture and dominate movement, to control it and to fix it, not to liberate it.

Would it be possible to say that our graphical user interfaces are virtualizations of pushing, pulling, pressing? The case of push-buttons might tell us some clues. As we know, push-buttons are almost ubiquitous in today's GUI. Buttons function along with pointers. The basic case of use is: the user manipulates the pointing device, she moves it and clicks on it (press, hold, release). These actions are represented on the screen: the pointer moves around the screen and, if it is accordingly positioned over an electronic representation of a button, it launches an action in the system. We believe one of the first virtualizations behind this simple scheme is the action of switching states and their associated processes.

The virtualization of pushing, pressing and pulling is at the heart of inventions such as the hammer and the bow. Many implementations of these actions can be found in objects such as springs, which were adapted for first mold-based locks in XVIII century. Other virtualizations can be found in pipe organs. During the XIV century, organs constituted one of the most complex inventions of that time. The basic components of pipe organs are very telling for us: the arrangement of pipes, a wind system and a key desk. The place where the user controlled the whole system was the key desk, and comprised manuals, pedals and stop controls. In order for the organist to perform a musical piece, some actions were performed. First there was a secondary user who fed the system with wind. Then the organist relied on the tracker action, which is the mechanical connection between the key desk and the wind system. The series of acts of pressing and pushing on manuals and pedals functioned along with the combination of stops, which was basically turning on or off the passage of air.

Yet another virtualization in the history of push-buttons can be seen in first electric telegraphs, which virtualized some operations and mechanisms of the pipe organ. Not only the user interface of the first telegraphs resembled pedals and manuals, but also the basic principle of switching on and off, however in this case the detection of electric current.

Switching states is one of the virtualizations behind push-buttons. But now let's consider the 'play button' as it exists in media players such as Apple Quicktime, in media authoring software such as Adobe After Effects, Autodesk Maya, Adobe Acrobat, and in programming environments such as Processing. It is possible to identify the play button as a remediation of previous buttons that appeared in recording devices that required to playback recorded signals. In this case, the act of switching on/off conveys movement from different angles: play a movie (QuickTime), preview a film montage (After Effects), go forward or go next (Acrobat) or compile a programming code (Processing). What happens now is that the action of pushing a button in an electronic environment is associated with larger series of processes and algorithms. This means that switching between 0 and 1 corresponds to modifying the entire system, from state A to state B, which may alter state C, and in turn state D.

To pursue our example, the task now would be to identify those processes and the virtualizations of actions, organs and things. But to do that it is necessary to conduct more research and to document empirical results. Today, media archaeology is still in its early stages. We need more projects that tackle the relationship between media and technology in an evolutionary perspective. We need to interrogate where do our tools come from? How are they related to past new media? What was at stake at the origin of the invention? How the invention altered other technologies? How media virtualizes us and things? An example of such endeavor is the Media Archaeology Lab, presented in 2011 by Lori Emerson. The project aims at documenting hardware, software, peripherals and individual collections that explain how tools were used in the past (MAL, 2013).

Second Dimension:
Standards-Conventional

There are a series of passages that occur in the life of inventions. The time in which those passages is accomplished could take years or even decades, and sometimes the passage might not take place until centuries later. Those passages go from the latent state to the manifest, from the virtual to the actual. The process starts in small scale. Gilbert Simondon has called the 'abstract object' to that moment of technical species when they are only known to their direct actors involved with the invention. Then, as the object interacts with others and the actualization of actions and transformations gets recognized, it could be that technical objects tend toward its 'concrete' phase. To be 'concrete' means that the object has evolved intrinsically and externally, within its parts and to its users and ecosystem. In the concreteness, the technical object couples in equal ontological manner with the user. No one is manipulated by the other, rather both cooperate for the same purpose.

The case of media design of course does not escape standardization and conventionalism, however we believe we are still far from the concreteness state of digital media. Standards and conventions allow media to consolidate a vocabulary, its syntax, its rules, its semantics; that allow to be communicated and foster the exchange of parts and modules. On the other hand, if pervasive virtual worlds would tend to full concreteness they would no longer be virtual, but possible, from the philosophical perspective that we discussed before. The point of virtual worlds is precisely to remain in constant dynamism and to motivate creative questions about them.

In the last section we borrowed from Zielinski the terms 'built constructs' and 'media forms of expression and realization' with the intention to make evident the distinction between media container and media content, respectively. As we will see, conventions and standards exist for both forms.

Let's take a brief look at conventions in media content. The investigation about conventions in film, radio, TV, games and other kinds of mass media has been done mainly in the field of humanities and social sciences, particularly in media studies, communication, information, humanities, literature, etc. From the moment a technical object or a new media is released to public at large, there has been noted a gap of thirty years until the first conventions appear. Alexander Galloway calls this gap the 'thirty-year rule', starting from the invention of a medium and ending at its ascent to proper and widespread *functioning in culture at large* (Galloway, 2006:85). In film studies, to mention an example, we can observe this gap between the introduction of the cinématographe, by Louis and Auguste Lumière in 1895, and the use of visual narrative techniques by David W. Griffith in a film like "The Birth of a Nation" (1915) or in rules of montage posited by Sergei Einsenstein in films such as "The Battleship Potemkin" (1925).

We use the notion of convention in similar terms as Janet Murray does: "social practices and communication formats shared by members of a culture or subculture, as well as media formats shared by artifacts within the same genre" (Murray 2012:415). This definition also considers the distinction between media content and media containers. For Murray, digital media is still in its immature phase, so its conventions have not yet fully been settled. As it has not yet passed the thirty-year rule. While other more established fields look for refinement, media designers deal with invention: "inventing something for which there is no standard model" (Murray 2012:3).

According to Murray, the move towards convention must follow a direction in which the four affordances of digital media are best exploited. These affordances are: encyclopedic, spatial, procedural and participatory. The method to follow is to design media by doing new media and, at the same time, to search for an increase of awareness in design choices, cultural traditions, cultural values, human needs and media specific conventions.

While all these questions are deeply important, we also suggest that pervasive virtual worlds should adopt an open point of view in regard of conventions. Virtualization and actualization require to be informed by actions, organs, components of the widest range, even going further than human perception.

Murray is right in adopting a more professional standpoint where conventions need to solve human needs. Do we really have needs? Instead of debating around questions that go beyond the scope of this chapter, we prefer to review three existent models that seem oriented toward the installation of conventions in digital media, if not fully in content and container, at least focused on the latter, the 'built constructs'.

First, perhaps the most advanced efforts on standardizing digital media come from software guidelines and specifications, best-practices, international recommendations, consortiums and, more recently, design patterns. Among the most acclaimed software guidelines we may cite the Macintosh Human Interface Guidelines, later changed to Apple's Human Interface Guidelines and more recently also making available the iOS Human Interface Guidelines. In those documents, Apple describes the notions of WYSIWYG, metaphors, direct manipulation and how to use the interface elements (i.e. menus, windows, dialog boxes, controls, icons, colors, behaviors and language) the Mac way (Apple Computer Inc., 1993). Regarding specifications, in 1993 the International Organization for Standardization released the ISO 9241 titled Ergonomic requirements for office work with visual display starting with requirements for Visual Displays and Keyboards. Today, ISO 9241 covers ergonomics of human-computer interaction around eight levels, going from software ergonomics to environment ergonomics and tactile and haptic interactions (ISO 2014). Another example of standardization is the World Wide Web Consortium (W3C), initiated by Tim Berners-Lee in 1994, and which is focused on standards for the World Wide Web:

languages, technologies, protocols and guidelines (W3C 2014). Finally, in a more user-oriented and content-oriented fashion, we have seen recently the development of design and programming patterns. An example is the online repository Yahoo Design Pattern Library which categorizes user interface patterns around layout, navigation, selection, rich interaction and social categories. A pattern, in terms of Yahoo, "describes an optimal solution to a common problem within a specific context (Yahoo! Developer Network, 2014). Any pattern is defined by a title, a problem, a context and a solution". Although Yahoo gathers and promotes the resources, it is a social-driven catalog, where users can submit and contribute with their own discoveries.

Second, one of the underlying principles that has allowed media software to flourish and expand is the availability to interchange files and data between applications and operating systems. This is possible because data structures and data formats are common in several environments. For example, although the Graphics Interchange Format (GIF) started as a proprietary technology developed and owned by CompuServe in 1987, it can be used free today, that is to say that the technique of data-compressing with the algorithm LZW and its packaging in a GIF file can be freely used by developers. As we know, GIF animated images have gained popularity with the explosion of web-based social networks so they can be opened, distributed, embedded and produced with many different software. Conversely, the MP3 format (MPEG-1 Audio Layer III), popular for compressing audio files, is not free and media software developers would need to pay a license to the Fraunhofer Society in order to distribute or sell encoders/decoders. This is one of the reasons why, for instance, a web browser like Mozilla Firefox does not support MP3 files. Instead, Firefox relies on the open format Ogg Vorbis.

Third, it seems that many required professional skills to access to job positions influence on the establishment of 'de facto' standards. This is also true for other cultural and conventional factors such as popularity and acceptance. We can refer once again to Adobe Photoshop as an example. Despite de fact that it is proprietary and commercial media software, it remains the number one choice among graphic designers, photographers and visual artists. Recently we have witnessed that alternative solutions exist, tools developed by the open-source community: the GIMP or the online Pixlr editor. However, the Adobe culture is still dominant.

The importance of taking a look at conventions and standards from the point of view of the design of pervasive virtual worlds is to embrace a reflexive thinking about our practices and tools. If we make the effort to detach ourselves from the continuum of everyday life and conventions, we can reinvigorate a critical and creative posture of our media. This is like natural language in culture, we don't often realize when a change was produced and suddenly we are using the same convention.

We would like to observe a final case that we believe makes the bridge with the following section. A large part of contemporary web design is done through content management systems (also called by the acronym CMS), for example WordPress; they can be extended with frameworks, plugins and libraries like Bootstrap. In the end, it seems like the design of web sites is based extensively on models and de facto standards. As a result, the web experience is more or less the same in a navigation session. Against the use of conventions, we react sometimes delighted when we see a piece of net art while navigating the web. As it occurred in the twentieth century with the installations by artists like Marcel Duchamp and Nam June Paik, who questioned and rearranged everyday objects, technologies and media, today media artists constitute an important community that questions the conventions of our electronic worlds.

Third Dimension: Cultural-Cognitive

In this section we adopt an approach more centered on the design of media software, and not on the design of media with software. The main focus is now on tools to create software. As we have seen, media is designed with software and this software constitutes the vision of actors that conceive a way of acting and accessing the world. We will now explore the design of software especially created for media production.

Media software can be broadly divided into media player software and authoring media software (Wardrip-Fruin, 2009). In this section we will focus on the latter and more specifically in those systems designed for desktop computers, instead of portable devices. The reason of this choice is twofold. On the one hand, software applications for desktop computers have existed for a larger time, so there are more lessons that can be learned from the implementation of computing forms, processes and interfaces. On the other hand, we believe mobile applications is an exciting field that requires a deeper investigation and we should accord it its own space in a further contribution.

Authoring media software, as we mentioned, inherit visions from pioneers who understood the computer as a media machine. We have also said that media software is a combination of conventions from past new media with properties exclusive of digital treatment of signals and information. In that manner, not only the established conventions should now be accessed and manipulated through graphical user interfaces, but also those conventions are informed by techniques from other domains and create new forms of designing media. Lev Manovich, in his recent book "Software Takes Command" (Manovich, 2013), observes how filters in Photoshop are varied and combined techniques from photography, painting and drawing such as blur and artistic effects. And there are also other filters that borrow actions developed in electrical engineering such as noise.

The design of media software is complex because there is always a dialectic relationship between conventions and new features. For instance, if we create a plugin, a script or a new menu for an experimental feature in already existing software, we must make it available through the given arrangement of the software. Conventions such as menus and submenus, property panels and inspectors, buttons and icons, are closely related to the operating system and middleware available to access components of the computer.

The case of software for media art is appealing because we have seen different conceptions of how to be in the world. The cooperation between digital artists and software developers has produced prominent examples of how to remediate past new media, to access to their features and to add new combinations, actions and processes. Software like Pure Data (1996), SuperCollider (1996), Processing (2001), Cinder (2010), NodeBox (2010), qualify in this category. Reas and Fry account for the importance of software in arts: "software holds a unique position among artistic media because of its ability to produce dynamic forms, process gestures, define behavior, simulate natural systems, and integrate other media including sound, image, and text" (Reas & Fry, 2007). Reas and Fry not only talk about media and software but they are also the beginners and main developers of Processing, a programming tool specifically created for artists and designers.

In their book, Reas and Fry dedicate a useful appendix to present other development tools oriented toward art and design; and they are all programming languages. Media art software could be then better seized if understood as an authoring system where software applications and programming languages interrelate and cooperate. As we know, the great majority of software applications users mainly communicate with it though its GUI, but a lot of those programs can also be extended with scripts and computer code. This means that GUI and programming languages lay in the same container; they are like two creative modes and/or layers that can be used separately or integrative.

We must add another remark regarding this particular software dedicated to create media art. Artists have always explored and combined new materials (Shanken, 2009). In the digital terrain this often means hacking, modifying, disrupting, connecting, and remixing software components, scripts, source code and binary files (besides hardware and devices). In that form, media artists may consider any software as a potential environment and laboratory to create media artworks, even if it is an accounting application or an office suite.

What are the effects of media art software? One of the pioneers of digital art, Jack Burnham, curated in 1970 one of the first exhibitions devoted to digital art: "Software, Information Technology: Its New Meaning for Art". As Edward Shanken points out, Burnham's idea of software was of a metaphor for art: "He conceived of 'software' as parallel to the aesthetic principles, concepts, or programs that underlie the formal embodiment of the actual art objects, which in turn parallel 'hardware'" (Shanken, 1998). We agree. Most studies on art movements understand art mainly from the aesthetics standpoint, concentrating on the experiences from the visitor side, on the dialogue that was established, and the altered effects that remain at the end of the day (most of the time in the viewer, and for Burnham, also in the manipulated artwork).

Is it possible to say the similar about media art software? Is there something like an aesthetics of media art software? To tackle this question we have to direct our discussion towards 'software criticism', which completes the aesthetic approach. Software critics reflect on ethical, political and socio-historical questions.

For example, Matthew Fuller understands software as a form of digital subjectivity (Fuller, 2003). The accent is put on the human-computer interface as the window and mirror of software, but also of a series of ideological, historical, and political values attached to it. To study the HCI implies to investigate power relations between the user and the way the software acts as a model of action. This idea goes along, although not exactly formulated as software criticism, with Winograd and Flores: "We encounter the deep questions of design when we recognize that in designing tools we are designing ways of being" (Winograd & Flores, 1986).

In a recent essay, Alexander Galloway thinks about the question of interfaces and claims that they are not objects, but rather processes and effects (Galloway, 2013). He observes the computer as a set of actions that relate to the world, so he embraces the philosophical standpoint of ethics to develop his arguments. For the author, the interface is a functional analog to ideology. Hence, the interface is not the object, but it is within it. It is manifested at the surface level of digital media, devices, and graphical representations.

Later, Galloway claims that software inherits some properties from interfaces. Software would be an allegorical analogy to ideology, i.e. more a simulation than a vehicle of ideology: "What is crucial in software is the translation of ideological force into data structures and symbolic language" (Galloway, 2013).

These brief insights into software criticism allow to think about 'media art software' differently. First, following Galloway, software functions in a dialectical fashion that requires visibility and invisibility. While computing code might be hidden as it is, only to be interpreted and parsed, at the same time, the artist/developer has a high degree of declarative reflexivity (variables, functions, etc.). This resonates with our earlier coupling of software applications and programming languages: media art can also have two entry points for software criticism and should take into account the dialectical logic between invisibility and syntax formalism.

Second, following Fuller, our practice as media artists could also be thought in terms of 'speculative software'. If software simulates ideology, then such simulations might be interrogated. Speculative software would be software that reveals its processes as it enacts them:

What characterizes speculative work in software is, first, the ability to operate reflexively upon itself and the condition of being software (…) to make visible the dynamics, structures, regimes, and drives of each of the little events which it connects to. Second, (…) to make the ready ordering of data, categories, and subjects spasm out of control. Third, it is to subject the consequences of these first two stages to the havoc of invention (Fuller, 2003).

Finally, let's come back to digital subjectivity. Nake and Grabowski seem to summarize Fuller and Burnham. They see 'aesthetic computing' as the introduction of subjectivism into computing… with all its consequences. They recall a very important aspect of software and computers:

… the computer does not directly operate on the pixels on the screen. It operates on their representations in the display buffer, and further down on this scale of manipulability are representations of other entities that form the real stuff of programs (Nake & Grabowski, 2008).

For any speculative effort on software, it seems necessary to go further down the GUI. The more we know the software, the more we can interrogate its simulations. But before simulations, there are bits and bytes, functions and classes, visual representations, etc. How can we access to them? How they relate between them? These are some questions that need to be addressed by designers of digital media and media software.

To summarize, the design of pervasive virtual worlds demands to ask deeper questions about the selection of processes and data formats that we implement in any project. Software is the reflection of cultural choices by its designers, who often take into account the cognitive framework of the final user. As we have showed with the example of media art software, the development of our tools should be accompanied by a reflective thinking that looks at ethical, political and aesthetical considerations. Furthermore, it is also pertinent to be aware of recent research on cognitive sciences and cognitive semiotics because they consider the coupling of meaning, mind and perception. Unfortunately we are not aware of any empirical project that links software design and cognitive semiotics, however we can point to studies that are interested on 'translations' from the visual to the audio realm by using software (AGI, 2014).

Fourth Dimension: Computational-Digital

The fourth dimension in the design of media software puts attention on software and its computational aspects. It is about understanding software and computation themselves, as an object of study. So far we have traced a line of study that goes from the archaeology of media to conventions and standards to cultural and ideological aspects of media software. In this part the focus is on material properties of software. If media is created with software and if we must regard how media software is designed, then a further step is to investigate which are the components of software and how they work.

Traditionally, this area has been the subject of computer science, which explores the theory and practice of computer systems, methods, languages, structures and processes. Most of the efforts in computer science have been directed toward the optimization and performance of computer systems. However, the implication of humanists and artists has also motivated creative innovations. The case of artists in residence, like David Em at NASA in the 70s, is an example of advances and uses from the creative and artistic standpoint.

For humanists and social scientists, perhaps one of the most notable crossings between computer science and history, literature, philosophy, and cultural studies, has been the emergence of the 'humanities computing', or as it is known today: digital humanities. The first practices that emerged from this interdisciplinary convergence were based on text and its statistical processing in order to distinguish patterns and features that could assist in issues of stylometry and lexicography. More recently, digital humanities increasingly use computing methods to produce information visualization, network analysis, text mining, databases, digital publishing and even the design of software especially dedicated to assist the work of digital humanists.

As it can be perceived, art, social and human sciences hold a close relationship with computer science. Humanities have made contributions in the sense of reflecting on the human effects and consequences of computing. Recently, Bruno Latour has insisted on considering the effects of the digital on the environment (Latour 2014). For Latour the materiality required by digital data has often been neglected and created a myth around the immateriality of the digital. Digital media is very material. To put it simply, software and data are stored in devices that process information. This information can be digital, saved as binary data, but in the end it needs to be rendered analogically for human consumption. The acquisition, processing and restitution from digital to analog requires electricity to power up computers and this source of energy has direct incidence in the environment: nuclear plants, massive hangars to store hard drives and servers, together with all infrastructure necessary to maintain our current state of affairs. Materiality cannot be disregarded any longer, but in this section we will inspect another type of materiality of software, the 'real stuff', in terms of Nake and Grabowski. These material properties are their constituent elements.

Where to start in order to grasp the complexity of software and its place within the computer sciences? As an entry point we will use the Computing Classification System elaborated by the Association for Computing Machinery (ACM, 1998) with the objective to index articles and publications in conferences, journals and books edited by the ACM Press. The ACM has a three-level classification system and their descriptors. At the top level there are eleven domains: A. General Literature, B. Hardware, C. Computer system organization, D. Software, E. Data, F. Theory of computation, G. Mathematics of computing, H. Information systems, I. Computing methodologies, J. Computer applications and K. Computing milieux.

As the computing machinery field has evolved and as researchers have published and documented their results, the categories and subcategories have grown. Is it possible to say that subcategories represent refinement in the domain? Can we say that the computing filed is dynamic instead of static, i.e. in continuous expansion? Which are those categories where refinement has taken place? Figure 1 shows a flow diagram connecting the first level with the second.

As we can see, I. Computing methodologies is the largest region and has 7 subcategories at the second level. From these subcategories, the most abundant are I.2 Artificial intelligence, I.4 Image processing and computer vision, and I.3 Computer graphics. The second largest category is D. Software, with 4 stronger subcategories within D.2 Software engineering. The third largest is B. Hardware, which has 8 subcategories mainly concentrated in B.4 Input/output and data communications, B.1 Control structures and B.6 Logic design.

In Figure 2 we show a network map with the connections between the first level and the last one, that is the descriptors. In this diagram it will interesting to note how descriptors appear in several different categories. For example, Interactive systems, Nonprocedural languages, and Standards exist both in I. Computing methodologies and D. Software. The link between I. Computing methodologies and B. Hardware is given by the descriptors Algorithms and Parallel. D. Software and B. Hardware are related by Diagnostics, Simulation, and Virtual memory. It would be curious

to note there is no single descriptor that relies the three largest domains (I, D and B). The only descriptor that relies more than two domains is Standards, which is the link between C. Computer system organization, D. Software, I. Computing methodologies and K. Computing milieux. A deeper analysis will have to investigate what and why are those relationships? What are the topics and problems that scientific papers regard? Or, is it possible that more links between domains appear in the future?

While a brief analysis like this can help approaching trends in computer science, we can also try to explore a different angle directly related to media software. For this matter we will follow Manovich's definition of media: *media = data structures + algorithms* (Manovich, 2013). For him, the most fundamental constituents of media software are algorithms and data structures. For his formula, Manovich declares inspiration from Niklaus Wirth, designer of the programming language Pascal, and particularly from his book "Algorithms Plus Data Structures Equals Programs "(1975). Our intention at present will be precisely to explore data structures and algorithms in more detail.

Which are the major algorithms? And which are those algorithms particularly dedicated to media, for example images? Which techniques have been introduced by those algorithms? What kinds of data structures they use? What is the relationship between data structures and algorithms for digital imaging? How have they influenced our conception of digital media and the operations we can perform with them? Is there a place for virtualization of digital media?

Algorithms and data structures are in constant development. A field such as computational geometry, for instance, considers among its interests the systematic study of geometry algorithms, observing the "realization that classical characterizations of geometric objects are frequently not amenable to the design of efficient algorithms (…) computational geometry must reshape –whenever necessary- the classical discipline into its computational incar-

Figure 1. Flow diagram of first two levels of ACM classification system (Everardo Reyes, 2014).

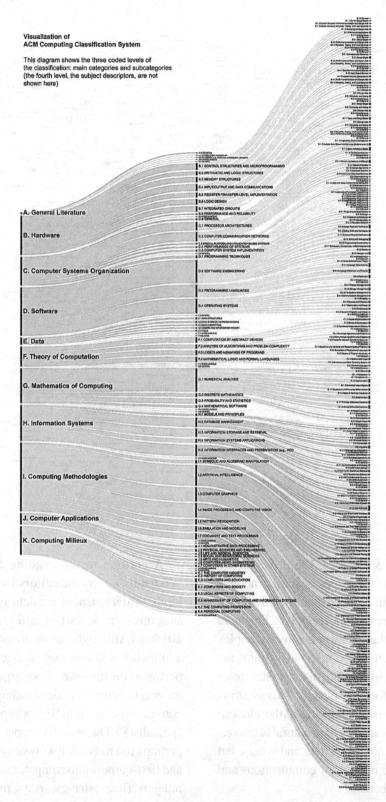

Figure 2. Network diagram of ACM classification system (Everardo Reyes, 2014).

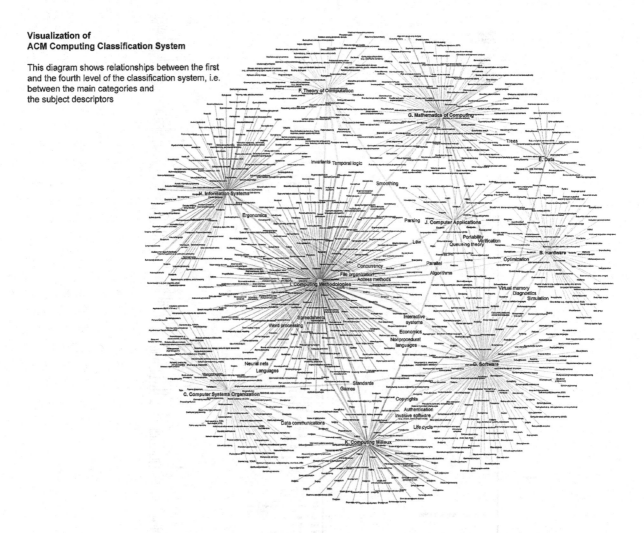

nation" (Preparata & Shamos, 1985). So far, we can say that the existing types of data structures are more reduced in number than the amount of algorithms. For computational geometry, Preparata and Shamos recall that the most common complex objects in the design of geometric algorithms are sets and sequences, so they must use data structures particularly suited for these objects. This situation can be explained in a similar manner as the relationship between letters and words in natural language. There is a limited number letters and words, but a relatively infinite number of combinations and techniques to use them.

According to the ongoing classification by Wikipedia's users and editors, there are five major kinds of data structures: data types, linear data structures, trees, hashes, and graphs (Wikipedia 2014a). (Although the information available in Wikipedia is in constant change, we believe it is pertinent for the sake of our argument because it reflects the current understanding of the field by a community constituted by both specialists and non-specialists.) The primitive types of data types are perhaps the most well-known types to beginners and first-comers into computer science: Booleans, integers, floats, strings, arrays, matrices, bitmaps.

Other lesser-known structures are: trees, heaps, tries, hashes and graphs. It is important to notice that data structures determine how information is structured and stored, in order to be processed by algorithmic techniques.

Algorithms, as it can be guessed, have larger types and classifications. Following Wikipedia, algorithms are classified in five types: 1) combinatorial (network analysis, routing for graphs, graph search, string metrics, etc.); 2) computational mathematics (collision detection, triangulation, discrete logarithms, computation of PI, eigenvalues, etc.); 3) computational science (algorithms of astronomy, bioinformatics, geoscience, linguistics, medicine, physics, and statistics); 4) computer science, and 5) software engineering (database, operating systems, memory allocation, distributed systems -all of them are interesting entry points to search deeper the relation between the ACM's categories B. Hardware and I. Computing methodologies evoked before) (Wikipedia 2014b).

The fourth category of algorithms, called computer science, is particularly exciting to study because it contains many operations behind techniques in software for media design. Within the subcategory of 'digital signal processing', for example, we find image processing algorithms: contrast enhancement, dithering and half-toning, feature detection, segmentation, which are familiar in digital graphic design and scientific visualization. Other media techniques can be found in different subcategories, computer graphics algorithms (clipping, ambient occlusion, beam tracing, ray tracking), shading algorithms, coding theory algorithms (image and video compression).

The manner in which these algorithms act and are implemented in software is varied: it could be through the graphical user interface; or it could be in parallel or in sequential series; or they can be invoked by the click of one or a combination of buttons; or by parametric adjustments; or even automatically programmed upon an indirect action. Within this context, virtualizations of media may arrive by combining different algorithms and data structures. But at another level, virtualizations might also occur in the creation of new data structures and new algorithms. To put an example, let's imagine an engine to visualize the fourth spatial dimension. How to represent something that goes beyond the grasp of our senses and cognition?

TWO EXERCISES IN THE DESIGN OF PERVASIVE VIRTUAL WORLDS

In this part we present a couple digital works developed by us. The intention is to inform the reader on the creative strategies put in practice behind our productions. In all the cases, we have tried to question standard and conventional paradigms of information visualization. Our practice is thus more related to speculative computing, aesthetic provocations, design by disruption, experimentation and media art.

Messages vers le Futur

'Messages vers le futur' was an installation presented at the event 'La nuit de chercheurs' at the IUT Bobigny, Paris, in September 28, 2012. The main intention of the event was to introduce science and technology to public in general. We decided to propose an installation consisting on a video projection and a computer station. In the projection the visitor saw the representation of a hyperbolic figure floating in a dark digital 3D environment. This figure was inspired from the theoretical concept of 'wormhole' in physics, coined by John Wheeler in 1967, also known as the Einstein–Rosen bridge, described as *a hypothetical shortcut for travel between distant points in the Universe* (Thorne, 1994:484).

The idea of 'Messages vers le futur' was to invite visitors to metaphorically send a message to the future. Through the computer station or through their mobile devices, they could send a message about they feelings or sensation of the present time: something appealing to them, or a recent event they lived, or something they would like to do in the future. This message could contain de hashtag #messagesfutur and so it appeared on screen in form of a 3D sphere along with the text of the message. The sphere crossed the wormhole and then disappeared from the projection. For every message sent, the user registered her email address and received the message sent one year later into her email inbox. Figure 3, shows a screenshot of the electronic wormhole and a message passing by.

Technically speaking, the projection was made with Processing, enhanced with the libraries Twitter API, TwitterStream, PeasyCam and Box2D. For the design of the hyperbolic figure we translated into the Processing language the mathematical formula of super-quadratic figures. We started from the main algorithm by Kostas Terzidis (Terzidis, 2009), who kindly agreed to be used as the base for 'Messages vers le futur'. Some assistance should also be credited to Eleanor Dare, who made suggestions to refine the algorithm and implementation in Processing.

The metaphor of space-time traveling was interesting to be studied. During the exhibition, it was well-received mainly by young visitors (teenagers and younger) who got the idea immediately. We received few questions about the graphical rendering. Instead, the questions were about the content of the message: what can I write? As the answer is open, users evoked the fact of messaging to a future self.

Another thing to note was the implementation of mathematical formulae. Because Processing does not have a function to draw a one-sheet hyperboloid, it was necessary to code the figure. This single aspect led to think on what other mathematical figures and surfaces does not have a computational representation though software. What are we missing because there is no access through software? Where can find alternatives

Figure 3. Graphical projection from then installation Messages vers le future (Everardo Reyes, 2014).

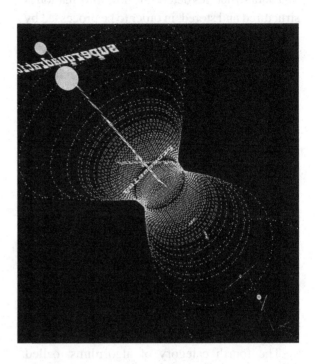

to standardized software which already proposes different figures than those in Euclidean geometry? And ultimately, can we represent a fourth spatial dimension? This has been a real question in science and astronomy. Recent research at UC Santa Barbara demonstrated that, at very small nano scales, there are particles that exist in two places at the same time (Cho, 2010) or that time moves slower as we separate from the Earth's surface (Reinhardt, 2007).

In any case, what is interesting to evoke at this point is that virtualization of digital media has an opportunity with computers and electronic representation. Designers can obtain inspiration from the vantage point of objects and environment. How do objects perceive? What is like for an environment to be connected with multiple devices at the same time? How does the environment perceive the transmission of signals?

Disrupting 3D Models

3D models are generally considered as digital objects made of geometry that simulate width, height and depth inside a computational environment. Although their origins can be traced to computer graphics during the 60s, when pioneers created computer simulations, virtual reality, virtual worlds and visual effects in film, nowadays we encounter them in graphic design, video games, architecture, art, advertising, Web, industrial design, scientific visualizations, and digital humanities.

In 2012 we have developed a simple application that allows users to interact with 3D models. Technically speaking, we used Processing with ModelBuilder and ControlP5 libraries. The application basically takes a STL model and renders it in the 3D digital environment. For us, the importing process implies to read the original geometry in the STL file and to render it in its organized 3D spatial layout in form of a series of points or a formation of polygonal shapes (triangles). Once a file has been loaded, the user is able to interact inside the 3D view environment. A series of GUI sliders indicate modifications upon three factors. Additional buttons apply transformations, change mode view (points or triangles), and reset

the model to its original state. Figure 4 shows an original model, the user interface and the resulting transformation.

The idea of the system is to invite users to perform transformations on the models. The resulting images from transformations are basically non-figurative. Some would be appealing but disrupting at the same time. They show how the same quantity of triangles in a model may be recomposed. Of course because STL relies heavily on tessellation, triangles are never broken apart. That means, geometry is not spread, they rather create new solid forms. If a transformation is made on the view mode of POINTS, then the result looks like a particle explosion.

As we mentioned earlier, we used Processing to develop our viewing/transformation system. Regarding the acquisition of 3D models, we used several different software applications depending on the input kind of model. Before developing our own application, we asked ourselves if it was possible to produce our generative transformations with existing software. Although Maya and Blender, among others, allow to enhance their functionalities with scripting code, we decided to create our own system mainly because we wanted to deploy a simple user interface to interact with objects. Indeed, Maya and Blender are complex environments that cover

Figure 4. Disrupting 3D models
Everardo Reyes, 2014).

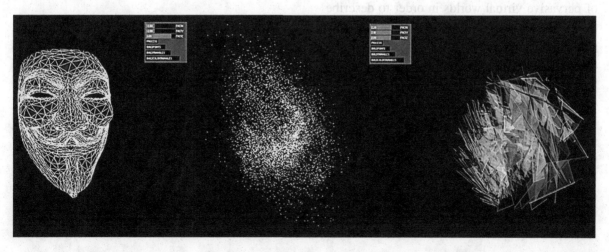

topics from modeling to animation and rendering. Furthermore, they handle their own file formats. It is possible to export/import to other formats but the main workspace remains the same. For us, we used STL format, which is widely adopted for 3D printing and would accordingly satisfy the desire of printing a complex and disordered model. But perhaps the main reason behind the production of this experimental system was the cultural practices that it supported. A complex and integrated environment, such as Maya in the case of 3D modeling, is suited for many tasks required by cultural industries but not precisely for a particular artistic approach and research need.

How could the approach on disruption be used for virtual worlds? We believe disrupting software could foster creative practices, but in a virtual world we can also disrupt reality, or the simulations of the physical world, or even fictions, plots and sequences of events. The task would be to challenge human perception, to adopt existing processes from other fields (science, astronomy, neurology, archaeology, etc.). But because software and digital media have the inherited intention of extending our senses, we have to consider the world at large, beyond our senses and experiences, from the transcendental perspective.

CONCLUSION

In this contribution we have explored the notion of pervasive virtual worlds in order to describe the analogical and electronic world that is mixed, extended and mediated through media. Media was understood in its largest sense: as technique and technology. Pervasive virtual worlds are composed of concrete and simple forms, but also of abstract and complex ones, produced by the interaction of heterogeneous elements: individuals, things, objects, machines; these forms can be physical but immaterial as well. Furthermore, recalling the idea of the world as larger than human perception and understanding, some forms can even be unknown for some actors of the world.

Pervasive virtual worlds is an idea aiming at opening opportunities for new design and communication processes. Virtual worlds are pervasive because there is an ever-increasing quantity and types of devices connected between them: from mobile handhelds to ambient intelligence to the internet of things. But simulation, communication, extension and virtualization do not depend on those artifacts to flourish, principally because they are latent. As we have seen, organs and actions are being virtualized in artificial worlds from the perspective of human beings, but there is still a lot of work to do if we approach virtualization from the vantage point of things in general, for example.

We proposed to study the design of media with software and the design of media software by taking into account four perspectives:

1. Media archaeological;
2. Standards and conventions;
3. Cultural;
4. Computational.

The main intention was to rethink media within a larger context and to point to design strategies for new media in creative manners. Media are the result of the vision of a series of actors, they are manifest in the form of representations, simulations, devices, graphical interfaces. These are for us examples of pervasive worlds that can be virtualized and actualized.

REFERENCES

ACM. (1998). *The 1998 ACM computing classification system*. Retrieved July 14, 2014, from http://www.acm.org/about/class/1998/

AGI. (2014). *Accessible graphics initiative*. Retrieved July 14, 2014, from http://perceptual-artifacts.org/agi/

Apple Computer Inc. (1993). *Macintosh human interface guidelines*. New York: Addison-Wesley.

Bogost, I. (2013). *Alien phenomenology, or what it's like to be a thing.* Minneapolis, MN: University of Minnesota Press.

Bolter, J. D., & Grusin, R. (1999). *Remediation: Understanding new media.* Cambridge, MA: MIT Press.

Boulanger, P. (2008, March). *Virtual reality and the arts: A critical review.* Keynote at Computer Art Congress 2008 [CAC.2]. Mexico City, Mexico.

Cho, A. (2010). The first quantum machine. *Science, 330*(6011), 1608–1609. doi:10.1126/science.330.6011.1604 PMID:21163978

Darwin, Ch. (1859). *The origin of species.* London: Signet Classics.

De Landa, M. (2002). *Intensive science and virtual philosophy.* London: Bloomsbury Academic.

Deleuze, G. (1968). *Différence et Répétition.* Paris: PUF.

Fuller, M. (2003). *Behind the blip: Essays on the culture of software.* New York: Autonomedia.

Galloway, A. (2006). *Gaming: Essays on algorithmic culture.* Minneapolis, MN: University of Minnesota Press.

Galloway, A. (2013). *The interface effect.* Cambridge, UK: Polity Press.

Giedion, S. (1948). *Mechanization takes command.* Minneapolis, MN: University of Minnesota Press.

Grau, O. (Ed.). (2010). *MediaArtHistories.* Cambridge, MA: MIT Press.

ISO. (2014). Retrieved July 14, 2014, from http://www.iso.org

Kittler, F. (2009). *Optical media.* Cambridge, UK: Polity Press.

Latour, B. (2014, July). *Rematerializing humanities thanks to digital traces.* Keynote at Digital Humanities 2014, Lausanne, Switzerland.

Lévy, P. (1998). *Qu'est-ce que le virtuel?* Paris: La Découverte.

MAL. (2013). *Media archaeology lab.* Retrieved October 9, 2014, from http://mediaarchaeologylab.com/

Manovich, L. (2013). *Software takes command.* London: Bloomsbury Academic.

McLuhan, M. (1964). *Understanding media: The extensions of man.* New York: McGraw Hill.

Meillassoux, Q. (2012). *Après la Finitude: Essai sur la Nécessité de la Contingence.* Paris: Seuil.

Murray, J. (2012). *Inventing the medium: Principles of interaction design as a cultural practice.* Cambridge, MA: MIT Press.

Nake, F., & Grabowski, S. (2008). The interface as sign and as aesthetic event. In P. Fishwick (Ed.), *Aesthetic computing.* Cambridge, MA: MIT Press.

Parikka, J. (2012). *What is media archaeology.* Cambridge, UK: Polity Press.

Preparata, F., & Shamos, M. (1985). *Computational geometry: An introduction.* New York: Springer-Verlag. doi:10.1007/978-1-4612-1098-6

Reas, C., & Fry, B. (2007). *Processing: A programming handbook for visual designers and artists.* Cambridge, MA: MIT Press.

Reinhardt, S., Saathoff, G., Buhr, H., Carlson, L. A., Wolf, A., Schwalm, D., & Gwinner, G. et al. (2007). Test of relativistic time dilation with fast optical atomic clocks at different velocities. *Nature Physics, 3*(12), 861–864. doi:10.1038/nphys778

Reyes, E. (2011). Pervasive virtual worlds. In G. Mura (Ed.), *Metaplasticity in virtual worlds: Aesthetics and semantic concepts.* Hershey, PA: IGI Global. doi:10.4018/978-1-60960-077-8.ch004

Shanken, E. (1998). The house that jack built: Jack Burnham's concept of "software" as a metaphor for art. *Leonardo Electronic Almanac, 6*(10). Retrieved July 14, 2014, from http://www.artexetra.com/House.html

Shanken, E. (Ed.). (2009). *Art and electronic media*. London: Phaidon Press.

Simondon, G. (1989). *Du mode d'Existence des Objets Techniques*. Paris: Aubier.

Terzidis, K. (2009). *Algorithms for visual design*. Indianapolis, IN: Wiley Publishing.

Thorne, K. (1994). *Black holes and time warps*. Norton & Co.

W3C. (2014). *World wide web consortium (W3C)*. Retrieved July 14, 2014, from http://w3.org

Wardrip-Fruin, N. (2009). *Expressive processing*. Cambridge, MA: MIT Press.

Wikipedia. (2014a). *List of data structures*. Retrieved July 14, 2014, from https://en.wikipedia.org/wiki/List_of_data_structures

Wikipedia. (2014b). *List of algorithms*. Retrieved July 14, 2014, from https://en.wikipedia.org/wiki/List_of_algorithms

Winograd, T., & Flores, F. (1986). *Understanding computers and cognition: A new foundation for design*. New York: Addison Wesley.

Yahoo Developer Network. (2014). *Yahoo design pattern library*. Retrieved July 14, 2014, from https://developer.yahoo.com/ypatterns/

Zielinski, S. (2006). *Deep time of the media: Toward an archaeology of hearing and seeing by technical means*. Cambridge, MA: MIT Press.

KEY TERMS AND DEFINITIONS

Analytical Maps: A material and graphical support that tries to make evident and easy to identify patterns and trends about a domain. It consists of digital processing of data and its rendering in visual form. It is a tool for research and study. It could assist researchers that work in digital humanities, speculative computing, aesthetic provocations, design by disruption, experimentation and media art. The projects and experiments in analytical maps, as well as other forms of graphical representations, might also serve as conceptual tools to think about the virtualization processes and archaeology.

Computing Medium: Also related to the notion of 'software as medium'. It describes the computer as a media machine, that is, an virtualizing tool for creating media content, but also as a tool to create media software (software to create other media). The complexity of the computing medium relies in its combination of conventions from past new media with properties exclusive of digital treatment of signals and information. In that manner, not only the established conventions are now accessed and manipulated through graphical user interfaces, but also those conventions are informed by techniques from other domains and create new forms for designing media.

Media Archaeology: A recent approach elaborated within media studies that investigates the several virtualizations of actions, organs, and things as well as their implementation through technological means throughout historical periods. It assumes that there are actions that have already been virtualized and that those virtualizations have been translated into technical objects and then, more recently, to computing forms. It asks, among other questions: where do our tools come from? How are they related to past new media? What was at stake at the origin of the invention? How the invention altered other technologies? How media virtualize us and virtualize things?

Pervasive Virtual Worlds: A vision of the world from a creative and innovative standpoint, mainly for design and communication. It considers the emerging environment that combines analog and electronic media as the ground and sandbox to experiment with new forms of design and communication. It is an attempt to describe the analogical and electronic world that is mixed, extended and mediated through media. A pervasive virtual world is complex. It recalls the importance of taking into account concrete and simple forms, but also of abstract and complex ones, produced by the interaction of heterogeneous actors: individuals, things, objects, machines; these forms can be physical but immaterial as well. Furthermore, recalling the idea of the world as larger than human perception and understanding, some forms can even be unknown for some actors of the world.

User-Interface Convention: Generally referred as those graphical elements that have been embraced and acknowledged because they facilitate using a computer and software by a common person. Broadly speaking, UI conventions can be elements from the WIMP paradigm: windows, icons, mouse, pointers. But they is also related to visual and language metaphors, where the software applications reside: operating systems, middleware, etc. The most famous metaphor related to the computing medium remains the desktop, but others can emerge in a time when portable devices, ambient intelligence and different kind of artisanal and experimental software develop.

Virtual World: In its traditional meaning, informed by the computer sciences, it can also be referred to as 'artificial worlds' or 'virtual environments'. From a different perspective, that is, from a philosophical one, a virtual world is approached as a state of being. Following the work by Pierre Lévy, Gilles Deleuze, Henri Bergson, there are four states of being: the real, the possible, the actual and the virtual. The virtual and the possible are latent, while the real and the actual are manifest. The main difference between the virtual and the possible is that the virtual questions a creative solution to a problem: it tries to problematize it again, while the possible only executes and repeats already existing solutions.

Virtualization: The passage from the actual state of being to the virtual. The actual is a manifest state that tries to solve a problem in a creative manner, but when this creative solution is questioned again it is re-articulated and virtualized. It is a process of dematerialization but at the same time of thinking, inspiring, reasoning, and connecting different (and often non-obvious) actors.

Section 2
Education

Chapter 11
Making It for the Screen:
Creating Digital Media Literacy

Paul Chilsen
Carthage College, USA

ABSTRACT

We are immersed in a culture of spoken media, written media, and now irrevocably, digital screen media. Just as writing and speaking skills are keys to functioning in society, we must consider that the world increasingly demands proficiency in "mediating" as well. Doing anything less leaves this powerful medium in the hands of a relative few. By offering instruction in what digital screen media is, how it is effectively created, how the Internet continues to alter communication, and how this all informs everyday teaching and learning, digital media literacy can become more broadly understood and accessible. This chapter follows a program developed by the Rosebud Institute and looks at how—using simple, accessible technology—people can become more digital media literate by creating screen products themselves. The creation process also enables deeper, more authentic learning, allowing us all to communicate more effectively, to self-assess more reflectively, and to thrive in a screen-based world.

DIGITAL MEDIA: LITERACY ON SCREEN

You may well be reading this text on paper, but it remains increasingly likely that you are reading some or all of it on a screen right now. In many cases, as you read this chapter, it seems not that big of an issue. After all, it is simply words on a page and the medium of delivery may not be all that crucial. Inverting the classic phrase of communication scholar Marshall McLuhan for a moment, the medium does not really seem to alter or affect the message all that much in this particular case.

However, with the tectonic media shift in which we find ourselves, the lines we think we know, and think we can count on, seem to be blurring. The myriad machinations and goings on in our convergent media world, while a fascinating and rich topic, understandably extend beyond the scope of

DOI: 10.4018/978-1-4666-8205-4.ch011

this chapter. Rather the focus here is to look more at what we are doing now. Now that the explosive growth and pervasive penetration of new media is upon us, are we doing the best that we can to get a firmer grip on the reins? The wave of buying and handing out expensive devices designed to merely access the conversation continues to grow and swell, threatening to eat up shrinking resources. In light of that, what are steps that can be taken to move beyond the latest techno wizardry and instead convey real skills that allow more people to effectively join in, to make clear meaning, and to affect the change they seek?

One way is to take a step back – get back to basics a bit and begin to give people some simple tools that they can use to more effectively be a part of the burgeoning world of what is happening on screens around the world. Yet another related approach is to seek out existing resources and systems that are already in place, but are ripe for innovation, change and a refreshed perspective. As mentioned, you may be looking at a screen right now but if not, you have probably looked at one if not several already today and most certainly – unless you make a concerted effort to the contrary – you will be bombarded with screen images all day, telling you what to do, what to think, what to like – even what to say.

And that trend continues to grow with abandon. As Eva and John Waterworth state in their discussions on mediated presence "Our everyday lives are more and more pervasively experienced through media… There are very few places where one is out of reach of [these] devices…" (Waterworth & Waterworth, 2010)

This ever-expanding world of screen-based electronic media encompasses such an understandably and incredibly broad array of media types, paradigms, and histories that even finding a name or term to refer to it all can prove difficult. Under the auspices of the

Rosebud Institute, introduced in the next section, we have used the term broader term 'digital media' as well as the more specific 'screen media'.

These terms work somewhat interchangeably to describe media specifically produced, created for, and unfolding on the screen yet are general enough to encompass a broad array of different media, both moving (film, video, television, and gaming) as well as those which are generally more static (websites, social media, blogs). As mentioned, this chapter has a necessarily refined scope. It looks at a very practical and doable approach that is giving people a baseline way to become more active and informed members of a screen media world. Interestingly, it is in this more simple approach that the potential becomes highly expansive, giving people the tools to literally go wherever they want, much like the effect of teaching a person to write or to read.

But what *people* or *persons* are we talking about? In attempting to define who really needs to be digital media literate, to say *everyone* may well elicit a raised eyebrow or two but literally, digital media literacy is so crucial that virtually everyone will need some baseline understanding of what it is and how it works. This is not a new concept of course. The term media literacy has been around since the 1970's and in 1988, one of the most relevant and enduring quotes comes from a former president of the Carnegie Foundation for the Advancement of Teaching, Ernest Boyer: "It is no longer enough to simply read and write. Students must also become literate in the understanding of visual images" (Boyer, 1988). What is new however, is how far-reaching and therefore undeniable the screen has become. If screen media is virtually everywhere, then its literacy is in demand virtually everywhere if we are to have an informed and literate public. "The ability to both read and write visual information; the ability to learn visually; to think and solve problems in the visual domain—will, as the information revolution evolves, become a requirement for success in business and in life." (Gray, 2008) That said, keeping the sites of this chapter on achievable goals and not biting off more than is manageable, the immediate audience addressed mostly herein are students and educators – both in a K-12 environment and in post-secondary education as well.

Without delving too deeply into program specifics, we will outline a broadly prescriptive approach that we have pursued and continue to develop – a program that takes achievable steps towards reducing and addressing what has been referred to as our rampant media *illiteracy* (Baker, 2012). While the method is simple enough, there have been some speed bumps and even roadblocks along the way but the promise of a more informed, empowered, and literate digital citizenry seems a worthy enough cause to overcome the obstacles.

Toward the end of the chapter, there is a look at ongoing program efficacy and the exploration of ideas for growth, refinement, and expansion, giving attention to where things can go and furthering the mission of creating digital media literacy for all.

THE NEW DIGITAL DIVIDE

It has been said that those who control the media, control the future. Setting aside a more manipulative connotation of "control," and focusing rather on an interpretation more aligned with understanding and effective use, it seems a natural, logical extension that in order to more positively affect our future we must not only increase the *number* of future media makers, but we must also increase the number who are truly and more fundamentally literate (Chilsen & Wells, 2012).

If you accept this "proliferating mediation of our everyday lives" (Waterworth & Waterworth, 2010) as perpetual and expanding, and embrace the intrinsic notion that we are therefore irreversibly immersed in a screen media culture, then one could argue that just as we are taught and know how to write and speak in a text-based society, now, in order to function competently in a screen-based society, we all would do well to start becoming more proficient at "mediating" as well.

Given the massive realignment that continues to unfold in the broad world of digital media, it seems both right and pressing that we realign the thinking and approach taken towards defining what screen media is, who ought to know how it works and how we can democratize the understanding and use of these powerful and exploding media.

Unlike fashionable pedagogical trends, the need for screen media literacy and ability is here to stay. Embracing and expanding what Elizabeth Daley, of USC's School of Cinema-Television once called "the greatest digital divide," the approach outlined herein seeks to close the chasm between those who can read and write in screen media, and those who cannot (Van Ness, 2005). Put simply, because so many now have access to and can therefore create media for the screen, everyone ought to be learning the basics of how to read and write in its unique language. To do anything less leaves this awesome and expanding power in the hands of a relative few and by virtue of its relevance and importance, a *new* digital divide has opened before us.

The term 'digital divide' has been around since the 1990s and originally defined technology's haves and have-nots (Richtel, 2012). According to the World Economic Forum in a 2014 report on global information technology, the original divide is still a problem and progress is slow (Cann, 2014). However, not unlike the way phone service or even electrical service eventually found its way to wherever it could reasonably go, this seems more an economic question rather than an ideological concern. As with phone and electricity, it may seem callous to say but there's simply too much money to be made for high speed internet to not also eventually reach everywhere it can logically go. Eventually screens will literally be everywhere and like the current internet joke about Afghan rebels being able to send a video from a mountain cave when we can't get cell service in our living rooms, everyone will be using its power. Since the mid 1990s, many have expropriated the digital divide term, refining it as the issues continue to morph. But one of the earliest realignments of the term has followed the logic that since eventually most all will have the access, what do we *do* with it now? This is truly a new divide.

It is from this wellspring of possibilities that the Rosebud Institute was formed. Given the somewhat prescriptive nature of this chapter, it seems prudent to at least briefly discuss this umbrella organization, in the interest of giving a point of reference for the approach taken. To that end, it is important to point out the Rosebud Institute is at least partly inspired in name and independent spirit by the enigmatic and prodigious filmmaker Orson Welles, (*Citizen Kane, The Magnificent Ambersons, Touch of Evil*). The institute seeks to embody both Welles' revolutionary approach to motion pictures as well as a sort of can-do, hands-on approach to addressing a growing need – a need to better equip future media makers in a world virtually drowning in images on the screen.

ROSEBUD INSTITUTE: MISSION

Even five or six years ago, things looked quite different in the increasingly intersecting worlds of media and education. At the time, most were grappling with how and whether to effectively put the expanding technologies to work in the classroom. The Rosebud Institute was formed around this time, at least in part as a response to the call for more technology in schools. Schools were doing a decent job of "infusing technology in schools" but the general notion could be summed up with a "now what?" mentality – now that it's here, how can we make better, more comprehensive use of the technology to enhance teaching and learning (NEA, 2008). The Rosebud Institute found an appropriate and constructive association at Carthage College in Kenosha, Wisconsin, a private, liberal arts institution, nestled between the twin metro areas of Chicago and Milwaukee. The newest department at Carthage is Communication and Digital Media (CDM). Tangentially affiliated with CDM, the Rosebud Institute found obvious alignment with a substantial portion of the department's stated mission in that CDM is devoted to the advancement and development of a student's knowledge and ability with media on the screen. Grounded in the liberal arts, and taking a modest, non-film-school approach – just far enough away from the trappings of the entertainment industry – the Rosebud Institute seeks an appropriate combination of exploring where and how education may change in the area of digital media literacy. It is neither an easy nor insular task, and challenges, encouragement, input and even inspiration are sought from every corner. Even the very name Rosebud Institute – as mentioned, inspired by a Wellesian sensibility – has a geographic alignment; Orson Welles was born in Kenosha and lived there for the first formative years of his life.

Irrespective of any ethereal inspiration Welles may provide, it is the broader notion that all students need at least a basic, core knowledge of creating media, wherein exists a powerful motivator – for Carthage, for the Communication and Digital Media department, and for the Rosebud Institute. This motivation lead to action and the Rosebud Institute was formed. Since then, the institute has developed and expanded a program that is finding better ways to teach and utilize digital media literacy. Building on this, and collaborating with a large and robust Education department as well as Office of Graduate and Professional Studies, the Rosebud Institute's larger, more universal mission – defining and exploring screen media literacy for all in order to better equip individuals to communicate and thrive – seems connected at Carthage College, both in ideal and setting.

Rosebud continues to seek and find new associations and connections, both at Carthage and beyond. Later in the chapter we will look at new curricular programs being explored that are highly interdisciplinary, leveraging the almost inborn tendency of students to want to blend sources, texts and technologies in order to more fully explore their world and more deftly direct their own learning. New affiliations will be looked at with Library and Information Services at Carthage, (LIS) where the development of a Center For Digital Literacy is being imagined that begins to grapple with the changing role of libraries in a technology-centric and media-centric society. Additionally, there are new initiatives in the surrounding communities – outreach programs to organizations, workshops for professionals, and effective K-12 programs being instituted. All of these enterprises function to more fully bring digital media literacy literally out of the dark and into the mainstream where technological advancement has already placed its many and varied tools.

A MEDIAFESTO: PLEASE "LIKE" THIS...

When one currently teaches writing or speaking, it is not necessarily to create great novelists or orators. That may happen, but the main driver is literacy and all that comes with it – especially cultural, social and political literacy and along with that cultural, social and political efficacy. As Carl Casinghino (2011) asserts in the preface of his text *Moving Images*, we do not teach math to young students in order to prepare them all to become professional mathematicians. Similarly, we are not teaching motion picture studies to crank out a new generation of Spielbergs. Instead we are "helping learners to develop cooperative skills, to enhance their problem-solving abilities, and to participate in cultural and social processes as capable, engaged interpreters" (Casinghino, 2011). Rosebud is interested in pushing the idea of skills development further, insisting that both reading and *writing* in screen media are important, and intrinsically interconnected.

In short, we need both. It seems increasingly a given that education needs to improve student understanding of how screen media work, how they make meaning, and how they construct (or

reconstruct) reality. But more and more are coming to understand that true screen media literacy must also provide students with the ability to *create* media products. (Baker, 2012). With the written word, we know that people are better readers if they have at least a working understanding of how to write, and the same seems to hold true for media.

The notion of cultural context pushes the importance further still. David Buckingham (2007) in his piece on Digital Media Literacies, extracts this notion from the discourse on "multiliteracies": that literacy education cannot simply be confined to the acquisition of skills but rather must include a framing by cultural and social contexts. In media for the screen, there is always a maker and there is always an audience. Without an understanding of who made what, for whom, and for what reason, there will always exist a danger of painting media with too broad a brush. With due respect to the late Roger Ebert, especially with matters of the screen, we live in a "thumbs up-thumbs down" world where it seems everyone has an opinion and the conversation quickly gets judgemental, political, even vituperative. In a world where we are merely asked to "like" something, and aren't really all that well trained or even asked to look at the who or why behind what we see, media products get passed off as temporary, mundane and far too easily dismissible. When discussing media, tangential arguments surface on all sides, a good portion of which come under the "media is too…" lead in: media is too violent, it's too much about entertainment, it's too difficult, it's too expensive, it's too liberal, it's too sexy and perhaps the biggest one in education circles: it's just too much more for teachers to teach. However, one could easily make the argument that media is simply too important – too important now to just let it go.

If you take a moment to look around the American mediated landscape, you may quickly come to the conclusion that the average teenager seems to do precious little thinking outside of the four walls of the screen. Given the chance, they will let the addictions of Facebook, YouTube and Twitter usurp their time (along with any number of current online trends, e.g., Instagram, Pintrest, StumbleUpon) But we currently give them no formal training to navigate these byways even in the most basic of ways, to say nothing of inculcating them with any sense of how best to spend their time there. An increasing number end up simply "wasting time," and the reality is only increasing that a computer's "use for education or meaningful content creation is minuscule compared to its use for pure entertainment" (Richtel, 2012)

It's not surprising given that we are unrealistically expecting young people to develop an enlightened sensibility on their own, basically giving them the keys to drive without requiring they obtain any kind of license. By comparison, if we took an average child, but one who had been given no formal training in any of the disciplines of reading, writing and speaking, and set them down anywhere in a modern culture, leaving them to their own devices, expecting them to develop a culturally recognized proficiency solely from the multiple channels of stimuli around them, would they be able to function in society? Some of them certainly would, eventually, but intrinsically, we recognize that many of them would not function all that well, and that overall, their proficiencies would remain at the lower end of that functionality. Just as a rising tide lifts all boats, in this case, the opposite is also true. Our reasons for teaching any basic literacy may seem to be a given to many, but in this case it requires a retrospective, even deconstructed look. We teach these basic literacies for many reasons, not the least of which is to elevate our society and level the playing field, as it were. The more who know the language of the land, the more who are able to come to, and participate at, the tables of meaningful discourse. If we accept the fact that digital screen media is here to stay, in perpetuity, and recognize that its literacy is important and unique, then it stands to reason that we must take a more formal approach to its pedagogy (Chilsen & Wells, 2012). Media on the screen has become, in effect, how we communicate…now.

And yet, in at least the broadest sense, in this culture of *like*, we are generally taking the opposite approach. "Most uses of computers in schools signally fail to engage with the complex technological and media-saturated environment in which children are now growing up. For the most part, they are narrowly defined, mechanical and unimaginative" (Buckingham, 2007). If that is still the case – and it appears that little has changed in that arena – then what we are doing is leaving it up to the surrounding stimuli to teach our children how to read and write in this pervasive, growing medium. In that way, students – and the general public – are developing a skewed and undiscerning way of relating to screen media in general. A University of Wisconsin and North-western University colleague, Laura Kipnis, has referred to this phenomenon as a "marginally-trained sensibility" – one based almost entirely on the unregulated consumption of commercial television, film and internet programming in a comparatively indiscriminate fashion. If the educational system produces students with little or no formal training in digital media literacy, we are passing on that legacy and sending them out into the world as comparative babes in the wood, rather ill-equipped to function at the level the rapidly-converging world demands. Filmmaker, George Lucas has been quoted as saying "If people aren't taught the language of sounds and image, shouldn't they be considered as illiterate as if they left college without being able to read and write?" (Lucas, 2004). This may seem a strong and biased opinion but it raises a valid point. If we can begin to address the often-vast differences in a student's understanding of how screen media is made, how its language works, and how it affects change in ourselves and the culture around us, we will start students on a path of developing and refining the tools they need to function as capable, engaged individuals in a digitally mediated world.

As the downward trend in cost and the con-current upward trend in quality in consumer electronics continue to expand both the reach and cultural power of screen media technology, the core knowledge of making media is even further democratized. And as accessibility continues to spread, so do the expectations of a modern culture. The whole idea of "media making" becomes a lingua franca of the future. In order to keep up, people – students and their teachers – need a basic tool kit of these specific skills as they venture out into the real and professional world, regardless of their eventual vocation. It is a new literacy – a language that continues to be accessible and used by greater numbers of people. It is a natural step then to guide, educate, and form the possible ways students can use this language across virtually all professions, in a more engaged, enlightened and effective manner (Chilsen & Wells, 2012).

Creating Those Who Can

The challenge for the Rosebud Institute has been to translate its mission and ideals into action and come up with an approach that can address a need in current and future pedagogy. A pilot program launched in June 2010 lead the way to develop a curricular series called *Media and the Moving Image*. Building off these beginnings, a number of offshoot programs, explorations and successes have grown, and reviewing them here is at least one way to look at both the importance and the possibilities of what can be done about digital media literacy and even fluency.

Originally offered under Rosebud's program header *Summer Series for Teachers*, Media and the Moving Image (MMI) is now a regular offering at Carthage College both in the summer and during the regular academic year. Using current resources at Carthage College and remaining affiliated programmatically with the Education Department as well as the Office of Graduate and Professional Studies, the courses can still target elementary, middle and high school teachers who are interested in learning to better understand digital media themselves and want to be able to teach it in their classrooms.

The core instruction takes place in a highly regulated and rigorous classroom component. Available also to graduate students, the course is designed to address new approaches for teaching media literacy by exploring the basics of reading and writing in the language of screen media. Outside of the education ties, the course has also become a sought after offering for many across the disciplines. It offers students not only an opportunity to re-explore their creativity, but the ePortfolio segment gives them a much needed baseline in setting up a professional representation of their work and what kind of employee they can be.

Following a dynamic yet simple hands-on approach, participants learn a two-pronged approach to screen media. They each create two somewhat modest media pieces designed to help them begin to find their own voice in the often-cacophonous world of digital media. Participants conceive of a simple, relevant motion picture project, which they write, film and edit, trying their own hand at using basic narrative, cinematic language to tell a simple, visual story. Alongside the film project, they each build an eFolio website of their own design, creating a timely, accessible and expandable way to display, manage, and share their projects, their ideas and even themselves. The film is not simply a slideshow movie and the eFolio is not simply another website repository, but rather both projects carry the weight of audience and are a true expression of what one can call the maker's 'digital self'. While the projects may seem modest in scope, they are rife with importance and significance. The gratification of getting a solid grip on using technology more effectively, coupled with the thrill of truly creating something from nothing, lends a palpable air of accomplishment to the work. All of the projects are done in a guided, supportive learning environment where collective work, feedback, interaction, and sharing are all fostered and encouraged.

Creating a short first film of this nature seems to give most people a heightened sense of ownership along with the empowering feeling of "I can do this." They get to see how it is done, and – contrary to their assertions at the beginning of the course – they learn to become *better* watchers of film and television, not "ruined" as they often fear. An additional benefit of both projects is a deeper, richer and more authentic learning experience. We have found this to be even more significant in younger students but literally, one cannot help but learn something more deeply by going through the process of having to create a piece about it for the screen. The very creation process itself, seems to imbue the creator with knowledge and insight that reportedly surpasses any number of pedagogical activities. As inverted classrooms and project-centered learning continue to grow in importance and efficacy, this is one of the areas we are most excited about exploring further.

As mentioned, both projects have a strong sense of audience – the idea of *who is watching*. In an attempt to address this issue even further, we give some focus to eFolios as a form of self-distribution. Again, these are not simply a way to show work, but rather ePortfolios can also give the maker a sense of the potential power and reach of their creations. This is not art or expression created in a vacuum. This is work that potentially the world can see, and that is a lot of power and responsibility to consider.

The motion media component, while relying on basic precepts of moviemaking, is decidedly removed from a Hollywood mode and instead approaches film grammar as new language of expression and making meaning. To lay the groundwork for effective communication, the coursework introduces a process encompassing fundamental aspects of

1. **Preproduction:** Treatments, scripting, storyboarding and planning,

2. **Production:** Basic camera use, angles and filming, and

3. **Postproduction:** Importing and editing clips, exporting, and delivery, as well as addressing issues of aesthetics, ethics and cultural impact.

The eFolio component extends communication beyond creation and into the arenas of audience and distribution via internet presentation. Participants build a base of knowledge with which to create their own purposeful, comprehensive collection of work and information. Through the process of building their own site throughout the course, they learn about the collaborative potential of online portfolios as well as the means by which they are able to create, upload and share their own original media in the form of video and audio podcasts.

With the pervasive spread of social networking, and its ever-younger-skewing clientele, a concurrent and integrated approach to creating, managing and distributing digital assets seems a viable, connected and crucial initiative to pursue. The additional benefit is to stimulate teachers to think about instructing their students on some of the how and why – and need – of managing their digital personae…their digital selves. As stories continue to hit the news about school-age sexting and other inappropriate interactions on the web, and as employers, schools and organizations increasingly support their personnel decisions by what they find on someone's Facebook site (Hechinger, 2008), the time seems perhaps even a bit overripe for educating students in the art of representing themselves appropriately in virtual reality, at a young enough age to begin building essential and culturally suitable lifelong skills. Of course the hope is that eventually there will come a day when most everyone is able to instantly capture, identifiably own, intelligently store, and instinctively know what to do with their digital assets (Chilsen & Wells, 2012), but until that time, we need to guide, to prod, even to insist.

As the discussion of mediating continues to unfold, a natural progression continues to build towards presentation; the dovetailing of eFolios or other Web 2.0 interfaces with motion media is a natural occurrence and a means of distributing originally created digital media via the use of a well-designed, well-placed, and well-managed websites. As designed, anyone can simply take the course for their degree, their enrichment or their professional development, but teachers taking the class have the additional option of coming away with interrelated curriculum modules which they may want to use in their own classrooms.

As the MMI program continues to modestly expand its reach, building from the baseline notion of how best to communicate on the screen, several other related affiliations and connections continue to present themselves. The courses are finding connections with a much broader array of constituencies beyond education, such as professional development and undergraduate distribution coursework.

One way this has been successfully explored, at least in its initial stages is with a Rosebud program launched as a pilot with a local high school in spring 2011. Dubbed the Intensive Onsite Training Approach (IOTA), the program gives individuals working within their organizations the chance to work closely with Rosebud Institute instructors to implement their own version of teaching the MMI series directly in their schools. Five highly successful IOTA programs have been completed to date including an Illinois College professional development program working under a 2011 Mellon grant.

Another exciting measure of the program's success is an ongoing program by one of the IOTA graduate students, Cindy Renaud. As a teacher, Ms. Renaud implemented a modified version of the Rosebud screen media approach at her high school, launching new coursework in the fall of 2012 at Harborside Academy, an Experiential Learning (EL) school in Wisconsin. The program continues to this day and has been successfully implemented throughout the school. Ms. Renaud may not seem the rule, in that she is a very driven teacher who is drawn specifically to more intentional use of technology in the classroom, but highly effective classroom teachers are out there in great numbers and it is up to the educational structures to give them the training and support to more fully utilize the tools they – and their students – are being handed. A growing number of teachers recognize that "technology is a tool, not a solution. [and] what really matters in the classroom is teacher quality" (Day, 2014). As a quality classroom teacher, Renaud's words are convincing and cut to the core of a broader necessity for more integrated screen media instruction:

Today's students will live their lives in a competitive, technology-driven global society. The ability to create relevant, content-specific, professional quality products using screen media will give students a foundation for being proficient digital citizens.... The aim of today's educator, then, is to engage the media-centric population of youth and prepare them for the competiveness of a global society and economy. (Renaud, 2012)

Another approach and angle that Rosebud programming has pursued is going directly to younger students by launching a summer camp for students ages 13-17. Originally called *Screen Media Boot Camp*, and now being reworked under a more structured summer program at Carthage College as the *Summer Media Experience*, this weeklong overnight camp essentially takes the same type of program offered to the adults, tweaks the coursework and activities for a younger audience, and takes kids through the steps to make their own movies and eFolios with intentionality and purpose.

The Department of Communication and Digital Media at Carthage College (CDM) continues to grapple with these emerging issues. Under new leadership at many levels, the college and the department are working to find a balance between what students seem to want, what employers seem to need and what the future of education seems to demand. As educators, programmer and administrators, it seems increasingly important to get the balance right. Education has never really relied on what's trending well with students in the hope of figuring out what they need, and we really only can depend on employers to know what they need today. Therefore, it must be up to educators to look to the near and upcoming futures and try to educate and prepare students for those futures. We need to be aware of the trends and try to stay ahead of them as much as we can, but ideally, we are building not only their practical skills, but we are giving students essential understandings and protocols so they can re-tool and modify their abilities as the world inevitably shifts under their feet.

As core curricular choices, clarifications and enhancements are contemplated, some startup interdisciplinary initiatives show great promise at Carthage. Working with Modern Languages Professor Matt Borden, two different courses have been implemented that effectively draw on the notion of communicating and learning by creating with media. One course is called *Filming Don Quixote*, where students read the full text of Quixote and also extract and create a couple short films throughout the term as adaptations of inspiring or interesting aspects of what they have read. The results of the initial offering garnered some attention in tangential academic circles and have given the program some needed feedback and insight from international colleagues (Borden & Chilsen, 2012).

The other is a course called *Filming Cultures: Explorations Beyond Tourism*, which is originally designed as a month-long course that has a two-week study tour component where students travel to a foreign country and are then required to interact with the culture, cuisine and commerce of the target destination. The student participants film all the interactions –interviews, personal digital essays, student travel, etc – and the results are edited together and shown upon returning to campus. The success of the course has lead to the development of a semester-long version that will hopefully be launched in the near future.

Another of the more promising and new explorations has come in the form of working with Dr. Todd Kelley of Library and Information Services at Carthage (LIS). Originally invited as part of a Rosebud panel at the popular Charleston Conference, a gathering of all things library, Dr. Kelley has been a strong supporter of creating learning environments that allow students to become not only literate, but *proficient* with digital media. In a follow-up series of articles called *Digital Conversations*, in the industry trade bimonthly *Against The Grain*, Kelley is sharing his department's exploration of how to manage the necessary change that libraries must go through to remain current and viable. As libraries buckle under the strain of new and varied uses by a screen-driven society (Crawford, 2011), Kelley sees the need to shift our understanding of what a library is and what it can be. Far from eschewing the strong traditions of a library, Kelley sees a necessary blending of mission. He is strongly aligned with the idea that media spaces need to literally and figuratively come out of the basement – out of the small dark rooms that are typically associated with media creation – and up into the bright and common areas where everyone can see their existence and understand that these newly imagined "maker spaces" are for their use and for their creating. The ultimate hope is for the eventual establishment of something preliminarily called the *Center for Digital Literacy*, a new and visionary part of the academic library, further asserting that these are not ideals housed in a single department or discipline, but are foundational components of how we teach and learn (Chilsen & Kelley, 2014).

All of these interdisciplinary and cross-curricular initiatives – the programming, the outreach, the camp, the library – are highly intentional and are attempting to address what is seen by more and more as a core necessity. As screen time increases for students, up to one quarter of their day and rising (Herring & Notar, 2011), the need to educate to, through and with screen media is becoming crucial. With this in mind, the current Rosebud approach, albeit developing, offers recurring rotation of courses, enabling participants to expand both their own skills in making media, as well as guide and assess the work of their peers, graduates and students. When applicable, course credit has been configured for the necessary flexibility in today's transfer-laden and professional development landscape. Additionally, other options offer more choices for virtually anyone seeking general professional development, giving individuals and teachers more – and more media-savvy – options that can apply toward advancement, and licensure renewal, extending their abilities, their strengths and their own digital media literacy.

With the IOTA onsite exceptions mentioned above, most classes and initiatives are currently somehow related to or physically located on the campus of Carthage College. But as the IOTA and other programs demonstrate, the courses and ideals are a movable feast of sorts, able to go virtually anywhere and effectively instruct at almost any level. Altered as appropriate for various constituencies, programs attempt to offer realistic and useful options for participants, giving them differing viewpoints and ideas through a number of atypical sessions including film screenings, story circles, panel discussions, emerging technology lectures, and relevant supplemental coursework. What has been witnessed in programs thus far is that the close-knit structure of the course and the necessity to collaborate offers ample opportunity for participants to work and learn together while networking and sharing with their peers.

In a tangential fashion, the veritable explosion of social networking, self-promotion, and digital media distribution via the internet creates another opportunity for learning. As mentioned above, the sheer accessibility of virtually anything, anywhere at anytime necessitates that students learn to build, discern, shape, maintain, organize, and share their own *original* selves through the creation and management of their online presence. Additionally, it is increasingly in the nature of younger students to want to pull together all the elements they can get their hands on, in an effort to better understand and communicate in the world as they see it. They don't really have any formal training or guidance, hardly even in the basic issues of ethics and the law that quickly arise in these endeavors, but they are venturing forth, with or without our help. Especially for young people, it is important to "think twice about the online personae they are presenting to the world" (Coutu, 2007). What they post or even expropriate today, will be available for years, and they may not understand this until they are sitting in a job interview years from now, and the potential employer opens a file that includes their résumé as well as their latest online rantings and party photos (Coutu, 2007). In short, students must manage and contextualize their digital selves, and if they do not, someone will begin to do it for them.

By offering instruction in these areas, focusing on what screen media is, how its language is constructed, what it looks like, how to make it, how it impacts the culture around us, and how it informs everyday teaching, learning, discourse and commerce, Rosebud Institute programs and initiatives are seeking to make screen media literacy more broadly understood and accessible, allowing us all to communicate and thrive in an increasingly media-saturated world (Chilsen & Wells, 2012).

FASTFORWARDING

How do we keep moving forward? Just as the tendrils of digital media pervade all channels and insistently drive and necessitate a literacy entirely its own, how do we approach the need for a more global paradigm shift? This is not a disciplinary expansionist view nor is it intended to simply add to the increasingly overwhelming cacophony and unrelenting focus on technology tools, interface, and software. Rather, it is an assertion and potential solution towards a refocus – a shift towards communicating rather than simply responding, embracing a baseline process that is inherently multi-platform and upgrade-proof rather than chasing the newest toys, a step that puts technology's tools to work for our learning and efficacy and sets aside the notion of like.

Recognizably, this is almost as challenging and exciting as arriving at this point in the first place. The interconnected nature of this kind of literacy exploration – a pioneering attempt to define, codify and teach a basic screen language and the subsequent digital and screen media literacy it will hopefully engender – is most certainly not an isolated undertaking, nor should it be. Instead, it demands input, guidance and molding not only from the ongoing development of learning technologies and teaching, but from the many other pursuits – academic, social, and professional – which will continue to shape its content as well as its analysis.

Therefore a look forward involves not only assessing the results of the ongoing and expanding programs of the Rosebud Institute – their overall acceptance, efficacy and usefulness according to the participants – but also seeking and considering a veritable multitude of other viewpoints and approaches. As mentioned earlier, just as screen media is not created in a vacuum, so too, the analysis, definition and program development toward broader digital media literacy – even the most basic grammar, syntax and structure of the language as well as how best to teach this literacy – is an ongoing and multi-dimensional subject which, like most areas of study across the academy, will thrive best as it becomes part of the rich discourse on how we now communicate, interact and get along.

A growing number of academics, theorists, educators and pundits from varied walks of life are seeing the need. MIT Computer Scientist Mitch Resnick embodies many of the same baseline ideals with his assertion that it is crucial to teach kids to code, so they can do more than just "read"

new technologies (Resnick, 2013). Popular Kansas State anthropologist and self-proclaimed digital ethnographer Michael Wesch touts similar ideals, asserting that critical thinking is having to share its importance with the need for educators to create learning environments where students can harness and leverage this screen-driven world, allowing them to learn to not only examine and question it, but be able to re-create it as well (Wesch, 2012). The innovative education portal Edutopia often espouses similar views and seems based on a notion of access *and* ability, recognizing that students need to see these new devices as more than merely toys, but as useful learning tools that their teachers and parents also know how to use and can help guide them (Day, 2014).

These are critical issues; would that they were a sitting target. They are not, and complicating the discourse is the fact that it's all changing, often before we can grasp what happened yesterday. Kathryn Montgomery, noted theorist and pundit on children and youth interactions with media, pointed out over a decade ago that "the explosion of the new digital media culture is occurring so rapidly that its growth is surpassing the ability of scholars…and educators to grasp fully its nature, its direction and its impact…" (Montgomery, 2000). And it's only getting worse.

All the more reason it seems, to work to get a better understanding of it now. In the interest of not chasing the elusive dragon of expanding media portals and their pervasive, seemingly unruly effects on our culture, the Rosebud Institute programs are attempting to take a more stripped-down, basic approach. How can educators arm themselves in what many see as a battle for attention in an ever-dizzying cacophony?

One way is by realizing that there is a *me* in media. As the personal increasingly becomes public, it will be the clearer voices that rise above the din. As with any form of communication, if you want to be heard you must strive to be the more effective communicator. More and more, what the world seems to want and even demand are unique and personal views. Witness how the phenomenon of "mommy blogging" continues as an important resource for those in search of the best consumer goods. As with the voyeuristic attraction of cinema, the more personal someone is on the screen, the more drawn in the viewers seem to become. Why else would the seeming mundanity of Twitter be so engaging for so many? The aproach outlined herein is designed to give individuals the tools they need to find their voice and become more effective "mediators." The approach is simple. The equipment is accessible. The results are measurable (Chilsen & Wells, 2012).

Initial, pre-course feedback from Rosebud Institute program participants thus far reveals that a general and pervasive fear of technology poses a significant initial hurdle, especially among established professionals who are looking for fewer challenges in their busy days, not more. *Digital Natives* – kids who grew up with technology, and "spent their entire lives surrounded by and using computers…phones, and all the other toys and tools of the digital age" (Prensky, 2001) – seem to have a great deal less of this anxiety. In many cases they are naturals, but it still does come up. In view of this fear, it is important to continue to assess the effectiveness of the coursework's attempt at demystifying and deemphasizing the technical interface, in favor of a more basic exploration of reading and writing in the language of the screen. Is the program ultimately encouraging participants to first embrace and then look beyond the technical, towards a future that will eventually equate camera and screen technology with pencil-to-paper technology? Can cloud computing, where digital assets and computing resources are delivered over the web, be accepted by educators as a natural extension of teaching, learning and self-assessment? Will we be willing to start down the road of affirming that "writing" with a camera in a basic cinematic language or communicating with images on a website, are no more or less "natural" than depositing ink on the page or even painting on the walls of a cave?

Ongoing analysis of post-coursework comments and survey results indicate that many aspects of the offerings are finding an effective and relevant niche. Comments such as the following are representative:

- "I'm getting a lot of ideas that I can take back to the classroom."
- "The ePortfolio portion of the course was also inspiring."
- "I learned more technology here than I've learned in my whole life. It's been an amazing class."
- "I think it's interesting that every single person in this class is going to do something different with what they've learned once they leave."
- "I was afraid of this stuff at first. But when my work heard I took this course, they asked me to make a film for our company website; I did, and they loved it!"
- "I was not getting any response from job applications until I included a link from my new ePortfolio. I got three calls the next week and have now landed a job!"

These comments seem to indicate that the general structure of the program is headed in the right direction and is garnering the kind of ownership, engagement and buy-in initially hoped for.

Further assessment, refinement and development of the coursework and its results will also include investigation of participants' responses to and incorporation of the ongoing application of what they learn. How the participating teachers deploy program elements in their classrooms, how professionals use their new skills to communicate more effectively with their constituencies, even how graduating seniors use these skills to land a job – all of these are important and measurable indicators of people's capacity and willingness to inject digital media literacy and fluency into the ebb and flow of their lives.

The creation of more streamlined and organizationally specific approaches that can be remapped onto different circumstances according to need also seems a critical component of expansion. Potential school in-service visits to directly introduce, assess, and promote further program application and efficacy should be further explored. The hope is that such follow-up activities will nurture a more complete, ongoing acceptance and integration of the foundational principles that the programs espouse and embody.

Continuing the look forward, program outcomes are extrapolated across visions for further coursework modification, integration and expansion in order to continue to effectively meet the needs of professionals, both within education and outside of it, as well as the mediated learning abilities of their constituencies.

TEACHING CONVERGENCE

A few final thoughts revolve around perhaps somewhat overrun notion of convergence – that we indeed find ourselves nearing what feels to many like an apex in mediating, a veritable disolution of old ways and a tumultuous, aggressive and often calamitous scramble for finding a new modus operandi. While access to technology remains an issue, it seems to be turning more into a matter of effectively accessing one's own voice. "When people talk to me about the digital divide, I think of it not being so much about who has access to what technology as who knows how to create and express themselves in this new language of the screen" (Lucas, 2004). Even more so today, with phones becoming cameras and cameras becoming mobile devices and iPods becoming iPads and tablets and movie screens and televisions, and everyone scrambling to reach the almighty consumer where they live, eat, breath and sleep, the time does indeed seem to be now. While not everyone agrees how this will unfold, most are clear that as the crescendo ensues, the best way to use this new power and reach cannot be left to its own devices:

Learning depends crucially on the exact character of the activities that learners engage in with a program, the kinds of tasks they try to accomplish, and the kinds of intellectual and social activity they become involved in…technology may provide interesting and powerful learning opportunities, but these are not taken automatically; teachers and learners need to learn how to take advantage of them. (Salomon & Perkins, 1996)

Since simply having technology in the classroom "does not automatically inspire teachers to rethink their teaching or students to adopt new modes of learning" (Hiltzik, 2012), handing out $2000 pencils is not enough. Technology is here to stay and digitally native students relate to it differently. We therefore need a different approach (Chilsen & Wells, 2012). We can't simply add screen media literacy "to the curriculum menu, hiving off 'information and communication technology' into a separate subject" (Buckingham, 2007). Rather, in a world that is increasingly dominated by media and even basic communication on the screen, we need to reconceptualize our definition of *literacy*. We have both the ability and the duty to educate young and old alike in the language of the screen; to do anything less would be to leave them unprepared in an often hostile world – a world where the immediacy, manipulation and message of today's media have the potential to dramatically alter the classic modes of teaching, learning and communicating.

REFERENCES

Baker, F.W. (2012). *Media literacy in the K-12 classroom*. International Society for Technology in Education – ISTE.

Borden, M & Chilsen, PJ, (2012, March 2). *Don't just watch*. Paper presented at the International Society for Social Studies, Miami, FL.

Boyer, E. (1988). *Media literacy.* Retrieved from http://www.medialiteracy.com/sayings.htm

Buckingham, D. (2007). Digital media literacies: Rethinking media education in the age of the internet. *Research in Comparative and International Education,* *2*(1), 43–55. doi:10.2304/rcie.2007.2.1.43

Cann, O. (2014, April 23). *Addressing new digital divide key for balanced growth.* Retrieved from http://www.weforum.org/news/addressing-new-digital-divide-key-balanced-growth

Casinghino, C. (2011). *Moving images: Making movies, understanding media.* Delmar Cengage Learning.

Chilsen, PJ, & Kelley, T (2014, February - November). Digital conversations. *Against The Grain,* (1, 2, 4).

Chilsen, P. J., & Wells, C. R. (2012, June). *Media and the moving image: Creating those who thrive in a screen media world.* Paper presented at Ed-Media World Conference on Educational Media & Technology, Denver, CO.

Coutu, D. (2007, June). We Googled you. *Harvard Business Review,* *85*(6), 37–47. PMID:11184976

Day, L. (2014, April 13). *Bridging the new digital divide.* Retrieved from http://www.edutopia.org/blog/bridging-the-new-digital-divide-lori-day

Gray, D. (2008, May 22). *Web log message.* Retrieved from http://www.davegrayinfo.com/2008/05/22/why-powerpoint-rules-the-business-world/

Hechinger, J. (2008, September 18). College applicants, beware: Your Facebook page is showing. *Wall Street Journal,* p. D1.

Herring, D. F., & Notar, C. F. (2011). Show what you know: ePortfolios for 21st century learners. *College Student Journal,* *45*(4), 786.

Hiltzik, M. (2012, February 4). Who really benefits from putting high-tech gadgets in classrooms? *Los Angeles Times,* p. B1.

Lucas, G. (2004, September 14). Life on the screen: Visual literacy in education. *Edutopia.* Retrieved from http://www.edutopia.org/life-screen

McLuhan, M. (1964). *Understanding media: The extensions of man.* New York: McGraw-Hill.

Montgomery, K. (2000). Youth and digital media: A policy research agenda. *Journal of Adolescent Youth,* *27S,* 61–68. PMID:10904209

NEA. (2008). *An NEA policy brief.* Washington, DC: NEA Education Policy and Practice Department.

Prensky, M. (2001). Digital natives, digital immigrants. *On the Horizon,* *9*(5). Retrieved July 16, 2012 from http://www.marcprensky.com/writing/

Renaud, C. (2012). *Creating a digital media curriculum for the high school.* (Unpublished master's thesis). Carthage College, Kenosha, WI.

Resnick, M. (2013, June 25). *Keynote address.* Paper presented at EdMedia World Conference on Media and Technology.

Richtel, M. (2012, May 29). Wasting time is the new digital divide. *New York Times.*

Salomon, G., & Perkins, D. N. (1996). Learning in wonderland: What computers really offer education. In S. Kerr (Ed.), Technology and the future of education (pp. 111-130). Chicago: University of Chicago Press.

Thompson, R., & Bowen, C. J. (2009). *Grammar of the shot* (2nd ed.). Amsterdam: Focal Press.

Van Ness, E. (2005, March 6). Is a cinema studies degree the New M.B.A.? *New York Times,* p. M1.

Waterworth, E., & Waterworth, J. (2010). Mediated presence in the future. In C. C. Bracken & P. D. Skalaski (Eds.), *Immersed in media: Telepresence in everyday life* (pp. 183–196). New York, NY: Routledge.

KEY TERMS AND DEFINITIONS

Digital Asset: An originally created piece of work that has been imported or converted into digital format and therefore can be deployed in any number of digital media. Digital assets can include but are not limited to: photos, videos, music, blog entries, podcasts, files, résumés, and/or any other work created in an academic setting.

Digital Divide: Originally a term to define the gap between those who have access to internet and related computer technologies and those who do not.

Digital Immigrant: A person born before the existence or current pervasive nature of digital technologies who is not naturally familiar or instinctively comfortable and therefore must adapt to using digital technology, interfaces, and software.

Digital Media Literacy: The acquired ability to understand, access, evaluate, and analyze types and avenues of information created online or with available software and hardware to communicate and participate in civic life as competent media consumer, contributor, and creator of media in the online community.

Digital Native: A person who is indigenous to the digital world, has grown up with and uses a wide variety of available and continually evolving technology with an inborn, instinctive sense of how to communicate, record, understand and share in society.

eFolio (Also ePortfolio): A website created for or by an individual, that manages their digital assets and online presence, communicating learning or professional progress, which continues to change as long as its creator continues to develop and refine the content to reflect current experience, skill, and/or career focus.

Media Convergence: The natural, continual, accelerating evolution of technology resulting in a more integrated, inescapable coming together of multiple avenues of information, entertainment and online communication.

Mediate: To create original work for and effectively communicate through the technology, tools, and language of the screen.

Screen Media: Any media that is produced for or distributed via the screen, including the entire spectrum of what constitutes 'the screen': the cinematic screen, the television screen, the computer screen, and the small screens accessed on a smartphones and other handheld devices.

Chapter 12
Using Virtual Environments to Achieve Learner Outcomes in Interprofessional Healthcare Education

Michelle Aebersold
University of Michigan, USA

Dana Tschannen
University of Michigan, USA

ABSTRACT

The use of simulation in the training of healthcare professionals has become an essential part of the educational experience. Students and practitioners need to learn a variety of technical, interpersonal, and clinical judgment skills to be effective healthcare practitioners. Virtual simulation can provide an effective training method to facilitate learning and can be targeted to develop specific skills in the area of Interprofessional Education (IPE). This chapter reviews the literature around simulation techniques and outlines a development process that can be used to develop virtual simulations to meet a variety of learning objectives including IPE. Specific issues and solutions are also presented to ensure a successful educational experience.

INTRODUCTION

Quality and safety are ongoing concerns in the healthcare environment. A recent article in the Journal of Patient Safety found 210,000 patients die each year from preventable medical errors (James, 2013). The Joint Commission (2013) attributes over 70% of these errors to failures in communication, with the majority of failures oc-

curring between various disciplines. This has led to an increase focus in the area of interdisciplinary or interprofessional education (IPE). The World Health Organization (WHO) defines interprofessional education as "When students from two or more professions learn about, from and with each other to enable effective collaboration and improve health outcomes" (WHO, 2010, p.7) In May 2011, the Interprofessional Education Col-

DOI: 10.4018/978-1-4666-8205-4.ch012

laborative published a set of core competencies for interprofessional education, which included competencies related to values/ethics, roles/responsibilities, interprofessional communications and teams/teamwork (Interprofessional Education Collaborative Expert Panel, 2011). Many academic and practice institutions have struggled with the implementation of these competencies due to a variety of challenges in both space and cost barriers. One promising methodology that may assist in attainment of these core competencies includes simulation. This chapter will provide an example of the use of one type of simulation method; virtual simulation to address the growing need for IPE to improve competencies in the area of communication.

BACKGROUND

Patient safety is currently one of the most urgent issues facing our health care systems. Beginning with the Institute of Medicine's (IOM) (Kohn, Corrigan, & Donaldson, 2000) report on patient safety in which it was reported up to 98,000 people die each year because of medical errors, patient safety has become an urgent concern for both health care administrators and those educating the future generation of health care providers. The IOM (2003) has made recommendations on health care education focused around their vision, "All health professionals should be educated to deliver patient-centered care as members of an interdisciplinary team, emphasizing evidence-based practice, quality improvement approaches and informatics" (http://www.nap.edu/catalog/10681.html, p. 3). In particular their recommendations around teamwork include the need to develop skills around communication and collaboration. Evidence has shown that effective team performance requires team members effectively communicate with each other and have a shared goal; such as improving patient care (AHRQ, 2003). Additionally communication failures are at the

root cause of many sentinel events analyzed by The Joint Commission (a regulatory agency that accredits hospitals) (http://www.jointcommission.org/sentinel_event.aspx). Many factors including how different professions train their students to communicate create the challenges in communication that currently exist between physicians and nurses in particular (Leonard, Graham, & Bonacum, 2004).

As a result of this focus on fostering IPE many health science schools have focused efforts on utilizing simulation as a means to achieve competencies in this area. Several studies have been published in this area utilizes different approaches. In a study by Liaw and colleagues (2014) nursing and medical students engaged together in simulations using standardized patients and high-fidelity computerized mannequin simulators. The students played their respective roles in caring for a patient who was going in to septic shock and becoming quite ill. Students were able to practice skills such as roles, communication, teamwork and handoffs; meeting several IPE competencies. Pre/Post evaluation showed a significant improvement in self-confidence with no significant differences between groups and the participants were highly satisfied with their learning. In another study by Dillion, Noble and Kaplan (2009) nursing and medical students engaging in a mock cardiac arrest code blue simulation to determine their perception of the value of simulation as an IPE learning experience. The results showed the experience to be a positive one and an increase in understanding of both their own roles and the other person's roles were found. In other areas IPE is met through a combination of curricular activities and simulation activities.

Simulations as proposed in this chapter could be defined as educational simulations. Aldrich (2009) considers educational simulations as a subset of immersive learning simulations. He also classifies serious games as subset of immersive learning simulations as well as games. This is part of his overall taxonomy in which sims are the broad category that includes computer games for entertainment and immersive learning simulations for formal learning programs. Educational simulations are different from computer games because they do not have a goal of being necessarily fun but do focus on engagement. They are focused on specific learning goals and strive to increase the participant's skill level in the real world whereas serious games increase awareness of real-world topics and can be used for both entertainment and learning (Aldrige, 2009).

VIRTUAL REALITY SIMULATION IN HEALTH CARE

Creating a virtual reality simulation program to support IPE in health care requires the consideration of many factors to ensure a successful outcome. These factors include a thorough understanding of the skills needed by those in the health care profession, an understanding of educational pedagogies, the ability to develop virtual environments and simulations scenarios, and most importantly how to evaluate their effectiveness.

Required Skills

Health care practitioners need a variety of clinical skills, cognitive skills, and interpersonal skills to be effective in their roles. Clinical or technical skills generally involve learning how to do procedures and often simple repetitive practice can enable a high degree of proficiency. This practice can usually be set up in a skills lab area or in the patient care area where they can practice skills such as inserting a urine catheter or administering intravenous medications. Cognitive and interpersonal skills may require more complex training due to their complex nature and need to vary depending on the situation. Cognitive skills such as clinical reasoning is the process of collecting cues, processing information, coming to a an understanding of the patient problem or

situation, planning and implementing interventions, evaluating outcomes and finally reflecting upon and learning from the process (Hoffman, O'Donnell, & Kim, 2007; Levett-Joneseta, et al., 2010; Tanner, Padrick, Westfall, & Putzier, 1987). It allows the nurse or healthcare practitioner to build upon previously acquired knowledge and past experiences in order to deal with new or unfamiliar situations (Lapkin, Levett-Jones, Bellchambers, & Fernandez, 2010). Educating professionals to acquire the necessary skill set requires not only technical knowledge but artistry. Artistry is a kind of knowing that is different from professional knowledge. Some would say artistry is based on intuition or even pattern recognition and is found in nurses practicing at an expert level. There is recognition that both the art and science of health care is needed by practitioners to perform effectively (Schon, 1983). The greatest challenge for educators is often in teaching the artistry. Educators are also challenged with bridging the gap between the classroom and the clinical area. Health care practitioners need to make the connections between the didactic material they hear in lecture or other training venues with the actual patient care setting in which they care for patients. Health care can be chaotic and doesn't always conform to typical textbook clinical signs and symptoms. Initially students and beginning health care practitioners often engage in very deliberate problem solving efforts focusing on one issue at a time. Situational awareness or sense of salience allows health care practitioners to problem solve in novel situations using their professional knowledge base. The ability to focus on important aspects of a patient situation, ignore those that don't apply and be able to use their professional knowledge in addressing the situation is called salience (Benner et al. 2009) or situational awareness (Aldridge, 2009). Salience or situational awareness is usually a hallmark of an expert practitioner and develops over time given the right circumstances to support this learning. For example, a patient who has a serious blood stream infection will exhibit a constellation of signs and symptoms that include a low blood pressure, a high heart rate, a fever and a low urine output. That same patient may also have lung congestion that is not part of the signs and symptoms of the blood stream infection itself. A beginner will assess all the signs and symptoms and recognize they are abnormal but may not be able to separate out which ones go together to support the diagnosis of blood stream infection. An expert will be able to look at the entire constellation of signs and symptoms and recognize the patient has sepsis (a blood stream infection) that might be secondary to pneumonia (as noted by the lung congestion). They must develop these key skills to become an effective practitioner and in addition they must also learn to become an effective member of the health care team.

Health care practitioners also need key interpersonal and communication skills because they do not practice alone but are part of a team. Although they can learn about effective communication skills through a lecture or other didactic approach, only after 'practicing' these skills in a simulated environment can they gain the proficiency necessary for effective use in the high stakes, complex clinical environment. Several programs have been developed to educate practitioners around effective communication strategies. Crew Resource Management (CRM) (originally developed in the airline industry) has become a popular training methodology for nurses and physicians. Various communication techniques are taught in CRM including how to 'go up the chain of command' and get someone to address a critical patient situation. TEAMSTEPPS is another training program developed by the Agency for Healthcare Research and Quality (AHRQ). The focus of this training is on teamwork skills with effective communication being one of those skills. The training identifies key communication strategies that have been found effective in health care and uses demonstrations, role play and debriefing to teach these strategies. Teamwork itself is another critical interpersonal skill. Nurses and other health care practicitoners

need to know how to be team leaders as well as good followers. They often need to move between roles depending on the situation and can do that several times a day, often in very challenging and intense situations. All of these skills will enhance patient outcomes and patient safety and poor skills in these areas will potentially lead to poor patient outcomes (Mazzocco et al., 2009). Acquisition of these skills is often challenging as students and healthcare practitioners are not always exposed to the 'right' patient care experiences which will foster the development of these skills.

Conceptual Framework

The development of these skills requires an integrative learning environment where students and health care practitioners can learn didactic information and then use that information in the practice environment to attain proficiency of these crucial skills. In the field of healthcare nurses and other health care practitioners are expected to become, at the minimum competent in their work. New nurses are considered beginners trying to achieve a level of competency and the ability to provide safe care to their patients with some support from nurses at a higher level of expertise. Nurses need to quickly progress to a competent level. Although one could remain at the competent level, nurses need to continue on to become experts in their field to support the highest level of patient care outcomes possible. To do this requires more than just experience. Although experience alone will initially improve the nurse's skills, it is not sufficient to continue the growth and over time skills may decay. It is the opportunity to 'practice' their skills in a meaningful way that will contribute to the progression towards mastery. This is in line with the educational pedagogy developed by Ericsson, which supports that acquisition of skills requires practice.

Ericsson's (2004) expertise framework is based on the assumption that to acquire expert performance one must engage in deliberate practice activities that are focused on improving some aspect of performance. This expert performance will include clinical or technical skills, cognitive skills and interpersonal skills and a sense of salience or situational awareness. This experiential learning (learning by doing) framework is helpful in guiding educators in facilitating focused experiential learning opportunities. Health care professionals improve their skills with experience, however, Ericsson's theory posits that experts are those individuals who continue to improve beyond the level needed to perform adequately and become recognized as experts in their domain. This level of expertise is gained through deliberate efforts focused on improving selected skills or tasks. Schon's (1983) work highlights the need for professionals to reflect upon experiences in order to gain knowledge. Ericsson states this occurs when individuals are instructed to improve certain aspects of their performance for a well defined task and then given immediate detailed feedback on their performance which they can reflect upon and continue to practice during subsequent training sessions. This is based on the ability of educators and trainers to determine the types of representative tasks (knowledge and skills) that define the domain of practice. Individuals who do not engage in deliberate practice activities experience the decay or their skills over time or their skills can be outdated as new knowledge about practice is discovered. This framework of deliberate practice to educate and train professionals can be achieved through the use of educational simulations and serious games.

Simulation

Simulation is a technique currently being used by many educators in a variety of fields. Simulation has long been used in the military, aviation and nuclear power industries as part of their overall training and readiness programs. Health care facilities, medical and nursing schools have recently incorporated simulation in an effort to enhance learning related to procedural training, team training and individual learner training. Simulation in health care increases patient safety, improves clinical judgment and can be used to teach/evaluate specific clinical skills (Bearnson & Wiker, 2005).

In the world of medical simulations there are three classifications of simulations used: low-fidelity (non-computerized trainers that teach a specific task such as intravenous catheter insertion), mid-fidelity (standardized patients, computer programs, video games), and high-fidelity (computerized human patient simulator mannequins that respond to treatments) (Harder, 2010). Simulation is a practical and successful model which can be used to teach a variety of skills; psychomotor (technical), cognitive (clinical reasoning, decision making), and interpersonal (communication, teamwork). A key benefit to using simulation is its ability to mimic real life situations without putting patients at risk (Nehring & Lashley, 2004; Morgan, Cleave-Hogg, McIlroy, & Devitt, 2002). The benefits of simulation are well established in the literature (Buckley & Gordon, 2010; Harder, 2010; Lapkin, Levette-Jones, Bellchambers, & Fernandez, 2010; McGaphie, Issenberg, Petrusa, & Scalese, 2010; Orledge, Phillips, Murray & Lerant, 2012; Shearer, 2013; Cumin, Boyd, Webster & Weller, 2013).

In addition simulation can help health care professionals learn how to apply previously learned knowledge in novel situations. Research has shown that participation in simulations is effective in helping students manage scenarios they had not previously encountered when compared to other forms of education (Owen, Mugford, Follows, & Plummer, 2006). This also occurs in the area of skill transfer from a simulation environment to the actual practice environment. In a study on advanced life support training it was found that physicians who participated in simulations designed to teach them how to be an effective leader in a situation where a patient was experiencing a cardiac arrest, performed better during actual cardiac arrests

(Wayne et al., 2008). Simulation also provides opportunities for students and nurses to engage in deliberate practice using evidence-based or best practice guidelines (Aebersold, 2010). In addition, simulation has shown to improve student's level of confidence or self-efficacy (Scherer, Bruce, & Runkawatt, 2007; Morgan & Cleave-Hogg, 2002).

Virtual Simulation

Although much is known about simulation using high-fidelity mannequins, research is just starting to emerge around the use of virtual reality environments for simulation in health care. Educators are using a variety of platforms to build virtual reality environments to support simulations. Much of the work done has been in Second Life (SL), which to date, is the most popular and mature multi-user virtual environment used in education (Warburton, 2009). SL provides an accessible environment for learners to participate in simulation scenarios with other learners through the use of avatars (a virtual on-line persona) in a realistic setting that fosters learning. Using SL is not without its challenges (which will be discussed later), but it can support certain types of simulations without significant start up costs providing educators have access to an 'island' or space within SL to set up their learning environment. Through the use of avatars, learners can gain a feeling of being 'physically present' in the environment, yet it is still a safe, controlled setting where students can practice their skills and make mistakes without harming patients (Burgess, Slate, Rojas-LeBouef, & LaPrairie, 2010). The virtual environment has an advantage over traditional role play in a classroom because we can mimic the setting in which the learner will practice (i.e. hospital unit, emergency room, operating room, clinic). Conradi and colleagues (2009) found that paramedic students using SL for problem based learning, indicated the environment was more authentic and collaborative than paper-based problem solving scenarios. Our own work in SL has shown that

learners are more likely to take risks in using new skills or problem solving novel situations because it is their avatar doing the work and they have a degree of anonymity. Early research is showing that simulations conducted in virtual reality can be just as effective for learning as those done with traditional high-fidelity simulation using human patient simulators (Youngblood, Harter, Srivastava, Moffett, Heinrichs, & Dev, 2008).

Virtual simulations have a role to play in overall education of health care practitioners. They can be used effectively for creating deliberate practice scenarios for skill development such as cognitive and interpersonal skills. In particular they are useful for communication and teamwork skill development. The next section will describe how we developed our virtual environment using SL and how simulations are developed using a standardized process supported by Ericsson's (2004) deliberate practice framework.

Virtual Environment Development

Land in Second Life—owned by the University of Michigan Medical School—was used to create a space for training students in cognitive and interpersonal skills. An eight-bed virtual hospital unit occupies one floor of the six-story hospital building. To create a sense of realism, patient rooms are equipped with wall-mounted blood pressure gauges, bedside cardiac monitors, medical supply cabinets, a sink, a computer desk, and chairs. Additional equipment on the unit includes central desk and computer workspace, crash cart, medication dispensing unit, x-ray view boxes and wheelchairs. Although the hospital unit was initially set up for nursing students to use for virtual simulations, the environment is well suited for inter-professional education. Specifically, the space supports several avatars in each patient room at one time (8-10 avatars), with additional observation space on the exterior deck of the building (translucent wall so that observers can see into the unit).

Several SL features provide opportunities for information sharing and interaction among the interprofessional learners. For example, objects can be created for learners to interact with in order to gain clinical information about their patients, such as health history, current vital signs and assessment parameters. Notecards—developed prior to the educational session—can be shared with learners to give them information or cues to aid them during the simulation. The voice chat function also allows for synchronous communication among the interprofessional learners. In summary, the overall environment provides a realistic, dynamic space for active learning. The environment can quickly be adapted to support educational objectives for a variety of simulations, while still maintaining fidelity and a sense of realism.

Second Life Scenario Development Process

A standardized process for simulation development is needed to maximize fidelity of the simulation process. The five step process includes

1. Key concept identification,
2. Competency and standard mapping,
3. Scenario building,
4. Debriefing development, and
5. Beta testing and refinement (as needed) of the scenario (Tschannen & Aebersold, 2010).

This process has been successfully used for the development of simulations for diverse settings, including ambulatory care, acute care, community prevention and professional educational settings (Tschannen, Aebersold, Sauter & Funnel, 2013). For the purpose of this chapter, a detailed description of each phase in the process will be given. In addition, an exemplar will be developed using the phases in the process. The exemplar will focus on the use of effective communication strategies among the interprofessional healthcare team. Although the setting is within the

healthcare environment, it can be applied to many other business-related industries where transfer of communication is critical.

Phase 1: Key Concept Identification

In Phase 1, key concepts or behaviors that are needed for success in a particular industry must be identified. This step requires the review of current industry standards of practice and key competencies. For healthcare, this includes the Institute of Medicine Reports, the Quality and Safety in Education (Cronenwett, et al., 2007) standard, the *Essentials of Baccalaureate Education for Professional Nursing* (2009), the Accreditation Council for Graduate Medical Education (ACGME) competencies (http://www.acgme.org/acgmeweb/Portals/0/PFAssets/ProgramRequirements/CPRs2013.pdf), and the Interprofessional Education Collaborative (Interprofessional Education Collaborative Expert Panel, 2011). As noted in these publications, interprofessional communication is a core competency for both physicians and nurses.

- **Exemplar:** One of the most critical aspects in healthcare delivery is communication among the healthcare team. According to The Joint Commission, miscommunication is one of the primary root causes for sentinel events (The Joint Commission, 2013). When communication is effective among nurses and physicians, patient and professional outcomes improve, such as improved quality of care (Hamric & Blackball, 2007; Kramer & Schmalenberg, 2003) increased patient and professional satisfaction (Hamric & Blackball, 2007; Boyle & Kochinda, 2004) and greater intent to stay (Boyle & Kochinda, 2004; Krairiksh & Anthony, 2001). Breakdowns in communication between nurses and physicians can often result in errors, many of which are preventable (Solet, Norvell,

Rutan, & Frankel, 2005). For this reason, every opportunity to 'practice' communication among members of the healthcare team is important.

Phase 2: Competency and Standard Mapping

The key concepts are mapped in phase 2 to clinical standards and competencies to ensure that the simulation focus is in alignment with current requirements. This phase is critical to ensuring the approach taken within the simulation scenario will assist in the development of the preferred competency.

- **Exemplar:** The concept of communication is in alignment with many professional standards and core competencies. The Interprofessional Education Collaborative identified interprofessional communication as one of three competency domains. Specifically, members of the healthcare team must "Communicate with patients, families, communities, and other health professionals in a responsive and responsible manner that supports a team approach to the maintenance of health and the treatment of disease (pg 23)." Similarly, the *Essentials of Baccalaureate Education for Professional Nursing* (2009), which addresses stakeholders' recommendations for required core knowledge of all health care providers, identified communication as a critical component of education. Within the document, nine essentials are included covering a range of topics, including Essential (VI) which describes incorporation of "effective communication techniques, including negotiation and conflict resolution to produce positive professional working relationships (American Association of Colleges of Nursing, 2009,

pg 22)." In the medical profession, residents must 'demonstrate interpersonal and communication skills that result in the effective exchange of information and collaboration with patients, their families, and health professionals (pg 9)."

Understanding the types of communication techniques required for competent practice for the interprofessional team (e.g. collaboration, conflict management, and negotiation) helps in determining the type of scenario that needs to be presented. In this case, it is clear that the ability to communicate pertinent patient information in a succinct and efficient manner is necessary for safe and effective patient care. For this reason, the scenario should require a succinct patient communication between a nurse and physician.

Phase 3: Scenario Building

Scenario building (Phase 3) includes brainstorming clinical scenarios that will stimulate the desired response/behavior. To ensure successful development of a scenario, it is important to have experts in the field (related to the scenario topic) assisting with the scenario building. In an interprofessional education session, this requires engagement of all stakeholders (e.g. nurses and physician faculty). This helps with ensuring the fidelity or 'degree of realism' of the developed scenario through each stakeholder lense. An important next step is to decide the background needed for the scenario (in this case where in SL should the scenario be run?) and which roles are played by learners and which are played by facilitators or 'actors'. A storyboard outlining the key aspects of the scenario is needed to build the scenario. Elements of the storyboard should include the following: Key concepts, prerequisites, timeframe, setting, participants, scenario design and timeline, and debriefing questions.

Once the simulation has been developed, the process in which students or learners will be evaluated on their performance must be considered. Educators can use standardized scales such as the Emergency Medicine Crisis Resource Management (EMCRM) tool, developed by Youngblood et al. (2008) or the Capacity to Rescue Instrument (CRI) developed by Aebersold (2008). The EMCRM was developed to evaluate the participant's crisis management skills and assesses their team leadership skills, including knowledge of the environment, utilization of information and resources, and overall ability to communicate and facilitate task completion. The CRI identifies key assessments and interventions that need to be performed in the simulation scenario to ensure a good patient outcome. Educators can also develop their own set of behaviors based on 'best practice' standards or current evidence-based practice guidelines. Performance, which can be measured individually or as a team, can then be reviewed during the debriefing session after the completion of the simulation scenario.

- **Exemplar:** Prior to the simulation, medical and nursing students should be provided some pre-learnings related to the education content, which in this case, is communication among the interprofes-

sional team. There are a variety of training programs available that focus on communication, including Medical Team Training, Crew Resource Management, and Team Strategies and Tools to Enhance Performance and Patient Safety (TEAMSTEPPS). CRM, for example, was developed by the National Center for Patient Safety at the VA (Sculi, 2010). Part of this training program provides an overview of key behaviors and strategies that are used by leaders and subordinates to ensure that effective teamwork and communication takes place, especially when safety is in question. The training also provides an overview of the effective followership algorithm shown in Figure 1. Effective Followership Algorithm, which includes specific communication strategies. Upon completion of the pre-learning, students can 'practice' the communication strategies identified in the training session while incorporating the specific experiences needed for the student to become competent (as deemed by industry standards).

Figure 1. Effective followership algorithm
© 2011, Fortis Business Media, LLC and Gary L. Sculli. Used with permission.

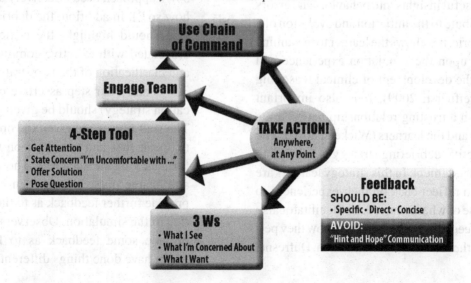

A storyboard of the scenario should be developed. For the purpose of this exemplar, a storyboard, overviewing each element of the scenario was developed (Appendix). Once the storyboard has been developed, review of the scenario by experts in the field (e.g. communication and patient safety) should be conducted. Such feedback will aid in ensuring realism and fidelity in the scenario, as well as to ensure the most relevant evidence related to the themes are being highlighted in the scenario.

For the purpose of this scenario, a specific evaluation tool was not developed. The faculty should consider the student performance in relationship to the evidence based communication strategies learned in the CRM (i.e. effective followership algorithm). For example, did the nurse use the 3W's? The 4-step communication process? Was hinting and hoping avoided? Additionally, performance should be discussed during the debriefing session, which would occur at the conclusion of the simulation scenario.

Phase 4: Debriefing Development

This phase of the development is critical for success. Debriefing sessions provide an opportunity for participants to reflect on their performance (as well as the performance of other team members) and gain useful insights into behaviors and errors that contribute to the initiation and evolution of a crisis. Debriefing allows the learner to reexamine or reflect upon the simulation experience and supports the development of clinical reasoning skills (Dreifuerst, 2009). It is also important to establish a trusting relationship between the facilitator and the learners (Wickers, 2010). The most effective debriefing strategy is debriefing with good judgment. In this strategy learners are required to reflect back on their experiences to make sense of what occurred. The facilitator also provides feedback to the learner on how they performed in the scenario (Rudolf, Simon, Dufresne,

Raemer, 2006). According to a study conducted by Day and colleagues (2009), feedback provided during simulation has been shown to significantly improve performance over feedback given in the actual clinical site. Debriefing can also include feedback to participants based on their individual or group performance in the scenario as compared to a standardized measurement scale or a list of expected behaviors.

- **Exemplar:** At the completion of the simulation, all participants would need to participate in the debriefing, which usually occurs in a classroom or conference room (e.g. unit conference room on SL unit). For this scenario, a focus would be on understanding how the interaction transpired. The debriefing should begin with a focus on the aspects of the simulation that went well (e.g. 'what do you feel went well during this scenario?'). Once positive aspects of the simulation are discussed, the facilitator should ask questions focused on the key concept of the simulation ('How would you describe the interaction between Nancy, the staff nurse, and Tracey, the physician?' What might the nurse have done differently? Was the 3W's approach used effectively and if not, how so?'). In addition, the debriefing session should highlight the critical points associated with effective communication, and clarification of the two strategies (e.g. 3 W's and Four step assertive communication strategy) should be given if needed. The staff nurses are given the opportunity to speak first and to reflect on their performance in the scenario. The physician and charge nurse should then be able to provide further feedback as to their reflection of the simulation. Observers may also provide some feedback as to how they might have done things differently.

Phase 5: Beta Testing and Further Refinement

The simulation should be beta tested with a group of individuals familiar with the topic of interest prior to implementation. In interprofessional simulations, it is important to ensure the diverse professions are accounted for in the beta test group. A diverse group will provide feedback to the fidelity of the scenario from all stakeholder perspectives. The beta test is an opportunity to 'test' the simulation and should be conducted in a manner similar to how one expects to implement the simulation to the targeted population. For example, if the scenario developed requires certain pre-work or supplies, all of this should be provided to the participants in the beta test. This helps to determine the effectiveness of the anticipated implementation process, as well as the overall fidelity of the scenario. This step in the process requires participants to provide feedback on all aspects of the simulation (i.e. scenario, implementation process, fidelity, etc). This feedback is then used to revise the scenario and the implementation process as needed.

- **Exemplar:** For the purpose of the exemplar, the scenario should be beta tested with both nurse and medical faculty who also have completed the Crew Resource Management training. The purpose of the beta testing would be to test the process of setting up and running the scenarios and to pilot test the actual scenario with the interprofessional group. Faculty participating in the beta test would be brought to the simulation setting, provided the notecards (e.g. instructions) for the different roles, and provided the same instructions as noted in the scenario (Appendix A). The simulation should run over approximately 15 minutes, with an additional 15 minutes allotted for the debriefing session. Faculty should be asked to share their input as to the fidelity and effectiveness of the implementation of the simulation used in the beta test. Specifically, questions related to the 'realness' and flow should be discussed (e.g. 'What (if any) changes would you make in the scenario of the implementation of the scenario when we implement this with our students?'). Feedback obtained from the beta test of the exemplar may include changes in wording and flow of the simulation

Scenario Implementation

Once the scenarios have been developed and adjustments made after the beta testing, they are ready to be used by learners. The virtual simulations are scheduled and 'run' by a trained facilitator who can oversee the simulation and effectively manage the debriefing directly after the simulation. Content experts may also be present to add to the experience during debriefing. The effectiveness of simulations can be evaluated by using standardized scoring templates during the scenario, having learners take a knowledge test or following the learners in the actual clinical site and observe their performance. Virtual simulations, as with all simulations are evaluated carefully during their execution for areas that might need further improvement.

ISSUES, CONTROVERSIES, PROBLEMS

Challenges occur in any new type of learning particularly when it includes technologies outside of the educator's control. There are advantages to using SL for educational purposes; it is free to users, can be downloaded on most computers without difficulty and basic navigation skills are easy for most people to learn. When using it for virtual simulations the learners usually only need basic navigation skills and do not require more advanced skills such as building objects or writing scripts. The educators, however, need to have access to space they can use which usually means having an island available and some type of building or structure to implement the virtual simulation. Many universities and even several health systems have invested in purchasing space (islands) in SL for training and education (both formal and informal). Challenges around using the space at a university or heath system are usually related to technology infrastructure and firewall issues. Computer labs on campus or training rooms often have closed systems that do not allow for the installation of programs such as SL without permission and support from the information technology (IT) departments. For example, prior to one of the virtual simulation days, a new version of SL was required prior to use of the software. We were unable to download the new version, thus the simulations were postponed (adding to student frustration). On the health system side, privacy issues exist as health care systems need to ensure protection of private health information and therefore several IT security measures and firewalls are in place, limiting the ability to incorporate a new software program such as SL.

Additional issues include skill set of the faculty or educator who is interested in using SL. As with many new technologies on campus that may be used by innovators or early adopters there is usually no internal IT support available. Often IT staff are not even familiar with the product. It then becomes the faculty/educator's responsibility to set up the space and manage the technology, including assisting students or learners with issues in downloading and using the program. Faculty/educators need to have skills to build their environments within SL and basic scripting skills are a minimal requirement for many virtual simulations. While it is possible to purchase many items that are needed, a working knowledge of Prims (basic building blocks in SL)

and scripting (to program object interactions) are usually necessary to understand how objects work. Faculty and educators find themselves functioning in several roles; developing the SL environment, developing and running the virtual simulations, and providing IT support to learners. One particular technology challenge for our work has been in getting learners to use the voice chat function. We found it necessary to use headsets to reduce the amount of background noise found with using laptop microphones. Learners often had difficulty getting their headsets to work and sometimes lost functionality part way through the simulations. Again some of this was due to using university/health system computers that faculty/educators did not have administrative access to so troubleshooting problems was difficult. It is also necessary for them to develop some skills with their avatars ahead of time to make full use of the training time.

Other concerns include privacy for participants during the virtual simulations and during the debriefing. In simulation, learners are encouraged to take risks and try new behaviors and skills that they have not mastered. During debriefing, learners are given critical feedback on their performance and it is sometimes very emotional, particularly if they did not do well and their 'virtual patient' did not have a positive outcome. When running simulation in a simulation lab using human patient simulators there are usually only the learners and faculty present. Even simulations that take place in situ (in the actual health care environment-hospital unit, emergency room) there is still a limited number of people around to observe. In SL if you are running the virtual simulation on an open island, any avatar can 'drop in' and watch. Even on a closed island, avatars that have permission to be on that island can observe or 'hear' or see what is happening. There are ways to mitigate this by placing up signs/barriers that tell other avatars there is a simulation in progress and it would be preferable not to have others observing.

SOLUTIONS AND RECOMMENDATIONS

Despite the challenges in using SL there are ways to minimize them and take full advantage of the benefits of SL for virtual simulations. One recommendation is getting the IT department involved in the beginning. You can add an IT member on your development team and encourage them to learn the program so they can be supportive. It is important that they understand this is a learning tool, not a game—such is the case with other forms of technology (i.e. clickers, video conferencing). Early research on the benefits of virtual simulation to learner development can be helpful in convincing others this is educational and not just 'fun'. Getting small grants from internal sources that support new types of learning or new uses for technology can also be helpful to educators/ faculty in getting started. This money can be used to purchase items in SL or hiring a 'builder' or 'designer' to help with setting up the environment and even scripting objects.

In addition, thought must be given to the process of orienting students or learners to SL. We developed podcasts and an on-line orientation manual to use to assist learners in getting started. Learners would get instructions at the beginning of class or a few weeks ahead of training on downloading the program and setting up their avatars. This allows the learners time to practice navigation skills and getting to their destination for training so when they are scheduled for their virtual simulations time is not wasted on getting avatars ready to participate.

Finally the issue of privacy during virtual simulations and debriefing need to be addressed. Using SL exposes student to the potential of other avatars overhearing the conversations that occur. This can be mitigated by putting up a notification that simulations are in progress and please do not disturb. Local chat can be used and voice chat should be limited to the area needed by the participants.

FUTURE RESEARCH DIRECTIONS

Simulation is becoming integral to many areas of health professional education including IPE both in the classroom setting and in the work environment. The research is beginning to show the tremendous benefits of human patient simulation in helping learners develop both clinical/ technical skills, cognitive skills (clinical reasoning) and interpersonal skills. Research in the area of virtual simulation is still very new. It is important as educators use technology like this to evaluate its effectiveness as a learning pedagogy in addition to evaluating technical aspects. Institutions will be more likely to fund and support virtual reality programs like SL if the benefits can be shown from a solid research and cost/ benefit perspective. Future research is needed to identify the impact of virtual simulations on actual performance in the clinical setting. Our work has shown improvement in interpersonal skills using virtual simulation, but we are currently considering a methodology for following these students into the clinical setting to assess performance.

CONCLUSION

Simulations have been demonstrated to be a safe way to train health care practitioners and are used in a variety of settings. Virtual simulations, in particular, can provide an effective teaching methodology for use in health care practitioner education. The technology required can be easily obtained but requires planning and IT support to ensure it runs smoothly and learners are not frustrated by the technology challenges. The scenario development process outlined here can be used to develop simulations for a variety of settings including health care and IPE and can help faculty and educators design and conduct effective simulations.

REFERENCES

Aebersold, M. (2008). *Capacity to rescue: Nurse behaviors that rescue patients*. Retrieved from http://hdl.handle.net/2027.42/60718

Aebersold, M. (2010). Using simulation to improve the use of evidence-based practice guidelines. *Western Journal of Nursing Research*. doi:10.1177/0193945910379791 PMID:20876552

Aldridge, C. (2009). *The complete guide to simulations and serious games: How the most valuable content will be created in the age beyond Gutenberg to Google*. San Francisco, CA: Pfeiffer.

American Association of Colleges of Nursing. (2009). *The essentials of baccalaureate education for professional nursing practice faculty toolkit*. Author.

Bearnson, C. S., & Wiker, K. M. (2005). Human patient simulators: A new face in baccalaureate nursing education at Brigham Young University. *The Journal of Nursing Education*, *44*, 421–425. PMID:16220650

Benner, P., Sutphen, M., Leonard, V., & Day, L. (2009). *Educating nurses: A call for radical transformation*. Carnegie Foundation.

Boyle, D. K., & Kochinda, C. (2004). Enhancing collaborative communication of nurse and physician leadership: Two intensive care units. *JONA*, *34*(2), 60–70. doi:10.1097/00005110-200402000-00003 PMID:14770064

Buckley, T., & Gordon, C. (2011). The effectiveness of high fidelity simulation on medical–surgical registered nurses' ability to recognise and respond to clinical emergencies. *Nurse Education Today*, *31*(7), 716–721. doi:10.1016/j.nedt.2010.04.004 PMID:20573428

Burgess, M. L., Slate, J. R., Rojas-LeBouef, A., & LaPraire, K. (2010). Teaching and learning in second life: Using the community of inquiry (CoI) model to support online instruction with graduate students in instructional technology. *The Internet and Higher Education*, *13*(1-2), 84–88. doi:10.1016/j.iheduc.2009.12.003

Conradi, E., Kavia, S., Burden, D., Rice, A., Woodham, L., Beaumont, C., & Poulton, T. et al. (2009). Virtual patients in a virtual world: Training paramedic students for practice. *Medical Teacher*, *31*(8), 713–720. doi:10.1080/01421590903134160 PMID:19811207

Council for Graduate Medical Education. (n.d.). Retrieved from http://www.acgme.org/acgmeweb/Portals/0/PFAssets/ProgramRequirements/CPRs2013.pdf

Cronenwett, L., Sherwood, G., Barnsteiner, J., Disch, J., Johnson, J., Mitchell, P., & Warren, J. et al. (2007). Quality and safety education for nurses. *Nursing Outlook*, *55*(3), 122–131. doi:10.1016/j.outlook.2007.02.006 PMID:17524799

Cumin, D., Boyd, M. J., Webster, C. S., & Weller, J. M. (2013). A systematic review of simulation for multidisciplinary team training in operating rooms. *Simulation in Healthcare: Journal of the Society for Simulation in Healthcare*. doi: 10.1097/SIH.0b013e31827e2f4c

Day, T., Iles, N., & Griffiths, P. (2009). Effect of performance feedback on tracheal suctioning knowledge and skills: Randomized controlled trial. *Journal of Advanced Nursing*, *65*(7), 14–23. doi:10.1111/j.1365-2648.2009.04997.x PMID:19457007

Dillon, P., & Noble, K. (2009). Simulation as a means to foster collaborative interdisciplinary education. *Nursing Education Perspectives*, *30*(2), 87–90. PMID:19476071

Dreifuerst, K. T. (2009). The essentials of debriefing in simulation learning: A concept analysis. *Nursing Education Perspectives, 30*(2), 109–114. PMID:19476076

Ericsson, K. A. (2004). Deliberate practice and the acquisition and maintenance of expert performance in medicine and related domains. *Academic Medicine: Journal of the Association of American Medical Colleges, 79*(10Suppl), S70–S81. doi:10.1097/00001888-200410001-00022 PMID:15383395

Hamric, A. B., & Blackhall, L. J. (2007). Nursing-physician perspectives on the care of dying patients in intensive care units: Collaborations, moral distress, and ethical climate. *Critical Care Medicine, 35*(2), 422–429. doi:10.1097/01.CCM.0000254722.50608.2D PMID:17205001

Harder, N. B. (2010). Use of simulation in teaching and learning in health sciences: A systematic review. *The Journal of Nursing Education, 49*(1), 23–28. doi:10.3928/01484834-20090828-08 PMID:19731886

Hoffman, R., O'Donnell, J., & Kim, Y. (2007). The effects of human patient simulatiors on basic knowledge in critical care nursing with undergraduate senior baccalaureate nursing students. *Simulation in Healthcare, 2*, 110–114. doi:10.1097/SIH.0b013e318033abb5 PMID:19088615

Interprofessional Educational Collaborative Expert Panel. (2011). *Core competencies for interprofessional collaborative practice: Report of an expert panel*. Washington, DC: Interprofessional Education Collaborative.

IOM Health Professions Education. (n.d.). *A bridge to quality (free executive summary)*. Retrieved from http://www.nap.edu/catalog/10681.html

Joint Commission. (n.d.). Retrieved from http://www.jointcommission.org/sentinel_event.aspx

Kohn, L. T., Corrigan, J., & Donaldson, M. S. (Eds.). (2000). *To err is human: Building a safer health system*. Washington, DC: National Academy Press.

Krainkish, M., & Anthony, M. K. (2001). Benefits and outcomes of staff nurses' participant in decision making. *JONA, 31*(1), 16–33. doi:10.1097/00005110-200101000-00005

Kramer, M., & Schmalenberg, C. (2003). Securing good nurse/physician relationships. *Nursing Management, 34*(7), 34–38. doi:10.1097/00006247-200307000-00013 PMID:12843717

Lapkin, S., Levett-Jones, T., Bellchambers, H., & Fernandez, R. (2010). Effectiveness of patient simulation mannequins in teaching clinical reasoning skills to undergraduate nursing students: A systematic review. *Clinical Simulation in Nursing, 6*(6), e207–e222. doi:10.1016/j.ecns.2010.05.005

Leonard, M., Graham, S., & Bonacum, D. (2004). The human factor: The critical importance of teamwork and communication in providing safe patient care. *Quality & Safety in Health Care, 13*(suppl 1), i85–i90. doi:10.1136/qshc.2004.010033 PMID:15465961

Levitt-Jones, T., Hoffman, K., Dempsey, Y., Jeong, S., Noble, D., & Norton, C. et al.. (2010). The "five rights" of clinical reasoning: An educational model to enhance nursing students' ability to identify and manage clinically "at risk" patients. *Nurse Education Today, 30*(6), 515–520. doi:10.1016/j.nedt.2009.10.020

Liaw, S., Zhou, W., Lau, T., Siau, C., & Chan, S. (2014). An interprofessional communication training using simulation to enhance safe care for a deteriorating patient. *Nurse Education Today, 34*(2), 259–264. doi:10.1016/j.nedt.2013.02.019 PMID:23518067

Mazzocco, , Petitti, D. B., Fong, K. T., Bonacum, D., Brookey, J., Graham, S., & Thomas, E. J. et al. (2009). Surgical team behaviors and patient outcomes. *American Journal of Surgery*, *197*(5), 878–685. doi:10.1016/j.amjsurg.2008.03.002 PMID:18789425

McGaghie, W. C., Issenberg, S. B., Petrusa, E. R., & Scalese, R. J. (2010). A critical review of simulation-based medical education research: 2003-2009. *Medical Education*, *44*(1), 50–63. doi:10.1111/j.1365-2923.2009.03547.x PMID:20078756

Medical Teamwork and Patient Safety: The Evidence-Based Relationship. (2003). Agency for Healthcare Research and Quality.

Morgan, P. J., & Cleave-Hogg, D. (2002). Comparison between medical students' experience, confidence and competence. *Medical Education*, *36*(6), 534–539. doi:10.1046/j.1365-2923.2002.01228.x PMID:12047667

Morgan, P. J., Cleave-Hogg, D., McIlroy, J., & Devitt, J. H. (2002). Simulation technology: A comparison of experiential and visual learning for undergraduate medical students. *Anesthesiology*, *96*(1), 10–16. doi:10.1097/00000542-200201000-00008 PMID:11752995

Nehring, W. M., & Lashley, W. R. (2004). Current uses and opinions regarding human patient simulators in nursing education: An international survey. *Nursing Education Perspectives*, *25*(5), 244–248. PMID:15508564

Orledge, J., Phillips, W. J., Murray, W. B., & Lerant, A. (2012). The use of simulation in healthcare: From systems issues, to team building, to task training, to education and high stakes examinations. *Current Opinion in Critical Care*, *18*(4), 326–332. doi:10.1097/MCC.0b013e328353fb49 PMID:22614323

Owen, H., Mugford, B., Follows, V., & Plummer, J. L. (2006). Comparison of three simulation-based training methods for management of medical emergencies. *Resuscitation*, *71*(2), 204–211. doi:10.1016/j.resuscitation.2006.04.007 PMID:16987587

Rudolf, J. W., Simon, R., Dufresne, M. S., & Raemer, D. B. (2006). There is no such thing as non-judgmental debriefing: A theory and method for debriefing with good judgment. *Simulation in Healthcare*, *1*(1), 49–55. doi:10.1097/01266021-200600110-00006 PMID:19088574

Scherer, Y. K., Bruce, S. A., & Runkawatt, V. (2007). A comparison of clinical simulation and case study presentation on nurse practitioner students' knowledge and confidence in managing cardiac event. *International Journal of Nursing Education Scholarship*, *4*(1), 22. doi:10.2202/1548-923X.1502 PMID:18052920

Schon, D. A. (1983). *The reflective practitioner: How professionals think in action*. San Francisco, CA: Jossey Bass.

Sculi, G. L. (2010). *Nursing crew resource management*. VA National Center for Patient Safety.

Shearer, J. E. (2013). High-fidelity simulation and safety: An integrative review. *The Journal of Nursing Education*, *52*(1), 39-45. doi:10.3928/01484834-20121121-01

Solet, D. J., Norvell, J. M., Rutan, G. H., & Frankel, R. M. (2005). Lost in translation: Challenges and opportunities in physician-to-physician communication during patient handoffs. *Academic Medicine*, *80*(12), 1094–1099. doi:10.1097/00001888-200512000-00005 PMID:16306279

Tanner, D. A., Padrick, K. P., Westfall, U. E., & Putzier, D. J. (1987). Diagnostic reasoning strategies of nurses and nursing students. *Nursing Research*, *36*(6), 358–365. doi:10.1097/00006199-198711000-00010 PMID:3671123

Tschannen, D., & Aebersold, M. (2010). *Second Life: Innovative simulation development-making it REAL!* Meaningful Play.

Tschannen, D., Aebersold, M., Sauter, C., & Funnell, M. M. (2013). Improving nurses' perceptions of competency in diabetes self-management education through the use of simulation and problem-based learning. *Journal of Continuing Education in Nursing*, *44*(6), 257–263. doi:10.3928/00220124-20130402-16 PMID:23565600

Van Sickle, K. R., McClusky, D. A., Gallagher, A. G., & Smith, C. D. (2005). Construct validation of the ProMIS simulator using a novel laparoscopic suturing task. *Surgical Endoscopy and Other Interventional Techniques*, *19*(9), 1227–1231. doi:10.1007/s00464-004-8274-6 PMID:16025195

Wayne, D. B., Didwania, A., Feinglass, J., Fudala, M. J., Barsuk, J. H., & McGaghie, W. C. (2008). Simulation-based education improves quality of care during cardiac arrest team responses at an academic teaching hospital: A case-control study. *Chest*, *133*(1), 56–61. doi:10.1378/chest.07-0131 PMID:17573509

Wharburton, S. (2009). Second Life in higher education: Assessing the potential for and the barriers to deploying virtual worlds in learning and teaching. *British Journal of Educational Technology*, *40*(3), 414–426. doi:10.1111/j.1467-8535.2009.00952.x

Wickers, M. P. (2010). Establishing the climate for a successful debriefing. *Clinical Simulation in Nursing*, *6*(3), e83–e86. doi:10.1016/j.ecns.2009.06.003

World Health Organization (WHO). (2010). *Framework for action on interprofessional education & collaborative practice*. Geneva: World Health Organization. Retrieved August 30, 2014 from http://www.who.int/hrh/resources/framework_action/en/

Youngblood, P., Harter, P. M., Srivastava, S., Moffett, S., Heinrichs, W. L., & Dev, P. (2008). Design, development, and evaluation of an online virtual emergency department for training trauma teams. *Simulation in Healthcare*, *3*(3), 146–153. doi:10.1097/SIH.0b013e31817bedf7 PMID:19088658

ADDITIONAL READING

Anderson, P., & Stephens, M. (2008). Wolverine Island. *EDUCAUSE Review*, *43*(5). http://www.educause.edu/EDUCAUSE+Review/EDUCAUSEReviewMagazineVolume43/WolverineIsland/163175 Retrieved November 19, 2009

Boulos, M. N. K., Hetherington, L., & Wheeler, S. (2007). Second Life: An overview of the potential of 3-D virtual worlds in medical and health education. *Health Information and Libraries Journal*, *24*(4), 233–245. doi:10.1111/j.1471-1842.2007.00733.x PMID:18005298

Cheal, C. (2009). Second life: Hype or learning? *On the Horizon*, *15*(4), 204–210. doi:10.1108/10748120710836228

Clark, C.C. (1976) Simulation gaming: a new teaching strategy in nursing education. *Nurse Educ.*, Nov-Dec;1(4):4-9.

Fanning, R. M., & Gaba, D. M. (2007). The role of debriefing in simulation based learning. *Simulation in Healthcare*, *2*(2), 115–125. doi:10.1097/SIH.0b013e3180315539 PMID:19088616

Gaba, D. M. (2004). A brief history of mannequin-based simulation and application. In W. F. Dunn (Ed.), *Simulators in critical care and beyond* (p. 130). Des Plaines, IL: Society of Critical Care Medicine.

Gaba, D. M., Howard, S. K., Fish, K. J., Smith, B. E., & Sowb, Y. A. (2001). Simulation-based training in anesthesia crisis resource management (ACRM): A decade of experience. *Simulation & Gaming, 32*(2), 175–193. doi:10.1177/104687810103200206

Garrison, D. R., Cleveland-Innes, M., & Fung, T. S. (2010). Exploring causal relationships among teaching, cognitive andsocial presence: Student perceptions of the community of inquiry framework. *The Internet and Higher Education, 13*(1-2), 31–36. doi:10.1016/j.iheduc.2009.10.002

Issenberg, S. B., McGaghie, W. C., Petrusa, E. R., Lee, G. D., & Scalese, R. (2005). Features and uses of high-fidelity medical simulations that lead to effective learning: A BEME systematic review. *Medical Teacher, 27*(1), 10–28. doi:10.1080/01421590500046924 PMID:16147767

Jeffries, P. R. (2005). A framework for designing, implementing, and evaluating simulations used as teaching strategies in nursing. *Nursing Education Perspectives, 26*(2), 96–103. PMID:15921126

Kamel-Boulos, M., Hetherington, L., & Wheeler, S. (2007). Second Life: An overview of the potential of 3-D virtual worlds in medical and health education. *Health Information and Libraries Journal, 24*(4), 233–245. doi:10.1111/j.1471-1842.2007.00733.x PMID:18005298

Kapp, K. M., & O'Driscoll, T. (2010) *Learning in 3D: Adding a New Dimension to Enterprise Learning and Collaboration*. NY: Wiley. Retrieved from: http://books.google.com/books?id=d6lSyf3HNLIC

Kirriemuir, J. (2010). UK university and college technical support for second life developers and users. *Educational Research, 52*(2), 215–227. doi:10.1080/00131881.2010.482756

Kuiper, R. A., Heinrich, C., Matthias, A., Graham, M. J., & Bell-Kotwall, L. (2008). Debriefing with the OPT Model of Clinical Reasoning during High Fidelity Patient Simulation. *International Journal of Nursing Education Scholarship, 5*(1), 1–14. doi:10.2202/1548-923X.1466 PMID:18454731

Leong, J., Kinross, J., Taylor, D., & Purkayastha, S. (2008). Surgeons have held conferences in Second Life. *BMJ (Clinical Research Ed.), 337*(jul08 2), a683. doi:10.1136/bmj.a683 PMID:18614495

Mah, J. W., Bingham, K., Dobkin, E. D., Malchiodi, L., Russell, A., Donahue, S., & Kirton, O. C. et al. (2009). Mannequin simulation identifies common surgical intensive unit teamwork errors long after introduction of sepsis guidelines. *Society of Simulation in Healthcare, 4*(4), 193–199. doi:10.1097/SIH.0b013e3181abe9d6 PMID:21330791

Mayo, P. H., Hackney, J. E., Mueck, J. T., Ribaudo, V., & Schneider, R. (2004). Achieving house staff competence in emergency airway management: Results of a teaching program using a computerized patient simulator. *Critical Care Medicine, 32*(12), 2422–2427. doi:10.1097/01.CCM.0000147768.42813.A2 PMID:15599146

Medley, C. F., & Horne, C. (2005). Using simulation technology for undergraduate nursing education. *Educational Innovations, 44*(1), 31–34. PMID:15673172

Minocha, S., & Reeves, J. (2010). Design of learning spaces in 3D virtual worlds: An empirical investigation of Second Life. *Learning, Media and Technology, 35*(2), 111–137. doi:10.1080/17439884.2010.494419

Nehring, W. M., & Lashley, F. R. (2009). Nursing Simulation: A Review of the Past 40 Years. *Simulation & Gaming*, 40(4), 528–552. doi:10.1177/1046878109332282

Oblinger, D. (2006). *Learning Spaces*. London: EDUCASE.

Pfeil, U., Ang, C. S., & Zaphiris, P. (2009). Issues and challenges of teaching and learning in 3D virtual worlds: Real life case studies. *Educational Media International*, 46(3), 223–238. doi:10.1080/09523980903135368

Rosen, K. R. (2008). The history of medical simulation. *Journal of Critical Care*, 23(2), 157–166. doi:10.1016/j.jcrc.2007.12.004 PMID:18538206

Stephens, M., & Chapman, C. (2009). *The Virtual First Responder: Exploring Virtual Reality in the Context of Medical Education*. Poster Presentation. Presented at Campus Technology. *USC Institute for Creative Technologies* (homepage). Retrieved from: http://ict.usc.edu/

University of Michigan Health Sciences Libraries. (2008). *HSL Videos - Second Life and Public* Health - Video | Health Sciences Libraries | MLibrary.

Wayne, D. B., Didwania, A., Feinglass, J., Fudala, M. J., Barsuk, J. H., & McGaghie, W. C. (2008). Simulation-based education improves quality of care during cardiac arrest team responses at an academic teaching hospital: A case-control study. *Chest*, 133(1), 56–61. doi:10.1378/chest.07-0131 PMID:17573509

KEY TERMS AND DEFINITIONS

Clinical Reasoning: The ability for the learner to use previous knowledge and skills and apply those to a new situation.

Effective Communication: Communication between two or more individuals that results in a good outcome.

Exemplar: An example that highlights the specific action you want the learner to replicate.

Learning Framework: A guide to use when developing learning activities.

Patient Safety: Patients do not suffer any harm during their care.

Simulation: A technique used to re-create a realistic environment for learners to practice skills.

Virtual Simulations: Simulations conducted in an on-line, 3D computer environment.

APPENDIX

Scenario Storyboard: Nurse-Physician Communication using Crew Resource Management Strategies

- **Key Concepts:**
  - ○ Interpersonal relations.
  - ○ Communication.
  - ○ Teamwork.
- **Prerequisites:** Completion of Crew Resource Management Training.
- **Timeframe:** 15 minute (scenario); 15 minute (de-briefing).
- **Setting (In Second Life):**
  - ○ Participants begin in unit conference room.
  - ○ Patient care to occur in the Patient room.
- **Participants:**
  - ○ RN,
  - ○ Physician,
  - ○ Charge Nurse.

Scenario Design and Timeline

Assign participants to roles within the scenario. Additional participants can be assigned an observer role. Once assignments in roles are complete, pass out the SL notecards, which provide guidance to the roles.

- **Staff Nurse Notecard:** You will be the primary nurse on a general medicine unit, working the night shift. You have been assigned four patients, one of which is Mr. Howard. Further instructions will be given by the facilitator at the beginning of the simulation. Please note that you may speak with the charge nurse or physician at anytime during the scenario.
- **Charge Nurse Notecard:** You will be available as a resource for the staff nurse. If the nurse calls for your assistance, you should recommend calling the physician (based on the patient's current assessment findings).
- **Physician Notecard:** During the course of the scenario, the nurse will contact you with a specific request related to Mr. Howard. If the nurse clearly articulates her concern and wants (e.g. uses the 3Ws...What I see, What I am concerned about, What I want), consider ordering some of her requests (but not all). If the nurse does not clearly articulate her concern and wants, be vague in your response and only order fluids if you see fit. Regardless of the nurse's effectiveness at communicating needs, refuse to come to the unit to assess the patient or transfer the patient to the ICU.

Once roles are assigned and notecards distributed, the facilitator should introduce the simulation and give context to the simulation, including the environment and role-specific instructions (as needed).

- **Facilitator Introduction:** "Hello and welcome. As you know, communication among the health care team is critical for high quality of care. For this reason, we are going to have an opportunity to 'practice' our communication skills. Sometime during the scenario you may find it necessary to communicate to other members of the healthcare team. If the situation arises, consider using the communication strategies you learned in the Crew Resource Management training you recently completed. The scenario begins with shift report on a general medicine unit. Nancy (who is the participant playing the role of the staff nurse), you have just received report on your four patients. One of the patients you will be caring for is Mr. Howard. Mr. Howard is a 55 year old who suffered a stroke 10 days ago, his baseline is oriented to person only, left sided weakness, chronic a-fib (a heart dysrythmia), and hypertension. He has a tracheostomy (a breathing tube in his neck) and has been requiring every four hour suctioning for moderate amounts of secretions. In addition he has had a temperature around 100.2F and oxygen saturation (i.e. level of oxygen in the blood, want above 90%) has been running around 95% on 30% trach mask. It is now 2AM and you are heading into Mr. Howard's room to assess him. Please use your charge nurse and physician as a resource (as needed). Tom and Tracey (who are playing the role of charge nurse and physician, respectively), you can wait in the conference room and be available if Nancy asks for your assistance. Nancy, you may begin."
- **Phase I (Nurse Assessment):** The staff nurse (Nancy) will 'assess' the patient, using the notecard function in SL. Specifically, the notecard will provide current vital signs and assessment findings. Upon review of the assessment data, the Nancy would find Mr. Howard's condition to have deteriorated since the initial report. Specifically, Mr. Howard would have difficulty breathing, increased blood pressure and heart rate, lots of secretions needing to be suctioned, high temperature, and mental status changes. Upon assessment, Nancy would see the need for closer observation and would more than likely identify the need to call the physician. She may also speak with the charge nurse, who has been instructed to mention the need to call the physician.
- **Phase 2 (Nurse-Physician Interaction):** Nancy would contact the physician (Tracey) to describe Mr. Howard's current status. The primary expectation of the staff nurse includes use of the 3 Ws:
  - What I see,
  - What I am concerned about, and
  - What I want (VA National Center for Patient Safety).

The nurse should state her needs clearly without 'hinting' about what she wants (i.e. "Mr. Howard needs to be transferred to the ICU" versus "Mr. Howard is going to require a lot of care"). When the physician does not comply to her wishes (if she sees the need to transfer the patient), she should re-state her needs, using either the 3 W's again or use a more assertive communication strategy:

- State the name or position (to get the individuals attention),
- State concern ('I am uncomfortable with…'),
- Offer an alternative, and
- Pose a question to get a resolution ('Do you agree?') (Sculi, 2010).

This phase may require a couple interactions with the physician, as the initial response from the physician will not be transferring to the ICU. The simulation will continue until the staff nurse uses one of the methods above in an effective manner (e.g. no 'hinting or hoping') to obtain the transfer order as needed or time is up. (maximum timeframe of 15 minutes).

De-Brief Questions

1. What went well during the scenario?
2. How would you describe the interaction between Nancy, the staff nurse, and Tracey, the physician?
3. What might the nurse have done differently?
4. Was the 3W's approach used effectively and if not, how so?
5. How do you believe use of the communication strategies can impact patient care?

Chapter 13
Digital Media in the Classroom:
Emergent Perspectives for 21st Century Learners

Kathy Sanford
University of Victoria, Canada

Liz Merkel
University of Victoria, Canada

Tim Hopper
University of Victoria, Canada

ABSTRACT

The purpose of this chapter is to highlight the engagement, social connectivity, and motivation to learn observed in two classes of students, one a grade 9/10 information technology class, the other a grade 3 class of learners classified with learning disabilities. The common factor in the two classes was the way the teachers were rethinking literacy for the 21st century learning by simultaneously engaging students in an event of creating computer programing to address a competition task whilst also addressing curriculum demands. The chapter explores the way the teachers were learning to develop the conditions for emergent learning systems in their classrooms as the first steps to reform the current education system. Drawing on complexity theory, the authors suggest that these students are offering two microcosmic examples of where global systems are heading. The goal of the chapter is to help shift school teaching from its present disconnect between the real world outside students' classrooms and the contrived, dated world of typical school-based curriculum practices.

INTRODUCTION

In the fall of 2006 our ethnographic research study began in a response to increasing social concern regarding adolescent (dis)engagement in school literacy practices. We began data col-

lection in a grade 9/10 Information Technology (IT) class wherein students were in the process of creating their own videogames as a way to learn programming. The work with these initial participants spurred the proliferation of several strands of subsequent research, and only inspired

DOI: 10.4018/978-1-4666-8205-4.ch013

more questions about the ways in which youth are immersed in gaming and programming. With our work with the grade 9/10 class, we began to understand videogames have the potential for immersive, emergent learning where relationships develop to become more fluid, organic interconnections where the students and teacher are both learning and guiding each other. Our theoretical perspectives shifted to frame our research with emergent and complexity theories (Hopper, 2012; Merkel & Sanford, 2009; Sanford & Hopper, 2009; Sanford & Merkel, 2011; Sanford, Merkel & Madill, 2011). The initial work with the IT class was the impetus from which a longitudinal study began, investigating ongoing engagement with videogames by a core group of students. In 2014 this study continues to morph as said participants are now in university and in the work force and currently conduct study groups as our 'in-house expert' research assistants. This multitudinous research has also inspired the curriculum design and perspective in a grade three classroom in which one of the current researchers teaches. Below are two vignettes to consider, from the 2006 initial study with grade 9 students and from a 2013 grade 3 classroom, respectively:

2006: The lab is bustling. Students are seated--sort of--searching through a variety of windows open on their computers. Fingers click and clack keys, and there are murmurs of "Oh! I just died!" and calls from across the room: "Sam! I just figured it out!" Some students get up and peer over the shoulder at a friend's computer. Where is the teacher? He is working one-on-one with a student and there is a list on the board where students may sign up if they would like some guidance from the teacher, but otherwise they are on their own. Alone, that is, with their friends, the internet, software tutorials and 'cheats', blog and wiki sites, game forums, YouTube and of course, their past experiences with technology and/or gaming. The students approach problem solving in a multiplicity of ways (Squire, 2008) and realize that their expertise is

developing in order to make them more capable. One student, Sam, is immersed, working through a problem and we are surprised that he has yet to ask for help from the teacher: "Ok, never during this time have you raised your hand for help," one of us points out. Sam replies: "No, I don't know if the teacher could figure it out anyway. Might be able to, but I want to figure it out myself 'cause what am I going to learn if I just let him do it." The students are all working at different paces and timelines, on different steps and problems, and on different projects of their own choice but with the same software, the same initial challenge to create a video game. They are engaged, immersed, and are both teachers and learners in not only their individual learning process, but also the collective learning and knowledge acquisition of the class.

* * *

2013: The classroom is bustling. Students are seated—sort of—searching through a variety of computer programming tools on their computer screen to solve an exploratory problem-based learning task. These are grade 3 students, grouped in pairs and their task is to move a robotic car with a computer program. These particular students are faced with a personal challenge they will experience for their lives in schools -- they all have been diagnosed with language based learning disabilities. They are given a few simple directions and told "the only way to learn how to make your robot move is to try and fail and then fix it—go ahead!" Up for the challenge, they fill numbers in boxes.

"Okay, let's try 3 units for rotation—I think that will get the robot to knock the block off", says one student, Isabelle. Isabelle and her partner download the program they have created, disconnect the robot from the computer and place it on a testing ground, a large square platform. They want their robot to move from the centre of the square to the edge where it should knock a block off, but

will itself stay on the platform. Isabelle starts the robot and it starts to move from the centre. The girls cheer as it starts to move and then, just as passionately, boo as it falls over the edge. They look at each other. "It's two! It's two rotations! Not three!" Isabelle and her partner race back to their computer to try again. The teacher/researcher stands back, without knowing the correct answers herself about how many rotations it will take to get the robot to the edge. It is an experiment for all involved, and the kind of teaching she can offer here is to encourage risk taking, to praise determination and creativity and to affirm that this is very serious play, indeed. This empowering process of teaching and learning is a relatively new one for these 8 year olds in a classroom setting. However, similar to the 15 year old students in 2006, the students are all working at different paces and timelines, on different steps and problems, and on different projects of their own choice but with the same software. They are engaged, immersed, and are both teachers and learners in not only their individual learning process, but also the collective learning and knowledge acquisition of the class.

The engagement, social connectivity and motivation to learn in the above scenarios do not represent the majority of classrooms in North America that often still value and practice hegemonic structures and conventional schooling. Most typical schools are caught in transition, trying to prepare students for the 21st century workforce with traditional literacy skills, whilst mediating the ever-morphing world of technology and information to which students have access. Gee and Levine (2009) claim that schools are not meeting the learning needs of students who are deeply engaged in learning outside of school using technological advances like the ones the IT students were accessing in order to develop their games. Gee and Levine suggest that both teachers and students "witness a disconnect between the real world outside their classrooms and the contrived, dated world that exists within" (p.

51). Further, Shaffer, Halverson, Squire and Gee (2005) remind us of this when they compare the internal motivation of students in the classroom and in the gaming world:

Whereas schools largely sequester students from one another and from the outside worlds, games bring players together, competitively and cooperatively, into the virtual world of the game and the social communities of game players. In schools, students largely work along with school-sanctioned materials; avid gamers seek out news sites, read and write FAQ's, participate in discussion forums, and most important, become critical consumers of information (p. 5).

In developing our research questions we felt it integral that, as Gee and Levine (2009) suggest, "[a] crucial first step in promoting student engagement is to rethink literacy for the 21st century" (p. 49). Developing the conditions for emergent learning systems is critical to the success and reform of the current education system, and the complex ways in which these students are already informally working serve as a microcosmic example of where global systems are heading. In Snyder's (2013) recent OECD Education working paper, he states, in regard to international education systems, "[a] shift in emphasis is needed away from the analysis of individuals and outcomes to an analysis of processes and a shift in institutional culture toward greater systemic engagement amongst all actors and levels" (p. 13). His viewpoint is not unusual; all over the world nations are racing to keep up with the exponentially increasing access to information students have and their creative capacities to prepare for the 21st century job market (Greenhow, Robelia & Hughes, 2009; Trilling & Fadel, 2009). The seemingly simple vignettes we present show examples of emergent systems created from students that facilitate these 21st century needs and argue for Snyder's case for a shift in perspectives in how we view learning. To this end, Snyder quotes Kuhn (2008) saying:

A complexity approach acknowledges that all levels of focus, whether this is the individual, class, school, national or international associations, reveal humans and human endeavour as complex, and that focusing on one level will not reduce the multi-dimensionality, non-linearity, interconnectedness, or unpredictability encountered" (as cited in Snyder, 2013, p. 13).

The data collected in this current paper highlights the multi-dimensionality, non-linearity, interconnectedness and unpredictability youth experience and create through video game play/creation and programming a robot. In our presentation we draw upon the work of John Holland (1998), well-referenced author of the seminal work *Emergence: From chaos to order.* Holland provides emergence markers that are as follows: Mechanisms and Perpetual Novelty; Dynamics and Regularities; Hierarchical Organizations. In addition we support insights from Holland with current ideas on complexity theory (Cochran-Smith, Ell, Ludlow, & Aitken, 2014; Davis, Sumara, & Luce-Kapler, 2008; Hopper, 2013; Mason, 2008; Ovens, Hopper, & Butler, 2012). This paper will demonstrate how the students in our original 2006 group were engaged in a powerful, *emergent* learning experience, and one that concretely demonstrates a working example for school reform as many educational systems seek new structures to meet the demands for a 21st century learning model. Additionally, the practical application of the emergent framework in an entirely different environment, a 2013 grade three special education classroom, demonstrates the potential of generalization of emergence theory across diverse educational groups.

BACKGROUND

Context and Participants

The initial example was situated in a high school with a population of approximately 1300 students. Two technology teachers chose to use videogames as motivational entry points for students to learn the abstract concepts of computer programming. The Information Technology grade 9 and 10 classes used the open source software called *Game Maker* that has built-in programming language and enable students to create a variety of types of videogames. The students ranged in ability and experience with videogames and technology; some students had rarely played videogames, while others were considering careers in the videogame industry. The majority of students were male in both classes. In the IT class the teachers set the task of creating a video game based on a local competition developed by a regional group of IT teachers. The goal was as a class to create different games that could be entered into the competition. The teachers indicated that the work would be assessed for completion and workability by implementing a rubric that was shared with the students at the outset.

The subsequent example was situated in a small, independent school designed for students from kindergarten to grade 10 who had been unsuccessful in the regular school system and had been diagnosed with one or more learning challenge. The class involved in this project was students in grade 3. Again, the students had a range of experience with computers and with videogames as well as with project-based inquiry learning. The teacher set the task, using collaborative competition (district wide robot programming project) as a motivator, to use computer programming to move a robotic car.

In both instances, competition (individual and collective) as an attractor provided a level of commitment, engagement, and fun – the challenge was to figure out how to solve the problem set by the teacher in a supportive environment that supported multiple trials and many mistakes. The sense of 'event' that was created through friendly competition encouraged the students to continue on to completion, so that they could feel a sense of completion and also an opportunity to share their learning with others in the class and beyond. And although the students were required to complete these tasks as part of their formal learning, they were inspired by the challenge to learn and apply new knowledge. All students had enough time and support to complete the task successfully, to collaborate with their peers, to share their learning, and to make multiple attempts. Some of the mistakes, in both situations, created funny, crazy outcomes that needed to be solved so that the game would work appropriately or that the robotic car would move with appropriate actions to solve the task.

Unlike other school-based learning, the assessment of the students' learning was successful completion of the task – all students were able to achieve the goals set, and were able to share their completed projects and the different approaches used in each instance. Students themselves valued their work and their learning, as well as the teachers, and the learning process was valued as highly as the final product.

It is important to note that in each instance, the teachers had developed a learning environment in their classes, where the students trusted and respected the teachers, drawing on their expertise as needed but able and willing to try themselves. The learning environment enabled sharing, learning from each other, and celebrating each other's successes, rather than focusing on the 'winner' in an individualistic competitive model.

Methods of Data Collection

Beginning in the fall of 2006 our research team began to visit the IT classes, all the while taking extensive observational notes, photographs and video recordings of the students, formally interviewing the participating students twice, as well as collecting their videogame artifacts. The teachers were interviewed on two occasions, once individually and once together; additionally, they engaged in a follow up meeting to discuss the research findings. Demonstrations of participants creating videogames and describing the game creation process have been videotaped and screen captured using *Camtasia* (2008) in an attempt to more clearly understand the thinking behind the participants' actions as creators and in relation to their experiences as players.

Our analysis process included hand coding the transcripts of the interviews; each transcript was hand coded by two researchers. Then the transcripts were uploaded and coded using the NVivo software program where more specific coding was completed. The main themes from the hand coding are reported in a previous paper (Sanford, Starr, Merkel, & Bonsor Kurki, 2015), whilst this paper describes a further analysis using emergent theory to support our current thinking.

Below is an excerpt from an interview with a student, Sam, wherein he explains to a researcher his problem solving process as he creates his videogame in class. Through student interviews and narratives we can provide the reader with a rich analysis drawing on a framework based on emergence theory, as articulated primarily by Holland (1998). Sam comments:

OK, so pretty much what I was doing was, there was a problem where my character wasn't stopping if the other character was moving. So, both of them had to stop or else the one character wouldn't stop. So I was trying to make it so they would stop by themselves. So basically what's happening right here is, I'm testing it for the first time just about to realize that what's going on right now is so bad… and there my friend there is trying to figure out what's going on and he can't figure it out so none of us can figure it out…so then I go back and… they stop when they hit a wall by themselves so I copied what was happening when he hit a wall to stop him then the problem was when you hit a wall you bounce off of it a little bit and so if you only tap the button you bounce off of yourself…off of nothing pretty much. So, that wasn't working. So, yeah here I'm copying and pasting everywhere back and forth changing numbers.

Beginning in 2011 Liz started teaching at an alternative school for students with learning and language challenges. Reflecting on her experiences in the earlier research project she consciously tried to develop her practice around principles related to complexity thinking. Her data collection took the form of a reflective journal and conversations with her co-authors in this paper who visited her classroom. Using cross-case analysis, these reflections were compared to the data collected in the earlier study. Extracts from her journal are used in this paper to highlight the application of ideas original presented in Sanford & Merkel (2011).

Theoretical Framework: Emergence and Complexity

Although this paper uses notions of emergence as the framework from which we analyze complex and sophisticated learning with digital media, this exploration must begin with a (too) brief discussion of the encompassing theories of complexity science under which emergence is a key element. A body of work is continuously developing that uses complexity science as a meaningful and transformative lens through which to see learning (Barab, et al. 1999; Cochran-smith et al., 2014; Collins & Clarke 2008; Davis & Simmt, 2003; Davis & Sumara 2006; Davis, Sumara & Luce-Kapler,

2008; Doll, 2008; Sanford & Hopper, 2009). As complexity theory is interdisciplinary, interconnected, intricate, complicated, and not matured in the field of education, researchers must develop markers with which to study complex phenomena (Ricca, 2012). Sanford and Hopper (2009) present such complexity framework markers for understanding videogame play and Hopper (2012) has used it to interpret the learning in a teacher education class.

Complex systems are made up of agents that Mennin (2010) defines as "something that takes part in an interaction and is itself subsequently changed: a person, a society, a molecule, a plant, a nerve cell." In addition, "individual agents interact at the local level and cannot know the system as a whole nor does a central agent have responsibility for overall control of the system." Such agents come together around an attractor, something that draws them together in a way that is "determined by the interactions among the multiple variables in the environment" (p. 838).

For this paper we understand complexity science, as defined by Davis & Simmt [2003], as "the science of learning systems, where *learning* is understood in terms of the adaptive behaviours of phenomena that arise in the interactions of multiple agents" [p. 7, italics in original]. This implies that both adaption and emergence are integral to such learning. Adaption indicates a continuous assessment and response by an individual or individuals (agents) within a system to fit the needs of the whole, an adjusting that, by nature, transforms the system itself as it self-organizes around the common intent. Emergence, more difficult perhaps to define, is the interaction and dynamics between "agents" or mechanisms in the system that allows a new and different system to arise: "much coming from little" (Holland, 1998, p. 1).

As described by Davis et al., (2008) bringing a complexity sensibility to learning demands that we attend to both the diversity of the agents within a system (greater the diversity the more intelligence the system exhibits), as well as a redundancy or degree of commonality between agents. In complex systems organization unfolds from the bottom-up through a process of recursive elaboration within a system set-up by simple rules that creates nested experiences of knowing. Once agents of a system are bound by a common intent the complex systems exhibit decentralized control, wherein hierarchical positions are in flux and often negotiated for the needs of the whole through a process of neighborly interactions allowing information, ideas and actions to be exchanged in the service of a common project. These actions of a complex system may be consider as non-linear, dynamic and random but they are limited and enabled by what Davis' (2004) terms as "guidelines and limitations" defined as liberating constraints, which allow agents to move freely within boundaries or rules that maintain the collective objective. The actions of the agents in a system are modulated by a variety of feedback loops that amplify (positive) or dampen (negative) their collective actions "that takes part of a system's output and feeds it back as input" (Davis et al., 2008, p. 204). Finally, the system retains a memory of previous actions as part of its structuring retaining and discarding experiences as needed; this last marker Sanford and Hopper (2009) present as learning being 'distributed'. This recognizes that concepts like cognition or skill associated with "knowing and learning are situated in physical and social contexts, social in nature, and distributed across persons and tool" (p. 12, Putnam & Borko, 2000) and throughout the system. For a fuller discussion, refer to Sanford & Hopper, *Videogames and Complexity Theory: Learning through Game Play*, 2009].

John Holland (1998), author of the seminal work *Emergence: From chaos to order*, agrees that even he has difficulty in giving a definition of the complex and complicated science of emergence but that he can "provide some markers that stake out the territory" (p. 3). This paper uses Holland's markers as a backbone to *begin* to understand the complex learning demonstrated by these grade 9 IT students as they create videogames and these grade 3 students as they program their robot cars. Holland's emergence markers are as follows: Mechanisms and Perpetual Novelty; Dynamics and Regularities; and Hierarchical Organizations. These markers and the science of emergence are underpinned by the use of models and modeling, which is (not coincidentally) also a property of game design and exploratory learning. The following serves as a reciprocal presentation of not only the emergent theoretical framework with which to view a young person's learning experience, but also, in the spirit of emergent theory, exemplifies videogame creation and exploratory problem-solving as a beginning model for emergent markers.

EMERGENT MARKERS

Mechanisms and Perpetual Novelty

SONIA: *Descartes was the primary architect of the view that sees the world as a clock. A mechanistic view that still dominates most of the world today. And, it seems to me, especially you politicians.*

JACK: *"Mechanistic?" Is that a real word?*

THOMAS: *Mechanistic, mechanical, mechanics, yeah, it's a good word.*

SONIA: *Mechanistic, as if nature functioned like a clock. You take it apart, reduce it to a number of small simple pieces, easy to understand, analyze them, put them all back together again and then understand the whole.*

(From the film *Mindwalk*, 1990, based on the book The *Turning Point*, by Fritjof Capra)

The Cartesian view of the world is one challenged by theories of emergence and complexity science, though, sculpted through Newtonian science of mechanics, is a view often taken up to make meaning of a complex and unpredictable world. Wheatley (1999) states:

... this reduction into parts and the proliferation of separations has characterized not just organizations, but everything in the world during the past three hundred years. Knowledge was broken into disciplines and subjects, engineering became a prized science, and people were fragmented - counseled to use different "parts" of themselves in different settings. (p. 27)

Reductionism seems the most straightforward way to understand life and how it works, but falls short in explaining phenomena that result from the interaction of agents in the collective and unexpected behaviour of complex systems such as ant colonies (Johnson, 2001; Hofstadter, 1979; Holland, 1998). Reductionism would tell us that by examining an individual ant we would be able to predict and understand the behaviour of two ants, three ants or an entire colony: "Yet the colony exhibits a flexibility that goes far beyond the capabilities of its individual constituents" (Hofstadter, 1979). Hofstadter's metaphor of the ant colony is a seminal example of such systems and helps us to see how emergence theories provide a framework to better understand like phenomena, in this case, the phenomenon of creating a videogame or programming a robot. Emergent systems also reveal that Cartesian and Newtonian mechanistic theory has a place, but that those simple mechanisms are combined and in interaction with other mechanisms that create something novel.

Mechanistic theories alone neglect the world as an ever-changing, adapting and interacting environment. Emergence depends on the "ever-changing flux of patterns" (Holland, 1998, p. 4) in the interactions of simple mechanisms. Each change within a system creates a new whole that grows from nested experiences that enable the present systems behaviour. That is, something novel is perpetually emerging as the world and environment constantly shifts and changes at a mechanistic level: Hence, the term "perpetual novelty". Morowitz (2002) concurs that, in our

understanding of emergence, "the real gain is that both reduction and novelty can exist together in the same framework" (p. 20). In fact, reduction and novelty can *and do* exist together, according to Holland. Thus, in regards to the writing and reading of this text, mechanisms and perpetual novelty must implicate and influence the other. The following excerpt from the grade 9 IT class highlights the recombining of mechanisms in order for a new whole entity to emerge:

I have changed something, but it's no good. If you hold down the keys it works fine, but if you just want to move a little bit it doesn't work at all... you just like bounce all over the place. So that was me typing in umm 32...so that was me trying to jump to position if I wasn't aligned with the grid. See I've got a grid....32 by 32 pixels that I keep aligning with so if I clicked one it would move me over so at a speed of four....so now I'm testing it here and it just doesn't work.

Students change one mechanism of the game program, sometimes the speed, the grid or the commands to try and solve the problem of the avatars not stopping independently of the other. There is an aspect of unpredictability here, of how the avatars or robots will respond to the change, to the other mechanisms and how the game or robot itself will change as a result of previous edits.

The girls cheer as it starts to move and then, just as passionately, boo as it falls over the edge. They look at each other. "It's two! It's two rotations! Not three!" Isabelle and her partner race back to their computer to try again.

Recalling the grade 3 example aforementioned Isabelle recognizes that by changing a number by one degree, her experiment with her robot would produce entirely different results. Isabelle and her partner hypothesized that changing the wheel rotation number from three to two would have the robot move from the centre, knock the block off, but not crash over the side of the platform. These examples demonstrate Johnson's (2001) assertion that mechanisms in the system "act locally, but their collective action produces global behaviour" (p. 74). The whole is more than the sum of its parts; its behaviour is also a product of the interaction of the parts. One high school participant asserts that game design "teaches you that logic of how to jumble things around like that, and not be afraid to move it around, and then go back and redo it if you have to because that kind of thing happens a lot" (James, participant). Those "things" that are jumbled around are individual mechanisms that, put in combination with other mechanisms, exhibit collective emergent properties. Said in another way, this jumbling allows for *perpetual novelty*.

As Holland describes, mechanisms can be thought of as building blocks, generators or agents within a system. Building blocks "range from mechanisms in physics to the way we parse the environment into familiar objects" (p. 224). Generators might be explained as the rules, principles or constraints playing within a system. Agents then perform a mechanism "that processes input to become output" (pp. 123-124). These mechanisms are parts of systems that can be scrutinized individually by decomposing the system. However, changing/altering/replacing one of these mechanisms will combine in a different way with the other mechanisms, creating a different outcome: "the whole is greater than the sum of its parts in these generated systems. The interactions between the parts are nonlinear, so the overall behaviour *cannot* be obtained by summing the behaviours of isolated components" (Holland, 1998, p. 225). It is as Bateson (1972, p. 107) asserts, "series of *symmetrical* patterns, in which people respond to what others are doing by themselves doing something similar" that connects. It is these patterns that connect that make the difference in our generated systems. It is the *interaction* between agents and the combinations of building blocks/generators/agents that allow for a new behaviour or system to arise, emerge, from simple mechanisms.

Dynamics and Regularities

Holland offers that "[e]mergent phenomena in generated systems are, typically, persistent patterns with changing components" (p. 225). That is, there are both dynamics and regularities within emergent systems that interplay with one another, changing roles at times. There are patterns that are observed or generated by the combining of certain building blocks, which when they become recurring, are considered to be rules, or regularities within the system. As students work through problems, they look for those patterns, those regularities, which might generate a configuration that works: "So, I'm just looking at all the different possibilities" (Sam – a participant in video game study). Recognizing patterns and discrepancies in patterns shows great sophistication in any field of study. Students need to make critical choices and discard irrelevant detail as they come closer to successfully creating a working videogame or a successful robot task.

As one of the researchers pondered, "[these students must] look at all the different steps involved to see how each step affects the other step" (Kathy). Holland calls this moving through the "tree of moves", or "tree of possibility." This metaphor of the tree is helpful in visualising the branching off in different directions when a new choice is made, or a new building block is added: "The root of the tree is the game's initial state, the first branches lead to the states that can be attained from the root, the branches on those branches lead to the states that can be attained by two moves…" (Holland, 1998, pp. 34-38) and so on. In short, the decisions made influence and manipulate the possibility, prediction, and situation of next decision, and perhaps create the grounds for innovation or, as Whitehead (1920/1971) writes, "the creative advance of novelty." The state of the situation/game changes through the succession of choices or new arrangements leading to new and newer states. This process is guided by a few simple rules (enabling constraints) and students work with the software given and the discoveries/regularities found by trying out certain combinations of building blocks. Through testing and experience, programmers exhibit skills in deciding what data is irrelevant to the problem and discards appropriately: "We learn what is irrelevant to 'handling' or understanding situations, and we refine our building blocks accordingly. We also learn to use rules [and regularities] to project the way in which the blocks will shift and recombine as the future unfolds" (Holland, p. 26). Such experiences become memories that can be discarded but then recalled later when elements of previous experiences are recombined in a new task (distributed cognition). Choices are also made by the contextual significance of certain patterns: "context places boundary conditions on the particular meanings that occur" (Barab, et al., 1999, p. 226; see also Holland, 1998). The regularities are not always reliable, but they serve as tools to inform those choices or moves to future states. As Davis and Simmt (2003) concur, "decisions around planning are more about setting boundaries and conditions for activity than about predetermining outcomes and means—proscription rather than prescription" (p. 147). Feedback loops become important to agents within a system in setting those boundaries and conditions (Johnson, 2001; Bateson, 1979).

These 'enabling constraints' (Davis & Sumara, 2006) highlight the importance of creating and engaging in activities free enough to enable exploration but focused enough for specific outcomes to be generated by the rules of the system, in this case, game design. As Gee (2003) describes, games are designed to lead players to form good guesses about how to proceed when they face more challenging problems at later stages of the game. In this way, students work not only to 'play' within the rules of game design and coding, but also they anticipate how the game would be played and the enabling constraints set up for consumers of the game to use in order to engage in the game.

Hierarchical Organizations

The students who were involved in game design and in robot programming, respectively, seemed genuinely engaged and immersed in the work they were doing. One high school student decided that though he was struggling with this glitch in his game, he was determined to solve it out of class time: "I've got my next class that I'm done all the assignments so I'm gonna work on it in that class too. I'm gonna work on it until this is done."

As students continue to select and combine mechanisms, they will observe the way that they interact, and perhaps begin to recognize familiar patterns. Over time and with "enhanced persistence" (Holland, 1998), those patterns become generators themselves. In other words, a programmer will not have to recombine certain mechanisms together to get the same result as she expects them to interact in similar fashion. She can now treat those patterns as a collective mechanism. This concept is referred to by Holland as "hierarchical organization" as experiences become nested within each other, connected by a common intent.

As more and more patterns emerge, and the complexity of the tasks increases, students have more possibilities of combinations to make. "Nonlinear interactions, and the context provided by other patterns...both increase the competence [of an emergent system]. In particular, the number of possible interactions, and hence, the possible sophistication of response, rises extremely rapidly (factorially) with the number of interactants" (Holland, 1998, p. 227). Consider the following example of the game *SimCity* given by Steven Johnson (2001):

Each block in SimCity obeys a set of rigid instructions governing its behaviour, just as our cells consult the cheat sheet of our genes. But those instructions are dependent on the signals received from other blocks in the neighbourhood, just as cells peer through gap junctions to gauge the state of their neighbours. With only a hand-

ful of city blocks, the game is deathly boring and unconvincingly robotic. But with thousands of blocks, each responding to dozens of variables, the simulated cityscape comes to life, sprouting upscale boroughs and slums, besieged by virtual recessions and lifted by sudden booms. As with ant colonies, more is different. (pp. 88-89)

A hallmark of emergent phenomena is that systems with very few, but firm, rules can produce a multiplicity of complex and unpredictable possibilities, "much coming from little". As more agents enter the system under the constraints of those firm rules, more unpredictability arises, with more possibility for innovation. The grade 3 students are bound by the rules of tasks given and the computer software used. As these young programmers add more mechanisms to the program (e.g., wheel rotation; moving the robot forward and back, left and right; moving arms), they discover more possible situations and capabilities within the design; they hypothesize what might be possible. This is a messy, non-linear process and one that involves much play, tinkering and dreaming. As Wheatley and Kellner-Rogers (1996) assert: "All this messy playfulness creates relationships that make available more: more expressions, more variety, more stability, more support" (p. 18). To find the best-fit solution, students must proceed using this messy method, guided by the teacher showing through demos and examples from peers as needed and as successes emerge, so that students develop combinations of mechanisms that, together, exhibit new and collective properties. In this way, learning through digital media is generally not a short term, test-based event wherein students achieve an objective and then moves on to the next disconnected objective. Rather they are involved in deep, layered learning wherein mechanisms/parts become coupled or collective, building on past knowledge and experience. For the grade 3 students the project spread over 8 weeks in short but regular periods between other lessons, for the grade 9 the lessons happened during a four-week module towards the end of the term.

IMPLICATIONS

Educational reform is never a completed task, and as information technology continues to expand at a rapid pace and be an integral part of life for 21st century children, the implications for ways to prepare children in classrooms become increasingly significant. Snyder (2013) reports that higher level thinking systems and expertise are necessary for educational reform. He adds that the world at large is not a simple or complicated system, but it is a complex one in which a complexity theory, or in our case, an emergence theory and lens is critical. Our students' experiences present in-depth and rich case studies to demonstrate an emergent system. They learn in ways that are challenging, rewarding and engaging. The emergent understanding and competence developed for both our grade 9 and grade 3 students could not have happened if the learning/exploration environments did not afford them the opportunity. Consider some of the common elements of the environments and curriculum of the described class scenarios:

1. **Process Based Learning:** Students in both classes were working on long term projects (respective to their age groups) wherein they worked through steps under their own timelines, contributing to their knowledge of digital media and appropriate software. Although they were working with an end goal in mind, they worked in a multiplicity of ways with a multiplicity of resources in order to solve problems throughout the process. These open ended goals present rules or constraints (e.g., using particular software and creating a videogame), but the product details are unknown as students value the learning along the way and use hierarchical organizations in further steps as novel situations emerge. The outcome of the project is not easily assessed with traditional methods as students adapt as new information arises through the interaction of

mechanisms. Students, as the best assessors of their own learning and problem solving, should be consulted in the assessment of such long-term projects in which they are invested and hold expertise.

2. **Decentralized Control:** Newtonian thinking has led western society to falsely rely on determinism and predictability (Wheatley, 1999), and that the teacher is expert, the student the apprentice. This is in contrast to emergent thinking that "the phenomenon at the cent[re] of each collective is not a teacher or a student, but the collective phenomena of shared insight" (Davis & Simmt, 2003, p. 153). What might emerge from different interactions isn't something the teacher could anticipate, nor could the students without trying some different combinations of mechanisms. Within the classes there seemed to be a collective approach to all the games being created wherein friends and teachers would add insight to game design in order to reach the best possible fit for solving problems. The ways in which we observe young people interacting with/in digital worlds, both on and off-line, create great possibility to view learning and knowing in other, more democratic ways: "the alchemy between youth and digital media has been distinctive; it disrupts the existing set of power relations between adult authority and youth voice" (Ito, et al., 2008, p. ix). Young video game players are often experts in this field and are more than capable of engaging in critical conversation about their practices with/in new media. The individuals we have observed in video game play are active participants in their learning, exploring and taking on multiple roles as fits the context (Sanford & Bonsor Kurki, 2014).

3. **Participatory Culture:** (Jenkins, 2006) Represents the 'active and circular' shifting of roles individuals take in the consumption and creation of media content in this flow.

The aforementioned notion of decentralized control that is often exercised within these realms allows for students to become teachers and vice versa (see Sanford & Madill, 2007). Decentralized control readily lends itself to disrupting conventional views of teaching and learning, offering a space in which young people, who are already exploring a multiplicity of roles within digital worlds, are empowered (Bennett, 2008). This shifting of power dynamics through new media challenges our taken-for-granted notions of schooling and teacher-as-expert, and presents new opportunities for educational researchers to adjust conventional thinking about schooling through their research related to youth and media use. The students felt empowered to be working *with* teachers instead of *for* teachers. Emergent learning does not move in teleological paths wherein an end goal can be predicted and assessed. In this way, perpetual novelty is valued as an outcome of experimental systems. Students author their own knowledge in such systems and contribute to the collective. Teachers-as-facilitators allow students to be innovative, to take risks, and to feel confident in experimenting. In this way expertise is valued in every member of a class community and is used to generate collective knowledge.

4. **Choice:** Students were given choice in the theme of their project and how they approached problems. They developed great confidence by being able to choose the right path for the problem presented, looking for patterns that offered them both dynamics and regularities to manipulate. Students were involved in projects that were meaningful to their lives and their expertise. Meaningful learning was situated in their experiences outside of the classroom, and then transferred inside the context of their own storyline and innovations in a classroom setting. In such classes, responsibility is on the student to

make the choices that will best suit her or his project, and these choices are respected and supported by the teacher.

5. **'The Pattern That Connects' That Makes the Difference (Bateson, 1972):** Key is creating the conditions for meaningful patterns to emerge, where learning does not happen in the student but in system of teacher, student and subject matter interactions. Failure to do this means, as Ricca (2013) states, "Students, because they are presented only the unchanging canon of a discipline, find very little with which to interact" (p. 40). When this happens, as is too often the case in schools, "Students fail to learn what is truly important about a discipline...do not see the wonder that those who practice the discipline see...the disciplines themselves become cut off from the daily living of most people" (p. 41). This focus on emergent interactions means that the teacher has to plan to improvise rather than merely develop a series of steps to be followed. The teacher may plan for anticipatory events and prepare the learning conditions accordingly (materials, room set-up, wording of tasks, etc.), but planning now entails preparing the teacher to recognize the "growth nature" (Ricca (2013) of student learning. In this way each student's learning is recognized as a "bringing forth" of learners learning as they engage, reflect and transform as an autopoetic being in interaction with other autopoetic beings around a common pursuit (Varela, Thompson, & Rosch, 1991). By autopoetic we refer to the self-structuring ability of human beings in relation to their environment. Assessment of learning is then focused on helping students recognize their own learning in the service of a task, 'the patterns that connect', so that they can call upon this skill or knowledge and develop further its application in order to advance the pursuit of a goal.

6. **Modeling:** As a complex and chaotic system there are always more problems to solve in the world, be they concerns regarding world population, war and conflict, environmental devastation, energy crisis or space exploration. The ability to develop hypotheses and test through models is a critical learning skill to have as a 21st century learner. Underpinning John Holland's markers for emergent properties is the concept of modeling: "Models, especially computer-based models, provide accessible instances of emergence, greatly enhancing our chances in understanding the phenomenon. Moreover the model can be started, stopped, examined and restarted under new conditions, in ways impossible for most real dynamic systems" (p. 12). Human beings develop and look to models to make meaning of the world in a variety of disciplines. Holland's study on emergence is based on models like games (e.g., checkers), neural networks, weather patterns, and computer science. Further, in *Learning and Games*, Gee (2008) reminds us of model use in engineering (model planes), architecture (blueprints and model buildings/towns), and videogames (avatars and model environments/universes), for a few examples. Models give opportunity to imagine, to consider all possibilities, to experiment with design and play, and to acquire hypotheses about phenomena that may be too big, complex, expensive, dangerous to manipulate and/or understand. Models are often simplified and/or focused on specific properties of these phenomena, which allow more accessibility than the real phenomena/system itself. Students involved in computer programming are developing models, strategies and patterns that can be transferred to larger, more abstract problems. The robots built by the grade three children are not going to move objects on Mars, but the seemingly simple model has great implications for the

future. The patterns, principles, testing and movements of the model robots are not unlike the Mars Rover on a very simplistic level.

FUTURE RESEARCH DIRECTIONS

Gee and Levine (2009) support the notion that "[a] key challenge is to overcome traditional barriers to integrating the informal media that young people love into the more formal settings of schools" (p. 49). Teachers must become familiar with new literacies and be supportive in their uses. It is not good enough to rely on traditional teaching methods if the students recognize that they are not meaningful or engaging. Teachers must also honour that their students often (but not always) hold expertise in some or many new literacies. Instead of seeing this as unfavourable to a teacher/student relationship, teachers must perceive this as an opportunity for students to become engaged with schooling, to be innovative and to be part of a social community of learning. The grade 3 classroom is a particularly relevant and demonstrative example of how 21st century literacies can enable the creativity, complexity and innovation for future generations. As alluded to previously, all the students in the class were diagnosed with learning disorders. These include, but are not limited to: dyslexia, reading disorders, dysgraphia, Autism Spectrum Disorder, Attention Deficit Disorders. The students who participated in the robot programming sessions were most often engaged and literate in relation to the task. Contrary to their experiences in more traditional classrooms where reading and writing textbooks were privileged as the primary literacy skills, these students demonstrated a diversity of strengths in problem solving, spatial awareness, patterning, computer science, creative thinking and innovation. The workforce of the 21st century promises to be an extremely diverse spectrum where new occupations and fields of study will be created (Greenhow, Robelia, & Hughes, 2009; Ricca,

2012; Trilling & Fadel, 2009), and rather than being subscribers to traditional roles, students will be expected to innovate and develop these type of diverse skill sets. .

Over the past eight years our research as shifted and transformed over its own emergent pathways. The fifteen year old students we met in 2006 are now in their early twenties and a few are now assisting our projects as co-researchers reflected in their work on the Blended Gaming website set up as a social network hub to explore video gaming and the development of civic engagement (Blended-Gaming, 2014). We have delved into video game play, in and out of the classroom, and we have inquired into game play within boy and girl groups. The emergent frameworks developed in initial studies have carried over into other community groups, notably into the curriculum development of one of the current author's grade 3 classroom. What is the job of educators in the 21st century? How do we prepare students for the multi-dimensional, non-linear, interconnected, and unpredictable world? According to Synder quoting Johnson:

Currently, many methods of investigating the educational outcomes of individual schools...are based on linear algorithms that simplify and break down systems into isolated component parts. The premise of such linear models is that inputs into the system will result in predictable outcomes. While appropriately predictive of some static, closed systems, these models fail to adequately predict the behaviour of or capture the essence and emergent properties of complex systems involving three or more interacting components. (Johnson as cited in Synder, 2013, p. 5-6).

The implications presently put forth, underpinned by Holland's emergent framework, can be generalized to diverse communities of learners in the 21st century. Whether they are teenagers in an IT class or eight year olds in a special education classroom, these students show sophisticated engagement with digital media that challenge traditional, linear concepts of schooling, learning and literacy. There is a resonating understanding throughout the world that the future is not simplistic, and that future generations will depend on innovation, creation, imagination and on the ability to learn how to learn.

REFERENCES

Barab, S., Cherkes-Julkowski, M., Swenson, R., Garrett, S., Shaw, R., & Young, M. (1999). Principles of self-organization: Learning as participation in autocatakinetic systems. *Journal of the Learning Sciences, 8*(3&4), 349–390. doi:10.1080/10508406.1999.9672074

Bateson, G. (1972). Steps to an ecology of mind. San Francisco, CA: Chandler.

Bennett, W. L. (2008). Changing citizenship in the digital age. In W. L. Bennett (Ed.), *Civic life online: Learning how digital media can engage youth* (pp. 1–24). Cambridge, MA: The MIT Press.

Blended-Gaming. (2014). *Explore the potential for democratic/civic engagement among future citizens who engage with video gaming.* Retrieved August 8, 2014 from http://blendedgaming.com/

Camtasia. (2008). *Screen capture software.* Retrieved from http://www.techsmith.com/camtasia.html

Cochran-smith, M., Ell, F., Ludlow, L., & Aitken, G. (2014). Article. *The Challenge and Promise of Complexity Theory for Teacher Education Research, 116*(May), 1–38.

Cohen, A. (Producer), & Capra, B. (Director). (1990). *Mindwalk* [motion picture]. America: Paramount.

Collins, S., & Clarke, A. (2008). Activity frames and complexity thinking: Honouring both the public and personal agendas in an emergent curriculum. *Teaching and Teacher Education, 24*(4), 1003–1014. doi:10.1016/j.tate.2007.11.002

Davis, B., & Simmt, E. (2003). Understanding learning systems: Mathematics education and complexity science. *Journal for Research in Mathematics Education, 34*(2), 137–167. doi:10.2307/30034903

Davis, B., & Sumara, D. (2006). *Complexity and education.* Mahwah, NJ: Lawrence Erlbaum Associates, Inc.

Davis, B., Sumara, D., & Luce-Kapler, R. (2008). *Emerging minds: Changing teaching in complex times* (2nd ed.). New York: Routledge.

Doll, W. (2008). Complexity and the culture of curriculum. *Educational Philosophy and Theory, 40*(1), 191–212. doi:10.1111/j.1469-5812.2007.00404.x

Gamemaker 7.0. (2008). *Yoyogames.* Retrieved January 20, 2015, from https://www.yoyogames.com/studio

Gee, J. (2003). *What videogames have to teach us about learning and literacy.* New York: Palgrave Macmillan.

Gee, J. (2008). Learning and games. In K. Salen (Ed.), *The ecology of games: Connecting youth, games and learning* (pp. 21–40). Cambridge, MA: MIT Press.

Gee, J., & Levine, M. (2009). Welcome to our virtual worlds. *Educational Leadership,* 48–52.

Greenhow, C., Robelia, B., & Hughes, J. E. (2009). Learning, teaching, and scholarship in a digital age: Web 2.0 and classroom research: What path should we take now? *Educational Researcher, 38*(4), 246–259. doi:10.3102/0013189X09336671

Holland, J. (1998). *Emergence: From chaos to order*. Reading, MA: Addison-Wesley.

Hopper, T. F. (2010). Complexity thinking and creative dance: Creating conditions for emergent learning in teacher education. *PHEnex*, *2*(1), 1–20.

Hopper, T. F. (2013). Emergence in school integrated teacher education for elementary PE teachers: Mapping a complex learning system. In A. Ovens, T. Hopper, & J. Butler (Eds.), *Complexity thinking in physical education: Reframing curriculum, pedagogy and research* (pp. 151–163). London: Routledge.

Ito, M., Davidson, C., Jenkins, H., Lee, C., Eisenberg, M., & Weiss, J. (2008). Foreword. In W. L. Bennett (Ed.), *Civic life online: Learning how digital media can engage youth* (pp. vii–ix). Cambridge, MA: The MIT Press.

Johnson, S. (2001). *Emergence: The connected lives of ants, brains, cities and software*. New York: Simon & Schuster.

Mason, M. C. (2008). What is complexity theory and what are its implications for educational change? *Educational Philosophy and Theory*, *40*(1), 35–49. doi:10.1111/j.1469-5812.2007.00413.x

Mennin, S. (2010). Complexity and health professions education: A basic glossary. *Journal of Evaluation in Clinical Practice*, *16*(4), 838–840. doi:10.1111/j.1365-2753.2010.01503.x PMID:20659212

Merkel, L., & Sanford, K. (2009). Complexities of gaming cultures. *In Proceedings. DiGRA*. London: DiGRA.

Merkel, L., & Sanford, K. (2011). Complexities of gaming cultures: Adolescent gamers adapting and transforming learning. *E-Learning and Digital Media*, *8*(4), 397. doi:10.2304/elea.2011.8.4.397

Morowitz, H. (2002). The emergence of everything: How the world became complex. New York: Oxford.

Murray, J. (1997). *Hamlet on the holodeck: The future of narrative in cyberspace*. Cambridge, MA: The MIT Press.

Ovens, A., Hopper, T. F., & Butler, J. I. (2012). *Complexity thinking in physical education: Reframing curriculum, pedagogy and research* (A. Ovens, T. F. Hopper, & J. I. Butler, Eds.). London: Routledge.

Putman, R., & Borko, H. (2000). What do new views of knowledge and thinking have to say about research on teacher learning? *Educational Researcher*, *29*(1), 4–15. doi:10.3102/0013189X029001004

Ricca, B. (2012). Beyond teaching methods: A complexity approach. *Complicity: An International Journal of Complexity and Education*, *9*(2), 31–51.

Salen, K. (2008). Toward an ecology of gaming. In K. Salen (Ed.), *The ecology of games: Connecting youth, games and learning* (pp. 1–17). Cambridge, MA: MIT Press.

Sanford, K., & Bonsor Kurki, S. (2014). Videogame literacies: Purposeful civic engagement for 21st century youth learning. In K. Sanford, T. Rogers, & M. Kendrick (Eds.), *Everyday youth literacies: Critical perspectives for new times* (pp. 29–45). London: Springer. doi:10.1007/978-981-4451-03-1_3

Sanford, K., & Hopper, T. (2009). Videogames and complexity theory: Learning through game play. *Loading...*, *3*(4). Retrieved October 31, 2009, from http://journals.sfu.ca/loading/index.php/loading/article/view/62

Sanford, K., & Madill, L. (2007). Understanding the power of new literacies through videogame play and design. *Canadian Journal of Education, 30*(2), 421–455. doi:10.2307/20466645

Sanford, K., & Madill, L. (2007b). Critical literacy learning through video games: Adolescent boys' perspectives. *E-Learning and Digital Media, 4*(3), 285–296.

Sanford, K., & Merkel, L. (2011). Emergent/see: Viewing adolescents' video game. In E. Dunkels, G.-M. Frånberg, & C. Hallgren (Eds.), Interactive media use and youth: Learning, knowledge exchange and behavior (p. 102). Hershey, PA: IGI Global.

Sanford, K., & Merkel, L. (2012). The literacies of videogaming. In K. James, T. Dobson, & C. Leggo (Eds.), *English in secondary classrooms: Creative and critical advice from Canadian teacher educators*. UBC.

Sanford, K., Merkel, L, & Madill, L. (2011). "There's no fixed course": Rhizomatic learning communities in adolescent videogaming. *Loading Journal..., 5*(8).

Sanford, K., Starr, L., Merkel, L. & Bonsor-Kurki, S. (2015). Serious games: Videogames for good? *E-Learning and Digital Media Journal, 12*(1). doi:10.1177/2042753014558380

Shaffer, D., Squire, K., Halverson, R., & Gee, J. (2005). Video games and the future of learning. *Phi Delta Kappan, 87*(2), 104–111. doi:10.1177/003172170508700205

Snyder, S. (2013). *The simple, the complicated, and the complex: Educational reform through the lens of complexity theory* (OECD Education Working Papers, No. 96). Paris: OECD Publishing.

Squire, K. (2008). Open-ended video games: A model for developing learning for the interactive age. In K. Salen (Ed.), *The ecology of games: Connecting youth, games and learning* (pp. 167–198). Cambridge, MA: MIT Press.

Squire, K. (2008b). Video game literacy: A literacy of expertise. In J. Coiro, M. Knobel, C. Lankshear, & D. Leu (Eds.), *Handbook of research on new literacies* (pp. 635–669). New York: Lawerence Erlbaum Associates.

Trilling, B., & Fadel, C. (2009). *21st century skills: Learning for life in our times*. San Francisco, CA: Jossey-Bass.

Varela, F. J., Thompson, E., & Rosch, E. (1991). *The embodied mind*. Cambridge, MA: The MIT Press.

Wheatley, M. (1999). *Leadership and the new science: Discovering order in a chaotic world* (2nd ed.). San Francisco, CA: Berrett-Koehler.

Wheatley, M., & Kellner-Rogers, M. (1996). *A simpler way*. San Francisco, CA: Berrett-Koehler.

Whitehead, A. (1971). *The concept of nature*. Cambridge, UK: Cambridge University Press. (Original work published 1920)

ADDITIONAL READING

Black, R., & Steinkuehler, C. (2009). Literacy in virtual worlds. In L. Christenbury, R. Bomer, & P. Smagorinsky (Eds.), *Handbook of adolescent literacy research* (pp. 271–286). New York: Guilford Press.

Buckingham, D. (Ed.). (2008). *Youth, identity and digital media. (The John D. and Catherine T. MacArthur Foundation Series on Digital Media and Learning)*. Cambridge, MA: The MIT Press.

Capra, F. (1982). *The turning point: Science, society and the rising culture*. New York: Simon and Schuster.

Capra, F. (1996). *The web of life: A new scientific understanding of living systems*. New York: Anchor Books.

Capra, F., & Luigi Luisi, P. (2014). *The Systems View of Life: A Unifying Vision* (p. 472). New York: Cambridge University Press. doi:10.1017/CBO9780511895555

Cilliers, P. (2000). *Complexity and postmodernism: Understanding complex systems*. London: Routledge.

Cohen, J., & Stewart, I. (1994). *The collapse of chaos: Discovering simplicity in a complex world*. NY: Penguin.

Coiro, J., Knobel, M., Lankshear, C., & Leu, D. J. (Eds.). (2008). *Handbook of new literacies research*. New York: Lawrence Erlbaum Associates.

Davis, B., & Sumara, D. (2006). Complexity and education: Inquires into learning, teaching and research (p. 202 ST – Complexity and education: Inquires into). London: Lawrence Erlbaum.

de Castell, S., & Jenson, J. (2004). Paying attention to attention: New economies for learning. *Educational Theory*, *54*(4), 381–397. doi:10.1111/j.0013-2004.2004.00026.x

Doll, W. Jr. (1986). Prigogine: A new sense of order, a new curriculum. *Theory into Practice*, *25*(1), 10–16. doi:10.1080/00405848609543192

Doll, W. (1993). *Postmodern perspective on curriculum*. New York: Teachers College Press.

Doll, W., Fleener, J., Trueit, D., & St. Julien, J. (Eds.). (2005). *Chaos, complexity, curriculum, and culture: A conversation*. New York: Peter Lang.

Gee, J. (2005). Learning by design: Games as learning machines. *Telemedium: The Journal of Media Literacy*, *52*(1&2), 24–28.

Gee, J. (2007). *Good video games and good Learning*. New York: Peter Lang.

Gee, J. (2007). Are video games good for learning? In S. de Castell & J. Jenson (Eds.), *Worlds in play: International perspectives on digital games research* (pp. 323–335). New York: Peter Lang.

Goodwin, B. (1994). *How the leopard changed its spots: The evolution of complexity*. NY: Scribner.

Hopper, T., Butler, J., & Storey, B. (2009). *TGfU... Simply good pedagogy: Understanding a complex challenge*. Ottawa: Physical Health Education Canada.

Hopper, T., Sanford, K., & Clarke, A. (2009). Game-as-teacher and game-play: Complex learning in TGfU and videogames. In T. Hopper, J. Butler, & B. Storey (Eds.), *TGfU...Simply good pedagogy: Understanding a complex challenge* (p. 246). Ottawa: Physical Health Education (Canada).

Hopper, T. F., & Sanford, K. (In press). Occasioning moments in game-as-teacher: Complexity thinking applied to TGfU and videogaming. In J. Butler & L. Griffin (Eds.), *Second TGfU book: Theory, research and practice*. Windsor: Human Kinetics.

Jenkins, H. (2000). Art form for the digital age: Video games shape our culture. It's time we took them seriously. *Technology Review*, 117–120.

Jenkins, H. (2006). *Convergence culture*. New York: New York University Press.

Kauffman, S. (1992). *Origins of order: self-organization and selection in evolution*. Oxford: Oxford University Press.

Kress, G. (2003). *Literacy in the new media age*. London, UK: Routledge. doi:10.4324/9780203164754

Lankshear, C., & Knobel, M. (2003). *New literacies: Changing knowledge and classroom learning*. Buckingham, UK: Open University Press.

Lewin, R. (1992). *Complexity: Life at the edge of chaos*. NY: Macmillan.

Mason, M. (2008). *Complexity theory and the philosophy of education* (p. 239). Hong Kong: Wiley-Blackwell. doi:10.1002/9781444307351

McPherson, T. (Ed.). (2008). *Digital youth, innovation, and the unexpected. (The John D. and Catherine T. MacArthur Foundation Series on Digital Media and Learning)*. Cambridge, MA: The MIT Press.

Ovens, A., Hopper, T., & Butler, J. (2012). Reframing curriculum, pedagogy and research. In Complexity Thinking in Physical Education: Reframing curriculum, pedagogy and research (pp. 1–13). New York: Routledge: Taylor and Francis group.

Pearce, C. (2006). Productive play: Game culture from the bottom up. *Games and Culture*, *1*(1), 17–24. doi:10.1177/1555412005281418

Prigogine, I., & Allen, P. (1982). The challenge of complexity. In W. Schieve & P. Allen (Eds.), *Self-organization and dissipative structures: Applications in the physical and social Sciences* (pp. 3–39). Austin: University of Texas Press.

Waldrop, M. (1992). *Complexity: The emerging science on the edge of order and chaos*. NY: Simon & Schuster.

KEY TERMS AND DEFINITIONS

Adaption: Individual agents or collectives of agents continually alter their work/role/play within a system in order to maintain the needs of the whole; thus transforming the system itself.

Complexity: An interdisciplinary lens through which to articulate the learning behaviours in/ of systems wherein perpetual emergence and adaption occurs. Central to the understanding of complexity is the notion that individual agents within the system are involved in continuously negotiated and in-flux self-organization and decentralized control.

Decentralized Control: Hierarchical positions and/or centres of expertise that are in constant flux and, through regular feedback loops, negotiated their actions base on the needs of the whole.

Emergence: The occurrence of new phenomena generated unpredictably by the interaction of simple rules and individual mechanisms that are in constant flux and interaction. Emergence suggests something novel is perpetually emerging at a systems/global level as the world and environment constantly shifts and changes at a mechanistic/local level.

Liberating Constraints: Rules or boundaries generated and acknowledged collectively that allow for individual agents to interact and innovate within a system whilst maintaining the context that the environment affords. This definition is extended from Davis' (2004) "guidelines and limitations" in complex systems.

Mechanisms: A broad title pertaining to the individual elements and/or simple structures within complex systems that can be identified by decomposing the system. The emerging system as a whole becomes unpredictable when mechanisms interact with and adapt to other mechanisms.

New Literacies: A broad term developed to articulate literacy practices made available through the advent of new and multi-media, particularly (though not exclusively) pertaining to digital advances. Examples of such digital advances include: blogs, fan fiction, video games, websites, online social networking, etc. (For more see: Coiro, J., Knobel, M., Lankshear, C., & Leu, D. J. (Eds.) (2008). *Handbook of new literacies research*. New York: Lawrence Erlbaum Associates.).

Chapter 14
Using Spatial Reasoning for Creative Design:
Merging Engineering and Mathematics Practices

D. Craig Schroeder
Fayette County Public Schools, USA

Carl W. Lee
University of Kentucky, USA

Margaret J. Mohr-Schroeder
University of Kentucky, USA

ABSTRACT

With the adoption and implementation of the Common Core State Standards for Mathematics and the Next Generation Science Standards, teachers are being called upon now more than ever before to regularly utilize and incorporate mathematics, science, and engineering practices in order to deepen students' understanding of the content they are learning, make broader connections to the STEM disciplines, and to ultimately help to strengthen the STEM pipeline. This chapter describes how teachers can use SketchUp as a tool to implement the practices through creative design into their own classrooms. The premise and basics of SketchUp are shared as well as a rich creative design project that develops spatial reasoning in middle grades students.

INTRODUCTION

Every person is born with a certain amount of innate spatial reasoning; it is an essential part of our everyday life. While we use it regularly by positioning and orienting ourselves in everyday environments, it is important to continue to develop it, especially when visualizing and moving between 3-dimensional objects to 2-dimensional and conversely.

DOI: 10.4018/978-1-4666-8205-4.ch014

Transforming mental images is a spatial skill that engineers and designers depend on. When a hiker pauses with a map and compass, it is the spatial intelligence that conceptualizes the path. Through the spatial sense, a painter "feels" the tension, balance and composition of a painting. Spatial ability is also the more abstract intelligence of a chess master, a battle commander, or a theoretical physicist, as well as the familiar ability to recognize objects, faces and details. (Grow, 1990, para. 2)

Spatial reasoning is formally introduced in school curricula and standards as early as kindergarten. For example, throughout the Common Core State Standards for Mathematics [CCSSM] (Council of Chief State School Officers [CCSSO], 2010), one would find multiple emphases placed on "modeling", "decomposing", and "applying" concepts to real world situations (e.g., M.GM-1, H.GM-1) – terms that we often use to be more explicit in what we mean by "spatial reasoning". Moreover, there is an explicit focus on spatial reasoning, especially modeling, through the intentional use and structure of the eight Standards for Mathematical Practice.

In combination, the Next Generation Science Standards [NGSS] (NGSS Lead States, 2013) emphasize not only the eight Standards for Mathematical Practice through cross-cutting concepts, but also lay out the eight Science and Engineering Practices (Table 1). Students need to be exposed not only to the scientific facts, but also the processes that engineers and scientists use in developing knowledge and understanding the world around them. Through interaction and exploration with the world around them, students gain valuable understanding of how the scientific community performs their work.

The purpose of this book chapter is to provide a rich example of developing spatial reasoning in middle grades students, especially regarding 2- and 3-dimensional relationships, through the use of SketchUp (http://www.sketchup.com) in a real-world engineering design problem. This chapter will provide detailed information regarding the implementation of SketchUp in a public school middle grades classroom, including directions and challenges to help guide students to increasing their spatial reasoning, especially between 2- and 3-dimensional objects. The chapter will highlight a culminating project in which the students used their reasoning abilities to create a 3-dimensional project employing the NGSS Engineering Practices (National Research Council [NRC], 2011) as well as the CCSSM Standards of Mathematical Practice (CCSSO, 2010).

Spatial Reasoning

One could argue that every second we are using spatial reasoning. How far away is the fork in my hand? How far do I need to move it to pierce this piece of steak? Will the piece fit in my mouth? All of these movements require spatial reasoning within

Table 1. Standards for mathematical practice and science and engineering practices

Standards for Mathematical Practice [CCSSM]	Science and Engineering Practices [NGSS]
1. Make sense of problems and persevere in solving them. 2. Reason abstractly and quantitatively. 3. Construct viable arguments and critique the reasoning of others. 4. Model with mathematics. 5. Use appropriate tools strategically. 6. Attend to precision. 7. Look for and make use of structure. 8. Look for and express regularity in repeated reasoning.	1. Asking questions (for science) and defining problems (for engineering). 2. Developing and using models. 3. Planning and carrying out investigations. 4. Analyzing and interpreting data. 5. Using mathematics and computational thinking. 6. Constructing explanations (for science) and designing solutions (for engineering). 7. Engaging in argument from evidence. 8. Obtaining, evaluating, and communicating information.

the immediate environment. Today's workplace is requiring workers to interact with and use software programs that render 3-dimensional designs on a 2-dimensional screen. In order to successfully navigate this work environment and creatively design it is essential to have developed the skill of creating a 2-dimensional drawing of a 3-dimensional object, or conversely using a set of 2-dimensional representations to create a 3-dimensional object.

Spatial reasoning can be shown as an innate skill at a young age (Piaget & Inhelder, 1973). For instance a young child trying to use a shape sorter must use spatial reasoning to place the shapes in the sorter. In many situations spatial reasoning is necessary to make sense of and solve real-world problems. In viewing objects a person with a well-developed sense of spatial reasoning is able to create a mental image that allows for mental manipulation of the object (La Pierre & Fellenz, 1988). To develop students who can design creatively, educators must actively develop these skills through the integration of new technologies in the classroom involving real-world problems and activities. National Council of Teachers of Mathematics [NCTM] (2000) foresaw this need in the *Principles and Standards for School Mathematics*:

Some students may have difficulty finding the surface area of three-dimensional shapes and their two-dimensional representations because they cannot visualize the unseen faces of the shapes. Experience with models of three-dimensional shapes and their two-dimensional "nets" is useful in such visualization...Students should build three-dimensional objects from two-dimensional representations. (p. 237)

More recently NCTM has expounded on the need for more technology in the 21st century classroom; specifically interactive geometry applications and modeling tools that can be used to explore three-dimensional objects in engaging "what if" explorations, such as those offered by SketchUp (NCTM, 2014).

Modeling and Transformations

The CCSSM also recognizes the key role of mathematical modeling in the learning of mathematics. It establishes modeling as one of the eight Standards for Mathematical Practice, explicitly weaving appropriate settings for modeling throughout all grade levels. Engineering design elements can be found throughout the modeling language in the CCSSM:

Mathematically proficient students who can apply what they know are comfortable making assumptions and approximations to simplify a complicated situation, realizing that these may need revision later. *They are able to identify important quantities in a* practical situation *and map their relationships using such tools as diagrams, two-way tables, graphs, flowcharts and formulas. They can analyze those relationships mathematically to* draw conclusions. *They routinely interpret their mathematical results* in the context of the situation *and reflect on whether the results make sense, possibly* improving the model *if it has not served its purpose.* (CCSSO, 2010, p. 7, emphasis added)

The process of mathematical modeling rises in prominence at the high school level as a co-equal in value with content courses. The CCSSM states that modeling should be consciously incorporated into all of the courses at this level. Of course, mathematical modeling is much broader than just making physical or virtual models of geometrical objects. But this is certainly one important aspect of modeling, with a long, rich tradition in mathematics and mathematical visualization. Modeling with geometry offers powerful opportunities to bring geometric concepts to bear on applications in our everyday lives. For example, the high school geometry standards include modeling with geometry (G-MG), including "use geometric shapes, their measures, and their properties to describe objects (e.g., modeling a tree trunk or a human torso as a cylinder)", "apply concepts of density based on area and volume in modeling situations (e.g., persons per square mile, BTUs per cubic foot)", and "apply geometric methods to solve design problems (e.g., designing an object or structure to satisfy physical constraints or minimize cost; working with typographic grid systems based on ratios)" (CCSSO, 2010, p. 72-73).

The CCSSM places a central emphasis on rigid motions and similarity transformations to approach congruence and similarity. Focused encounters with such transformations occur in the middle grades.

Students use ideas about distance and angles, how they behave under translations, rotations, reflections, and dilations, and ideas about congruence and similarity to describe and analyze two-dimensional figures and to solve problems. (CCSSO, 2010, p. 52)

High school students must then build upon this foundation.

The concepts of congruence, similarity, and symmetry can be understood from the perspective of geometric transformation. Fundamental are the rigid motions: translations, rotations, reflections, and combinations of these, all of which are here assumed to preserve distance and angles (and therefore shapes generally).... Similarity transformations (rigid motions followed by dilations) define similarity in the same way that rigid motions define congruence, thereby formalizing the similarity ideas of 'same shape' and 'scale factor' developed in the middle grades. (CCSSO, 2010, p. 74)

With free software such as SketchUp, students and citizens have access to Computer-Aided Design (CAD) software that can create models, such as those described in the CCSSM, that have applications to many fields, including those involved in engineering.

Engineering Design

The NGSS (NGSS Lead States, 2013) calls for Engineering and Science Practices to be combined with core ideas and crosscutting concepts to derive performance expectations. Not only must students know science concepts but they also must be able to "solve meaningful problems through engineering design." (p. 1, Appendix F). The eight engineering practices are

1. Defining problems.
2. Developing and using models.
3. Planning and carrying out investigations.
4. Analyzing and interpreting data.
5. Using mathematics and computational thinking.
6. Designing solutions.
7. Engaging in argument from evidence.
8. Obtaining, evaluating, and communicating information.

As educators begin to address these performance needs, a change in assessment practices will be necessary. Multiple-choice knowledge tests do not provide feedback as to the engineering knowledge needed to successfully solve problems. These hands-on experiences are lacking in most middle school classrooms and may result from teachers' inexperience or lock of mastery of engineering practices and design. Teachers need accessible assessment and teaching projects that allow students to practice the engineering practices without necessitating a high-level of knowledge of engineering core ideas. Creating simple, yet engaging projects that draw on multiple subject areas and allow for student creativity and autonomy will give teachers the opportunity to readily adopt new instructional strategies and assessments. Technology can help to make these engineering design projects accessible to all students, even at younger ages and in schools with limited resources.

Additionally, K12 students need regular opportunities to acquire and foster the 21st century skills that industry values and advocates for today. Engaging in instruction that utilizes the engineering practices provides opportunities for active engagement in STEM and helps to foster student interest in STEM fields. The knowledge and skills acquired through classrooms that regularly incorporate engineering design are intended to deepen student interest while growing responsible citizen across communities. Ultimately, doing so will provide a gateway to STEM careers for all students.

CREATIVE DESIGN SKETCHUP PROJECT

This project was conceived by the authors, a middle school STEM teacher and a university mathematics professor, through a joint-discussion about utilizing dynamic mathematics software to increase students' use of engineering design in order to further develop their spatial reasoning skills. The authors had prior experience in using SketchUp for creative design projects in the classroom (see Schroeder & Lee, 2013) but wanted to further the design process by integrating the NGSS Engineering Practices through creative design. Prior to the project, the researchers developed a set of examples and exercises to introduce students to the numerous features and tools in SketchUp.

The activities described took place in an urban upper South middle school (population ~ 1100) during an integrated 7th grade science - high school geometry class (called 7th grade STEM) (n=21). The course's scope and sequence was a transdisciplinary approach to formalized Euclidean proof-based Geometry and the new NGSS Integrated Science Standards for 7th Grade. The students were in the classroom for approximately 2.5 consecutive hours with numerous cross-curricular projects and activities meant to address standards for each subject throughout the year. This course was a pilot program to measure the effectiveness of teaching the subjects in a formally combined classroom. The activities described took place in the final two months of the academic year when the students had completed most the curricular requirements (approximately eight weeks of instruction). The class met each day for 137 minutes in the afternoon. The students had been exposed to traditional manipulatives, integrated STEM instruction, the mathematical, science and engineering practices, group activities, and project-based instruction throughout the year prior to this creative design project. While the students were advanced in their coursework, they lacked any formal instruction in transformations or 3-dimensional manipulations and structures prior to this course. The students were instructed on solids and the surrounding constructs in the instructional unit immediately prior to this activity.

The instruction relied on documents distributed through Edmodo, which had been utilized by the class throughout the year and all students were familiar with its navigation. All project files were uploaded through this site and the end of project survey was also distributed in this manner.

SketchUp Overview

SketchUp is well suited to simultaneously address the CCSSM transformations and modeling standards, as well as the NGSS Engineering Practices and the CCSSM Mathematical Practices. It is a 3D geometric modeler powered by a rich set of geometric transformation tools. SketchUp Make is freely available from http://www.sketchup.com. It is focused on practical real world design, but also readily lends itself to both 2D and 3D mathematical constructions and explorations. At its heart it is a 3D modeling environment that can be populated by complex shapes created by the user from basic elements through a sequence of transformations. In addition, there is a vast library of pre-constructed models (in the "3D Warehouse") that the user can import and incorporate into the design. In addition, SketchUp offers the option of exporting models

Figure 1. 3D printed puzzle created in SketchUp

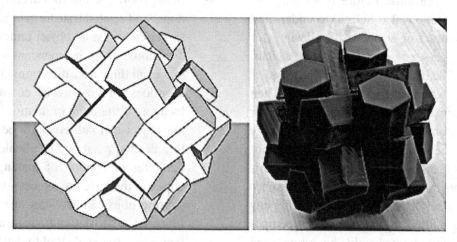

in file formats suitable for 3D printing. Figure 1 shows a puzzle assembled from 12 individually printed pieces.

A considerable collection of tutorials and educational resources for SketchUp already exists, some available directly from the SketchUp website, with many contributors at all levels of K-12 and college experience.

- **Environment:** SketchUp operates within a 3D work environment, equipped with a set of axes. The user can use tools such as Orbit, Pan, Zoom, and Walk to change the observer's viewpoint, even to the extent of entering and moving around in spaces (such as rooms) in the design. Further, by setting the precise location and time of day on earth, the program can correctly compute and display the location of shadows. One can place individual elements of a design onto different "layers," and these layers can be selected and deselected for viewing in various combinations. For example, by placing the basic physical design of a classroom on one layer, and its furnishings (such as desks and chairs) on a second layer, it becomes easy to view the classroom with or without its furnishings.

- **Elements:** The basic elements of SketchUp are lines and curves, two-dimensional shapes bounded by lines and curves, and three-dimensional objects composed of two-dimensional shapes. The designer can embellish the shapes with various colors and textures. Tools for lines and curves include Line (for straight line segments), Freehand (for general curves), Arc and 2-Point Arc (for circular arcs). SketchUp offers various means of control over locations of points (for example, by exact or relative coordinates, by key points of previously constructed shapes, and by establishing guide lines) and locations of segments (by length or coordinates). When these elements enclose a planar region, the program will then create an inferred 2D shape. For drawing 2D shapes the designer can use Rectangle (including squares and golden rectangles), Circle, Polygon (for regular polygons with specified numbers of sides), and Pie (for segments of circles). Again, there is considerable control of locations of points and sizes of objects.

The real power of SketchUp becomes immediately apparent with its set of transformation tools to construct ever more complicated three-dimensional shapes from simpler elements, as described below.

- **Transformations:** Before describing the transformations it is helpful to understand that a subset of elements of a design (for example, a set of elements forming a chair, or the side of a box) may be fused together into a "group" or a "component." Then transformations can act on these groups or components as single entities. The primary difference between a group and a component is that if a component is replicated by, say, moving or rotating it, the new copies act as a set "clones" in the sense that any further editing of any one of the components will immediately be propagated to each clone. This is very convenient in modeling. For example, if one is designing a set of chairs, modifications and improvements to one chair apply to all of them automatically.

- **Move Tool:** With this tool one can move or copy an object from one location to another. Thus one can affect the 'translation' rigid motion. SketchUp offers several ways to determine the direction and distance of the translation, and the user can also create a specified number of multiple copies simultaneously. Note that if the user moves only part of given shape, the results can be interesting and perhaps unexpected. For example, starting with a rectangle, not fused into a group or component, and moving one side along itself using the Auto-Fold option, results in a shearing transformation producing a parallelogram. In a similar way one can construct general parallelepipeds by shearing rectangular parallelpipeds.

- **Rotate Tool:** To 'rotate' an object in three dimensions with the Move tool the user selects an axis, a starting reference point, and an ending reference point. Again, there are some options for specifying the extent of the rotation, and the object can be either rotated or copied into the new position.

- **Scale Tool:** Use this tool to carry out 'dilations' and related transformations. The designer can scale an object uniformly in all directions, or by independent scaling factors in all three axes directions. Though the user does not have precise control over the location of the point of dilation, the resulting object can subsequently be translated to a desired position. The Scale tool does not offer the option of making a scaled copy of the original object—leaving the starting object intact—but one can easily first use the Move tool to make a copy, and then apply the Scale tool to that copy.

- **2D Simulation:** The Move and Rotate tools are, of course, designed for a 3D environment. But for pedagogical purposes a teacher may wish to consider the power of these tools when limited to 2D. One can simulate this in SketchUp by selecting the Parallel Perspective, Top Camera View and restricting the design to two-dimensional shapes. As mentioned before, it can be helpful to create "groups" of some of these shapes before acting upon them. It is now easy to work with the rigid motions in the plane. Use the Move tool to carry out 'translations' in a very natural way. For 'rotations' select the axis by selecting a point; the actual axis is pointing up at the observer vertically, but this will not be evident. 'Reflections' are more interesting: one can use the Rotate tool and select the axis of rotation by clicking and dragging along the desired line of reflection. Moving a reference point of the figure to the other side of the line results in the reflection of the object. But what is actually happening? Though it will not be obvious from this viewpoint, the object is rotating through the third dimension and coming to rest back in the plane. This is the traditional "flip" view of reflections in the plane—invoking the presence of a third dimension to carry out the reflection continuously. Pedagogically this is perhaps not the best way to view or define a reflection in the plane. For example, how will one then define reflection across a plane? It is indeed possible to make reference to a "flip" through a fourth dimension, but this is an unnecessary complication at the K-12 level. It should be noted that SketchUp also offers a Flip command, which will result in reflecting the object in place across a plane parallel to a selected coordinate plane. But one has less control over the location of the reflecting plane. Also, if the user applies the Scale tool along a single direction with a scaling factor of -1, the resulting object will be a reflection of the original.

- **Push/Pull Tool:** Using this tool the designer can select any two-dimensional shape and "extrude" it in a perpendicular direction to create a three-dimensional solid. Mathematically one can regard this as a '(right) prism' transformation. Because this tool operates on arbitrary 2D shapes, even those that are already parts of solids, it is extremely useful as well as empowering.
- **Follow Me Tool:** In some ways this tool is a generalization of the Push/Pull tool. The designer can use this tool to extrude a 2D shape along the path of any line or curve. In particular, by extruding a planar region along the path of a circle, one can generate a solid of revolution.
- **Some Additional Tools:** This list of tools and capabilities is not exhaustive. There are numerous other tools to assist in 3D design and modeling, including those to measure and mark lengths and angles, to calculate area and surface area, to introduce cross-sectional planes for cut-away views, and to add text and images.

Examples of Exploring Mathematics with SketchUp

As design software grounded upon transformations, SketchUp is well positioned as a sophisticated, yet intuitive, technological tool to explore mathematical concepts of the CCSSM and the engineering design practices in the NGSS. Here is a brief, representative list of examples.

- Describe how various objects can be defined by means of transformations.
  - **Regular Polygon:** Appropriately rotate a radius of the polygon.
  - **Parallelogram:** Rotate a triangle about the midpoint of one of its sides or create a rectangle and sheer it by moving one of the sides.
  - **Ellipse:** Scale a circle in a single direction.
  - **Rectangular Prism:** Extrude a prism over a rectangle.
  - **Cylinder:** Extrude a prism over a circle; construct the volume of revolution of a rectangle.
  - **Sphere:** Construct the volume of revolution of a circle about a perpendicular circle of the same center.
  - **Torus:** Construct the volume of revolution of a circle about a suitably sized perpendicular circle with a different center.
  - **Pyramid or Cone:** Create a prism and then apply a scaling with small positive scaling factor (e.g., 0.001) to one of the bases only.
  - **Hyperboloid:** Create a circular cylinder and rotate just one of the bases (e.g., power plant cooling tower).
- Describe the symmetries of various objects by means of transformations.
  - Isosceles triangles, regular polygons, rectangles, rhombi, kites, (mapped to themselves via certain rotations and reflections).

- ○ Platonic solids, prisms (mapped to themselves via certain 3D rotations and reflections across planes).
- Develop two-dimensional area formulas via dissection and transformation arguments
  - ○ Dissect the starting object, turn appropriate pieces into groups and then apply some combination of translations, rotations, and reflections.
- Develop surface area formulas for three-dimensional objects
  - ○ For polyhedra use 3D rotations to unfold the faces into the plane to make nets.
- Develop volume formulas for three-dimensional objects
  - ○ Approximate objects by piles of cubes; use cross-sectional planes to illustrate Cavalieri's principle to match volumes of rectangular and nonrectangular parallelepipeds, and to match the volume of a hemisphere with that of a cylinder with an inverted cone removed.
- Motivate the effect of scaling on length, area, surface area, and volume
  - ○ Scale planar regions superimposed on grids of unit squares, and scale three-dimensional structures composed of unit cubes.
- Illustrate congruence via combinations of rigid motions and similarity via combinations of scalings and rigid motions
  - ○ Given two planar figures, test congruence by attempting to move one to exactly match the other through a sequence of appropriate transformations.
- Tessellations - create a tile as a component, replicate it multiple times, and move the copies around to tile the plane.
- Illustrate the Pythagorean Theorem - make a model of one of the dissection proofs.

- Construct and visualize solids through intersections and unions
  - ○ Construct two perpendicular cylinders with crossing axes, use the Intersect Faces command to compute all of the intersections of two dimensional elements, delete away the portions that are not in the common 3D intersection.

Outline of SketchUp Sessions: Content and Assessments

Work began with the students in March 2013. During the SketchUp sessions the class gathered in a computer lab at the school. Each student had a computer, and the lab was equipped with a projector and computer for the presenters. The university faculty member met with the class and taught with the class teacher seven times over a period of five weeks, each session lasting about 45 minutes. A typical session began with the demonstration of a set of tools, examples of their applications, and recommendations for constructions to attempt. Certain specific constructions called "challenges" were assigned as homework. In addition, the class teacher worked with the students for an additional 3 weeks, providing some additional challenges and giving students time to complete some of the projects.

One important consideration was to deliberately introduce a collection of the SketchUp tools in an appropriate sequence to gradually unfold its capabilities. The facilitators provided written notes, which they updated throughout the project. The latest version is posted at the website http://tinyurl.com/k2lr9sf. We summarize here the sequence of activities, which will also provide an overview of some of SketchUp's capabilities that were described in the previous section. (Note that the numbering is for convenience, and the numbers do not correspond precisely to specific sessions.)

1. After a brief introduction to the nature of SketchUp the students began experimenting with a basic working set of tools.

2. **Orbit:** This tool enables the student to change the direction of view, and seeing this in action for the first time immediately drew the students into the program. Mathematically this corresponds to a rotation of the camera.

3. **Zoom, Zoom Extents, and Pan:** These provide other convenient means to modify the point of view of a scene. Panning corresponds to translating the camera.

4. **Select:** With this the student can select an element or collection of elements of the current construction for manipulation.

5. **Rectangle:** This provides a quick way to create rectangles of desired dimensions.

6. **Line:** This tool constructs line segments, and thus the student can also, for example, draw polygonal regions.

7. **Push/Pull:** This powerful tool provides the capability to "extrude" regions into three-dimensional shapes, and is one of the most powerful elements of SketchUp. Its demonstration is immediately enticing and attractive. Pulling a base polygon results in a prism, but any region can be extruded outward or inward.

8. **Circle:** Circles in SketchUp are actually many-sided polygons. Of course, students can extrude circles into cylinders.

9. **Polygon:** With this students can easily draw regular polygons with specified numbers of sides.

10. **Paint Bucket:** By now students were creating a wide variety of shapes, and they used this tool to adorn them with textures and colors.

11. **Shadows:** This is designed to illuminate the scene and cast shadows. Students can even select lighting corresponding to particular locations and times of day.

12. **Move:** Once students have constructed a collection of scene elements, they may wish to move (translate) or duplicate them.

The facilitators took special care to use appropriate geometric vocabulary throughout. Student progress during the initial session was rapid and impressive, and by the end of this session most students had made substantial progress on, or completed, the first challenge problem:

Challenge #1: Make your own "still life" with a cube, a rectangular prism, a pentagonal prism, a prism with a base that is not a regular polygon, and a cylinder.

The challenge problems were used as formative assessment throughout the project to ensure the students were gaining skill and comfort with the program. Throughout the challenge problems, the facilitators introduced new tools, allowing the students to explore and become familiar with the different features SketchUp had to offer to aid in their creative design.

1. **Warehouse:** SketchUp has established a virtual warehouse of objects, now populated by an overwhelming searchable collection of creations submitted by users around the world. Students found this resource invaluable in their modeling, drawing upon instances of desks, chairs, doors, windows, bookcases, etc., to furnish their rooms. Students in turn submitted some of their own constructs to the warehouse for others to use, including a wad of gum to be placed beneath a desk.

2. **Arc:** Students use this to draw arcs of circles.

3. **Freehand:** This tool draws general freehand curves.

4. **Copy:** This is a modification of the move tool with which students can make a copy or array of copies of a given object. For one homework assignment students started by creating arrays of open-top boxes, and then strategically deleted sides of certain cubes to create mazes that they could then walk through virtually.

5. **Rotate:** Students can select an object, specify an axis and angle, and then rotate the object about that axis. There is also the option to create a rotated copy or array of copies of the original object.

6. **Scale:** Students can easily scale objects in different ways: uniformly (dilation), uni-directionally, and bi-directionally. Negative scaling factors are allowable, which can be used to create reflections of objects through points and planes.

7. **Follow Me:** There is no specific tool in SketchUp to make a sphere. But to make one it suffices to draw a circle and sweep out a sphere by having it follow the path of a certain perpendicular circle. The Follow Me tool is useful this way, and in general students can make any two-dimensional region follow any curve and thereby sweep out an unlimited family of three dimensional shapes.

8. **Tape Measure:** This virtual tape measures lengths in the model, and can also set up guide lines for the placement of objects. There is also a protractor for measuring angles.

9. The facilitators introduced various other tools as well, such as those used for creating cross-sections of objects, animations of scenes, and virtual walk-throughs of scenes.

Once the students accomplished a challenge, another challenge was introduced that was more rigorous (for more on the challenges and examples of their results see Schroeder & Lee, 2013 and also http://tinyurl.com/k2lr9sf). This continued until the researchers felt the students were ready for the initial project. The initial task for the students was to model a current classroom in the school. Students visited the classroom, took pictures and measurements, and then returned to the lab to create a virtual model of the classroom. This provided practice in using SketchUp to create an accurate model of a room (see Figure 2). The culminating creative design project was to have each student create an accurate virtual model of their "dream" classroom. The students were given the freedom to design the room for any given subject and no constraints were placed on the design. The facilitators dedicated most the time during the final set of sessions to completing the room modeling project. Lab time was characterized by active student collaboration and mutual assistance.

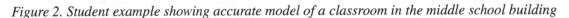

Figure 2. Student example showing accurate model of a classroom in the middle school building

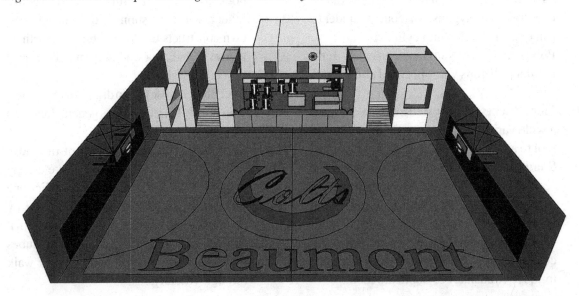

Even in the face of learning a new piece of software, the students in the class were persistent and demonstrated a high level of ingenuity (see Figure 3). The work sessions and challenges dedicated to this project were sufficient and allowed students to be successful initially (by completing each challenge) that in turn inspired a certain degree of confidence and willingness to persevere.

SOLUTIONS AND RECOMMENDATIONS

At the end of the project the students were asked to reflect on the project by responding to a short survey regarding their dispositions toward the project and the mathematics they understood to be central to the SketchUp project. In the pre/post design, the students reported an average growth of 2 points on a scale from 1 (lowest) to 5 (highest) in their knowledge of the SketchUp program. The enjoyment level was 4.875 on the same Likert scale. These self-responses indicate a strong level of learning and enjoyment with the project for all students.

In addition the students were asked to "describe at least three geometry concepts and skills you used as a part of this project." Responses included:

- Spatial Thinking;
- Proportionality;
- I used area to create certain dimensions for a particular amount of square footage;
- I made nets of 3-D shapes;
- Similar Shapes;
- Area;
- Volume;
- Properties of 3-D objects;
- I used angles to determine how much to rotate a figure;
- I used ratios to solve the amount I needed to scale a figure;
- I used inequalities to see if I had enough room to put a certain amount of a figure there.

The students were then asked to "describe the design process you used to design your own room. (List steps)." This question was a basis for eliciting their knowledge of the creative design process and Engineering Practices inherent in designing their own room. Some sample responses were:

Figure 3. Student example of dream classroom design

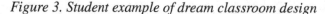
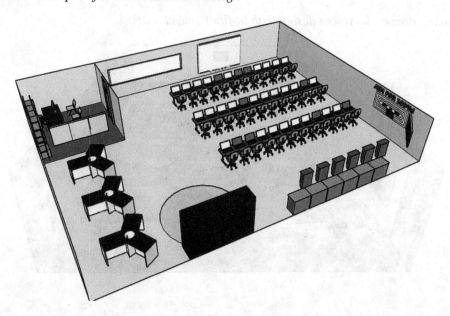

- **Student 1:**
  - Decide what type of classroom you wish to build (I did an Anatomy/Chemistry room).
  - Go to Google images for inspiration on other rooms of the same subject.
  - Collect 2-3 pictures of your liking before making a rough sketch on paper of your room (tables mostly).
  - Begin your classroom and add the simple structures.
  - Research on equipment used in your classroom and either make or add it in (I had autoclaves, freezers, incubators, microscopes, bacterial shakers etc.) [sic].
  - Place equipment and tweak to your liking.
- **Student 2:**
  - Think out what the class it was going to be and what I need in the room.
  - Plan out where things were going to be.
  - Make the room itself (rectangular prism without top).
  - Add things need in a classroom (created myself or from the 3D warehouse).
  - Change some things.
  - Make scenes.

It is obvious the students were identifying the problem, researching and developing a solution, and then creating and testing their design and then revamping it to meet their needs. These are displays of the Engineering Practices (NGSS Lead States, 2013).

The students were asked to design their "dream classroom" and many took this to the extreme while others found it hard to think outside of their current model of classroom space. There were additions of marine tanks for a specially designed Biology room as well as actual offices for teachers that were separate from the student classroom (We think students understand the need for teacher privacy!). The most unique design involved the use of student desks that were recessed in the floor of the classroom (see Figure 4). These allowed students a better vantage point of all sides of the classroom, but they were also designed to swivel so the students had access to all sides of the room and could quickly form working groups with other students. The desks moved with a gear system similar to the teacups at the local fair. This is the creative and ingenuity we were hoping to spark in our students!

Figure 4. Student dream classroom design with in-floor swivel seats

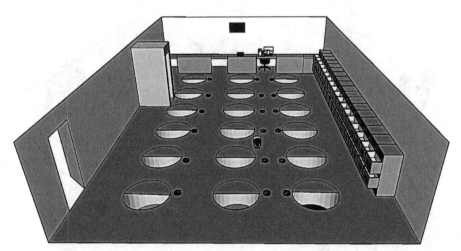

Finally the students were asked about other uses for SketchUp outside of the project. They listed such things as building a new house, and rearranging or reorganizing a room, which have been typical responses in previous iterations of this project. In addition one student reported it could be used in architectural design. Another mentioned using the program for arts and crafts through building an object, unfolding it into a digital net, printing, and then folding the object. Yet another student described using the program to make a model of a place described in a literary story, another mentioned using it to create a model to represent a problem, and one student stated he would use it to create a digital 3D design to use along with his science fair presentation. Finally, a student mentioned that he would just use it to tinker and have fun.

All students reported that they would enroll in an elective course that was based solely on using SketchUp. At the same time all students reported that they used geometry concepts they learned during the year in the project. Additionally, they all also felt confident they could use the program to design their own home. Finally, all students reported the confidence to teach another student how to use SketchUp to create their own design.

Student Impact

This project was the second iteration for the researchers and the addition of an engineering design component was a large success. As was true in previous studies (Schroeder & Lee, 2013), the students readily enjoyed the use of SketchUp to design their rooms. The students continually asked for time to work on the project and often worked on their designs at home in their free time.

The mathematical impact evident was students' ease in moving from 3-dimensional views to 2-dimensional representations of objects. In modeling the current rooms at the school, the students drew on their spatial reasoning to create digital replications of desks, tables, and filing cabinets. This spatial reasoning ability is necessary for engineering design outside of this project in the fields of engineering and construction and is a skill these students have mastered.

In addition the students were able to implement the Science and Engineering Practices to solve a problem. This authentic task engaged the students in the process. The highlight was not only that the students were able to use the steps, but that they were able to dictate and describe the steps. This level of conceptual knowledge is evidence the students understand the practices and are not simply implementing them haphazardly. This is the performance evidence necessary to meet the new NGSS standards.

FUTURE RESEARCH DIRECTIONS

The purpose of this project was to build on the previous pilot project and to implement the new Science and Engineering Practices in a middle school STEM classroom. The SketchUp software has been proven to be elementary and user-friendly. Students require as little as 2 hours of instruction to actively create their own building and form a net.

Student reflections showed that they were explicitly aware of the geometry concepts and skills they are using during the geometric modeling process. More formal research studies could be used to pinpoint and determine the specific impact on student learning and retention. Conceptually, however, the students do show understanding of the skills they are employing to complete their design.

In regard to the Science and Engineering practices, the students showed conceptual understanding of the process. Refining their skills and use of this process is a future goal of the instruction. How can we implicitly design the instruction so the students develop these skills?

Based on this project, the next step is to develop the project on a larger scale. The researchers believe a multiple school study and refinement of the curriculum is in order based on the positive results of the current research. Teachers will need training prior to the implementation, but the project lends itself to any school working with the CCSSM and NGSS.

CONCLUSION

The hope is that the information provided in this chapter is ample to help a current teacher to implement this creative design SketchUp project in their classroom. The sharing and collaboration of successful instruction is pivotal to students' creating and designing using spatial reasoning. Instructors should be looking for ways to develop projects and activities that allow students to think creatively, tinker, and design in an effort to create practical applications that employ formalized mathematical skills.

REFERENCES

Council of Chief State School Officers (CCSSO). (2010). *Common core state standards for mathematics*. Retrieved from http://www.corestandards.org

Grow, G. (1990). *Writing and multiple intelligences*. Paper presented at the Annual Meeting of the Association for Educators in Journalism and Mass Communication. Retrieved June 10, 2012, from http://www.longleaf.net/ggrow

La Pierre, S. D., & Fellenz, R. A. (1988). *Spatial reasoning and adults*. Bozeman, MT: Center for Adult Learning Research, Montana State University.

National Council of Teachers of Mathematics (NCTM). (2000). *Principles and standards for school mathematics*. Reston, VA: NCTM.

National Council of Teachers of Mathematics (NCTM). (2014). *Principles to actions: Ensuring mathematical success for all*. Reston, VA: NCTM.

National Research Council (NRC). (2011). *A framework for K-12 science education*. Washington, DC: The National Academies Press.

Next Generation Science Standards (NGSS) Lead States. (2013). *Next generation science standards: For states, by states*. Washington, DC: The National Academies Press.

Piaget, J., & Inhelder, B. (1973). *Memory and intelligence*. London: Routledge and Kegan Paul.

Schroeder, D. C., & Lee, C. (2013). Integrating digital technologies for spatial reasoning: Using Google SketchUp to model the real world. In D. Polly (Ed.), *Common core mathematics standards and implementing digital technologies* (pp. 110–127). Hershey, PA: IGI Global. doi:10.4018/978-1-4666-4086-3.ch008

KEY TERMS AND DEFINITIONS

Computer-Aided Design (CAD): The use of computer software to create virtual representations of objects in 2- or 3-dimensional space.

Dynamic Geometry Software: Interactive software in which the user can create and manipulate geometric constructions.

Engineering Design: The process of creating, designing, implementing, and revisiting a plan to help create a product that has specified performance goals.

Geometry: The school study of Euclidean plane and solid geometry, both with and without coordinates.

Modeling: "Modeling is the process of choosing and using appropriate mathematics and statistics to analyze empirical situations, to understand them better, and to improve decisions" (CCSSO, 2011, p. 72).

SketchUp: A software package for three-dimensional modeling and computer-aided design currently available at http://www.sketchup.com/.

Spatial Visualization: The process of constructing and manipulating mental models of 2- and 3-dimensional objects and locations.

Chapter 15
An Empirical Study about the Use of the Internet and Computer Games among Croatian Children

Sanja Tatalović Vorkapić
University of Rijeka, Croatia

Elma Polanec
Kindergarten "Little Sparow", Croatia

ABSTRACT

This book chapter is dedicated to theoretical and empirical review of media among children. Empirical results about computer presence in family homes, IT literacy with different computer programmes among parents, as well children are described. In addition, attitudes of parents and preschool and school-aged children about using Internet and computer games as well as attitudes toward the Internet violence are analysed. The results of games types that children play as well as frequency of playing and children's emotions evoked by them are shown. Finally, the results about presence of significant others as well as their conversation with children are shown. All of the above are interestingly studied in the frame of correlation analysis to research relations between some socio-demographic variables (sex, age, the level of education, and presence of computer in family home), so certain future research guidelines can be established.

DOI: 10.4018/978-1-4666-8205-4.ch015

INTRODUCTION

Somehow I was always attracted people in different disciplines -

psychology, sociology, anthropology -

things are looked at comprehensively. They are intrigued me

who stood to the side and tried to answer the question

What is this really happening to human behaviour that

outside sometimes seems so confusing and hard to understand?

Mihaly Csikszentmihalyi (1990)

Digital world, internet and computer games have become great and inevitable in the life of preschool and school aged children. Nevertheless, parents could ask themselves how it influences on his/her child. A lot of questions are asked: How does it influence on child's health?; How to get a child familiar with a computer,?; Is there time limitation in playing computer games?; Does a child get access to some networks not provided for their age?, Is a child exposed to any internet violence?; What about the content of computer games?; What kind of emotions child experience at the same time?. To all these questions, there is an interesting question about difference in perception between parents and children. In any way, existing digital age inflicts new situations and requirements to children as well as parents and experts in the purpose of educational work with children (Tatalović Vorkapić & Milovanović, 2013). Therefore, it is essential to implement systematic and continuous empirical research in the purpose of more adequate adoption to modern world and maximal preservation of psychological

health of children, as well as happy childhood. By putting aside their shared computer time, parents can give their children the chance to develop the full range of skills—technical and social—they'll need to succeed in our digital age. Parents can also help ensure children not to overload themselves on screen time, and buffer the flow of stress chemicals in their over stimulated systems. Despite parental fretting, technology isn't going away, and simply cloistering our children from it is neither beneficial nor practical (Letourneau & Joschko, 2014).

Child's free time is increasingly devoted to playing different indoor games, among them computer games. Dr. Clements (2007) determined that children in the early 2000s, as compared to a generation ago:

1. Spend less time playing outdoors;
2. Participate in different activities outdoors (e.g. fewer street games and more organized youth sports); and
3. Participate in more indoor than outdoor play activities.

Furthermore, Dr. Donald Roberts and his colleagues (2005) and Rideout and Hamel (2006) investigate media in the lives of children 6 months to 6 years of age, as well as in the lives of 8 to 18 years old. These studies were conducted in association with the Kaiser Family Foundation and involved various research techniques. Both studies took place during the school year and measured recreational (non-school) using of media, including TV and videos, music, video games, computers, movies, and print. A few of the key findings highlighted in these reports include the following. Young people today experience a substantial amount of electronic media. Children between the ages of 6 months and 6 years spend an average of 1.5 hours with electronic media on a daily basis, whereas children between the ages of 8 and 18 years spend an average of nearly 6.5 hours a day with electronic media. What is happening with computer games? The computer activity grows up as findings say. The National Association for the Education of Young Children, NAEYC (1996) sets forth attitude that development suitability should have to be integrated in usual context of learning. In accordance to them, computer should have to supply not to replace very valuable activities and stimulations in early childhood as art, blocks, sand, water, books, experiments with art and literacy. Furthermore, Cole (1996) described different ways in which computers could be incorporated in child's imaginary games. There are numerous studies, which demonstrated the main advantages of computer usage in early childhood and game (Yelland, 2005; Flintoff, 2002; Cassell & Ryokai, 2001; Pillay, 2003). However, how many are family homes and parents familiar with it?

BACKGROUND

The term "computer games" is usually identified with the term of video game. Actually, there is no significant difference except that computer games are used by computer but videogames are used by console (for instance play station) which is connected to TV set. However, computer games are more widespread because the computer has a wider use and is not just for playing games, unlike the console which it is the only purpose (Bilić, Gjukić & Kirinić, 2010). The first videogame appeared in 1971 and it was named *Pong*.

The first multimedia computer game, which was available to public, was made in 1958. In that way, the first generation of its computer game development had begun. Their author was William Higinbotham and the name of that game was *Tennis for Two*. The development of media makes more significant questions about the influence of media on users, especially children which are the most sensitive part of population.

What kind of computer games do different age children play? What are all these games? This question is answered by the classification created by authors Bilić and his associates

(2010). Shooting games are based on player who can win if he destroys all enemies using different weapons (rifles, cannons with plasma, etc.). Fighting games are characterized on fight with naked hands or traditional weapon against a big number of enemies. Strategies are kind of games in which player plays against computer or a friend (it can be single or more, usually to eight). For instance, popular strategy game *Starcraft* has a status of national symbol in South Korea. These kind of games are usually popular between young players as they play with their friends, its permanency is significantly prolongs. Role-playing game or RPG serves illusion of moving in three-dimensional space and player chooses personal symbolic display (Avatar). But here is in relation to the dominant action games. A player involves in an adventure of searching, discovering as well a game can be enriched by adding new rules or parts. The success is recorded by points-experiences. Massively multiplayer online role-playing game (MMORPG) is a kind of game which is played over internet in the presence of a big number of players in a big virtual world. When it was told about that kind of the game, it was conducted the research from January 2002 to January 2012, on nine databases (AMED, ASSIA, Cochrane Database of Systematic Reviews, CINAHL, Embase, MEDLINE, OTDatabase, ProQuest, and PsycINFO) in order to identify relevant literature. MMORPG was searched concurrently with mental health along with the alternatives psychosocial, well-being, and health status. The results found that MMORPG playing became "pathological" for some adolescents and was significantly associated with three intrapersonal variables: real-ideal self-discrepancy, negative mood, and escape from itself (Kwon, Chung & Lee, 2013).

Within that field of an early and preschool development, it is a well-known fact how much playing is important in children's life. As it was previously mentioned, playing is not only enjoyed and spontaneous activity but also significantly contributes to psychological development of child

(Verenikina, Haris & Lysaght, 2003). Numerous characteristics were identified by which play is quite different from other forms of human activity (Garvey, 1990). The play is marked as spontaneous, self-initiated and self-regulated activity of younger children which does not expose a child to a risk and is not necessarily subject to somebody (Duran, 2003). The play is intrinsically motivated: it is common for children to have a deliberate desire and interest to get involved in the game, actively involved in the creation of your game and have it under control. Essential property of child's play is act dimension. It means that the action and interaction are imaginary in style "what if…". Such game contains some rules and symbolic use of objects which contributes significantly to the psychological development of the child in terms of the development of symbolic thought (Vygotsky, 1977; Bodrova & Leong 1996; Leontiev, 1981; Nikolopolou, 1993).

In explaining issues about relation among child and computer games, the theory of cognitive development of Lev S. Vigotsky is very important. The theory of Lev Vigotsky is classified in early theories of social constructivism which assumes that for the development of higher thinking functions is essential the social environment in which the child acquires more experience. Besides, theory postulates that learning takes place in symbolic of the gradual sequence identical to all children, what is similar with the content of Piaget's theory (Miljković, Rijavec & Vizek-Vidović, 2003). According to Vygotsky, the basis of cognitive development is learning of symbol system what enables child a reconstruction meaning of the phenomena from his environment. In computer games there are different people who move, speak, do all actions as a child or an adult by in that way they use symbols through letters, numbers, different codes. A child tries to reconstruct these codes. Every child does that in a unique way so it gives unique seal to his personality. It can be said that cognitive development is encouraged by cooperation among child, adults and peers mov-

ing direction of the externally controlled behavior toward behavior which the child independently operated inside (Vizek Vidović, Vlahović Štetić & Miljković, 2003).

Cognitive development is encouraged by cooperation child with adult and is moving direction of the externally controlled behavior toward behavior which the child independently operated inside (Vizek Vidović, Vlahović Štetić & Miljković, 2003). Contrary to conventional believes that playing video games is intelectually lazy and sedating, it turns out that playing these games promotes a wide range of cognitive skills (Granic, Lobel & Engels, 2014).This is particularly true for shooter video games (often called "action" games by researchers), many of which are violent in nature (Granic, Lobel & Engels, 2014).Preliminary research has also demonstrated that these cognitive advantages manifest in measurable changes in neural processing and efficiency. For example, a recent functional magnetic resonance imaging (fMRI) study found that the mechanisms that control attention allocation (e.g. the fronto-parietal network) were less active during a challenging pattern-detection task in regular gamers than in nongamers (Bavelier, Achtman, Mani & Föcker, 2012). The authors also mention that enchanced cognitive performance is not documented for all computer games. In addition to spatial skills scholars have also speculated that video games are excellent means for developing problem solving skills (Prensky, 2013). American studies (Granic, Lobel & Engels, 2014) have mentioned creativity in the process of playing games. For example, among a sample of almost five hundred 12-year-old students in the United States of America video game playing was positively associated with creativity (Jackson, Witt, Games, Fitzgerald, von Eye & Zhao, 2012). On the other hand, this study's cross-sectional design has made it unclear whether playing video games develops creative skills or creative people prefer video games (or both).

In using computer games, most of users use short-term or working memory. Short-term memory is the stage of memory that retains data for a period of 20 seconds after the disappearance of traces and if it is not repeated (Vizek Vidović, Vlahović Štetić & Miljković, 2003). However, one of the ways to keep information in short-term memory, perhaps permanently, is their repetition. If informations are repeated, they stay in memory as long as they want. It means if preschool or school aged child plays a game more times, there is a greater possibility that this game will be remembered and also given information to another child and peers. But there is an opposite effect with regarding that the offer of computer games changes all the times in the aim of necessities of the market.

The primary motivation in using technology is a conviction that technology will support superior forms of learning. Because of that, theory and research in learning enables very important source of data. Advances in cognitive psychology have strengthened our understanding of nature practiced intellectual performances and created the foundation for the creation of an environment that is conductive learning.

Besides socio-cultural aspect of the play there is also correlation with psychological aspect of the play. According to Vygotsky (1977, 1978), playing is very important for development and is contained in concentric form such that all developmental tendencies in the focus are increased (Vygotsky, 1977, 1978).

Vygotsky makes sure us that imaginary play is socially and culturally determined. Playing role of real life for example a mum or a doctor, a child achieves and creates mental performance of social roles and roles of societies. Toys and moves with child's play are seen as significant artefact from social and cultural settings. So, in that way, children get the tools and new meaning of culture.

The pace of life imposes new rules of children's game. One of them is technology modernism, which has a characteristic of a new tool and a new meaning of culture. It tells about computer games and a new computer age. It becomes everyday activity to preschool and school aged children. When assessing the quality of certain parts of the software for children, researchers point to the developmental appropriateness. Software designers are focused on presenting educational game content as attractive and accessible to a younger audience. However, there is a relative lack of focus on the value of using the computer as a game per se. If a computer game is becoming an important part of the lives of children, it is necessary to take into account the developmental value from the same perspective that is taken when considering the importance of play in child development (Verenikina, Haris & Lysaght, 2003).

NAEYC (1996) points out that a developmentally appropriate play should be integrated in a common environment for learning and use it as an option that supports the learning environment. According to them, the computers should complement and not replace very valuable activity and incentives in early childhood, such as art, blocks, sand, water, books, exploring the visual and literary works (NAEYC, 1996).

Michael Cole (1996) has described different ways in which computer could be incorporated in children's imaginary play. It was elaborated in evening school *Information Technology and Literacy Program,* designed for children from five to twelve years and is known as *The fifth Dimension.* The design of program originates from Vygotsky's theory (1977). The project is structured around computer and telecommunication which supports specially chosen software as using the Internet. The aim of this project is to reinforce learning at the same time, including various computer software content in imaginary games and communication with peers and adults in a position of acting (Verenikina, 2006; Verenikina & Belyaeva, 1992).

Computer games and imaginary play are two different matters and there is a question: "Where is correlation among these two games?" The question is whether there is a correlation – only in case if the artificially created as in the case of evening school project. Other cases implied at the negative connotations of computer games. There are numerous studies that illustrate the benefits of using computers in early childhood and game (Yelland, 2005; Flintoff, 2002; Cassell & Ryokai, 2001; Ko, 2002; Pillay, 2003).

Computer games can be useful in strengthening capacity of memory, attention concentration and in solving strategic problems of younger children so due to which it can indirectly affect their academic achievements (Verenikina, 2006; Flintoff, 2002). Computer games in the form of symbols and pictures represent symbolic game, in some way.

Internet gives a great number of possibilities and risks. Young people can search information, talk to friends or unknown people, create own programme or music and many other things. It is possible to be named new kind of pedagogical media where a lot of attention is paid to the role of parents and educators (Comer, Furr, Beidas, Weiner & Kendall, 2008; Kerawalla & Crook, 2002; Lenhart, 2005; Young, 2008) as well as politicians (Furlong & Morrison, 2000; Livingstone, 2003), just to protect children and teens from certain risks as give them a chance to develop its own personality over the Internet (Livingstone & Haddon, 2008; Mitchell, Becker-Blease & Finkelhor, 2005).

Except social and cognitive skills, computer games also influence on language skills. A larger number of computer games offer a complete content in different languages: English, German, Portuguese, French, etc. But in most cases it is preferred to play games in English - players have the option respective possibility to select the language in which they want to serve during the games of your computer. In desire to have a game that a child likes, preschool and school aged child will exert extra effort in learning new foreign phrases. Step by step, using the eu-dict dictionary and other various dictionaries, starting with a

certain playroom or a foreign language course, will create excellent conditions for learning a foreign language, and thus create a virtual communication with children from different parts of the world.

In other words, a simple computer program teaches children to different sounds that can dramatically boost their hearing ability. It allows them to advance from two weeks to two years, as the creators claim games (Graham, McCabe & Sheridan, 2003). An example of this is the game called *Phenomena*, created by David Moore of the University of Oxford, in order to help children who have language difficulties. He added that these games can help any child (Graham, McCabe & Sheridan, 2003).

Free time and computer games are connected. In their free time, school or preschool child stays at home and play computer games. A child spends more and more free time in computer games but less with friends and hunting games. It is not interesting because they are thought as children of the 21st century and want to behave in accordance with this fact. Leisure can be defined as the totality of time, situation and activities that are not conditioned by biological, social or professional necessity, despite the undeniable human participation in certain activities (Previšić, 2000).

FAMILY ROLE IN CHILDREN'S USE OF A COMPUTER AND THE INTERNET

Family is important institution in all societies, which is very high on the scale of life values (Rijavec, Miljković & Brdar, 2008). In accordance with GfK researches, it is determined that 67% of households have personal computer. In accordance with Livingstone and Bober (2006) research, one third says that their parents play direct social role supporting the Internet in the way they help (32%), one third propose web pages which their children would visit (32%) in general, and one third share their experience about computer usage (31%).

Parents give a different view in the context of using the Internet of a child. Most of them report that they have direct role in sharing and supporting his/her child for usage of computer. 81% parents claim that they have asked a child: "What do you do on the computer?" (57% claims that they help a child online (compared with 32%) and 32% claims that they sit down with a child when the child is online (in that point 31% children agree with parents). Parents play a very important role in child's education as well as its access to virtual world, computer games and virtual friends. How will the children distinguish between positive and negative characteristics of computers, between fiction and reality, or choose specific content and understand the meaning of the presented content is depending on many factors, but mainly depends on the parents, with whom young people live. Parental influence on a young person will be surely different, what mainly depends on the group of characteristics such as: parental education methods, parental competencies to intervene properly and in a time, depend on their personality and many other factors (Radetić–Paić, Ružić Baf & Dragojlović, 2010).

In addition, parents are responsible for their child's security so they have to look for a way to control child's growing independence as well as privacy rights what is very important. The second, children and parents agree that children are more qualified in using the Internet than parents (Livingstone & Bober, 2006). Overall, this study shows that children enjoy the opportunities which internet provides to them in a game of identity, relationships, research, and communication as they might not want to share with their parents.

Livingstone and Bober (2006) have empirically recognized a big gap among parental and child's experience, so it brings efficient regulation of child using the Internet in a family home. It seems that parents overestimate the risks to which children may be exposed due to the use of the Internet or playing games. On the other hand, children overestimate the regulatory rules that their parents are trying to implement. Parental concern leads to the ill-informed and in a way, poor efficiency in upholding the rules. Children's enthusiasm for this new media results in risky behaviors.

Maleš and Kučević (2011) emphasized that women employment directly influences on the number of children who spend their time without parental presence and care. In daily fight for acquisition of basic incomes, parents spend less and less time with their children, so a shortcut to optional way of care is the computer use. Then social isolation of children and possible problems inside family relations appear. Warning signs are constant prolongation of game; development of tolerance on stimulus; restlessness and irritability when the game is disrupted; inability to control the playing and stopping; break with earlier relevant activities; lying about playing; continuing playing despite prohibitions; conflicts with parents, friends and school problems (Bilić, Gjukić & Kirinić, 2009). The role of the family in children's computer and the Internet use is very important because parents are essential to their children's academic success. The parents usually do all the best to help their children in education, growing up. The computer can connect family and a child. Parents have high educational aspirations for their children (Spera, Wentzel & Matto, 2009). One of the most effective ways is that parents and other caregivers can help their children achieve ambitious educational goals is to become involved in their children's education. Research shows that children whose parents and other caregivers are knowledgeable about and engaged in their homework assignments, talk to them about school, and help planning their education to achieve higher test scores, make better grades, have better school attendance, and demonstrate better behavior at school and at home (Henderson & Mapp, 2002). So, computers and sometimes computer games can effectively enhance communication between the home and school, engage families in learning with their child, inform parents about student academic performance and attendance promote beneficial educational practices and make family relaxed.

Attitudes toward Computer and the Internet Use

Definitely, it is interesting to explore attitudes of parents, children and experts toward computer games which are more widespread, available and make an integral part of life regardless of whether that parents and children want or not. It is revealed that there are distinctions between parent's and children's attitudes. A special note is provided to the views of experts on the application of computer games. In early childhood, children speak fluently "digital language", language of videogames and the Internet, so they develop hypertextual mind. For them, the computer is a window into their world, which weighs your intelligence with artificial intelligence (Tatković, 2011).

Since it is very important regarding the possibility of predicting their behavior (Santrock, 1997), it is very interesting to investigate what do teachers think about computer and the use of the Internet? It was investigated by Turkish EFL teachers' attitudes towards ICT use. The data collected from English teachers (n=70) working in public schools in Turkey. The study used SPSS Version 18 to analyze the responses to the computer attitude scale. The scale tapped on af-

fective, cognitive and behavioral components as Albirini (2006) maintained that exploring these aspects would yield reliable ideas about teachers' attitudes. The analyses revealed that the participants in this study had significantly positive attitudes towards ICTs with an overall means the score of 4.20. As Table 1 indicates, a great majority of the participants (81.7%) responded positively to the affective (mean: 4.18), cognitive (mean: 4.18) and behavioral (mean: 4.26) aspects of computer attitudes scales. With regard to the affective domain, 80% of the participants reported feeling comfortable with the recent increase in the number of computers and using computers. As to the cognitive aspect, the study found that 81.1% of the participants agreed or strongly agreed that computers were effective educational tools saving precious classroom time and fostering students' motivation by enabling easy access to information.

What are the parents' attitudes about computer? Parents play an important role in child's education, in access to virtual world, computer games, and virtual friends. The 21st century is highlighted by IC era, using computers, mobiles, laptops, tablets and other informational equipment. For parents, information era is something quite new, something what they must learn, acquire

Table 1. The list of emotions in accordance with Lazarro

Emotions	Common Themes and Triggers
Fear	Threat of harm, object moving quickly to hit player, sudden fall or loss of support, possibility of pain.
Surprise	Sudden change. Briefest of all emotions, does not feel good or bad, after interpreting event this emotion merges into fear, relief, etc...
Disgust	Rejection as food or outside norms The strongest triggers are body products such as feces, vomit, urine, mucus, saliva, and blood.
Naches/kvell	Pleasure or pride at the accomplishment of a child or mentee. (Kvell is how it feels to express this pride in one's child or mentee to others).
Fiero	Personal triumph over adversity. The ultimate Game Emotion. Overcoming difficult obstacles players raise their arms over their heads. They do not need to experience anger prior to success, but it does require effort.
Schadenfreude	Gloat over misfortune of a rival. Competitive players enjoy beating each other especially a long-term rival. Boasts are made about player prowess and ranking.
Wonder	Over whelming improbability. Curious items amaze players at their unusualness, unlikelyhood, and improbability without breaking out of realm of possibilities.

(Lazzaro, 2013).

new concepts and get along in a world that is completely new to them. In that way, children can help them to whom computer application is simple and attractive. Parental concern is mostly directed to children's internet usage specially related on values, commercialization, privacy and first of all, sexual material (Livingstone, 2002). Parents understand that use of computer has a lot of positive sides such as memory development, learning methods, skills of problem solving and self-confidence (Radetić–Paić, Ružić Baf & Dragojlović, 2010). Also, parents have more positive attitudes to internet application for educating purposes, creativity development and acquiring new knowledge than as a mean of fun. Parents are ready to invest considerable resources in informatical education for his/her child, and buy necessary equipment. However, there is another medal of this story. Playing computer games becomes a strong resource, even frustrating for parents as well as children in the situation trying to adopt computer in their lives and homes. These challenges assume a certain financial means, informatical knowledge, installation and upgrading computer, manners in which computer is used. The most important are cultural and cognitive questions related on media, internet and literacy (Livingstone & Bober, 2006). Kovačević's research (2007), displays the research results about correlation of free time and playing computer games among elder primary school children. For example, parental attitudes toward child are playing computer game show that 9.9% pupils are aware of the fact that their parents do not approve their way of spending free time. The rest of 76.8% participants emphasize that their parents approve playing computer games in their free time (Kovačević, 2007). Frustrations caused by playing computer games, parents can solve by entering the virtual world of computer games, take free time with their child to play a game. Then it creates a bond and better opportunity to talk to your child. Many experts make statements about computer games, such as authors Buljan-Flander and Karlović (2004) who consider that parents pay

too little and too less devoted time to their child and also have too little control under child's spending time because of the bustle of everyday life, various commitments and problems. This leaves a space where children can engage in a threatening or dangerous activity. Just to set clear rules and boundaries, give the child a sense of security and protection, and reduces the likelihood that the child would be found in a potentially dangerous situation (Buljan-Flander & Karlović, 2004).

An important goal of educational technology is to develop positive attitudes in relation to their peers and understanding of working with others. Technological activities have the potential that allows all children to succeed. Children develop respect for each other because they realize that anyone can engage in technological activities. It encourages nurturing learning environment. Children need opportunities to work on the activities in which people grow, but also the place to be offered challenges, where place can certainly manage risk and failure analysis (Stables, Benson & de Vries, 2011).

Lemke's third positive attitude refers to that "technology in schools can also be an excellent relationship between scientists and the creation of the Professional Practice Areas" (Salpeter, 1999). Lemke explains that, for example, mathematics and science courses are performed in different ways today than how they are used. He says: "Today's practicing mathematicians and scientists in many cases does not require an answer, but the whole cup responses through the design and simulation models." Let's prepare our students for their future exposing them the newest area of practice" (Salpeter, 1999, p.10). To prepare children for the future, the use of technology should begin in early childhood. It is believed that teaching children these skills at an early age is quite correctly. Stables says: "There is an increasing acceptance that the general technological competencies are more appropriate for younger children in such a rapidly technological society than the specific skills" (according to Salpeter, 1999, p. 11). Lemke's fifth way is that technology has a positive impact on education because the technology enhances teaching. He says that it is powerful learning tool that adds a teacher's repertoire. Technology can be a powerful tool for teachers to use, if they know how to use it. Kay Stables (according to Salpeter, 1999) commented that when the first computer technology came on the market, many teachers were confused. They were not sure what computer technology means, applied science or craft work. He says that very few teachers received training on technological education, and recommends four key areas to assist teachers to move forward, which are shown in Figure 1. Connecting the idea of learning Bayesian causal maps enabled computer experts to build the effective expert systems. Causal models are called Bayesian networks (Gopnik, 2011). Famous Turing test is the fact that sitting in front of a computer terminal, trying to discover whether communicate to a computer or to another man. Turing, who invented the modern computer, says that if you cannot notice the difference, it is necessary to verify that the computer has a mind. Servers like Hotmail implemented Turing test, asking the user to recognize the written Word to make sure that your email address will not get the computer spammers. But that would be really compel the Turing test would have to be tightened. In the original work, he also talks about the test computer child. The computer should do the same things as an adult, but at the same time must be able to learn to do those things as a child (Gopnik, 2011).

In addition, research of pediatrics from American University in Ohio (2011) have shown that young children who are occupied with computers in their own home or in home of any relative, have better results in intelligence test and tests for enrollment of primary school unlike their peers who have no access to computer (http://www.roda.hr/article/read/utjecaj-kompjutera-na-iq-djece).

In explaining attitudes toward computer and the Internet use, it is good idea to understand gender-differences in computer experience and its influence on computer attitudes. Namely, the study in Duquesne University in Pittsburg, USA have found that there are significant gender differences in computer attitudes and experience, based on a sample of college students. The study found that males are more interested in computers than were females and had more self-confidence in working in computers (Shashaani, 1997). According to early studies males believed that computers were more appropriate for males (Voogt, 1987; Kiesler, Sproull & Eccles, 1983). The other important outcome of Shashaani's study (1997) was related to the parents' role in influencing participant's attitudes toward computers. Yee and Eccles (1998) found that although boys and girls perfomed equally well in maths, their parents held different beliefs about their sons' and daughters' ability and effort. So, the association between computer attitudes and computer experience was stronger for males than females.

Computer Games and Their Effect on Children's Emotions

"Our average level of subjective well-being is largely determined by what we do and what we do is heavily influenced by our genetic structure. We continue to follow the path paved by our grandparents, or we can apply direction, at least to some extent. The conclusion to which I came was similar to what our grandmothers were saying: Happy is the one who makes himself happy" (Lykken, 1997, p. 8.). In explaining and connecting positive emotions and influence of computer games on positive emotions, the first matter would be the question what are the positive emotions? What is the role of positive or negative emotions? What do they mean for preschool and school aged child in his play with virtual world? Positive affective states are associated with more activity than with thinking (it is easier to encourage exercise and

Figure 1. Four key areas in the application of technology in education
(Stables, Benson & de Vries, 2011).

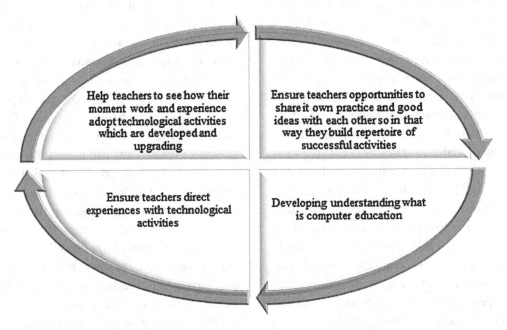

socializing than thinking). Relating the increase of the frequency of positive emotions and moods (exercise, activity, company) and computer games, it could be seen that computer games and positive emotions are common gateways where computer games increase the frequency of positive emotions, no matter how much school and preschool aged child love, enjoy and is happily, while it is in the virtual world. The question is whether this is a false sense of happiness, sufficient to preschool and school-aged child. People feel the best when they are physically and socially active. The inverse: people prefer to exercise more and look for the company when they are feeling good. This is not the case within engagement in virtual world of computer games...

Computer games are a great source of pleasure for children of preschool and school aged children. Children enjoy because they exclude from the outside world where there is no ban, where they can do what they really want, where they can learn what they want, and what they do not want, do not have to do. So, the world of

entertainment and it is deprived of the obligations and responsibilities. Because the world does not exist in perfection and computer games have their sore point. It would be interesting to find out what happens to the children's emotions during the game are, how the game affects behaviour, physical health? What does really happen when a child plays game continuously for several hours, every day, every week, and every month? Muijs & Roe (1998) found justification for linking frequent players with social isolation and less positive behaviour towards society in general, while Gupta and Vensky (1996) pointed to indications that frequent players gamble more than players who play less. Self-esteem is an important issue (Cesaroni, 1998; Roe & Muijs, 1998; Colwell & Payne, 2000). Roe and Muijs (1998) found that increased skills in computer games offers players a temporary sense of power, control and achievements, which were previously felt to be lacking. Such artificially increasing self-esteem can lead to interaction with computer games become a substitute for social relationships.

For impact of computer games on children's emotions it is inevitable to mention the health problems that may occur and as such influence the emotions of a child, because physical health has a link with psychological health. Players who complain of pain in the eyes, headaches, shoulder pain, fatigue and behavioral changes (Tazawa, Soukalo, Okada & Takada, 1997). Medical experts are concerned because of metabolic and heart problems (Dorman, 1997; Emes, 1997). It is frequently associated with gaming health problems like tendonitis and repetitive injuries dislocations (Emes, 1997; Cleary, McKendrick & Sills, 2002), and computer games may trigger seizures in susceptible individuals (Funk, 1992, 1993; Emes, 1997; Ricci & Vigevano, 1999; Singh, Bhalla, Lehl & Sachdev, 2001). A possible reason for this is that the user is sitting close to the screen (Kasteleijn-Nolst Trenite, Trenite, da Silva, Ricci, Binnie, Rubboli, Tassinari & Segers, 1999).

A few experimental studies suggest that playing violent video games, even for a short period, can cause current transmitted effects of increased aggression in children's free play (Cooper & Mackie 1986; Irwin & Gross, 1995; Schutte, Malouff, Post-Gorden & Rodasta, 1988; Silvern & Williamson, 1987), increased aggressive/hostile responses to the ambiguous, open-closed questions (Kirsh, 1998). For example, Kirsh reported that children of the third and fourth grade who have played *Mortal Kombat 2*, a violent game away violently responded to the open-closed questions as opposed to children who play basketball games. Children who like and prefer aggressive game also show some prosocial behaviour as donating money or helping someone (Chambers & Ascione, 1987; Wiegman & van Schio, 1998).

Chris Bateman (2008) gathered data from a DGD2 survey with 1,040 responses and ranked the top 10 emotions as reported by computer-game players. It is a list of estimation and "This isn't a strict scientific measure, as such, but the highest scoring emotions are those for which the majority of people not only recognised having that emotion while playing games, but recognised it enhanced their enjoyment." (Bateman, 2008, p. 9). Bateman (2008) goes on to theorize about possible biological mechanisms that were responsible for each emotion, attributing the feeling of bliss to serotonin for example. For the emotions of relief and naches Bateman is not certain enough to speculate on the chemicals responsible, guessing relief "may be the experiential analogue of the hormone cortisol". Therefore, Bateman (2008) connect with serotonin. He thinks that it would be good to make a mix of neurotransmitters and emotions what is shown in Figure 2 (Bateman, 2008, p. 9).

In XEODesign's study, Lazzaro (2013) identified seven major emotions by observing facial expressions, body language and verbality. Although this is not the most scientific method of interpreting emotion the list is interesting. The emotions are fear, suprise, disgust, naches/kvell, fiero, schandenfeude and wonder as it is shown in Table 1.

INTERNET VIOLENCE

First, it must be clear what does it actually mean internet violence? Internet violence comprehends exposure to inappropriate content and/or direct communication with the person who asks inappropriate relationships, encouraging group hatred, the spread of violent and abusive comments, impersonation, sending malicious and unpleasant contents to others, breaking in someone else's e-mail address and many other things (web.ffos.hr/serv/psih.php?file=380).

As is true in any community, the internet has light safe side and a dark, dangerous side (Axelrod, 2009). We live in the world which is very technologically advanced but on the other hand, it does not mean that our children are spared of its influence of media and technology, especially the negative

Figure 2. Emotions grouped by biomechanisms responsible (Bateman, 2008).

side of that media. The media is unfortunately not always aware of responsibility in modelling life attitudes and values directed to children and young people (Mandarić, 2012). From different institutions, police forces, state attorney, scientists who did researches about this topic, family. Acting as if we were reconciled to the fact that there is internet violence is not good. But in the past, it is discussed how to remediate the consequences of internet violence. It means that people are reconciled to a new technology world, do not want to leave that world despite there are a lot of serious problems. Perhaps, people believe that all these problems will be solved out. So, there is no fear. Technology is here. It must be seriously discussed about technology, here written internet. It must be because our children will be caught in the internet network and parents will not have password to enter that network. *Caught in network* means that children are exposed to internet violence. Once when child experiences internet violence, there

is no return. There is no return for a child. There is no return for parents. Any magical password will not be able to help. Child's mental health is at risk and could be damaged.

Axelrod (2009) speaks out a kind of internet violence. It is interpersonal violence and crime on internet. Interpersonal crime on the internet is not a new phenomenon, but that in general has not been widely examined or explored (Axelrod, 2009). In fact, many people often minimize the importance and impact of interpersonal violence and crime on internet because they are not physical and people sitting in front of their computers are viewed as being safe within the walls of their home (Axelrod, 2009). Most researchers define media violence as visual portrayals of acts of physical aggression by one human or human-like character against another (Huesmann, 2007).

Most theorists would now agree that the short-term effects of exposure to media violence are mostly due to:

1. Priming processes,
2. Arousal processes, and
3. The immediate mimicking of specific behaviours.

Priming is the process through which spreading activation in the brain's neural network from the locus representing an external observed stimulus excites another brain node representing a cognition, emotion, or behavior. Arousal is the extent that mass media presentations arouse the observer aggressive behaviour may also become more likely in the short run for two possible reasons excitation transfer and general arousal. Mimicry is the third short term process, imitation of specific behaviors, and can be viewed as a special case of the more general long-term process of observational learning.

In order to understand the empirical research implicating violence in electronic media as a threat to society, an understanding of why and how violent media cause aggression is vital. In fact, psychological theories that explain why media violence is such a threat are now well established. Furthermore, these theories also explain why the observation of violence in the real world – among the family, among peers, and within the community – also stimulates aggressive behavior in the observer (Huesmann, 2007).

Violence in entertainment media is also considered by many to be a major contributor to aggressive and violent behaviour in real life (see Donnerstein & Smith, 1997; Huesmann, Moise & Podolski, 1997; Anderson & Bushman, 2002; Sparks & Sparks, 2002).

Relationships between a preference for violent video games, attitudes towards violence, and empathy were examined in research with 52 sixth graders (Funk, Buchman, Schimming, & Hagan, 1998). Participants completed Bryant's Index of Empathy for Children and Adolescents (Bryant, 1982) and the Attitudes toward Violence Scale (Funk, Elliott, Urman, Flores, & Mock, 1999).

Funk (2004) made a research about empathy and attitudes towards violence. Empathy, the capacity to perceive and to experience the state of another, is critical to the process of moral evaluation (Tangney & Fischer, 1995; Eisenberg, 2000; Hoffman, 2000). Attitudes contribute to the process of moral evaluation, especially attitudes towards violence. The formation of attitudes towards violence is probably influenced by many factors including the amount of exposure to violence in real-life and the media, and the attitudes of peers and parents (Rule & Ferguson, 1986; Vernberg, Jacobs, & Hershberger, 1999). When it tells about study, the participants were 150 students recruited from primary schools and a daycare center located in a mid-sized, Midwestern city. The measure instruments were: 4 questionnaires (order counterbalanced): a background questionnaire with demographic information and questions about media use and preferences; a survey with questions about real-life violence exposure across different settings; an assessment of children's attitudes towards violence; and a measure of children's empathy. Empathy was assessed by the Children's Empathy Questionnaire (CEQ) – a 15-item self-report questionnaire. Similar to the ATVC, children are instructed to read each statement and endorse one of four possible response choices reflecting their agreement with that statement (1=No, 2=Maybe, 3=Probably, 4=Yes). Items include statements such as "When I see a kid who is upset it really bothers me and If two kids are fighting, someone should stop it". A total score is calculated across all items, with higher scores indicating more empathy. The results show that there is positive correlation between empathy and gender (r=0.33, p=0.01), but negative correlation between empathy and searching the internet (r=-0.17, p=0.05). That means that more searching on internet reduce the level of empathy. Also, it is found negative correlation on gender and attitudes toward computer games (r=-0.21, p=0.05).

The research (Ybarra, Diener-West, Markow, Leaf, Hamburger & Boxer, 2008) showed exposure to violence in the media, both online and offline, were associated with significantly elevated odds for concurrently reporting seriously violent behaviour.

One of the most interesting researches was done in Croatia about internet violence. It was conducted by Child Protection Zagreb and Hrabri Telefon (Brave Phone) (2008) with 2700 participants (11-18 years old, 44% of boys and 56% girls) from different Croatian cities. In a question about experience in internet violence, the participants said: "15% - one he wrote and published secrets or lies about me, 5% - someone has put my pictures or movies and is accompanied by unpleasant comments, 20% - someone posing as me and speak / write in my name, 18% - someone insisted on meeting in person, who did not want to". In the question about exposure to inappropriate questions and comments of a sexual nature during communication via the Internet (chat, MSN, ICQ, blog, forum...), the answers of participants are: 67% - questions about sex, love, and sexual experiences, 31% - questions about intimate body parts, 29% - questions about the experience of masturbation, 42% - questions about clothes, 39% - an invitation to meet or sex. Otherwise, Hrabri Telefon (Brave Telephone) is a nongovernmental, nonprofit organization founded in 1997. It was registered in 2000th year. The organization was established to provide direct assistance and support to abused and neglected children and their families, but also work to prevent child abuse and neglect as well as unacceptable behavior in children and adolescents. In their work, Hrabri Telefon has principles such as accessibility (all activities and services are free to end users); confidentiality (information about customers is used solely for statistical processing and analysis and are not available to the public) and the best interests of the child (counseling and support orientated this principle).

THE CORRELATES OF ATTITUDES TOWARD COMPUTER AND INTERNET USE

Attitudes toward computers, computer self-efficacy and usage of computers play an important role in children's ability to identify a computer as a valuable mean of learning as well as necessity for professional development in 21st century. Accepted opinion of many researchers is that parental attitude has significant impact on children's attitude about learning and work at the school. In explaining some significant attitude correlations with computer application and its effects on children's development, it is began with correlates related on sex, age, level of parent's education.

The Luba Zuk Levy's dissertation (2007) presents results about the attitude toward computers, self-efficacy and usage in children and parents regarding sexual and age differences of their children ages 10–14 years residing in the Tarrant County area. The instruments used by parents in that study were: Computer Self-Efficacy Scale (CSE), Parents' Attitudes toward Computers (PAC), and the Parental Computer Usage and Demographics Questionnaire. Children were administered: Computer Self-Efficacy Scale (CSE), the Computer Attitude Questionnaire (CAQ - child), and the Child Computer Usage and Demographic Questionnaire. Quantitative methodology was utilized to collect and interpret the data. CAQ questionnaire is a questionnaire where the respondents have been examined on Likert scale of 5 degrees by entering the appropriate numerical values depending on to what extent you agree or disagree with the above statement. It is constructed to measure attitudes towards people, things and dispositions. Findings revealed a significant positive correlation between parents and their children's attitude toward computers, indicating that parents who had higher computer attitudes tended to have children who had higher computer attitudes. Parents and their children had statistically similar self-efficacy scores. There was no statistically significant positive relationship between parents' computer usage and their children's computer usage. Children's computer usage during the week totaled an average of 9.56 hours. Parents' average computer usage during the week was 24.42 hours. Investigation of the role that gender plays in children's and their parents' computer attitude, self-efficacy, and usage did not show statistically significant differences between boys and girls or between male and female parents. There was, however, a gender difference in the child's favorite and worst academic subjects. The results failed to reveal any significant predictors for child computer attitudes, self-efficacy or usage Luka Zuk Levy's finding (2009) show a difference between male and female attitudes toward computer and self-efficacy.

Lack of significant correlation between parental knowledge of computers and their attitudes about computers can represent positive outcome. There is a very interesting research about computer games which connects emotions and attitudes. It tells about dissertation made by Allen (2013). The dissertation uses primary researches to get different opinions of different aged people who play video games daily or regularly. In accordance with collected data, (2013) the study predicts that there will no be correlations between violence in video games and real life (physical violence), although the conclusion can not be taken because of small sample. The first, gamers are roughly split 50:50 in the opinion that games can cause violence, but if the over 50% yes responses reflects the thoughts of the UK adult population. The second, the answer for question "Do You Feel Any Of These Emotions While Playing Violent Video Games?" is given by illustration 7-Frustration and enjoyment are by far the most felt emotions while playing violent video games followed by disgust, humiliation and rage. Emotions mentioned in this dissertation are next: disgust, humiliation, enjoyment, fear, rage, distress and frustration. In his dissertation (Allen, 2013) has posed The Lövheim cube of emotion which is a theoretical model of explaining the relationship

between monoamines (serotonin, dopamine and noradrenaline) and mood, emotions and behavior.

The Social learning theory (Griffiths, 1999) presumes that people learn from each other via observation and imitation, so playing video games leads to simulation of aggressive behavior. In contrary with this theory, Catharsis theory (Griffiths, 1999) presumes that playing video games has relaxing effect by feeding latent aggression (Allen, 2013). Except the connection between attitudes and emotions, Allen (2013) connects video games with player's health. Research shows that games teach children; this of course can be used as either for good or for bad. There are many games that are suitable for children that can teach them a variety of lessons including learning about consequences, hand-eye co-ordination, keeping fit and healthy or playing a musical instrument. In today's age, obesity is a major problem and playing games could improve the health of today's children. In his conclusion, Allen (2013) says that violent video games can be linked to violent behaviour in some circumstances and using the Lövheim cube of emotion a theoretical link was made between the chemical dopamine, produced when humans feel certain emotions, and violent behaviour.

MAIN FOCUS OF THE CHAPTER

Considering presented theoretical frame and previous relevant research studies, it can be helpful to present findings of conducted empirical research in Croatia and propose new research of that topic in other countries especially for preschool and school aged children. So, that research can be a background for further research in other European on non-European countries. Generally, there is a lack of systematic and detailed empirical research about computer and internet use among (pre)school children perceived from children's and parents' point of view. Therefore, this study is aimed to investigate the computer presence in family homes, IT literacy with different computer programmes in parents as well in children. Besides, as it was described before, attitudes of parents and (pre)school aged children about using internet and computer games as well attitudes of internet violence are explored. Since, there was a small amount of studies on games types that children play as well frequency of playing them; this kind of analysis is included here too. The parental control seems to be very important, so the level of control in use of internet and computer games for children and the results about presence of others as well conversation are presented here. Furthermore, the frequency and types of computer games which children play as well type of emotions provoked by these games are analysed. Finally, all relevant correlates such as socio demographic variables (sex, age, the level of education, and presence of computer in family home) of computer and internet use are taken into discussion, so some important future guidelines about this matter could be drawn.

Therefore, the main aim of this study was to explore the computer and internet use among (pre)school children from children's and parents' perception with all relevant correlates. The basic design of this study is correlational, so it cannot provide answers about causal-consequential relations among explored variables. Nevertheless, an objective and reliable correlations could be definitely revealed and used for some future research designs.

From this study aim, the following research problems have been defined:

1. To examine parents' perception of computer and internet use among children by exploring:
   a. The general data about parents (gender, age, family structure, education level, computer use, number of computers in the home, internet content explanation by a parent, the use of words from the internet) from the perception of parents of preschool and school children.
   b. The informatics knowledge of parents.
   c. The internet use of children from the parents' perception.
   d. Parents' attitudes toward internet use.
   e. Parents' attitudes toward internet violence.
   f. Parents' perception of the frequency of internet use in the presence of adults.
   g. Parents' perception of the conversation about internet with a child.
   h. Parents' perception of playing computer games and the correlated emotions.

2. To examine preschool children's perception of computer and internet use among them by exploring:
   a. The general data about preschool children (gender, age, family structure, food consumption while playing computer games, institutional care and education).
   b. Children's perceptions of their internet use.
   c. Children's perceptions of their internet use in the presence of adults.
   d. Children's perceptions of their playing computer games and the correlated emotions.
   e. Children's perceptions of their activities in the situations of internet violence.

3. To examine school children's perception of computer and internet use among them by exploring:
   a. The general data about school children (gender, age, family structure, food consumption while playing computer games, class in the primary school).
   b. Children's perceptions of their internet use.
   c. Children's perceptions of their internet use in the presence of adults.
   d. Children's perceptions of their playing computer games and the correlated emotions.
   e. Children's perceptions of their activities in the situations of internet violence.

4. To examine the correlations between all variables of parents' and (pre)school children's perception of computer and internet use and relevant socio-demographic variables.

On the basis of findings of previous research and relevant literature research hypotheses:

H1: It is expected to determine high presence of computer in family homes and its influence on children's behaviour. In addition, it is expected that parents have a certain informatical knowledge, have positive attitudes toward computers and internet but not significant control as well as make conversation about internet content. It is expected that they are aware of violence on internet and that they will evaluate their children computer play as frequent and experienced with both, positive and negative emotions.

H2: It is expected that preschool aged children use computer and internet, to consume food while playing, have positive attitudes toward computer, to use in the presence of adults more than school aged children, to experience different emotions during playing computer games, and to show different ways of reactions in the case of violence on internet.

H3: It is expected that school aged children use computer and internet, to consume food while playing, have positive attitudes toward computer, to use in the presence of adults less than preschool aged children, to experience different emotions during playing games, to show different ways reactions on violence on internet.

H4: It is expected significant positive correlation between number of computers in home, positive attitudes of parents, control and making conversation in the relation on quantity of playing games, and emotions experienced by playing games. Also, it is expected significant difference in perception among parents,

preschool and school aged children with regarding IT literacy, internet and computer usage, making conversation about internet content in the favour of school aged parents for whom it is expected to use much more computer, internet and computer games. As far as children's perception, it is expected sex difference at higher level of aggressivity in boys as well as age difference in the meaning less expressed negative feelings at elder children.

METHODS

Participants

The study was conducted on the sample of N=199 children. Of these, N=100 children of preschool aged children (M=46, F=54), mean age M=4.97 (SD=0.92) in the range of 4-7 years, and N=99 children of primary school aged children (M=47, F=52), mean age M=9.50 (SD=2.13) in the range of 7-14 years.

In addition to children, participated in the study: N=199 of their parents. Parents of preschool aged children was N=100 (M=26, F=74), mean age M=33.51 (SD=5.7) ranging from 23 to 50 years. Parents of school aged children is N=99 (M=27, F=71), mean age, M=37.15 (SD=4.40) in the range of 26-50 years. Of the total sample of preschool aged children, 25 of them live in Mačkovec and 75 in Šenkovec, while all school aged children live in the municipality Šenkovec.

Measurement

The study used three surveys created for the purpose of carrying out research. Basis for the development of the survey is theoretically grounded. It covered the area relating to the subject matter of the research findings related to computer games, as well as previous studies. It was used to create questions about parents' attitudes towards computer games by web search on the surveys. General Data were collected through closed-type questions in a way that respondents choose a category offered. Variables associated with IT literacy, attitudes towards the use of Internet and internet violence, and emotions related to computer games were assessed by Likert-type scale of 5 degrees. Subjects were instructed to give the appropriate numerical values depending on to what extent you agree or disagree with the above statement (1=completely disagree, 2=partially disagree, 3=neither agree nor disagree, 4=partially agree, 5=strongly agree).

Procedure

The survey was conducted in schools and early and preschool institutions, and partly as part of graduate work at Faculty of Teacher Education in Rijeka. Based on requests for cooperation in the conduct of research is allowed entrance into kindergartens and primary school early 2014th year. Research process lasted about four weeks into the school, and included N=99 children and their parents and by steam grades: second, fourth, sixth and eighth. In kindergartens lasted three months, and by randomized schedule included N=100 children and their parents. The survey was conducted only after obtaining the written consent of their parents and the participation of their children in the study where anonymously and confidentiality is guaranteed. Upon completion of the research promise is to give feedback on the survey results. During the study, there were several telephone inquiries regarding the questionnaire and the fear of parents related to the disclosure of the identity of children. It was explained that the research was conducted on group level with guaranteed anonymity.

Methods of statistical processing of the data included the statistical analysis of the collected data was performed using the statistical software package SPSS 18.0. In an attempt to answer the first and second issue was conducted descriptive analysis. In response to the third problem was used correlation analysis, and considering das in almost all measured variables showed significant deviations from normal distribution, applied non-parametric statistics. In other words, the analysis applied Spearman correlation coefficient correlation, and to analyze the significance of differences Mann-Whitney or Kruskall-Wallis test.

SOLUTIONS AND RECOMMENDATIONS: THE MAIN RESEARCH FINDINGS

Considering the fast and huge technology development, especially the development of computer and internet use from the one side, and from the other related behaviours that parents and children are displaying according to that, it is very important to perform various empirical studies. As it could be seen in the previous sections, this subject matter is more than complex, since numerous variables effect children's behavior on different ways. With the aim of systematic and deep investigation in this field, the perceptions of parents of preschool and school aged children, and of the children themselves were explored. Within these three perceptions (parents, preschool children and school aged children), various variables that are closely related to computer and internet use were taken into consideration. Therefore, even though this research has clear correlational design, its main contribution lies in the fact that it could reveal much better understanding of this subject matter due to measuring almost all relevant variables.

Parents' Perception of Computer and Internet Use among Their Children

To examine parents' perception of computer and internet use among children by exploring:

1. The general data about parents (gender, age, family structure, education level, computer use, number of computers in the home,

internet content explanation by a parent, the use of words from the internet) from the perception of parents of preschool and school children.

2. The informatics knowledge of parents.
3. The internet use of children from the parents' perception.
4. Parents' attitudes toward internet use.
5. Parents' attitudes toward internet violence.
6. Parents' perception of the frequency of internet use in the presence of adults.
7. Parents' perception of the conversation about internet with a child.
8. Parents' perception of playing computer games and the correlated emotions.

As it could be observed in Table 2, with respect to the structure of the family, parents have responded that (1.0%) of children are living with one parent, (68.8%) of them with both parents, (5.0%) with his grandparents and one parent, and (26.0%) of them with both parents and grandparents. On the issue of family members, parents responded that they have one member (1.0%), two members (6.1%), 3 members (11.1%), 4 members (53.5%), five members (14, 1%), six members (10.1%), eight members (1.0%) and nine members (3.0%). On the issue of the number of male children, the parents enrolled the following: a male child (39.4%), two male children (25.3%), and three male members (10.1%), four male members (1.0%), of these 31% are missing. In the issue of girls: no girl child (1.0%), one female child (46.5%), two female children (22.2%), three female children (7.1%), four female children (3.0%), missing (20.2%). On the issue of mother's education, parents responded that ended: primary school (8.1%), high school (71.7%), College (17.2%), master's (3.0%) of these missing (1.0%). On the issue of father's, education parents responded that ended: primary school (10.1%), secondary school (72.7%), master's degree (12.1%) missing (5.1%). Considering the family structure, parents reported that

majority of children live within their nucleus families, as it could be observed in the Table 2. Much smaller number of children is living with their extended families and the lowest number of them live with only one parent. This family structure in the sample was expected, and it was similar between subsamples of preschool aged children's parents and school aged children's parents. Also expected, the average of total number of family members is four, even though the range is from two to nine family members. Considering the educational level of mothers as comparing to the educational level of fathers, it could be seen that they have higher education level. The same difference between determined frequency could be seen between mothers and fathers of preschool children as comparing to mothers and fathers of school aged children, what could be explained with generation differences between these two subsamples of parents. Furthermore, in the analyses of the independent children's use of the computer, parents of preschool children reported similar number of children who use or not use independently computer, what could be explained definitely by their preschool age.

On the other side, the independence in the computer use rise with the age, because parents of school aged children reported that 85 children use computer independently and only 13 if them not. This finding was also expected since the computer use if more frequent in the school ages due to numerous school tasks and bigger informatic knowledge that children gain. Considering the family status regarding the number of computers that each family has in their home, this finding definitely confirmed previous findings about significant presence of computers in our homes. As it could be observed in Table 1, just six parents of preschool children reported about having no one computer in their home, and that number is even smaller as reported by parents of school aged children. The interesting finding is also the one related to the parents' reports about having two or three computer in the home – these frequencies

Table 2. Descriptive parameters (frequencies, means (M), standard deviations (SD) and ranges) of socio-demographic variables, informatics knowledge, the internet use of children, the use of internet in the presence of other and conversations with children about internet content from the parents' perception (all parents, parents of preschool children and parents of school aged children)

Data Collected from Parents (N=199)		
All Parents (N=199)	**Parents of Preschool Aged Children (N=100)**	**Parents of School Aged Children (N=99)**
Gender	F=145 M=53 Missing=1	F=74 M=26	F=71 M=27 Missing=1
Age	35.48 (SD=4.93); 23-50	33.58 (4.87); 23-47	37.15 (4.4); 26-50
The child is living with:	1. with one parent=5 2. with both parents=133 3. with grandparents=0 4. with one parent and grandparents=14 5. with both parents and grandparents=47	1. with one parent= 1 2. with both parents= 68 3. with grandparents=0 4. with one parent and grandparents=5 5. with both parents and grandparents=26	1. with one parent=4 2. with both parents=65 3. with grandparents=0 4. with one parent and grandparents=9 5. with both parents and grandparents=21
The average of total number of family members	M=4.16 (SD=1.19); 2-9	M=4.04 (SD=0.98); 2-9	M=4.27 (SD=1.36); 2-9
The educational level of mother	Primary education=10 Secondary education=129 Higher education=52 Master degree=7 Doctoral degree=0 Missing=1	Primary education=2 Secondary education=58 Higher education=35 Master degree=4 Doctoral degree=0 Missing=1	Primary education=8 Secondary education=71 Higher education=17 Master degree=3 Doctoral degree=0
The educational level of father	Primary education=11 Secondary education=146 Higher education=33 Master degree=3 Doctoral degree=0 Missing=6	Primary education=1 Secondary education=74 Higher education=21 Master degree=3 Doctoral degree=0 Missing=1	Primary education=10 Secondary education=72 Higher education=12 Master degree=0 Doctoral degree=0 Missing=5
Does your child use computer independently?	YES=128 NO=70 Missing=1	YES=43 NO=57	YES=85 NO=13 Missing=1
How many computers do you have in your home?	No one=9 One=99 Two=59 Three=32	No one=6 One=55 Two=25 Three=14	No one=3 One=44 Two=34 Three=18
Do you explain to your child the content from the internet?	YES=168 NO=28 Missing=3	YES=89 NO=9 Missing=2	YES=79 NO=19 Missing=1
Does your child use the words from the internet content?	YES=123 NO=73 Missing=3	YES=65 NO=32 Missing=3	YES=58 NO=41

continued on following page

implied at equalizing the family members with the number of computers in the home, more independent computer use without any parental or other control. Further question about explaining to the child the content from the internet resulted with expected higher frequencies about that parents are providing those explanations. Nevertheless, since this question implies at socially desirable answers, it is the question how much the parents were honest about it?

Table 2. Continued

	Data Collected from Parents (N=199)		
Parents' informatics knowledge M(SD)	1.Microsoft Power Point	2.78 (1.37)	2.94 (1.34)	2.61 (1.39)
	2. MsOffice Word	3.48 (1.52)	3.67 (1.47)	3.27 (1.56)
	3. Google	3.71 (1.65)	3.94 (1.55)	3.47 (1.72)
	4. E-mails exchange	3.68 (1.53)	3.88 (1.53)	3.46 (1.52)
	5.Adobe Reader Flash Player	3.09 (1.34)	3.34 (1.29)	2.81 (1.35)
	6.Skype	3.01 (1.5)	3.32 (1.46)	2.68 (1.48)
	7.Windows Live Messenger	2.78 (1.31)	2.85 (1.27)	2.7 (1.36)
	8.Windows Media Player	3.18 (1.44)	3.22 (1.48)	3.13 (1.41)
	9.Other	0.42 (1.29)	0.65 (1.55)	0.18 (0.9)
	Total	26.63 (9.6)	28.12 (9.65)	24.99 (9.33)
Parents' perceptions of children internet use M(SD)	10.Playing games	3.18 (1.07)	2.94 (1.03)	3.43 (0.99)
	11.Internet search	2.43 (1.26)	1.76 (1.03)	3.15 (1.07)
	12. E-mails exchange	1.37 (0.86)	1.02 (0.2)	1.73 (1.11)
	13.Chat	1.58 (1.14)	1.1 (0.52)	2.08 (1.37)
	14.Facebook	1.84 (1.32)	1.16 (0.63)	2.53 (1.48)
	15.Twitter	1.08 (0.34)	1.01 (0.1)	1.16 (0.48)
	16.Skype	1.65 (1.05)	1.36 (0.84)	1.95 (1.16)
	17.You tube	2.87 (1.27)	2.49 (1.27)	3.26 (1.16)
	18.Google Earth	1.62 (0.96)	1.22 (0.58)	2.04 (1.09)
	19.Windows Live Messenger	1.17 (0.51)	1.02 (0.2)	1.33 (0.66)
	20.Other	0.13 (0.62)	0.18 (0.66)	0.08 (0.57)
	Total	18.69 (6.35)	15.18 (3.73)	22.66 (6.37)
Frequency of internet use with others M(SD)	Alone	2.97 (1.28)	2.54 (1.28)	3.42 (1.11)
	Mom	2.79 (1.24)	2.81 (1.3)	2.77 (1.18)
	Dad	2.78 (1.22)	2.84 (1.27)	2.71 (1.16)
	Brother	2.4 (1.36)	2.26 (1.37)	2.56 (1.33)
	Sister	2.39 (1.38)	2.24 (1.46)	2.56 (1.26)
	Cousin	2.21 (1.23)	2.09 (1.22)	2.35 (1.23)
	Family friend	2.08 (1.2)	1.86 (1.14)	2.31 (1.23)
	School friend	2.14 (1.22)	1.74 (1.09)	2.53 (1.22)
	Grandparents	1.47 (0.85)	1.52 (0.83)	1.41 (0.87)
	Total	16.96 (5.59)	16.21 (6.06)	17.84 (4.88)
Frequency of conversations with children about internet use M(SD)	About Facebook friends	2.37 (1.38)	1.77 (1.1)	2.95 (1.39)
	How to use internet	3.51 (1.17)	3.43 (1.21)	3.6 (1.14)
	About search of permitted internet contents	3.05 (1.5)	2.67 (1.5)	3.43 (1.4)
	E-mails exchange with friends	2.23 (1.35)	1.89 (1.28)	2.57 (1.34)
	Internet shopping	2.25 (1.48)	1.89 (1.39)	2.62 (1.48)
	Total	13.3 (5.4)	11.49 (4.99)	15.16 (5.2)

Finally, considering the question: 'Does your child use the words from the internet content?' it could be seen that there is the influence of the internet content regarding the use of the words which children read from the internet. It is interesting that this influence is more perceived by the parents of preschool children than in the subsample of the parents of school aged children. This difference could be explained by the fact that preschool children are indeed more vulnerable and non-critic to their environment than older children, what should be taken into account while creating some guidelines for parental education about computer and internet use. The second reason is purely developmental, since there is a big difference in cognitive development of preschool and school aged children.

Furthermore, parents showed medium informatics knowledge about computer and internet use. Testing the differences between parents of preschool and school aged children with the non-parametric Mann-Whitney U test, results showed significant difference between the informatics knowledge of these two subsamples of parents (z=-2.083, p=0.037). In other words, parents of preschool children showed significantly higher level of informatics knowledge than the parents of school aged children (Figure 3), what could be explained by the fact that parents of preschool children are younger. This explanation is confirmed by the later determined negative correlation coefficient between parents' age and their informatics knowledge (Table 2), younger parents showed significantly higher level of informatics knowledge than older parents. At the same Table and Figure it could be observed that children use of computer and internet is medium too. However, there is a significant difference in that use between parents' perception of preschool and school aged children's use (z=-8.112, p=0.001). School aged children significantly more use computers and internet than preschool children do, what was expected to be determined. Moreover, there was a significant difference in the presence of others

when children use computer and internet between parents' perception of preschool and school aged children. Parents of school aged children reported significantly more than their children use computer and internet alone (z=-4.857, p=0.001) and significantly less in the presence of others (z=-2.368, p=0.018) than parents of preschool children did. Finally, in general, parents reported that they discuss about internet content with their children in a medium amount. In addition, parents of preschool aged children talk significantly less with their children than parents of school aged children do (z=-4.710, p=0.001) what has got not so good implications concerning the development of constructive use of computer and internet.

Within the analysis of parents' self-rated attitudes toward internet use, which are displayed by the means of each individual item and by the mean of total scale in Table 3, it could be seen that they have in general positive attitudes toward internet use. As it was shown in the Figure 3, there were no significant difference in these attitudes between parents of preschool children and parents of school aged children (z=-0.495, p=0.621). In addition, there were no significant difference determined in the knowledge and attitudes about internet violence between parents of preschool children and parents of school aged children (z=-1.781, p=0.075). However, it must be emphasized that parents' knowledge about Internet violence is not sufficient as measured in this study, what definitely implied at the need for their education and development of more critical attitudes about internet violence. Parents' attitudes about computer games and the internet give a completely different picture of seeing the world of computer games. Parents of school children perceive computer games and the internet as a tool where children can develop their skills and quality of children spend time online than watching television. The dissertation Luba Zuk Levy (2009) examined attitudes about computers, self-efficacy and use of children and parents, with regard to gender and age differences in children

Figure 3. Means of focused variables in this study rated by parents of preschool children and school aged children

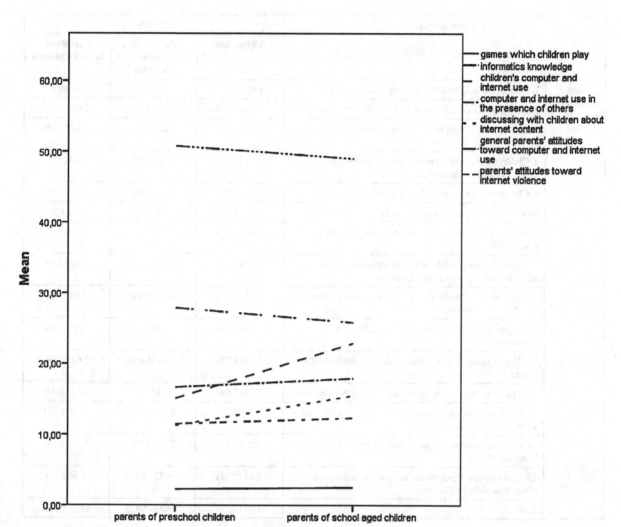

ages ten to fourteen, lived and stayed in the area of Tarrant County. Parents and children had statistically similar results in self-efficacy, but there is no statistically significant positive relationship between parent and child using a computer.

Parents of preschool children perceive computer games and the internet as a way of making friends and means where children can develop their skills using games on the computer. It is interesting in this debate to mention the views of students on part-time study early and pre-school education, where most of the parents, have attitude:

"I think it is important that the media no matter what it is you do not take control over the habits and lives of the people, indicating the importance of control over children playing."

Considering the descriptive analysis of parental perception of which computer games do they children play and what emotions they experience while playing them, determined results could be observed in the Table 4 and Figure 4. For better understanding, ratings of parents of preschool children will be explained first. In the issue of evaluation of frequency of playing above in the

Table 3. Parents' attitudes toward Internet use and Internet violence (all parents, parents of preschool children and parents of school aged children)

Parents' Attitudes		M (SD)		
		All Parents	**Parents of Preschool Children**	**Parents of School Children**
Toward Internet use	1. Internet can help children in doing schoolwork	1.81 (0.85)	1.93 (.92)	1.69 (0.76)
	2. Internet usage contributes to better communication	2.66 (1.11)	2.65 (1.1)	2.67 (1.13)
	3. Children spend their time on internet instead playing with peers	2.31 (1.34)	2.27 (1.31)	2.34 (1.37)
	4. Children can develop much better itw on abilities by means of games on internet.	3.34 (1.26)	3.38 (1.32)	3.30 (1.2)
	5. Children are less occupied with sport because of internet.	1.89 (1.26)	1.93 (1.15)	1.86 (1.36)
	6.Internet enables making new friends	3.21 (1.28)	3.35 (1.2)	3.07 (1.35)
	7. Internet enables to spread rumors, gossip and intrigue among children.	1.67 (1.02)	1.79 (1.11)	1.54 (.91)
	8. It is useful that a child can meet people of different interests from different parts of regions	2.78 (1.23)	2.87 (1.16)	2.68 (1.3)
	9. Using internet, children learn to be more independent in searching information.	2.17 (1.03)	2.39 (1.04)	1.94 (.96)
	10. Bigger usage of internet can evoke separation from parents and friends.	1.54 (0.89)	1.64 (.92)	1.44 (.86)
	11. Thanks internet usage, children develop intellectually faster.	2.74 (1.12)	2.81 (1.06)	2.67 (1.19)
	12. Thanks internet usage, children reach creative solutions	2.79 (1.04)	2.83 (1)	2.74 (1.09)
	13. It is better that children search explanations of unknown words in books than on internet.	2.22 (1.12)	2.24 (1.09)	2.20 (1.16)
	14. Children spend more quality time on internet than watching TV.	3.04 (1.11)	2.98 (1.04)	3.10 (1.19)
	15. Children who regularly use internet are in danger to create dependency of internet.	1.64 (0.91)	1.72 (.87)	1.56 (.95)
	Total	49.43 (7.1)	49.78 (7.63)	49.07 (6.52)

continued on following page

issue of frequency rating mentioned computer games which preschool child shows (Table 4) for logical games, the frequency is below than average, so M=2.87 (SD=1.25), but displayed emotions such as motivation for learning is M=0.53 (SD=0.56), emotion pleasure M=0.34 (SD=0.48), emotion happiness is M=0.27 (SD=0.45), emotion boredom is M=0.07 (SD=0.36), emotion anger is M=0.10 (SD=0.39), variable aggressive behavior M=0.03 (SD=0.30), variable readiness for quarrel M=0.06 (SD=0.42), indicate that preschool

aged children do not show special interest for that type of computer game. In second game-arcade game, the frequency is lower in relation to other games, so M=1.93 (SD=1.12) variable emotion which preschool aged child show such as motivation for learning is M=0.08 (SD=0.27) emotion pleasure M=0.22 (SD=0.42) variable happiness M=0.14 (SD=0.35), variable boredom M=0.09 (SD=0.29), variable anger M=0.10 (SD=0.40), variable aggressive behaviour M=0.10 (SD=0.18) and variable readiness for quarrel M=0.03

Table 3. Continued

Parents' Knowledge		Yes/No		
		All Parents	**Parents of Preschool Children**	**Parents of School Children**
about internet violence	Internet violence is illegal and harassing content (photos of children who fight, quarrel and consume alcohol.)	Yes=150 No=48 Missing=1	Yes=86 No=14	Yes=64 No=34 Missing=1
	Internet violence is searching pornography contents.	Yes=113 No=85 Missing=1	Yes=63 No=37	Yes=50 No=48 Missing=1
	Internet violence is sending harassing messages by e-mails or over chat.	Yes=146 No=52 Missing=1	Yes=77 No=23	Yes=69 No=29 Missing=1
	Internet violence is false identification as other child	Yes=114 No=83 Missing=2	Yes=61 No=39	Yes=53 No=44 Missing=2
	Internet violence is announcing private data or false data on chat, blog or internet site.	Yes=121 No=75 Missing=3	Yes=69 No=30 Missing=1	Yes=52 No=45 Missing=2
	Internet violence is theft of password for e-mail or nickname on chat	Yes=103 No=94 Missing=2	Yes=55 No=45	Yes=48 No=49 Missing=2
	Internet violence is form of pedophilia.	Yes=156 No=41 Missing=2	Yes=79 No=20 Missing=1	Yes=77 No=21 Missing=1
	Internet violence is ending virus to e-mail.	Yes=98 No=99 Missing=2	Yes=54 No=46	Yes=44 No=53 Missing=2
	Internet violence is sending harassing messages to e-mail.	Yes=147 No=51 Missing=1	Yes=76 No=24	Yes=71 No=27 Missing=1
	Internet violence is other	Yes=1 No=196 Missing=2	Yes=0 No=100	Yes=1 No=96 Missing=2
	Total	12.16 (2.98)	11.79 (2.8)	12.55 (3.12)

(SD=0.17), what indicates that type of computer game is not interesting as previous. In the third game, action game, frequency rating is below an average M=1.97 (SD=1.25) a variable emotions what a child shows such as motivation for learning is M=0.11 (SD=0.31), pleasure M=0.15 (SD=0.34), happiness M=0.15 (SD=0.36), variable boredom is M=0.05 (SD=0.22) what indicates that the most expresses variable is happiness. The range from minimum to maximum for action game is 1 to 5. The rating of these variables indicate that anger M=0.09 (SD=0.29) is more

expressed than variable aggressive behavior. M=0.07 (SD=0.36) and variable readiness for quarrel M=0.07 (SD=0.26). The fourth game is fun game at which the frequency of playing is mean average M=3.13 (SD=1.26). Emotions what a child show in this game is motivation for learning M=0.06 (SD=0.24), pleasure M=0.36 (SD=0.48) happiness M=0.50 (SD=0.50) boredom M=0.01 (SD=0.10) what indicates that positive emotions as happiness and pleasure are more frequent. The range for fun game is from 1 to 5, but other mentioned variables are from 0 to 1. The frequency of

Table 4. Descriptive parameters of computer games type children play and emotions which they experience while playing them perceived by their parents (all parents, parents of preschool children and parents of school aged children)

Games	Different Parents' Samples	The Frequency of Games M(SD)	Tick Emotions that Your Child Experiences during Playing Games						
			Motivation M(SD)	Pleasure M(SD)	Happiness M(SD)	Boredom M(SD)	Anger M(SD)	Aggression M(SD)	Quarelling M(SD)
Logical games	All parents	2.89 (1.25)	0.49 (0.53)	0.35 (0.48)	0.24 (0.43)	0.06 (0.3)	0.07 (0.31)	0.03 (0.23)	0.04 (0.31)
	Parents of preschoolers	2.87(1.25)	0.53(0.56)	0.34(0.48)	0.27 (0.45)	0.07 (0.36)	0.10 (0.39)	0.03(0.30)	0.06 (0.42)
	Parents of schoolers	2.92 (0.13)	0.44 0.5	0.35 0.48	0.21 0.41	0.05 0.22	0.12 0.56	0.1 0.55	0.04 0.2
Arcade games	All parents	2.08 (1.2)	0.08 (0.32)	0.26 (0.44)	0-13 (0.34)	0.09 (0.28)	0.11 (0.48)	0.07 (0.41)	0.04 (0.18)
	Parents of preschoolers	1.93 (1.12)	.08 .27	.22 .42	.14 .35	.09 .29	.10 .4	.10 .18	.03 .17
	Parents of schoolers	2.25 (1.27)	.07 .36	.29 .46	.12 .33	.08 .27	.12 .56	.10 .54	.04 .2
Action games	All parents	2.1 (1.36)	0.07 (0.26)	0.16 (0.37)	0.15 (0.35)	0.08 (0.26)	0.09 (0.28)	0.08 (0.32)	0.07 (0.25)
	Parents of preschoolers	1.79 (1.25)	.11 .31	.13 .34	.15 .36	.05 .22	.09 .29	.07 .356	.07 .26
	Parents of schoolers	2.23 (1.46)	.03 .17	.19 .4	.14 .35	.10 .3	.08 .27	.08 .27	.08 .27
Fun games	All parents	3.18 (1.23)	0.07 (0.25)	0.33 (0.47)	0.5 (0.5)	0.03 (0.17)	0.03 (0.16)	0.07 (0.35)	0.02 (0.14)
	Parents of preschoolers	3.13 (1.26)	.06 .24	.36 .48	.50 .5	.01 .1	.03 .17	.10 .46	.03 .17
	Parents of schoolers	3.23 (1.2)	.07 .26	.30 .46	.51 .5	.05 .22	.02 .14	.03 .17	.01 .1
Sport games	All parents	2.68 (1.4)	0.08 (0.27)	0.3 (0.46)	0.27 (0.44)	0.05 (0.22)	0.06 (0.24)	0.07 (0.35)	0.04 (0.18)
	Parents of preschoolers	2.59 (1.41)	.09 .288	.34 .48	28 .45	.04 .18	.04 .2	.07 .36	.03 .17
	Parents of schoolers	2.75 (1.41)	.07 .26	.27 .444	.26 .438	.06 .240	.08 .274	.06 .345	.04 .198
Car games	All parents	2.38 (1.37)	0.07 (0.25)	0.24 (0.43)	0.23 (0.42)	0.07 (0.26)	0.09 (0.29)	0.04 (0.25)	0.07 (0.35)
	Parents of preschoolers	2.27 (1.43)	.07 .26	.23 .42	.23 .42	.05 .22	.08 .27	.02 .14	.07 .36
	Parents of schoolers	2.48 (1.3)	.06 .24	.24 .43	.23 .42	.09 .29	.10 .3	.05 .33	.06 .34
Old games	All parents	2.03 (1.14)	0.06 (0.24)	0.23 (0.42)	0.2 (0.4)	0.14 (0.34)	0.04 (0.2)	0.01 (0.1)	0.03 (0.16)
	Parents of preschoolers	2.17 (1.78)	.07 .26	.27 .45	.21 .41	.12 .33	.05 .22	.01 .1	.03 .17
	Parents of schoolers	.19 (1.07)	.05 .22	.19 .4	.19 .4	.15 .36	.03 .17	.01 .1	.02 .14

continued on following page

Table 4. Continued

Games	Different Parents' Samples	The Frequency of Games M(SD)	Tick Emotions that Your Child Experiences during Playing Games						
			Motivation M(SD)	Pleasure M(SD)	Happiness M(SD)	Boredom M(SD)	Anger M(SD)	Aggression M(SD)	Quarelling M(SD)
Adventure games	All parents	2.3 (1.32)	0.11 (0.31)	0.24 (0.43)	0.25 (0.44)	0.07 (0.25)	0.04 (0.2)	0.02 (0.12)	0.05 (0.33)
	Parents of preschoolers	2.13 (1.25)	.12 .327	.23 .423	.22 .416	.08 .273	.05 .219	.02 .141	.09 .452
	Parents of schoolers	2.47 (1.36)	.09 .29	.24 .43	.28 .45	.05 .22	.03 .17	.01 .1	.01 .1
Board games	All parents	2.28 (1.31)	0.26 (0.6)	0.2 (0.4)	0.19 (0.39)	0.09 (0.28)	0.04 (0.18)	0.03 (0.16)	0.05 (0.32)
	Parents of preschoolers	2.42 (1.35)	.31 .58	.19 .39	.19 .39	.06 .24	.03 .17	.02 .14	.07 .42
	Parents of schoolers	2.15 (1.26)	.20 .61	.20 .4	.19 .4	.11 .32	.04 .2	.03 .17	.02 .14
Children games	All parents	3.26 (1.31)	0.19 (0.51)	0.37 (0.48)	0.41 (0.49)	0.05 (0.21)	0.03 (0.17)	0.01 (0.1)	0.03 (0.16)
	Parents of preschoolers	3.43 (1.28)	.21 .41	.38 .49	.50 .50	.02 .14	.05 .22	.01 .1	.02 .14
	Parents of schoolers	3.09 (1.32)	.17 .59	.35 .48	.32 .47	.07 .26	.01 .1	.01 .1	.03 .17
Shooting games	All parents	1.73 (1.1)	0.06 (0.43)	0.11 (0.4)	0.08 (0.27)	0.06 (0.23)	0.11 (0.32)	0.1 (0.3)	0.09 (0.29)
	Parents of preschoolers	1.58 (1.04)	.02 .14	.07 .26	.05 .22	.03 .17	.13 .34	.11 .32	.11 .32
	Parents of schoolers	1.88 (1.14)	.09 .59	.15 .50	.11 .32	.08 .27	.09 .29	.09 .29	.07 .26
Total	All parents	2.4 (0.81)	1.47 (1.97)	2.76 (2.75)	2.67 (2.49)	0.75 (1.46)	0.7 (1.65)	0.49 (1.16)	0.49 (1.33)
	Parents of preschoolers	2.38 (0.84)	1.64 1.79	2.74 2.68	2.76 2.46	0.63 1.16	0.76 1.74	0.49 1.05	0.61 1.38
	Parents of schoolers	2.43 (0.77)	1.31 2.13	2.77 2.84	2.58 2.53	0.88 1.7	0.65 1.57	0.49 1.26	0.37 1.27

emotion anger is M=0.03 (SD=0.17), aggressive behaviour is M=0.10 (SD=0.46) readiness for quarrel M=0.03 (SD=0.17) what indicates that the parents have mostly perceived aggressive behavior.

The fifth game is sport game where the frequency of playing is below than average so is M=2.59 (SD=1.41), variable motivation for learning is M=0.09 (SD=0.29), pleasure M=0.34 (SD=0.48), happiness M=0.28 (SD=0.45), boredom M=0.04 (SD=0.18). The range for this game is 1 to 5 but other mentioned variables are

from 0 to 1. The frequency of emotion anger is M=0.04 (SD=0.20), aggressive behavior is M=0.07 (SD=0.36), readiness for quarrel M=0.03 (SD=0.17) what indicates that the parents have perceived aggressive behaviour in sport game. Car game is the sixth game where the frequency is below than average M=2.27 (SD=1.43), emotions that a child show such as motivation for learning is M=0.07 (SD=0.26), pleasure M=0.23 (SD=0.42), happiness M=0.23 (SD=0.42) boredom M=0.05 (SD=0.22), it indicates more frequent appearing of

Figure 4. Means of emotions that children experience while playing computer games perceived by parents of preschool children and parents of school aged children

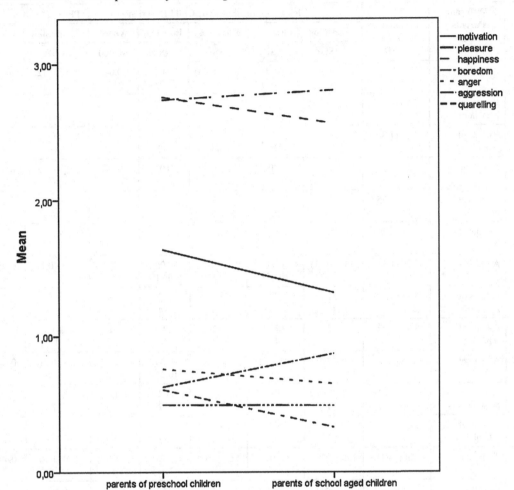

positive emotions such as pleasure and happiness. The range is from 1 to 5 but for other variables is 0 to 1. Higher frequency rating of emotions has anger M=0.08 (SD=0.27) in relation to aggressive behaviour M=0.02 (SD=0.14) and readiness for quarrel M=0.07 (SD=0.36). The seventh game is old game where the frequency is below tna an average so is M=2.17 (SD=1.78) and the rating show that positive emotions (pleasure and happiness), have the highest rating. Motivation for learning is M=0.07 (SD=0.26), pleasure M=0.27 (SD=0.45), happiness M=0.21 (SD=0.41), boredom M=0.12 (SD=0.33), anger M=0.05 (SD=0.22), aggressive behaviour M=0.01 (SD=0.10) and readiness for

quarrel M=0.03 (SD=0.17). The eight game is adventure game where the frequency rating of playing is below than an average so is M=2.13 (SD=1.25), but rating show the highest frequency have pleasure and happiness, motivation for learning is M=0.12 (SD=0.33), pleasure M=0.23 (SD=0.42), happiness M=0.22 (SD=0.42), boredom M=0.08 (SD=0.27), anger M=0.05 (SD=0.22), aggressive behaviour M=0.02 (SD=0.14) readiness for quarrel M=0.09 (SD=0.45).

The ninth game is board game where the frequency has an approximate average M=2.42 (SD=1.35), but the highest frequency has pleasure and happiness; motivation for learning M=0.31

(SD=0.58), pleasure M=0.19 (SD=0.39), happiness M=0.19 (SD=0.39) boredom M=0.06 (SD=0.24), anger M=0.03 (SD=0.17), aggressive behaviour M=0.02 (SD=0.14) readiness for quarrel M=0.07 (SD=0.42). The tenth game children game is with rating M=3.43 (SD=1.28) what indicates more frequent level of playing such as motivation for learning M=0.21(SD=0.41) pleasure M=0.38 (SD=0.49), happiness M=0.50 (SD=0.50), boredom M=0.02 (SD=0.14), anger M=0.05 (SD=0.22), aggressive behaviour M=0.01 (SD=0.10) readiness for quarrel M=0.02 (SD=0.14), what indicate the highest frequency have happiness and pleasure. The eleventh game is shooting game where the frequency of playing is very below an average so is M=1.58 (SD=1.04), the rating of emotions such as motivation for learning is M=0.02 (SD=0.14), pleasure M=0.07 (SD=0.26), happiness M=0.05 (SD=0.22), boredom M=0.03 (SD=0.17), anger M=0.13 (SD=0.34), aggressive behaviour M=0.11 (SD=0.32) readiness for quarrel M=0.11 (SD=0.32) what indicates the appearance of negative emotions such as anger and aggressive behaviour. From mentioned, it is clear that children game as the highest rating of frequency at preschool aged children and the most usual emotions are comfort and happiness. Specific quality has shooting game in accordance with results, preschool and school aged children do not play often. Other researches such as Bateman (2013) indicate appearance of emotions such as fear, surprise, disgust, pride, triumph, hilarity and wonderment.

Ratings of Parents of School Aged Children

In the issue of frequency rating mentioned games and emotions at school aged children (Table 4), the issue of logical game, the frequency of playing is average M=2.92 (SD=0.13), emotions what children show are motivation for learning M=0.47 (SD=0.50) emotion pleasure M=0.35

(SD=0.48) emotion happiness M=0.21 (SD=0.41) emotion boredom M=0.5 (SD=0.22), emotion anger is M=0.12 (SD=0.56), variable aggressive behaviour M=0.10 (SD=0.55), readiness for quarrel M=0.04 (SD=0.20) what indicates that motivation for learning is the most frequent emotion at school aged children. The second game is arcade game where frequency of playing is below than an average so is M= 2.25 (SD=1.27). The highest rating of frequency has emotion pleasure as you can see from the attached: emotion motivation for learning M=0.07 (SD=0.36), pleasure M=0.29 (SD=0.46), variable happiness M=0.12 (SD=0.33), variable boredom M=0.08 (SD=0.27), variable anger M=0.12 (SD=0.56), variable aggressive behaviour M=0.10 (SD=0.54) and variable readiness for quarrel and M=0.04 (SD=0.20). In the third game, action game, the frequency of playing is below than an average mean rating has positive emotions pleasure and motivation for learning M=0.3 (SD=0.17) emotion pleasure M=0.19 (SD=0.40), emotion happiness M=0.14 (SD=0.35), variable boredom M=0.01 (SD=0.30). The range of action game is 1 to 5 but for other variables is 0 to 1. For variable anger is M=0.08 (SD=0.27), variable aggressive behaviour M=0.08 (SD=0.27) and variable readiness for quarrel is M=0.06 (SD=0.24). The fourth game is fun game where frequency rating is higher in relation to others so is M=3.23 (SD=1.20). Emotions that a child show in this game are: motivation for learning M=0.07 (SD=0.26), pleasure M=0.30 (SD=0.46), happiness M=0.51 (SD=0.50). boredom M=0.05 (SD=0.22) what indicates that positive emotions (pleasure and happiness). The range for fun game is 1 to 5 but for other is 0 to 1. For variable anger M=0.02 (SD=0.14), variable aggressive behaviour M=0.03 (SD=0.17) readiness for quarrel M=0.01 (SD=0.10). The fifth game is sport game where the frequency is below than an average so is M=2.75 (SD=1.41). Emotions what school aged children are significantly identified are motivation for learning M=0.07 (SD=0.26), pleasure M=0.27 (SD=0.44), happiness M=0.26

(SD=0.44), boredom M=0.06 (SD=0.24) but pleasure and happiness have approximate ratings and usually appeared at school aged children. The range for sport game is from 1 to 5, but for other 0 to 1. Variable anger is M=0.08 (SD=0.27), aggressive behaviour is M=0.06 (SD=0.34), readiness for quarrel M=0.04 (SD=0.20). Car game where frequency rating is mean M=2.48 (SD=1.30). Emotions that school aged children show as motivation for learning M=0.06 (SD=0.24), pleasure M=0.24 (SD=0.43).happiness M=0.23 (SD=0.42),boredom M=0.09 (SD=0.29) it indicates that the most frequent are pleasure and happiness. In emotion anger M=0.10 (SD=0.30), aggressive behaviour M=0.05 (SD=0.33), readiness for quarrel M=0.06 (SD=0.35), it is obvious that the most frequent emotion is anger for this game. The seventh game is old game where frequency is rare M=0.19 (SD=1.07). Emotions that a child shows are significantly identified such as M=0.05 (SD=0.22), pleasure M=0.19 (SD=0.40), happiness M=0.19 (SD=0.40), boredom M=0.15 (SD=0.36), anger M=0.03 (SD=0.17), aggressive behavior M=0.01 (SD=0.10) and readiness for quarrel M=0.02 (SD=0.14). It indicates that emotions such as pleasure and happiness are most frequent emotions at school aged children. The eight game is adventure game where is below an average M=2.47 (SD=1.36) and emotions such as motivation for learning M=0.09 (SD=0.29), pleasure M=0.24 (SD=0.43), happiness M=0.28 (SD=0.45), boredom M=0.05 (SD=0.22), anger M=0.03 (SD=0.17), aggressive behaviour M=0.01 (SD=0.10) readiness for quarrel M=0.01 (SD=0.10) what indicates that positive emotions predominance negative emotions again. The ninth game is board game where the frequency of playing is below an average M=2.15 (SD=1.26). Emotion such motivation for learning is M=0.20 (SD=0.61), pleasure M=0.20 (SD=0.40), happiness M=0.19 (SD=0.40) boredom M=0.11 (SD=0.32), anger M=0.04 (SD=0.20), aggressive behaviour M=0.03 (SD=0.17) readiness for quarrel M=0.02 (SD=0.14). It indicates that the most frequent

emotions are pleasure and happiness. The tenth game is children game where frequency rating is higher so M=3.09 (SD=1.32). Emotions shown by school aged children are: motivation for learning M=0.17 (SD=0.59), pleasure M=0.35 (SD=0.48), happiness M=0.32 (SD=0.47), boredom M=0.07 (SD=0.26) anger M=0.01 (SD=0.10), aggressive behaviour M=0.01 (SD=0.10) readiness for quarrel is M=0.03 (SD=0.17). The shown emotions indicate that positive emotions have predominance. The eleventh game is shooting game where rating frequency is lower M=1.88 (SD=1.14), the rating of emotions: motivation for learning M=0.09 (SD=0,59), pleasure M=0.15 (SD=0.50) happiness M=0.11 (SD=0.32), boredom M=0.08 (SD=0.27), anger M=0.09 (SD=0.29), aggressive behaviour M=0.09 (SD=0.29) readiness for quarrel M=0.07 (SD=0.26). The results show that positive emotions have predominance but not insofar as previous games. The interest of results at school aged children correspond preschool aged children's results. The highest ratings have children game and fun game and in this case positive emotions have predominance.

Analysing all games in total and related children's emotions, it could be seen that it was determined lower levels of motivation (M=1.63, SD=1.80), while the average value of pleasure M=2.73 (SD=2.69) as well as happiness M=2.76 (SD=2.46). The values of other parameters for the emotions are as below average, so far, M=0.63 (SD=1.16), anger M=0.76 (SD=1.74), aggression M=0.50 (SD=1.05), quarreling M=0.61 (SD=1.38). The results are generally in line with our expectations and the children have shown an average level of positive emotions such as pleasure and happiness. To substantiate the results of this study, we observe them in relation to others that we also confirm the relevance of the obtained results. A list of emotions by Bateman (2013), which addresses the emotions of pleasure, happiness, pride, triumph, surprises but the difference is that unlike this study will be supported. Bateman connects emotions to biological mechanisms.

Similar research was conducted by Lazzaro (2003) where he had discussed the emotions of fear, surprise, triumph, pleasure, pride and even disgust. In addition, there were no significant difference between ratings of computer games type by parents of preschool and school aged children (z=-0.571, p=0.568). Considering the related children's emotions, parents did differentiated significantly in their ratings only about children experienced motivation during playing (z=-2.520, p=0.012), what could be observed in the Figure 4. Therefore, parents of preschool children reported that their children experienced significantly more motivation for computer games than parents of school aged children, what is very interesting. There were no other significant differences regarding other related emotions.

Preschool and School Aged Children's Perception of Computer and Internet Use

With the aim of examining preschool and school aged children's perception of computer and internet use, several variables have been measured:

1. The general data about preschool children (gender, age, family structure, food consumption while playing computer games, institutional care and education);
2. Children's perceptions of their internet use;
3. Children's perceptions of their internet use in the presence of adults;
4. Children's perceptions of their playing computer games and the correlated emotions; and
5. Children's perceptions of their activities in the situations of internet violence. All general data were presented in the Table 5.

Besides previously described children's gender and age, other relevant general data showed that all examined preschool children went to a kindergarten. Regarding the school children, 17.6% of

them were enrolled at the second grade, 18.6% of them at the fourth grade, 4.5% of them at the sixth grade and 8.5% of them at the eighth grade. More than half of the preschool children eat food during playing on the computer, while approximately one third of the school aged children have the same behavior while using computer. In both subsamples, the level of the food consumption during computer use is rather high, what is not good from two perspectives: for development of bad eating habits and for development of sedentary and dependent behavior. This finding should be taken into account when creating educational workshops with parents. Moreover, considering children's internet activities, it could be observed that they show numerous activities, but playing favourite games is the most desirable and popular activity regardless of their age. Also, there was no significant difference between Internet activities mean between preschool and school aged children. Very interesting finding as reported by children is the one related with their ratings about their internet use in the presence of adults. Preschool children reported that they are more frequently spending their computer time alone, than in the presence of other, and significantly more than school aged children (z=-7.889, p=0.001). As it was previously reported, there was no significant difference between parents of preschool and school aged children. It is even more interesting, that parents' and children's ratings are significantly different in the same question. Parents of preschool children reported that their children spend less time alone with the computer than their children themselves. On the other side, parents of school aged children reported that their children spent more time alone with a computer than the children themselves. Since, this variable of the presence of others during children's computer and internet use is very important regarding the parental control and because of that, it has very socially desirable potential, it is very hard to be interpreted and discussed. We can ask ourselves: "What is the truth?" Even though this findings

Table 5. Descriptive parameters (frequencies, means (M), standard deviations (SD) and ranges) of socio-demographic variables, food consumption, Internet activities of children, the use of Internet in the presence of others (preschool children and school aged children)

Data Collected from Children (N=199)		
	Preschool Children (N=100)	**School Aged Children (N=99)**
Gender	F=54 M=46	F=52 M=47
Age	M=4.97 (SD=0.92); 2-7	M=9.50 (SD= 2.13); 7-14
Do you consume food during playing on the computer?	Yes=50 No=46 Missing=4	Yes=37 No=59 Missing=3
Circle what you attend	Kindergarten=100	PS 2ND Class =35 PS 4TH Class =37 PS 6 TH Class =10 PS 8TH Class =17
Internet activities. M(SD) — Visit Facebook, Twitter/ visit specialized sites for friendship (Facebook, Myspace etc..)	1.66 (1.2)	2.46 (1.56)
Search coloring pages, games. surf website and search interesting	2.93 (1.38)	2.51 (1.15)
Search interesting topic (dinosaurs various animals, plants). search content which can help in writing homework, articles or lecture.	2.57 (1.44)	2.41 (1.22)
Talk with friends over skype or Facebook/search additional literature about school and schoolwork	1.87 (1.31)	1.84 (0.92)
Play favourite games/visit forums and different chat rooms	3.15 (1.44)	1.39 (1.01)
Send e-mails to friends, family members/visit sites for adults	1.36 (0.98)	1.25 (0.72)
Total	13.58 (4.78)	12.02 (3.96)
Frequency of internet use with others M(SD) — Alone	3.29 (1.42)	1.22 (1.84)
Mom	1.87 (1.29)	3.56 (1.44)
Dad	1.96 (1.28)	2.17 (1.2)
Brother	1.89 (1.42)	1.92 (1.32)
Sister	1.9 (1.39)	1.86 (1.29)
Cousin	2.04 (1.36)	1.99 (1.16)
Family friend	2.53 (1.43)	1.78 (1.02)
School friend	2.33 (1.48)	2.35 (1.33)
Grandparents	1.68 (1.15)	1.41 (0.95)
Total	15 (5.59)	16.96 (5.59)

could be interpreted as the presence of very small parental control overall, no matter to children's age due to data discrepancy, tt this moment, it only could be concluded that these findings are not congruent, and this variable should be measured in different way in future studies.

Furthermore, Table 5 shows the feelings of preschool aged children while playing games on the computer. In the issue of assessment how the preschool aged child feels while playing games on the computer, in a sense *I am very keen on playing computer* average response was both agree and disagree M = 3.21 (SD = 1.41). In a sense *I am glad playing on the computer*, the average response was disagree M = 3.66 (SD = 1.40).

Children are on the 'item I want to play for a long time on the Internet', express agreement and disagreement, M = 3.29 (SD = 1.50). In the assertion I constantly search on the internet what I want to play, preschool aged children express agreement and disagreement M = 3.19 (SD = 1.57). In the assertion 'playing on internet motivate me for learning' the average response is M = 2.22 (SD = 1.33). In the assertion 'playing on the computer helps me develop my creative abilities' M = 2.52 (SD = 1.57). In the assertion 'I am bored playing on the computer' preschoolers expressed disagreement M = 1.58 (SD = 1.11), on the issue 'I am angry if I play for a long time on the computer', preschoolers expressed disagreement M = 1.36 (SD = 0.90). Regarding assertion 'I quarrel with parents if parents will not let me play more' children have expressed disagreement M = 1.51 (SD = 0.95), the claim 'if my parents did not let me play as much as I want, in defiance not want anything else' to do response of preschool aged children was disagree M = 1.36 (SD = 1.08) and with assertion that 'I am aggressive if someone interferes while playing' M = 1.86 (SD = 1.26), the claim 'I feel a lot better to be out with friends than playing games on the computer, the answer is that preschool aged children are very disagreed M = 4.26 (SD = 1.28). The range of variables all emotion is from 1 to 5. For descriptive indicators for preschool aged children experienced emotions while playing various computer games, preschool aged children showed the most agreement on claims much better to me to be out with friends than playing games on the computer and make them happy play games on the computer, it may be desirable and good for preschoolers.

When it is asked to estimate how school aged child feels while playing games on the computer followed by responses that are shown in Table 6. In assertions, 'I am very keen playing on the computer', the average response was agree and disagree M = 3.35 (SD = 1.27), with claims 'It pleases me playing on the computer' average response was agree and disagree M = 3.74 (SD = 1.08), with claims 'I want to play for a long time on the Internet', the average response was M = 2.68 SD = 1.42. in the assertion 'I constantly search on the internet what I want to play' the average response was M = 2.66 (SD = 1.29), with claims of 'playing on the internet motivates me to learn', we got an answer and I agree I disagree M = 1.76 (SD = 1.08), the 'assertion playing on the computer helps me develop my creative abilities' average response was agree and disagree M = 2.23 (SD = 1.24), in assertions 'I am bored playing on the computer', school aged children partly expressed disagreement M = 2.23 (SD = 1.24), with assertion 'I am angry if I play on the computer for a long time', school aged children expressed disagreement M = 1.99 (SD = 1, 27) in this assertion 'I quarrel with parents if they will not let me play longer', school aged children have expressed disagreement M = 1.60 (SD = 1.15), in assertion 'if my parents did not let me play as much as I want, in defiance not want anything else to do', it is expressed disagreement M = 1.76 (SD = 1.14). In assentation 'if my parents did not let me play as much as I want, in defiance not want anything else', school aged children expressed agreement and disagreement M = 2.24 (SD = 1.42), in an assertion 'I am aggressive if someone disturbed while playing', school aged children partly expressed disagreement M = 1.74 (SD = 1.03); in saying 'a lot better to me to be out with friends than playing games on the computer', the answer was agree and disagree M = 3.03 (SD = 1.10). The range of these variables from is 1 to 5. For descriptive indicators for school aged children experienced emotions while playing various computer games, the greatest agreement is on the assertion 'I am very keen playing on the computer and I am happy to play on the computer', at least matching the claim playing on the computer motivates me to learn. It shows that school aged children do not perceive the computer as an aid in school activities. There are significant

Table 6. Descriptive parameters of children's feelings during playing computer games and children's activities in the situations of internet violence (preschool and school aged children)

	M (SD)	
	Preschool Children	**School Aged Children**
1. I am very thrilled with playing on the computer.	3.21 (1.41)	3.35 (1.27)
2. I am happy to play on the computer.	3.36 (1.40)	3.74 (1.08)
3. I show o a wish to play longer on the computer.	3.29 (1.5)	2.68 (1.42)
4.I always search on the internet what I want to play	3.19 (1.57)	2.66 (1.42)
5. Playing on the computer motivate me for learning.	2.22 (1.33)	1.76 (1.08)
6.Playing on the computer helps me to develop my creative abilities	2.52 (1.57)	2.23 (1.24)
7.It is boring to play on the computer	1.58 (1.11)	2.23 (1.24)
8.I get angry when I play longer	1.36 (0.9)	1.99 (1.27)
9. I quarrel with parents if they do not to allow me play longer.	1.51 (.95)	1.55 (1.06)
10. If parents do not allow to play as I want, in my grudge I do not want to do anything else.	1.36 (1.08)	2.24 (1.42)
11. I am aggressive someone disturbes me while playing	1.86 (1.26)	1.74 (1.03)
12. I feel much better to spend time outside with my friends than playing computer.	4.26 (1.28)	3.03 (1.10)
Total	23.02 (7.89)	25.84 (7.36)
When someone had been violent over internet, I would say it my parents	3.61 (1.81)	3.26 (1.42)
I would not visit that site more. Block a person who insults me.	1.54 (1.16)	3.35 (1.56)
I would say a friend	1.84 (1.34)	2.81 (1.43)
I would show it an adult person.	2.43 (1.64)	2.88 (1.58)
I would say brother or sister.	2.53 (1.76)	2.51 (1.47)
I would officially report (administrator of the site, police…)l	2.17 (1.64)	2.14 (1.42)
I would say to preschool teacher or teacher.	2.7 (1.81)	2.4 (1.5)
I would do the same.	1.2 (0.72)	1.91 (1.27)
I would smile to this	1.09 (0.51)	1.63 (1.11)
I would not do anything.	1.29 (0.97)	1.65 (1)
I would not visit internet more.	2.55 (1.42)	1.85 (1.19)
Total	33.5 (6.86)	33.45 (7.41)

research on emotions of school aged children, says research Kirsh (2009), who reported that the children of the third and fourth grade who have played Mortal Kombat 2, a violent game away violently responded to the open-closed questions as opposed to children who play basketball. Also, relevant research for school aged children was carried out in Croatia by association Tić (tested the 2072 pupils). There are no significant differences in feelings of preschool and school aged children.

To examine children's perception of their activities in the situations of internet violence it could be observed that no matter to children's age they would act appropriately in the situations of the internet violence. Preschool children showed more passive strategies due to lower levels of their informatics knowledge and more strategies that include telling others. On the other side, school aged children showed more active and independent strategies in these situations, what is expected considering their age. The results show good average rating for saying parents about Internet violence (M=3.61, SD=1.81) for preschoolers and M=3.26 (SD= 1.42) for schoolers. It is interesting that there are differences in interpreting results about visiting that site more or blocking a person who insults child. The preschool aged children have below average (M=1.54, SD=1.16) and school aged children M=3.35 (SD=1.56). Below average is also shown in variables such as 'doing the same' M=1.2 (SD=0.72) for preschool aged children, M=1.91 (SD=1.27) for school aged children 'smiling to this' M=1.09 (SD=0.51) for preschool aged children M=1.63 (SD=1.11) for school aged children, 'doing nothing' M=1.29 (SD=0.97) for preschool aged children M=1.65 (SD=1) for school aged children. The results are in accordance with expected results. To corroborate results of this research, it would be observed in respect to other researches and findings. Similar results are from nongovernmental association Hrabri telefon about findings of internet violence: 15% - someone wrote and published secrets or lies about me 5% - someone has put my pictures or movies and is accompanied by unpleasant comments 20% - someone posing as me and speak / write in my name 18% - someone insisted on meeting in person, whom I did not want. There are a lot of other researches about internet violence but do not talk about children's reactions.

CORRELATIONAL ANALYSIS OF ALL VARIABLES OF PARENTS' AND (PRE)SCHOOL CHILDREN'S PERCEPTION OF COMPUTER AND INTERNET USE AND RELEVANT SOCIO-DEMOGRAPHIC VARIABLES

Considering very complex correlational design of this empirical research, several correlational analysis were run, all of them by calculating Spearman's correlation coefficients. The results from the first one, which included correlations between socio-demographic variables, informatics knowledge, the internet use of children, the use of internet in the presence of other and conversations with children about internet content, general attitudes toward computer and internet use and knowledge about internet violence from the parents' perception, were presented in Table 6. Therefore, it could be seen, that fathers perceived playing computer games as more frequent than mothers did, what is interesting finding. Older parents reported significantly less informatics knowledge and less knowledge about internet violence of their own than younger parents. Besides, older parents perceived more computer use of their children. These findings definitely implied at the need for different educational workshops considering the parents' age. Interesting finding is the one related to the significant positive correlation between number of family members and parents' knowledge about internet violence. Parents from the family with more family members reported to have significantly higher levels of knowledge about internet violence, what could be explained by the fact that more family members have more information in general and greater sharing of those information. However, this finding deserves to be explored furthermore in the future studies.

The higher educational levels in mothers and fathers were significantly correlated with their higher informatics knowledge, perceived less children computer use, fewer discussions about internet application and less knowledge about internet violence. Besides, higher educated mothers perceived significantly less children's computer use in the presence of others. It seems that educational level of parents is very important factor, which moderates the ways of parental control in the situations of children's computer and internet use. Moreover, parents with a higher perception of more independent computer use by their children, also perceived less playing computer games, less computer use, less computer use in the presence of others, less discussions about internet application and more positive attitudes toward computer use by their children. Greater number of computer in their homes have those parents who showed significantly greater informatics knowledge but more negative attitudes toward computer use, what is very interesting. Parents who explained Internet content to their children more often, they have lees informatics knowledge, less discussion about Internet application and more knowledge about internet violence. Parents, who rated higher the children's word use form the internet, also perceived that their children were playing fewer games, that they have fewer informatics knowledge and fewer talks about internet application.

Parents, who perceived more frequent playing games in their children, also rated children's computer use as fewer, but more computer use in the presence of others and more talks about internet application. It is interesting that those parents who showed higher informatics knowledge also showed more negative attitudes toward children's computer use and less knowledge about internet violence. Higher computer use of children is positively correlated with more talks about Internet application, more computer use in the presence of others and less positive attitudes toward computer and Internet use in general. Overall, this analysis confirmed that parents' attitudes are strongly correlated with their overall behavior within their control of children's computer and Internet use. More negative attitudes resulted with more control as measured by several variables in this research.

Another problem concerns the relationship between some socio-demographic variables (gender, age, level of parental control over the use of computers) with frequency of different emotions while playing computer games for children of preschool and school-aged children. To clarify this issue it will be used correlation analysis, whose results are shown in Table 8 it is determined statistically significant negative correlation between age and their parents' perception of motivation among children experience of playing computer games ($r = -0.22$, $p = 0.01$). In other words, younger parents are significantly more perceived experience of motivation in their

children during the playing of computer games as opposed to older parents. Relevant correlative research of students (Warschauer, 1996) included a correlation with the personal aspects of motivation. Multivariate analysis of variance (MANOVA) between sex and 30 motivational issues and whether or not they have a computer showed no significant relationship. Nevertheless, the third factor indicated that students feel that their computer can help them learning better and be independent within their learning process.

There was a statistically significant negative correlation between the estimated motivation of children and parents' assessments of explaining the contents of the program, which is his / her perceived on the internet ($r = -0.17$ $p = 0.05$), which means that as more parents explained the contents of the program, (pre) school aged children are less experienced motivation. There was a statistically significant negative correlation between feelings of wellbeing in preschool and school aged children and parental perception of words that a child benefits from the content that is viewed on the internet ($r = -0.21$, $p = 0.01$). In other words, as more as parents estimate children use words from the internet their level of wellbeing is being over estimated. This finding is logical, given that children are more likely to repeat and imitate those contents (in this case, words) that experience comfortable and accept. There was a statistically negative correlation between the estimated level of aggression of children and parental perceptions of independent computer use ($r = 0.16$ $p = 0.05$), with the level of aggression increases with independent use of computers among children. This finding may be explained by the lower external control present in the independent use of computers, and then the possibility of higher levels of aggression increased. Relevant research by Allen (2013) predicts that there will be no correlation between violence found in video games and real life (physical violence), but maintains that the conclusions cannot be drawn because of the relatively small sample size.

Table 7. Correlation matrix of socio-demographic variables, informatics knowledge, the Internet use of children, the use of Internet in the presence of other and conversations with children about Internet content, general attitudes toward computer and Internet use and knowledge about Internet violence from the parents' perception

		Games	Informatics Knowledge	Computer Use	Others	Talks	Attitudes	Violence
Parents' gender	rho	-,223**	-,079	,000	-,043	,019	,085	,029
	p	,004	,298	,995	,633	,795	,254	,691
Parents' age	rho	-,101	-,187*	,215**	-,029	,105	,017	-,167*
	p	,232	,020	,006	,766	,189	,827	,031
Family members	rho	,012	-,082	,033	-,007	-,063	,054	,142*
	p	,877	,281	,658	,935	,399	,471	,049
Edu. Level mothers	rho	-,146	,374**	-,211**	-,193*	-,222**	-,083	-,252**
	p	,061	,000	,004	,033	,003	,268	,000
Edu. Level fathers	rho	-,035	,240**	-,182*	-,099	-,254**	-,049	-,247**
	p	,655	,002	,015	,280	,001	,517	,001
Indep. use	rho	-,284**	-,091	-,611**	-,261**	-,324**	,241**	-,003
	p	,000	,231	,000	,003	,000	,001	,972
Computer number	rho	,073	,331**	,091	,115	,088	-,155*	-,103
	p	,348	,000	,222	,203	,234	,036	,152
Explanations	rho	-,019	-,168*	,090	-,036	-,186*	,036	,235**
	p	,805	,026	,229	,694	,012	,628	,001
Words use	rho	-,212**	-,180*	-,050	-,087	-,217**	,118	,040
	p	,007	,018	,503	,344	,003	,113	,581
Games	rho	1,000	,121	,255**	,418**	,345**	-,156	,046
	p		,144	,001	,000	,000	,055	,568
Inf. knowledge	rho		1,000	-,088	-,034	,098	-,200*	-,210**
	p			,261	,720	,215	,010	,006
Computer use	rho			1,000	,449**	,421**	-,210**	,115
	p				,000	,000	,006	,126
Others	rho				1,000	,342**	-,001	,055
	p					,000	,992	,548
Talks	rho					1,000	-,140	-,040
	p						,069	,592
Attitudes	rho						1,000	,047
	p							,527
Violence	rho							1,000
	p							

**p<0,01; *p<0,05.

Table 8. Correlation matrix of socio-demographic variables from parents and emotions that children experience while playing the computer games

		Motivation	Pleasure	Happiness	Bored	Anger	Aggression	Quarrelling
Parents' gender	rho	,067	-,098	-,029	-,072	,022	,017	,024
	p	,351	,173	,682	,319	,761	,807	,742
Parents' age	rho	**-,217****	,040	-,004	,088	-,112	,103	-,145
	p	**,005**	,603	,957	,255	,145	,179	,060
Family members	rho	,080	-,034	-,009	-,075	,029	-,069	,075
	p	,265	,640	,903	,295	,683	,333	,295
Mothers' edu. level	rho	,067	,056	,120	-,140	-,033	-,055	,040
	p	,349	,435	,093	,051	,646	,444	,575
Fathers' edu. level	rho	,007	-,009	,102	-,082	,004	,099	,032
	p	,920	,902	,162	,260	,955	,173	,656
Independent use	rho	-,003	-,079	-,031	-,070	-,031	**,159***	,062
	p	,962	,270	,664	,327	,666	**,025**	,389
Computer number	rho	,022	-,007	,017	,046	,083	-,008	-,008
	p	,761	,920	,817	,525	,245	,913	,908
Explanations	rho	**-,167***	-,071	,026	,083	-,034	-,034	-,001
	p	**,020**	,324	,719	,247	,639	,632	,988
Words use	rho	-,129	**-,213****	-,089	-,036	-,136	-,003	-,101
	p	,074	**,003**	,220	,613	,059	,967	,159

**p<0,01; *p<0,05.

Table 9. Correlation matrix of parents perception of playing games, informatics knowledge, computer use in general, computer use in the presence of others, parental talks with children about Internet application, attitudes toward computer and Internet use and knowledge about Internet violence with emotions that children experience while playing the computer games

		Games	Informatics Knowledge	Computer use	Others	Talks	Attitudes	Violence
Motivation	rho	**,270****	,110	-,041	,066	**,160***	**-,177***	-,128
	p	**,000**	,149	,585	,471	**,032**	**,017**	,079
Pleasure	rho	**,381****	,136	-,014	,164	**,269****	**-,200****	**-,200****
	p	**,000**	,075	,850	,072	**,000**	**,007**	**,005**
Happiness	rho	**,379****	**,167***	,068	,093	,111	-,058	-,103
	p	**,000**	**,028**	,361	,307	,134	,435	,157
Boredom	rho	**,351****	,058	,097	,074	**,225****	-,043	-,049
	p	**,000**	,445	,194	,413	**,002**	,569	,498
Anger	rho	**,275****	,028	-,034	-,168	,116	,077	**-,215****
	p	**,000**	,713	,647	,063	,120	,305	**,003**
Aggression	rho	,082	-,070	-,112	-,085	,022	**,155***	-,078
	p	,296	,360	,134	,351	,765	**,037**	,284
Quarrelling	rho	,097	,017	-,115	,016	-,004	,145	-,048
	p	,217	,824	,123	,862	,961	,051	,507

**p<0,01; *p<0,05.

Table 10. Correlation matrix of parents perception of playing games, informatics knowledge, computer use in general, computer use in the presence of others, parental talks with children about internet application, attitudes toward computer and Internet use and knowledge about Internet violence with children internet activities, computer use in the presence of others, self-rated feelings about games and behaviours regarding the Internet violence

		Internet Activities_ PD	Presence of Others_PD	Feelings_ PD	Internet Violence_ PD	Internet Activities_ SC	Presence of Others_SC	Feelings_ SC	Internet Violence_ SC
Games	rho	,081	-,029	,146	,105	-,027	**,432****	-,015	-,027
	p	,467	,826	,206	,347	,821	**,002**	,903	,829
Infor. Knowl.	rho	,052	,075	,128	,102	-,057	,071	-,180	-,142
	p	,627	,569	,247	,344	,624	,623	,128	,255
Computer use	rho	**,252***	,048	,092	-,011	**,337****	**,470****	,044	,080
	p	**,014**	,703	,396	,919	**,003**	**,001**	,711	,515
Pres. of others	rho	-,071	-,044	,046	-,146	,103	1,000	-,077	-,074
	p	,577	,771	,724	,247	,451	.	,589	,617
Talks	rho	-,051	-,094	,038	,151	**,266***	**,296***	-,100	-,097
	p	,633	,469	,729	,155	**,015**	**,028**	,381	,418
Attitudes	rho	-,190	-,017	-,009	,068	-,043	-,053	-,026	-,033
	p	,072	,898	,932	,523	,698	,698	,821	,780
Violence	rho	-,097	,013	-,122	-,051	,144	-,130	,136	,067
	p	,347	,916	,254	,625	,187	,345	,225	,563

**p<0,01; *p<0,05. (PD=preschool children; SC=school aged children).

In Table 9 the data about relationship between parents perception of playing games, informatics knowledge, computer use in general, computer use in the presence of others, parental talks with children about Internet application, attitudes toward computer and Internet use and knowledge about Internet violence with emotions that children experience while playing the computer games, could be seen. Parents' rating of higher frequency of playing games among children is significantly related with higher levels of children's motivation, pleasure, happiness, boredom and anger. It is interesting that if children playing more games, they are experiencing not only positive but also negative emotions at higher levels. Furthermore, higher parents' informatics knowledge is closely related only with higher levels of children's happiness, what is very interesting. Those parents who

are discussing with their children about internet application, they also rated their children to experience more motivation, pleasure and boredom. The more positive attitudes toward computer and internet use parents have less motivation and pleasure their children are experiencing and more boredom. Finally, greater level of parents' knowledge about Internet violence is significantly correlated with fewer pleasure and anger in children, as perceived by parents.

The relationship between parents perception of playing games, informatics knowledge, computer use in general, computer use in the presence of others, parental talks with children about internet application, attitudes toward computer and Internet use and knowledge about Internet violence with children internet activities, computer use in the presence of others, self-rated feelings about games and behaviours regarding the internet violence, separately for preschool and school aged children could be observed in Table 10.

Correlational analysis revealed that parents' higher perception of more games playing is strongly related with more frequent computer use in the presence of other only rated by school aged children. The more parents perceived computer use in children, children have more frequent internet activities, no matter to age. Again, more frequent computer use perceived by parents is significantly correlated with more frequent computer use in the presence of others only rated by school aged children. Finally, discussion of parents about internet application is significantly higher only in more frequent internet activities and computer use in the presence of other among school aged children.

Last correlation analysis revealed results about socio-demographic variables of parents and children with children internet activities, computer use in the presence of others, self-rated feelings about games and behaviours regarding the internet violence, separately for preschool and school aged children (Table 11). According to children's ratings, preschool boys showed significantly more active behaviours against internet violence, what is very interesting. Since there is no significant relationship between this variable and children's age, it could be concluded that this kind of knowledge does not grow with the age, what is very interesting and concerning finding. To be efficiently protected from possible internet violence, children should be more critic and behaviourally more efficient with age. So, this should be taken into account within creating guidelines for educative workshops with children. On the other side, children showed a significant grow in internet activities and more positive feelings with the higher age. Concerning the variable of food consumption during computer and internet use it is determined that is significantly correlated with less internet activities and less knowledge about internet violence among preschool children. School aged children showed the same relationship with the addition

of negative relationship between higher level of food consumption and less Internet activities in the presence of others. The presence of others seems to be not only good way of parental control in the situations of pure computer and internet use but also in the situations of eating food while playing on the computer. Only school children rated significantly more frequent presence of mothers while playing computer games. Finally, independent computer use is significantly correlated only with variables of school aged children. It is significantly higher in school aged children with fewer Internet activities and less positive feelings about computer and internet use.

CONCLUSION AND FUTURE RESEARCH DIRECTIONS

Today's lifestyle imposes the need for frequent use of computers to find out what is going on in the world, in order to make a cake, how to buy a favorite book or perhaps a nice piece of jewelry. By the way, when you look in the computer world, you find that there is a world of computer games and that world of computer games increasingly plays an important role in the lives of children of preschool and school-aged children. Learn to play computer games has a positive effect on cognitive development, But for every bright side of the coin there is a dark side of the coin. In this case, it's the long hours playing computer games encourages preschool and school aged children to retreat into themselves and occupy in the world of computer games, it encourages negative emotions such as anger, readiness to fight. In addition, various studies indicate about computer games and the health problems that can be caused by playing computer games (problems seating cause obesity, problems with the spine, fist).

In order to examine the situation on the use of computer games in the Municipality of Šenkovec and Mačkovec in Croatia, conducted a study on children of preschool and school children as well

Table 11. Correlation matrix of socio-demographic variables of parents and children with children Internet activities, computer use in the presence of others, self-rated feelings about games and behaviours regarding the Internet violence

		Internet Activities_ PD	Presence of Others_ PD	Feelings_ PD	Internet Violence_ PD	Internet Activities_ SC	Presence of Others_ SC	Feelings_ SC	Internet Violence_ SC
Children's gender	rho	,057	-,031	,013	**-,306****	,021	-,060	,035	-,187
	p	,595	,819	,907	**,004**	,837	,634	,745	,068
Children's age	rho	**,757****	-,143	**,333****	,047	-,107	-,119	,018	,176
	p	**,000**	,289	**,002**	,669	,297	,342	,864	,087
Food consumption	rho	**-,227***	-,117	,030	**-,315****	**-,360****	**-,278***	**-,237***	-,062
	p	**,034**	,390	,792	**,003**	**,000**	**,027**	**,028**	,557
Grade	rho	**,731****	-,200	**,344****	,058				
	p	**,000**	,135	**,002**	,599				
Parents' gender	rho	-,010	-,106	-,107	-,030	,040	**,281***	,032	,010
	p	,923	,434	,345	,787	,700	**,022**	,768	,923
Parents' age	rho	,101	,077	,041	-,111	,025	-,164	,004	-,013
	p	,380	,586	,737	,348	,823	,231	,971	,908
Edu. Level of mothers	rho	-,168	,031	-,187	-,191	,076	,014	,049	,074
	p	,114	,821	,094	,078	,465	,912	,647	,477
Edu. Level of fathers	rho	-,050	,268	-,069	-,146	,024	,071	-,070	,073
	p	,648	,050	,546	,190	,817	,571	,513	,483
Ind. Computer use	rho	-,084	-,166	-,039	,097	**-,258***	-,177	**-,246***	-,109
	p	,432	,218	,732	,373	**,011**	,154	**,020**	,289
Computer number	rho	,118	-,078	-,106	-,080	,106	-,103	,133	,082
	p	,267	,562	,348	,463	,303	,409	,212	,425
explanations	rho	-,034	-,201	,019	,025	-,062	-,237	-,044	-,180
	p	,754	,137	,866	,818	,546	,058	,684	,080
Words	rho	-,070	-,162	-,085	,040	,012	,104	-,063	,027
	p	,511	,230	,448	,717	,908	,418	,563	,794

**$p<0,01$; *$p<0,05$. (PD=preschool children; SC=school aged children).

as parents, N = 399. The sample is representative for Croatia, since most of the participants are from the nucleus families with mean of family members of four and with the mean of parents' education level of secondary education. Regarding the parents' perception, which is coloured by mothers' perspective more, since just one-third of fathers were participated in the study, results showed mainly positive attitudes toward computer and internet use among their children. In addition, there was no significant difference in those attitudes between parents of preschool and school aged children. Generally, todays parents have mostly positive attitudes toward modern technology use, what is confirmed by the number if computer present in their homes. Also, all parents, with no differences between subsamples, have a middle level of knowledge about internet violence. From this study it could be seen that parents reported about their children mostly use computers and internet, they mostly explained internet content to them and children mostly use words from the internet. The significant effect of computers and internet in family homes is more than evident, what is confirmed by this study.

Furthermore, parents showed middle level of informatical knowledge and what was more interesting, parents of preschool aged children showed significantly more of that knowledge, what could be explained because they are younger. From the parents ratings it could be seen that children frequently use computer and internet and mostly for playing computer games, searching internet and YouTube. Parents were differed on this rating; since they reported that school aged children use computer and internet more than preschool children, what was expected. Considering parental control measured by children's computer and internet use in the presence of others, the study revealed that it was on the middle level and that school aged children are more alone than preschool children. These parents' reports are not congruent with self-ratings of preschool and school aged children, since preschool children reported that they use computers and internet alone significantly more than their parents said and then school aged children said. Since this variable is very important one in the whole study and very vulnerable to giving socially desirable answers, it is recommended to be measured in the future studies other than using self-reported measures. Due to more honesty in children, some advantage could be given to the children's answers, but this is still speculation, so some observation measures must be employed in future studies. Moreover, parents reported to have middle level of talks about internet application with their children, and parents of preschool children even less than that what was expected since internet chopping is not of the interest of the preschool child. Finally, in addition to parents' perception of games that their children are playing at the computer, they have re-

ported that children are experiencing positive and negative mentions during computer and internet use – mostly pleasure and happiness, what was expected. Children differed only on experiencing motivation, where parents of preschool children reported that they experience significantly more motivation than school aged children.

From the children's perspective it could be seen that they differed in their ratings only on the variable of the computer use in the presence of others. All other ratings are similar to those from their parents. So, children reported about food consumption while playing computer games, and preschool children more than school aged children. Furthermore, all children are very active in computer and internet use, and all of them experience positive emotions during computer activities, school aged children even more than preschool children. It is interesting that their overall behavior toward internet violence is similar, but strategies are rather different – preschool children are focused on getting others help, but school aged children are more active and independent in solving that kind of problems, if they experienced them.

Finally, detailed correlation analysis revealed lots of significant relations of examined variables. It could be concluded that most of the socio-demographic variables of parents play an important role in the overall parents' behavior and control toward their children's computer and internet use. This study clearly showed that and because of that it is of utmost importance to create educational workshops within kindergartens and primary schools for parents. The study clearly showed that parents' positive attitudes toward children's computer and internet use are strongly correlated with less positive and more negative emotions that children have experienced while they use computers and internet. Moreover, more parents know about informatics, less they show more negative attitudes toward computer and internet use. No matter to that, the number of computer in the family homes is constantly growing. This only could draw very important implication, than modern technology is more than present in family homes and contemporary childhood, but parents and children are not very well prepared how to implement them within positive growing up of their children.

That research shows results of preschool and school aged children in a municipality Šenkovec, Croatia, so it is told about single sample culture. In any way, that research has potential for wider impact than it is acknowledged. How? Namely, there is a small number of findings about usage of computer in preschool and school aged children in Europe, so scientists must join its own forces and make broad research in that topic. In some way, this manuscript is a message and invitation to do it and as a solid ground for continuing this kind of research on much diverse samples.

REFERENCES

Allen, M. (2013). *A study into video game violence and its effect on game player behaviour and attitudes.* University of Portsmouth, School of Creative Technologies.

Axelrod, E. A. (2009). *Violence goes to the internet (avoiding the snare of the net).* Charles C. Thomas Publisher.

Bateman, C. (2013). *Designing computer games preemptively for emotions and player types: New technology.* Arelius Sveinn.

Bateman, C. (2013). *Designing computergames preemptively for emotions and player types.* Arelíus Sveinn Arelíusarson. Accessed 04.05.2014. from http://www.olafurandri.com/nyti/papers2013/Designing%20Computer%20Games%20Preemtively%20for%20Emotions%20and%20Player%20Types.pdf

Bauerlein, M. (2008). *The dumbest generation: How the digital age stupefies young Americans and jeopardizes our future.* New York, NY: Tarcher/Penguin.

Bilić, V. (2010). The relation between media violence and aggressive peer behaviour. *Odgojne znanosti, 12*(2), 263-281.

Bilić, V., Gjukić, D., & Kirinić, G. (2010). Possible effects of playing computer and video games on children and adolescents. *Napredak, 151*(2), 195–213.

Bodrova, E., & Leong, D. J. (1996). *The Vygotskian approach to early childhood.* Merrill, Prentice Hall.

Bryant, J., Carveth, R. A., & Brown, D. (1981). Televison viewing and anxiety:An experimental examination. *Journal of Communication, 31*(1), 106–119. doi:10.1111/j.1460-2466.1981.tb01210.x PMID:7204618

Buchman, D. D., & Funk, J. B. (1996). Video and computer games in the '90s: Children's time commitment & game preference. *Children Today, 24*(1), 12-15, 31.

Buljan-Flander, G. & Karlović, A. (2004). *Izloženost djece zlostavljanju putem interneta.* God. X. Dvobroj 54/55: MEDIX.

Cassell, J., & Ryokai, K. (1999). *Making space for voice: Technologies to support children's fantasy and storytelling.* Cambridge, MA: MIT Media Lab.

Cassell, J., & Ryokai, K. (2001). Making space for voice: Technologies to support children's fantasy and storytelling. *Personal and Ubiquitous Computing, 5*(3), 169–190. doi:10.1007/PL00000018

Cesarone, B. (1998). *Video games: Research, ratings, recommendations.* ERIC DIGEST (217) 333-1386, (800) 583-4135.

Cleary, A. G., McKendrick, H. & Sills, J. A. (2002). Hand–arm vibration syndrome may be associated with prolonged use of vibrating computer games. *British Medical Journal, 324*(7332), 301.

Cohen L., Manion L. & Morrison K. (2007). *Metode istraživanja u obrazovanju*. Jastrebarsko: Naklada Slap.

Cole, M. (1996). *Cultural psychology: A once and future discipline*. Cambridge, MA: The Belknap Press of Harvard University.

Comer, J. S., Furr, J. M., Beidas, R. S., Weiner, C. L., & Kendall, P. C. (2008). Children and terrorism-related news: Training parents in coping and media literacy. *Journal of Consulting and Clinical Psychology*, 76(4), 568–578. doi:10.1037/0022-006X.76.4.568 PMID:18665686

Computer Application in Education. (n.d.). *Scope and challenge*. Accessed 04.05.2014 from http://criticalcompetency.wordpress.com/2011/11/06/computer-application-in-education-scope-and-challenges/

Cooper, J., & Mackie, D. (1986). Video games and aggression in children. *Journal of Applied Social Psychology*, 16(8), 726–744. doi:10.1111/j.1559-1816.1986.tb01755.x

Csikszentmihalyi, M. (1983). *Flow, the psychology of optimal experience*. Harper & Row.

David & Lucile Packard Foundation. (2000). The future of children. Los Altos, CA: Author.

Digital Opportunity for Youth Issue Brief Number 7. (2010, October). *Empowering parents through technology to improve the odds for children*. Retrieved from http://www.childrenspartnership.org/storage/documents/Publications/TCP-ParentTech-LowRezFinal.pdf

Djeca i računalo: Uloga računala u predškolskoj dobi. (n.d.). Accessed 30.03.2014, from http://www.istrazime.com/djecja-psihologija/djeca-i-racunalo-uloga-racunala-u-predskolskoj-dobi/

Do Sterotypic Images in Video Games Affect Attitudes and Behaviour? (n.d.). *Adolescent perspectives*. Accessed 17.05.2014., from http://www.academia.edu/371174/_Do_Stereotypic_Images_in_Video_Games_Affect_Attitudes_and_Behavior_Adolescent_Perspectives

Dorman, S. M. (1997). Video and computer games: Effect on children and implications for health education. *The Journal of School Health*, 67(4), 133–138. doi:10.1111/j.1746-1561.1997.tb03432.x PMID:9130190

Downey, S., Hayes, N., & O'Neill, B. (2004). Play and technology for children aged 4-12. In R. Gentile et al. (Eds.), Centre for social and educational research. Dublin Institute of Technology, Office of the Minister for Children.

Duran, M. (2003). *Dijete i igra*. Naklada Slap, Jastrebarsko. In Croatian

Eisenberg, N. (2000). Emotion regulation and moral development. *Annual Review of Psychology*, 51(1), 665–697. doi:10.1146/annurev.psych.51.1.665 PMID:10751984

Emes, C. E. (1997). Is Mr Pac Man eating our children? A review of the impact of video games on children. *Canadian Journal of Psychiatry*, 42(4), 409–414. PMID:9161766

Flintoff, J. P. (2002). *Children get smart with their computer games: Shooting baddies may help the development of academic skills*. London: Financial Times.

Floros, Siomos, K., Dafouli, E., Fisoun, V., & Geroukalis, D. (2012). Influence of parental attitudes towards Internet use on the employment of online safety measures at home. *Studies in Health Technology and Informatics*, 181, 64–70. PMID:22954830

Funk, J. B., & Buchman, D. D. (1995). Video game controversies. *Pediatric Annals, 24*(2), 91–96. doi:10.3928/0090-4481-19950201-08 PMID:7724256

Funk, J. B., Elliott, R., Urman, M. L., Flores, G. T., & Mock, R. M. (1999). The attitudes towards violence scale: A measure for adolescents. *Journal of Interpersonal Violence, 14*(11), 1123–1136. doi:10.1177/088626099014011001

Funk, J. B., Heidi, H. B., Pasold, T., & Baumgardner, J. T. (2004). Violence exposure in real-life, video games, television, movies and the internet: is there desensitization? Department of Psychology, The University of Toledo.

Furlong, M. J., & Morrison, G. M. (2000). The school in violence: Definition and facts. *Journal of Emotional and Behavioral Disorders, 8*(2), 71–82. doi:10.1177/106342660000800203

Garvey, C. (1990). *Play*. Cambridge, MA: Harvard University Press.

GFK. (2009). *Trajna dobra u kućanstvima Hrvatske*. Centar za istraživanje tržišta.

Gligora, M., Antić, M., & Rauker Koch, M. (2013). Proces razvoja multimedijske računalne igre. *Rijeka. Zbornik Veleučilišta u Rijeci, 1*(1), 151–163.

Gopnik, A., Meltzoff, A. N., & Kuhl, P. K. (2011). *The scientist in the crib: What early learning tells us about the mind*. EDUCA.

Graham, R., McCabe, H., & Sheridan, S. (2003). *Pathfinding in computer games*. School of Informatics & Engineering. Institute of Technology Blanchardstown.

Granic, I., Lobel, A., & Engels, R. C. M. E. (2014). The benefits of playing video games. *The American Psychologist, 69*(1), 66–78.

Griffiths, M. (1999). Violent video games and aggression: A review of the literature. *Aggression and Violent Behavior, 4*(2), 203–212. doi:10.1016/S1359-1789(97)00055-4

Griffiths, M. D. (2010). Computer game playing and social skills. A pilot study. *Aloma Revista de Psihcologia Ciencies del Educacio i del Esport, 27*, 301–310.

Gupta, R., & Derevensky, J. L. (1996). The relationship between gambling and video game playing behaviour in children and adolescents. *Journal of Gambling Studies, 12*(4), 375–395. doi:10.1007/BF01539183 PMID:24234157

Henderson, A. T., & Mapp, K. L. (2002). *A new wave of evidence: The impact of school, family, and community connections on student achievement*. Austin, TX: National Center on Family & Community Connections With Schools.

Higinbotham, W. (n.d.). *Tennis for two*. Retrieved from http://ahyco.ffri.hr

Hoffman, M. L. (2000). *Emapthy and moral development: Implications for caring and justice*. Cambridge Press. doi:10.1017/CBO9780511805851

Hrabri telefon-Savjetodavna linija za djecu. (n.d.). Accessed 30.03.2014, from https://www.google.hr/?gws_rd=ssl#q=hrabri+telefon

Huesmann, L. R., Moise-Titus, J., Podolski, C. L., & Eron, L. D. (2003). Longitudinal relations between children's exposure to TV violence and their aggressive and violent behavior in young adulthood: 1977–1992. *Developmental Psychology, 39*(2), 201–221. doi:10.1037/0012-1649.39.2.201 PMID:12661882

Huesmann, R. L. (2007). *The impact of electronic media violence: Scientific theory and research*. NIH Public Access. doi:10.1016/j.jadohealth.2007.09.005

Ilišin, V., Marinović Bobinac, A., & Radin, F. (2001). *Djeca i mediji. Uloga medija u svakodnevnom životu djece.* Zagreb: Državni zavod za zaštitu obitelji, materinstva i mladeži – Institut za društvena istraživanja.

Irwin, A. R., & Gross, A. M. (1995). Cognitive tempo, violent video games, and aggressive behavior in young boys. *Journal of Family Violence, 10*(3), 337–350. doi:10.1007/BF02110997

Istraživanje o iskustvima djece pri korištenju interneta. (n.d.). Accessed 30.05.2014., from http://www.tic-zadjecu.hr/index. php?option=com_content&view=article&id=3 1:istraivanje-o-iskustvima-djece-pri-koritenju-interneta&catid=2&Itemid=2

Izloženost nasilju putem internet. (n.d.). Retrieved from web.ffos.hr/serv/psih.php?file=380

Jackson, L. A., Witt, E. A., Games, A. I., Fitzgerald, H. E., von Eye, A., & Zhao, Y. (2012). Information technology use and creativity: Findings from the children and technology project. *Computers in Human Behavior, 28*(2), 370–376. doi:10.1016/j. chb.2011.10.006

Kapasi, H., & Gleave, J. (2009). *Because it's freedom: Children's views on their time to play.* NCB.

Kasteleijn-Nolst Trenite, D. G., da Silva, A. M., Ricci, S., Binnie, C. D., Rubboli, G., Tassinari, C. A., & Segers, J. P. (1999). Video-game epilepsy: A European study. *Epilepsia, 40*(s4Suppl 4), 70–74. doi:10.1111/j.1528-1157.1999.tb00910.x PMID:10487177

Kerawalla, L., & Crook, C. (2002). Children's computer use at home and at school: Context and continuity. *British Educational Research Journal, 28*(6), 751–771. doi:10.1080/0141192022000019044

Kirsh, S. J. (1998). Seeing the world through Mortal Kombat-colored glasses: Violent video games and the development of a short-term hostile attribution bias. *Childhood: A Global Journal of Child Research, 5,* 177-184.

Ko, S. (2002). An empirical analysis of children's thinking and learning in a computer game context. *Educational Psychology, 22*(2), 219–233. doi:10.1080/01443410120115274

Kovačević, S. (2007). Spare time and computer games. *Školski vjesnik, 56*(1-2), 49-63.

Kwon, J. H., Chung, C. S., & Lee, J. (2011). The effects of escape from self and interpersonal relationship on the pathological use of internet games. *Community Mental Health Journal, 47*(1), 113–121. doi:10.1007/s10597-009-9236-1 PMID:19701792

Lazzaro, N. (2013). *Designing computer games preemptively for emotions and player types: New technology.* Aurelius Sveinn.

Lenhart, A. (2005). *Teens and technology-youth are leading the transition to a fully wired and mobile nation.* PEW Internet & American Life Project.

Leontiev, A. N. (1981). *Problems of the development of the mind.* Moscow: Progress Publisher.

Levy, L. Z. (2009). *Computer attitudes, self-efficacy, and usage of children and their parents: Viewed through gender lens.* UMI Microform.

Livingstone, S. (2003). *Children's use of the internet: Reflections on the emerging research-agenda (online).* London: LSE Research Online.

Livingstone, S., & Bober, M. (2006). Regulating the internet at home: Contrasting the perspectives of children and parents. In *Digital generations: Children, young people and new media* (pp. 93–113). Mahwah, NJ: Lawrence Erlbaum.

Livingstone, S., & Helsper, E. (2008). Parental mediation and children's internet use. *Journal of Broadcasting & Electronic Media, 52*(4), 581–599. doi:10.1080/08838150802437396

Mandarić V. (2012). *Novi mediji i rizično ponašanje djece i mladih.*Katolički bogoslovni fakultet Sveučilišta u Zagrebu.

Milas, G. (2005). *Istraživačke metode u psihologiji i drugim društvenim znanostima.* Zagreb: Jastrebarsko.

Mitchell, K. J., Becker-Blease, K. A., & Finkelhor, D. (2005). Inventory of problematic internet experiences encountered in clinical practice. *Professional Psychology, Research and Practice, 36*(5), 498–509. doi:10.1037/0735-7028.36.5.498

NAEYC. (1996). *Technology and young children: Ages 3 through 8.* Retrieved from https://www.google.hr/?gws_rd=ssl#q=http:%2F%2Fwww.naeyc.org%2Fresources%2Fposition_statements%2Fpstech98.htm

National Association for the Education of Young Children (NAEYC). (1996). Technology and interactive media as tools in early childhood programs serving children from birth through. *Age,* 8.

Nikolopolou, A. (1993). Play, cognitive development and the social world: Piaget, Vygotsky, and beyond. *Human Development, 36*(1), 1–2. doi:10.1159/000277285

Parents Attitudes toward Computer Use by Young Children. (n.d.). Accessed 30.03.2014., from http://jrre.vmhost.psu.edu/wp-content/uploads/2014/02/2-4_1.pdf

Petz, B. (2004) *Osnove statističke metode za nematematičare.* Jastrebarsko: Naklada Slap.

Pillay, H. (2003). An investigation of cognitive processes engaged in by recreational computer game players: Implications for skills of the future. *Journal of Research on Computing in Education, 34*(3), 336–350.

Portal o e-learning u AHyCo.uniri.hr! (n.d.). Retrieved from http://ahyco.uniri.hr/portal/Pocetna.aspx

Previšić, V. (2000). Slobodnovrijeme između pedagogijske teorije i odgojne prakse. *Napredak, 4*(141), 403–411.

Radetić Paić, M., Ružić Baf, M., &Dragojlović, D. (2010). The role of parents and computer use of pupils perpetrators of criminal acts. *Metodički obzori, 10*(5), 7-20.

Ricci, S., & Vigevano, F. (1999). The effect of video-game software in video-game epilepsy. *Epilepsia, 40*(4), 31–37. doi:10.1111/j.1528-1157.1999.tb00904.x PMID:10487171

Rideout, V., & Hamel, E. (2006). *The media family: Electronic media in the lives of infants, toddlers, preschoolers, and their parents.* Kaiser Family Foundation. Retrieved from http://www.childrenandnature.org/research/volumes/C42/42/#sthash.LBYsTm0w.dpuf

Rijavec, M. (1994). Čuda se ipak događaju- psihologija pozitivnog mišljenja. Zagreb: IEP d.o.o.

Rijavec, M., & Brdar, I. (2001). Pozitivna psihologija. Zagreb: IEP d.o.o.

Rijavec, M., Miljković, D. & Brdar, I. (2008). *Pozitivna psihologija: Znanstveno istraživanje ljudskih snaga i sreće.* Zagreb: IEP d.o.o.

Roberts, D. F., Foehr, U., & Rideout, V. (2005). *Generation M: Media in the lives of 8 to 18 year olds.* Kaiser Family Foundation.

Roe, K., & Muijs, D. (1998). Children and computer games: A profile for the heavy user. *European Journal of Communication, 13*(2), 181–200. doi:10.1177/0267323198013002002

Ružić Baf, M. I., & Radetić Paić, M. (2010). The influence of computer games on young people and the use pegi tool. Život i škola, 56(24).

Salpeter, J. (1999). *How can technology benefit our students?* Technology and Learning Magazine.

Santrock, J. W. (1997). *Psychology* (5th ed.). Dubuque, IA: Brown & Benchmark Publishers.

Schutte, N. S., Malouff, J. M., Post-Gorden, J. C., & Rodasta, A. L. (1988). Effects of playing videogames on children's aggressive and other behaviors. *Journal of Applied Social Psychology*, *18*(5), 454–460. doi:10.1111/j.1559-1816.1988.tb00028.x

Scott, J., & Porter Armstrong, A. (2013). *Impact of multiplayer online role-playing games upon the psychosocial well-being of adolescents and young adults: Reviewing the evidence* (Vol. 2013). Psychiatry Journal. doi:10.1155/2013/464685

Shashaani, L. (1997). Gender differences in computer attitudes and use among college students. *Journal of Educational Computing Research Issue*, *16*(1), 37–51. doi:10.2190/Y8U7-AMMA-WQUT-R512

Silvern, S. B., & Williamson, P. A. (1987). The effects of video game play on young children's aggression, fantasy, and prosocial behavior. *Journal of Applied Developmental Psychology*, *8*(4), 453–462. doi:10.1016/0193-3973(87)90033-5

Singh, R., Bhalla, A., Lehl, S. S., & Sachdev, A. (2001). Video game epilepsy. *Neurology India*, *49*(4), 411–412. PMID:11799420

Sparks, J. A. (1986). *The effect of microcomputers in the home on computer literacy test scores.* Central Missouri State University.

Spera, C., Wentzel, K. R., & Matto, H. C. (2009). Parental aspirations for their children's educational attainment: Relations to ethnicity, parental education, children's academic performance, and parental perceptions of school climate. *Journal of Youth and Adolescence*, *38*(8), 1140–1152. doi:10.1007/s10964-008-9314-7 PMID:19636777

Stables, K., Benson, C., & de Vries, M. (2011). PATT 25: CRIPT 8: Perspectives on learning in design & technology education. Goldsmiths, University of London.

Tangey, J., & Fischer, K. W. (1995). *Self conscious emotions: The psyhology of shame, guilt, embarassement and pride.* New York: Guilford Press.

Tatalović Vorkapić, S. & Milovanović, S. (2013). Computer use in the preschool age: The attitudes of future preschool teachers. *Education 3-13: International Journal of Primary, Elementary and Early Years Education, 1-13.* 10.1080/03004279.2012.673003

Tatković, N. & Ružić Baf, M. (2011). Računalo –Komunikacijski izazov djeci predškolske dobi. *27 Informatologia, 44*(1), 27-30.

Tazawa, Y., Soukalo, A. V., Okada, K., & Takada, G. (1997). Excessive playing of home computer games by children presenting unexplained symptoms. *The Journal of Pediatrics*, *130*(6), 1010–1011. doi:10.1016/S0022-3476(97)70298-1 PMID:9202632

Utjecaj kompjutera na IQ djece. (n.d.). Accessed 12.1.2014, from (http://www.*roda*.hr/article/read/utjecaj-kompjutera-na-iq-djece).

Verenikina, I., & Belyaeva, A. (1992). *Sensitivity of preadolescents to complex activity in the computer mediated telecommunication environment.* Paper presented at East-West Human, Computer Interaction Conference, St.Petersburg, Russia.

Verenikina, I., Harris, P., & Lysaght, P. (2003). *Child's play: Computer games, theories of play and children's development.* University of Wollongong.

Verenikina, I., Harris, P., & Lysaght, P. (2008). *Child's play: Computer games, theories of play and children's development.* University of Wollongong, Faculty of Education.

Verenikina, I., & Herrington, J. (2006). *Computer play, young children and the development of higher order thinking: exploring the possibilities.* Faculty of Education, University of Wollongong.

Verenikina, I., Herrington, J., & Peterson, R. (2008). *The affordances and limitations of computers for play in early childhood.* University of Wollongong.

Verenikina, I., Lysaght, P., Harris, P., & Herrington, J. (2004). Child's play: Exploring computer software through theories of play. In L. Cantoni & C. McLoughlin (Eds.), *Proceedings of EdMedia 2004* (pp. 4070–4074). Norfolk.

Vygotsky, L. (1978). *Mind in society.* Cambridge, MA: Harvard University Press.

Vygotsky, L. S. (1977). Play and its role in the mental development of the child. In *Play: Its role in development and evolution.* New York: Basic Books.

Warschauer, M. (1996). Computer assisted language learning: An introduction. In *Multimedia language teaching* (pp. 3–20). Tokyo: Logos International.

Warschauer, M. (1996). *Motivational aspects of using computers for writing and communication.* Retrieved from http://nflrc.hawaii.edu/NetWorks/NW01/NW01.html

Where Do We Start? (n.d.). Accessed 30.02.2014, from https://www.thinkuknow.co.uk/parents/Primary/Conversation-Starters/)

Ybarra, M., Diener-West, M., Markow, D., Leaf, P. J., Hamburger, M., & Boxer, P. (2008). Linkages between internet and other media violence with seriously violent behavior by youth. *Pediatrics*, *122*(5), 929–937. doi:10.1542/peds.2007-3377 PMID:18977970

Yelland, N. (2005). The future is now: A review of the literature on the use of computers in early childhood education (1994–2004). *AACE Journal*, *13*(3), 201–232.

Young, K. (1996). Psyhology of the computer use.XL.addictive use of the internet: A case that breaks the stereotype. *Psychological Reports*, *79*(3), 899–902. doi:10.2466/pr0.1996.79.3.899 PMID:8969098

KEY TERMS AND DEFINITIONS

Attitude: Presents one of the determining factors in predicting an individuals' behaviour and it has been defined as positive and negative disposition to behave in certain ways towards some person, groups or objects.

Attitudes toward Computer and Internet Use: Individual's general evaluations or feelings of favour or antipathy towards computer technologies and specific computer-related activities.

Child Development: Presents normal progression that includes numerous changes with children age. These changes could be observed in three major aspects: motor/physical, cognitive and socio/emotional.

Computer Games: The term "computer games" is usually identified with the term of video game, only while playing computer games children are using only by computer. Computer games are more widespread because they can be used for fun and for learning. Usually, they have been categorized as: Shooting games, Fighting games, Strategies, Role-playing game or RPG and Massively multiplayer online role-playing game (MMORPG).

Emotions: Defined as very complex psychological states, which include three distinct components: physiological state and response, subjective experience based on cognitive interpretation of emotion and behavioral answer. There are six universal and basic emotions: fear, disgust, anger, surprise, happiness and sadness.

Family: A group of people related by blood, marriage or adoption, whose members live together, they cooperate economically and care for offspring. Family is dynamic system in which each member affects other members. Family has transaction nature, i.e. event or change in any part of the family affects everyone.

Informatic Knowledge: The understanding, knowledge and ability to efficient use of computers and related technology. Besides basic knowledge and abilities, this term includes also the individuals' comfort level of using computer and applications related to computers.

Internet Violence: Defined as any kind of violet act, like as any harm or harass other people in a deliberate manner, by using information technology, i.e. internet on computers.

Section 3
Communication and Innovation

Chapter 16
Tools for the Process:
Technology to Support Creativity and Innovation

Rachel Heinen
Creighton University, USA

Joshua Fairchild
Creighton University, USA

Salvatore A. Leone
Creighton University, USA

Lily Cushenbery
Stony Brook University, USA

Samuel T. Hunter
The Pennsylvania State University, USA

ABSTRACT

Technology exerts an all-encompassing impact on the modern workplace, and has a strong influence on how designers approach creative problem solving. Such technologies can be valuable tools for organizations seeking to develop creative solutions to maintain a competitive advantage. However, with the rapid pace of technological development, it can be difficult for organizations to remain up-to-date and ahead of the competition. There is much that is still unknown about the ways in which novel technologies influence creative performance. The chapter attempts to provide insight on this topic by utilizing a process model of creative endeavors to predict how various types of technology may be used to enhance organizational creativity and innovation. Recommendations for future research and practice in the realms of technology and innovation are also discussed.

INTRODUCTION

Technology is an integral part of modern life, and its influence continues to grow. New and developing technologies, such as smartphones and social media, have transformed many aspects of our daily life, influencing how we interact with others and how we share and consume information. Most individuals have experienced the transformative power of technology in their personal lives, and this influence is equally strong in the business world, where competitive pressures demand that organizations continually innovate to stay ahead of the competition (DeFillipi, Grabher, & Jones, 2007; Florida, 2002).

Increasingly then, organizations must turn to new and emerging technologies in order to break free from the status quo and develop innovative

DOI: 10.4018/978-1-4666-8205-4.ch016

solutions (Bonnardel & Zenasni, 2010; Edmonds & Candy, 2002). Indeed, creative organizations can rarely succeed without harnessing the power of technology (Edmonds & Candy, 2002). However, successful innovation is not simply a matter of adopting new technologies and applying them to creative design. In fact, research suggests that most attempts to adopt new technologies meet with substantial resistance and often fail (Rizzuto & Reeves, 2007).

Therefore, to best utilize technology tools, implementation strategies are key. We argue that successful implementation involves matching the appropriate technology with the correct phase of the creative design process (e.g., Fairchild, Cassidy, Cushenbery, & Hunter, 2011; Hunter, Cushenbery, Ginther, & Fairchild, 2013). Specifically, technology can be invaluable in overcoming a number of creative design issues, but only when appropriately applied. In a prior review (cf. Fairchild et al., 2011), we have discussed several ways in which technology can enhance innovation. However, new advancements in technology demand additional evaluation. For instance, smartphones and tablet computers are now ubiquitous devices, and social media has become a pervasive aspect of our society, utilized by everyday citizens and corporations alike. In particular, a large proportion of new technologies directly or indirectly serve to influence interpersonal communication. Throughout this chapter, we will explore various ways in which such technology-mediated communication may be beneficial in enhancing the creative process.

BACKGROUND

This chapter aims to explore the influences novel technologies have on the creative process. Although "creativity" or "creative behavior" represents a complex, integrated process, comprising for the sake of application, we will utilize a commonly accepted definition of 'creativity' as ideas that are both novel (original or unexpected) and useful (practical and serving a specific purpose) (Runco & Jaeger, 2012). 'Creative performance', then is the behavioral act of generating such novel and useful ideas. 'Innovation' is commonly accepted to be implementation of creative ideas (West & Altink, 1996). Additionally, we use the term 'designer' as a generic phrase to indicate a person who engages in the creative process (thus producing some form of creative design).

Finally, within this chapter, we adopt a definition of 'technology' from Aziz (1995), referring to any "tools or tool systems by which we transform parts of the environment, derived from human knowledge, to be used for human purposes" (Aziz, 1995, p.478). 'Software', then, will be defined concretely as electronic applications that users interact with through a technological system.

Bearing these definitions in mind, the present chapter provides insight into how organizations may capitalize on such developing technologies in order to enhance their creative performance and facilitate innovation. We adopt a process perspective on creativity and innovation (e.g., Mumford et al., 1991), through which we examine the impact of new and emerging technologies on creative tasks. A visual depiction of Mumford and colleagues' (1991) model of the creative process is presented in Figure 1.

USING PROCESS MODELS TO UNPACK THE EFFECTS OF TECHNOLOGY

The knowledge economy is driven by constantly changing ideas, often resulting in a great deal of uncertainty and ambiguity (Madsen, Miller, & John, 2005). Likewise, creative endeavors themselves necessitate addressing ambiguous, poorly defined problems and situations (Mumford et al., 1991). At the same time, however, competitive pressures necessitate that employees maintain stable control over generating innovative products (Boatman & Wellins, 2011).

Figure 1. Diagram of Mumford and colleagues' (1991) creative process model

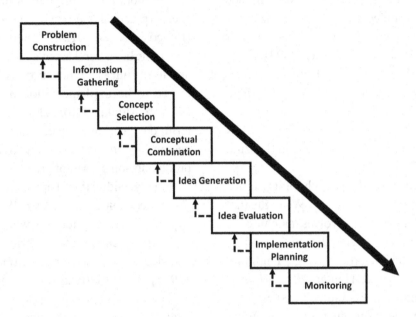

Therefore, the application of technology is challenging as the needs of the project can change as users explore the problem space. Innovation is not the result of a single activity, but rather the culmination of a complex series of interconnected stages (Hunter et al., 2006; Fairchild et al., 2011; Mumford et al., 1991). Utilizing the wrong tools at various points in the design process can lead to wasted resources as well as poor quality or unoriginal solutions. Therefore, a framework of social, cognitive, and psychological processes can illustrate how technology can aid in the innovation.

An Eight-Stage Model of the Creative Process

In this chapter, we adopt an eight-stage model of the creative process first proposed by Mumford and colleagues (e.g., Baughman & Mumford, 1995; Mumford et al., 1991). This model acknowledges that the creative process is not necessarily linear, where early activities can influence later performance and later stages can lead to designers revisiting earlier stages as well (Mumford et al., 1991; Hunter et al., 2006). There are numerous

process-oriented models of creativity and innovation, but Mumford and colleagues' model has been selected for the present chapter due to its specificity of the discrete stages at which technology may have an impact.

1. In **Problem Construction:** Designers must first identify the nature of the specific problem that will be addressed by their ensuing work. As previously stated, the creative process inherently involves ill-defined, ambiguous problems (Mumford et al., 1991; Simon, 1973), and problem framing will have a lasting impact on their creative performance. Thus, a key task during problem construction is determining what exactly the problem at hand is, and determining what the criteria for successful resolution (Hunter et al., 2006; Mumford et al., 1991).

2. Next, in **Information Gathering:** Designers must search broadly for information that could help address the identified problem (Hunter et al., 2006; Mumford, Baughman, Supinski, & Maher, 1996b). The information gathered in this stage forms a foundation

for later creative thought, as it provides the initial information that designers will use to develop creative solutions (Mumford et al., 1996b).

3. In **Concept Selection:** The emphasis shifts from gathering raw information to identifying which pieces of information appear most relevant to the problem at hand, and organizing such information into categories (Hunter et al., 2006).

4. Then, in **Conceptual Combination:** Designers combine concepts from multiple sources to come up with new, innovative collections of ideas (Hunter et al. 2006). After forming novel conceptual groups, designers proceed to

5. **Idea Generation:** In which the primary goal is to take concepts and hone them into concrete, potential solutions to the identified problem (Hunter et al., 2006). After generating a number of potential solutions, designers proceed to

6. **Idea Evaluation:** In which ideas are vetted in order to eliminate impractical solutions and determine which are most likely to be successful. (Hunter et al. 2006). Idea evaluation concludes with the selection of a solution to pursue, which is further expanded in

7. **Implementation Planning:** In this phase, designers build a framework for bringing the proposed solution to fruition. This involves building the idea from an abstract concept to a concrete product, and then successfully bringing it to market (Hunter et al., 2006). Finally, in

8. **Monitoring:** The implemented solution continues to be evaluated with regard to its ongoing performance.

Often, there are problems or limitations that are not noted until the product has been released, at which time the designers need to utilize feedback to make any adjustments necessary for the product's ongoing success (Hunter et al., 2006). Each of these stages will now be discussed in greater detail, and examples of technologies that may be beneficial will be discussed at each juncture.

Problem Identification and Construction

As previously discussed, creative problem solving is an inherently open-ended process, in which problems do not have clearly defined boundaries or specifications. Therefore, in order to develop effective creative solutions, it is important to begin the creative process by providing structure to the situation (Mumford, Baughman, Threlfall, Supinski, & Costanza, 1996a; Reiter-Palmon, 2009). The first stage in the creative process, 'problem identification and construction', is critical to the subsequent development of innovative solutions, as designers must determine what will constitute a successful solution. At the same time, it is critical that the problem is not too narrowly defined that it could restrict potential innovation (Simon, 1973). Navigating this stage entails identifying a problem to be solved, determining the criteria will establish an idea as a creative solution, and determining the criteria for success of the solution. Successfully identifying and structuring the problem to be addressed is vital to the success of the subsequent stage of the creative process (e.g., Hunter, Friedrich, Bedell, & Mumford, 2006; Mumford et al., 1996a).

Mumford and colleagues (Mumford et al., 1996a) demonstrated that constructing an initial framework of the problem to be addressed contributed to an increase in the production of creative solutions. Developing such a structure includes identifying the nature of the problem, including goals, procedures, and any constraints or restrictions that must be applied to the solution (Mumford et al., 1996a, Reiter-Palmon, 2009). Restrictions are boundaries that eliminate impractical or unfeasible ways of framing the problem. Identifying such boundary conditions during problem construction also helps direct the subsequent information search toward new ways of working around such limitations. In turn, this can assist in developing new, effective, and surprising solutions (Baughman and Mumford, 1995; Mumford et al., 1996a; Reiter-Palmon, 2009). Technology can identify limitations and constraints on the upcoming design process by providing additional sources of information and facilitating communication among designers in framing the problem.

The use of Computer-Aided Design (CAD) is one example of how technology can facilitate problem identification and construction by uncovering constraints. CAD is a family of programs that enables designers to develop three-dimensional models of proposed designs. CAD also enables users to review models built by others to address related problems. By examining such models, designers can gain insight into the effective and ineffective elements of prior designs (Wang & Horvath, 2013). As such, CAD models can add useful constraints to an ambiguous problem by specifying which elements should be changed or retained. This in turn creates a clearer picture of the problem at hand, enabling creators to focus on a shared understanding of the situation. For instance, Heesom and Mahdjoubi (2004) note that CAD models have been demonstrated to be effective tools for helping individuals with diverse backgrounds and skillsets develop shared perspectives on a large-scale construction task.

Similarly, successful navigation of this first stage of the creative process requires reaching a consensus about the nature of the problem. Therefore, effective communication among team members is vital. At the outset of the creative process, successful problem construction involves listening to and integrating various conceptualizations of the problem. Due to the ambiguous nature of creative problems (Mumford et al., 1991, 1996a), early in the creative process, each member of a design team may have a different impression of what the problem is. At this point, successful problem identification and construction requires

that designers work together to arrive at a common creative direction (Mumford et al., 1996a; Mumford, van Iddekinge, Morgeson, & Campion, 2008). Thus, technologies that support team communication are one set of beneficial tools in this part of the process. Computer programs, such as video conferencing software (e.g., Skype, Facetime, and Adobe Connect) are common tools for facilitating efficient communication. Furthermore, because these software programs are available on a variety of mobile platforms (e.g., smartphones, laptops, and tablet computers), designers can communicate remotely at any time of the day – time and physical distance do not need to be roadblocks to team-based problem construction.

Social media platforms, such as Facebook, Twitter, and Instagram, are another set of communication tools that can play a powerful role in problem construction. As of 2011, 73% of Fortune 500 companies were actively engaging with the public on Twitter, and this figure has grown rapidly. Social media has the potential to impact numerous phases of the creative process (e.g., Geho & Dangelo, 2012), but with regard to this initial stage, a critical effect stems from its ability to provide valuable information about problems the public wants to address. For example, Kalatzis and colleageus (2014) have noted that social media platforms provide unique opportunities for facilitating communication between groups who would otherwise not be able to directly communicate. With the advent of social media, members of the public can easily share their thoughts, ideas, and reactions in a free-flowing, natural manner (Geho & Dangelo, 2012; Heath, Singh, Ganesh, & Taube, 2013). Such narrative can provide valuable information for designers seeking to figure out what specific problems need to be addressed (Heath et al., 2013; Kietzmann, Hermkens, McCarthy, & Silvestre, 2011). For instance, Berthon and colleagues (Berthon, Pitt, Plangger, & Shapiro, 2012) note that information obtained from consumers via social media can be highly valuable for developing creative business plans.

Information Gathering

Once designers have a clear picture of the problem to be addressed, they need to acquire the information necessary to proceed. In the 'information gathering' stage of the creative process, designers seek out information needed to support creative thought. A primary goal in this stage is to acquire a wide range of information related to the problem at hand to serve as the basis of subsequent problem solving (Alves, Marques, Saur, & Marques, 2007; Mumford, Baughman, Supinski, & Maher, 1996b). A high-quality solution requires information about the problem domain as well as a breadth of information from *outside* the domain (e.g., Leiponen & Helfat, 2010). That is, if designers only build their solutions using information drawn from the problem's primary domain, the results will likely follow a familiar pattern and not be innovative (Leiponein & Helfat, 2010).

However, it is rare for a single individual to possess sufficient depth and breadth of knowledge about a problem space to develop an innovative solution him or herself. Instead, successful innovation is typically the result of a group of highly trained individuals with diverse skillsets (Reiter-Palmon, Wigert, & de Vreede, 2012). Indeed, having a range of functional backgrounds and knowledge bases among team members typically enhances the team's creative performance (Reiter-Palmon et al., 2012; van Knippenberg & Schippers, 2007). Therefore teamwork and collaboration are critical activities that provide access to a greater pool of knowledge. At this stage of the creative process, technology can be useful by increasing both the quantity and variety of information available to the designers, provide instant access to such information, and facilitate communication and knowledge sharing with colleagues and geographically dispersed experts (e.g., Fruchter, 2004).

As previously discussed, technology can increase the quantity and diversity of information available to an innovator (Hunter et al., 2006). By increasing this pool of ideas, innovators gain access to a greater array of ideas to incorporate into concepts and potential designs in subsequent phases of the creative process. One example of software used to maximize this information pool is Google Scholar, which has become widely used both by the general public and professional researchers. Antell and Strothmann (2013) note that professional researchers have acknowledged Google Scholar as a leading search tool for academic and professional information, and they tend to use it more frequently than most other subscription-based abstracting and indexing (A&I) services. Google Scholar indexes scholarly information from a wide range of disciplines, in contrast to discipline-specific databases such as PubMed or PsychINFO. This variety allows innovators easier access to information outside of their domain that they may be less familiar with. Easy access to such diverse information may prove useful in developing novel and unexpected solutions in later phases of the creative process (e.g., Antell & Strothmann, 2013; Mumford et al., 1991). In addition to Google Scholar, popular search engines like Google, Yahoo, and Bing allow users access to information to assist in developing solutions.

Although information from such search engines is unfiltered, and much of it may be irrelevant, such tools provide designers with yet another way to supplement their own knowledge and expertise as they gather information to address a creative problem. However, the unfiltered nature of information from general search engines requires care in what information is chosen as it has the potential to be irrelevant or incorrect. That is, technology should serve to supplement, rather than replace, the human element in information gathering. When used appropriately, these tools provide near instant access to a wide range of information, allowing designers to rapidly expand their knowledge base during information gathering. By reducing the time necessary to acquire information, designers can potentially navigate this stage more quickly, thus leaving more time available for subsequent stages of the creative process.

As previously stated, technology should serve to enable creative designers to exercise their skills and knowledge. In general, the design process in most organizations is highly collaborative, and effective teamwork is typically necessary in order to succeed in creative endeavors (e.g., Ellemers, De Gilder, & Haslam, 2004; Mumford et al., 2008; Skilton & Dooley, 2010). Early in the creative process, such as in the information gathering stage, effective communication is critical in order to ensure that team members are on the same page regarding the direction their project is taking.

Having come to a consensus regarding the definition of the problem in the previous stage, team members should share their individual knowledge and skills in order to jointly develop a pool of information during the information gathering stage. Therefore, technologies that facilitate or supplement interpersonal interaction can be vital. For instance, videoconferencing software, such as Skype, Apple Facetime, and Adobe Connect enable users who may not be located in the same space to communicate in real time. With the ubiquity of mobile devices, such as smartphones, laptops, and tablet computers, designers are able to stay in contact using high-fidelity software, even on the go. Furthermore, many of these digital communications tools enable recording and reviewing interactions, allowing creative problem solvers to return to their interactions to identify good ideas that may have gone overlooked in the live discussion. Cutler and Colleagues (2002) have demonstrated that not only are remote meeting programs useful for facilitating distributed communication, but recordings of such interactions can provide valuable information to enhance team performance in the future.

Creative success in the information gathering stage can be further enhanced by cross-disciplinary collaborations. Greg Satell, a Forbes journalist, states "By thoroughly examining their domain, [experts] become aware of a variety of techniques, alternative approaches and different philosophies. The larger the creative toolbox, the greater the possibility for creative excellence" (Satell, 2014, *2. Searching the Domain*). In other words, experts in one field can utilize knowledge and skills from other fields to solve complicated issues (Gayraud, 2005). Collaboration between individuals from various disciplines enhances divergent thinking – the capacity to generate a large variety of potential, unconventional solutions to a problem. Therefore, such cross-disciplinary collaborations expand this creative toolbox to allow for the generation of new creative ideas as the creative process progresses. Similarly to facilitating communication among members of a design team, videoconferencing technologies are highly beneficial in gathering and sharing cross-disciplinary information (Fruchter, 2004). In short, the easier it is for team members to communicate, the more effective they will be at sharing information and experiences with one another, which increases the pool of information available to fuel creative endeavors (Mumford et al., 2008). Furthermore, as information is gathered from a range of sources, team members begin to sort and organize this information, giving rise to the next stage on the creative process: concept selection (Mumford, Supinski, Threlfall, Baughman, 1996c).

Concept Selection

After navigating the information gathering stage of the creative process, designers are faced with a fresh challenge, as they must decide how best to organize the large quantity of raw data available to them (e.g., Fairchild et al., 2011; Mumford et al., 1991, 1996c). Therefore, 'concept selection' constitutes an important phase of the creative process. In this stage, a key task is taking the large quantity of information gathered in the preceding phase and grouping or organizing it into a smaller body of related categories. By forming such categories and organizing information, designers position themselves to subsequently uncover novel, high quality ideas (Mumford et al., 1996c). In fact, concept selection can be seen as a "turning point," the creative process, in which information starts to converge, and designers begin to develop a more specific direction for working toward the end result (King & Sivaloganathan, 1999). Nearly 60-80% of the cost in design processes is committed at this stage (Duffy et al., 1993), and so any tools that reduce cost or increase efficiency of organizing concepts are highly valuable.

In this step, the central challenges lie in recognizing which pieces of information are most relevant and useful for addressing the problem at hand, and then grouping such information and key themes or categories (Mumford et al., 1996c). Individuals' analytical ability is likely a critical characteristic in helping designers to navigate this stage. This trait involves critical thinking ability, as well as the capacity to sort and organize a wide variety of information (Sternberg, O'Hara, & Lubart, 1997). Individuals who can clearly organize ideas and identify the concepts most pertinent to the current situation are more successful in generating a large number of creative ideas (Hunter et al., 2006). Therefore, during 'concept selection', technology can create a framework narrowing the breadth of information by supporting, sorting, organizing and cataloging information (Hunter et al., 2006).

Online databases, such as Google Scholar, online libraries, and other broad-based electronic records management systems prove to be valuable tools to for helping designers filter, organize, and analyze information. Although their use may be more immediately apparent for information gathering, the myriad information management options present in such databases can be extremely useful in concept selection. With options for advanced searches, information can be filtered by key words and themes, specific subjects, specified date ranges, and field of study. Keyword searches (based on previously gathered information) in particular are potentially valuable tools that allow designers to identify related groups of topics. Additionally, some databases, such as Web of Science, include features that let users visualize connections among

topics or extant literature. By identifying connections, these databases can further help users to identify connections among various sources and pieces of information, particularly if information has been drawn from multiple disciplines (Gautam & Yanagiya, 2012).

This information can be further filtered and sorted through information management and productivity software (such as *Evernote* and Microsoft *OneNote*). Once stored in such a program, designers can continue to sort, annotate, and organize information into discrete clusters based around user-defined themes. Such platforms also allow users to share their notes and organized information with others, enabling multiple designers to more efficiently collaborate during the concept selection process. Unlike more traditional information management systems, these programs can store large volumes of a variety of information types (e.g., text, photographs, and audio) with text recognition software and geo-location tags that allow for quick search and retrieval.

As in the preceding creative process stages, such collaboration continues to be vital for successful creative performance. In the concept selection state, effective communication allows team members to suggest connections between key concepts that enhance organization and categorization efforts. Individual designers may have distinct cognitive maps of the information they have absorbed (Kearney & Kaplan, 1997) and group discussion can create a shared mental model (Klimoski & Mohammed, 1994; Mathieu, Heffner, Goodwin, Salas, & Cannon-Bowers, 2000; Mohammed & Dumville, 2001). Such shared mental models constitute patterns of cognition that are shared among members of a team, including an understanding of the role each member plays and the knowledge each person has (Mohammed & Dumville, 2001). This shared understanding can help team members organize concepts from raw information. Therefore, additional technologies that can aid in this phase of the creative process include any tools that facilitate or enhance communication among team members. This includes videoconferencing software, email, and smartphones, all of which allow for fast, easy contact and information sharing. In general, engaging in such deliberate information sharing has been shown to enhance innovative outcomes for an organization (e.g., Lin, 2007).

Once designers have drawn on available information to develop a set of concepts, they can progress to the next stage of the creative process, in which concepts are refined and reassembled to develop the seeds of new ideas.

Conceptual Combination

'Conceptual combination', the fourth step of the eight-process model, involves designers combining information and concepts from multiple sources to come up with new, innovative patterns of information (Hunter et al., 2006). In contrast to the preceding stage, in which raw information was categorized based on similarity or related features, conceptual combination involves reassembling clusters of ideas in unexpected ways that have not been utilized before. Such combinations lead to new ways of addressing a problem and bring new solutions to the forefront (Hunter et al., 2006; Mumford, Baughman, Maher, Costanza, & Supinski, 1997a). Conceptual combination is essential for divergent thinking (e.g. Runco, 1991), which can result in a greater variety of unconventional, out-of-the-box ideas (Mumford et al., 1997a).

At the individual level, the capacity to develop such unusual ideas stems from synthetic ability. This ability, closely associated with creative potential, describes an individual's capability to develop new concepts by identifying previously untapped connections among existing concepts (Sternberg et al., 1997; Sternberg & O'Hara, 1999) and integrating them in new ways.

Although a baseline level of synthetic ability is critical (e.g., Sternberg et al., 1997; Sternberg & Lubart, 1996), technology can play a valuable supplemental role during the conceptual com-

bination phase of the creative process. Specifically, tools can assist with extracting novel and abstract conceptual combinations from groupings of seemingly unrelated ideas (Sternberg et al., 1997). Specialized software, known as "mind-mapping technologies" can aid in this process. Mind-mapping is the method of linking concepts together through diagrams, images, and lines that link one idea to another. Such visualization tools have the potential to greatly enhance the design process, as designers often deal with complex concepts that are best understood (and more easily combined) when relationships among them can be depicted graphically (Cañas et al., 2005). For example, *Popplet* allows users to break down ideas into smaller concepts, which can then be combined into a new idea or solution in subsequent creative process stages (Smith, 2013). This mind-mapping method can be useful to the creative process in that it provides an opportunity for the innovator to visualize new connections between associated ideas.

Critically, users must be careful to remain focused on combining *concepts*, rather than directly trying to use these programs to visualize final design prospects (Fairchild et al., 2011). Since conceptual combination is a relatively early creative process stage, if users focus too closely on an imagined "end result," they may experience design fixation, a cognitive error that can cause users to overlook novel, potentially successful concepts that do not fit with their established ideas (Jannsen & Smith, 1991). Therefore, mind-mapping software has the further benefit of helping users stay "in the moment," by depicting fine-grained clusters of ideas, rather than emphasizing an end result. This way, designers can mentally "zoom in" on connections among ideas without prematurely worrying where they may lead. An empirical investigation by Buisine and colleagues (2007) suggests that using software such as this may facilitate better group communication and participation in the creative process, potentially enhancing creative performance at later stages.

In addition, computer aided design software (CAD) allows users to load examples of established ideas and designs and interact with them in three dimensions. Whereas mind-mapping software allows users to visualize hypothetical connections among concepts, CAD software allows users to visualize object representations themselves, and physically fit models of such objects together. CAD enables users to break apart and reassemble existing elements, which enables designers to collaboratively test ideas before implementing them. By allowing users to explore models of various concepts in three dimensions, they may be able to discover combinations that would not be immediately apparent. For instance, two elements that may not seem to fit together can be rotated in the CAD model to test whether the combination is feasible. Not only can this allow users to identify novel combinations to pursue, but it also allows designers to rule out combinations that would be ineffective or impractical before substantial resources are spent on production. This in turn can streamline the creative process, saving time and money in the long run.

As with the preceding stages of the creative process, conceptual combination is a social process where interpersonal communication is essential for acquiring new knowledge structures (Hertzum & Pejterson, 2000). Consequently, technology that facilitates intra-team communication is likely to enhance creative performance (Warr & O'Neill, 2005). Specifically, during conceptual combination, technology can be used to build a framework for interaction and information sharing among designers to combine effective ideas. Along these lines, Dossick and colleagues (2014) have identified that collaborative virtual environments enable designers to integrate unique perspectives to address a novel problem. In addition to previously described communication software, technologies that aid in visualizing and sharing concepts with others during discussion include large-screen displays that will help develop this framework for discussion. Additionally, collaborative writing and visualization tools, such as Google Docs and similar online platforms allow for groups to collaborate and combine concepts more easily from remote locations.

Idea Generation

Once various pieces of existing information and concepts have been gathered and combined, the next stage of the creative process, termed 'idea generation', involves taking these combined concepts and using them to generate novel potential solutions. In this stage, concepts are shaped into more concrete ideas (Baughman & Mumford; 1995; Hunter et al., 2006; Mumford et al., 1991). However, the goal of idea generation is not only to create as many potential solutions as possible, but also to produce ideas of both high quality and high novelty. As these potential solutions may be developed through subsequent creative process stages and eventually implemented, idea generation plays a critical role in the creative process (Giotra, Terweisch, & Ulrich, 2010).

A classic strategy used to facilitate idea generation is brainstorming. Originally proposed by Osborn (1957), brainstorming involves generating as many eccentric ideas as possible in a group setting and then improving or combining proposed ideas. According to Osborn (1957), a key element of brainstorming is that team members avoid criticizing or dismissing ideas offhand. Having an encouraging, unstructured environment is more likely to support the generation of numerous high quality and unconventional ideas. However, several studies (e.g., Bouchard, Drauden, & Barsaloux, 1974; Diehl & Stroebe, 1987; Taylor, Berry & Block, 1958) suggest drawbacks to group brainstorming. In one early study, individuals who generated ideas alone produced more novel and high quality ideas than group brainstorming, suggesting that group participation can inhibit creative thinking (Taylor, Berry, & Block, 1958). Explanations for this inhibition center around the concepts of 'production blocking' (e.g., Diehl

&Stroebe, 1987; Lamm & Trommsdorff, 1973) and 'evaluation apprehension' (e.g., Collaros &Anderson, 1969; Connolly, Jessup, & Valacich, 1990), which contribute to a drop in performance when generating ideas in a group setting.

Production blocking occurs because group brainstorming typically allows only one member to speak at a time. This structure can contribute to blocking the productivity of other members, causing some to forget ideas as they listen to teammates or withhold ideas as they become irrelevant when a conversation moves forward (Diehl & Stroebe, 1987; Lamm & Trommsdorff, 1973). However, most organizations use teams for creative work despite obstacles to creativity and efficiency (Coutu, 2009). Therefore, successful idea generation requires understanding and circumventing potential barriers to innovation.

Brainstorming could also result in evaluation apprehension, where team members fear contributing to the discussion because the group may react negatively to their ideas. In a study by Collaros and Anderson (1969), participants placed in a 4-person group setting were led to believe that their group consisted of no experts in the topic, one expert, or all experts and then asked to generate ideas together. The results of the study showed that participants placed in the all-expert group felt the most inhibited to participate and generated the least original and practical ideas of the three groups. Additionally, participants led to believe all other members of their group were experts reported they "sensed disapproval from other members" (Collaros & Anderson, 1969, p. 162) and felt less inclined to voice their ideas. Additionally, Connolly and colleagues (1990) found that groups working anonymously generated more ideas than non-anonymous groups, suggesting higher average participation from members. These studies describe the disadvantages of group-based brainstorming due to fear of negative reactions to ideas. If not held in check, this evaluation apprehension can lead to an overall drop productivity.

To avoid evaluation apprehension, it is important for teams and organizations to foster a culture of openness to new and risky ideas. That is, the group members need to experience 'psychological safety' within the team or organization. Psychological safety involves a perception by members of a team that it is safe to share one's ideas, even if they are unconventional or counter to the norm (Edmondson, 1999). This entails a sense of confidence within the team members that any novel or eccentric ideas will not be met with hostility or ostracism from other members of the team or other forces within the organization (Baer & Frese, 2003; Edmondson, 1999). Furthermore, in psychologically safe teams, discussion and debate about ideas is viewed constructively, rather than as personal attacks (e.g., Baer & Frese, 2003; Edmondson, 1999, 2003). Teams with high psychological safety have less fear of evaluation and greater willingness to share unconventional ideas (Edmondson, 2003; Howell & Boies, 2004). Conversely, teams with low psychological safety may produce fewer or lower quality ideas.

Technology offers tools to help increase creative performance of group-based performance brainstorming by reducing barriers to sharing unconventional ideas. The following strategies actively facilitate better group-based productivity by using computers, the Internet, smartphone applications (apps), or other communication programs to decrease the negative group effects of production blocking and evaluation apprehension. A particularly useful modern brainstorming tool is referred to as "Brainwriting" or "Electronic Brainstorming" (EBS).

Electronic Brainstorming allows participants to generate ideas in a group setting, but still act relatively individually. Usually, participants sit at a computer and type their ideas as they think of them. The ideas are submitted anonymously to the EBS program so that other users can read them as often as they want, and at their own pace. The EBS system then allows a user to see a "bank" of the groups' ideas and thus reference past ideas without waiting or actively try to remember each detail other group members say (Ardiaz-Villanueva, Nicuesa-Chacon, Brene-Artazcoz, de Acedo Lizarraga, & de Acedo Baquedano, 2011; Michinov 2012). Michinov has demonstrated that this approach decreases production blocking as each member of the team can express ideas without needing to take turns and risking forgetting or self-censoring an idea (Michinov, 2012). Additionally, the anonymity reduces evaluation apprehension (Collaros & Anderson, 1969), which can lead to a greater diversity of generated ideas (Collaros & Anderson, 1969).

In a theoretical EBS program, as each user types their ideas, they can see other group members doing the same. Thus each member has a constant access to a free-flowing and growing bank of generated ideas, such as in a chat-room or instant message board. The added benefit, then, is the ability to visualize and then combine others' ideas in real time, thus further increasing the amount of ideas generated. Researchers have found evidence of the positive effects of EBS, with a meta-analysis claiming "EBS groups are superior to face-to-face groups with respect to creative idea generation...there is little reason to employ traditional face-to-face brainstorming" (DeRosa, Smith, & Hantula, 2007, p. 1574).

Additionally, EBS programs can be advantageous to groups because they can utilize modern communication routes, namely the Internet, to give groups the additional option of not physically meeting. With the option of virtual meetings, participants can retain higher levels of anonymity, as they are not required to be physically visible in the EBS session. This increase in anonymity can reduce evaluation apprehension and facilitate better idea generation.

A good example of an EBS system is the *Google Docs* family of online programs. A user can create an online document and share the link with other group members, who may edit the document anonymously. While multiple individuals are logged on to the same document or spreadsheet, each can input their idea into the file while others either watch or work at their own pace. The programs allow users to leave comments on specific lines of text, make changes, or work on their own as they please. *Google Docs* also allows individuals to work simultaneously by typing in different fields of the same document. Thus, production blocking is decreased as no member of the team needs to wait before inputting their ideas. As mentioned previously, *Google Docs* also acts to decrease evaluation apprehension because team members do not need to login with personal information, and may participate in the EBS session as an anonymous user.

With new technology, such as smartphones and tables, the EBS framework is no longer restricted to desktop and laptop computers. For example, recent apps such as CoMapping and SpiderScribe allow users to create and organize ideas into maps that can be shared or edited with other users in real time. By allowing users to access, contribute to, and modify ideas in an EBS system on-the-go, they are no longer restricted to interacting with their peers' ideas at set times or locations. As such, if a user has an idea at night, or while commuting to work, he or she does not need to wait to share it, and risk forgetting it, as can often occur with creative ideas (Dennis & Valascich, 1993). It should also be noted that Google has created smartphone apps of their GoogleDocs programs, allowing teams access anywhere with the use of mobile data plans. However, it is important to note that some benefits of the EBS process may be overstated in the current literature.

A common theme in group brainstorming is the process of 'buildup' (Girotra and Ulrich, 2010). Buildup (often referred to as "building off" of an idea) is the process of adding a new concept or other, newer, elements into a previously-generated idea. Although buildup was generally considered to improve quality and quantity of generated ideas, more recent research suggests otherwise. Girotra and Ulrich (2010) found that buildup of ideas has no beneficial consequences to the team in terms of quantity or quality of ideas generated. In fact, the researchers reported that the action of idea buildup is counterproductive to the group, as they waste time building up a few, lesser quality ideas instead of developing new, higher quality concepts. To prevent this loss in productivity, the researchers recommend a "hybrid structure" to brainstorming. In this hybrid approach, brainstorming team members first work independently to generate ideas on their own, and then meet with the larger group to continue their efforts, as opposed to working either entirely together, or entirely separately.

Hybrid-structured brainstorming has been found to be more effective for generating more ideas, higher quality ideas, and "better discerning the quality of the ideas they generated" (Girotra & Ulrich, 2010, p.1). The increase in productivity seen in these hybrid teams may be due to the issues of counter-productivity found in traditional team settings. For instance, both production blocking and evaluation apprehension are related to creativity-diminishing factors of working in a team setting (fear of negative reactions, and inability to simultaneously communicate). The hybrid structure, however, allows each member to work individually at first, and thus effectively acts to diminish both of these pitfalls.

Theoretically, pitfalls could further be avoided by applying the hybrid brainstorming model with current EBS applications discussed previously. For instance, group members could individually and simultaneously input their ideas into an "idea bank app", such as a *GoogleDoc*. However, the main difference is all submitted ideas are hidden from the other members of the group until after the individual brainstorming session is complete. Afterwards, the ideas of other members are revealed, and additional brainstorming continues. By combining strategies, this theoretical app can retain the advantages of EBS while diminishing the counter-productivity of buildup. First, EBS programs can work via the internet or smartphones to allow for geographically dispersed teams. Then,

because group members work simultaneously and individually, production blocking is decreased and no time is wasted waiting for others to finish their ideas. Similarly, because the EBS programs allows for anonymous users, team members feel less evaluation apprehension while contributing. Finally, the hybrid structure prevents buildup of ideas as group members do not see others' work until after the first session of brainstorming is complete.

Smartphones and tablets can be particularly useful, as other applications and features can be used peripherally or can be combined to continue idea generation. For example, after an idea generation session, the team then has the option to meet virtually through video conferencing software such as Skype, Oovoo, or Google Hangouts using the front-facing camera on most modern smartphones and tablets. Here, after the group has "broken the ice" with anonymously sharing ideas, they can go into more detail, clarify points, and discuss how to move forward. This gives team members the opportunity to elaborate on generated ideas, propose new combinations of ideas, or begin to determine which possible ideas might best address the identified problem. This process feeds directly into the next stage of the creative process, 'idea evaluation'.

Idea Evaluation

After numerous and high quality ideas have been generated, innovators move on to the next step in the creative process, Idea Evaluation. The activities in this stage are used as operations of idea implementation planning, as previously generated ideas are considered in the context of practicality for future idea implementation (Hunter et al. 2006; Lonergan, Scott, & Mumford, 2004; Mumford, Peterson, & Childs, 1999). The goal in this stage is to eliminate impractical ideas and determine which concepts are most likely to be successfully implemented in light of the restrictions on the current resources available to innovators (Hunter et al., 2006). During the evaluation process the idea is compared against external standards (such as novelty, popularity, usefulness, etc.) to determine both the idea's potential impact once implemented, and the likelihood of the innovators pursuing the implementation (Lonergan, Scott & Mumford 2004; Csikszentmihalyi, 1999). Finally, this stage involves the continuous gathering of information and generation of new ideas as limitations on resources or other obstacles force innovators to develop novel solutions to overcome barriers to the idea's eventual implementation (Mumford, Zaccaro, Harding, Jacobs, & Fleishman, 1991; Lonergan, et al. 2004).

Successful idea evaluation starts with forecasting. This operation involves predicting how an idea will fare in a particular context (Lonergan et al. 2004). In this step, innovators must think beyond the idea itself to its full implementation in order to consider the potential outcomes and consequences. If the possible outcomes of the idea's implementation seem desirable, the idea is pursued, while undesirable outcomes force innovators to discard or revise the idea being evaluated (Lonergan et al. 2004; Hammond, 1990). Even after the initial evaluative forecasting, however, the remaining novel ideas tend to still be undeveloped and unstructured, leading innovators to revisit the idea generation stage to revise, improve, or reject the idea being evaluated (Lonergan et al. 2004; Mumford, Scott, & Gaddis, 2003).

Technology in this stage can assist innovators in estimating the resources necessary to bring the idea to implementation, including identifying flaws and shortcomings, and determining if additional elaboration of the idea is necessary. Such technology can be helpful because innovators are able to avoid devoting time or resources to the pursuit of an idea which could potentially be impossible to fully implement, or which would not likely lead to a successful solution (Hunter et al. 2006; Csikszentmihalyi, 1999). Furthermore, efficient evaluation of ideas can help determine the time and resource commitment associated necessary for

their implementation; ideas that would be resource prohibitive to implement can then be discarded or revised to reduce sunk costs. A traditional and effective strategy applied in many business and marketing settings to determine the viability of an idea as a potential solution is Cost-Benefit Analysis (CBA). This strategy estimates the strengths and weaknesses of various ideas and provides information concerning the innovator's return or gain on the resources expended on the idea's implementation and/or development (Ngulube & Dube, 2013). The CBA is particularly useful as it allows innovators to retain available resources and evaluate ideas without moving forward into the idea implementation stage. Although CBA does not explicitly require technology, numerous software programs and templates exist to streamline the process of conducting such an analysis.

Another technique innovators use to evaluate ideas is called 'rapid prototyping'. Rapid prototyping involves using models created with CAD software to produce a printed three-dimensional scale model of the final product faster than a full development of the final product (Wang & Horvath, 2013). Such "3d-printed" models are then used to extrapolate information about the resources necessary to implement the full version of the idea on a wider scale and test for possible design flaws (Tripp & Bichelmeyer, 2014). For example, the amount of materials, manpower, software, or time needed to create the scale model can determine the needed resources for the full product. Similarly, faulty parts, ineffective design, or other errors can be identified and addressed before the final product is implemented. Prototyping has the benefit of saving time and resources that can be devoted to anticipating other barriers of implementation. Furthermore, designers can go beyond visualization and actually manipulate and interact with the prototype to examine how it functions (Chua, Leong, & Lim, 2003; Fairchild et al., 2011). Indeed, rapid prototyping is important in the evaluation stage because it "reduces development costs, decreases communication problems, lowers operation's costs, slashes calendar time, and produces the right system for the designated task" (Lantz, 1986; Tripp & Bichelmeyer, 2014, p. 36).

In contrast to virtual prototyping systems, traditional rapid prototyping techniques often use a form of polymer (ABS plastic) as the printing medium (Chua et al., 2003; Grimm, 2004). This material is cheap and relatively durable for simple prototypes, but has functional limitations. Specifically, the material itself can be brittle, and cannot hold a large deal of weight (Grimm, 2004). Furthermore, these models did not allow users to examine interactions among different materials, often a necessity in effective evaluation of complex designs.

However, advances in 3D printing technology create models even faster, more accurately, and with a variety of materials including plastics, nylon, metal, glass, and even living tissue (Mills, 2014). With a variety of materials to choose from, innovators can use these 3D printers to create more accurate representations of the final design, which in turn can enhance their ability to estimate the necessary resources or structural weaknesses or flaws in the idea. This can help evaluate ideas by determining which idea can or cannot be implemented with the available resources, and whether further revisions or modifications are necessary.

In addition to helping designers directly visualize their proposed solutions, evolutions in rapid prototyping equipment can enable designers to solicit feedback from consumers. 3D printing technology is becoming increasingly widespread, with companies such as Microsoft, and startups such as MakerBot selling personal 3D printers and software to the general public (Hachman, 2013). With this technology, a designer could send a computer model to outside colleagues or consumers, who are then able to print the product on their own personal 3D printer for further evaluation. Thus, using personal 3D printers, developers can potentially receive feedback on scale models of their product from a variety of evaluators fairly easily. This is important for idea

evaluation as several studies have shown that positive feedback facilitates further creative thinking (Carson and Carson, 1993; Zhou, 2003; George and Zhou, 2007). Lowering the cost of design can translate to a cheaper product for consumers. That is, instead of physically producing a product, companies could simply develop the design and a three-dimensional CAD model, and then sell these printing specifications to consumers to 3D print for themselves, saving resources for the developers.

Beyond rapid prototyping, communication with consumers has a great deal of benefits during idea evaluation. With the massive increase and cultural integration of social media websites such as Facebook and Twitter, innovators in business and marketing settings are now able to easily gauge consumer reactions to proposed products and ideas. For instance, comments posted on open forums such as Facebook can include product ideas, unsatisfied consumer needs, and new ideas or features that consumers want to see included in their products. Similarly, companies can get a sense of how proposed products or services would be received by monitoring consumer reaction over a social media service like Twitter. Consumers re-posting or endorsing a status update can give organizations information on how well their proposed products or services are being received by consumers (Kaplan & Haenlein, 2010). This provides useful input, as designers can then decide if a product is ready to be produced, or if additional revision and improvement is necessary.

Such collaboration with consumers was previously discussed with regard to problem identification, but at this later stage of the creative process, such rapid consumer feedback is perhaps even more valuable. At this late stage in the creative process, an important nuance is that the individuals providing this feedback are real consumers giving unbiased opinions on their preferences and reactions to a real proposed product. Chen and colleagues (Chen, Marsden, & Zhang, 2012) note that Internet-mediated feedback from consumers can be valuable for enhancing innovative outcomes. For instance, this interaction can result in designers realizing that a seemingly good idea is not worth pursuing in its current form, or could justify proceeding with an expensive or complex design if there is sufficient demand. This may reveal that a high-cost product may be more profitable than a cost efficient product. Conversely, the organization may find very little demand for a product they planned on implementing. Using the feedback gained from social media, they can revisit the idea generation stage to develop new ideas or modify the current design to align with consumer wants.

This designer-consumer collaboration is indicative of another key advantage of social media: rapid feedback. As previously mentioned, receiving greater quantities of positive feedback can enhance creativity (Carson & Carson, 1993; Zhou, 2003; George and Zhou, 2007). With the use of social media, organizations can receive a very large quantity of feedback from actual consumers (Kaplan & Haenlein, 2010). A major obstacle to this process, however, lies in separating the quality responses from consumers from the responses of lesser quality. That is, designers need to be able to determine which feedback is meaningful through all the noise.

An algorithm developed by Agichtein and colleagues (Agichtein, Castillo, Donato, Gionis, & Mishne, 2010) may be useful in filtering such feedback. In a recent study, this algorithm was able to identify Yahoo! Answer responses of high quality and separate them from responses of lower quality. This system analyzes and combines information from several sources and accurately rated the quality of responses on Yahoo! Answers forum (Agichtein et al., 2010). Presumably, this process could be applied to other feedback tools for consumer idea evaluation. This feedback, then, facilitates further creative thinking for the developers, which may result in a more innovative final product.

Another recent development involving collaboration between designers and consumers is 'crowd funding'. Championed by the website *Kickstarter.*

com, crowd funding allows anyone to propose an idea online and generate interest for implementing it. Designers then ask for a specified amount of money to complete their project, and donations are solicited from members of the general public who express an interest in the project. No fees are charged to designers unless the project meets its stated funding goal, and so it is a very low-risk way for designers to gain funding for a project. Likewise, the service provides limited risk for interested consumers, as donators (called "backers") can pledge any amount of money to the project (as little as a dollar), and they are only charged if the project reaches its funding goal. Since its inception, Kickstarter has become a major source for crowd funding creative projects. Indeed, in 2013 alone, three million backers pledged approximately $480 million, and nearly twenty thousand projects were successfully funded (Kickstarter.com, 2013).

Though at first glance, such a platform seems useful for preparing to implement an idea (as is indeed the case, and will be discussed shortly), it also has a great deal of value as a feedback tool. By monitoring the project's progress toward its goal, designers can get a sense of how much enthusiasm there is toward the proposed product. Furthermore, Kickstarter provides a comment form for each project where consumers can ask questions, leave feedback, or provide constructive criticism to help shape the project. Indeed, although Kickstarter's original purpose was to provide innovators with the opportunity to develop their product via donations, several high-profile projects credit their success to the comments and feedback they received from backers. For instance, Brian Fargo, CEO of a video game company, launched a project that has become one of the largest Kickstarter successes, raising almost $3 million dollars through the service. More so than the money, however, Fargo credits the success of the project to feedback and insight received from backers over the course of the product. He states that backer feedback was instrumental in shaping the direction and quality of his company's final product (Griffiths, 2013). Indeed, technology's role as an enabler of designer-consumer interaction may be one of its most critical benefits during idea evaluation.

Implementation Planning

After designers have determined which idea is most likely to succeed, and made any necessary revisions or modifications, the planning of the concept's implementation begins (Anderson & Gasteiger, 2007; Fairchild et al., 2011). At this stage, designers should have a sense of their available resources and develop a strategy for using them effectively (Hunter et al., 2006; Mumford et al., 1991). Furthermore, they should ensure that implementation is consistent with the organization's broader goals and objectives (Hunter et al., 2006).

Similarly to idea evaluation, this planning stage involves further refining ideas as designers work toward an innovative solution. However, the focus at this point is narrower – unrealistic or otherwise ineffective ideas should have already been eliminated, and the goal is instead to add details necessary for full implementation of more promising ideas (Sharma, 1999; Osburn & Mumford, 2006). The planning stage, then, acts to fill in missing details that ultimately allow the developers to bring the product to market.

As touched upon previously, this particular stage in the creative process may facilitate the return to previous stages in the model. For example, because the planning process inherently involves anticipating both the failure and success of the product's potential implementation (Hammond, 1990), in this stage revisiting idea generation may be necessary. That is, developers need to be prepared for obstacles such as unmet deadlines, change of situation, or necessary revisions to the idea (Osburn & Mumford, 2006). New ideas generated in this phase must be integrated into the plan, creating a cycle of generation, refinement (evaluation), and further planning for the idea's eventual execution (Mumford, Schultz, & Van Doorn, 2001).

As discussed previously, a culture of psychological safety both within the creative team and organization as a whole is important in the creative process (Edmondson 1999; Madjar, 2008). A lack of perceived psychological safety in this stage is a barrier to implementation as an idea met with doubt or disapproval will be less likely to be implemented (Janssen, 2003; Da Silva & Oldham, 2012; Axtell et al. 2006). With a psychologically safe climate, innovators in the planning stage are more resistant to the effects of failure and negative feedback, and can have a wider variety of implementation procedures to choose from leading to an increased chance of successful implementation.

Technologies particularly useful in this stage can increase resources for a potential product, increase the pool of potential implementation strategies available to designers, and facilitate cross-disciplinary collaboration to aid in the idea's implementation. Social media can once again be a powerful tool for developers in this stage. As was discussed in the previous phase, such interaction with potential consumers can yield valuable feedback, which may provide insight into last-minute changes. Critically, companies can also use platforms such as Facebook and Twitter to quickly and easily spread the word and build excitement over upcoming products via Tweets and Facebook statuses, increasing the chances that their product will be successful on the market (Thackeray, Neiger, Hanson, & McKenzie, 2008; Barwise & Meehan 2010).

Crowd funding platforms like Kickstarter can also be extremely useful in implementation planning. As previously discussed, because Kickstarter does not charge a fee to designers or backers unless a proposed product meets its chosen goal, it is a very low risk investment for designers. In exchange for some time and care in crafting an effective pitch designers stand to gain a substantial amount of money from individuals who care about the product's success. This is important to organizations, as a significant increase in resources allows innovators to take more risks with their ideas or experiment. Additionally, a product that meets or exceeds a funding goal creates more support for further refinement (Adams, 2014; Kosner, 2012). For example, The Pebble smart watch and OUYA open-source gaming console were two ideas posted on Kickstarter which received overwhelming support. The Pebble smartwatch raised over $10 million in under three months, and OUYA raised over $8 million in a similar time frame (Adams, 2014; Kosner, 2012). This support has subsequently suggested a market for a wide range of similar products.

Additionally, research has demonstrated that increased knowledge within a domain facilitates creative performance (e.g., Mumford & Gustafson, 1988; Rietzschel, Nijstad, & Stroebe 2006). Therefore, as designers are preparing to implement a new idea, it is beneficial to broaden their knowledge through discussions with other professionals, developers, and researchers within various domains (Perry-Smith & Shalley, 2003).

With this exchange of information, innovators can incorporate more refined solutions and improve the implementation plan with cross-disciplinary information (Mumford & Gustafson, 1988; Andrews & Smith, 1996; Perry-Smith & Shalley, 2003). With advances in telecommunications, modern technology can facilitate such information sharing. For example, videoconferencing software discussed earlier, such as Skype, Facetime, or Google Hangouts allows for geographically dispersed collaborators to communicate effectively in real time. Google Hangouts has the added advantage of being compatible across multiple devices such as a laptops, tablet computers, smart phones, and the new wearable-technology Google Glass (Cipriani, 2013).

Indeed, these advancements in technology increase the ease and capability for innovators to collaborate and share new information. Through effective communication, both with potential consumers and within the creative team, organizations can enhance their implementation planning efforts. Videoconferencing programs increase the innovators' information pool, which can allow them to maximize resources by incorporating this new information into the implementation plan, a critical step in this stage. Similarly, social media and crowdfunding websites allow them to generate excitement and gather additional resources for the implementation. At the conclusion of this stage, designers should have a fully-developed product, with a suitable plan to bring it to market (Hunter et al., 2006).

Monitoring

Once an idea has been implemented, it must still be continuously monitored and re-evaluated to ensure a successful implementation, such as success on the market and consumer satisfaction (Fairchild et al. 2011; Hunter et al., 2006; Mumford et al., 1991). Therefore, gathering and analyzing feedback regarding the product's performance, failures, and any necessary modification is crucial for this stage (Hunter et al. 2006). Research suggests that feedback is extremely important to the success of the creative process (Zhou, 1998; Oldham & Cummings, 1996; Deci and Ryan, 1987; Baker et al, 2013). For instance, Carson and Carson (1993) found preliminary feedback on a creative task was related to increased creativity in subsequent tasks. These findings are significant, as they imply that even after launching a product, creative performance can still be further enhanced by listening to feedback and incorporating it into future innovations. That is, feedback and past hands-on experience implementing similar products can enhance future innovative efforts (Andrews & Smith, 1996; Wu et al., 2005). More specifically, experienced designers may have a better sense of the costs of future ideas, and be better able to identify barriers to implementation. Indeed, developing greater expertise is associated with improved innovative performance (Fairchild, Eubanks, & Hunter, 2013). Effective monitoring, then, should not only help designers gauge the relative success of a new creative product, but should also provide feedback that can enhance future creative work.

As innovators receive both positive and negative feedback, they need to be prepared to transition back to other stages of the creative process in order to make the necessary modifications to their product and ensure a continuously successful implementation (Hunter et al. 2006). As such, technology useful in this stage focuses on the rapid collection of consumer feedback, evaluation, and reception. Such tools have the added benefit of providing feedback that can also serve as useful sources of information for future creative endeavors (as discussed previously in the 'information gathering' stage). These tools are useful in monitoring as they allow developers to rapidly receive this feedback and then act to either resolve consumer issues with the product, or modify and update future the design for future products. Once again, social media websites and Internet marketplace sites can be used as a tool for innovators in this stage. The latter typically have sections dedicated to consumer comments and reviews on products. Social media platforms provide additional unstructured evaluative feedback on their implemented products extremely quickly, as consumers can post about the products as soon as they are purchased.

For example, Amazon reviews offer both potential consumers and designers valuable information on personal experiences with the product. Studies have shown that consumer reviews do influence other consumers buying decisions, with one study finding that an improvement in a books' reviews on sites such as Amazon and Barnes and Noble led to an increase in the book's sales in its respective site (Chevalier & Mayzlin, 2006). Conceivably, this pattern would hold for other forms of products as well. Thus, innovators are able to track both sales and positive/negative reviews on their products to determine how well consumers report the product performs. Developers can then adjust their product accordingly to prevent future negative consumer experiences.

Indeed, the power of social media and other internet networks have already been recognized, with many companies devoting resources to monitor discussions on forums, chat rooms, and review posts (such as Amazon). In an interview, Senior Consumer Report Editor Todd Marks described how organizations attempt to "intercept a potentially negative discussion and rectify a problem before it goes viral" (Landsman, 2013). Marks continues the discussion, describing the "snowballing effect" on sites such as Twitter, where the ability to retweet a potentially negative review of a product may hurt sales for an organization (Landsman, 2013). Such platforms provide a vital avenue for designers to initiate an ongoing dialog with consumers. Adam Root, CTO and co-founder of web application developer *Hiplogiq,* says that platforms such as Facebook are the "tool of choice for small business owners wanting to connect and maintain relationships with customers" (Root, 2014).

However, it is critical that designers and their organizations do not lose sight of a critical fact regarding social media: Simply posting or occasionally viewing customer comments does not constitute effective use. An important characteristic of social media usage for this stage, then, is maintaining a live stream of continuous consumer reviews and reactions. For example, many companies will raise awareness for a product by including a specialized, identifiable search term (called a "hashtag") on Twitter. However, an important detail that organizations must not overlook is that, when consumers reply using this same hashtag, their feedback or reactions are linked back to the company (Boko, 2014). The hashtag allows organizations to sift through feedback received in relation to their initial post. This strategy can be utilized effectively by an organization by monitoring the trending hashtag, and thus collecting not only evaluation on their product, but also ideas and suggestions for further improvements and future products (Boko, 2014).

Technology provides many opportunities for innovators to succeed in monitoring. By using the social media strategies described, organization can track both general reactions to their products, as well as specific points to improve upon. One of the main advantages, however, stems from how widespread social media is in today's culture. Any consumer can leave a comment or tweet for an organization, and the process for doing so requires only a trivial time commitment. Using this technology, organizations can successfully monitor their products as soon as they are released, and use consumer evaluative information to improve the overall quality of their products.

FUTURE RESEARCH DIRECTIONS

Despite advancements in research, there is still much we do not know about how emerging technologies will impact the creative process. Technology continues to develop at an incredible rate, but there is still a dearth of empirical investigations regarding the effects of technology on the creative process. Much of the evidence regarding the benefits or pitfalls of technology are anecdotal, and in many cases, our discussion is speculative; thus, more carefully controlled studies would help to better understand the mechanisms by which technology impacts each stage of the creative process.

Furthermore, we must acknowledge that majority of the discussion included in this chapter draws on examples from engineering and related fields. This is primarily because much of the relevant research has been conducted by engineering scholars or social scientists studying engineers or those in similarly design-oriented disciplines. However, the creative process applies to any innovative endeavor, be it in engineering, education, the arts, or other fields. Therefore, future research should investigate the ways in which technology may facilitate creative performance in domains where successful performance may take a different form, such as in education or in the arts.

FUTURE DIRECTIONS FOR PRACTICE

By taking a process perspective on creativity and innovation, it becomes clear that organizations seeking to enhance their creative performance need to pay close attention to the activities that designers are engaging in throughout the creative process. As previously discussed, different technologies will have varying effects on different creative process stages.

A central, critical theme throughout most stages, however, is the importance of fostering effective communication among members of a design team. Regardless of the technologies utilized to support innovation, the creative process will fail if designers are not effectively sharing information and ideas, and working together to develop and evaluate solutions. Therefore, fostering a psychologically safe culture (Edmondson, 1999) is vital to the creative process. Not only does having a psychologically safe culture enhance creative performance (Edmondson, 1999; West & Anderson, 1996), but it facilitates team learning (Edmondson, 1999), which can help designers more effectively adopt new technologies as a team.

Another common theme in examining the role of technology in the creative process is the ubiquity of social media. This technological phenomenon has permeated every aspect of individual and organizational life, and its influence continues to grow. Though most companies utilize social media, many may not be using it effectively. In order to enhance creative performance, organizations need to go beyond posting information and counting followers and focus on actively engaging with customers. Customer reviews, postings on Facebook, and comments on Twitter, among other formats, often constitute meaningful and efficient feedback that can be used to enhance creative solutions.

Finally, we most note that, although a majority of our discussion draws examples from engineering and related design fields, the ways in which we suggest technology may enhance the creative process will likely apply to individuals or groups engaging in creative pursuits within a much broader range of disciplines. In particular, many of the communication-facilitating effects of emerging technologies are likely discipline-agnostic.

CONCLUSION

In closing, it is clear that novel technologies can exert a valuable transformative impact on the creative process, if they are properly applied. Such careful application requires an understanding of creativity from a process perspective, as different technologies can exert different effects at each stage. For example, CAD software, social media websites, and EBS programs offer different advantages at different stages, due to their wide range of possible applications. CAD is useful in the problem identification and construction stage as it allows innovators to find limitations in their designs. This feature also makes CAD useful in later stages such as idea evaluation and implementation planning as it allows developers to test the product for design flaws without first having to fully implement the concept.

Similarly, social media can be used effectively in the idea evaluation stage as these websites offers the opportunity for the collection of feedback from more consumers than ever before. This aspect of social media also makes it a useful tool in the monitoring stage where the focus is continuous collection of performance reviews and potential modifications for future products. As organizations effectively make use of the feedback on their products or services, customer-company relationships are enhanced while members of the public become a part of the creative process (Vivek, Beatty, & Morgan, 2012).

It is also critical to understand that the stages of the creative process, while distinct, influence one another (Mumford et al., 1991), and effects at one stage can feed into subsequent stages. Furthermore,

the creative process is recursive (Mumford et al., 1991; Baughman & Mumford, 1995). That is, at any point in the model, should it be necessary, innovators may cycle back to previous stages to address problems that come to light (Mumford et al 1991). Through such cyclical interrelationships, the positive effects facilitated by technology at one stage to impact other stages.

For example, information gathering tools such as Google Scholar and other search engines increase the knowledge pool available to researchers. This increased knowledge pool is then useful to innovators later in the implementation planning stage as cross-disciplinary information can aid developers in forecasting necessary resources or obstacles. Similarly, technology that facilitates idea generation will lead to the increase of quantity and quality of ideas conceived and discussed among innovators at this stage. Later in the idea evaluation stage, innovators now have a larger pool of ideas to pull from, analyze, or revise, allowing them to choose the most appropriate solution for the given situation.

It is also important that we point out that the technologies discussed in this chapter are meant primarily to serve as illustrative examples, rather than a definitive list of technologies that can impact each stage of the creative process. That is, there are many other tools available, and even more that will come to market in the near future. Though a good deal of extrapolation and speculation is necessary to envision how certain completely new technologies might impact the creative process, future developments will clearly continue to have a transformative impact. For instance, virtual reality technologies appear to be on the rise, with high-profile devices from Google, Sony, and Oculus VR among others coming to market.

The latter in particular, a device known as the Oculus Rift (itself a Kickstarter success) may revolutionize how teams and navigate the design process. Indeed, Ford Motor Company is planning to implement the Oculus Rift as a tool for next-generation automotive design, letting users explore CAD models in three dimensions (King, 2014). As this technology continues to develop, it will be interesting to see how such equipment impacts the creative process. For instance, will 3D visualization enhance idea generation?

Further research will be necessary to investigate these and a host of other questions. What is clear, however, is that technology is inexorably embedded in modern organizations, and will continue to exert enormous impact on the creative process. By continuing to study its effects, we can gain further understanding of this relationship, and can help creative organizations to flourish in this technological age.

REFERENCES

Agichtein, E., Castillo, C., Donato, D., Gionis, A., & Mishne, G. (2008). Finding high-quality content in social media. *WSDM*, *08*, 183–193. doi:10.1145/1341531.1341557

Alves, J., Marques, M. J., Saur, I., & Marques, P. (2007). Creativity and innovation through multidisciplinary and multisectoral cooperation. *Creativity and Innovation Management*, *16*(1), 27–34. doi:10.1111/j.1467-8691.2007.00417.x

Anderson, N., & Gasteiger, R. M. (2007). Helping creativity and innovation thrive in organizations: Functional and dysfunctional perspectives. In J. Langan-Fox, C. L. Cooper, & R. J. Klimoski (Eds.), *Research companion to the dysfunctional workplace: Management challenges and symptoms* (pp. 422–440). Cheltenham, UK: Edward Elgar Publishing. doi:10.4337/9781847207081.00032

Antell, K., Strothmann, M., Chen, X., & O'Kelly, K. (2013). Cross-examining google scholar. *Reference and User Services Quarterly*, *52*(4), 279–282. doi:10.5860/rusq.52n4.279

Ardaiz-Villanueva, O., Nicuesa-Chacón, X., Brene-Artazcoz, O., Sanz de Acedo Lizarraga, M. L., & Sanz de Acedo Baquedano, M. T. (2011). Evaluation of computer tools for idea generation and team formation in project-based learning. *Computers & Education*, *56*(3), 700–711. doi:10.1016/j.compedu.2010.10.012

Axtell, C., Holman, D., & Wall, T. (2006). Promoting innovation: A change study. *Journal of Occupational and Organizational Psychology*, *79*(3), 509–516. doi:10.1348/096317905X68240

Aziz, A. (1995). Defining technology and innovation markets: The DOJ's antitrust guidelines for the licensing of intellectual property. *Hofstra Law Review*, *24*(2), 476–513.

Baer, M., & Frese, M. (2003). Innovation is not enough: Climates for initiative and psychological safety, process innovations, and firm performance. *Journal of Organizational Behavior*, *24*(1), 45–68. doi:10.1002/job.179

Baker, A., Perreault, D., Reid, A., & Blanchard, C. M. (2013). Feedback and organizations: Feedback is good, feedback-friendly culture is better. *Journal of Canadian Psychology*, *54*(4), 260–268. doi:10.1037/a0034691

Barwise, P., & Meehan, S. (2010, December). The one thing you must get right when building a brand. *Harvard Business Review*, 63-68.

Baughman, W. A., & Mumford, M. D. (1995). Process-analytic models of creative capacities: Operations influencing the combination and reorganization process. *Creativity Research Journal*, *8*(1), 37–62. doi:10.1207/s15326934crj0801_4

Berthon, P. R., Pitt, L. F., Plangger, K., & Shapiro, D. (2012). Marketing meets web 2.0, social media, and creative consumers: Implications for international marketing strategy. *Business Horizons*, *55*(3), 261–271. doi:10.1016/j.bushor.2012.01.007

Boatman, J., & Wellins, R. S. (2011). *Global leadership forecast*. Pittsburgh, PA: Development Dimensions International, Inc.

Bonnardel, N., & Zenasni, F. (2010). The impact of technology on creativity in design: An enhancement? *Creativity and Innovation Management*, *19*(2), 180–191. doi:10.1111/j.1467-8691.2010.00560.x

Bouchard, T. J., Drauden, G., & Barsaloux, J. (1974). A comparison of individual, subgroup, and total group methods of problem solving. *The Journal of Applied Psychology*, *59*(2), 226–227. doi:10.1037/h0036336

Buisine, S., Besacier, G., Najm, M., Aoussat, A., & Vernier, F. (2007). Computer-supported creativity: Evaluation of a tabletop mind-map application. *Engineering Psychology and Cognitive Ergonomics*, *4562*, 22–31. doi:10.1007/978-3-540-73331-7_3

Cañas, A. J., Carff, R., Hill, G., Carvahlo, M., Arguedas, M., Eskridge, T. C., & Carvajal, R. et al. (2005). Concept maps: Integrating knowledge and information visualization. In S.-O. Tergan & T. Keller (Eds.), *Knowledge and information visualization* (pp. 205–219). New York, NY: Springer. doi:10.1007/11510154_11

Carson, P. P., & Carson, K. D. (1993). Managing creativity enhancement through goal-setting and feedback. *Creativity Research Journal*, *27*(1), 36–45.

Chen, L., Marsden, J. R., & Zhang, Z. (2012). Theory and analysis of company-sponsored value co-creation. *Journal of Management Information Systems*, *29*(2), 141–172. doi:10.2753/MIS0742-1222290206

Chevalier, J. A., & Mayzlin, D. (2006). The effect of word of mouth on sales: Online book reviews. *JMR, Journal of Marketing Research*, *43*(3), 345–354. doi:10.1509/jmkr.43.3.345

Chua, C. K., Leong, K. F., & Lim, C. S. (2003). *Rapid prototyping: Principles and applications* (2nd ed.). Singapore: World Scientific Publishing. doi:10.1142/5064

Collaros, P. A., & Anderson, L. R. (1969). Effect of perceived expertness upon creativity of members of brainstorming groups. *The Journal of Applied Psychology*, *53*(2, Pt.1), 159–163. doi:10.1037/h0027034 PMID:5790809

Connolly, T., Jessup, L. M., & Valacich, J. S. (1990). Effects of anonymity and evaluative tone on idea generation in computer-mediated groups. *Management Science*, *36*(6), 689–703. doi:10.1287/mnsc.36.6.689

Culnan, M., McHugh, P., & Zubillaga, J. (2010). How large U.S. companies can use twitter and other social media to gain business value. *MIS Quarterly Executive*, *9*(04), 243–259.

Cutler, R., Rui, Y., Gupta, A., Cadiz, J., Tashey, I., He, L., . . . Silverberg, S. (2002). Distributed meetings: A meeting capture and broadcasting system. In *Preceedings of the 10th ACM International Conference on Multimedia* (pp. 503-512). ACM.

Da Silva, N., & Oldham, G. R. (2012). Adopting employees' ideas: Moderators of the idea generation-idea implementation link. *Creativity Research Journal*, *24*(2-3), 134–145. doi:10.1080/10400419.2012.677257

DeFillippi, R., Grabher, G., & Jones, C. (2007). Introduction to paradoxes of creativity: Managerial and organizational challenges in the cultural economy. *Journal of Organizational Behavior*, *28*(5), 511–521. doi:10.1002/job.466

Dennis, A. R., & Valascich, J. S. (1993). Computer brainstorms: More heads are better than one. *The Journal of Applied Psychology*, *78*(4), 531–537. doi:10.1037/0021-9010.78.4.531

Derosa, D. M., Smith, C. L., & Hantula, D. A. (2007). The medium matters: Mining the long-promised merit of group interaction in creative idea generation tasks in a meta-analysis of the electronic group brainstorming literature. *Computers in Human Behavior, 23*(3), 1549–1581. doi:10.1016/j.chb.2005.07.003

Diehl, M., & Stroebe, W. (1987). Productivity loss in brainstorming groups: Toward the solution of a riddle. *Journal of Personality and Social Psychology, 53*(3), 497–509. doi:10.1037/0022-3514.53.3.497

Dossick, C. S., Anderson, A., Azari, R., Iorio, J., Neff, G., & Taylor, J. E. (2014). Messy talk in virtual teams: Achieving knowledge synthesis through shared visualizations. *Journal of Management Engineering.*

Duffy, A. H. B., Andreasen, M. M., MacCallum, K. J., & Reijers, L. N. (1993). Design co-ordination for concurrent engineering. *Journal of Engineering Design, 4*(4), 251–261. doi:10.1080/09544829308914785

Edmonds, E., & Candy, L. (2002). Creativity, art practice, and knowledge. *Communications of the ACM, 45*(10), 91–95. doi:10.1145/570907.570939

Edmondson, A. (1999). Psychological safety and learning behavior in work teams. *Administrative Science Quarterly, 44*(2), 350. doi:10.2307/2666999

Edmondson, A. (2003). Managing the risk of learning: Psychological safety in work teams. In M. West, D. Tjosvold, & K. Smith (Eds.), *International handbook of teamwork and co-operative working* (pp. 255–276). West Sussex, UK: John Wiley & Sons. doi:10.1002/9780470696712.ch13

Ellemers, N., De Gilder, D., & Haslam, S. A. (2004). Motivating individuals and groups at work: A social identity perspective on leadership and group performance. *Academy of Management Review, 29*(3), 459–478.

Fairchild, J., Cassidy, S., Cushenbery, L., & Hunter, S. (2011). Integrating technology with the creative design process. In A. Mesquita (Ed.), *Technology for creativity and innovation: Tools, techniques and applications* (pp. 26–51). Hershey, PA: IGI Global. doi:10.4018/978-1-60960-519-3.ch002

Fairchild, J., Eubanks, D., & Hunter, S. T. (2013). Effects of intuition, positive affect, and training on creative problem solving. In E. G. Carayannis (Ed.), *The encyclopedia of creativity, invention, innovation, and entrepreneurship* (pp. 562–567). New York, NY: Springer. doi:10.1007/978-1-4614-3858-8_363

Florida, R. (2002). *The rise of the creative class.* New York: Basic Books.

Fruchter, R. (2004). Global teamwork: Cross-disciplinary, collaborative, geographically-distributed e-learning environment. In J. Bento, J. P. Duarte, M. V. Heitor, & W. J. Mitchell (Eds.), *Collaborative design and learning: Competence building for innovation* (pp. 265–297).

Gallupe, R. B., Dennis, A. R., Cooper, W. H., Valacich, J. S., Bastianutti, L. M., & Nunamaker, J. F. (1992). Electronic brainstorming and group size. *Academy of Management Journal, 35*(2), 350–369. doi:10.2307/256377

Gautam, P., & Yanagiya, R. (2012). Reflection of cross-disciplinary research at creative research institution (Hokkaido University) in the web of science database: Appraisal and visualization using bibliometry. *Scientometrics, 93*(1), 101–111. doi:10.1007/s11192-012-0655-3

Gayraud, Y. (2005). *Cross-disciplinary report in FET.* Academic Press.

Geho, P. R., & Dangelo, J. (2012). The evolution of social media as a marketing tool for entrepreneurs. *Entrepreneurial Executive, 17*, 61–68.

George, J. M., & Zhou, J. (2007). Dual tuning in a supportive context: Joint contributions of positive mood, negative mood, and supervisory behaviors to employee creativity. *Academy of Management Journal, 50*(3), 605–622. doi:10.5465/AMJ.2007.25525934

Girotra, K., Terwiesch, C., & Ulrich, K. T. (2010). Idea generation and the quality of the best idea. *Management Science, 56*(4), 591–605. doi:10.1287/mnsc.1090.1144

Griffiths, D. N. (2013). Words from the wasteland: InXile CEO Brian Fargo talks tides and torments. *Forbes.com*. Retrieved from http://www.forbes.com/sites/danielnyegriffiths/2013/04/03/brian-fargo-interview-torment-tides-of-numenera-kickstarter/

Grimm, T. (2004). *User's guide to rapid prototyping*. Society of Manufacturing Engineers.

Hammond, K. J. (1990). Case-based planning: A framework for planning from experience. *Cognitive Science, 14*(3), 385–443. doi:10.1207/s15516709cog1403_3

Heath, D., Singh, R., Ganesh, J., & Taube, L. (2013). Building thought leadership through business-to-business social media engagement at infosys. *MIS Quarterly Executive, 12*(2), 77–92.

Heesom, D., & Mahdjoubi, L. (2004). Trends of 4D CAD applications for construction planning. *Construction Management and Economics, 22*(2), 171–182. doi:10.1080/0144619042000201376

Hertzum, H., & Pejtersen, A. M. (2000). The information-seeking practices of engineers: Searching for documents as well as for people. *Information Processing & Management, 36*(5), 761–778. doi:10.1016/S0306-4573(00)00011-X

Howell, J., & Boies, K. (2004). Champions of technological innovation: The influence of contextual knowledge, role orientation, idea generation, and idea promotion on champion emergence. *The Leadership Quarterly, 15*(1), 123–143. doi:10.1016/j.leaqua.2003.12.008

Hunter, S., Freidrich, T., Badell, K., & Mumford, M. (2006). Creative thought in real–world innovation. *Serbian Journal of Management, 1*, 29–39.

Hunter, S. T., Cushenbery, L., Ginther, N., & Fairchild, J. (2013). Leadership, innovation, and technology: The evolution of the creative process. In S. Hemlin, C. M. Allwood, B. R. Martin, & M. D. Mumford (Eds.), *Creativity and leadership in science, technology, and innovation* (pp. 81–110). New York, NY: Routledge.

Jannsen, D. G., & Smith, S. M. (1991). Design fixation. *Design Studies, 12*(1), 3–11. doi:10.1016/0142-694X(91)90003-F

Janssen, O. (2005). The joint impact of perceived influence and supervisor supportiveness on employee innovative behaviour. *Journal of Occupational and Organizational Psychology, 78*(4), 573–579. doi:10.1348/096317905X25823

Kalatzis, N., Liampotis, N., Roussaki, I., Kosmides, P., Papaioannou, I., Xynogalas, S., & Anagnostou, M. et al. (2014). Cross-community context management in cooperating smart spaces. *Personal and Ubiquitous Computing, 18*(2), 427–443. doi:10.1007/s00779-013-0654-2

Kaplan, A. M., & Haenlein, M. (2010). Users of the world, unite! The challenges and opportunities of social media. *Business Horizons, 53*(1), 59–68. Retrieved July 2 2014. doi:10.1016/j.bushor.2009.09.003

Kearney, A. R., & Kaplan, S. (1997). Toward a methodology for the measurement of knowledge structures of ordinary people: The conceptual content cognitive map (3CM). *Environment and Behavior, 29*(5), 579–617. doi:10.1177/0013916597295001

Kickstarter.com. (2013). *The year in Kickstarter: 2013*. Retrieved from https://www.kickstarter.com/year/2013/

Kietzmann, J. H., Hermkens, K., McCarthy, I. P., & Silvestre, B. S. (2011). Social media? Get serious! Understanding the functional building blocks of social media. *Business Horizons, 54*(3), 241–251. doi:10.1016/j.bushor.2011.01.005

King, A. M., & Sivaloganathan, S. (1999). Development of a methodology for concept selection in flexible design strategies. *Journal of Engineering Design, 10*(4), 329–349. doi:10.1080/095448299261236

King, L. (2014). Ford, where virtual reality is already manufacturing reality. *Forbes.com*. Retrieved from http://www.forbes.com/sites/leoking/2014/05/03/ford-where-virtual-reality-is-already-manufacturing-reality/

Klimoski, R., & Mohammed, S. (1994). Team mental model: Construct or metaphor? *Journal of Management, 20*(2), 403–437. doi:10.1016/0149-2063(94)90021-3

Kulkarni, D., & Simon, H. A. (1998). The process of scientific discovery: The strategy of experimentation. *Cognitive Science, 12*(2), 139–175. doi:10.1207/s15516709cog1202_1

Lamm, H., & Trommsdorff, G. (1973). Group versus individual performance on tasks requiring ideational proficiency (brainstorming): A review. *European Journal of Social Psychology, 3*(4), 361–388. doi:10.1002/ejsp.2420030402

Leiponein, A., & Helfat, C. E. (2010). Innovation objectives, knowledge sources, and the benefits of breadth. *Strategic Management Journal, 31*, 224–236.

Lin, H. (2007). Knowledge sharing and firm innovation capability: An empirical study. *International Journal of Manpower, 28*(3/4), 315–332. doi:10.1108/01437720710755272

Lonergan, D. C., Scott, G. M., & Mumford, M. D. (2004). Evaluative aspects of creative thought: Effects of appraisal and revision standards. *Creativity Research Journal, 16*(2-3), 231–246. doi:10.1080/10400419.2004.9651455

Madjar, N. (2008). Emotional and informational support from different sources and employee creativity. *Journal of Occupational and Organizational Psychology, 81*(1), 83–100. doi:10.1348/096317907X202464

Madsen, S. R., Miller, D., & John, C. R. (2005). Readiness for organizational change: Do organizational commitment and social relationships in the workplace make a difference? *Human Resource Development Quarterly, 16*(2), 213–234. doi:10.1002/hrdq.1134

Mathieu, J. E., Heffner, T. S., Goodwin, G. F., Salas, E., & Cannon-Bowers, J. A. (2000). The influence of shared mental models on team process and performance. *The Journal of Applied Psychology, 85*(2), 273–283. doi:10.1037/0021-9010.85.2.273 PMID:10783543

Michinov, N. (2012). Is electronic brainstorming or brainwriting the best way to improve creative performance in groups? An overlooked comparison of two idea-generation techniques. *Journal of Applied Social Psychology, 42*, E222–E243. doi:10.1111/j.1559-1816.2012.01024.x

Mohammed, S., & Dumville, B. (2000). Team mental models in a team knowledge framework: Expanding theory and measurement across disciplinary boundaries. *Journal of Organizational Behavior, 22*(2), 89–106. doi:10.1002/job.86

Mumford, M. D., Baughman, W. A., Maher, M. A., Costanza, D. P., & Supinski, E. P. (1997a). Process-based measures of creative problem-solving skills: IV. Category combination. *Creativity Research Journal, 10*(1), 59–71. doi:10.1207/s15326934crj1001_7

Mumford, M. D., Baughman, W. A., Supinski, E. P., & Maher, M. A. (1996b). Process-based measures of creative problem-solving skills: II. Information encoding. *Creativity Research Journal, 9*(1), 77–88. doi:10.1207/s15326934crj0901_7

Mumford, M. D., Baughman, W. A., Threlfall, K. V., Supinski, E. P., & Costanza, D. P. (1996a). Process-based measures of creative problem-solving skills. I. Problem construction. *Creativity Research Journal, 9*(1), 63–76. doi:10.1207/s15326934crj0901_6

Mumford, M. D., Connelly, S., & Gaddis, B. (2003). How creative leaders think: Experimental findings and cases. *The Leadership Quarterly, 14*(4-5), 411–432. doi:10.1016/S1048-9843(03)00045-6

Mumford, M. D., & Gustafson, S. B. (1988). Creativity syndrome: Integration, application, and innovation. *Psychological Bulletin, 103*(1), 27–43. doi:10.1037/0033-2909.103.1.27

Mumford, M. D., Schultz, R. A., & Doorn, J. R. (2001). Performance in planning: Processes, requirements, and errors. *Review of General Psychology, 5*(3), 213–240. doi:10.1037/1089-2680.5.3.213

Mumford, M. D., Supinski, E. P., Threlfall, K. V., & Baughman, W. A. (1996). Process-based measures of creative problem-solving skills: III. Category selection. *Creativity Research Journal, 9*(4), 395–406. doi:10.1207/s15326934crj0904_11

Mumford, M. D., Zaccaro, S. J., Harding, F. D., Jacobs, T., & Fleishman, E. A. (2000). Leadership skills for a changing world: Solving complex social problems. *The Leadership Quarterly, 11*(1), 11–35. doi:10.1016/S1048-9843(99)00041-7

Mumford, T. V., Van Iddekinge, C. G., Morgeson, F. P., & Campion, M. A. (2008). The team role test: Development and validation of a team role knowledge situational judgment test. *The Journal of Applied Psychology, 93*(2), 250–267. doi:10.1037/0021-9010.93.2.250 PMID:18361630

Oldham, G. R., & Cummings, A. (1996). Employee creativity: Personal and contextual factors at work. *Academy of Management Journal, 39*(3), 607–634. doi:10.2307/256657

Oldham, G. R., & Silva, N. D. (2013). The impact of digital technology on the generation and implementation of creative ideas in the workplace. *Computers in Human Behavior, 1*, 1–7.

Osburn, H., & Mumford, M. (2006). Creativity and planning: Training interventions to develop creative problem-solving skills. *Creativity Research Journal, 18*(2), 173–190. doi:10.1207/s15326934crj1802_4

Perry-Smith, J. E., & Shalley, C. E. (2003). The social side of creativity: A static and dynamic social network perspective. *Academy of Management Review, 28*(1), 89–106.

Qin, Y., & Simon, H. A. (1990). Laboratory replication of scientific discovery processes. *Cognitive Science, 14*(2), 281–312. doi:10.1207/s15516709cog1402_4

Reiter-Palmon, R. (2009). A dialectic perspective on problem identification and construction. *Industrial and Organizational Psychology: Perspectives on Science and Practice, 2*(3), 349–352. doi:10.1111/j.1754-9434.2009.01157.x

Reiter-Palmon, R., Wigert, B., & de Vreede, T. (2012). Team creativity and innovation: The effect of group composition, social processes, and cognition. In M. D. Mumford (Ed.), *Handbook of organizational creativity*. London, UK: Elsevier. doi:10.1016/B978-0-12-374714-3.00013-6

Rietzschel, E. F., Nijstad, B. A., & Stroebe, W. (2006). Relative accessibility of domain knowledge and creativity: The effects of knowledge activation on the quantity and originality of generated ideas. *Journal of Experimental Social Psychology*, 43(6), 4–14.

Rietzschel, E. F., Nijstad, B. A., & Stroebe, W. (2006). Productivity is not enough: A comparison of interactive and nominal brainstorming groups on idea generation and selection. *Journal of Experimental Social Psychology*, 42(2), 244–251. doi:10.1016/j.jesp.2005.04.005

Rizzuto, T., & Reeves, J. (2007). A multi-disciplinary overview of person-related barriers to technology implementation. *Consulting Psychology Journal: Practice and Research*, 59(3), 226–240. doi:10.1037/1065-9293.59.3.226

Root, A. (2014). Your business needs to tweet – Here's how to make it worth your while. *Forbes.com*. Retrieved from http://www.forbes.com/sites/theyec/2014/07/02/your-business-needs-to-tweet-heres-how-to-make-it-worth-your-while/

Runco, M. A. (1991). *Divergent thinking*. Westport, CT: Ablex Publishing.

Runco, M. A., & Jaeger, G. J. (2012). The standard definition of creativity. *Creativity Research Journal*, 24(1), 92–96. doi:10.1080/10400419.2012.650092

Sharma, A. (1999). Central dilemmas of managing innovation in large firms. *California Management Review*, 41(3), 146–164. doi:10.2307/41166001

Silva, N. D., & Oldham, G. R. (2012). Adopting employees' ideas: Moderators of the idea generation-idea implementation link. *Creativity Research Journal*, 24(2-3), 134–145. doi:10.1080/10400419.2012.677257

Simon, H. (1973). The structure of ill structured problems. *Artificial Intelligence*, 4(3-4), 181–201. doi:10.1016/0004-3702(73)90011-8

Skilton, P. F., & Dooley, K. J. (2010). The effects of repeat collaboration on creative abrasion. *Academy of Management Journal*, 35, 118–134.

Sternberg, R. J., & Lubart, T. I. (1996). Investing in creativity. *The American Psychologist*, 51(7), 677–688. doi:10.1037/0003-066X.51.7.677

Sternberg, R. J., & O'Hara, L. A. (1999). Creativity and intelligence. In R. J. Sternberg (Ed.), *Handbook of creativity* (pp. 251–272). Cambridge, UK: Cambridge University Press.

Sternberg, R. J., O'Hara, L. A., & Lubart, T. I. (1997). Creativity as investment. *California Management Review*, 40(1), 8–21. doi:10.2307/41165919

Taylor, D. W., Berry, P. C., & Block, C. H. (1958). Does group participation when using brainstorming facilitate or inhibit creative thinking? *Administrative Science Quarterly*, 3(1), 23–47. doi:10.2307/2390603

Thackeray, R., Neiger, B. L., Hanson, C. L., & McKenzie, J. F. (2008). Enhancing promotional strategies within social marketing programs: Use of web 2.0 social media. *Health Promotion Practice*, 9(4), 338–343. doi:10.1177/1524839908325335 PMID:18936268

Tripp, S. D., & Bichelmeyer, B. (1990). Rapid prototyping: An alternative instructional design strategy. *Educational Technology Research and Development*, 38(1), 31–44. doi:10.1007/BF02298246

Van Knippenberg, D., & Schippers, M. (2007). Work group diversity. *Annual Review of Psychology, 58*(1), 515–541. doi:10.1146/annurev.psych.58.110405.085546 PMID:16903805

Vivek, S. D., Beatty, S. E., & Morgan, R. M. (2012). Customer engagement: Exploring customer relationships beyond purchase. *Journal of Marketing Theory and Practice, 20*(2), 127–145. doi:10.2753/MTP1069-6679200201

Wang, Y., & Horvath, I. (2013). Computer-aided multi-scale materials and product design. *Computer Aided Design, 45*(1), 1–3. doi:10.1016/j.cad.2012.07.013

Warr, A., & O'Neill, E. (2005). Understanding design as a social creative process. In *Proceedings of the 5th Conference on Creativity & Cognition* (pp. 118-127). New York: ACM Press. doi:10.1145/1056224.1056242

West, M. A., & Altink, W. M. (1996). Innovation at work: Individual, group, organizational, and socio-historical perspectives. *European Journal of Work and Organizational Psychology, 5*(1), 3–11. doi:10.1080/13594329608414834

West, M. A., & Anderson, N. R. (1996). Innovation in top management teams. *The Journal of Applied Psychology, 81*(6), 680–693. doi:10.1037/0021-9010.81.6.680

Wu, C. H., Cheng, Y., Ip, H. M., & Mcbride-Chang, C. (2005). Age differences in creativity: Task structure and knowledge base. *Creativity Research Journal, 17*(4), 321–326. doi:10.1207/s15326934crj1704_3

Zhou, J. (1998). Feedback valence, feedback style, task autonomy, and achievement orientation: Interactive effects on creative performance. *The Journal of Applied Psychology, 83*(2), 261–276. doi:10.1037/0021-9010.83.2.261

Zhou, J. (2003). When the presence of creative coworkers is related to creativity: Role of supervisor close monitoring, developmental feedback, and creative personality. *The Journal of Applied Psychology, 88*(3), 413–422. doi:10.1037/0021-9010.88.3.413 PMID:12814291

KEY TERMS AND DEFINITIONS

Brainstorming: An idea generation process in which individuals or groups are instructed to generate ideas without criticizing or censoring themselves or one another.

Computer-Aided Design: A family of software programs that enable the generation of two- and three-dimensional virtual models.

Creativity: Ideas that are both novel (original or unexpected) and useful (practical and serving a purpose).

Crowd Funding: A method of resource gathering where interested potential customers pledge money to innovators for a product that has not yet been created.

Innovation: The production or manufacture of creative ideas into a useful solution.

Production Blocking: Phenomenon which occurs in a group brainstorming setting where only one member is allowed to speak at a time, causing other members to forget earlier ideas shared or prevent members from sharing their current immediate thoughts.

Psychological Safety: A perception that team members' contributions will be encouraged, and that disagreement or criticism will not be met with negative reactions, even if the contribution is radical or goes against the established norms of the group.

Rapid Prototyping: A family of technologies that enable the relatively fast and low-cost production of products for testing and evaluation purposes.

Software: Electronic technologies that enable users to interact with a technological system.

Technology: Tools or systems that provide support for some human activity.

Chapter 17
Digital *Parrhesia* 2.0:
Moving beyond Deceptive Communications Strategies in the Digital World

François Allard-Huver
Sorbonne University, France

Nicholas Gilewicz
University of Pennsylvania, USA

ABSTRACT

Deceptive communications strategies are further problematized in digital space. Because digitally mediated communication easily accommodates pseudonymous and anonymous speech, digital ethos depends upon finding the proper balance between the ability to create pseudonymous and anonymous online presences and the public need for transparency in public speech. Analyzing such content requires analyzing media forms and the honesty of speakers themselves. This chapter applies Michel Foucault's articulation of parrhesia—the ability to speak freely and the concomitant public duties it requires of speakers—to digital communication. It first theorizes digital parrhesia, then outlines a techno-semiotic methodological approach with which researchers—and the public—can consider online advocacy speech. The chapter then analyzes one case of astroturfing, and one of sockpuppeting, using this techno-semiotic method to indicate the generalizability of the theory of digital parrhesia, and the utility of the techno-semiotic approach.

INTRODUCTION

This chapter aims to analyze a variety of deceptive communication strategies and practices taking place in the digital world. Examining phenomena of astroturfing done by corporate actors to sockpuppet comments and other misconduct by private actors, we try to understand how deceptive communications practices are further problematized in the digital space, where ethos depends on a finding a proper balance between the ability to create pseudonymous or anonymous online presences, and the public need for transparency in public speech.

DOI: 10.4018/978-1-4666-8205-4.ch017

Among these deceptive communication practices we include, astroturfing—fake grassroots campaigns about matters of public interest—presents a special problem to researchers, particularly to those interested in studying the content of advocacy speech. Specifically, the content may be true, and even compelling, but if the honesty of the speaker is questionable, that truth may be a house of cards. This concern is heightened because of the fake accounts or false posts used by so-called "sockpuppets." In recent years, these wrongdoings even extended to the private sphere with the multiplication of fake social network accounts used for cyberbullying or cyberharassment. These deceptive communication practices threaten the prospect that the Web could function as a public sphere and therefore need to be taken into account in our analysis.

In previous work, we expanded Pramad K. Nayar's application of *parrhesia* to digital space (2010), relying, as did Nayar, on Foucault's articulation of this ancient Greek concept (Foucault, 2001). In this chapter we further develop our previous research on *parrhesia* and digital *parrhesia* (Gilewicz and Allard-Huver, 2012) Thus, we not only derive a model for analyzing the credibility of digital advocacy speech and a model for truth-telling in the digital public sphere, but also implement a theoretical and pragmatic method for understanding ethos and its implication on the web. *Parrhesia*, or the ability to speak freely, implies three public duties for speakers: to speak the truth, to sincerely believe that truth, and to honestly represent themselves when speaking. Astroturfing, sockpuppets or other online misbehavior that conceals identities in order to reduce the risks of speaking truth to power—or to the public—always fails the latter duty.

In networked space, however, pseudonymous and anonymous speech can work both democratically and propagandistically. We think that the legitimate need to speak the truth in this space does not forbid the right to protect your identity in specific situation, but the examples we chose to explore here show abusive use of pseudonyms or anonymity. This chapter proposes that digital *parrhesia* helps evaluate deceptive communication strategies and helps understand why such evaluation matters. By using digital *parrhesia* to analyze these online communication practices, this chapter's analytic model aims to contribute to the preservation—and maybe the revivification of—a culture of truth-telling.

BACKGROUND: BEEKEEPING OR ASTROTURFING?

Recently an important phenomenon of bee mortality has been observed around the globe. Every year, nearly 30-60% of the bee colonies are unable to survive the winter, a phenomenon called "CCD - Colony Collapse Disorder" by scientific experts (Evans et al., 2009). As some observers raise the specter of a total disappearance of bees in the forthcoming years, several scientific hypotheses have been advanced to explain CCD. The first is related to the multiplication of colonies diseases – such as parasites, mites or fungus. Another one blames the current agricultural system and intensive agriculture leading to bee malnutrition. Intensive beekeeping and selection of more docile but more fragile species are part of the assumptions. However, one of the main explanations given by scientists is that crop protection products – pesticides – play a determining role in the general weakness and therefore mortality of beehives (Henry et al., 2012) but is also subject to harsh fights between scientists (Cresswell & Thompson, 2012). Nonetheless, the insecticide class of neonicotinoids, such as imidacloprid, fipronil or thiamethoxam, is suspected to disorient and weaken the bees. These three insecticides are respectively sold under the commercial name Gaucho, Regent TS and Cruiser by Bayer, BASF and Syngenta, three of the world largest chemical and agricultural companies. Many sound science studies argue that these pesticides are at least one factor in CCD, but crop protection companies often deny any link, blaming misuse of their products not the products themselves. In December 2013, after numerous studies pointing out the critical role of neonicotinoids in the CCD, the European Union decided to temporarily ban the use of these insecticides. This decision has revived the controversy and led to judicial arm-wrestling between the EU and the big companies.

In this simmering conflict, the Bee Biodiversity Network (BBN) was created in 2007 to gather French beekeepers, growers and other agricultural professionals. The BBN supports the idea that CCD's most plausible explanations are parasites or bee malnutrition. They promote numerous innovative programs for helping the bees, particularly the creation of so-called "jachère apicole" (bee fallow land), the goal of which "is to create a pantry for bees and thus contribute effectively to the survival of bees and maintaining biodiversity." (Bee Biodiversity Network, 2012). The promotion of these programs also led the BBN to organize, every year since 2012, "The European Bees and Pollination Week" with help of European Parliament members, on the grounds of the European Parliament. The BBN also developed a lot of online action and has an active website.

The BBN raised attention within the online community and watchdog websites such as Corporate Europe and Lobbypedia started to investigate. What surprised these actors was that the BBN suggested that alimentation would be the major causes of the CCD without mentioning pesticide as a factor. They even discharged industry responsibility, an odd and unique position among beekeepers. Further investigation led the NGOs to discover the website was in fact funded and publicly endorsed by BASF. Where the Bee Biodiversity Network website is vague about its members, partners, and funders, BASF's Web site promotes "The French Bee Biodiversity Network" as something

the corporation initiated, and the Web site of the network credits its chairman and founder, Philippe Lecompte, who is identified as a "professional organic beekeeper in France." (Bee Biodiversity Network, n.d.). Nowhere does the network's web site identify BASF as a creator or a partner, (Corporate Europe Observatory, 2012). In fact, BASF only appears on the BBN site with its corporate logo, in small font, in the bottom right corner of an invitation to a biodiversity conference in Brussels. The industry thus officially started to support and endorse such public actions (Campagnes et environnement, n.d.) in order to promote its corporate responsibility (Mennessier, 2010), while, at the same time, concealing its role as a prime mover for the BBN in the first place.

A core concern of the circulation and presentation of information in public space is one central to the question of authorship and credibility: astroturfing. In this case, what began as a simple action in the public space and through a website ended in astroturfing practices being exposed by digital media observers.

This clear case of astroturfing—and how it was uncovered—allows us to observe the interrelationship between astroturfing, digital media use, and the exposure of other deceptive communication practices. In Europe, much as in the United States, citizens are accustomed to controversies and debate. The BBN raised concern and became a center of attention not because it was making a point in the debate about CCD. The astroturf was exposed as such because the BBN misled, hiding who in reality spoke through it and from where its discourses and ideas originally emerged—that is, from the pesticide industry. These beekeepers violated what we see as a fundamental factor governing digital communication space: *parrhesia*, in which the public duty of speakers is to speak the truth, to sincerely believe that truth, and to honestly represent themselves when speaking.

BUILDING A THEORY OF
DIGITAL *PARRHESIA*

Growing access to the tools of digital media production, from email to Web site design to video, have created new communication spaces and communities. Citizens, corporations, and governments all have enhanced abilities to engage in public dialogue about their beliefs, products, and intents—and enhanced abilities to conceal their identities while doing so. Thus, digital communication space introduces new problems for ethos; this realm depends on a proper balance between the ability to create pseudonymous or anonymous online presences, and the public need for transparency in public speech.

The act of astroturfing may be thought of as manufacturing support for an issue, or attempting to mislead politicians, news media, or citizens about the origins of such support. The use of the term dates at least to 1985, when United States Senator Lloyd Bentsen said, about receiving letters that promoted insurance companies' interests, that, "A fellow from Texas can tell the difference between grass roots and Astroturf. This is generated mail" (qtd. in Sager, 2009). Astroturfing attempts to leech the legitimacy held by grassroots movements, pretending that it is a response from below to governance from above.

Among online deceptive communication strategies, sockpuppetry has raised a lot of attention and concern in online civil society and is often seen as a major threat to ethical online discussion. Sockpuppetry can be seen as a related online astroturfing strategy. It creates false online identities, not for the legitimate purpose of protecting true identity—anonymity or pseudonymity can be understood as an "alternate" identity operating as a protective mask—but to defend an axiological or ideological point of view that a person or an organization would not normally publically defend. Phony Facebook or Twitter accounts, comments under another name in a forum discussion or even false

product reviews are the most common form of sockpuppetry in the web. But, how can we distinguish between sockpuppetry and regular and legitimate communication, especially those involving alternate identities?

Pseudonymity and anonymity surely have their place, for they accommodate truthful comments from individuals who may have valid reasons—from fear of community disapproval to the fear of being "disappeared" by a government—to conceal their identity. Yet, corporations, governments, and their public relations or advertising companies can exploit that same anonymity. What may be legitimately defensive for an individual becomes a public relations tactic for an organization attempting to reduce the risk of advocacy. But if in the digital era, astroturfing is easier than ever, so is learning the true identity of astroturfers, as seen in the Bee Biodiversity Network case.

In order to fully understand the role of digital communications in astroturfing, and to develop a method to analyze digital astroturfing, this chapter turns to Foucault's articulation of the ancient Greek concept *parrhesia* (2001). Commonly translated as "free speech," *parrhesia* implies that when one has the ability to speak freely, one also has the public duty to speak the truth, to sincerely believe that truth, and to honestly represent oneself when speaking—criteria worth repeating, and to which this chapter will repeatedly return.

This concept was first ported to digital space to make an affirmative argument for the value of the Web site WikiLeaks as a defender of "the agora of information" and a culture of digital truth-telling (Nayar, 2010). The argument is compelling, but the implications of digital *parrhesia* are both wider and deeper than simply defending WikiLeaks, because, according to Nayar himself, digital cultures generate new communities: "Digital cultures create a new communications culture, which generates a new community, the global civil society . . . and the globalisation of conscience. [WikiLeaks] is an embodiment of this new form of communications-leading-to-community, a digital *parrhesia*" (Nayar, 2010, p. 29). Under this view, new communities emerge whose participants may be judged by whether they adhere to the duties implied by *parrhesia*. Discourse under *parrhesia* centers on truth-telling in the service of community. Digital *parrhesia* is then a necessary component of digital communities, like *parrhesia* was a necessity in the Greek agora.

Risk balances the duty to speak truthfully in digital *parrhesia*, and in what Foucault calls the "parrhesiastic game," speakers balance the risk to themselves with the duty to speak the truth. "In *parrhesia*, the speaker uses his freedom and chooses frankness instead of persuasion, truth instead of falsehood or silence, the risk of death instead of life and security, criticism instead of flattery, and moral duty instead of self-interest and moral apathy" (Foucault, 2001, p. 19-20). If engaging in the parrhesiastic game is courageous, then undermining and exploiting the game is cowardly. Moreover, doing so suspends or negates the rule of the game, and thus suspends—and threatens—the role of the society as a discursive community as well.

Digital *parrhesia*, then, may be considered a discursive space where a wide range of individuals can engage in truth-telling practices, and a space whose boundaries—the duty to speak the truth, to believe that truth, to honestly represent oneself, all though online media—also provide the beginnings of a critical framework for assessing the credibility of digital texts. Clearly, identifying digital *parrhesia* as a discursive space and defining the boundaries of that space is useful; it allows us to distinguish between digital actors who seek to reveal the truth, or to conceal it. Getting there, however, requires a clear methodology. And the importance of good methods here cannot be overstated; accusing an author of astroturfing or sockpuppetry, under digital *parrhesia*, is tantamount to accusing that author of propagandistic lying.

Digital *parrhesia* lends itself to semiotic analysis because it identifies different levels of speech. At each level, truth-claims hinge on the medium where the speech occurs, how the speech is distributed, the content of the speech, and the identity of the speaker herself. People who have the ability to speak freely in digital culture also have the obligation to become Bentsen's "fellow from Texas" who can distinguish between grassroots content that emerges from below, and content that is astroturfed down from above. Distinguishing between the two often is contingent on questions of authorship and discourse. In order to help researchers make this distinction, the next section operationalizes digital *parrhesia* by integrating the author and the medium into what we call a "techno-semiotic" method of analysis.

Building a Techno-Semiotic Method for Digital *Parrhesia*

The idea that every human construct has different levels of meaning is the basis of semiotics, which itself can be a key that unlocks the structure of communication by revealing patterns of meaning at those levels. Semiotics aims to build builds a coherent approach for analyzing units of meaning. The goal of this chapter is not to solve questions asked by generations of semioticians, from the foundational work (Saussure, 1977; Barthes, 1968; Morris, 1964; Greimas, 1989) to scholars of today (Eco, 1976; Klinkenberg, 2000; Veron, 1988), but rather to operationalize their theoretical work into an easily applied method. The different steps of this method have much in common with the analytical skills used in the humanities and literature studies. And the "techno" part of the techno-semiotic method does not require advanced technical knowledge, but rather awareness that a medium itself is a complex object or condition.

In this way, we propose to understand online statements and the systems in which they evolve. Of the object of research—in the case of this chapter, an advocacy statement that may or may not be astroturfing—four questions must be asked:

Figure 1. Levels of meaning and questions

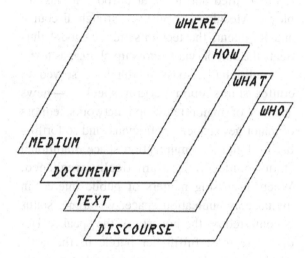

1. Where does the statement occur?
2. How is the statement enunciated?
3. What does the statement say?
4. And who said it?

These questions correspond to different levels of meaning: the medium, the document, the text, and the discourse (see Figure 1). In the techno-semiotic method, the levels, while having separate and identifiable characteristics, are not isolated from each other. Rather, each level plays a role and influences, and is influenced by, the other levels. So each level must be considered through two points of view: looking at properties intrinsic to each specific level of meaning, and looking at how the levels of meaning can and do interact.

First, the practice of semiotics in social science, communication and media studies has shown that exhaustive analyses must not restrict themselves only to content—the technical apparatus of communication must be considered as well. Davallon, for example, suggested that what makes objects of communication research unique is their "techno-semiotic weight" (2004). From the sheet of paper to the PDF document, every document has material features that transform the way we receive and perceive signs, but also influences our research

practices and the meanings we give to objects. This is but one aspect of the method—particularly significant at the level of the medium—which is highly influential, but not deterministic, because as Wright suggested, a technical apparatus does not determine communicative processes, which are themselves social, not technological, in nature (1986). Thus, the first step in describing an object is to describe the technical apparatus and the system that produces it. For example, this method always asks: are articles published in *The New York Times* newspaper and on nytimes.com the same? Is a 1933 speech by United States President Franklin Delano Roosevelt the same when heard on the radio then, and when read in a history textbook today? These are the types of questions that the techno-semiotic method prompts: Where does the statement occur? And how does the medium in which it occurs affect the meaning of the statement? These questions serve to avoid the pitfall of technological determinism, while still insisting that a statement's technological context affects its meaning.

The second step of this method takes us to the level of how a statement is enunciated. This is closely related to the where, or to the medium, but is distinct. Rather than looking at the medium and its systems—the differences between New York Times stories in print or online, or the differences between a contemporaneous radio speech and a textbook—the second step turns to the document itself, and the process by which it comes into being. The question of how a statement is enunciated regards how statements become text and how those texts are disseminated. For example, an author rarely publishes handwritten drafts of her work. Instead, she uses word processing software, then sends a copy—sometimes digital, sometimes paper—to her editor, who may send it along for further review by peers and copyeditors, until the document is transformed into a printable version for the printers. Thus, techno-semiotic analysis requires that attention be paid to how documents are produced and distributed, and to how those processes affect and inform the meanings of statements.

Of course, analyses of communication texts are commonly concerned with the content of statements, which is our third level: what the statement says, returning to the classic core question of finding meaning in a text. A news story viewed on YouTube will be different than the same news story viewed during a CNN broadcast. Neither will be understood in exactly the same way, nor will they be understood the same way as the script of the broadcast, or the audio track heard without the video. The medium informs this level, because audiences receive different media differently. Nonetheless, texts—particularly news and digital advocacy—have claims. Those claims must be identified and evaluated, and understood in the context of the previous two levels: to what extent the medium informs those claims, and to what extent how those claims are presented and distributed affects their reception.

The final level of meaning to investigate is the discourse. The analysis of discourse can be as complex as the definition of the term itself. In the techno-semiotic method, research into the content of the message requires gathering some information about the speaker, in order to understand his intentions and purposes. When considering a statement, the question of who said it is then a more global question about the speaker and her relation to the statement. Analysis at the level of discourse is closely and strongly interrelated with the other levels of meaning. Through analysis at the levels of the technics of the medium, of the production and distribution of a text, and of the content of a text, a holistic understanding of a statement and its meaning begins to emerge. To paraphrase and expound upon Marshall McLuhan, if the message is the medium, then we can say that the discourse is the medium: analysis of the medium reveals the space in which the discourse can evolve, can be

influenced and transformed, but also for whom it was crafted and to what purpose it was deployed. Meaning is conveyed through discourse and its intent; the techno-semiotic model thus treats the author, via authorship claims, as text.

Traditionally, mass media have served to confer status upon certain speakers—news anchors of major television networks, editors of major newspapers, politicians, and so forth—but in digital communication space, traditional status conferral is dramatically weakened. When discussing matters of public interest in digital communication space, we argue, status is conferred by the honesty of the speaker. Her discourse must fulfill her public parrhesiastic duties, which, again, are: to speak the truth, to sincerely believe that truth, and to honestly represent herself when speaking. As we will see in the examples that follow, analyzing the last of these—honest representation—is at the crux of determining whether advocacy speech is astroturfing.

ASTROTURFING THE EUROPEAN COMMISSION: FROM PUBLIC CONSULTATION TO RISK MANIPULATION

In a previous project, Allard-Huver tried to understand how negotiating the concept of risk in the European public sphere transformed advocacy communications (2011). He analyzed the public deliberation from 2002 to 2009 surrounding the 91/414 European Directive regulating pesticides, finding that some public feedback was surprisingly similar, considering letters were supposedly from individuals writing individually. Using the techno-semiotic method, it quickly became clear that an astroturfing attempt was being made within the European legislative process.

During its public consultation for the report *Thematic strategy on the sustainable use of pesticides*, the European Commission invited pesticide stakeholders to send comments, suggest modifications, put forward reservations and criticize the commission's work (European Commission, 2009). Some feedback that initially seemed to be from individuals appeared to be a part of a coordinated campaign, when seen through the prism of digital *parrhesia* and evaluated by the techno-semiotic method. These questions followed from the method:

First, is the European Commission Web site, as a digital public sphere, more subject to astroturfing attempts? The first level of inquiry focuses on the Web site—the media layer—of the European Commission, its functions, and the ways it created a digital public sphere. The site functioned in three ways: it served as a medium that raised public awareness of the problems of pesticides; it built a digital discussion space for public participation in debates about pesticide use; and now, it serves as a public archive for a completed process. Each function makes clear that the Web site is a mediator between different publics. The site, by enunciating the perspectives of European legislators as well as those of other stakeholders, suggests that the rules of *parrhesia* are at work; in turn, stakeholders, by participating in the process, imply that they accept those rules. But the physical and material distance introduced by Internet communication itself must not be forgotten. On the commission's Web site, distinguishing speakers can be difficult, and one can easily submit false information, or falsify an identity; this admits the possibility of astroturfing into the process. Nevertheless, because the site also plays the role of an archive, the public—and researchers—can investigate the advocacy speech therein, and how *parrhesia* operates in these debates.

Now, we can look at the third level of meaning: the content of the documents. The principal element of our interrogation is that some of the stakeholder texts are remarkably similar. The text of Birgitt Walz-Tylla's letter is almost the same as the text sent by Carlo Lick, B. Birk and Joseph Haber. For example, all four letters include this exact text: "As a scientist who has dedicated most of his career to researching and developing crop protection products, I believe there are a number of elements of this strategy that need to be further considered," even Walz-Tylla, a woman who, humorously, also "dedicated most of *his* career" (emphasis ours) (European Commission, 2009). Here, the content analysis is less the analysis of signs themselves, and more the recognition that the texts are the same. And these seams—like Birgitt Walz-Tylla's apparent claim to manhood, and our ability to quickly compare texts—suggest that these letters are part of a coordinated astroturfing campaign.

So, *who* then is the speaker? The person who signed these letters? The person or people who wrote the original text, which was then distributed to these four scientists? These questions go directly to the third duty of a speaker in the realm of digital *parrhesia*: the duty to honestly represent oneself when speaking. These four letters share the same content, but differ slightly in their presentation and the ways in which their authors present themselves publically. All identify themselves as scientists, and some sign their letters with their academic titles, laying a public claim to be experts in their fields. The letters from Birk and Lick clearly state their professional affiliations; both work for BASF, a chemical company with interests in pesticide production. Walz-Tylla and Haber do not provide their professional affiliations. But no matter: a simple Google search revealed that at the time of the report, Walz-Tylla was an employee of Bayer CropScience, and Haber was an employee of BASF. Both companies are industry stakeholders.

Thus, what separately seem to be legitimate individual positions of experts are revealed to be the direct participation of industry. This discourse does not arise from the individual concern of scientists, but from what appears to be coordinated industry propaganda. An industrial agent almost certainly wrote the original text, and suggested the campaign to other industrial stakeholders. This actor, in fact, is the true author of the discourse, but stays in the shadows, uses different identities, and ultimately leaves its intention unclear—is the issue one of good science, or good business? In this debate, then, we can say that these four scientists—and whomever wrote their letters for them—do not respect *parrhesia*. While they may have attempted to exploit the ease of submitting digital feedback, the realm of digital *parrhesia* also affords the opportunity to uncover their campaign. Therefore, digital *parrhesia* and the techno-semiotic method reveal what we believe to be a clear case of astroturfing.

SOCKPUPPETING PINELLAS COUNTY, FLORIDA: SECRETING RACISM

Astroturfing can be professional, well-styled, and coordinated, as seen in the BASF and Bayer-CropScience employees submitting letters as individual stakeholders, even though the content thereof is so similar as to suggest a coordinated campaign by industrial stakeholders. Astroturfing can also be petty, but still astroturfing, when a public official spreads individual social biases and political accusations under pseudonyms. In its previous iteration, the following example was discussed in terms of petty astroturfing; in fact, it bears greater resemblance to sockpuppeting: the creation of an online account controlled by a user of a different name or reputation, in an attempt to conceal the identity of that user while simultaneously providing him with a mouthpiece for his views.

In 2010 and 2011, a commenter on the Web site of the *St. Petersburg Times*, a daily newspaper in Florida, posted a number of controversial comments under the pseudonym "Reality." The commenter complained about "race pimps" who would "walk around looking like an idiot thug trying to hold your pants up. Whitie isn't to blame for your ignorance" (*sic*.). Reality also criticized what he saw as St. Petersburg's outsized number

of "thug shootings" and "prostitute beatings," and also attacked two Pinellas County commissioners—in one case alleging that a commissioner helped a "developer friend" access funds from the county (DeCamp, 2011b).

A reporter noticed that Reality often ended comments with the phrase "just say'n," a phrase also used by another Pinellas County commissioner named Norm Roche, and he noticed that Reality announced a new Web site in a comment—a Web site registered to Roche. Initially, this might not seem to be a case of astroturfing; after all, Roche was not manufacturing wide support for racism. However, when confronted by a reporter, Roche admitted that he posted both as "Reality" and as "Norm Roche," suggesting a desire to distance his public persona from the views of "Reality"—revealing that "Reality" was Roche's digital sockpuppet. And when critiquing elected officials, including his colleagues, he again used a pseudonym to distance Norm Roche from Reality. Even if the Reality persona was consistent and the author of Reality's comments believed them to be true, that one person operated two personae, whose opinions did not fully align (at least in public), suggested an effort to mislead or misdirect readers of those comments.

The word "secreting" has two meanings: concealing in a hiding place, and forming then emanating a substance. Here, Roche used a pseudonym to conceal the origins of his controversial comments, and possibly to conceal his own controversial views. (It must be noted, however, that Roche has publicly denied being a racist or a homophobe.) At the same time, he used a pseudonym to distribute those controversial comments, and to do so, used a medium that permitted pseudonymous comments and integrated them with news stories. In this case, the journalist who uncovered the relationship between Reality and Norm Roche used something akin to the techno-semiotic method to do so, and we argue that the method works very well to analyze speech in this situation.

As per the method, we first address issues related to the medium. Here, Roche's speech required a news product that offered an online commenting system. Such a system permits an exchange of ideas between readers who participate, and sometimes between readers and journalists, should journalists choose to respond to comments. Immediately, we see that these texts are polysemous—different readers interpret the meaning of news stories differently, including inscribing their own, sometimes divergent, meanings onto those texts.[1] At the same time, we see how these texts become polyvocal—for readers who do not comment, the news product is the story *plus* the comment threads. Within such polyvocal texts, voices that threaten the peace of the community can easily be identified. In this case, a reporter identified outlandish claims by a commenter. These claims could not exist without the newspaper offering a comment thread, which offering, in turn, introduced polyvocality into its news product. The digital text therefore has the ability to reveal through its medium the plurality of voices that create and recreate new texts.

Second, we address questions related to how the speech is distributed. In the case of these comment threads, reader comments are attached to the end of a news story. Online, the *St. Petersburg Times* publishes stories along with the comments; at the end of the story, the reader must click a link reading "Join the discussion: Click to view comments, add yours." While other content exists on the page, ranging from advertisements to copyright information to links to other news stories, only links to the comments, or links that help readers repurpose the story by sharing or printing it, are directly connected to the story itself. When commenting, a reader becomes a reader-author; when sharing a story by email or on a blog, the reader becomes a reader-publisher. In both cases, a participating reader implicates herself in a case of digital *parrhesia*, especially because she must agree to "Comment policy and guidelines" which include, among others, the requirement that

"Your comments must be truthful. You may not impersonate another user or a tampabay.com staff member by choosing a similar screen name. You must disclose conflicts of interest" (Tampabay. com, 2012). Finally, other commenters indicated a parrhesiastic situation, because they implicitly interrogated and summoned the criteria of digital *parrhesia*. On the story revealing that Reality was Norm Roche, many of the 137 comments debated whether the publication had violated its own promises of privacy to its commenters, whether the reporter had used honest techniques to uncover this story, and whether a commenter should take responsibility for his comments by posting them under his real name.

Next, we address questions about the content of the speech. The comments by Reality were often incendiary, supporting biases of some commenters and provoking outrage among others. Reader comments, in fact, operate as at least three different texts. First, comments exist in relation to the news story—expanding it, criticizing it, and opining on it. Second, comments exist in relation to other comments; they respond to previous comments while anticipating future ones. Third, comments exist as part of a complete news product, one that includes news story and all comments, that is served to non-commenting readers. The digital text is at the crossroads of the journalist's production of meaning and the public's reception and sometimes re-appropriation of it. The reporter who revealed Reality as Roche did so by understanding the first two content interrelationships—by identifying commonalities between supposedly different voices, and ultimately revealing them to be the same.

Finally, we consider the speaker himself. All four of the levels of the techno-semiotic method interrelate, but questions of discourse are perhaps the most pervasive of all. Above, we have seen how online commenting systems promote polyvocal texts, and thus create opportunities for deviant speech. We also have seen that by posting comments, readers become reader-authors, and in doing so, implicate themselves in a parrhesiastic system. Further, even the most cursory look at the content of reader comments reveals that understanding their intertextual and multitextual nature allows us to see the different ways in which content may be deployed. Discourse, then, is overlaid on all of these. The question of who is commenting and why may be the fundamental question of digital ethos in online texts such as these. In this case, once the reporter marshaled his evidence and asked Roche if he was Reality, Roche admitted that his reasons for concealing his identity (at least part of the time) were entirely discursive. He told the reporter, "A lot of it can be rhetoric and rants. Unfortunately it's part of our communication base now, and you have to be part of it, you have to track it" (Decamp, 2011a).

Thus, we see how a reporter used a process much like the techno-semiotic method to break a news story about a politician who concealed his identity while making possibly racist comments about his constituents. And we also see how different layers of meaning generated through the medium, its distribution, its content, and its author are all available to analyze the credibility of online speech.

CONCLUSION: DIGITAL *PARRHESIA* AND DIGITAL COMMUNICATION TEXTS

Clearly, an application of digital *parrhesia* has the potential to evaluate and assess digital astroturfing and sockpuppeting. Under the *parrhesia* model, truth-claims are reviewed in three ways: whether they are true, whether the speaker believes that they are true, and whether the speaker is honestly representing herself. Again, *parrhesia* accommodates pseudonymous and anonymous speech because honesty does not require mapping a name onto a real speaker, but rather requires that the speaker honestly believes in and argues for her truth claims. The techno-semiotic method accounts for this, but it also has wider implications.

As Nayar suggested, digital communication constitutes new communities (2010). This is not a new phenomenon—we have seen it before in the old bulletin board systems and chat rooms, and we see it today in online communities ranging from 4chan to Facebook groups. These communities, as all communities do, develop their own behavioral norms and mores. These norms help define the discursive space of digital *parrhesia*; the risks to a speaker for violating those norms—in the digital space, ranging from chastisement to banishment—help determine when and how the speaker will fulfill her duties to speak the truth, to believe that her truth-claim is indeed true, and to honestly represent herself and her belief. For astroturfers, the risk is that a secret propaganda campaign will be revealed, with consequences ranging from public shame to criminal liability. For sockpuppeteers, the risk is that their false representations and true identities will be revealed and that they have thus violate the mores or norms of the discursive space in which they operate. Most directly in the case of cyberbullying or cyberharrassment, fake accounts only show the perpetrators' cowardice as they serve the purpose to evade the law or to avoid direct confrontations with "targets," using the technosemiotic layer as a cover.

To operationalize digital *parrhesia*—to make it useable not only for academic critics, but to make a model that can be used to consider digital communication more broadly—we have integrated the medium and the speaker into our techno-semiotic method. Doing so solves a major problem with the sender-receiver model of communications, which manages to persist even when it is not appropriate. Under a sender-receiver model, texts can be recognized as univocal and polysemous—that is, readers can negotiate their own meanings with texts, even meanings that run counter to the preferred reading of a univocal author. But when texts become *polyvocal*, and when the medium itself—for example, an online news story with comments—creates polyvocality, the sender-receiver model falters.

Considering polyvocality in digital media facilitates the exposure of astroturfers and sockpuppeteers. In this chapter alone, we have a scholar (Allard-Huver, 2011) and a journalist (DeCamp, 2011a; DeCamp, 2011b) use observations made through or use techniques reliant upon digital media to expose astroturfing and sockpuppeting that, themselves, were at least partially executed through digital media. This suggests that polyvocal media and polyvocal texts, when functioning in a parrhesiastic way (that is to say, when discussing community issues in ways that hinge on acts of truth-telling), are especially appropriate subjects for the techno-semiotic analysis outlined in this chapter.

The cases outlined here—how the distribution of the PDF of a European Commission report compiling the feedback of stakeholders regarding pesticide use facilitated the revelation of astroturfing by pesticide manufacturers; and a journalist revealing that an elected official clandestinely used a digital sockpuppet to stoked the fires of racism in Florida—suggest the versatility of both digital *parrhesia* as a theory and the techno-semiotic method as a method.

REFERENCES

Allard-Huver, F. (2011). *Transformation and circulation of the notion of "risk" in the European Commission*. (Unpublished Master Thesis). University of Paris-Sorbonne, Paris, France.

Barthes, R. (1968). *Elements of semiology*. New York: Hill and Wang.

Bee Biodiversity Network / Le Réseau Biodiversité pour les Abeilles. (2012). *Give a flower to the bees*. Retrieved April 24, 2014 from http://www.reseau-biodiversite-abeilles.com/?page_id=1169

Conseil supérieur de l'audiovisuel. (2011, October 18). *Convention de la chaîne M6*. Retrieved February 12, 2012, from http://www.csa.fr/Espace-juridique/Conventions-des-editeurs/Convention-de-la-chaine-M6

Cresswell, J., & Thompson, H. (2012). Comment on "A Common Pesticide Decreases Foraging Success and Survival in Honey Bees". *Science*, *337*(6101), 1453. doi:10.1126/science.1224618 PMID:22997307

Davallon, J. (2004). Objet concret, objet scientifique, objet de recherche. *Hermes*, *38*, 30–37.

DeCamp, D. (2011a, November 17). Pinellas county commissioner Norm Roche has alter ego for online comments. *St. Petersburg Times*. Retrieved January 22, 2012, from http://www.tampabay.com/news/localgovernment/article1202065.ece

DeCamp, D. (2011b, November 18). Norm Roche's anonymous online snark strains city, county relations. *St. Petersburg Times*. Retrieved January 22, 2012, from http://www.tampabay.com/news/politics/local/norm-roches-anonymous-online-snark-strains-city-county-relations/1202287

Eco, U. (1976). *A theory of semiotics*. Bloomington, IN: Indiana University Press.

European Commission. (2009). Towards a thematic strategy on the sustainable use of pesticides. *Environment*.

Evans, J. D., Saegerman, C., Mullin, C., Haubruge, E., Nguyen, B. K., Frazier, M., & Pettis, J. S. et al. (2009). Colony collapse disorder: A descriptive study. *PLoS ONE*, *4*(8), e6481. doi:10.1371/journal.pone.0006481 PMID:19649264

Foucault, M. (2001). *Fearless speech*. Los Angeles, CA: Semiotext(e).

Freenews. (2011a, May 17). *La Freebox à l'honneur dans E=M6 (MàJ)*. Retrieved February 12, 2012, from http://www.freenews.fr/spip.php?article8300

Freenews. (2011b, October 11). *Reportage bidon sur la Freebox dans E=M6: intervention du CSA*. Retrieved February 12, 2012, from http://www.freenews.fr/spip.php?article9131

Gilewicz, N., & Allard-Huver, F. (2012). Digital parrhesia as a counterweight to astroturfing. In S. Apostel & M. Folk (Eds.), Online credibility and digital ethos: Evaluating computer-mediated communication (pp. 215-227). Hershey, PA: IGI Global.

Greimas, J. (1989). *The social sciences: A semiotic view*. Minneapolis, MN: University of Minnesota Press.

Henry, M., Béguin, M., Requier, F., Rollin, O., Odoux, J.-F., Aupinel, P., & Decourtye, A. et al. (2012). A common pesticide decreases foraging success and survival in honey bees. *Science*, *336*(6079), 348–350. doi:10.1126/science.1215039 PMID:22461498

Klinkenberg, J.-M. (2000). *Précis de sémiotique générale*. Paris: Seuil.

McLuhan, M. (1994). *Understanding media: The extensions of man*. Cambridge, MA: MIT Press.

Morris, C. W. (1964). *Signification and significance: A study of the relations of signs and values*. Cambridge, MA: MIT Press.

Nayar, P. K. (2010, December 25). Wikileaks, the new information cultures and digital parrhesia. *Economic and Political Weekly*, *52*(45), 27–30.

Sager, R. (2009, August 18). Keep off the astroturf. [Electronic version]. *The New York Times*. Retrieved January 22, 2012, from http://www.nytimes.com/2009/08/19/opinion/19sager.html

Saussure, F. (1977). *Course in general linguistics*. Fontana: Collins.

Tampabay.com. (2012). *Comments policy*. Retrieved January 22, 2012, from http://www.tampabay.com/universal/comment_guidelines.shtml

Veron, E. (1988). *La sémiosis sociale: Fragments d'une theorie de la discursivité*. París: Presses Universitaires de Vincennes.

Wright, C. R. (1986). *Mass communication: A sociological perspective*. New York: Random House.

KEY TERMS AND DEFINITIONS

Discourse: A sum of proposition and enunciation that creates a body of knowledge. The circulation of this discourse via media and other form of organization is called "discursive formation" in Foucault's discourse.

Semiotics: Literally the science of the signs, semiotics is the study of the meaning in every form. Here the perspective adopted is to study communication as an exchange, a construction and a negotiation of sign *via* the media.

Technological Determinism: A doctrine focusing on the technological evolution of information and communication system rather than on their interaction and their subordination to the society that developed them.

Techno-Semiotic: A way to understand and analyze media and communication phenomenon as being at the crossroad between a construction and a circulation of knowledge and signification, and information and communication technologies seen a *savoir-faire* serving and accompanying this circulation.

ENDNOTE

[1]   A phenomenon readily seen in comment threads following all political stories, for example.

Chapter 18
BOLD Ideas for Creative Social Networking:
An Invitational Discussion

Wei Zhang
Peking University, China

Cheris Kramarae
University of Oregon, USA

ABSTRACT

To further open the conversation about women's empowerment and global collaborations using new networking technologies, this chapter problematizes some prevalent ideas about creativity and social networking, notes suggested change that carry anti-feminist sentiments throughout the world, and suggests a number of ways that women and men can all benefit from an opening of queries about innovative ways of working together online. With the suggested expansions, the authors welcome more inclusive and invitational discussion about future digital media research and development.

INTRODUCTION

We are aware of dramatic technological changes, as more and more of us live in media-saturated cultures. The innovative practices of designers and practitioners of digital media technologies have provided millions of people with new and valuable means for obtaining and exchanging information and skills, and for building networks across many geographical and social boundaries. We read and hear about, and often experience, so-called "revo-

lutionary" changes in social networking practices that enable increasing number of people to share and process information in innovative digital forms. And yet, according to several recent reports, women's representation in technology continues to be low in general, and even the small number of women in technical fields are often isolated from influential social networks (Simard & Gammal, 2012). Given these barriers, we wonder just who is listening to whom, and we wonder if some critical "revolutionary" ideas are being refused or ignored.

DOI: 10.4018/978-1-4666-8205-4.ch018

In the current mainstream discourse on women's use of social networking technologies, we find prevalent assumptions that presuppose that, compared with men's uses, women's ideas and activities on the social Web are deficient and less serious. The assumption that women are not capable of generating creative and Big Ideas (about anything) is entrenched in much mainstream consciousness and unconsciousness, and appears in many guises. This fundamentally serious problem has been, for several decades, stated, illustrated and reiterated by feminists, without much, if any, fundamental changes. This is a discouraging situation, for everyone. If this situation is to change, for the benefit of all, women will need to be included, at every level, in the discussions and design of the digital media technologies. But not just included, in a perfunctory, numerical way, but in ways that acknowledge the complex history of gender inequalities in digital media work, and that acknowledge the challenging, creative and bold offerings women can bring to the work. At the moment, in terms of the recognition of their creativity, women seem to be hidden online.

In an effort to further open the conversation about women's empowerment on the Internet and global collaborations using new social networking technologies, we look at some of the ways that some current narrow ideas, usually unexplored, are carrying anti-feminist sentiments online throughout the world. If left unscrutinized, the misleading ideas can result in very limited notions of what access, equality, and interactive cultures can be. Here, we are not going to review and explore all the studies of creativity and gender. Rather, we problematize some prevalent ideas, stress that the social climate is an important element of what is accepted as creativity, and suggest a number of ways that men and women can all benefit from an opening of queries about innovative ways working together online. With our suggested expansions below we offer a number of thoughts about how to encourage fresh ideas about future digital media research and development. While not the only areas that need to be spotlighted, they can provide beneficial beginnings of more inclusive and invitational discussions.

IDEAS, EXPANSIONS, AND INVITATIONAL DISCUSSIONS

Can We Expand Prevalent Ideas of Online Creative Practices?

Women have a slight edge over men in terms of group communication skills; when women are included they generally improve the collective intelligence of a group (see studies cited in Kamberidou, 2013). In explaining the rising collective intelligence in groups with more women, Woolley and Malone (2011) point out that women are more inclined to "listen to each other. They share criticism constructively. They have open minds. They're not autocratic" (p. 2). Despite all these values women bring to innovative practices, women have not been widely recognized as having Big Ideas or of being creative in general (see the review in Zhang & Kramarae, 2012). Even when women in some locations are seen as somehow catching up to men's better efforts on the social Web, women are not seen as equals in creativity, or as offering many valuable ideas and examples about how the new social networking technologies can work. Kaliya Hamlin observed that of the fifty "brilliant thinkers" recognized at Ideas Project, a site on big ideas of the future of the social Web and collaboration, only seven were women (July 27, 2009). Our own experiences at conferences and workshops on new technologies confirm her observation: In most sessions, women are encouraged to be primarily listeners, and women's issues are rarely singled out as topics for discussion. As media critic Soraya Chemaly (April 18, 2013) summarizes, "The technology sector dresses itself up as progressive when in reality it shows every indication of being, at its core, powerfully retrograde." Chemaly warns that the ghettoized status of women and minorities in media and technology work "means that our attempts to express ourselves are limited, misrepresented and repackaged to make what we say palatable to a sexist status quo." She points out that this is not an indictment of white men as individuals but, rather, a description of systemic problems that we need to confront in order to arrive at creative, systemic solutions.

Not that solving these problems will be quick and simple. Some of the reasons affecting the perceived creativity and judgment of women are outlined by Baer (1999) and include differences in schooling opportunities and expectations (societal and academic) of women and men, and the fact that accomplishments in a variety of fields are judged by standards that have been controlled primarily by men. Many assessments of creativity are, of course, very subjective. Even in empirical studies the evidence does not reveal any simple, general conclusions about gender differences in scores on creativity tests (Baer & Kaufman, 2008) or even about what creativity is. We note that there are many areas and components of creativity, including flexibility, imagination, technical, and procedural expertise.

We also call attention to the fact that what is considered "knowledge," "analysis," or "rationality" is often set in opposition to "emotion." Yet, Raia Prokhovnik (2007) reminds us that language "is saturated with value (triggering personal and intellectual resonances, social norms, intellectual values and power relations) so that we respond to language with *both* reason and emotion" (p. 21, our emphasis). Prokhovnik writes, "Emotion is not an added extra, but... a necessary feature of all reasoning" (p.14). (See also Illouz & Finkelman, 2009.) If this one idea was really considered, it would be a Big Shift in the way that reasoning is primarily associated with, and glorified by, men, while emotion is often associated with women and often less valued.

We note that Wikipedia, a prominent online repository of contemporary knowledge, has been written predominantly by men about men's thoughts and actions; the technological accomplishment, and much more, of women have not been acknowledged at this widely used and cited repository. Working collaboratively and creatively in wikistorming sessions, many writers involved with technology, science and feminism have designed a "shared pedagogical activity" to help contribute to Wikipedia, "help revolutionize its culture," and help create a "more equitable and inviting space." (See discussion at http://femtech-net.newschool.edu/wikistorming/.)

There are, of course, many other examples of women's shared inventiveness online. In China, women are active in exploring new terms of address that do not always accord with the mainstream values and ideas regarding women. A good example is the evolution of the Chinese equivalent for "lesbian." In recent years, a playful innovative use of 同志 (comrade) that draws on local linguistic resources, has been widely used as an alternative for 同性恋, directly translated from "homosexuals," a general term of address for lesbians and gays. To differentiate from gays, Chinese women from online lesbian communities have created a new term, 拉拉 (pronounced as [la: la:]), which adapts the English word "lesbian" with Chinese characters. Innovatively pulling from both the local and international linguistic resources, Chinese lesbians have created their glocal identity (Zhang & Kramarae, 2008). A more recent example is about the popular new address term '女汉子' ('woman man' or 'wo-man'), a creative combination of the Chinese characters '女' ('female') and '汉子' ('man'). First invented by Li Ai, a fashion model and TV hostess, in a discussion initiated on her microblog, the address term became one of the top catchwords in China in the year of 2013. The term '女汉子' ('woman man' or 'wo-man') is now used to represent women who are both gentle and tough and are able to shift freely between the traditional gender roles associated with woman and man. The invention and the spread of the term '女汉子' reveals women's creative power in developing new forms of address that reflects and shapes desirable gender identities of Chinese women (Feng & Zhang).

Recognizing diverse forms of creativity women have presented in their practices online, shall we broaden the traditional conception of creativity and pay more critical attention to how women's ideas and practices of creativity might contribute to gender equity that benefit all people?

Can We Expand Ideas about Networking?

Web-based social networks allow participants to share ideas, interests, events and plans with others. One of the promises of social networking technology is the potential of expanding our social networks in everyday life by connecting to women and men across disciplinary, background, state, and cultural borders. But there are social and political complications that affect both women and men.

In many cases, to communicate with people from different countries, English literacy is almost indispensable. In countries where English is used as a foreign language, English may be the shared language primarily of elites. For many women who have limited English literacy skills, it may be quite difficult to expand their social networks across national borders. Or even within the borders. In some newly industrialized countries such as India, the high rate of illiteracy especially for women is further complicated by traditional cultural values that view a computer as masculine technology (Shuter, 2012). In a 2010 study, only 23% of Internet users in India were women and only 8% of married women with children used the Internet (Johnson, 2010). Mobile phones are more plentiful than computers in India. A system using vocal synthesis, icons, and customized avatars symbols enables women and men who are unable to read and write to send and read text messages; however, researchers have reported that families restricted and monitored text messaging by women much more than text messaging by men, creating a gender text-messaging divide (Shuter, 2012).

The difficulties of interacting online with others with diverse experiencers are present even when there is a shared language and more ready access to social media. Members of online communities, women and men, are more likely to connect with people similar to themselves in offline communities. As noted in Eszter Hargittai et al. (2008), our membership in online communities seems to mirror our identities in offline communities. Strong cohesiveness of divergent cultures or subcultures, values, and affiliations may hamper the development of national or global networks. For instance, Chen Yaya (2008) has observed that members of mainstream feminists' online communities in China are mainly metropolitan women academics in the field of sociology and other areas of social sciences; few communities involve women in the field of natural sciences, and women who belong to marginal social groups. Although there are vibrant online lesbian communities, the voices of these communities tend to be ignored in the discussions of the mainstream feminist communities. Further, similar to offline social communities, online social communities often have their own history, their own interests and goals, and their own norms of interaction, which may make it difficult for outsiders to step in, despite good intentions of participants.

Given this situation, can online technologies and practices be better planned to enable connections among diverse social groups? What can we learn from women's effort to use social media for new ways of interacting?

Women's communication networks are not, of course, a new cultural form. In many parts of the world, for decades feminists have created alternatives to mainstream media coverage as a method to give public voices to women. Without formal institutional bases of power, women have pulled together many groups with multiple (often changing) leaders, have made problems of hunger and unemployment more visible, and they have shown an ability to link to each other across many boundaries for particular actions (Hawkesworth, 2006, pp.70-72). For example, the organizers and participants in some of the new online communities have been resisting the kind of consumerist and entertainment-focused individualism of the Internet one sees so frequently in Europe, North America, and Asia. They are documenting the threats made to women and minorities and providing collective spaces to diverse social movements for the purposes of networking and information sharing (Desai, 2009, p.84). We have observed a growing number of blog communities that deal with gender and identity issues directly. A few examples can be found at the woman blog directory Blogged.com (http://www.blogged.com/directory/society/culture/women), a California-based blog search engine: Black Feminista, Feministing, Girlfriends Get-Together, Bad Girls Guide, and Feminist Philosophers, Appetite for Equal Rights, Above Average Jane, and BlogHer (See http://informedvoters.wordpress.com/2007/10/04/a-list-of-100-women-blogging-on-politics).

Moreover, women have often made new global networks while still keeping roots in local cultures and politics, in what Arturo Escobar (1999) has called the feminist political ecology of cyberspace. For example, we have witnessed the ways that some women in the Middle East have utilized traditional as well as new media for activism, and democratization. Because often women have to devise ways of countering not only government restrictions but also the everyday heavy-handed policing of women's bodies, they have devised creative ways of using social media, creating new forms of leadership and empowerment in the process (Eltantawy, 2013).

Being aware of what women have achieved in using new social networking technologies, shall we pay more critical attention to how everyone might benefit from learning more about women's networking ideas and skills?

Can We Expand Current Dominant Ideas of Online Gender Representation?

It is no secret that technology can be gendered, and is now deeply involved in gender relations. Much attention has been on how women and men are presented and present themselves on social media, given the ubiquitous sexualization of girls and women on social networking sites and the online bullying of those people and interests that are "different". Some research has focused on how masculinity is so often portrayed online—especially in games—as violence and power. Other research has focused on the ways that women throughout the world are leading the way at not only voicing their resentment of the ways that gender-based violence has been legitimized, but also showing how the skewed social norms prevent the growth and health of citizenship and nations (Skalli, 2013).

While gay men and their masculinities have been a reoccurring theme in digital media studies, there are few studies that deal, in general, with heterosexual masculinities and digital media (Light, 2013, p. 247). Young activist women are illustrating the ways that quite varied masculinities and femininities exist within any culture, even as the design and use of social network sites often continue to insist on binary gender roles (Carstensen, 2009). These and other feminist discussions and studies point out that there are many similarities across cultures in the ways in which patriarchal ideologies are being reinvented on the very online so-called liberation technologies that people are using to help obtain equality and justice (Diamond, 2010). An often-neglected issue related to the potential of new media for equality, justice, and democracy is that much thinking prioritizes the so-called public sphere, placing it as the center of social reality and significance, with a disregard for gender inequalities issues. The so-called private topics and interactions, involving such as household, family and education concerns, and sexist representations of women, are often, if inaccurately, believed to be of concern only for women and are regarded as less important, less newsworthy (see Youngs, 2008).

For years, women have been criticized for focusing on personal and social uses of technologies, as if these are of minor importance. Blog studies in the US, Africa, and Britain seem to confirm the personal and social nature of many women's blogs. In the U.S., Susan Herring and her colleagues (2004) have found that, while men tend to focus their comments on news and politics, and on distributing their knowledge in their blogs, women tend to focus on personal lives, emotions, and relationship building. This finding is echoed in studies on British blogging behavior (Pedersen & Macafee, 2007) and African women bloggers (Somolu, 2007). Oreoluwa Somolu (founder of Blogs for African Women) writes, "although many of the blogs featured are not overtly pushing for women's empowerment and gender equality, the fact that women are able to write about issues of interest to them" is indeed an important step for many women in gaining a sense of empowerment (2007, p.1487). Such observations are making a challenge to prevalent ideas about who can speak in public. Cultural barriers persist, and girls and women have, for example, experienced intense surveillance and risk harsh social judgment if they seem to become too "public". Girls' interest in, and ability to engage in defiant gender performances often exposes them to possibility of harsh judgments from boys (Bailey, Steeves, Burkell & Regan 2013, p.108). These blogs and actions are certainly "political," and we are all the poorer when ideas about women's and men's "places" and topics online remain sharply divided into private and public categories of differing value.

There are other ways in which current issues of online gender representation can be usefully questioned and challenged. Girls and young women, especially, are participating in online social media, in large numbers. So some critics who think that gender equity is primarily a matter of numbers may think that all is now well, that girls and women can say what they wish to the same extent as can boys and men. Indeed, girls and women have been early and avid users of social networking. And some people have noted that the new media cultures often have values such as creativity, cooperation and informality that have been considered as "typically feminine," and have thought that women would certainly not only be able to access and use the technology but also be a valued part of the designing group (Fernànez, 2013). Yet they are not often on the designing teams. This is true even as, in the U.S. for example, women now earn a good percentage of science and engineering Ph.D.s, but are less than a quarter of the STEM — science, technology, engineering and mathematics — work force. (See for example http://www.nsf.gov/funding/pgm_summ.jsp?pims_id=5383.)

Can paying attention to this research about online gender representation provide discussions that can assist us in questioning, in fundamental and demystifying ways, the methods that our digital media are being used to reproduce old gendered divisions, and the ways the research suggests methods of change?

Can We Expand Ideas of Freedom of Speech?

The openness of social networking sites has increasingly been abused by destructive individuals or groups that often target women, people of color, and other marginal social groups with hate speech, threats of violence, and attacks that ruin the reputation or privacy of the victims (Citron, 2009). Most of the time, victims cannot do much except go offline, limit certain functions of interactions (e.g., turning off the commenting function of a blog), or even close down their spaces.

YouTube, since its launch in 2005, has become a space with many displays of problematic behaviors including violence, abuse, hate speech and harassment. The site does have "Community

Guidelines," which defend free speech while also addressing behaviors not permitted; in this self-governing system, users can report instances of guideline violations, which are then reviewed and sometimes removed (Wotanis & McMillan, 2014). However, while the site claims to have no tolerance for abusive behaviors, many users still make harassing comments, prompting the question, "Is this new technology producing new social relations—or a rerun of old-style social relations with which we are all too familiar?" (Miller, 2009, p.427) and prompting the observations that there is relatively little minority content on YouTube, and girls and young women producing and appearing in videos are often judged according to how well they fit terms of gendered norms. (See discussion in Wotanis & McMillan, 2014.)

Social networking sites are not just cool new applications used for personal enjoyment, they are also sites of public discussion, which often comes with a polarity of opinions. As noted by Zhang Yiwu (2011), it is very common for people "to curse at disagreeable opinions on Weibo," one of the most popular microblogging platform in China. The seemingly broad and open space for discussion has turned into sites of polarized opinions, which might even develop into virtual attacks. Virtual attacks, which are often multimodal, can seem very real to those who are attacked. "Griefing" (incidences of avatar harassment, assault, racism, and homophobia) in virtual communities, as well as harassment on MySpace and Facebook sites can seem very dangerous to those who have experienced unwanted, hateful speech and other actions that can have very real consequences for those attacked. An official of Linden Lab, which created Second Life, has acknowledged that sexual harassment and assault exist in that virtual world, but she would mute criticism by adding that virtual assault "cannot cause physical harm" and the avatar's controller can teleport elsewhere or leave the online premises if s/he wishes. However, as Michael Bugeja (2007) has pointed out, this discussion needs to be continued: You can also leave the premises in "real life" when someone

makes a racist, sexist or other offensive remark, but such incidents are still considered very serious and can result in legal actions.

The abusive individual or groups often defend themselves with words about the importance of freedom of speech. And yet, in an article suggesting that we might usefully consider sexist discourse as hate speech, Donna Lillian (2007) has pointed out that most discussions of "free speech" in the U.S. revolve around interpretations of the First Amendment. Framing this large, world-wide problem of hate speech in U.S. legal terms may blind U.S. analysts, in particular, to the possibility of deeper consideration of how to respond to virtual abuse. Further, the issue is complicated. The notion of "virtual abuse" itself can be abused as a convenient excuse to achieve political purposes. For example, in some countries, politically "inconvenient" websites are sometimes labeled as "pornography sites" and blocked from user access.

Gender-blind policies and technologies cannot be assumed to lead "naturally" to women's involvement. Research has demonstrated that such issues as security, privacy, and safety are important areas of gender concerns, with women more concerned about these areas than are men. The dangers of censorship are acknowledged by many women's organization, but they also make clear that discussions, debates, practices and policies regarding censorship policies need to include women and their critical experiences (Michota, 2013).

While generalizations should always contain qualifications, we note that women often take a longer-term perspective. Many critiques focus on very current issues. The potential of social media *could* be seen as primarily in the support of civil society, with change measured in years and decades rather than weeks or months.

Realizing that traditional patriarchal ideology has reinvented itself in part by appropriating the new communication technologies, can a reconceptualization of the notion of freedom of speech help develop a more inclusive civil society in the social media spaces?

Can We Expand Ideas of Social Mobilizing for Change?

A lot of attention has been focused on men's use of social networks during the Arab Spring. Generally ignored in the many accounts of the men's use of social media for organizing actions are the differing ways women combined on-the-ground mobilization with cyber activism in ways that prompted new kinds of uses of new communication technologies and social networks (Skalli, 2013). Because of various restrictions and dangers, the women were less visible than men in the streets but played robust roles in cyberspace during the uprisings (Radsch & Khamis, 2013, pp. 883-884). For women, the streets were particularly dangerous; during the days of mass protests, there were almost 100 reported cases of sexual assault and rape of women in Cairo's Tahrir Square (Compendium, 2013).

Many women considered the assaults and heavy harassment of women as expression of gendered power threatening all women's mobility, and limiting their practice of full citizenship. They have tried to use social media not only to unite, embracing a diversity of class, race, gender, ethnicity, age and sexual orientation, but also to defy the conspiracy of silence condoned not only by the state but by much of mainstream media and society. The women have combined what they have learned in their more traditional methods of advocating for legislation to criminalize violence (face-to-face, radio and TV), with innovative methods involving SMS messages and uses of online maps to report, document and text about "hotspots" of violence. Harassmap, for example, quickly gained more than 17 thousand Twitter followers through the use of these and other innovative strategies (Skalli, 2013, pp. 6-8).

Similarly, some women in Morocco used traditionally sexist media portrayals of women to send forth a "scream of anger" on Facebook, deliberately provoking controversy and gaining attention for their arguments and initiatives (Almi-raat, 2011). In China, feminist NGOs appropriated the official microblog of Shanghai No. 2 Metro Company as a site for the Chinese component of the global SlutWalks, mobilizing broader publics for actions against sexual harassment in China, using traditional and social media resources, online and offline pathways and strategies (Zhang & Kramarae, 2014).

It is not only women's expertise with the new social media that enables them to open up dialogue, but also their knowledge about, and experiences with challenging the dominant, traditional stereotypes and myths. Historical and material conditions are key components for understanding the design and uses of online activities and communities of women and men, and these are often quite different. Because so many women are accustomed to having to define and defy many political, economic, and social structures (accustomed to facing not only government dictatorships but also sexism) might they be especially qualified to offer innovative ways of bringing about more holistic change?

CONCLUSION

We have looked at and questioned some current ideas about women's work and creativity that are spreading anti-feminist sentiment. If left unscrutinized, these misleading ideas can dampen creativity, and result in very limited notions of what online access, equality, and interactive cultures can be.

In our discussion we have referred to women and men as separate categories. Yet we certainly do not encourage the limiting division of the world into dual categories. Rather, we are acknowledging the frequent and troublesome ways that so many people use inappropriate stereotypes and actions when dealing with women and men, and some of the resulting limitations, for everyone, on the creativity in digital media work. Meanwhile, we are also calling for innovative ways to address the fluidity of gender beyond the dual categories of women and men. We have not, in this Chapter, focused on all the other exclusionary divisions of people such as those based on their race or ethnicity, religion, language, nationality, age, physical and mental abilities, and income, in part because we are aware that women are usually more acutely affected by exclusion across these various cultural categories and divides. Our efforts are, in the long run, to de-emphasize gender, by the very calling attention to current divisions and resulting evaluations.

We do emphasize that many women are using new social networking technologies to deal with this inequality and many other global problems in creative ways. We note that feminists, often looking for social change, are more likely to see possibilities for change, and therefore may provide especially innovative, interdisciplinary approaches to digital media research and development. As one researcher states, "Feminism is a natural ally to interaction design, due to its central commitments to issues such as agency, fulfillment, identity, equity, empowerment and social justice" (Bardzell, 2010, p.1301).

Yet not many of these concerns seem to be included in most discussions of digital media and creative technologies. In noting the continual way that women and their ideas about technology and creativity ideas are so often ignored, slighted, or mocked, we are not arguing that this process is always, or even usually, conscious. Research on unconscious human behaviors is making clear that reflective reactions based on stereotypes (including gender stereotypes) are often persistent, even if they run counter to our conscious beliefs of equality and fairness. The ability to regulate our behavior depends, in good part, on our ability to identify and then try to overcome the stereotypical, more automated, impulses that influence us every day (Bargh, 2014). Our suggestions above for the consideration of some alternative perspectives are designed to call into question our employment of stereotypes, and

binaries (such as male/female and good/bad), in order to help diversify and thus strengthen future work on creatively devising and applying digital media. Decades of research from organizational psychology, psychology, economy, and sociology shows that informational and social diversity, which includes racial, gender, and other dimensions of diversity, has unique value in arriving at greater innovation (Phillips, September 16, 2014).

Feminists have been active for decades in reframing the mainstream ideas about the creative use of digital technologies. Despite the potentials of local, national, and global social networking technologies in helping women generate and promote social enriching ideas, often these ideas are not readily recognized as "Big" or useful. The enduring ideas about the inadequacies of women's ideas and social networking are connected to the systematic disparities in the evaluation of others whose ideas are not considered important, online or off, including not only women but also men who are poor, with less formal education, older, or "ethnic". The Internet can provide the means for information, skills and networks. But we need to look at whose interests, access and ideas are being considered important in general, in order to understand whose words are credited as Big ideas.

Before researchers, policy makers and other critics make or accept many assumptions about women's social networking online, we need also to look at the enormous variation in informal kinship and friendship networks in many places. For example, in many western countries, the erosion of social welfare support and the breakup of households has meant that for many people the household, the dwelling, the home, social life, resources, and the family are no longer available in one place, and the kinds of networks and resources needed have changed (Healey, 2006, p.107). All kinds of networks need to be studied in order to understand what networks are wanted and will work.

Of course, it's not only men who may need some of the cautions we suggest about hidden assumptions. Some women who become successful in terms of, say, employment and economic security, are encouraged—perhaps by class disdain, racism, and a façade of equal opportunity as portrayed by popular culture and the media—to believe that they no longer need the support of each other. And those who are not "successful" may be lead to believe that they fail because they just don't have the necessary motivation and ambition, or have made too many "bad choices" (such as having children).

We worry about the assumptions that there is now a meritocracy operating with the new media technologies, such as that a relatively few individual women are enjoying the same visibility as many men do. We suggest that faulty assumptions about the politics of the Internet and social networking that ignore or repudiate the realities of women's lives throughout the world will not be useful to technology diffusion and gender equality, and thus not useful to the planning for the new social media spaces. At the same time, we suggest that looking at the kind of networking that women are doing and at the words and ways they are using can be very helpful in understanding the potentials of the new communication technologies.

In asking these questions about women's and men's ideas, interests, and practices on the social Web, we are trying to help reframing ideas about creative social networking. What seems clear is that the mainstream discourse about social networking is deeply gendered. Many people have raised concerns about some of the negative effects of digital and mobile media. Here, we point out that we have available opportunities to see not only the risks, but also opportunities of social media, if we pay attention to what women, in particular, are saying about social media. Digital inequities can't be adequately addressed until women's ideas are well considered, and utilized.

REFERENCES

Almiraat, H. (2011). Morocco: SlutWalk gets a toehold. *Global Voices*. Retrieved October 16, 2014, from http://globalvoicesonline.org/2011/09/07/morocc-slutwalk-gets-a-toehold/

Baer, J. (1999). Creativity and gender differences. In M. A. Runco & S. R. Pritzker (Eds.), *Encyclopedia of creativity* (pp. 753–758). San Diego, CA: Academic Press.

Baer, J., & Kaufman, J. C. (2008). Gender differences in creativity. *The Journal of Creative Behavior*, *42*(2), 75–105. doi:10.1002/j.2162-6057.2008.tb01289.x

Bailey, J., Steeves, V., Burkell, J., & Regan, P. (2013). Negotiating with gender stereotypes on social networking sites: From 'bicycle face' to Facebook. *The Journal of Communication Inquiry*, *37*(2), 91–112. doi:10.1177/0196859912473777

Bardzell, S. (2010). Feminist HCI: Taking stock and outlining an agenda for design. In *Proceedings of the SIGCHI Conference on Human Factors in Computing Systems* (pp. 1301-1310). ACM. doi:10.1145/1753326.1753521

Bargh, J. (2014). Our unconscious mind: Unconscious impulses and desires impel what we think and do in ways Freud never dreamed of. *Scientific American*, *310*(1), 30–37. doi:10.1038/scientificamerican0114-30 PMID:24616968

Bugeja, M. (2007). *Second Life, revisited: Which should take precedence in a virtual-reality campus: Corporate terms of service or public-disclosure laws?* Retrieved January 6, 2014, from http://0-chronicle.com.janus.uoregon.edu/weekly/v54/i12/12c00101.htm

Carstensen, T. (2009). Gender trouble in web 2.0: Gender relations in social network sites, wikis and weblogs. *International Journal of Gender, Science and Technology, 1*(1), 106-127. Retrieved January 16, 2013, from http://genderandset.open.ac.uk/index.php/genderandset/article/viewFile/18/31

Carter, C., Steiner, L., & McLaughin, L. (Eds.). (2014). *The Routledge companion to media and gender*. Abingdon, UK: Routledge.

Chemaly, S. (April 18, 2013). Facebook's big misogyny problem. *The Guardian*.

Chen, Y. Y. (2008). 网络的力量:女性主义者跨界合作的新途径[The power of the Internet: New means of feminist collaborations across communities.] Retrieved January 10, 2013, from http://www.mediawatch.cn/GB/75728/7151326.html

Citron, D. (2009, February). Cyber civil rights. *Law Review, 89*(1), 61–125.

Compendium. (2013). *Sexual assault and rape in Tahrir Square and its vicinity: A compendium of sources 2011-2013*. Retrieved January 3, 2014, from http://nazra.org/en/2013/05/sexual-assault-and-rape-tahrir-square-and-its-vicinity-compendium-sources-2011-2013

Desai, M. (2009). *Gender and the politics of possibilities: Rethinking globablization*. Lanham, MD: Rowman & Littlefield.

Diamond, L. (2010). Liberation technology. *Journal of Democracy, 21*(3), 63–83.

Eltantawy, N. (2013). From veiling to blogging: Women and media in the Middle East. *Feminist Studies, 13*(5), 765–769. doi:10.1080/14680777.2013.838356

Escobar, A. (1999). Gender, place and networks: A political ecology of cyberculture. In W. Hartcourt (Ed.), *Woman@Internet: Creating new cultures in cyberspace* (pp. 31–54). London: Zed Books.

Feng, L., & Zhang, W. (manuscript in preparation). *"Wo-Man" in China: Exploring the changing gender identities of young Chinese women*.

Fernànez, A. (2013). Internet in the feminine: Using feminine strategies in hacker culture. *Catalan Social Sciences Review, 3*, 93–112.

Hamlin, K. (July 27, 2009). *Missing: Privileged account management for the social web*. Retrieved January 6, 2014, from http://www.identitywoman.net/at-the-ideas-project-apparently-women-dont-have-any-ideas

Hargittai, E., Gallo, J., & Kane, M. (2008). Cross-ideological discussions among conservative and liberal bloggers. *Police Choice, 134*(1-2), 67–86. doi:10.1007/s11127-007-9201-x

Hawkesworth, M. (2006). *Globalization and feminist activism*. Rowman & Littlefield.

Healey, P. (2006). Collaborative planning: Shaping places in fragmented societies (2nd ed.). Houndsmills, UK: Palgrave.

Herring, S. C., Kouper, I., Scheidt, L. A., & Wright, E. L. (2004). Women and children last: The discursive construction of weblogs. In L. J. Gurak, S. Antonijevic, L. Johnson, C. Ratliff, & J. Reyman (Eds.), *Into the blogosphere: Rhetoric, community, and culture of weblogs*. Retrieved October 6, 2014, from http://blog.lib.umn.edu/blogosphere/women_and_children.html

Illou, E., & Finkelman, S. (2009). An odd and inseparable couple: Emotion and rationality in partner selection. *Theory and Society, 38*(4), 401–422. doi:10.1007/s11186-009-9085-5

Johnson, V. (2010). Women and the internet: A micro study in Chennai, India. *Indian Journal of Gender Studies, 17*(1), 151–163. doi:10.1177/097152150901700107

Kamberidou, I. (2013). Women entrepreneurs: "We cannot have change unless we have men in the room. *Journal of Innovation and Entrepreneurship*, 2(6). Retrieved from http://www.innovation-entrepreneurship.com/content/pdf/2192-5372-2-6.pdf

Light, B. (2013). Networked masculinities and social networking sites: A call for the analysis of men and contemporary digital. *Masculinities and Social Change*, 2(3), 245–265.

Lillian, D. (2007). A thorn by any other name: Sexist discourse as hate speech. *Discourse & Society*, 18(6), 719–740. doi:10.1177/0957926507082193

Michota, A. (2013). Digital security concerns and threats facing women entrepreneurs. *Journal of Innovation and Entrepreneurship*, 2(7). Retrieved from http://www.innovation-entrepreneurship.com/content/2/1/7

Miller, T. (2009). Cybertarians of the world unite: You have nothing to lose but your tubes! In P. Snickars & P. Vonderau (Eds.), *The YouTube reader* (pp. 424–440). Stockholm: National Library of Sweden.

Pedersen, S., & Macafee, C. (2007). Gender differences in British blogging. *Journal of Computer-Mediated Communication*, 12(4), 1472–1492. doi:10.1111/j.1083-6101.2007.00382.x

Phillips, K. (2014, September 16). How diversity makes us smarter. *Scientific American*.

Prokhovnik, R. (2007). Rationality. In G. Blakeley & V. Bryson (Eds.), *The impact of feminism on political concepts and debates* (pp. 12–24). Manchester, UK: Manchester University Press.

Radsch, C., & Sahar, K. (2013). In their own voice: Technologically mediated empowerment and transformation among young Arab women. *Feminist Media Studies*, 13(5), 881–890. doi:10.1080/14680777.2013.838378

Shuter, R. (2012). *When Indian women text message: Culture, identity, and emerging interpersonal norms of new media*. Retrieved October 16, 2014, from http://epublications.marquette.edu/cgi/viewcontent.cgi?article=1109&context=comm_fac

Simard, C., & Gammal, D. (2012). *Solutions to recruit technical women*. Retrieved December 1, 2014, from http://anitaborg.org/wp-content/uploads/2014/01/AnitaBorgInstitute_SolutionsToRecruitTechnicalWomen_2012.pdf

Skalli, L. (2013). Young women and social media against sexual harassment in North Africa. *Journal of North African Studies*, 18(5), 244–258.

Somolu, O. (2007). "Telling our own stories": African women blogging for social change. *Gender and Development*, 15(3), 477–490. doi:10.1080/13552070701630640

Woolley, A., & Malone, T. (2011). What makes a team smarter? More women. *Harvard Business Review*, 89(6), 32–33. PMID:21714385

Wotanis, L., & McMillan, L. (2014). Performing gender on YouTube. *Feminist Media Studies*, 14(6), 1–17. doi:10.1080/14680777.2014.882373

Youngs, G. (2008). Public/private: The hidden dimensions of international communication. In K. Sarikakis & L. R. Shade (Eds.), *Feminist interventions in international communication: Mind the gap* (pp. 17–29). Lanham, MD: Rowman & Littlefield.

Zhang, W., & Kramarae, C. (2008). Feminist invitational collaboration in a digital age: Looking over disciplinary and national borders. *Women & Language*, 36(2), 9–19.

Zhang, W., & Kramarae, C. (2012). Women, big ideas, and social newtworking technologies: Hidden assumptions. In R. Pande, T. van der Weide, & N. Flipsen (Eds.), *Globalization, technology diffusion and gender disparity: Social impacts of ICT* (pp. 70–82). Hershey, PA: IGI Global.

Zhang, W., & Kramarae, C. (2014). "Slutwalk" on connected screens: Multiple framings of a social media discussion. *Journal of Pragmatics*, *73*, 66–81. doi:10.1016/j.pragma.2014.07.008

Zhang, Y. W. (July 5, 2011). 网络时代也要好好说话 [Speaking with civility in social media age]. *Beijing Morning Post*. Retrieved January 16, 2014, from http://www.donews.com/net/201107/526203.shtm

KEY TERMS AND DEFINITIONS

Creativity: Traditionally, definitions of creativity have focused on individual achievements as perhaps resulting in a one-man show; what is considered creative, flexible, energetic, forward thinking, and interesting differs depending on one's world view, set of values, and a perception of what is valuable for social change.

Cyber Activism: Online actions and campaigns that aim to influence public opinion and major social/political processes; what is considered activism often varies from society to society.

Freedom of Speech: Often considered one of the basic human rights, freedom of speech is the legal or natural right to seek, receive and impart information and ideas without the fear of being punished.

Gender: A contested, sliding term often used to refer to the attitudes, feelings and behaviors that a given society considers appropriate to a person's biological sex, which may not be the same as one's gender identity.

Invitational Discussion: A non-judgmental conversational means to create relationships rooted in equality and dignity, and welcoming of others' perspectives.

Knowledge: What thoughts and understandings are considered knowledge depends on the prevailing ideas of domination and resistance.

Social Networking: Practices of gathering and managing a network of friends with specific interests; it means different things to different people, depending on their goals, their access to, and their use of varying communication technologies.

Chapter 19
Smart CCTV and the Management of Urban Space

Jung Hoon Han
University of New South Wales, Australia

Scott Hawken
University of New South Wales, Australia

Angelique Williams
University of New South Wales, Australia

ABSTRACT

This chapter briefly describes the proliferation of CCTV over the last few decades with particular reference to Australia and discusses the limits of the technology. It then focuses on new image interpretation and signal processing technologies, and how these advanced technologies are extending the reach, power, and capabilities of CCTV technology. The advent of "Smart" CCTV has the ability to recognize different human behaviours. This chapter proposes a typology to assist the application and study of Smart CCTV in urban spaces. The following four typologies describe different human behaviours in urban space: 1) Human-Space Interaction, 2) Human-Social Interactions, 3) Human-Object Interactions, and 4) Crowd Dynamics and Flows. The chapter concludes with a call for future research on the legal implications of such technology and the need for an evidence base of risk behaviours for different urban situations and cultures.

I. INTRODUCTION

Smart Cities aim to make urban areas more livable, efficient and safe through the integration of information and communication technology (ICT). Smart technologies within Smart Cities can either act as new innovative infrastructure in their own right, or more frequently, are implemented to transform the way traditional infrastructure and services are accessed and used. ICT facilitates networking and engagement with the urban system, and can improve the quality of life for people in urban areas (Han & Lee, 2013; Lee, at al. 2014; Neirotti, et al. 2014). A range of these smart technologies have been adapted to transform urban infrastructure into "smart" infrastructure.

DOI: 10.4018/978-1-4666-8205-4.ch019

Examples include the city-wide collection of digital data on parking spaces and urban services; security cameras that identify pedestrian risk behaviours; and GPS systems that identify traffic congestion, taxi locations and traffic lights. Such advances give urban residents access to real-time information so they can make better decisions whether it be: selecting the fastest driving route and avoiding congestion, or identifying and visiting nearby services, or avoiding crime or disaster scenes (Yigitcanlar & Han, 2010). Smart technology is changing the way urban residents use traditional cities and urban infrastructure. The range of smart technology is proliferating rapidly with new software and algorithms transforming technology that has been around for many decades.

One such technology, in the process of being transformed, is Closed Circuit Television (CCTV). This chapter briefly discusses the use CCTV technology during the last few decades and outlines the limits of its effectiveness. It then focuses on the transformation of this technology by new innovations. Finally a four category typology to help with the application of this technology in urban space is proposed. The categories that make up the typology are:

1. Human-Space Interaction;
2. Human-Social Interactions;
3. Human-Object Interactions; and
4. Crowd-Dynamics and Flows.

Traditional CCTV technology consists of two parts:

1. The camera or sensor, and
2. The interpretation or signal processing of the image sequence that the video camera takes.

There have been recent advances in both these areas. Image interpretation and signal processing technologies are now employing advanced algorithms to capture changes in the images recorded by the sensors, and the sensors themselves are also becoming more sensitive and so extending the reach, power and capabilities of CCTV technology. These two aspects of CCTV technology are significant for the continued rollout of new CCTV technology and the transformation of existing technology already deployed in cities around the world.

II. THE PROLIFERATION OF CCTV IN GLOBAL CITIES

The emergence of Closed Circuit Television (CCTV) systems occurred in the 1960s, Its subsequent proliferation in the 1980s and 1990s, has been documented by various authors (Fyfe and Bannister, 1996; Norris, Moran and Armstrong, 1998; Webster, 2004a). Especially since 9/11, CCTV technology has been adopted by urban governments. This reflects growing pressures to guarantee community and public safety in urban spaces, and changing socio-political government agendas. In Australia uses of CCTV technology have been most prevalent in the law and order context (Australian Institute of Criminology, 2004). The attractiveness of CCTV as a tool for the management of urban spaces can be explained by reference to three categories of justification: first, as having a predictive, preventative or deterrent function; second, in assisting on-the-spot responses to emergency situations as they occur; and third, in forensically identifying what has occurred in the past (Waters, 1996). Further attention is devoted to these applications of CCTV technology later in the chapter.

Sociologists have recognized that the increasing ubiquity of CCTV has been propelled by broader socio-economic and political forces which characterise the changing urban spaces of post-industrial cities (McCahill, 2013). Specifically, technological advances in mass surveillance coincided with economic restructuring and associated private outsourcing of government functions, which occurred in neo-liberal states from the 1970s (Webster, 2004b; McCahill, 2013). The phenomenon of modern "surveillance societies" has been accounted for by drawing together three theoretical strands: first, the 'electronic panopticon' (Giddens, 1987; 1990); second, 'post-Fordism' (Harvey, 1989); and third, the 'risk society' (Beck, 1992).

In terms of the 'electronic panopticon', new surveillance technologies such as CCTV have altered the Benthamite architectural norm for social discipline by removing traditional spatial and temporal barriers, and dispensing with the need for the physical co-presence of the observer. This technological innovation suited changed socioeconomic and political conditions in urban spaces from the 1970s. Following from this, post-Fordist literature suggests that such changes encouraged local business and local elites to utilise surveillance technology to protect and facilitate commercial exchange in new urban areas of consumption (McCahill, 2013).

And lastly, changing attitudes towards risk have occurred in law and order politics within Western neo-liberal states from the early 1990s. Government-industry cooperation in providing 'proactive intelligence-led policing' present a new paradigm of urban space management through a focus on crime (Webster, 2004a; Griffin, Trevorrow & Ialpin, 2007). A particular characteristic of this new approach is the promotion of social exclusionary practises. Analysing the installation of CCTV systems in the city centre of Liverpool, England, Coleman and Sim (2000) note the centrality of the private sector in 'constructing definitions of risk and danger in the city and who should be targeted to avoid these risks and dangers' (2000: 627).

In accordance with this political-economic philosophy of urban space management through 'intelligence-led policing', it can be observed how the embrace of mass surveillance technologies in global cities has additionally been influenced by Beck's theory of the 'risk society' (Beck, 1992). According to Beck's theory, actuarial reasoning

and technology are linked and operationalized in the management of urban criminogenic spaces. The database that results from such methods in turn produces informational intelligence to support the development of strategies for situational crime prevention.

Extensive British-based public perception surveys, undertaken for technology companies (Crockard & Jenkins, 1996; Ross & Hood, 1998), as well as by the Home Office (Honess & Charman, 1992; Brown, 1995) and independent academics (Bennet & Gelsthorpe, 1996; and Ditton, 2000) have indicated the community's support for the presence of CCTV, which is perceived to be necessary for crime reduction. Despite general public support for CCTV in overseas contexts, Australian social scientists have acknowledged the privacy implications for civil liberties that are associated with the 'real-time' surveillance capacity of CCTV in public areas (Brown, 1995). Indeed, in the absence of public perception studies to quantify the assumed populist support for CCTV in Australian urban spaces, it is relevant to note the considerable criticisms of civil libertarians in this field.

Concerns raised by civil libertarians concerning the unacceptable invasions of privacy perpetrated by privately owned and operated CTTV cameras in urban spaces were clearly voiced in the case of *SF v Shellharbour City Council* [2013] NSWADT 94, Australia. This case involved an application in the New South Wales Administrative Decisions Tribunal by a Nowra resident who had objected to police use of live footage in the Nowra city area. In particular, it was argued that the respondent council had breached various Information Protection Principles under the *Privacy and Personal Information Act 1998* (NSW) ("PPIA Act"). The court held in favour of the applicant, finding that the respondent council had failed to provide sufficient information in signage concerning the information collection process and the purposes for the information collected, in contravention of relevant privacy principles under the PPIA Act. This case demonstrates the important legal parameters within which CCTV footage can be lawfully applied. Further, it demonstrates legal recognition of the importance of striking a balance between the communal good and privacy concerns when considering uses of CCTV in urban space management.

III. CCTV AS A TOOL FOR THE MANAGEMENT OF URBAN SPACE

As the previous section indicates, despite its drawbacks, CCTV has been enthusiastically taken up in various cities, London being the best known example. In London CCTV technology is used to detect and deter both criminal and anti-social behaviour (ASB). It is important to note that anti-social behaviour is a contested concept and largely depends on a society's "behavioural expectations for a particular space and time" (Millie 2008, p.379). Anti-social behaviour is therefore culturally specific. ASB can be defined as behaviour that causes alarm or distress to others not in the same household as the perpetrator but nevertheless that such behaviour is a) not prohibited by the criminal law and b) in isolation such behaviour constitute relatively minor offences (Millie 2008). As a tool to facilitate urban crime detection, prevention and prosecution, as well as a technology to manage urban anti-social behaviour, the adoption of CCTV technology is based on the premise that formal surveillance modifies the urban environment in such a manner as to deter crime and anti-social behaviour due to an increased risk of detection (Clarke, 2004; Baum et al., 2014).

In addition to this crime and anti-social behaviour prevention role, CCTV cameras in urban spaces have the pro-active function of encouraging potential victims to take security precautions (Armitage, Smyth & Pease, 1999). Two prominent theories, the routine activities theory (Cohen & Felson, 1979) and the rational choice theory (Clarke & Cornish, 1985), underpin these

justifications for the role of CCTV in reducing crime. First, the occurrence of a crime depends on the convergence of three factors: a motivated offender, a suitable victim and the absence of a capable guardian (Cohen & Felson 1979). Second, the characteristics of a motivated offender typically include some degree of rational decision-making in the immediate situational context of crime (Clarke & Cornish 1985). In summary CCTV increases opportunity for detection of the crime, thus de-motivating the offender, making potential victims more security conscious and allowing for the quicker response rate of emergency services.

The sense of social control inspired by the installation of CCTV cameras, can beneficially generate community cohesion and pride, thus decreasing crime through more positive methods (Welsh & Farrington, 2002). In the Australian context, this explanation has been extended to include theories which link CCTV guaranteed safety to urban rejuvenation and to stimulation in local trade and investment (Coleman & Sim, 1998, 2000; Mackay, 2003; Martin, 2000; Reeve, 1998). This position was made clear in the City of Perth's 2001 CCTV Information Kit, which explained the context for the installation of CCTV systems in terms of economically-desirable safety goals: "The Central Business District was suffering a retail decline in the mid-1980s and the best efforts of the Council to rejuvenate the area were often offset by emotional stories in the media which generated an undesirable image of the city" (City of Perth, 2000).

IV. THE LIMITS OF TRADITIONAL CCTV TECHNOLOGY AND THE NEED FOR SMART TECHNOLOGY

The relevance of smarter uses of CCTV systems in Australian cities is highlighted by the concession made in the literature as to the questionable effectiveness of traditional CCTV as a singular tool for crime prevention (Kruegle, 2011). For example whilst the deterrence effect of CCTV can be strong in the initial installation period, it is acknowledged that this factor is difficult to sustain in the longer term. The effectiveness of CCTV systems can be improved by progressively modifying it for particular situations and types of anti-social behavior according to changing requirements. There are ways of fine tuning CCTV's impact. For example "smart" algorithms may be applied to CCTV systems for purposes of detecting entry into prohibited areas, loitering, vandalism, aggressive human exchanges, "man-down" situations, and pedestrian-vehicular accidents. CCTV technology has the potential to become a key component of digital policing strategies designed to more efficiently coordinate early emergency responses for serious incidents.

In the US, research has found that the deployment of CCTV on city streets has the potential to reduce crime. For instance Baltimore city government gains $1.06 in cost avoidance for every $1 spent on CCTV (Urban Institute, 2011). However this reduction is dependent on how the surveillance system is set up and monitored. Although the presence of CCTV has been found to reduce crime, if there is a perception that cameras are not monitored, such technology has little impact. This has led to a call for a more intelligent deployment, integration and monitoring of such systems. The study area included Baltimore, Chicago and Washington, D.C. and compared the monthly average crime reports in areas with CCTV. The cameras were deployed to areas of similar crime volume, land use and demographics. The report generally showed that urban crime decreased following introduction of CCTV, even controlling for an overall reduction in crime. However, CCTV had no effect in West Garfield Park, Chicago as the residents have a perception that "police do not watch the cameras" in their neighborhood. The mismatch between the widespread deployment of CCTV technology and human capacity to monitor the images captured by the cameras has been documented in behavioural studies. Generally a

human's maximum attention span, when faced with the visual challenge of monitoring such screens, is 10 minutes before there is a sharp decrease in ability to identify visual anomalies within image sequences (Medina, 2014; Dukette & Cornish, 2009).

The study that investigated the effectiveness of CCTV also found that the impact of such technology may be limited by the methods of deployment. Cameras had no effect on crime in Washington D.C. due the deployment of the technology. CCTV in the area was not able to capture significant crime scenes due to inappropriate pre-programmed panning functions and inadequate resolution that did not allow for enlargement of crime scenes captured on the cameras (Urban Institute, 2011). Although CCTV technology enables the deployment of hundreds of "eyes" focused upon the city, if there is no mechanism for interpreting such data the net result is visual "noise". A common sight in security and urban management departments around the world are enormous banks of monitors being fed images from different locations. Such monitor arrays produce meaningless data unless these images are able to be processed, interpreted and monitored effectively.

Smart CCTV (SCCTV) systems are based on integrating emerging signal processing technologies with more traditional CCTV technology to empower the interpretative power of urban authorities and limit the production of "noise streams". SCCTV technology reduces the likelihood of human error and oversight through the use of sophisticated algorithms designed to identify anomalies within image sequences and trigger a range of alarms. For example a SCCTV might identify a traffic incident with a pedestrian, call an ambulance, determine the best route for the ambulance and redirect traffic away from the incident area.

SCCTV systems integrate a series of cameras that are networked through a sophisticated wireless infrastructure to a control room, where images captured are recorded, monitored and stored. In addition traditional CCTV technology has evolved from static, low-resolution sensors, to high quality sensors capable of panning, tilting and zooming in accordance with complex behavioural-based algorithms set by remote operators. The broad adoption of SCCTV technology has occurred against an institutional backdrop that increasingly favours problem-oriented monitoring of space (Clarke, 2004; Goldstein, 2003). In this context, SCCTV has functioned as an integrated way to manage urban space issues such as crime detection, disaster response, and traffic incidents prevention (Ratcliffe, 2008).

V. THE INTEGRATION OF CCTV WITH SMART IMAGE RECOGNITION AND SIGNAL PROCESSING TECHNOLOGY

SCCTV can be applied to the process of human behaviour recognition. Typologies of such behaviour may be devised to distinguish between different urban situations and human actions. This chapter proposes a typology to assist the application and study of Smart CCTV in urban spaces. The following four typologies describe different human behaviours in urban space:

1. Human-Space Interaction;
2. Human-Social Interactions;
3. Human-Object Interactions; and
4. Crowd-Dynamics and Flows.

In the last decade numerous advances have been made in image or "signal processing" that promise new, more powerful ways to use CCTV to monitor and manage urban space. The application of smart technologies for the management of human behaviour in urban space varies according to the type of human behaviour under investigation. Thus, technologies facilitating motion detection are suited to Human Space Interaction. Alternatively, technologies that provide action

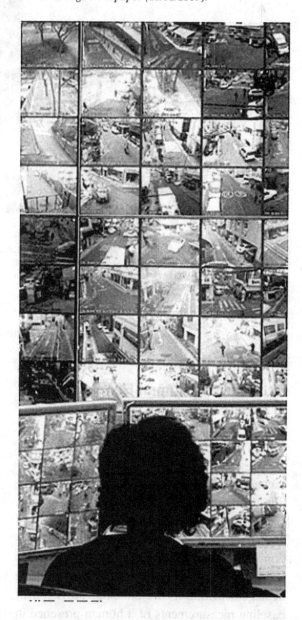

Figure 1. One police officer monitors 412 CCVTs in South Korea
Source: Donga Newspaper (20/02/2009).

recognition may be utilised to monitor Human-Social Interaction and Human-Object Interaction. Finally, technologies that seek to track objects are relevant to Crowd-Dynamics and Flows. The application of such technologies to the various situations of human behaviour in urban spaces is discussed below.

Figure 2. Typologies of the different situations of human behaviour in urban spaces

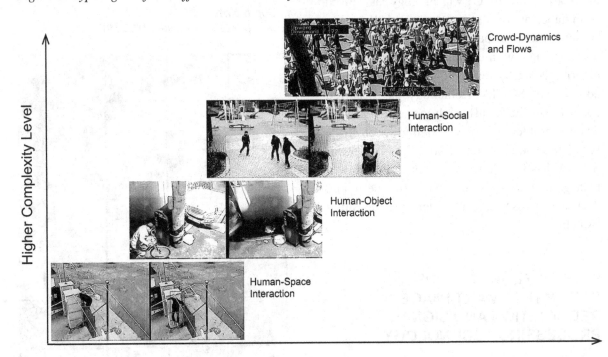

Situations of Human Behaviour in Urban Spaces

1. Human-Space Interaction

Signal processing technologies, which target motion detection and generate digital intelligence, can be used to inform policy-makers of relevant human interactions in urban spaces. Human motion information collected from CCTV cameras is of interest for the purposes of urban space management due to the potential provision of baseline measurements of a human presence in public as opposed to private areas. Motion detection can indicate the movement of humans from a private area (i.e. city office) to a public space (i.e. train station).

Motion detection in video images aims to segment regions corresponding with a person from the rest of an image. Motion segmentation is a notoriously difficult task. Several conventional approaches to motion detection include background subtraction (Haritaoglu, Harwood & Davis, 2000); statistical methods (Kim, Sakamoto, Kitahara, Toriyama, & Kogure, 2007); temporal distancing (Bayona, SanMiguel, & Martínez, 2010); and optical flow (Shibata, Yasuda & Ito, 2008).

Background subtraction requires a raw subtraction to be performed in relation to a target in stationary scenes (Sheikh, Javed & Kanade, 2009). Due to the constant changes that occur in dynamic scenes, a morphological operation must further be applied in order to obtain accurate detection (Camplani & Salgado, 2011). The statistical method represents a developed form of background subtraction, with such strategies as dual foreground involving the application of statistics to individual pixels or a group of pixels (Porikli, Ivanov & Haga, 2008). This method is sufficiently robust to tolerate illumination changes and occlusion, as well as deal with environmental conditions including noise and shadow (Ibid).

In order to identify human moving targets from other possible non-human moving targets across successive frames, temporal distancing is utilised. Under this approach, the current image frame is subtracted from either the preceding or the following frame of the image sequence (Bayona et al., 2010). Through the application of thresholds to remove pixel changes across successive image sequences, this method successfully adapts to a dynamic scene (Ibid). Figure 3 shows that different algorithms apply to the areas divided by a gate. The human activity moving from the 'outside' (left image) to the 'inside' of the gate (right image) is programmed to signal an alert with the presence of an intruder.

Finally, the optical flow method operates as a strategy to measure the spatial arrangement of objects based on their individual velocities, and is used for both motion detection and object detection (Denman, Chandran & Sridharan, 2007). The method is based on optical flow vectors, which are analysed to determine the apparent velocities of movement derived from patterns of brightness in an image (Ibid). Specialised hardware such as FPGA and GPU cards are required for the operation of the optical flow method in order to satisfy the demands of the processes computationally data-intensive nature (Ishii, Taniguchi, Yamamoto & Takaki, 2010).

As indicated in the above discussion, strategies for motion detection face various challenges in the analysis of dynamic scenes. Further in-novation is required in order to minimise issues associated with illumination changes, occlusion and environmental changes caused by noise and shadow. Furthermore, additional limitations are represented by the computational data-intensive nature of strategies such as optical flow.

2. Human-Social Interaction and 3. Human-Object Interaction

Significant insights into the social and object-based interactions of humans in urban spaces may be obtained through technologies that provide human activity recognition. Uses of technology to facilitate signal processing of CCTV footage may, for instance, reveal both positive and negative patterns of human social interaction within a particular urban space. Positive interactions that may be captured through SCCTV include hand-shaking and sitting in grouped clusters, so as to infer the conduciveness of a particular urban space to cordial greetings and informal human social gatherings. Alternatively, SCCTV may be programmed to identify aggressive encounters, including fighting and burglary, in turn indicating events of inter-personal aggression and conflict in urban spaces.

Behavioural analysis obtainable through smart technological manipulation of CCTV data for urban space management extends not only to social patterns, but also to patterns of human interactions

Figure 3. Intruder Alert! human space interaction
Source: National Information Society in Korea (2013).

Figure 4. Motion detection of garbage dumping
Source: National Information Society in Korea (2013).

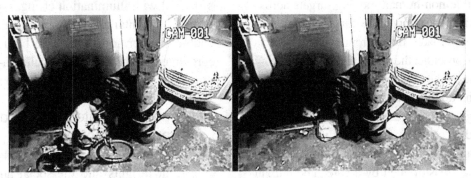

with inanimate objects. Particularly relevant to the context of Human-Object Interactions in urban spaces are architectural discourses, which enable post-occupancy assessment of urban design features. In addition, more ad hoc situations of human object-based interactions may be monitored, such as dumping of rubbish and suspicious objects in urban spaces. The algorithm applied in SCCTV detects when an unidentified object appears in the monitoring site. It is programmed to alarm (left photo image) if the possessor leaves the site and does not return within a set time (refer to Figure 4).

When using image processing technology in the application of human interaction identification in urban spaces, it is necessary to note that approaches to human activity recognition can be divided into two broad categories: non-hierarchical and hierarchical (Aggarwal & Ryoo, 2011). The non-hierarchical approach is divided into two classes: a space-time approach (Bobick & Davis, 2001) and a sequential approach (Darrell & Pentland, 1993). Three classes apply to the hierarchical approach: statistical (Zhang et al., 2006; Nguyen et al, 2005), syntactic (Ivanov & Bobick, 2000), and description-based (Intille & Bobick, 1999) approaches.

In analysing the overall advantages of respective hierarchical and non-hierarchical approaches to individual human and crowd activity recognition, strengths lie in the capacity of the strategies to model either periodic or non-periodic and

more complex activities. Thus, spatial-temporal approaches have been shown to be effective in recognising periodic actions, whereas description-based approaches are better adapted to identifying more complex, multiple and concurrent human activities.

Digital modelling of CCTV systems in order to generate an understanding of human behaviours seeks to isolate and analyse the normality or abnormality of individual human behaviours. This modelling requires a combination of the signal processing techniques outlined above, as well as artificial intelligence techniques (Leordeanu and Collins, 2005). Suspicious or endangering behaviour is "detected" through appropriate algorithms and rules, which are modelled according to different categories of human activities (Lalos and Anagnostopoulos, 2009). Various taxonomies have been developed for the purpose of classifying a hierarchy of human actions. For example, Moeslund et al (2006) propose the following abstract levels of an observable suspicious behaviour: action-primitive; action; and activity. An action-primitive may involve "raising the left hand", an action may involve "waving the hand", and an activity may involve "punching someone". Thus, in this example, the raising, waving and punching actions converge in the one course of conduct (Ibid). Action recognition algorithms developed for SCCTV accordingly alert human operators to such crimes as burglary and group fighting in public places (affray). Figure 5 shows an example of a conflict event.

Figure 5. Person falls down as a result of fight
Source: *National Information Society in Korea (2013).*

Algorithms are developed to distinguish between playing and serious violent activities. The left image shows that SCCTV alerts when a person falls down after the other person punches him.

4. Crowd-Dynamics and Flows

Initial uses of computer technology as part of the advancement of smarter CCTV involved the estimation of global properties of urban crowds, including density and flow (Davies, Yin and Velastin, 1995). Development of individual human tracking technology provided a platform for the study of the movement of individuals within a dynamic crowd scene. Such SCCTV applications are beneficial for policy-makers in the field of urban space management due to the generation of useful information relating to group and individual human behaviours in "rush-hour" type situations (Davies & Velastin, 2005). In particular, benefits include the provision of data crucial in informing policy related to threat assessment, emergency response procedures, and amenity/resource allocation in various public urban spaces, such as train stations. Figure 5 illustrates SCCTV crowd monitoring.

Figure 6. Crowd monitoring
Source: *www.evitech.com.*

Crowd density can be estimated by a ratio that measures the 'background area' against the 'crowd area' in a single area covered by the footage. Where densities are low, the individual 'edges' of all pedestrians may be extracted from the image (Velastin et al., 2006). For purposes of crowd density, basic motion data can be obtained by use of a gradient method to monitor changes in colour brightness from one image to the next, expressed as a vector field. Block matching the pixels in alternate images further produces similar results for monitoring crowd flows. Digital models for assessing both crowd density and flow are to be distinguished on the basis that they establish general models of crowd behaviour and do not seek to isolate individual behaviours (Davies, Yin and Velastin, 1995).

Technologies focusing on the tracking of individual human targets within a dynamic crowd scene aim to maintain the identity of the moving human target (Aggarwal and Cai, 1999; Haritaoglu et al., 2000). The tracking process typically establishes a correspondence between the image structure of two consecutive frames in what is referred to as a 'sliding window' approach (Benfold & Reid, 2011). This involves taking measurements from the scene of interest at a discrete time, and making a distinction between a target and all unwanted movements (referred to as clutter), so as to deduce information about the object being tracked (Cavallaro, Steiger & Ebrahimi, 2005).

Algorithms to track objects can be classified into six categories (Vishwakarma & Agrawal, 2013). First, algorithms can track objects by identifying variations in the image regions that correspond to the moving object (Meyer & Bouthemy, 1994; Schmaltz et al., 2012) Second, algorithms can provide for contour-based non-rigid object tracking (Yokoyama & Poggio, 2005; Yilmaz et al., 2006). Third, maths tools can be used to support both static (Comaniciu et al., 2003) and dynamic (Lin et al. 2009) feature-based object tracking. Fourth, model recognition can be used to track human motion (Gavrila & Davis, 1996). Fifth, hybrid tracking can be utilised, and has involved the combination of feature and model-based approaches (Lalos & Anagnostopoulos, 2009). Sixth, optical flow-based tracking may be achieved through intensive computation (Denman et al., 2005; Ince & Konrad 2008).

Hybrid tracking has been suggested as a particularly robust approach to dealing with occlusions of tracked entities (Vishwakarma and Agrawal, 2013). In order to minimise prob-

Figure 7. Tracking children in outer school zones
Source: National Information Society in Korea (2013).

lems associated with changes in the velocity of the object, referred to as 'occlusion', use of a Kalman filter can be applied to provide estimates of future trajectories in an occluded zone (Corvee, Velastin & Jones, 2003). Alternatives to the avoidance of occlusion issues include Bayesian random-sampling techniques (Narayana & Haverkamp, 2007), the adaptive background subtraction method (Luo, Li & Gu, 2007) and a perspective multi-scale approach (Nieto, Ortega, Cortes & Gaines, 2014). In addition to overcoming problems of occlusion, hybrid tracking may furthermore remove problems associated with background clutter and loss of an object due to rapid movements. Figure 7 demonstrates tracking technology in the context of school zones. It first identifies the school children (blue squares in the photo image) and then traces their pathways with a zoom-in (left image).

VI. DISCUSSION AND CONCLUSION

As this chapter notes, the shortcomings of traditional CCTV systems are well documented in scholarly literature. The increasing presence of CCTV in public places globally and the large amounts of money spent on its deployment warrant a comprehensive analysis of both the effectiveness of such technology and the legal implications of such technology. It is no longer so much a question of applying an unblinking surveillance gaze in search of a simple security fix, but more a question of what should be watched, and why, and by whom. SCCTV technology provides the technological means to address these questions through its increased precision and capabilities.

Considering current investment trends in urban security it is likely that Smart CCTV systems will develop as an integral component of Smart Cities in order to address the limitations of traditional CCTV. SCCTV systems have the potential to play a substantial role in the management of urban space through intelligence led policing. In applying this smart technology attention must be devoted to associated risks, such as the potential for false alarms and privacy breaches. Nevertheless when compared to conventional CCTV, intelligence-led policing via SCCTV offers a more flexible and focused approach through targeting specific risk behaviours. Rather than the unfiltered monitoring of urban space offered by traditional CCTV, SCCTV provides the technology to select specific risk behaviours and generate appropriate alarms. To achieve this, an evidence base of risk behaviours needs to be compiled in the form of a database. The four categories proposed in this chapter offer an initial framework for such a database. However beyond these four categories the culturally specific nature of urban space and behaviour, pose limitations for the application of this technology in urban areas globally. Any database must be adjusted to account for the different human behaviours, evident in different geographic contexts and different cultures. SCCTV itself has the potential to assist in generating this evidence base of urban human behaviour through a systematic program of research preceding the rollout of the technology.

The advent of SCCTV indicates a substantial increase in the power and sensitivity of traditional CCTV technology and the potential to transform both the management and design of urban space. This power needs to be guided by a technological vision of city-wide data management within a sophisticated legal framework cognisant of the culturally specific nature of urban space.

Figure 8. Evaluation of CCTV image interpretation technologies

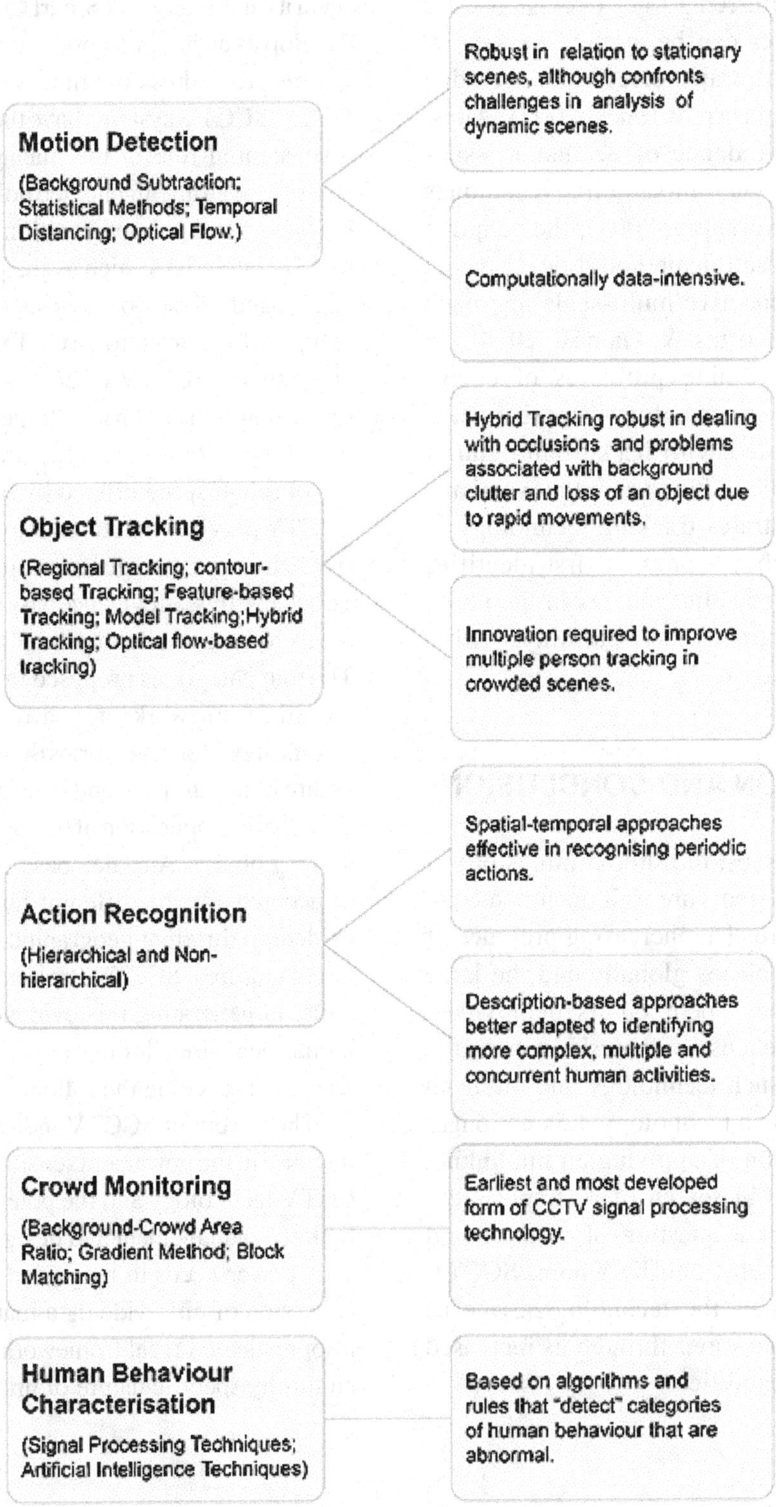

Motion Detection

(Background Subtraction; Statistical Methods; Temporal Distancing; Optical Flow.)

Robust in relation to stationary scenes, although confronts challenges in analysis of dynamic scenes.

Computationally data-intensive.

Object Tracking

(Regional Tracking; contour-based Tracking; Feature-based Tracking; Model Tracking; Hybrid Tracking; Optical flow-based tracking)

Hybrid Tracking robust in dealing with occlusions and problems associated with background clutter and loss of an object due to rapid movements.

Innovation required to improve multiple person tracking in crowded scenes.

Action Recognition

(Hierarchical and Non-hierarchical)

Spatial-temporal approaches effective in recognising periodic actions.

Description-based approaches better adapted to identifying more complex, multiple and concurrent human activities.

Crowd Monitoring

(Background-Crowd Area Ratio; Gradient Method; Block Matching)

Earliest and most developed form of CCTV signal processing technology.

Human Behaviour Characterisation

(Signal Processing Techniques; Artificial Intelligence Techniques)

Based on algorithms and rules that "detect" categories of human behaviour that are abnormal.

REFERENCES

Aggarwal, J. K., & Cai, Q. (1999). Human motion analysis: A review. *Computer Vision and Image Understanding, 73*(3), 428–440. doi:10.1006/cviu.1998.0744

Aggarwal, J. K., & Ryoo, M. S. (2011). Human activity analysis: A review. *ACM Computing Surveys, 43*(3), 1–43. doi:10.1145/1922649.1922653

Armitage, R., Smyth, G., & Pease, K. (1999). Burnley CCTV evaluation. In K. Painter & N. Tilley (Eds.), *Surveillance of public space: CCTV, street lighting and crime prevention* (pp. 225–250). Monsey, NY: Criminal Justice Press.

Australian Institute of Criminology. (2004). Closed Circuit Television (CCTV) as a crime prevention measure. *AICrime Reduction Matters, 18*, 1.

Baum, S., Arthurson, K., & Han, J. H. (2014, July). Tenure social mix and perceptions of antisocial behaviour: An Australian example. *Urban Studies (Edinburgh, Scotland), 22*. doi:10.1177/0042098014541160

Bayona, A., SanMiguel, J. C., & Martínez, J. M. (2010). Stationary foreground detection using background subtraction and temporal difference in video surveillance. In *Proceedings of IEEE 17th Int. Conf. on Image Processing*. IEEE. doi:10.1109/ICIP.2010.5650699

Beck, U. (1992). *Risk society: Towards a new modernity*. London: Sage.

Benfold, B., & Reid, I. D. (2011). Stable multi-target tracking in real-time surveillance video. In *Computer vision and pattern recognition* (pp. 1–8). Colorado Springs, CO: CVPR.

Bennett, T., & Gelsthorpe, L. (1996). Public attitudes towards CCTV in public places. *Studies on Crime and Crime Prevention, 5*(1), 72-90.

Bobick, A. F., & Davis, J. W. (2001). The recognition of human movement using temporal templates. *IEEE Transactions on Pattern Analysis and Machine Intelligence, 23*(3), 257–267. doi:10.1109/34.910878

Brown, B. (1995). *CCTV in town centres: Three case studies*. London: HMSO.

Camplani, M., & Salgado, L. (2011). Adaptive background modelling in multicamera system for real-time object detection. *Optical Engineering (Redondo Beach, Calif.), 50*(12), 1–17. doi:10.1117/1.3662422

Cavallaro, A., Steiger, O., & Ebrahimi, T. (2005). Tracking video objects in cluttered background. *IEEE Transactions on Circuits and Systems for Video Technology, 15*(4), 575–584. doi:10.1109/TCSVT.2005.844447

City of Perth. (2000). *Closed circuit TV information kit*. Perth, Australia: Perth City.

Clarke, R. V. (2004). Technology, criminology and crime science. *European Journal on Criminal Policy and Research, 10*(1), 55–63. doi:10.1023/B:CRIM.0000037557.42894.f7

Clarke, R. V., & Cornish, D. B. (1985). 'Modelling offenders' decisions: A framework for research and policy. In M. Tonry & N. Morris (Eds.), *Crime and justice* (pp. 147–185). Chicago: University of Chicago Press.

Cohen, L. E., & Felson, M. (1979). Social change and crime rate trends: A routine activity approach. *American Sociological Review, 44*(4), 588–608. doi:10.2307/2094589

Coleman, R., & Sim, J. (2000). You'll never walk alone: CCTV surveillance, order and neo-liberal rule in Liverpool city centre. *The British Journal of Sociology, 51*(4), 623–639. doi:10.1080/00071310020015299 PMID:11140887

Colman, R., & Sim, J. (1998). From the dockyards to the Disney stores: Surveillance, risk and security in Liverpool city centre. *International Review of Law Computers & Technology, 12*(1), 27–45. doi:10.1080/13600869855559

Comaniciu, D., Ramesh, V., & Meer, P. (2003). Kernel-based object tracking. *IEEE Transactions on Pattern Analysis and Machine Intelligence, 25*(5), 564–577. doi:10.1109/TPAMI.2003.1195991

Corvee, E., Velastin, S. A., & Jones, G. A. (2003). Occlusion tolerant tracking using hybrid prediction schemes. *Acta Automatica Sinica, 29*(3).

Crockard, S., & Jenkins, D. (1998). *An independent evaluation of Chelmsford town centre CCTV scheme*. Chelmsford: Anglia Polytechnic University.

Darrell, T., & Pentland, A. (1993). Space-time gestures. In *Proceedings of IEEE Computer Society Conf. on Computer Vision and Pattern Recognition* (pp. 335–340). IEEE.

Davies, A. C., & Velastin, S. A. (2005). A progress review of intelligent CCTV surveillance systems. In *Proceedings of IDAACS 2005 Workshop*. IDAACS. doi:10.1109/IDAACS.2005.283015

Davies, A. C., Yin, J. H., & Velastin, S. (2005). Crowd monitoring using image processing. *Electronics and Communication Engineering Journal, 7*(1), 37–47. doi:10.1049/ecej:19950106

Denman, S., Chandran, V., & Sridharan, S. (2007). Adaptive optical flow for person tracking. *Pattern Recognition Letters, 28*(10), 1232–1239. doi:10.1016/j.patrec.2007.02.008

Ditton, J. (2000). Crime and the city: Public attitudes to CCTV in Glasgow. *The British Journal of Criminology, 40*(4), 692–709. doi:10.1093/bjc/40.4.692

Dukette, D., & Cornish, D. (2009). *The essential 20: Twenty components of an excellent health care team*. RoseDog Books.

Fyfe, N. R., & Bannister, J. (1996). City watching: Closed circuit television in public spaces. *Area, 28*(1), 37–46.

Gavrilla, D., & Davis, L. (1996). 3D model-based tracking of humans in action: A multi-view approach. In *Proc. of the Computer Vision and Pattern Recognition* (pp. 73–80). Academic Press.

Giddens, A. (1987). *Social theory and modern sociology*. Palo Alto, CA: Stanford University Press.

Giddens, A. (1990). *The consequences of modernity*. Cambridge, MA: Polity Press.

Goldstein, H. (2003). On further developing problem-oriented policing: The most critical need, the major impediments, and a proposal. In J. Knutsson (Ed.), *Problem-oriented policing: From innovation to mainstream* (pp. 13–47). Monsey, NY: Criminal Justice Press.

Griffin, D. (2007). *Trevorrow, P. and Halpin, E.* Amsterdam, Netherlands: Developments in E-Government.

Han, J. H., & Lee, S. (2013). Planning ubiquitous cities for social inclusion. *Int. J. of Knowledge-Based Development, 4*(2), 157–172. doi:10.1504/IJKBD.2013.054092

Haritaoglu, I., Harwood, D., & Davis, L. S. (2000). W4: Real-time surveillance of people and their activities. *IEEE Transactions on Pattern Analysis and Machine Intelligence, 22*(8), 309–330. doi:10.1109/34.868683

Harvey, D. (1989). From managerialism to enerpreneurialism: The transformation in urban governance in late capital-ism. *Geografisk annaler. Series B. Human Geography, 71*(1), 2–17.

Honess, T., & Charman, E. (1992). *Closed circuit television in public places: Its acceptability and perceived effectiveness.* London: Home Office.

Ince, S., & Konrad, J. (2008). Occlusion-aware optical flow estimation. *IEEE Transactions on Image Processing*, *17*(8), 1443–1451. doi:10.1109/TIP.2008.925381 PMID:18632352

Intille, S. S., & Bobick, A. F. (1999). A framework for recognizing multiagent action from visual evidence. In Proceedings of AAAI-99. AAAI Press.

Ishii, I., Taniguchi, T., Yamamoto, K., & Takaki, T. (2010). 1000 fps real-time optical flow detection system. In *Proc. SPIE*. SPIE.

Ivanov, Y. A., & Bobick, A. F. (2000). Recognition of visual activities and interactions by stochastic parsing. *IEEE Transactions on Pattern Analysis and Machine Intelligence*, *22*(8), 852–872. doi:10.1109/34.868686

Javed, O., & Shah, M. (2002). Tracking and object classification for automated surveillance. In *Proceedings of 7th European Conference on Computer Vision*. Springer. doi:10.1007/3-540-47979-1_23

Kim, H., Sakamoto, R., Kitahara, I., Toriyama, T., & Kogure, K. (2007). Robust silhouette extraction technique using background subtraction. *MIRU*.

Kruegle, H. (2011). *CCTV surveillance: Video practices and technology*. Boston: Butterworth-Heinemann.

Lalos, C., & Anagnostopoulos, V. (2009). Hybrid tracking approach for assistive environments. *Int. Conf. Proc. Series*, *39*(64), 5.

Lee, S. H., Leem, Y. T., & Han, J. H. (2014). Impact of ubiquitous computing technologies on changing travel and land use patterns. *International Journal of Environmental Science and Technology*.

Leordeanu, M., & Collins, R. (2005). Unsupervised learning of object features from video sequences. In Proceedings of IEEE Computer Society Conf. on Computer Vision and Pattern Recognition. IEEE. doi:10.1109/CVPR.2005.359

Lin, F., Chen, B. M., & Lee, T. H. (2009). Robust vision-based target tracking control system for an unmanned helicopter using feature fusion. In *Proceedings of 9th IAPR Int. Conf. on Machine Vision Applications* (vol. 13, pp. 398–401). IAPR.

Luo, R., Li, L., & Gu, I. Y. (2007). Efficient adaptive background subtraction based on multi-resolution background modelling and updating. Springer.

Mackay, D. (2003). Multiple-targets: The reasons to support town-centre CCTV systems. In M. Gill (Ed.), *CCTV* (pp. 23–25). Leicester, UK: Perpetuity Press. doi:10.1057/palgrave.cpcs.8140154

Martin, C. (2000). Crime control in Australian urban space. *Current Issues in Criminal Justice*, *12*(1), 79–92.

McCahill, M. (2013). *The surveillance web*. Devon, UK: Taylor and Francis.

Medina, J. (2014). *Brain rules: 12 principles for surviving and thriving at work, home, and school*. Pear Press.

Meyer, F., & Bouthemy, P. (1994). Region-based tracking using affine motion models in long image sequences. *CVGIP. Image Understanding*, *60*(2), 119–140. doi:10.1006/ciun.1994.1042

Millie, A. (2008). Anti-social behaviour, behavioural expectations and an urban aesthetic. *The British Journal of Criminology*, *48*(3), 379–394. doi:10.1093/bjc/azm076

Moeslund, T. B., Hilton, A., & Kruger, V. (2006). A survey of advances in vision-based human motion capture and analysis. *Computer Vision and Image Understanding*, *104*(2-3), 90–126. doi:10.1016/j.cviu.2006.08.002

Narayana, M., & Haverkamp, D. (2007). A Bayesian algorithm for tracking multiple moving objects in outdoor surveillance video. In *Proceedings of CVPR* (pp. 1–8). New York: IEEE Press.

National Information Society Agency. (2013). *2012 yearbook of information society statistics*. Retrieved from http://eng.nia.or.kr/english/eng_nia.asp/

Neirotti, P., Marco, A., Cagliano, A., Mangano, G., & Scorrano, F. (2014). Current trends in Smart City initiatives: Some stylised facts. *Cities (London, England)*, *38*, 25–36. doi:10.1016/j.cities.2013.12.010

Nguyen, N.T., Phung, D.Q., Venkatesh, S., Bui, H. (2005). Learning and detecting activities from movement trajectories using the hierarchical hidden Markov model. In *Proceedings of IEEE Computer Society Conf. on Computer Vision and Pattern Recognition* (vol. 2, pp. 955–960). IEEE.

Nieto, M., Ortega, J. D., Cortes, A., & Gaines, S. (2014). Perspective multiscale detection and tracking of persons. *LNCS*, *8326*, 92–103.

Norris, C., Moran, J., & Armstrong, G. (Eds.). (1998). *Surveillance, closed circuit television and social control*. Aldershot, UK: Ashgate.

Porikli, F., Ivanov, Y., & Haga, T. (2008). Robust abandoned object detection using dual foregrounds. *EURASIP Journal on Advances in Signal Processing*, (8): 197875.

Ratcliffe, J. H. (2008). *Intelligence-led policing*. Cullompton, UK: Witlan.

Reeve, A. (1998). The panopticisation of shopping: CCTV and leisure competition. In Surveillance, closed circuit television and social control. Aldershot, UK: Ashgate.

Ross, D., & Hood, J. (1998). Closed circuit television (CCTV) - The Easterhouse case study. In L. Montanheiro, B. Haigh, D. Morris, & N. Hrovatin (Eds.), *Public and private sector partnerships: Fostering enterprise* (pp. 497–516). Sheffield Hallam University Press.

Sheikh, T., Javed, O., & Kanade, D. (2009). Background subtraction for freely moving cameras. In *Proceedings of IEEE 12th Int. Conference on Computer Vision*. IEEE.

Shibata, M., Yasuda, Y., & Ito, M. (2008). Moving object detection for active camera based on optical flow distortion. In *Proc. of the 17th World Congress the International Federation of Automatic Control* (pp. 720–725). Academic Press.

Urban Institute. (2011). *Evaluating the use of pulic surveillance cameras for crime control and prevention* (Final Technical Report). Author.

Velastin, S., Boghossian, B., & Vicencio-Silva, M. (2006). A motion-based image processing system for detecting potentially dangerous situations in underground railway stations. *Trans. Research Part C*, *14*(2), 96–113. doi:10.1016/j.trc.2006.05.006

Vishwakarma, S., & Agrawal, A. (2013). A survey on activity recognition and behaviour understanding in video surveillance. *The Visual Computer*, *29*(10), 983–1009. doi:10.1007/s00371-012-0752-6

Waters, N. (1996). Street surveillance and privacy. *PLPR, 3,* 48.

Webster, W. R. (2004). *The policy process and governance in the information age: The case of closed circuit television*. (Unpublished PhD Thesis). Glasgow Caledonian University, Glasgow, UK.

Webster, W. R. (2004). The diffusion, regulation and governance of closed-circuit television in the UK. *Surveillance and Society*, *2*(2/3), 230-250.

Yigitcanlar, T., & Han, J. H. (2010). Ubiquitous eco cities: Telecommunication infrastructure, technology convergence and urban management. *International Journal of Advanced Pervasive and Ubiquitous Computing*, *2*(1), 1–17. doi:10.4018/japuc.2010010101

Yilmaz, A., Javed, O., & Shah, M. (2006). Object tracking: A survey. *ACM Computing Surveys*, *38*(4), 1–45. doi:10.1145/1177352.1177355

Yokoyama, M., & Poggio, T. (2005). A contour-based moving object detection and tracking. In *Proceedings of 2nd Joint IEEE Int. Workshop on Visual Surveillance and Performance Evaluation of Tracking and Surveillance* (pp. 271–276). IEEE. doi:10.1109/VSPETS.2005.1570925

Zhang, D., Gatica-Perez, D., Bengio, S., & McCowan, I. (2006). Modeling individual and group actions in meetings with layered hmms. *IEEE Transactions on Multimedia*, 8(3), 509–520. doi:10.1109/TMM.2006.870735

KEY TERMS AND DEFINITIONS

Closed Circuit Television (CCTV): CCTV refers to a surveillance camera which transmits an image to a specific place where it is displayed on a limited set of monitors. The digital signal is not openly transmitted but may employ point to point (P2P), point to multipoint, or mesh wireless links.

Human–Computer Interaction: Human-computer interaction refers to the intersection of computer science and behavioural sciences, involving planning and design of the interaction between people (users) and computers.

Image Processing: Image processing is any form of digital signal processing for which the input is an image, such as a photograph or video frame.

Motion Detection: The process of detecting a change in position of an object relative to its surroundings or moving objects, particularly people.

Smart CCTV: Smart CCTV builds knowledge in the form of testable explanations and predictions about human movement and actions by a set of algorithms that computers use to perform specific operations or to prevent urban crime and antisocial behaviours.

Smart City: Smart Cities uses digital technologies and technological convergence to reduce costs and resource consumption and enhance urban areas to achieve more livable, efficient and safe cities.

Chapter 20
Crafting Smart Cities in the Gulf Region:
A Comparison of Masdar and Lusail

Evren Tok
Hamad Bin Khalifa University, Qatar

Maha Al Merekhi
Qatar Foundation, Qatar

Jason James McSparren
University of Massachusetts, USA

Hanaa Elghaish
Hamad Bin Khalifa University, Qatar

Fatema Mohamed Ali
Hamad Bin Khalifa University, Qatar

ABSTRACT

This chapter looks at these trajectories by specifically focusing on the interstices of smart cities and competitiveness through the role played by communication technologies. An initial question to tackle pertains to the definition of a smart city, as this concept is used in diverse ways in the literature. Transforming the cities into smart ones is a newly emerging strategy to deal with the problems created by the urban population growth and rapid urbanization. Smart city is often defined as an icon of a sustainable and livable city. Why are Gulf countries investing in smart cities? Is the emergence of smart cities a mere reflection or neoliberal urbanization or are there other dynamics that we need to take into consideration? This chapter attempts to convey the message that smart cities are crucial means of building social capital and also attaining better governance mechanisms in the Gulf.

DOI: 10.4018/978-1-4666-8205-4.ch020

Lusail City is where Qatar's imagination comes to life

&

Masdar City...Highest quality of life with lowest environmental footprint...

INTRODUCTION

This study approaches the development of Smart Economic & Sustainable Cities in the GCC through the application of these ICT based infrastructural platforms in a comparative perspective. Qatar's Lusail Smart City and United Arab Emirates' (UAE) Masdar City constitute two of the most recent examples of smart cities in the Gulf Region. Although there is an increase in frequency of use of the phrase "smart city", there is still not a clear and consistent understanding of the concept among practitioners and academia. Only a limited number of studies investigated and began to systematically consider questions related to this new urban phenomenon of smart cities (Chourabi et al., 2012). Smart city forerunners like San Diego, San Francisco, Ottawa, Brisbane, Amsterdam, Kyoto, and Bangalore are all now setting a trend for others to follow (Allwinkle & Cruickshank, 2011).

The concept of smart city entails common characteristics that are key indicators of smartness in a city: a smart economy (sustainable economic growth), smart mobility, smart environment (wise management of natural resources), smart people, smart living (a high quality of life), and smart governance (participatory governance). In the literature, there are widely accepted measures of what a smart city constitutes. For instance, the smartness of a city should be measured by its participatory governance, its smart economy, its smart urban mobility, its smart environmental strategy and management of natural resources, and the presence of its self-decisive, independent, and aware citizens leading a high-quality urban life.

Three necessary conditions are defined to create a spatially enabled society: first, citizens have to be "spatially literate"; second, "a conducive environment" for sharing spatial data is needed; third, globally unified Geospatial standards are needed (Roche, 2013). The practical application of this view refers to the individuals' ability to use geospatial information and location technology as a means to improve the way they interact with the space and other individuals on/in/through space.

To illuminate the connection between smart cities and ICTs, Richard Florida's "Creative City" (2008, 2006, 2005, and 2002) thesis is a fertile analytical approach for understanding how cities, especially in periods of neoliberal globalization, have become central to the attainment of competitive advantage. Resulting from the internalization of neoliberal values by national governments, local authorities, municipal leaders and other actors, it is now possible to detect a form of "hollowed out" nation state (Jessop, 2002), or the downloading of the capacities, responsibilities and authority of nation states onto cities. Consequently, as Florida's "Creative City" thesis[1] illustrates, the real economic competition today plays out among cities, not nation states. Florida's thesis positions the three T's - Technology, Talent, and Tolerance – as responsible for attracting the "Creative Class", contributing to the national economy and establishing the requisite framework for sustaining competitive advantage. While communication technologies should not be perceived as the only determinant of "creativity", they are indicative of the "new technologies of power" which have arguably become the momentum behind the intensification of a neoliberal ethos in urban spaces. As such, Florida's creative city thesis and its accompanying buzzwords, "creative class" and "creative economy", celebrate the increasing hegemony of the neoliberal market mentality.

Nonetheless, this hegemony is a contested one, albeit in different forms, intensities and technologies. The mechanisms portrayed as making cities more competitive also inform us that, while competitiveness is a key neoliberal concern in the production of urban spaces and creative cities, innovative technologies work in two directions:

1. Deepening the hegemony of markets by marshalling creativity and communication technologies towards the deeper entrenchment of market logic; and
2. Impacting the way urban space is imagined, instituted and produced by the state.

Hence, the combination of 1 and 2 indicate that states and markets are interlinked in many different ways and market logic is not essentially at loggerheads with the state. The rise of smart cities in the Gulf region signify that states and markets engender new collaborations through the use of ICTs and investigation of the state as an entrepreneur under the times of neoliberal urbanization is a critical area that needs to be delved into.

NEOLIBERAL URBANIZATION AND STATE AS AN ENTREPRENEUR

First, let us start with what neoliberalization means for the city and why the city is itself important to processes of neoliberalization? Neoliberalization is a range of policies intended to extend market discipline, competition and commodification throughout society. It is a search for securing the "vital cycle of economic growth". Neoliberal mindset needs quality economic foundations, such as quality of life, financial capital, business climate, so and so forth, reassuring Florida's main thesis so that new people and ideas in the form of creativity fosters this cycle. In the current context, neoliberal doctrines have brought about the deregulation of state control over industry and markets, assaults on organized labor, the downsizing and/or privatization of public services and assets, the dismantling of welfare programs, the enhancement of international capital mobility

and the intensification of interlocality competition. Its implementation has relied on national restructuring projects (Peck, Theodore & Brenner, 2009), and the dominance of competitive logic over redistributive objectives has opened up new spaces of contestation among economic actors, institutions, municipalities, nation states and civil actors. This has had significant implications for localities given the risks and responsibilities of downloading.

When we stand back and try to decipher the dynamics behind the increasing hegemony of neoliberalism in redesigning, restructuring and reproducing urban spaces, it becomes possible to conceptualize this phenomenon as a state strategy for creating new conditions of capital accumulation. However, as Brenner and Theodore (2002) note, although neoliberal projects take place at different and tangled scales, it is cities and regions in which the contradictions and tensions of actually or already existing neoliberalism are manifested (pp. 120-130). Cities become the venues on which these tensions and contradictions are concretized and managed (or attempts at management of these tensions and contradictions are made). There is now, for example, increasing city level competition across national borders for foreign direct investment and for trade in city based services and urban assets. Increasingly, urban economic performance matters more than national economic outcomes.

These dynamics correspond to 'a gradual shift away from distributive policies, welfare considerations, and direct service provision' and mark the competitive state's movement 'towards more market-oriented and market dependent approaches aimed at pursuing economic promotion and competitive restructuring' (Swyngedouw, Moulaert & Rodriguez, 2002, p. 200). Through this process, supply-side economic logic privileges the production of urban 'spaces of spectacle' in which the consumption of, and access to, goods by the urban population exists as a source of political motivation for neoliberal ideas. In this sense, rather than attempting to shift the social inequities brought about by the neoliberal political economy, policy concerns are directed towards ensuring urban centers appear attractive to mobile-capital and elite consumers with the explicit goal of improving "the tax basis of the city via a sociospatial and economic reorganization of metropolitan space" (p. 204).

This increasing emphasis on the rise of cities and urban centers as the new spaces of capitalist accumulation also brings into the fold a variety of new or more diverse actors that collectively produce and reproduce urban spaces (Brenner, 2004). Thus, the rise of cities and the way in which cities are perceived as the new engines of neoliberal capitalism should be seen as a product of agency. This leads us to approach the attainment of competitiveness as part of the urban socio-spatial dialectic that is not limited to the realm of economics, but that exists in the realm of culture as well. For this reason, as the cases below from the Gulf Region will demonstrate, the use of new technologies of power is an effective tool for analyzing this intermingling and articulations between the markets and states.

There is no doubt that new urban technologies are important in harnessing creative capacities for the sake of producing more vibrant, more competitive and more livable cities. The role of communication technologies is indicative of structural dynamics in relation to the unfolding of the neoliberal vocabulary, which asserts that cities matter for accumulation of capital. Florida's creative city thesis, however, goes one step further and emphasizes that it is not just that cities matter, but that particular strengths and qualities of cities matter. There are greater incentives for cities and city regions to actively promote positive locational characteristics, including patterns of linkage and innovativeness, which can then assist cities in attaining competitive advantage and responding flexibly to changing market conditions. (Florida, 2006, p.11)

The interface between states and businesses has always been a subject of interest for scholars due to the different strategies adopted by governments in the age of increasing globalization. The different institutional arrangements exist in each country generate unique state-business relations (Nasra & Dacin, 2009, p.583). Within a changing environment a more critical role of state to ensure economic growth and development has emerged, making it a critical area for researches. This role "entails greater involvement and interaction with economic actors such as entrepreneurs and corporations" (Nasra & Dacin, 2009, p. 587). Generally, there is a significant body of literature on state/firm relationships and the role of state in economy. With regard to the role of states, literature demonstrates that the classical role of state is ensuring internal order and stability and regulating the market ((Nasra & Dacin, 2009). Nevertheless, states can also act as an entrepreneur, identifying opportunities, and as an institutional entrepreneur, building the necessary institutional infrastructure to exploit and capitalize on these opportunities (Nasra & Dacin, 2009, p. 601).

Through institutional entrepreneurship the state role as a change agent is activated. The implications of being a change agent have been explored in literature. For instance organizational scholars found positive impacts of the transformative role of states on employment and human resources practices, and organizational forms. Building institutional structures can facilitate the creation of new productive capacities and set further opportunities (Nasra & Dacin, 2009, pp. 586-87). Additionally, shaping institutions impacts international entrepreneurship, Ireland and Webb (2006) emphasizes that the role of the state is not confined to offering support to economic activities through regulations but also by mediating several factors including instability and uncertainty in the market. For example some of the means to attract foreign investments, as indicated by Johnasson (1994) have been the establishment of free zones and ports, thought they are not novel (as cited in Nasra & Dacin, 2009, pp.586-587).

The notion of 'resource mobilization' is central to the role of state as institutional entrepreneur. Resources are not necessary tangible, but definitely intangible such as the assets of networks and alliances with firms, merchants, corporations and trading community. The state as institutional entrepreneur should possess social and political skills to facilitate cooperation among the different actors. Furthermore, establishing institutional structure and enabling frameworks promotes entrepreneurship within the country itself (Nasra & Dacin, 2009, p. 596). Generally, creation of institutional infrastructure enables the country to establish and manage two types of legitimacies: national and international. This legitimacy contributes to a country's attractiveness for international entrepreneurs and political stability within the country and the region (Nasra & Dacin, 2009, p. 585).

Despite the fact that states in the GCC are represented by individuals due to the monarchical system, it is not a limitation as these actors have showed explicit willingness and latitude to create change (Nasra & Dacin, 2009, p.601). Smart cities as free zones are part of the processes of crafting an institutional infrastructure by the state, as the principal entrepreneur and a change agent with a transformative power.

SMART CITIES OF THE GULF REGION

The six countries in the Gulf region share several common features, such as a high per capita GDP, monarchical rule and central authority, and abundant financial wealth generated from their dependence on oil and gas. The abundant wealth has contributed to the "introduction of comprehensive administration reform and the need to provide more public services".(Khodr, 2012, pp. 150-151) The public policies have been formulated and implemented in different sectors. The Smart Cities, or the Specialized Cities as named by Khdor

(2012), in the region are "important sources of [policy] innovation and economic growth, as well as vehicles for globalization" (p. 152). There is a diffusion of smart cities phenomena occurring in the Gulf region. Indeed, governments are not different from individuals or organizations when it comes to innovation (Khodr, 2012, pp. 149, 172). Although there are several projects around the world similar to the smart cities in the Gulf, Silicon Valley and Kerala's Smart City for instance, smart cities in the GCC are built from the ground up and rapidly (Khodr, 2012, p.152). There are many projects in the region, such as Education City in Qatar, Healthcare City in Dubai and Masdar City in Abu Dhabi.

The concept of 'free zone' is crucial to the understanding of the smart city. "A free zone is one with multiple economic incentives, opportunities and benefits" (Khodr, 2012, p.155). The majority of smart cities in the Gulf are free zones. However, those without a population are mostly called enterprises, while others are called cities only for marketing purposes. Some smart cities are built for political, economic, religious, ethnic or education reasons. The use of terms such as bay and park in naming them is common (Khodr, 2012, pp. 155-156). Nevertheless, there are several internal determinants for such innovation. The first determinant is the political system. The rulers of this region are the policy entrepreneurs who have the greatest latitude to create change. Dependence on fossil fuels, which are finite resources, constitutes the second internal determinant. Overcoming social problems that emerged from dependence on foreign workforce and planning to improve the education and heath sectors are the third determinant (Khodr, 2012, p.173). On the other hand, the diffusion is a result of geographical proximity. Some states already adopted these innovation policies and proximate countries tend to have the same economic and social problems and aspects. It is also the result of high level of communication between governmental officials who learn from each other, but also compete with each other (Khodr, 2012, p.173).

Comparison of Masdar/Abu Dhabi/ UAE and Lusail/Doha/Qatar

In the past decade, Qatar has transformed itself into a major hub for numerous economic and cultural activities. What is more, Qatar has become extremely attractive as a place for foreign investment. Qatar's national vision for the year 2030 consists of basic foundations focused on the necessity of continuous social development in order to achieve a fair and safe society based on upholding human values and social welfare and aims to maintain and improve its economic standards in order to further strengthen its national economy and remain competitive, while continuing to secure and satisfy the needs of its citizens. Qatar plans on fostering investment in environmental development in order to maintain a balance between economic growth and environmental protection and awareness. The Lusail City project is planned, designed and implemented in accordance with Qatar's *National Vision 2030* because it blends modern facets of architecture with traditional values and norms. Above all, it is a project inspired by the mystique of Qatar's heritage. Qatari Diar Real Estate Investment Company was established in December 2004 to support Qatar's growing economy and to co-ordinate the country's real estate development priorities. With a mission to become the most effective and trusted real estate investment company in the world, Qatari Diar strives to create developments that are sustainable, quality-built, well-planned and ultimately desirable places to visit, work and live.

Lusail City is a futuristic project which will create a modern and ambitious society. The smart, peaceful and inspirational environment combines artistic elements of architecture with various practical and versatile services in order to satisfy all the needs of its residents and visitors. Lusail City extends across an area of 38 square kilometers and includes four exclusive islands and 19 multipurpose residential, mixed use, entertainment and commercial districts. It is a comprehensive arena with leisure spots, residential buildings, commercial towers, avenues and public ports. Lusail, a true city of the future, accommodates 200,000 residents and 170,000 employees; it will also welcome over 80,000 visitors. The total estimated population of Lusail will eventually reach 450,000 people. The city also includes numerous residential units, office buildings of various sizes and 22 hotels with different international star ratings, making it an element of attraction for investment in Qatar.

The United Arab Emirates is comprised of seven emirates. By 1971, when the U.A.E. officially declared itself an independent federation, Abu Dhabi was the natural choice for capital of the new country due to its wealth, its undisputed political clout as well as the strength of its leaders' local and foreign alliances (Nasra & Dacin, 2009). Although economic developments are ongoing in all emirates, most of the projects are concentrated in two of the emirates: Dubai and Abu Dhabi. UAE has started a process of "transforming oil wealth into renewable energy leadership, and has set the long-term goal of a transition from a 20th Century, carbon-based economy into a 21st Century sustainable economy" (Reiche, 2010). In early 2007, The UAE government had announced the government strategy for the coming years, outlining activities and ambitions. Similarly, different emirates have developed their own economic strategies, e.g., Abu Dhabi Economic Vision 2030 and Dubai Strategic Plan 2015.

Although the dynamics of policymaking might be different in Qatar and UAE, the planning regimes and general policy model is very similar. It all starts with a leadership vision in which decisions are made about general policies; then more specific policies are formulated, adopted, then implemented, and eventually evaluated. Channels of communication between the public and the government official are diverse, though the interactions between the stakeholders are unique, and the public participation and the institutional legislative power are deferent in scope, size, and nature. Furthermore, the participants operate in a special policy milieu and use mechanisms to affect the making of the policy that are specific to the country's political traditions and recent political developments (Khodr, 2010).

Businesses and governments are starting to recognize the role of technology in meeting the goals of urban infrastructure provisioning both today and in the long term that leads to increased reliance on smart cities in United Arab Emirates and Qatar. Masdar City is an eco-city, located in the vicinity of Abu Dhabi in the United Arab Emirates. It is a project of Abu Dhabi's state-run Masdar Corporation, in partnership with Foster + Partners, a prominent British architecture firm (Whitehead, 2009). Lusail City is one of the most ambitious and ground breaking concepts of Qatari Diar Real Estate Investment Company, which aspires to become the most internationally renowned company in real estate investment.

Three years before the government of UAE's announcement of the first renewable energy policy in 2009, Abu Dhabi made a decision to initiate 'Masdar Initiative' (Mezher & Park, 2012, p.73). Masdar means 'the source' (Snyder, 2009, p.2). This initiative aims to "advance renewable energy and sustainable technologies through education, R&D, investment and commercialization" as mentioned in Masdar website – About Masdar. Masdar City is part of Masdar Initiative. For implementation, Abu Dhabi created Abu Dhabi Future Energy Company (ADFEC), later called Masdar Company in 2006 (Mezher & Park, 2012, p.74). ADFEC is mandated to drive the initiative. Masdar was established by Mubadala Development Company; a public joint stock company founded by the government of Abu Dhabi (Perkins, 2009, p.11), and designed by Foster + Partners; a British architectural firm for feats technological wizardry (Ouroussoff, 2010). The city is "presented as a solution to the equally pressing current problems of resource depletion and climate change" (Snyder, 2009, p. 2). The city is a US $22 billion free zone located 17 km from Abu Dhabi's downtown (Mezher & Park, 2012, 74). The city is built to

meet different purposes such as, contributing to sustainable human development, changing the position of UAE as technology producer and developer, and, the main objective, expanding Abu Dhabi's role in the global energy market and economic diversification (Mezher & Park, 2012, p.74).

Indeed, the economy of the emirate is mainly dependent on exporting fossil fuels and the government has started to strengthen the knowledge-based economic sectors. Thus Masdar City will have a remarkable role in this transition period from carbon-based economy to sustainable economy. Climate change has also created a global demand for alternative sources of energy. Hence, Masdar City as the vital technological cluster in the region will make Abu Dhabi a global energy leader. From a policy perspective, Masdar City will provide the government of Abu Dhabi with an opportunity to contribute to global policy development (Reiche, 2010, p. 379).

The features of the city will include "apartments, laboratories, factories, movie theaters, cafes, schools and a fire station – everything a normal city contains" (Snyder, 2009, p. 5). Masdar City will become a homeland for a population of 90,000: 40,000 residents and 50,000 daily commuters (Reiche, 2010, p. 379). The city incorporates traditional Arabic architecture, central social space and an agricultural zone. "The city is raised 23 feet off the ground to allow for transportation and removal networks underneath." (Snyder, 2009, p. 5). Cars are prohibited in Masdar City (Snyder, 2009, p. 8); therefore, resident will use the personal rapid transports (PRTs) or can choose to walk or ride bicycles. Commuters will have to park in offsite lots and take light rail transportation into the city (Snyder, 2009, p. 6).

Masdar City is an eco-friendly metropolis whose designers embraced the *One Planet Living Principles (OPLP)*, which were developed by BioRegional and World Wide Fund for Nature. In accordance with the OPLP, Masdar City is designed to be a free-carbon zone that uses energy from renewable resources, minimizes and recycles waste, and creates sustainable transports. The plan also preserves culture and integrates health and happiness through the building and city design (Mezher & Park, 2012, p. 77). The urban sustainability strategy of Masdar City is both economic and environmentally sustainable. It capitalizes on real estate development, intellectual property ownership and human capital, while simultaneously operating on renewable energy, within green buildings, and moving by means of intelligent transportation. All of these components add to the social benefits generated from living in Masdar City (Mezher & Park, 2012, p.78).

Masdar has several subsidiary companies. Masdar Institute of Science and Technology is the key pillar of the City (Reiche, 2010, p. 380). Masdar Institute was established in 2007, in cooperation with Massachusetts Institute of Technology (MIT) (Mezher & Park, 2010, p. 76). This unit is the "Middle East's first graduate institution dedicated to the research and development of sustainability and renewable energy" (Perkins, 2009, p. 11). The building that houses Masdar Institute uses at least 70% less electricity and potable water than any similar conventional building (Mezher & Park, 2010, p. 76).

The concept of Masdar City will be replicated and supported by companies established within the city. Masdar Carbon aims to create a significant reduction in Abu Dhabi's carbon footprint. The unit will develop a "multi-dollar national carbon network". Masdar Carbon will be offering technological assistance, project owners, and carbon management and finance for other similar projects. Masdar Power invests in renewable energy projects. It will help power companies to add renewable energy to their generation mix, while supporting cleantech companies with expertise and capital (Mezher & Park, 2010, p. 75). Masdar Capital aims to build a portfolio of cleantech and renewable energy companies and to provide them with capital and expertise for expansion. It targets investment focused on clean energy and environmental resources and services (Mezher & Park, 2010, p. 76).

The actual objective of Masdar City is most commonly criticized. Some scholars believe that Masdar City is one of several projects and plans to show off and impress the world (Snyder, 2009, p. 14; Reiche, 2010, p. 380). The project of Masdar City only shows that the "region in more concerned with image than with environment sustainability per se" (Snyder, 2009, p. 14). Khodr (2012) argues that the major social aspects remain unclear and questions the ability of the city to attract 40,000 people to live within its boundaries (p. 160). Both Masdar and Lusail cities represents clearly what Kanter and Litow discussed about smart cities, where they "consider a smarter city as an organic whole—a network and a linked system. While systems in industrial cities were mostly skeleton and skin, postindustrial cities—smart cities—are like organisms that develop an artificial nervous system, which enables them to behave in intelligently coordinated ways" (Chourabi et al., 2012, pp. 2289-2297).

CONCLUSION

The globalization of neoliberal ideals have manifest in promoting the development of new markets across the globe. In the Gulf, as well as elsewhere, one product of globalization is the smart city. As people and capital move more feely around the world, people will have the option to choose which area to live. This creates competition among global cities. Lusail and Masdar Cities are being designed for that competition so to attract knowledgeable and entrepreneurial people from around the globe to their locals so that the state may benefit socially and economically from the ideas, goods and services provided by such people. The neoliberal market mentality is imbedded in the development of smart cities because of the competition for global talent, but not necessarily for the absence of government intervention.

Table 1. A Comparison of Lusail and Masdar City

Category	Masdar City	Lusail City
Country	United Arab Emirates	State of Qatar
City	Abu-Dhabi	Doha
Description	The design is based on a fusion of the traditional Arab walled city with innovative modern architecture	• A Futuristic project aim to create a modern and ambitious society. • Artistic elements of architecture with various practical and versatile services.
Vision	Promote renewable energies & Develop sustainable and renewable alternatives to fossil fuels	A show case for urban development. Lusail city is to be as a conscience of sustainable development
Target Segment	• Citizens • Investors and development partners.	• Citizens • Investors and development partners.
Competitive Advantage	• Carbon-Neutral • Zero-Waste City • Promoting sustainable energy	Integration to QNV 2030
Launching Year	2006	2008
Completion Year	2025	2019/20
Challenges	• The question of governance sustainability highly relevant; The social and Governance Responsibility is an ambiguity matter.(Khodor, 2012) • The challenge of substitution between natural resources and zero carbon economy (Whitehead, 2011) • Residents will not own cars, therefore this will result in severe limitation on personal freedom. (Snyder, 2009). • The dependence on Rail system will create a challenge for business shipments. (Snyder, 2099) • Some of the technologies Masdar city is designed to use have not been examined to sustain and work efficiently in harsh deserts conditions. (Snyder, 2009) • The heavily relying on ICTs remains a challenge for two reasons: The ICT changes and develops rapidly, and in case of natural disasters how would human react and live their lives. (Allwinkle & Cruickshank, 2011)	• The question of would the city attract the targeted number of residents and visitors? • Another challenge is how it will serve to mitigate the urban rapid population increase while it only serves a certain segment of the society, the elite of the community? • As Lusail is a city inside a city, would its infrastructure, prevent from inheriting the current situation of bureaucracy and work delay in some of the offices of the country? • Qatar may face the challenge of human resource employment not on worker level but in hiring levels. (Mansfield,2012) • The heavily relying on ICTs remains a challenge for two reasons: The ICT changes and develops rapidly, and in case of natural disasters how would human react and live their lives. (Allwinkle & Cruickshank, 2011)
Role of the State	• Power is mainly with in the ruling families and hence the full legal control of oil and gas resources is with local government. Therefore, the state in UAE has a great role. (Reiche, 2010) • The State is diversify the country's investment therefore inviting heavily in SC such as Masdar City, to protect its position as leading energy player in world and to help develop the country knowledge base economy. (Perkins, 2009) • The state of UAE is investing in Masdar smart city and other cities in other states in order to diversify the investment portfolio of the emirates. • Masdar smart city opens opportunities in the market by attracting international investors and joint ventures. Using this strategy is transforming the state role to be institutional entrepreneur and economically active player to cope with the globalization of the market. • The states uses the PPP approach as the constructions of the city is being done via international companies, joint ventures with British companies.(Reiche, 2010)	• Adopting this policy has embodied Qatar National Vision 2030 in the field of real estate development • It's a life evident of the government major initiatives towards building a diversified market, relying on non-hydrocarbons investments to maintain a sustainable welfare to its community. • The state is applying the approach of Private joint venture and Public private partnership through Qatari Diar and Lusail subsidiary. • As Qatari Diar being a subsidiary of Qatar Investment Authority, the state has guaranteed proper governance is taken in place and that the companies are operating us to the states standards and aligned with the national vision. • The state is adopting this policy to mitigate the problems generated by the urban population growth by connecting the infrastructure in a sustainable technology. • Throughout the deployment of ICTs, the state will improve its smart governance. (Chourabi *et al.*, 2012)

In the Gulf, finite natural resources have played a critical role in state-building and economic development and these have always been public-private enterprises. It is essential to realize that within the Gulf context, free market mechanisms have not been totally independent. The monarchies in the Gulf have utilized a brand of state-managed capitalism that includes cooperation between public and private enterprise to conceptualize, implement and operate national economic programs as well as, initiatives such as Lusail and Masdar Cities. Neoliberal market theory promotes minimizing the intervention of the government in business and economic affairs. Yet, in the Gulf, it is the government that often drives the policy process and solicits the business expertise of multinational corporations or of its own state owned enterprises to implement policy programs. The point is that the framework of competition, efficiency and economic incentive is associated with neoliberal free market theory, but the reality is that without state-entrepreneurship projects such as these smart cities would likely not come to fruition.

Smart cities in the Gulf hold much promise for states that are ambitious in their drive to modernization. This pursuit of national development is to ensure the quality of life for future generations of society as well as elevate these nations to positons of importance in the knowledge and service industries that will continue to drive globalized markets going forward.

Only time will tell whether the promise offered by smart cities as described in the second part of this study will bring with them the profound social, environmental and political changes in the form of sustainable economic growth, wise management of natural resources, a multi-cultural, tolerant society that shares a high quality of life within a participatory governance system. These qualities as described in this study are not necessarily natural outputs of a smart city, nor are they the natural product of a free market economy, but they *can* be promoted through the policy process put forth and executed by a government.

The construction of smart cities in the Gulf is a progressive idea that has the potential to meet the goals of these countries. The main reason for investing in smart cities would be to overcome the rising problems that are emerging with the rapidly growing population in the urban areas. The role of government as an 'entrepreneur' in crafting those cities is remarkable as it enables the economic growth through the public-private-partnerships. However, it is too soon to evaluate the success of the smart city program, so only time will tell if the promise will become reality.

A detailed comparison of Lusail City and Masdar City is provided in Table 1.

REFERENCES

Booz & Co. (2010). *Sustainable urbanization the role of ICT in city development*. [report], 1-16.

Castells, M. (1991). *Informational city: Information technology, urban restructuring and the urban regional process*. Oxford, UK: Blackwell Publishers.

Chourabi, H., Gil-Garcia, J., Pardo, T., Nam, T., Mellouli, S., Scholl, H., . . . Nahon, K. (2012). *Understanding smart cities: An integrative framework*. Paper presented at 45th International Conference on System Sciences, Hawaii, HI.

Cox, K. R. (1998). Spaces of dependence, spaces of engagement and the politics of scale, or: Looking for local politics. *Political Geography*, *17*(1), 1–23. doi:10.1016/S0962-6298(97)00048-6

Dacin, M., & Nasra, R. (2010). Institutional arrangements and international entrepreneurship: The state as institutional entrepreneur. *Entrepreneurship Theory and Practice*, *34*(3), 583–609. doi:10.1111/j.1540-6520.2009.00354.x

Evans, G. (2009). Creative cities, creative spaces and urban policy. *Urban Studies (Edinburgh, Scotland)*, *46*(5-6), 1003–1040. doi:10.1177/0042098009103853

Firmino, R. J., Duarte, F., & Moreira, T. (2008). Pervasive technologies and urban planning in the augmented city. *Journal of Urban Technology*, *15*(2), 77–93. doi:10.1080/10630730802401983

Florida, R. (2002). *The rise of the creative class*. New York: Basic Books.

Florida, R. (2005). *Cities and the creative class*. New York: Routledge.

Florida, R. (2006). *The flight of the creative class*. New York: HarperCollins Publishers.

Florida, R. (2008). *Who's your city?* New York: Basic Books.

Ghere, R. K., & Rismiller, L. S. (2001). Information technology's potential to improve urban neighborhoods: Some citizen planning dilemmas. *Journal of Urban Technology*, *8*(2), 39–60. doi:10.1080/106307301316904781

Glaeser, E. L. (2000). The new economics of urban and regional growth. In G. L. Clark, M. P. Feldman, & M. S. Gertler (Eds.), *The Oxford handbook of economic geography*. Oxford, UK: Oxford University Press.

Grundy, J., & Boudreau, J. A. (2008). Living with culture: Creative citizenship practices in Toronto. *Citizenship Studies*, *12*(4), 347–363. doi:10.1080/13621020802184226

Hamel, P., Boudreau, J. A., Keil, R., & Jouve, B. (2006). Arrested metropolitanism: limits and contradictions of municipal governance reform in Los Angeles, Montreal and Toronto. In H. Hubert & K. Daniel (Eds.), *Metropolitan governance in the 21st century: Governing capacity, democracy and the dynamics of place*. Routledge.

Ibrahim, A. (2011). *Economic clustering in emerging markets case study: The Gulf region*. Ross School of Business at the University of Michigan.

Jessop, B. (2002). Liberalism, neoliberalism and urban governance: A state-theoretical perspective. *Antipode*, *34*(3), 452–472. doi:10.1111/1467-8330.00250

Johansson, B., Karlson, C., & Stough, R. (2006). *The emerging digital economy*. Berlin: Springer. doi:10.1007/3-540-34488-8

Keil, R. (2002). Commonsense neoliberalism: Progressive conservative urbanism in Toronto, Canada. *Antipode*, *34*(3), 578–601. doi:10.1111/1467-8330.00255

Khodr, H., & Reiche, D. (2012). The specialized cities of the gulf cooperation council: A case study of a distinct type of policy innovation and diffusiondome. *Digest of Middle East Studies*, *21*(1), 149–177. doi:10.1111/j.1949-3606.2012.00131.x

Kim, T. J. (2008). Planning for knowledge cities in ubiquitous technology spaces: Opportunities and challenges. In Y. Tan, K. Velibeyoglu, & S. Baum (Eds.), *Creative urban regions: Harnessing urban technologies to support knowledge city initiatives*. New York: Hersey. doi:10.4018/978-1-59904-838-3.ch013

Laguerre, M. S. (2005). *The digital city*. New York: Palgrave MacMillan. doi:10.1057/9780230511347

Larner, W. (2000). Neo-liberalism: Policy, ideology, governmentality. *Studies in Political Economy*, 63.

Lefebvre, H. (1991). *The production of space*. Cambridge, MA: Blackwell.

Lewis, N. M., & Donald, B. (2010). A new rubric for Canada's creative cities. *Urban Studies (Edinburgh, Scotland)*, *47*(1). doi:10.1177/0042098009346867

Mahon, R., & Keil, R. (2006). *The political economy of scale: An introduction.* Manuscript.

McCann, E. (2007). Inequality and politics in the creative city-region: Questions of livability and strategy. *International Journal of Urban and Regional Research, 31*(1), 188–196. doi:10.1111/j.1468-2427.2007.00713.x

Mezher, T. (2012). Meeting the renewable energy and sustainability challenges. In M. A. Ramday (Ed.), *The GCC economies: Stepping up to future challenges* (pp. 69–84). New York: Springer. doi:10.1007/978-1-4614-1611-1_7

Ouroussoff, N. (2010). In Arabian desert, a sustainable city rises. *The New York Times.*

Peck, J. (1998). Geographies of governance: TECs and the neoliberalisation of local interests. *Space and Polity, 2*(1), 5–31. doi:10.1080/13562579808721768

Peck, J. (2007). Banal urbanism: Cities and the creativity fix. *Monu, 7.*

Peck, J., Theodore, N., & Brenner, N. (2009). Neoliberal urbanism: Models, moments, mutations. *SAIS Review, 29*(1).

Peck, J., & Tickell, A. (2002). Neoliberalizing space. *Antipode, 34*(3), 380–404. doi:10.1111/1467-8330.00247

Perkins, J. (2009). The role of Masdar initiative and Masdar Institute of Science and Technology in developing and deploying renewable technologies in emerging economies. *ATDF Journal, 5*(1/2), 10–15.

Polanyi, K. (2001). *Great transformation: The political and economic origins of our time.* Boston: Beacon Press.

Rami, Y. (2013). *Planning the city of the future in Qatar Lusail integrated transportation system.* Paper presented at QFIS.

Reiche, D. (2010). Renewable energy policies in the gulf countries: A case study of the carbon-neutral "Masdar City" in Abu Dhabi. *Energy Policy, 38*(1), 378–382. doi:10.1016/j.enpol.2009.09.028

Reiche, D. (2010). Renewable energy policies in the gulf countries: A case study of the carbon-neutral Masdar City in Abu Dhabi. *Energy Policy, 38*(1), 378–382. doi:10.1016/j.enpol.2009.09.028

Roche, S. (2013). *Four puzzle pieces for the spatially enabled smart campus.* Available at http://www.spatial.ucsb.edu/eventfiles/ASESC/docs/Roche-position.pdf

Sands, G., & Reese, L. A. (2008). Cultivating the creative class: And what about Nanaimo? *Economic Development Quarterly, 22*(1), 8–23. doi:10.1177/0891242407309822

Snyder, L. (2009). *Masdar City: The source of inspiration or uneconomical spending?* Repps Hudson.

Sohn, J., Kim, T. J., & Hewings, G. (2004). Intra-metropolitan agglomeration, information technology, and polycentric urban development. In R. Cappelo & P. Nijkamp (Eds.), *Contributions to economic analysis.* Elsevier. doi:10.1016/S0573-8555(04)66008-1

Swyngedouw, E., Moulaert, F., & Rodriguez, A. (2002). Neoliberal urbanization in europe: Large-scale urban development projects and the new urban policy. *Antipode, 34*(3), 542–577. doi:10.1111/1467-8330.00254

Whitehead, I. (2010). *Models of sustainability? A comparative analysis of ideal city planning in Saltaire and Masdar City.* Academic Press.

KEY TERMS AND DEFINITIONS

Creative City: Cities that utilize new development paradigms.

GCC: Gulf Cooperation Council, composed by Saudi Arabia, Qatar, United Arab Emirates, Oman, Kuwait and Bahrain.

Governance: Processes, relations and mechanisms of governing inclusive of multiplicity of actors.

ICT: Information Communication Technology.

Neoliberalism: Increasing use of market based mechanisms and attempts to minimize state capacity in accordance to economic liberalization.

Smart City: Cities that are using digital technologies in advancing the quality of life, economic and social organization as well as governing urban populations.

ENDNOTE

[1] The creativity of cities is attributed to various factors, including openness to diversity, level of tolerance and the peaceful coexistence of differences in a society. Levels of technological innovation and a population comprised of talented and innovative people are also believed to have a direct impact on the creativity and hence, development of a city. In his latest book, Florida (2008) asserts that people can now choose the cities in which they want to live in, and this choice is shaped by the characteristics of the cities. In an earlier text (Florida, 2002), two population indexes are developed. The creativity index measures the number of artists, musicians, and painters living in a city, (also called the bohemian index). The diversity index is itself composed of two indices, the first one is the melting pot index, the number and ratio of foreign born people and immigrants, and the second is the gay and lesbian index, measuring the tolerance of the community, as well as the region.

Compilation of References

(1969). *The Poetic Edda* (Vol. 1Dronke, U., Trans. & Ed.). Oxford, UK: Clarendon Press.

Abel, R., & Altman, R. (2002). *The sounds of early cinema.* Indiana University Press.

Acker, P. (Ed.). (2001). *The poetic Edda: Essays on old Norse mythology.* London: Routledge.

ACM. (1998). *The 1998 ACM computing classification system.* Retrieved July 14, 2014, from http://www.acm.org/about/class/1998/

Adria, E. N., Hoover, A. E. N., Harris, L. R., & Steeves, J. K. E. (2012). Sensory compensation in sound localisation in people with one eye. *Experimental Brain Research*, *216*(4), 565–574. doi:10.1007/s00221-011-2960-0 PMID:22130779

Aebersold, M. (2008). *Capacity to rescue: Nurse behaviors that rescue patients.* Retrieved from http://hdl.handle.net/2027.42/60718

Aebersold, M. (2010). Using simulation to improve the use of evidence-based practice guidelines. *Western Journal of Nursing Research.* doi:10.1177/0193945910379791 PMID:20876552

Aggarwal, J. K., & Cai, Q. (1999). Human motion analysis: A review. *Computer Vision and Image Understanding*, *73*(3), 428–440. doi:10.1006/cviu.1998.0744

AGI. (2014). *Accessible graphics initiative.* Retrieved July 14, 2014, from http://perceptualartifacts.org/agi/

Agichtein, E., Castillo, C., Donato, D., Gionis, A., & Mishne, G. (2008). Finding high-quality content in social media. *WSDM*, *08*, 183–193. doi:10.1145/1341531.1341557

Alberts, P. (2011). Responsibility towards life in the early Anthropocene. *Angelaki*, *16*(4), 5–17.

Aldridge, C. (2009). *The complete guide to simulations and serious games: How the most valuable content will be created in the age beyond Gutenberg to Google.* San Francisco, CA: Pfeiffer.

Allard-Huver, F. (2011). *Transformation and circulation of the notion of "risk" in the European Commission.* (Unpublished Master Thesis). University of Paris-Sorbonne, Paris, France.

Allen, M. (2013). *A study into video game violence and its effect on game player behaviour and attitudes.* University of Portsmouth, School of Creative Technologies.

Almiraat, H. (2011). Morocco: SlutWalk gets a toehold. *Global Voices.* Retrieved October 16, 2014, from http://globalvoicesonline.org/2011/09/07/morocc-slutwalk-gets-a-toehold/

Altman, R. (2007). *Silent film sound.* New York: Columbia University Press.

Altman, R. (Ed.). (1992). *Sound theory sound practice.* New York: Routledge.

Alves, J., Marques, M. J., Saur, I., & Marques, P. (2007). Creativity and innovation through multidisciplinary and multisectoral cooperation. *Creativity and Innovation Management*, *16*(1), 27–34. doi:10.1111/j.1467-8691.2007.00417.x

American Association of Colleges of Nursing. (2009). *The essentials of baccalaureate education for professional nursing practice faculty toolkit.* Author.

Anderson, N., & Gasteiger, R. M. (2007). Helping creativity and innovation thrive in organizations: Functional and dysfunctional perspectives. In J. Langan-Fox, C. L. Cooper, & R. J. Klimoski (Eds.), *Research companion to the dysfunctional workplace: Management challenges and symptoms* (pp. 422–440). Cheltenham, UK: Edward Elgar Publishing. doi:10.4337/9781847207081.00032

Anders, P. (1999). *Envisioning cyberspace*. New York, NY: McGraw-Hill.

Ansell Pearson, K. (2002). *Philosophy and the adventure of the virtual: Bergson and the time of life*. London, UK: Routledge.

Antell, K., Strothmann, M., Chen, X., & O'Kelly, K. (2013). Cross-examining google scholar. *Reference and User Services Quarterly, 52*(4), 279–282. doi:10.5860/rusq.52n4.279

Apple Computer Inc. (1993). *Macintosh human interface guidelines*. New York: Addison-Wesley.

Ardaiz-Villanueva, O., Nicuesa-Chacón, X., Brene-Artazcoz, O., Sanz de Acedo Lizarraga, M. L., & Sanz de Acedo Baquedano, M. T. (2011). Evaluation of computer tools for idea generation and team formation in project-based learning. *Computers & Education, 56*(3), 700–711. doi:10.1016/j.compedu.2010.10.012

Armitage, R., Smyth, G., & Pease, K. (1999). Burnley CCTV evaluation. In K. Painter & N. Tilley (Eds.), *Surveillance of public space: CCTV, street lighting and crime prevention* (pp. 225–250). Monsey, NY: Criminal Justice Press.

Ascott, R. (2005). Syncretic reality: Art, process, and potentiality. *Drain*. Retrieved from: http://drainmag.com/index_nov.htm

Ascott, R. (2003). *Telematic embrace: Visionary theories of art, technology and consciousness*. Berkeley, CA: University of California Press.

Ashby, W. (1957). *An introduction to cybernetics*. London: Chapman and Hall.

Atkins, B. (2003). *More than a game*. Manchester, UK: Manchester University Press. doi:10.7228/manchester/9780719063640.001.0001

Atkins, B., & Krzywinska, T. (2007). *Videogame, player, text*. Manchester, UK: Manchester University Press.

Atkinson, R. (2007, July 17). Do I want my sight back. *The Guardian*. Retrieved from http://www.guardian.co.uk/lifeandstyle/2007/jul/17/healthandwellbeing.health

Auden, W. H., & Taylor, P. B. (1983). *Norse poems* (2nd ed.). London: Faber & Faber.

Australian Antarctic Division. (2014). *Arts fellowship alumni*. Retrieved from http://www.antarctica.gov.au/about-antarctica/antarctic-arts-fellowship/alumni

Australian Institute of Criminology. (2004). Closed Circuit Television (CCTV) as a crime prevention measure. *AICrime Reduction Matters, 18*, 1.

Axelrod, E. A. (2009). *Violence goes to the internet (avoiding the snare of the net)*. Charles C. Thomas Publisher.

Axelrod, S. G., Roman, C., & Travisano, T. (Eds.). (2003). *The new anthology of American poetry: Traditions and revolutions, beginnings to 1900*. New Brunswick, NJ: Rutgers University Press.

Axtell, C., Holman, D., & Wall, T. (2006). Promoting innovation: A change study. *Journal of Occupational and Organizational Psychology, 79*(3), 509–516. doi:10.1348/096317905X68240

Aziz, A. (1995). Defining technology and innovation markets: The DOJ's antitrust guidelines for the licensing of intellectual property. *Hofstra Law Review, 24*(2), 476–513.

Bachelard, G. (1994). *The poetics of space* (M. Jolas, Trans.). Boston: Beacon Press. (Original work published 1958)

Baer, J. (1999). Creativity and gender differences. In M. A. Runco & S. R. Pritzker (Eds.), *Encyclopedia of creativity* (pp. 753–758). San Diego, CA: Academic Press.

Baer, J., & Kaufman, J. C. (2008). Gender differences in creativity. *The Journal of Creative Behavior, 42*(2), 75–105. doi:10.1002/j.2162-6057.2008.tb01289.x

Baer, M., & Frese, M. (2003). Innovation is not enough: Climates for initiative and psychological safety, process innovations, and firm performance. *Journal of Organizational Behavior, 24*(1), 45–68. doi:10.1002/job.179

Bailey, J., Steeves, V., Burkell, J., & Regan, P. (2013). Negotiating with gender stereotypes on social networking sites: From 'bicycle face' to Facebook. *The Journal of Communication Inquiry*, *37*(2), 91–112. doi:10.1177/0196859912473777

Baily, G., Corby, T., & Mackenzie, J. (2014). *Reconnoitre*. Retrieved from http://www.reconnoitre.net/index.php

Baker, F. W. (2012). *Media literacy in the K-12 classroom*. International Society for Technology in Education – ISTE.

Baker, A., Perreault, D., Reid, A., & Blanchard, C. M. (2013). Feedback and organizations: Feedback is good, feedback-friendly culture is better. *Journal of Canadian Psychology*, *54*(4), 260–268. doi:10.1037/a0034691

Barab, S., Cherkes-Julkowski, M., Swenson, R., Garrett, S., Shaw, R., & Young, M. (1999). Principles of self-organization: Learning as participation in autocatakinetic systems. *Journal of the Learning Sciences*, *8*(3&4), 349–390. doi:10.1080/10508406.1999.9672074

Barad, K. (2007). *Meeting the universe halfway: Quantum physics and the entanglement of matter and meaning*. Durham, NC: Duke University Press. doi:10.1215/9780822388128

Bardzell, S. (2010). Feminist HCI: Taking stock and outlining an agenda for design. In *Proceedings of the SIGCHI Conference on Human Factors in Computing Systems* (pp. 1301-1310). ACM. doi:10.1145/1753326.1753521

Bargh, J. (2014). Our unconscious mind: Unconscious impulses and desires impel what we think and do in ways Freud never dreamed of. *Scientific American*, *310*(1), 30–37. doi:10.1038/scientificamerican0114-30 PMID:24616968

Barker, M., & Munster, A. (2010). *Brainwaves of monks meditating on unconditional loving-kindness and compassion*. Retrieved February 04, 2015, from http://www.blakeprize.com/works/brainwaves-of-monks-meditating-on-unconditional-lovingkindness-and-compassion

Barlow, J. (1996). *A declaration of the independence of cyberspace*. Retrieved from https://projects.eff.org/~barlow/Declaration-Final.html

Barthes, R. (1968). *Elements of semiology*. New York: Hill and Wang.

Barthes, R. (1977). *Image, music, text*. London: Flamingo.

Bartosch, B. (1932). *(Animation Director), & Masereel, F. (Writer)*. France: The Idea. [Animated Film]

Barwise, P., & Meehan, S. (2010, December). The one thing you must get right when building a brand. *Harvard Business Review*, 63-68.

Bateman, C. (2013). *Designing computer-games preemptively for emotions and player types*. Arelíus Sveinn Arelíusarson. Accessed 04.05.2014. from http://www.olafurandri.com/nyti/papers2013/Designing%20Computer%20Games%20Preemptively%20for%20Emotions%20and%20Player%20Types.pdf

Bateman, C. (2013). *Designing computer games preemptively for emotions and player types: New technology*. Arelius Sveinn.

Bateson, G. (1972). Steps to an ecology of mind. San Francisco, CA: Chandler.

Baudrillard, J. (1994). *Simulacra and simulation*. Ann Arbor, MI: University of Michigan Press.

Bauerlein, M. (2008). *The dumbest generation: How the digital age stupefies young Americans and jeopardizes our future*. New York, NY: Tarcher/Penguin.

Baugh, B. (2003). *French Hegel*. New York: Routledge.

Baughman, W. A., & Mumford, M. D. (1995). Process-analytic models of creative capacities: Operations influencing the combination and reorganization process. *Creativity Research Journal*, *8*(1), 37–62. doi:10.1207/s15326934crj0801_4

Baum, M. (2001). Evidence-based art? *Journal of the Royal Society of Medicine*, *94*, 306–307. PMID:11387430

Baum, S., Arthurson, K., & Han, J. H. (2014, July). Tenure social mix and perceptions of antisocial behaviour: An Australian example. *Urban Studies (Edinburgh, Scotland)*, 22. doi:10.1177/0042098014541160

Bayona, A., SanMiguel, J. C., & Martínez, J. M. (2010). Stationary foreground detection using background subtraction and temporal difference in video surveillance. In *Proceedings of IEEE 17th Int. Conf. on Image Processing*. IEEE. doi:10.1109/ICIP.2010.5650699

Bearnson, C. S., & Wiker, K. M. (2005). Human patient simulators: A new face in baccalaureate nursing education at Brigham Young University. *The Journal of Nursing Education, 44,* 421–425. PMID:16220650

Beck, U. (1992). *Risk society: Towards a new modernity.* London: Sage.

Bee Biodiversity Network / Le Réseau Biodiversité pour les Abeilles. (2012). *Give a flower to the bees.* Retrieved April 24, 2014 from http://www.reseau-biodiversite-abeilles.com/?page_id=1169

Bek-Pedersen, K. (2011). The norns in old Norse mythology. Edinburgh, UK: Dunedin.

Benfold, B., & Reid, I. D. (2011).Stable multi-target tracking in real-time surveillance video. In *Computer vision and pattern recognition* (pp. 1–8). Colorado Springs, CO: CVPR.

Benjamin, A. (2004). *Disclosing spaces: On painting.* Manchester, UK: Clinamen Press.

Benner, P., Sutphen, M., Leonard, V., & Day, L. (2009). *Educating nurses: A call for radical transformation.* Carnegie Foundation.

Bennett, T., & Gelsthorpe, L. (1996). Public attitudes towards CCTV in public places. *Studies on Crime and Crime Prevention, 5*(1), 72-90.

Bennett, J. (2010). *Vibrant matter: A political ecology of things.* Durham, NC: Duke University Press.

Bennett, W. L. (2008). Changing citizenship in the digital age. In W. L. Bennett (Ed.), *Civic life online: Learning how digital media can engage youth* (pp. 1–24). Cambridge, MA: The MIT Press.

Bergson, H. (1920). *Creative evolution.* London, UK: Macmillan and Co. Ltd.

Bergson, H. (1991). *Matter and memory.* New York: Zone Books. (Original work published 1896)

Berthon, P. R., Pitt, L. F., Plangger, K., & Shapiro, D. (2012). Marketing meets web 2.0, social media, and creative consumers: Implications for international marketing strategy. *Business Horizons, 55*(3), 261–271. doi:10.1016/j.bushor.2012.01.007

Bilić, V. (2010). The relation between media violence and aggressive peer behaviour. *Odgojne znanosti, 12*(2), 263-281.

Bilić, V., Gjukić, D., & Kirinić, G. (2010). Possible effects of playing computer and video games on children and adolescents. *Napredak, 151*(2), 195–213.

Biocca, F. (1997). The cyborg's dilemma: Progressive embodiment in virtual environments. *Journal of Computer-Mediated Communication, 3*(2). Available at: http://jcmc.indiana.edu/vol3/issue2/biocca2.html

Biocca, F., Kim, T., & Levy, M. (1995). The vision of virtual reality. In F. Biocca & M. Levy (Eds.), *Communication in the age of virtual reality* (pp. 1–13). Hillsdale, NJ: Lawrence Erlbaum Associates.

Biocca, F., & Levy, M. (1995). Preface. In F. Biocca & M. Levy (Eds.), *Communication in the age of virtual reality* (pp. vii–viii). Hillsdale, NJ: Lawrence Erlbaum Associates.

Bisio, T. (2013). *Decoding the Dao: Nine lessons in Daoist meditation.* Denver, CO: Outskirts Press.

Blended-Gaming. (2014). *Explore the potential for democratic/civic engagement among future citizens who engage with video gaming.* Retrieved August 8, 2014 from http://blendedgaming.com/

Boatman, J., & Wellins, R. S. (2011). *Global leadership forecast.* Pittsburgh, PA: Development Dimensions International, Inc.

Bobick, A. F., & Davis, J. W. (2001). The recognition of human movement using temporal templates. *IEEE Transactions on Pattern Analysis and Machine Intelligence, 23*(3), 257–267. doi:10.1109/34.910878

Boden, M. (2004). *The creative mind: Myths and mechanisms.* London: Routledge. (Original work published 1990)

Boden, M. (2010). *Creativity and art: Three roads to surprise.* Oxford, UK: Oxford University Press.

Boden, M. (2014). A polymath at play. *American Journal of Play, 7,* 1–19.

Bodrova, E., & Leong, D. J. (1996). *The Vygotskian approach to early childhood.* Merrill, Prentice Hall.

Boellstorff, T. (2008). *Coming of age in Second Life: An anthropologist explores the virtually human.* Princeton, NJ: Princeton University Press.

Bogost, I. (2011). *How to do things with videogames.* Minneapolis, MN: University of Minnesota Press.

Bogost, I. (2013). *Alien phenomenology, or what it's like to be a thing.* Minneapolis, MN: University of Minnesota Press.

Bolter, J. D., & Grusin, R. (1999). *Remediation: Understanding new media.* Cambridge, MA: MIT Press.

Bonnardel, N., & Zenasni, F. (2010). The impact of technology on creativity in design: An enhancement? *Creativity and Innovation Management, 19*(2), 180–191. doi:10.1111/j.1467-8691.2010.00560.x

Booz & Co. (2010). *Sustainable urbanization the role of ICT in city development.* [report], 1-16.

Borden, M & Chilsen, PJ, (2012, March 2). *Don't just watch.* Paper presented at the International Society for Social Studies, Miami, FL.

Bosnak, R. (2007). *Embodiment: Creative imagination in medicine, art and travel.* Hove, East Sussex: Routledge.

Bostrom, N., & Sandberg, A. (2009). Cognitive enhancement: Methods, ethics, regulatory challenges. *Science and Engineering Ethics, 15*(3), 311–341. doi:10.1007/s11948-009-9142-5 PMID:19543814

Bouchard, T. J., Drauden, G., & Barsaloux, J. (1974). A comparison of individual, subgroup, and total group methods of problem solving. *The Journal of Applied Psychology, 59*(2), 226–227. doi:10.1037/h0036336

Boulanger, P. (2008, March). *Virtual reality and the arts: A critical review.* Keynote at Computer Art Congress 2008 [CAC.2]. Mexico City, Mexico.

Boyer, E. (1988). *Media literacy.* Retrieved from http://www.medialiteracy.com/sayings.htm

Boyle, D. K., & Kochinda, C. (2004). Enhancing collaborative communication of nurse and physician leadership: Two intensive care units. *JONA, 34*(2), 60–70. doi:10.1097/00005110-200402000-00003 PMID:14770064

Bramwell, T. (2013). *Is the most disturbing scene in GTA 5 justified?* Retrieved 16.09.2013 from erogamer.net: http://www.eurogamer.net/articles/2013-09-16-is-the-most-disturbing-scene-in-gta5-justified

Brennan, S., & Clark, H. (1996). Conceptual pacts and lexical choice in conversation. *Journal of Experimental Psychology. Learning, Memory, and Cognition, 22*(6), 1482–1493. doi:10.1037/0278-7393.22.6.1482 PMID:8921603

Brice, R. (1997). *Multimedia & virtual reality engineering.* Oxford, UK: Newnes.

Brodlie, K., Dykes, J., Gillings, M., Haklay, M., Kitchin, R., & Kraak, M. (2002). Geography in VR: Context. In P. Fisher & D. Unwin (Eds.), *Virtual reality in geography* (pp. 7–16). London: Taylor and Francis.

Brown, B. (1995). *CCTV in town centres: Three case studies.* London: HMSO.

Bryant, J., Carveth, R. A., & Brown, D. (1981). Televison viewing and anxiety:An experimental examination. *Journal of Communication, 31*(1), 106–119. doi:10.1111/j.1460-2466.1981.tb01210.x PMID:7204618

Büchler, D., Biggs, M., & Ståhl, L.-H. (2009). Areas of design practice as an alternative research paradigm. *Design Principles and Practices: An International Journal, 3*(2), 327–338.

Buchman, D. D., & Funk, J. B. (1996). Video and computer games in the '90s: Children's time commitment & game preference. *Children Today, 24*(1), 12-15, 31.

Buckingham, D. (2007). Digital media literacies: Rethinking media education in the age of the internet. *Research in Comparative and International Education, 2*(1), 43–55. doi:10.2304/rcie.2007.2.1.43

Buckley, T., & Gordon, C. (2011). The effectiveness of high fidelity simulation on medical–surgical registered nurses' ability to recognise and respond to clinical emergencies. *Nurse Education Today, 31*(7), 716–721. doi:10.1016/j.nedt.2010.04.004 PMID:20573428

Budd, M., & Kirsch, H. (Eds.). (2005). *Rethinking Disney: Private control, public dimensions.* Middletown, CT: Wesleyan University Press.

Bugeja, M. (2007). *Second Life, revisited: Which should take precedence in a virtual-reality campus: Corporate terms of service or public-disclosure laws?* Retrieved January 6, 2014, from http://0-chronicle.com.janus.uoregon.edu/weekly/v54/i12/12c00101.htm

Buisine, S., Besacier, G., Najm, M., Aoussat, A., & Vernier, F. (2007). Computer-supported creativity: Evaluation of a tabletop mind-map application. *Engineering Psychology and Cognitive Ergonomics, 4562*, 22–31. doi:10.1007/978-3-540-73331-7_3

Buljan-Flander, G. & Karlović, A. (2004). *Izloženost djece zlostavljanju putem interneta.* God. X. Dvobroj 54/55: MEDIX.

Bunkley, B. (2009). *Displaced animals 2004 – 06.* Retrieved April 30, 2011, from http://www.britbunkley.com/

Burgess, M. L., Slate, J. R., Rojas-LeBouef, A., & LaPraire, K. (2010). Teaching and learning in second life: Using the community of inquiry (CoI) model to support online instruction with graduate students in instructional technology. *The Internet and Higher Education, 13*(1-2), 84–88. doi:10.1016/j.iheduc.2009.12.003

Burrows, D. (2012). *Melbourne-A lifesize iceberg has landed in Melbourne, thanks to David Burrows and his modern day 'Viewmaster' 12 August 2012.* Retrieved from http://www.smartplanet.com/blog/global-observer/in-melbourne-a-touch-of-the-antarctic/?tag=main%3Bcarousel

Burrows, D. (2014). *Portfolio.* Retrieved from http://davidburrows.info/index.html

Cabanne, P. (1971). *Dialogues with Marcel Duchamp.* London: Thames and Hudson.

Cache, B. (2001). *Earth moves: The furnishing of territories.* Cambridge, MA: The MIT Press.

Cage, J. (Composer). (1979). Roaratorio, an Irish circus on Finnegans Wake [musical composition]. West German Radio.

Cage, J. (1961). *Silence: Lectures and writings.* Wesleyan University Press.

Cage, J. (1968). (*Composer/Performer*). Reunion: Ryerson Theater, Toronto, Canada. [musical composition/performance]

Cage, J. (1973). *Silence.* Hanover, CT: Wesleyan University Press. (Original work published 1961)

Cage, J., & Gena, P. (1982). After antiquity. In *A John Cage reader* (pp. 167–168). New York: Peters.

Calvino, I. (1997). *Invisible cities.* London: Vintage.

Campbell, J. (1982). *Creative mythology.* London: Penguin Books. (Original work published 1968)

Camplani, M., & Salgado, L. (2011). Adaptive background modelling in multicamera system for real-time object detection. *Optical Engineering (Redondo Beach, Calif.), 50*(12), 1–17. doi:10.1117/1.3662422

Camtasia. (2008). *Screen capture software.* Retrieved from http://www.techsmith.com/camtasia.html

Cañas, A. J., Carff, R., Hill, G., Carvahlo, M., Arguedas, M., Eskridge, T. C., & Carvajal, R. et al. (2005). Concept maps: Integrating knowledge and information visualization. In S.-O. Tergan & T. Keller (Eds.), *Knowledge and information visualization* (pp. 205–219). New York, NY: Springer. doi:10.1007/11510154_11

Candy, L., & Edmonds, E. (Eds.). (2002). *Explorations in art and technology.* London: Springer. doi:10.1007/978-1-4471-0197-0

Cann, O. (2014, April 23). *Addressing new digital divide key for balanced growth.* Retrieved from http://www.weforum.org/news/addressing-new-digital-divide-key-balanced-growth

Cardenna, M. (2008). *Becoming dragon.* Retrieved from https://www.youtube.com/watch?v=pHEDym1aOZs

Card, S., Mackinlay, J., & Shneiderman, B. (1999). *Readings in information visualization: Using vision to think.* San Francisco, CA: Morgan Kaufmann.

Carroll, L. (2011). *Through the looking glass, and what Alice found there.* Macmillan Children's Books. (Original work published 1871)

Carroll, N. (2010). *Philosophy of art.* London: Routledge. (Original work published 1999)

Carson, P. P., & Carson, K. D. (1993). Managing creativity enhancement through goal-setting and feedback. *Creativity Research Journal, 27*(1), 36–45.

Carstensen, T. (2009). Gender trouble in web 2.0: Gender relations in social network sites, wikis and weblogs. *International Journal of Gender, Science and Technology, 1*(1), 106-127. Retrieved January 16, 2013, from http://genderandset.open.ac.uk/index.php/genderandset/article/viewFile/18/31

Carter, C., Steiner, L., & McLaughlin, L. (Eds.). (2014). *The Routledge companion to media and gender*. Abingdon, UK: Routledge.

Casey, E. (2000). *Imagining: A phenomenological study*. Bloomington, IN: Indiana University Press.

Casinghino, C. (2011). *Moving images: Making movies, understanding media*. Delmar Cengage Learning.

Cassell, J., & Ryokai, K. (1999). *Making space for voice: Technologies to support children's fantasy and storytelling*. Cambridge, MA: MIT Media Lab.

Castells, M. (1991). *Informational city: Information technology, urban restructuring and the urban regional process*. Oxford, UK: Blackwell Publishers.

Catanese, P., & Truckenbrod, J. (2010). Tangiality of digital media. In G. Mura (Ed.), *Metaplasticity in virtual worlds: Aesthetics and semantic concepts*. IGI Global. doi:10.4018/978-1-60960-077-8.ch003

Catlow, R., Garrett, M., & Morgana, C. (Eds.). (2010). *Artists re: thinking games*. Liverpool, UK: Liverpool University Press.

Cavallaro, A., Steiger, O., & Ebrahimi, T. (2005). Tracking video objects in cluttered background. *IEEE Transactions on Circuits and Systems for Video Technology, 15*(4), 575–584. doi:10.1109/TCSVT.2005.844447

Cesarone, B. (1998). *Video games: Research, ratings, recommendations*. ERIC DIGEST (217) 333-1386, (800) 583-4135.

Charlton, J. (2010). *iForm*. Retrieved August 21, 2014, from http://idot.net.nz/?page_id=508

Chemaly, S. (April 18, 2013). Facebook's big misogyny problem. *The Guardian*.

Chen, Y. Y. (2008). 网络的力量:女性主义者跨界合作的新途径[The power of the Internet: New means of feminist collaborations across communities.] Retrieved January 10, 2013, from http:// www.mediawatch.cn/GB/75728/7151326.html

Chen, L., Marsden, J. R., & Zhang, Z. (2012). Theory and analysis of company-sponsored value co-creation. *Journal of Management Information Systems, 29*(2), 141–172. doi:10.2753/MIS0742-1222290206

Chevalier, J. A., & Mayzlin, D. (2006). The effect of word of mouth on sales: Online book reviews. *JMR, Journal of Marketing Research, 43*(3), 345–354. doi:10.1509/jmkr.43.3.345

Chief Council of State School Officers (CCSSO). (2010). *Common core state standards for mathematics*. Retrieved from http://www.corestandards.org

Chilsen, P. J., & Wells, C. R. (2012, June). *Media and the moving image: Creating those who thrive in a screen media world*. Paper presented at EdMedia World Conference on Educational Media & Technology, Denver, CO.

Chilsen, PJ, & Kelley, T (2014, February - November). Digital conversations. *Against The Grain*, (1, 2, 4).

Chion, M. (1994). *Audio-vision: Sound on screen*. (C. Gorbman, Trans.). New York: Columbia University Press.

Chion, M. (1999). *The voice in cinema*. (C. Gorbman, Trans.). New York: Columbia University Press.

Chion, M. (2009). *Film a sound art*. (C. Gorbman, Trans.). New York: Columbia University Press.

Cho, A. (2010). The first quantum machine. *Science, 330*(6011), 1608–1609. doi:10.1126/science.330.6011.1604 PMID:21163978

Chorafas, D., & Steinmann, H. (1995). *Virtual reality: Practical applications in business and industry*. Englewood Cliffs, NJ: Prentice Hall PTR.

Chourabi, H., Gil-Garcia, J., Pardo, T., Nam, T., Mellouli, S., Scholl, H., . . . Nahon, K. (2012). *Understanding smart cities: An integrative framework*. Paper presented at 45th International Conference on System Sciences, Hawaii, HI.

Chua, C. K., Leong, K. F., & Lim, C. S. (2003). *Rapid prototyping: Principles and applications.* Singapore: World Scientific. doi:10.1142/5064

Cincera, R. (1967). *Kinoautomat* [interactive audio-visual performance/film]. Czechoslovakia.

Citizen Sense. (2014). *About citizen sense.* Retrieved from http://www.citizensense.net/about/

Citron, D. (2009, February). Cyber civil rights. *Law Review, 89*(1), 61–125.

City of Perth. (2000). *Closed circuit TV information kit.* Perth, Australia: Perth City.

Clair, R. (Director). (1924). *Entr'acte* [film]. France.

Clarke, R. V. (2004). Technology, criminology and crime science. *European Journal on Criminal Policy and Research, 10*(1), 55–63. doi:10.1023/B:CRIM.0000037557.42894.f7

Clarke, R. V., & Cornish, D. B. (1985). 'Modelling offenders' decisions: A framework for research and policy. In M. Tonry & N. Morris (Eds.), *Crime and justice* (pp. 147–185). Chicago: University of Chicago Press.

Cleary, A. G., McKendrick, H. & Sills, J. A. (2002). Hand–arm vibration syndrome may be associated with prolonged use of vibrating computer games. *British Medical Journal, 324*(7332), 301.

Cochran-smith, M., Ell, F., Ludlow, L., & Aitken, G. (2014). Article. *The Challenge and Promise of Complexity Theory for Teacher Education Research, 116*(May), 1–38.

Cohen L., Manion L. & Morrison K. (2007). *Metode istraživanja u obrazovanju.* Jastrebarsko: Naklada Slap.

Cohen, A. (Producer), & Capra, B. (Director). (1990). *Mindwalk* [motion picture]. America: Paramount.

Cohen, L. E., & Felson, M. (1979). Social change and crime rate trends: A routine activity approach. *American Sociological Review, 44*(4), 588–608. doi:10.2307/2094589

Cole, M. (1996). *Cultural psychology: A once and future discipline.* Cambridge, MA: The Belknap Press of Harvard University.

Coleman, R., & Sim, J. (2000). You'll never walk alone: CCTV surveillance, order and neo-liberal rule in Liverpool city centre. *The British Journal of Sociology, 51*(4), 623–639. doi:10.1080/00071310020015299 PMID:11140887

Collaros, P. A., & Anderson, L. R. (1969). Effect of perceived expertness upon creativity of members of brainstorming groups. *The Journal of Applied Psychology, 53*(2, Pt.1), 159–163. doi:10.1037/h0027034 PMID:5790809

Collins, S., & Clarke, A. (2008). Activity frames and complexity thinking: Honouring both the public and personal agendas in an emergent curriculum. *Teaching and Teacher Education, 24*(4), 1003–1014. doi:10.1016/j.tate.2007.11.002

Colman, R., & Sim, J. (1998). From the dockyards to the Disney stores: Surveillance, risk and security in Liverpool city centre. *International Review of Law Computers & Technology, 12*(1), 27–45. doi:10.1080/13600869855559

Comaniciu, D., Ramesh, V., & Meer, P. (2003). Kernel-based object tracking. *IEEE Transactions on Pattern Analysis and Machine Intelligence, 25*(5), 564–577. doi:10.1109/TPAMI.2003.1195991

Comer, J. S., Furr, J. M., Beidas, R. S., Weiner, C. L., & Kendall, P. C. (2008). Children and terrorism-related news: Training parents in coping and media literacy. *Journal of Consulting and Clinical Psychology, 76*(4), 568–578. doi:10.1037/0022-006X.76.4.568 PMID:18665686

Compendium. (2013). *Sexual assault and rape in Tahrir Square and its vicinity: A compendium of sources 2011-2013.* Retrieved January 3, 2014, from http://nazra.org/en/2013/05/sexual-assault-and-rape-tahrir-square-and-its-vicinity-compendium-sources-2011-2013

Computer Application in Education. (n.d.). *Scope and challenge.* Accessed 04.05.2014 from http://criticalcompetency.wordpress.com/2011/11/06/computer-application-in-education-scope-and-challenges/

Connolly, T., Jessup, L. M., & Valacich, J. S. (1990). Effects of anonymity and evaluative tone on idea generation in computer-mediated groups. *Management Science, 36*(6), 689–703. doi:10.1287/mnsc.36.6.689

Conradi, E., Kavia, S., Burden, D., Rice, A., Woodham, L., Beaumont, C., & Poulton, T. et al. (2009). Virtual patients in a virtual world: Training paramedic students for practice. *Medical Teacher*, *31*(8), 713–720. doi:10.1080/01421590903134160 PMID:19811207

Conseil supérieur de l'audiovisuel. (2011, October 18). *Convention de la chaîne M6*. Retrieved February 12, 2012, from http://www.csa.fr/Espace-juridique/Conventions-des-editeurs/Convention-de-la-chaine-M6

Cooper, J., & Mackie, D. (1986). Video games and aggression in children. *Journal of Applied Social Psychology*, *16*(8), 726–744. doi:10.1111/j.1559-1816.1986.tb01755.x

Corby, T. (2008). Landscapes of feeling, arenas of action: Information visualization as art practice. *Leonardo*, *41*(5), 460–467. doi:10.1162/leon.2008.41.5.460

Corvee, E., Velastin, S. A., & Jones, G. A. (2003). Occlusion tolerant tracking using hybrid prediction schemes. *Acta Automatica Sinica*, *29*(3).

Council for Graduate Medical Education. (n.d.). Retrieved from http://www.acgme.org/acgmeweb/Portals/0/PFAssets/ProgramRequirements/CPRs2013.pdf

Courschesne, L. (1997). Landscape one. *Interactive Film Installation*. Available at: http://courchel.net/

Coutu, D. (2007, June). We Googled you. *Harvard Business Review*, *85*(6), 37–47. PMID:11184976

Cox, K. R. (1998). Spaces of dependence, spaces of engagement and the politics of scale, or: Looking for local politics. *Political Geography*, *17*(1), 1–23. doi:10.1016/S0962-6298(97)00048-6

Coyle, R. (Ed.). (2010). *Drawn to sound: Animation film music and sonicity*. London: Equinox Publishing Ltd.

Crafton, D. (1993). *Before Mickey: The animated film 1898-1928*. London: University of Chicago Press.

Cresswell, J., & Thompson, H. (2012). Comment on "A Common Pesticide Decreases Foraging Success and Survival in Honey Bees". *Science*, *337*(6101), 1453. doi:10.1126/science.1224618 PMID:22997307

Crockard, S., & Jenkins, D. (1998). *An independent evaluation of Chelmsford town centre CCTV scheme*. Chelmsford: Anglia Polytechnic University.

Crompton, R. (1922). *Just William*. London: George Newnes.

Crompton, R. (1927). *William in trouble*. London: George Newnes.

Cronenwett, L., Sherwood, G., Barnsteiner, J., Disch, J., Johnson, J., Mitchell, P., & Warren, J. et al. (2007). Quality and safety education for nurses. *Nursing Outlook*, *55*(3), 122–131. doi:10.1016/j.outlook.2007.02.006 PMID:17524799

Cross, L. (1999). Reunion: John Cage, Marcel Duchamp, electronic music and chess. *Leonardo Music Journal*, *9*, 35–42. doi:10.1162/096112199750316785

Crossley-Holland, K. (1996). *Norse myths: Gods of the vikings*. London: Penguin Books.

Csikszentmihalyi, M. (2008). *Flow: The psychology of optimal experience*. Harper Perennial Modern Classics.

Csikszentmihalyi, M. (1996). *Creativity*. New York: Harper Collins.

Culnan, M., McHugh, P., & Zubillaga, J. (2010). How large U.S. companies can use twitter and other social media to gain business value. *MIS Quarterly Executive*, *9*(04), 243–259.

Culture and Trends. (2009, February 21). *Verdens Gang*. [newspaper article]. Retrieved from http://www.vg.no

Cumin, D., Boyd, M. J., Webster, C. S., & Weller, J. M. (2013). A systematic review of simulation for multidisciplinary team training in operating rooms. *Simulation in Healthcare: Journal of the Society for Simulation in Healthcare*. doi: 10.1097/SIH.0b013e31827e2f4c

Cutler, R., Rui, Y., Gupta, A., Cadiz, J., Tashey, I., He, L., . . . Silverberg, S. (2002). Distributed meetings: A meeting capture and broadcasting system. In *Preceedings of the 10th ACM International Conference on Multimedia* (pp. 503-512). ACM.

Cytowic, R. E. (1989). *Synaesthesia: A union of the senses*. Berlin: Springer. doi:10.1007/978-1-4612-3542-2

Da Silva, N., & Oldham, G. R. (2012). Adopting employees' ideas: Moderators of the idea generation-idea implementation link. *Creativity Research Journal*, *24*(2-3), 134–145. doi:10.1080/10400419.2012.677257

Dacin, M., & Nasra, R. (2010). Institutional arrangements and international entrepreneurship: The state as institutional entrepreneur. *Entrepreneurship Theory and Practice*, *34*(3), 583–609. doi:10.1111/j.1540-6520.2009.00354.x

Damer, B. (1998). *Avatars! Exploring and building virtual worlds on the internet*. Berkeley, CA: Peachpit Press.

Darrell, T., & Pentland, A. (1993). Space-time gestures. In *Proceedings of IEEE Computer Society Conf. on Computer Vision and Pattern Recognition* (pp. 335–340). IEEE.

Darwin, Ch. (1859). *The origin of species*. London: Signet Classics.

Davallon, J. (2004). Objet concret, objet scientifique, objet de recherche. *Hermes*, *38*, 30–37.

David & Lucile Packard Foundation. (2000). The future of children. Los Altos, CA: Author.

Davies, A. C., & Velastin, S. A. (2005). A progress review of intelligent CCTV surveillance systems. In *Proceedings of IDAACS 2005 Workshop*. IDAACS. doi:10.1109/IDAACS.2005.283015

Davies, C. (1995). *Osmose: Virtual reality environment*. Available at: http://www.immersence.com/osmose/index.php

Davies, C. (1997). Changing space: Virtual reality as an arena of embodied being. In *Multimedia: From Wagner to virtual reality*. New York: W.W. Norton & Company. Available at: http://www.immersence.com

Davies, C. (1998). *Ephémère: Virtual reality environment*. Available at: http://www.immersence.com/

Davies, C. (2003). Landscape, earth, body, being, space, and time in the immersive virtual environments *Osmose* and *Ephemere*. In *Women, art and technology*. Cambridge, MA: MIT Press. Available at: http://www.immersence.com

Davies, P. J. (1997). *The politics of perpetuation: Trajan's column and the art of commemoration*. Archaeological Institute of America. Retrieved from http://www.jstor.org/stable/506249

Davies, A. C., Yin, J. H., & Velastin, S. (2005). Crowd monitoring using image processing. *Electronics and Communication Engineering Journal*, *7*(1), 37–47. doi:10.1049/ecej:19950106

Davis, B., & Simmt, E. (2003). Understanding learning systems: Mathematics education and complexity science. *Journal for Research in Mathematics Education*, *34*(2), 137–167. doi:10.2307/30034903

Davis, B., & Sumara, D. (2006). *Complexity and education*. Mahwah, NJ: Lawrence Erlbaum Associates, Inc.

Davis, B., Sumara, D., & Luce-Kapler, R. (2008). *Emerging minds: Changing teaching in complex times* (2nd ed.). New York: Routledge.

Day, L. (2014, April 13). *Bridging the new digital divide*. Retrieved from http://www.edutopia.org/blog/bridging-the-new-digital-divide-lori-day

Day, T., Iles, N., & Griffiths, P. (2009). Effect of performance feedback on tracheal suctioning knowledge and skills: Randomized controlled trial. *Journal of Advanced Nursing*, *65*(7), 14–23. doi:10.1111/j.1365-2648.2009.04997.x PMID:19457007

De Landa, M. (1999). Deleuze, diagrams, and the open-ended becoming. In E. Grosz (Ed.), *Becomings: Explorations in time, memory and futures*. London, UK: Cornell University Press.

De Landa, M. (2002). *Intensive science and virtual philosophy*. London: Bloomsbury Academic.

De Winter, J. (2009). Aesthetic reproduction in Japanese computer culture: The dialectical histories of manga, anime, and computer games. In J. E. Ruggill, K. S. McAllister, & J. R. Chaney (Eds.), *The computer culture reader* (pp. 108–124). Newcastle, UK: Cambridge Scholars Publishing.

DeCamp, D. (2011a, November 17). Pinellas county commissioner Norm Roche has alter ego for online comments. *St. Petersburg Times*. Retrieved January 22, 2012, from http://www.tampabay.com/news/localgovernment/article1202065.ece

DeCamp, D. (2011b, November 18). Norm Roche's anonymous online snark strains city, county relations. *St. Petersburg Times.* Retrieved January 22, 2012, from http://www.tampabay.com/news/politics/local/norm-roches-anonymous-online-snark-strains-city-county-relations/1202287

Defiance . (2013-). [television series]. Five and Dime/ Universal Cable: Syfy. USA.

DeFillippi, R., Grabher, G., & Jones, C. (2007). Introduction to paradoxes of creativity: Managerial and organizational challenges in the cultural economy. *Journal of Organizational Behavior, 28*(5), 511–521. doi:10.1002/job.466

Deleuze, G. (1991). *Bergsonism.* New York: Zone Books.

Deleuze, G. (1999). *Foucault.* London, UK: The Athlone Press.

Deleuze, G. (2000). *Cinema II.* London, UK: The Athlone Press.

Deleuze, G. (2001). *Difference and Repetition.* London, UK: Continuum Books.

Deleuze, G. (2002). *Cinema I.* London, UK: The Athlone Press.

Deleuze, G. (2002). *Desert islands.* Los Angeles, CA: Semiotext.

Deleuze, G. (2004b). *The logic of sense.* London: Continuum.

Deleuze, G., & Guattari, F. (1998). *What is philosophy?* London: Verso.

Deleuze, G., & Guattari, F. (2002). *A thousand plateaus.* London: Continuum.

Deleuze, G., & Guattari, F. (2004a). *Anti-Oedipus: Capitalism and schizophrenia.* London: Continuum.

Denman, S., Chandran, V., & Sridharan, S. (2007). Adaptive optical flow for person tracking. *Pattern Recognition Letters, 28*(10), 1232–1239. doi:10.1016/j.patrec.2007.02.008

Dennis, A. R., & Valascich, J. S. (1993). Computer brainstorms: More heads are better than one. *The Journal of Applied Psychology, 78*(4), 531–537. doi:10.1037/0021-9010.78.4.531

Derosa, D. M., Smith, C. L., & Hantula, D. A. (2007). The medium matters: Mining the long-promised merit of group interaction in creative idea generation tasks in a meta-analysis of the electronic group brainstorming literature. *Computers in Human Behavior, 23*(3), 1549–1581. doi:10.1016/j.chb.2005.07.003

Desai, M. (2009). *Gender and the politics of possibilities: Rethinking globablization.* Lanham, MD: Rowman & Littlefield.

Deutsch, S. (2008). Aspects of synchrony in animation. *The Soundtrack,* (1/2), 95–105. doi:.10.1386/st.1.2.95/1

Diamond, L. (2010). Liberation technology. *Journal of Democracy, 21*(3), 63–83.

Diehl, M., & Stroebe, W. (1987). Productivity loss in brainstorming groups: Toward the solution of a riddle. *Journal of Personality and Social Psychology, 53*(3), 497–509. doi:10.1037/0022-3514.53.3.497

Digital Opportunity for Youth Issue Brief Number 7. (2010, October). *Empowering parents through technology to improve the odds for children.* Retrieved from http://www.childrenspartnership.org/storage/documents/Publications/TCP-ParentTech-LowRezFinal.pdf

Dillon, P., & Noble, K. (2009). Simulation as a means to foster collaborative interdisciplinary education. *Nursing Education Perspectives, 30*(2), 87–90. PMID:19476071

Ditton, J. (2000). Crime and the city: Public attitudes to CCTV in Glasgow. *The British Journal of Criminology, 40*(4), 692–709. doi:10.1093/bjc/40.4.692

Dixon, S. (2007). *Digital performance: A history of new media in theater, dance, performance art, and installation.* Cambridge, MA: MIT Press.

Djeca i računalo: Uloga računala u predškolskoj dobi. (n.d.). Accessed 30.03.2014, from http://www.istrazime.com/djecja-psihologija/djeca-i-racunalo-uloga-racunala-u-predskolskoj-dobi/

Do Sterotypic Images in Video Games Affect Attitudes and Behaviour? (n.d.). *Adolescent perspectives*. Accessed 17.05.2014., from http://www.academia.edu/371174/_Do_Stereotypic_Images_in_Video_Games_Affect_Attitudes_and_Behavior_Adolescent_Perspectives

Doll, W. (2008). Complexity and the culture of curriculum. *Educational Philosophy and Theory*, *40*(1), 191–212. doi:10.1111/j.1469-5812.2007.00404.x

Don, A. (1990). Narrative and interface. In B. Laurel & S. Joy (Eds.), *The Art of human computer interface design* (pp. 383–391). Reading, MA: Addison-Wesley.

Donahue, N. H. (2005). *A companion to the literature of German expressionism*. New York: Camden House.

Doris, D. T. (2011). *Vigilant things, on thieves, yoruba anti-aesthetics, and the strange fate of ordinary objects*. Seattle, WA: University of Washington Press.

Dorman, S. M. (1997). Video and computer games: Effect on children and implications for health education. *The Journal of School Health*, *67*(4), 133–138. doi:10.1111/j.1746-1561.1997.tb03432.x PMID:9130190

Dorset Tourism. (2014). *Jurassic coast*. Retrieved from http://www.visit-dorset.com/about-the-area/jurassic-coast

Dossick, C. S., Anderson, A., Azari, R., Iorio, J., Neff, G., & Taylor, J. E. (2014). Messy talk in virtual teams: Achieving knowledge synthesis through shared visualizations. *Journal of Management Engineering*.

Dove, T. (2002). The space between: Telepresence, re-animation and the re-casting of the invisible. In New screen media: Cinema/art/narrative. London: BFI.

Dove, T. (2005). *Spectropia: Interactive feature film*. Available at: http://tonidove.com/

Dove, T. (2006). Swimming in time: Performing programmes, mutable movies - Notes on a process in progress. In Performance and place. Basingstoke, UK: Palgrave Macmillan.

Dove, T., & Mackenzie, M. (1993). Archaeology of the mother tongue: Virtual reality installation. Alberta, Canada: Banff Centre for the Arts. Available at http://www.banffcentre.ca/bnmi/coproduction/archives/a.asp

Downey, S., Hayes, N., & O'Neill, B. (2004). Play and technology for children aged 4-12. In R. Gentile et al. (Eds.), Centre for social and educational research. Dublin Institute of Technology, Office of the Minister for Children.

Doyle, D. (2000). *Wandering fictions 2.0: Eleni's journey*. (Unpublished MA Project). Coventry University, Coventry, UK.

Doyle, D. (2008). *Kritical works in SL*. Morrisville, NC: Lulu Publishing.

Doyle, D., & Kim, T. (2007). Embodied narrative: The virtual nomad and the meta dreamer. *The International Journal of Performance Arts and Digital Media*, *3*(2&3), 209–222. doi:10.1386/padm.3.2-3.209_1

Dreifuerst, K. T. (2009). The essentials of debriefing in simulation learning: A concept analysis. *Nursing Education Perspectives*, *30*(2), 109–114. PMID:19476076

Duffy, A. H. B., Andreasen, M. M., MacCallum, K. J., & Reijers, L. N. (1993). Design co-ordination for concurrent engineering. *Journal of Engineering Design*, *4*(4), 251–261. doi:10.1080/09544829308914785

Dukette, D., & Cornish, D. (2009). *The essential 20: Twenty components of an excellent health care team*. RoseDog Books.

Duran, M. (2003). *Dijete i igra*. Naklada Slap, Jastrebarsko. In Croatian

Durlach, N., & Mavor, A. (Eds.). (1995). *Virtual reality: Scientific and technological challenges*. Washington, DC: National Academy Press.

Eco, U. (1976). *A theory of semiotics*. Bloomington, IN: Indiana University Press.

Edmonds, E., & Candy, L. (2002). Creativity, art practice, and knowledge. *Communications of the ACM*, *45*(10), 91–95. doi:10.1145/570907.570939

Edmondson, A. (1999). Psychological safety and learning behavior in work teams. *Administrative Science Quarterly*, *44*(2), 350. doi:10.2307/2666999

Edmondson, A. (2003). Managing the risk of learning: Psychological safety in work teams. In M. West, D. Tjosvold, & K. Smith (Eds.), *International handbook of teamwork and co-operative working* (pp. 255–276). West Sussex, UK: John Wiley & Sons. doi:10.1002/9780470696712.ch13

Eisenberg, N. (2000). Emotion regulation and moral development. *Annual Review of Psychology, 51*(1), 665–697. doi:10.1146/annurev.psych.51.1.665 PMID:10751984

Eisenstein, S. (1991). Vertical montage. In R. Taylor & M. Glenny (Eds.), Towards a theory of montage (Vol. 2). London: British Film Institute. (Original work published 1939)

Elger, D. (2004). *Dadaism*. Cologne: Taschen.

Ellemers, N., De Gilder, D., & Haslam, S. A. (2004). Motivating individuals and groups at work: A social identity perspective on leadership and group performance. *Academy of Management Review, 29*(3), 459–478.

Ellis, C. (2004). *The ethnographic 'I': A methodological novel about autoethnography*. Walnut Creek, CA: Altamira Press.

Ellsworth, E., & Kruse, J. (Eds.). (2012). *Making the geologic now: Responses to material conditions of contemporary life*. Brooklyn, NY: Punctum Books.

Eltantawy, N. (2013). From veiling to blogging: Women and media in the Middle East. *Feminist Studies, 13*(5), 765–769. doi:10.1080/14680777.2013.838356

Emes, C. E. (1997). Is Mr Pac Man eating our children? A review of the impact of video games on children. *Canadian Journal of Psychiatry, 42*(4), 409–414. PMID:9161766

Engelbart, D. (1962) Augmenting human intellect: A conceptual framework. *Summary Report AFOSR-3233.*

Ericsson, K. A. (2004). Deliberate practice and the acquisition and maintenance of expert performance in medicine and related domains. *Academic Medicine: Journal of the Association of American Medical Colleges, 79*(10Suppl), S70–S81. doi:10.1097/00001888-200410001-00022 PMID:15383395

Escobar, A. (1999). Gender, place and networks: A political ecology of cyberculture. In W. Hartcourt (Ed.), *Woman@Internet: Creating new cultures in cyberspace* (pp. 31–54). London: Zed Books.

Etheridge, K. (2011). Maria Sibylla Merian: The first ecologist? In V. Molinari & D. Andreolle (Eds.), *Women and science: Figures and representations – 17th century to present* (pp. 35–54). Newcastle upon Tyne, UK: Cambridge Scholars Publishing.

Ettlinger, O. (2009). *The architecture of virtual space*. Ljubljana: University of Ljubljana.

European Commission. (2009). Towards a thematic strategy on the sustainable use of pesticides. *Environment.*

Evans, G. (2009). Creative cities, creative spaces and urban policy. *Urban Studies (Edinburgh, Scotland), 46*(5-6), 1003–1040. doi:10.1177/0042098009103853

Evans, J. D., Saegerman, C., Mullin, C., Haubruge, E., Nguyen, B. K., Frazier, M., & Pettis, J. S. et al. (2009). Colony collapse disorder: A descriptive study. *PLoS ONE, 4*(8), e6481. doi:10.1371/journal.pone.0006481 PMID:19649264

Fairchild, J., Cassidy, S., Cushenbery, L., & Hunter, S. (2011). Integrating technology with the creative design process. In A. Mesquita (Ed.), *Technology for creativity and innovation: Tools, techniques and applications* (pp. 26–51). Hershey, PA: IGI Global. doi:10.4018/978-1-60960-519-3.ch002

Fairchild, J., Eubanks, D., & Hunter, S. T. (2013). Effects of intuition, positive affect, and training on creative problem solving. In E. G. Carayannis (Ed.), *The encyclopedia of creativity, invention, innovation, and entrepreneurship* (pp. 562–567). New York, NY: Springer. doi:10.1007/978-1-4614-3858-8_363

Fanès, F. (2007). *Salvador Dalí: The construction of the image 1925–1930*. New Haven, CT: Yale University Press.

Fauconnier, G., & Turner, M. (2002). *The way we think*. New York: Basic Books.

Felton, N. (2014). *2011 annual report*. Retrieved August 19, 2014, from http://feltron.com/

Feng, L., & Zhang, W. (manuscript in preparation). *"Wo-Man" in China: Exploring the changing gender identities of young Chinese women.*

Fernànez, A. (2013). Internet in the feminine: Using feminine strategies in hacker culture. *Catalan Social Sciences Review, 3*, 93–112.

Findell, M. (2014). *Runes*. London: The British Museum Press.

Finke, R., Ward, T., & Smith, S. (1992). *Creative cognition: Theory, research, and applications*. Cambridge, MA: MIT Press.

Firmino, R. J., Duarte, F., & Moreira, T. (2008). Pervasive technologies and urban planning in the augmented city. *Journal of Urban Technology, 15*(2), 77–93. doi:10.1080/10630730802401983

Fischinger, O. (1932). *Sounding ornaments*. Deutsche Allgemeine Zeitung. Retrieved from http://www.centerforvisualmusic.org/Fischinger/SoundOrnaments.htm

Fisher, P., & Unwin, D. (2002). Virtual reality in geography: An introduction. In P. Fisher & D. Unwin (Eds.), *Virtual reality in geography* (pp. 1–4). London: Taylor and Francis.

Fleischmann, M., & Strauss, W. (1992). *Liquid views – Narcissus' mirror*. Retrieved from http://www.eculturefactory.de/CMS/index.php?id=419

Flintoff, J. P. (2002). *Children get smart with their computer games: Shooting baddies may help the development of academic skills*. London: Financial Times.

Florida, R. (2002). *The rise of the creative class*. New York: Basic Books.

Florida, R. (2005). *Cities and the creative class*. New York: Routledge.

Florida, R. (2006). *The flight of the creative class*. New York: HarperCollins Publishers.

Florida, R. (2008). *Who's your city?* New York: Basic Books.

Floros, Siomos, K., Dafouli, E., Fisoun, V., & Geroukalis, D. (2012). Influence of parental attitudes towards Internet use on the employment of online safety measures at home. *Studies in Health Technology and Informatics, 181*, 64–70. PMID:22954830

Foucault, M. (2001). Fearless speech. Los Angeles, CA: Semiotext(e).

Fowler, C. B. (1967, October). The museum of music: A history of mechanical instruments. *Music Educators Journal, 54*(2), 45–49. doi:10.2307/3391092

Foxman, P. (1976). Tolerance for ambiguity and self-actualization. *Journal of Personality Assessment, 40*(1), 67–72. doi:10.1207/s15327752jpa4001_13 PMID:16367248

Freenews. (2011a, May 17). *La Freebox à l'honneur dans E=M6 (MàJ)*. Retrieved February 12, 2012, from http://www.freenews.fr/spip.php?article8300

Freenews. (2011b, October 11). *Reportage bidon sur la Freebox dans E=M6: intervention du CSA*. Retrieved February 12, 2012, from http://www.freenews.fr/spip.php?article9131

Freud, S. (1913). *The interpretation of dreams*. (A. A. Brill, Trans.). London: Macmillan. doi:10.1037/10561-000

Frodeman, R. (2006). Nanotechnology: The visible and the invisible. *Science as Culture, 15*(4), 383–389. doi:10.1080/09505430601022700

Fruchter, R. (2004). Global teamwork: Cross-disciplinary, collaborative, geographically-distributed e-learning environment. In J. Bento, J. P. Duarte, M. V. Heitor, & W. J. Mitchell (Eds.), *Collaborative design and learning: Competence building for innovation* (pp. 265–297).

Fuller, M. (2003). *Behind the blip: Essays on the culture of software*. New York: Autonomedia.

Funk, J. B., Heidi, H. B., Pasold, T., & Baumgardner, J. T. (2004). Violence exposure in real-life, video games, television, movies and the internet: is there desensitization? Department of Psychology, The University of Toledo.

Funk, J. B., & Buchman, D. D. (1995). Video game controversies. *Pediatric Annals, 24*(2), 91–96. doi:10.3928/0090-4481-19950201-08 PMID:7724256

Funk, J. B., Elliott, R., Urman, M. L., Flores, G. T., & Mock, R. M. (1999). The attitudes towards violence scale: A measure for adolescents. *Journal of Interpersonal Violence, 14*(11), 1123–1136. doi:10.1177/088626099014011001

Furlong, M. J., & Morrison, G. M. (2000). The school in violence: Definition and facts. *Journal of Emotional and Behavioral Disorders, 8*(2), 71–82. doi:10.1177/106342660000800203

Fyfe, N. R., & Bannister, J. (1996). City watching: Closed circuit television in public spaces. *Area, 28*(1), 37–46.

Galloway, A. (2006). *Gaming: Essays on algorithmic culture*. Minneapolis, MN: University of Minnesota Press.

Galloway, A. (2013). *The interface effect*. Cambridge, UK: Polity Press.

Gallupe, R. B., Dennis, A. R., Cooper, W. H., Valacich, J. S., Bastianutti, L. M., & Nunamaker, J. F. (1992). Electronic brainstorming and group size. *Academy of Management Journal*, *35*(2), 350–369. doi:10.2307/256377

Gamemaker 7.0. (2008). *Yoyogames*. Retrieved January 20, 2015, from https://www.yoyogames.com/studio

Gane, N., & Beer, D. (2008). *New media: The key concepts*. New York: Berg.

Gardiner, J. (2009). Light years: Jurassic coast and immersive 3D landscape project. In *Proceedings of the 2009 International Conference on Electronic Visualisation and the Arts*. London: BCS.

Gardiner, J., & Head, A. (2013). *Light years projects: A collaboration between Jeremy Gardiner and Anthony Head*. Retrieved from http://www.lightyearsprojects.org/

Gardiner, V. (Producer). (2013a). *Jeremy Gardiner in conversation Simon Martin*. London Art Fair 2013 - duration 48 min. [Video file]. Retrieved from http://vimeo.com/69150062

Gardiner, V. (Producer). (2013b). *Unfolding landscape*. Kings Place Gallery 2013. [Video file]. Retrieved from http://vimeo.com/67286839

Garvey, C. (1990). *Play*. Cambridge, MA: Harvard University Press.

Gautam, P., & Yanagiya, R. (2012). Reflection of cross-disciplinary research at creative research institution (Hokkaido University) in the web of science database: Appraisal and visualization using bibliometry. *Scientometrics*, *93*(1), 101–111. doi:10.1007/s11192-012-0655-3

Gavrilla, D., & Davis, L. (1996). 3D model-based tracking of humans in action: A multi-view approach. In *Proc. of the Computer Vision and Pattern Recognition* (pp. 73–80). Academic Press.

Gayraud, Y. (2005). *Cross-disciplinary report in FET*. Academic Press.

Gee, J. (2003). *What videogames have to teach us about learning and literacy*. New York: Palgrave Macmillan.

Gee, J. (2008). Learning and games. In K. Salen (Ed.), *The ecology of games: Connecting youth, games and learning* (pp. 21–40). Cambridge, MA: MIT Press.

Gee, J., & Levine, M. (2009). Welcome to our virtual worlds. *Educational Leadership*, 48–52.

Geho, P. R., & Dangelo, J. (2012). The evolution of social media as a marketing tool for entrepreneurs. *Entrepreneurial Executive*, *17*, 61–68.

Geist, S. (1968). *Brancusi: A study of the sculpture*. New York: Grossman.

George, J. M., & Zhou, J. (2007). Dual tuning in a supportive context: Joint contributions of positive mood, negative mood, and supervisory behaviors to employee creativity. *Academy of Management Journal*, *50*(3), 605–622. doi:10.5465/AMJ.2007.25525934

GFK. (2009). *Trajna dobra u kućanstvima Hrvatske*. Centar za istraživanje tržišta.

Ghere, R. K., & Rismiller, L. S. (2001). Information technology's potential to improve urban neighborhoods: Some citizen planning dilemmas. *Journal of Urban Technology*, *8*(2), 39–60. doi:10.1080/106307301316904781

Gibson, W. (1984) *Neuromancer*. New York, NY: Ace.

Giddens, A. (1987). *Social theory and modern sociology*. Palo Alto, CA: Stanford University Press.

Giddens, A. (1990). *The consequences of modernity*. Cambridge, MA: Polity Press.

Giedion, S. (1948). *Mechanization takes command*. Minneapolis, MN: University of Minnesota Press.

Gilbert-Rolfe, J. (1999). *Beauty and the contemporary sublime*. New York: Allworth Press.

Gilewicz, N., & Allard-Huver, F. (2012). Digital parrhesia as a counterweight to astroturfing. In S. Apostel & M. Folk (Eds.), Online credibility and digital ethos: Evaluating computer-mediated communication (pp. 215-227). Hershey, PA: IGI Global.

Gill, S., Thompson, S. R., & Himberg, T. (2012). Body rhythmic entrainment and pragmatics in musical and linguistic improvisation tasks. In *Proceedings of the 12th International Conference on Music Perception and Cognition of the European Society for the Cognitive Sciences of Music*. Thessaloniki:Greece: Academic Press.

Gimzewski, J., & Vesna, V. (2003). The nanoneme syndrome: Blurring of fact and fiction in the construction of a new science. *Technoetic Arts: A Journal of Speculative Research, 1*(1), 7-24.

Girotra, K., Terwiesch, C., & Ulrich, K. T. (2010). Idea generation and the quality of the best idea. *Management Science, 56*(4), 591–605. doi:10.1287/mnsc.1090.1144

Glaeser, E. L. (2000). The new economics of urban and regional growth. In G. L. Clark, M. P. Feldman, & M. S. Gertler (Eds.), *The Oxford handbook of economic geography*. Oxford, UK: Oxford University Press.

Gligora, M., Antić, M., & Rauker Koch, M. (2013). Proces razvoja multimedijske računalne igre. *Rijeka. Zbornik Veleučilišta u Rijeci, 1*(1), 151–163.

Goldstein, H. (2003). On further developing problem-oriented policing: The most critical need, the major impediments, and a proposal. In J. Knutsson (Ed.), *Problem-oriented policing: From innovation to mainstream* (pp. 13–47). Monsey, NY: Criminal Justice Press.

Gombrich, E. (1960). *Art and illusion: A study in the psychology of pictorial representation*. London: Phaidon.

Gomery, D. (2005). *The coming of sound*. London: Routledge.

Gopnik, A., Meltzoff, A. N., & Kuhl, P. K. (2011). *The scientist in the crib: What early learning tells us about the mind*. EDUCA.

Graham, M. (2012). *Big data and the end of theory?*. Retrieved August 29, 2014, from http://www.theguardian.com/news/datablog/2012/mar/09/big-data-theory

Graham, R., McCabe, H., & Sheridan, S. (2003). *Pathfinding in computer games*. School of Informatics & Engineering. Institute of Technology Blanchardstown.

Granic, I., Lobel, A., & Engels, R. C. M. E. (2014). The benefits of playing video games. *The American Psychologist, 69*(1), 66–78

Grau, O. (2003). *Virtual art: From illusion to immersion*. Cambridge, MA: MIT Press.

Grau, O. (Ed.). (2010). *MediaArtHistories*. Cambridge, MA: MIT Press.

Gray, D. (2008, May 22). *Web log message*. Retrieved from http://www.davegrayinfo.com/2008/05/22/why-powerpoint-rules-the-business-world/

Gray, P. (2011). The decline of play and the rise of psychopathology in children and adolescents. *American Journal of Play, 3*, 443–463.

Greenberg, C. (1995). *The collected essays and criticism: Modernism with a vengeance, 1957-69* (Vol. 4). Chicago, IL: University of Chicago Press.

Greenfield, S. (2001). *The human brain: A guided tour*. London: Phoenix. (Original work published 1997)

Greenfield, S. (2009, February 12). Speech, House of Lords. In *Parliamentary debates [Hansard]* (Vol. 707, columns 1290–3). Retrieved 13.92.2009 from http://www.publications.parliament.uk/pa/ld200809/ldhansrd/text/902120010.htm#09021268000191

Greenhow, C., Robelia, B., & Hughes, J. E. (2009). Learning, teaching, and scholarship in a digital age: Web 2.0 and classroom research: What path should we take now? *Educational Researcher, 38*(4), 246–259. doi:10.3102/0013189X09336671

Green, M. C., Strange, J. J., & Brock, T. C. (Eds.). (2002). *Narrative impact: Social and cognitive foundations*. Mahwah, NJ: Lawrence Erlbaum.

Greimas, J. (1989). *The social sciences: A semiotic view*. Minneapolis, MN: University of Minnesota Press.

Grieveson, L., & Krämer, P. (2003). *The silent cinema reader*. Abingdon, UK: Routledge.

Griffin, D. (2007). *Trevorrow, P. and Halpin, E.* Amsterdam, Netherlands: Developments in E-Government.

Griffiths, D. N. (2013). Words from the wasteland: InXile CEO Brian Fargo talks tides and torments. *Forbes.com*. Retrieved from http://www.forbes.com/sites/danielnyegriffiths/2013/04/03/brian-fargo-interview-torment-tides-of-numenera-kickstarter/

Griffiths, M. (1999). Violent video games and aggression: A review of the literature. *Aggression and Violent Behavior*, *4*(2), 203–212. doi:10.1016/S1359-1789(97)00055-4

Griffiths, M. D. (2010). Computer game playing and social skills. A pilot study. *Aloma Revista de Psihcologia Ciencies del Educacio i del Esport*, *27*, 301–310.

Grimm, T. (2004). *User's guide to rapid prototyping*. Society of Manufacturing Engineers.

Gromala, D., & Sharir, Y. (1994). *Dancing with the virtual dervish: Virtual bodies*. Virtual Reality Installation. Banff Centre for the Arts. Available at: http://www.banffcentre. ca/bnmi/coproduction/archives/d.asp#dancing

Gropius, W. (Ed.). (1961). *Theatre of the Bauhaus*. Middletown, CT: Wesleyan UP. (Original work published 1925)

Grossberg, L. (2010). Affect's future: Rediscovering the virtual in the actual. In The affect theory reader (pp. 309-338). Durham, NC: Duke University Press.

Grosz, E. (1999). *Becomings: Explorations in time, memory and futures*. London, UK: Cornell University Press.

Grosz, E. (2000). Deleuze's Bergson: Duration, the virtual and a politics of the future. In I. Buchanan & C. Colebrook (Eds.), *Deleuze and feminist theory*. Edinburgh, UK: Edinburgh University Press.

Grosz, E. (2001). *Architecture from the outside: Essays on virtual and real space*. Cambridge, MA: MIT Press.

Grow, G. (1990). *Writing and multiple intelligences*. Paper presented at the Annual Meeting of the Association for Educators in Journalism and Mass Communication. Retrieved June 10, 2012, from http://www.longleaf.net/ggrow

Grundy, J., & Boudreau, J. A. (2008). Living with culture: Creative citizenship practices in Toronto. *Citizenship Studies*, *12*(4), 347–363. doi:10.1080/13621020802184226

Gunkel, D. (2000). Hacking cyberspace. *Jac*, *20*(4), 797–823.

Gunkel, D. (2003). Second thoughts: Toward a critique of the digital divide. *New Media & Society*, *5*(4), 499–522. doi:10.1177/146144480354003

Gunkel, D. (2010). The real problem: Avatars, metaphysics and online social interaction. *New Media & Society*, *12*(1), 127–141. doi:10.1177/1461444809341443

Gunning, T. (1986, September1). The cinema of attractions: Early film, its spectator and the avant-garde. *Wide Angle*, *8*, 63–70.

Gupta, R., & Derevensky, J. L. (1996). The relationship between gambling and video game playing behaviour in children and adolescents. *Journal of Gambling Studies*, *12*(4), 375–395. doi:10.1007/BF01539183 PMID:24234157

Gwilt, I. (2010). Compumorphic art - The computer as muse. In *Proceedings of the First International Conference on Transdisciplinary Imaging at the Intersections between Art, Science, and Culture* (pp. 72-76). Artspace. Available from http://blogs.unsw.edu.au/tiic/files/2011/04/TIICproceedings.pdf

Haidary, N. (2009). *In-formed*. Retrieved August 29, 2014, from http://nadeemhaidary.com/In-Formed

Hales, C. (2005). Cinematic interaction: From Kinoautomat to cause and effect. *Digital Creativity*, *16*(1), 54–64. doi:10.1080/14626260500147777

Halifax, J. (1979). *Shamanic voices: A survey of visionary narrative*. London: Arkana.

Hallowell, E. (2005). Overloaded circuits: Why smart people underperform. *Harvard Business Review*, *83*, 54–62. PMID:15697113

Hallowell, E., & Ratey, J. (1994). *Driven to distraction*. New York: Touchstone.

Hall, S. (1973). *Encoding and decoding in the television discourse*. Birmingham, AL: Centre for Contemporary Cultural Studies.

Hamel, P., Boudreau, J. A., Keil, R., & Jouve, B. (2006). Arrested metropolitanism: limits and contradictions of municipal governance reform in Los Angeles, Montreal and Toronto. In H. Hubert & K. Daniel (Eds.), *Metropolitan governance in the 21st century: Governing capacity, democracy and the dynamics of place*. Routledge.

Hamlin, K. (July 27, 2009). *Missing: Privileged account management for the social web*. Retrieved January 6, 2014, from http://www.identitywoman.net/at-the-ideas-project-apparently-women-dont-have-any-ideas

Hammond, K. J. (1990). Case-based planning: A framework for planning from experience. *Cognitive Science*, *14*(3), 385–443. doi:10.1207/s15516709cog1403_3

Hamric, A. B., & Blackhall, L. J. (2007). Nursing-physician perspectives on the care of dying patients in intensive care units: Collaborations, moral distress, and ethical climate. *Critical Care Medicine*, *35*(2), 422–429. doi:10.1097/01.CCM.0000254722.50608.2D PMID:17205001

Han, J. H., & Lee, S. (2013). Planning ubiquitous cities for social inclusion. *Int. J. of Knowledge-Based Development*, *4*(2), 157–172. doi:10.1504/IJKBD.2013.054092

Hanrahan, M. (2014, October 20). Tale of tales: Making a game for the gamers. *Gamesindustry.biz*. Retrieved from http://www.gamesindustry.biz/articles/2014-10-20-tale-of-tales-making-a-game-for-the-gamers

Hansen, M. (2004). *New philosophy for new media*. Cambridge, MA: MIT Press.

Hansen, M. (2006). *Bodies in code: Interfaces with digital media*. New York: Routledge.

Hanson, V. L. (2012). Amidst nanotechnology's molecular landscapes. *Science Communication*, *34*(1), 57–83. doi:10.1177/1075547011401630

Haraway, D. (1985). Manifesto for cyborgs: Science, technology, and socialist feminism in the 1980s. *Socialist Review*, *80*, 65–108.

Haraway, D. (1992). The promises of monsters: A regenerative politics for inappropriate/d others. In L. Grossberg, C. Nelson, & P. Treichler (Eds.), *Cultural studies* (pp. 295–337). New York, NY: Routledge.

Harder, N. B. (2010). Use of simulation in teaching and learning in health sciences: A systematic review. *The Journal of Nursing Education*, *49*(1), 23–28. doi:10.3928/01484834-20090828-08 PMID:19731886

Hargittai, E., Gallo, J., & Kane, M. (2008). Cross-ideological discussions among conservative and liberal bloggers. *Police Choice*, *134*(1-2), 67–86. doi:10.1007/s11127-007-9201-x

Haritaoglu, I., Harwood, D., & Davis, L. S. (2000). W4: Real-time surveillance of people and their activities. *IEEE Transactions on Pattern Analysis and Machine Intelligence*, *22*(8), 309–330. doi:10.1109/34.868683

Harrison, D. (2011). Crossing over: Oscillations between the virtual and the real. In *Proceedings of Cyberworlds 2011 Conference*. Academic Press.

Harris, P. (2005). Deleuze, folding architecture. In I. Buchanan & G. Lambert (Eds.), *Deleuze and space*. Edinburgh, UK: Edinburgh University Press.

Hartman, K. (2015). What to sense, how to select and use sensors in wearable electronics. *Make*, *43*, 38–41.

Harvey, D. (1989). From managerialism to enerpreneurialism: The transformation in urban governance in late capital-ism. *Geografisk annaler. Series B. Human Geography*, *71*(1), 2–17.

Haskins, R. (2012). *John Cage*. London: Reaktion Books.

Haus der Kulturen der Welt (HKW). (2014). *The anthropocene project*. Retrieved from http://www.hkw.de/en/programm/projekte/2014/anthropozaen/anthropozaen_2013_2014.php

Hawkesworth, M. (2006). *Globalization and feminist activism*. Rowman & Littlefield.

Hawkins, H. (2013). Geography and art: An expanding field: Site, the body and practice. *Progress in Human Geography*, *37*(1), 52–71. doi:10.1177/0309132512442865

Hayles, N. K. (1999). *How we became posthuman*. Chicago, IL: University of Chicago Press. doi:10.7208/chicago/9780226321394.001.0001

Head, A. (2011). 3D weather: Towards a real-time 3D simulation of localised weather. In *Proceedings of the 2011 International Conference on Electronic Visualisation and the Arts*. London: BCS.

Head, L. (2014). Contingencies of the anthropocene: Lessons from the 'neolithic'. *The Anthropocene Review*, *1*(2), 113–125. doi:10.1177/2053019614529745

Healey, P. (2006). Collaborative planning: Shaping places in fragmented societies (2nd ed.). Houndsmills, UK: Palgrave.

Heath, D., Singh, R., Ganesh, J., & Taube, L. (2013). Building thought leadership through business-to-business social media engagement at infosys. *MIS Quarterly Executive*, *12*(2), 77–92.

Hechinger, J. (2008, September 18). College applicants, beware: Your Facebook page is showing. *Wall Street Journal*, p. D1.

Heesom, D., & Mahdjoubi, L. (2004). Trends of 4D CAD applications for construction planning. *Construction Management and Economics*, 22(2), 171–182. doi:10.1080/0144619042000201376

Heidegger, M. (2001). *Poetry, language, thought.* London, UK: Harper Perennial.

Heim, M. (1993). *The metaphysics of virtual reality.* New York: Oxford University Press.

Heim, M. (1998). *Virtual realism.* Oxford, UK: Oxford University Press.

Helmholz, H. (1954). *On the sensations of tone* (3rd ed.). New York: Dover publications.

Henderson, A. T., & Mapp, K. L. (2002). *A new wave of evidence: The impact of school, family, and community connections on student achievement.* Austin, TX: National Center on Family & Community Connections With Schools.

Hendricks, T. (2006). Play reconsidered. Champaign, IL: University of Illinois Press.

Hendy, D. (Presenter). (2013, March 18). *Noise: A human history, echoes in the dark.* [Radio Broadcast]. BBC Radio 4.

Henry, M., Béguin, M., Requier, F., Rollin, O., Odoux, J.-F., Aupinel, P., & Decourtye, A. et al. (2012). A common pesticide decreases foraging success and survival in honey bees. *Science*, 336(6079), 348–350. doi:10.1126/science.1215039 PMID:22461498

Heritage, S. (2013, November 4). Grand Theft Auto 5? Sorry, I'm just a bit too Guardian. *The Guardian.* Retrieved from http://www.theguardian.com/commentisfree/2013/nov/04/grand-theft-auto-5-guardian-gta-v-car-game

Herring, S. C., Kouper, I., Scheidt, L. A., & Wright, E. L. (2004). Women and children last: The discursive construction of weblogs. In L. J. Gurak, S. Antonijevic, L. Johnson, C. Ratliff, & J. Reyman (Eds.), *Into the blogosphere: Rhetoric, community, and culture of weblogs.* Retrieved October 6, 2014, from http://blog.lib.umn.edu/blogosphere/women_and_children.html

Herring, D. F., & Notar, C. F. (2011). Show what you know: ePortfolios for 21st century learners. *College Student Journal*, 45(4), 786.

Hertzum, H., & Pejtersen, A. M. (2000). The information-seeking practices of engineers: Searching for documents as well as for people. *Information Processing & Management*, 36(5), 761–778. doi:10.1016/S0306-4573(00)00011-X

Heudin, J. C. (Ed.). (1999). *Virtual worlds: Synthetic universes, digital life and complexity.* Reading, MA: Perseus Books.

Higinbotham, W. (n.d.). *Tennis for two.* Retrieved from http://ahyco.ffri.hr

Hillis, K. (1999). *Digital sensations: Space, identity, and embodiment in virtual reality.* Minneapolis, MN: University of Minnesota Press.

Hiltzik, M. (2012, February 4). Who really benefits from putting high-tech gadgets in classrooms? *Los Angeles Times*, p. B1.

Hoffman, M. L. (2000). *Emapthy and moral development: Implications for caring and justice.* Cambridge Press. doi:10.1017/CBO9780511805851

Hoffman, R., O'Donnell, J., & Kim, Y. (2007). The effects of human patient simulatiors on basic knowledge in critical care nursing with undergraduate senior baccalaureate nursing students. *Simulation in Healthcare*, 2, 110–114. doi:10.1097/SIH.0b013e318033abb5 PMID:19088615

Holland, J. (1998). *Emergence: From chaos to order.* Reading, MA: Addison-Wesley.

Honess, T., & Charman, E. (1992). *Closed circuit television in public places: Its acceptability and perceived effectiveness.* London: Home Office.

Honko, L. (Ed.). (2000). *Thick corpus, organic variation and textuality in oral tradition.* Helsinki: Finnish Literature Society.

Hopkins, D. (2004). *Surrealism and Dada: A very short introduction.* Oxford, UK: Oxford University Press. doi:10.1093/actrade/9780192802545.001.0001

Hopper, T. F. (2010). Complexity thinking and creative dance: Creating conditions for emergent learning in teacher education. *PHEnex*, 2(1), 1–20.

Hopper, T. F. (2013). Emergence in school integrated teacher education for elementary PE teachers: Mapping a complex learning system. In A. Ovens, T. Hopper, & J. Butler (Eds.), *Complexity thinking in physical education: Reframing curriculum, pedagogy and research* (pp. 151–163). London: Routledge.

Horn, R. (1972). *Finger gloves*. Retrieved from http://rebeccahornart.blogspot.co.uk/2009/11/finger-gloves-1973.html

Howell, J., & Boies, K. (2004). Champions of technological innovation: The influence of contextual knowledge, role orientation, idea generation, and idea promotion on champion emergence. *The Leadership Quarterly, 15*(1), 123–143. doi:10.1016/j.leaqua.2003.12.008

Hrabri telefon-Savjetodavna linija za djecu. (n.d.). Accessed 30.03.2014, from https://www.google.hr/?gws_rd=ssl#q=hrabri+telefon

Huesmann, L. R., Moise-Titus, J., Podolski, C. L., & Eron, L. D. (2003). Longitudinal relations between children's exposure to TV violence and their aggressive and violent behavior in young adulthood: 1977–1992. *Developmental Psychology, 39*(2), 201–221. doi:10.1037/0012-1649.39.2.201 PMID:12661882

Huesmann, R. L. (2007). *The impact of electronic media violence: Scientific theory and research*. NIH Public Access. doi:10.1016/j.jadohealth.2007.09.005

Hultkrantz, Å. (1996). A new look at the world pillar in arctic and sub-arctic religions. In J. Pentikäinen (Ed.), *Shamanism and northern ecology* (pp. 31–51). Berlin: Mouton de Gruyter. doi:10.1515/9783110811674.31

Hunter, S. T., Cushenbery, L., Ginther, N., & Fairchild, J. (2013). Leadership, innovation, and technology: The evolution of the creative process. In S. Hemlin, C. M. Allwood, B. R. Martin, & M. D. Mumford (Eds.), *Creativity and leadership in science, technology, and innovation* (pp. 81–110). New York, NY: Routledge.

Hunter, S., Freidrich, T., Badell, K., & Mumford, M. (2006). Creative thought in real–world innovation. *Serbian Journal of Management, 1*, 29–39.

Husserl, E. (1931). *Ideas: General introduction to pure phenomenology*. (W. R. Boyce Gibson, Trans.). London: George Allen & Unwin Ltd.

Ibrahim, A. (2011). *Economic clustering in emerging markets case study: The Gulf region*. Ross School of Business at the University of Michigan.

Ihde, D. (2002). *Bodies in technology*. Minneapolis, MN: University of Minnesota Press.

Ihde, D. (2012). Can continental philosophy deal with the new technologies? *Journal of Speculative Philosophy, 26*(2), 321–332.

Iliinsky, N., & Steele, J. (2011). *Designing data visualizations*. Sebastopol, CA: O'Reilly Media Inc.

Ilišin, V., Marinović Bobinac, A., & Radin, F. (2001). *Djeca i mediji. Uloga medija u svakodnevnom životu djece*. Zagreb: Državni zavod za zaštitu obitelji, materinstva i mladeži – Institut za društvena istraživanja.

Illou, E., & Finkelman, S. (2009). An odd and inseparable couple: Emotion and rationality in partner selection. *Theory and Society, 38*(4), 401–422. doi:10.1007/s11186-009-9085-5

Ince, S., & Konrad, J. (2008). Occlusion-aware optical flow estimation. *IEEE Transactions on Image Processing, 17*(8), 1443–1451. doi:10.1109/TIP.2008.925381 PMID:18632352

Inside Out Rapid Prototype Exhibition. (2010). *Object gallery, Sydney, Australia*. Retrieved August 29 2014, from http://www.object.com.au/exhibitions-events/entry/inside_out_rapid_prototyping/

Interprofessional Educational Collaborative Expert Panel. (2011). *Core competencies for interprofessional collaborative practice: Report of an expert panel*. Washington, DC: Interprofessional Education Collaborative.

Intille, S. S., & Bobick, A. F. (1999). A framework for recognizing multiagent action from visual evidence. In Proceedings of AAAI-99. AAAI Press.

IOM Health Professions Education. (n.d.). *A bridge to quality (free executive summary)*. Retrieved from http://www.nap.edu/catalog/10681.html

Irwin, A. R., & Gross, A. M. (1995). Cognitive tempo, violent video games, and aggressive behavior in young boys. *Journal of Family Violence, 10*(3), 337–350. doi:10.1007/BF02110997

Ishii, I., Taniguchi, T., Yamamoto, K., & Takaki, T. (2010). 1000 fps real-time optical flow detection system. In *Proc. SPIE*. SPIE.

ISO. (2014). Retrieved July 14, 2014, from http://www.iso.org

Istraživanje o iskustvima djece pri korištenju interneta. (n.d.). Accessed 30.05.2014., from http://www.tic-zadjecu.hr/index.php?option=com_content&view=article&id=31:istraivanje-o-iskustvima-djece-pri-koritenju-interneta&catid=2&Itemid=2

Ito, M., Davidson, C., Jenkins, H., Lee, C., Eisenberg, M., & Weiss, J. (2008). Foreword. In W. L. Bennett (Ed.), *Civic life online: Learning how digital media can engage youth* (pp. vii–ix). Cambridge, MA: The MIT Press.

Ivanov, Y. A., & Bobick, A. F. (2000). Recognition of visual activities and interactions by stochastic parsing. *IEEE Transactions on Pattern Analysis and Machine Intelligence, 22*(8), 852–872. doi:10.1109/34.868686

Izloženost nasilju putem internet. (n.d.). Retrieved from web.ffos.hr/serv/psih.php?file=380

Jackson, P. (Director) (2001). *The Lord of the rings: The fellowship of the ring*. [Cinema]. USA: New Line Cinema.

Jackson, P. (Director) (2002). *The Lord of the rings: The two towers*. [Cinema]. USA: New Line Cinema.

Jackson, P. (Director) (2003). *The Lord of the rings: The return of the ring*. [Cinema]. USA: New Line Cinema.

Jackson, L. A., Witt, E. A., Games, A. I., Fitzgerald, H. E., von Eye, A., & Zhao, Y. (2012). Information technology use and creativity: Findings from the children and technology project. *Computers in Human Behavior, 28*(2), 370–376. doi:10.1016/j.chb.2011.10.006

Jannsen, D. G., & Smith, S. M. (1991). Design fixation. *Design Studies, 12*(1), 3–11. doi:10.1016/0142-694X(91)90003-F

Janssen, O. (2005). The joint impact of perceived influence and supervisor supportiveness on employee innovative behaviour. *Journal of Occupational and Organizational Psychology, 78*(4), 573–579. doi:10.1348/096317905X25823

Javed, O., & Shah, M. (2002). Tracking and object classification for automated surveillance. In *Proceedings of 7th European Conference on Computer Vision*. Springer. doi:10.1007/3-540-47979-1_23

Jentsch, E. (1906). *On the psychology of the uncanny*. Oxford, UK: Imprint.

Jessop, B. (2002). Liberalism, neoliberalism and urban governance: A state-theoretical perspective. *Antipode, 34*(3), 452–472. doi:10.1111/1467-8330.00250

Johansson, B., Karlson, C., & Stough, R. (2006). *The emerging digital economy*. Berlin: Springer. doi:10.1007/3-540-34488-8

Johnson, S. (2001). *Emergence: The connected lives of ants, brains, cities and software*. New York: Simon & Schuster.

Johnson, V. (2010). Women and the internet: A micro study in Chennai, India. *Indian Journal of Gender Studies, 17*(1), 151–163. doi:10.1177/097152150901700107

Joint Commission. (n.d.). Retrieved from http://www.jointcommission.org/sentinel_event.aspx

Jones, D. E. (2006). I, avatar: Constructions of self and place in second life and the technological imagination. *Gnovis, Journal of Communication, Culture and Technology*. Available at: http://gnovisjournal.org/files/Donald-E-Jones-I-Avatar.pdf

Jónsdóttir, A. (2003). *Pop press programme* [Radio]. RUV Icelandic State Broadcasting.

Joyce, J. (1999). *Finnegans wake*. London: Penguin. (Original work published 1939)

Julier, G. (2014). *The culture of design* (3rd ed.). London, UK: Sage Publications.

Juniper, A. (2003). *Wabi Sabi: The Japanese art of impermanence*. Tuttle Publishing.

Kafka, F. (1995). *The complete stories*. New York: Schocken Books.

Kafno, P., & Turpainen, M. (2007). *FP6 IST – 004124 – NM2 final evaluation report*. EC. Internal Report. Retrieved from www.ist-nm2.org

Kalatzis, N., Liampotis, N., Roussaki, I., Kosmides, P., Papaioannou, I., Xynogalas, S., & Anagnostou, M. et al. (2014). Cross-community context management in cooperating smart spaces. *Personal and Ubiquitous Computing*, *18*(2), 427–443. doi:10.1007/s00779-013-0654-2

Kamberidou, I. (2013). Women entrepreneurs: "We cannot have change unless we have men in the room. *Journal of Innovation and Entrepreneurship*, *2*(6). Retrieved from http://www.innovation-entrepreneurship.com/content/pdf/2192-5372-2-6.pdf

Kamenetz, A. (2013). *Why video games succeed where the movie and music industries fail*. Retrieved 07.11.2013 from The Fast Company http://www.fastcompany.com/3021008/why-video-games-succeed-where-the-movie-and-music-industries-fail

Kapasi, H., & Gleave, J. (2009). *Because it's freedom: Children's views on their time to play*. NCB.

Kaplan, A. M., & Haenlein, M. (2010). Users of the world, unite! The challenges and opportunities of social media. *Business Horizons*, *53*(1), 59–68. Retrieved July 2 2014. doi:10.1016/j.bushor.2009.09.003

Kasteleijn-Nolst Trenite, D. G., da Silva, A. M., Ricci, S., Binnie, C. D., Rubboli, G., Tassinari, C. A., & Segers, J. P. (1999). Video-game epilepsy: A European study. *Epilepsia*, *40*(s4Suppl 4), 70–74. doi:10.1111/j.1528-1157.1999.tb00910.x PMID:10487177

Kearney, A. R., & Kaplan, S. (1997). Toward a methodology for the measurement of knowledge structures of ordinary people: The conceptual content cognitive map (3CM). *Environment and Behavior*, *29*(5), 579–617. doi:10.1177/0013916597295001

Keil, R. (2002). Commonsense neoliberalism: Progressive conservative urbanism in Toronto, Canada. *Antipode*, *34*(3), 578–601. doi:10.1111/1467-8330.00255

Kerawalla, L., & Crook, C. (2002). Children's computer use at home and at school: Context and continuity. *British Educational Research Journal*, *28*(6), 751–771. doi:10.1080/0141192022000019044

Khodr, H., & Reiche, D. (2012). The specialized cities of the gulf cooperation council: A case study of a distinct type of policy innovation and diffusiondome. *Digest of Middle East Studies*, *21*(1), 149–177. doi:10.1111/j.1949-3606.2012.00131.x

Kickstarter.com. (2013). *The year in Kickstarter: 2013*. Retrieved from https://www.kickstarter.com/year/2013/

Kietzmann, J. H., Hermkens, K., McCarthy, I. P., & Silvestre, B. S. (2011). Social media? Get serious! Understanding the functional building blocks of social media. *Business Horizons*, *54*(3), 241–251. doi:10.1016/j.bushor.2011.01.005

Kim, H., Sakamoto, R., Kitahara, I., Toriyama, T., & Kogure, K. (2007). Robust silhouette extraction technique using background subtraction. *MIRU*.

Kim, K. E. (2011). The creativity crisis: The decrease in creative thinking scores on the Torrance tests of creative thinking. *Creativity Research Journal*, *23*(4), 285–298. doi:10.1080/10400419.2011.627805

Kim, T. J. (2008). Planning for knowledge cities in ubiquitous technology spaces: Opportunities and challenges. In Y. Tan, K. Velibeyoglu, & S. Baum (Eds.), *Creative urban regions: Harnessing urban technologies to support knowledge city initiatives*. New York: Hersey. doi:10.4018/978-1-59904-838-3.ch013

King, L. (2014). Ford, where virtual reality is already manufacturing reality. *Forbes.com*. Retrieved from http://www.forbes.com/sites/leoking/2014/05/03/ford-where-virtual-reality-is-already-manufacturing-reality/

King, A. M., & Sivaloganathan, S. (1999). Development of a methodology for concept selection in flexible design strategies. *Journal of Engineering Design*, *10*(4), 329–349. doi:10.1080/095448299261236

Kirsh, S. J. (1998). Seeing the world through Mortal Kombat-colored glasses: Violent video games and the development of a short-term hostile attribution bias. *Childhood: A Global Journal of Child Research, 5*, 177-184.

Kittler, F. (2009). *Optical media*. Cambridge, UK: Polity Press.

Klanten, R. (Ed.). (2008). *Data flow: Visualising information in graphic design*. Berlin, Germany: Gestalten.

Klanten, R., Ehmann, S., Tissot, T., & Bourquin, N. (Eds.). (2010). *Data flow 2: Visualizing information in graphic design*. Berlin, Germany: Gestalten.

Klimoski, R., & Mohammed, S. (1994). Team mental model: Construct or metaphor? *Journal of Management, 20*(2), 403–437. doi:10.1016/0149-2063(94)90021-3

Klinkenberg, J.-M. (2000). *Précis de sémiotique générale.* Paris: Seuil.

Knowles, E., & Partington, A. (1999). *The Oxford dictionary of quotations.* Oxford, UK: Oxford University Press.

Knowles, J. G., & Cole, A. L. (Eds.). (2008). *Handbook of the arts in qualitative research: Perspectives, methodologies, examples, and issues.* Thousand Oaks, CA: Sage Publications. doi:10.4135/9781452226545

Kohn, L. T., Corrigan, J., & Donaldson, M. S. (Eds.). (2000). *To err is human: Building a safer health system.* Washington, DC: National Academy Press.

Ko, S. (2002). An empirical analysis of children's thinking and learning in a computer game context. *Educational Psychology, 22*(2), 219–233. doi:10.1080/01443410120115274

Kostelanetz, R. (2003). *Conversing with Cage.* New York: Routledge. (Original work published 1987)

Kounios, J., Fleck, J., Green, D., Payne, L., Stevenson, J., Bowden, E., & Jung-Beeman, M. (2008). The origins of insight in resting-state brain activity. *Neuropsychologia, 46*(1), 281–291. doi:10.1016/j.neuropsychologia.2007.07.013 PMID:17765273

Kovačević, S. (2007). Spare time and computer games. *Školski vjesnik, 56*(1-2), 49-63.

Kozel, S. (1994). *Spacemaking: Experiences of a virtual body.* Available at: http://art.net/~dtz/kozel.html

Kozel, S. (2006). Virtual/virtuality. *Performance Research, 11*(3), 136–139.

Kozel, S. (2007). *Closer: Performance, technologies, phenomenology.* MIT Press.

Krainkish, M., & Anthony, M. K. (2001). Benefits and outcomes of staff nurses' participant in decision making. *JONA, 31*(1), 16–33. doi:10.1097/00005110-200101000-00005

Kramer, M., & Schmalenberg, C. (2003). Securing good nurse/physician relationships. *Nursing Management, 34*(7), 34–38. doi:10.1097/00006247-200307000-00013 PMID:12843717

Krauss, R. (2000). *A voyage on the north sea: Art in the age of the post-medium condition.* London, UK: Thames and Hudson Ltd.

Krauss, R. (2002). *The originality of the avant-garde and other modernist myths.* Cambridge, MA: The MIT Press.

Kristjánsson, J. (1988). *Eddas and sagas.* (P. Foote, Trans.). Reykjavík: hið íslenska bókmennta félag.

Krueger, M. W. (1977). Responsive environments. In K. Stiles & P. Selz (Eds.), Theories and documents of contemporary art: A sourcebook of artists' writings (pp. 473-486). Berkeley, CA: University of California Press, 1996. doi:10.1145/1499402.1499476

Kruegle, H. (2011). *CCTV surveillance: Video practices and technology.* Boston: Butterworth-Heinemann.

Kueffer, C. (2013). Ecological novelty: Towards an interdisciplinary understanding of ecological change in the anthropocene. In H. Greschke & J. Tischler (Eds.), *Grounding global climate change: Contributions from the social and cultural sciences* (pp. 19–37). Dordrecht, The Netherlands: Springer Verlag.

Kuhn, T. (1996). *The structure of scientific revolutions.* Chicago, IL: University of Chicago Press. doi:10.7208/chicago/9780226458106.001.0001

Kulkarni, D., & Simon, H. A. (1998). The process of scientific discovery: The strategy of experimentation. *Cognitive Science, 12*(2), 139–175. doi:10.1207/s15516709cog1202_1

Kwon, J. H., Chung, C. S., & Lee, J. (2011). The effects of escape from self and interpersonal relationship on the pathological use of internet games. *Community Mental Health Journal, 47*(1), 113–121. doi:10.1007/s10597-009-9236-1 PMID:19701792

Kwon, M. (1997). Notes on site specificity. Cambridge, MA: The MIT Press.

La Pierre, S. D., & Fellenz, R. A. (1988). *Spatial reasoning and adults*. Bozeman, MT: Center for Adult Learning Research, Montana State University.

Lacan, J. (1979). The seminar of Jacques Lacan, book XI: The four fundamental concepts of psychoanalysis 1964-1965. (J. A. Miller, Ed.; A. Sheridan, Trans.). Harmondsworth, UK: Penguin.

Lacan, J. (1977). *The four fundamental concepts of psychoanalysis*. London: The Hogarth Press.

Lacan, J. (1977). The mirror stage as formative of the function of the I as revealed in psychoanalytic experience. In *Ecrits: A selection* (A. Sheridan, Trans.). London: Routledge, Tavistock. (Original work published 1949)

Lacan, J. (2006). *Écrits*. New York, NY: W. W. Norton & Company.

Lagrandeur, L. (2013). *Androids and intelligent networks in early modern literature and culture: Artificial slaves*. New York: Routledge.

Laguerre, M. S. (2005). *The digital city*. New York: Palgrave MacMillan. doi:10.1057/9780230511347

Lakoff, G., & Johnson, M. (1980). *Metaphors we live by*. Chicago, IL: University of Chicago Press.

Lalos, C., & Anagnostopoulos, V. (2009). Hybrid tracking approach for assistive environments. *Int. Conf. Proc. Series*, *39*(64), 5.

Lamm, H., & Trommsdorff, G. (1973). Group versus individual performance on tasks requiring ideational proficiency (brainstorming): A review. *European Journal of Social Psychology*, *3*(4), 361–388. doi:10.1002/ejsp.2420030402

Langer, S. (1977). *Feeling and form: A theory of art*. New York: Scribner, Prentice Hall. (Original work published 1953)

Lapkin, S., Levett-Jones, T., Bellchambers, H., & Fernandez, R. (2010). Effectiveness of patient simulation mannequins in teaching clinical reasoning skills to undergraduate nursing students: A systematic review. *Clinical Simulation in Nursing*, *6*(6), e207–e222. doi:10.1016/j.ecns.2010.05.005

Larner, W. (2000). Neo-liberalism: Policy, ideology, governmentality. *Studies in Political Economy*, 63.

Latour, B. (2013). *Telling friends from foes at the time of the anthropocene*. Lecture prepared for the EHESS-Centre Koyré- Sciences Po symposium "Thinking the Anthropocene" Paris, 14th-15th November, 2013. EHESS-Centre Koyré- Sciences Po symposium. Paris. [PDF document]. Retrieved from http://www.bruno-latour.fr/sites/default/files/131-ANTHROPOCENE-PARIS-11-13.pdf

Latour, B. (2014, July). *Rematerializing humanities thanks to digital traces*. Keynote at Digital Humanities 2014, Lausanne, Switzerland.

Latour, B., & Weibel, P. (2002). *Iconoclash: Beyond the image wars in science, religion and art*. MIT Press.

Laurel, B., & Strickland, R. (1993). *Placeholder*. Virtual Reality Installation. Banff Centre for the Arts. Available at: http://www.banffcentre.ca/bnmi/coproduction/archives/p.asp#placeholder

Lawlor, R. (1991). *Voices of the first day, awakening in the aboriginal dreaming*. Rochester, VT: Inner Traditions.

Lee, S. H., Leem, Y. T., & Han, J. H. (2014). Impact of ubiquitous computing technologies on changing travel and land use patterns. *International Journal of Environmental Science and Technology*.

Lefebvre, H. (1991). *The production of space*. Oxford, UK: Blackwell Publishing.

Leger, F. (1972). *Functions of painting*. (A. Anderson, Trans. & Ed.). New York: Viking.

Leiponein, A., & Helfat, C. E. (2010). Innovation objectives, knowledge sources, and the benefits of breadth. *Strategic Management Journal*, *31*, 224–236.

Lenhart, A. (2005). *Teens and technology-youth are leading the transition to a fully wired and mobile nation*. PEW Internet & American Life Project.

Leonard, M., Graham, S., & Bonacum, D. (2004). The human factor: The critical importance of teamwork and communication in providing safe patient care. *Quality & Safety in Health Care*, *13*(suppl 1), i85–i90. doi:10.1136/qshc.2004.010033 PMID:15465961

Leonardo Almanac. (2011). Interview with Tom Corby, 'The Southern Ocean Studies'. *LEA - Digital Media Exhibition Platform*. Retrieved from https://www.flickr.com/photos/lea_gallery/sets/72157626603712256/comments/

Leontiev, A. N. (1981). *Problems of the development of the mind*. Moscow: Progress Publisher.

Leordeanu, M., & Collins, R. (2005). Unsupervised learning of object features from video sequences. In Proceedings of IEEE Computer Society Conf. on Computer Vision and Pattern Recognition. IEEE. doi:10.1109/CVPR.2005.359

Levitt-Jones, T., Hoffman, K., Dempsey, Y., Jeong, S., Noble, D., & Norton, C. et al.. (2010). The "five rights" of clinical reasoning: An educational model to enhance nursing students' ability to identify and manage clinically "at risk" patients. *Nurse Education Today*, *30*(6), 515–520. doi:10.1016/j.nedt.2009.10.020

Levy, L. Z. (2009). *Computer attitudes, self-efficacy, and usage of children and their parents: Viewed through gender lens*. UMI Microform.

Levy, P. (1998). *Becoming virtual: Reality in the digital age*. New York: Plenum Trade.

Lévy, P. (1998). *Qu'est-ce que le virtuel?* Paris: La Découverte.

Lewis, N. M., & Donald, B. (2010). A new rubric for Canada's creative cities. *Urban Studies (Edinburgh, Scotland)*, *47*(1). doi:10.1177/0042098009346867

Liaw, S., Zhou, W., Lau, T., Siau, C., & Chan, S. (2014). An interprofessional communication training using simulation to enhance safe care for a deteriorating patient. *Nurse Education Today*, *34*(2), 259–264. doi:10.1016/j.nedt.2013.02.019 PMID:23518067

Lichty, P. (2009). The translation of art in virtual worlds. *Leonardo Electronic Almanac*, *18*(12). Available at: http://www.leonardo.info/LEA/DispersiveAnatomies/DA_lichty.pdf

Licklider, J. (1960). Man-computer symbiosis. *IRE Transactions on Human Factors in Electronics*, *HFE-1*(1), 4–11. doi:10.1109/THFE2.1960.4503259

Light, B. (2013). Networked masculinities and social networking sites: A call for the analysis of men and contemporary digital. *Masculinities and Social Change*, *2*(3), 245–265.

Lillian, D. (2007). A thorn by any other name: Sexist discourse as hate speech. *Discourse & Society*, *18*(6), 719–740. doi:10.1177/0957926507082193

Lima, M. (2009). Information visualization manifesto. In *Visual complexity VC blog*. Retrieved April 11, 2011, from http://www.visualcomplexity.com/vc/blog/?p=644

Lin, F., Chen, B. M., & Lee, T. H. (2009). Robust vision-based target tracking control system for an unmanned helicopter using feature fusion. In *Proceedings of 9th IAPR Int. Conf. on Machine Vision Applications* (vol. 13, pp. 398–401). IAPR.

Lindstrand, T. (2007). Viva pinata: Architecture of the everyday. In Space time play: Computer games, architecture and urbanism - The next level. Basel: Birkhauser Verlag AG.

Lin, H. (2007). Knowledge sharing and firm innovation capability: An empirical study. *International Journal of Manpower*, *28*(3/4), 315–332. doi:10.1108/01437720710755272

Livingstone, S. (2003). *Children's use of the internet: Reflections on the emerging research-agenda (online)*. London: LSE Research Online.

Livingstone, S., & Bober, M. (2006). Regulating the internet at home: Contrasting the perspectives of children and parents. In *Digital generations: Children, young people and new media* (pp. 93–113). Mahwah, NJ: Lawrence Erlbaum.

Livingstone, S., & Helsper, E. (2008). Parental mediation and children's internet use. *Journal of Broadcasting & Electronic Media*, *52*(4), 581–599. doi:10.1080/08838150802437396

Lohr, S. (2011, December 18). The internet gets physical. *New York Times*, p. Sunday Review.

Lonergan, D. C., Scott, G. M., & Mumford, M. D. (2004). Evaluative aspects of creative thought: Effects of appraisal and revision standards. *Creativity Research Journal*, *16*(2-3), 231–246. doi:10.1080/10400419.2004.9651455

Lord, A. B. (1968). *The singer of tales*. New York: Atheneum. (Original work published 1960)

Lovink, G. (1994). Michael Heim: The metaphysics of virtual reality. *Mediamatic Magazine*, *8*(1). Retrieved from http://www.mediamatic.net/5623/en/heim

Lucas, G. (2004, September 14). Life on the screen: Visual literacy in education. *Edutopia*. Retrieved from http://www.edutopia.org/life-screen

Luo, R., Li, L., & Gu, I. Y. (2007). Efficient adaptive background subtraction based on multi-resolution background modelling and updating. Springer.

Luu, R., Mitchell, D., & Blyth, J. (2004). Thrombolites (Stromatolite-like microbialite) community of a coastal brackish lake (Lake Clifton) (D. o. C. a. L. Management, Trans.). Interim Recovery Plan 2004-2009. Wannero, WA: Western Australian Threatened Species and Communities Unit (WATSCU).

Lynn, G. (1998). *Folds, bodies and blobs*. Brussels, Belgium: Bilblioteque de Belgique.

Lyotard, J. (1991). *The inhuman: Reflections on time*. Stanford, CA: Stanford University Press.

MacDonald, K. (2012, March 13). Journey – review. *The Guardian*. Retrieved from http://www.theguardian.com/technology/gamesblog/2012/mar/13/journey-ps3-review

Mackay, D. (2003). Multiple-targets: The reasons to support town-centre CCTV systems. In M. Gill (Ed.), *CCTV* (pp. 23–25). Leicester, UK: Perpetuity Press. doi:10.1057/palgrave.cpcs.8140154

Madjar, N. (2008). Emotional and informational support from different sources and employee creativity. *Journal of Occupational and Organizational Psychology*, *81*(1), 83–100. doi:10.1348/096317907X202464

Madsen, S. R., Miller, D., & John, C. R. (2005). Readiness for organizational change: Do organizational commitment and social relationships in the workplace make a difference? *Human Resource Development Quarterly*, *16*(2), 213–234. doi:10.1002/hrdq.1134

Mahon, R., & Keil, R. (2006). *The political economy of scale: An introduction*. Manuscript.

MAL. (2013). *Media archaeology lab*. Retrieved October 9, 2014, from http://mediaarchaeologylab.com/

Malory, T. (1977). Le Morte d'Arthur. In E. Vinaver (Ed.), *Malory: Complete works*. Oxford, UK: Oxford University Press. (Original work published 1485)

Mandarić V. (2012). *Novi mediji i rizično ponašanje djece i mladih*.Katolički bogoslovni fakultet Sveučilišta u Zagrebu.

Manovich, L. (2002). *Data visualization as new abstraction and anti-sublime*. Retrieved from http://manovich.net/index.php/projects/data-visualisation-as-new-abstraction-and-anti-sublime

Manovich, L. (2000). What is digital cinema? In P. Lunenfield (Ed.), *The digital dialectic, new essays in new media* (pp. 172–198). Cambridge, MA: The MIT Press.

Manovich, L. (2001). *The language of new media*. Cambridge, MA: The MIT Press.

Manovich, L. (2011). What is visualisation? *Visual Studies*, *26*(1), 36–49. doi:10.1080/1472586X.2011.548488

Manovich, L. (2013). *Software takes command*. New York, NY; London: Bloomsbury.

Manovich, L., & Kratky, A. (2005). *Soft cinema: Navigating the database*. Cambridge, MA: MIT Press.

Manuksela, A. (Reviewer). (2001). *Helsingin Sanomat* [newspaper article]. Finland. Retrieved from http://www.hs.fi

Marks, L. E. (1978). *The unity of the senses: Interrelations among the modalities*. New York: Academic Press. doi:10.1016/B978-0-12-472960-5.50011-1

Marsching, J. D., & Polli, A. (2012). *Far field: Digital culture, climate change, and the poles*. Bristol, UK: Intellect.

Marshall, R. (2013). *History of tomb raider: Blowing the dust off 17 years of Lara Croft*. Retrieved 30.06.2014 from http://www.digitaltrends.com/gaming/the-history-of-tomb-raider/#!7LAR0

Martin, C. (2000). Crime control in Australian urban space. *Current Issues in Criminal Justice*, *12*(1), 79–92.

Mason, M. C. (2008). What is complexity theory and what are its implications for educational change? *Educational Philosophy and Theory*, *40*(1), 35–49. doi:10.1111/j.1469-5812.2007.00413.x

Massey, D. (2003). Some times of space. In Olafur Eliasson: The weather report. London: Tate Publishing.

Massumi, B. (2002). *Parables for the virtual: Movement, affect, sensation.* Durham, NC: Duke University Press. doi:10.1215/9780822383574

Mathieu, J. E., Heffner, T. S., Goodwin, G. F., Salas, E., & Cannon-Bowers, J. A. (2000). The influence of shared mental models on team process and performance. *The Journal of Applied Psychology, 85*(2), 273–283. doi:10.1037/0021-9010.85.2.273 PMID:10783543

Mayer-Schönberger, V., & Cukier, K. (2013). *Big data: A revolution that will transform how we live, work and think.* London, UK: John Murray.

Mazzocco, , Petitti, D. B., Fong, K. T., Bonacum, D., Brookey, J., Graham, S., & Thomas, E. J. et al. (2009). Surgical team behaviors and patient outcomes. *American Journal of Surgery, 197*(5), 878–685. doi:10.1016/j.amjsurg.2008.03.002 PMID:18789425

McCahill, M. (2013). *The surveillance web.* Devon, UK: Taylor and Francis.

McCandless, D. (2012). *Information is beautiful.* London, UK: Collins.

McCann, E. (2007). Inequality and politics in the creative city-region: Questions of livability and strategy. *International Journal of Urban and Regional Research, 31*(1), 188–196. doi:10.1111/j.1468-2427.2007.00713.x

McCosker, A., & Wilken, R. (2014). Rethinking 'big data' as visual knowledge: The sublime and the diagrammatic in data visualisation. *Visual Studies, 29*(2), 155–164. doi:10.1080/1472586X.2014.887268

McDonald, J., Teder-Sälejärvi, W., & Hillyard, S. (2000, October). Involuntary orienting to sound improves visual perception. *Nature, 407*(6806), 906–908. doi:10.1038/35038085 PMID:11057669

McGaghie, W. C., Issenberg, S. B., Petrusa, E. R., & Scalese, R. J. (2010). A critical review of simulation-based medical education research: 2003-2009. *Medical Education, 44*(1), 50–63. doi:10.1111/j.1365-2923.2009.03547.x PMID:20078756

McKinnell, J. (1993). Völuspá. In P. Pulsiano & K. Wolf (Eds.), *Medieval Scandinavia* (pp. 713–715). London: Routledge.

McKinnell, J. (2001). On Heiðr. *Saga-Book, 25*(4), 394–417.

McLuhan, M. (1964). *Understanding media: The extensions of man.* New York: McGraw Hill.

Meadows, M. S. (2008). *I, avatar: The culture and consequences of having a second life.* Berkeley, CA: New Riders.

Medical Teamwork and Patient Safety: The Evidence-Based Relationship. (2003). Agency for Healthcare Research and Quality.

Medina, J. (2014). *Brain rules: 12 principles for surviving and thriving at work, home, and school.* Pear Press.

Meillassoux, Q. (2012). *Après la Finitude: Essai sur la Nécessité de la Contingence.* Paris: Seuil.

Melville, S. (2001). *As painting: division and displacement.* Cambridge, MA: MIT Press.

Mennin, S. (2010). Complexity and health professions education: A basic glossary. *Journal of Evaluation in Clinical Practice, 16*(4), 838–840. doi:10.1111/j.1365-2753.2010.01503.x PMID:20659212

Merian, M. (2009). *Insects of Surinam* (K. Schmidt-Loske, Ed.). Cologne: Taschen GmbH.(Original work published 1705)

Merkel, L., & Sanford, K. (2009). Complexities of gaming cultures. *In Proceedings. DiGRA.* London: DiGRA.

Merkel, L., & Sanford, K. (2011). Complexities of gaming cultures: Adolescent gamers adapting and transforming learning. *E-Learning and Digital Media, 8*(4), 397. doi:10.2304/elea.2011.8.4.397

Merleau Ponty, M. (1968). *Phenomenology of perception.* London: Routledge.

Merleau-Ponty, M. (1964). Eye and mind. In The primacy of perception (C. Dallery, Trans.; pp. 159-190). Northwestern University Press.

Merleau-Ponty, M. (1968). The intertwining-The chiasm. In C. Lefort (Ed.), The visible and the invisible: Philosophical interrogation (A. Lingis, Trans.; pp. 130–155). Evanston, IL: Northwestern University Press.

Meyer, F., & Bouthemy, P. (1994). Region-based tracking using affine motion models in long image sequences. *CVGIP. Image Understanding, 60*(2), 119–140. doi:10.1006/ciun.1994.1042

Meyer, J., & Bochner, M. (2001). How can you defend making paintings now? In *As painting: Division and displacement*. Cambridge, MA: MIT Press.

Mezher, T. (2012). Meeting the renewable energy and sustainability challenges. In M. A. Ramday (Ed.), *The GCC economies: Stepping up to future challenges* (pp. 69–84). New York: Springer. doi:10.1007/978-1-4614-1611-1_7

Michinov, N. (2012). Is electronic brainstorming or brainwriting the best way to improve creative performance in groups? An overlooked comparison of two idea-generation techniques. *Journal of Applied Social Psychology, 42*, E222–E243. doi:10.1111/j.1559-1816.2012.01024.x

Michota, A. (2013). Digital security concerns and threats facing women entrepreneurs. *Journal of Innovation and Entrepreneurship, 2*(7). Retrieved from http://www.innovation-entrepreneurship.com/content/2/1/7

Milas, G. (2005). *Istraživačke metode u psihologiji i drugim društvenim znanostima*. Zagreb: Jastrebarsko.

Miller, D. (2010). *Stuff*. Cambridge, UK: Polity.

Miller, T. (2009). Cybertarians of the world unite: You have nothing to lose but your tubes! In P. Snickars & P. Vonderau (Eds.), *The YouTube reader* (pp. 424–440). Stockholm: National Library of Sweden.

Millie, A. (2008). Anti-social behaviour, behavioural expectations and an urban aesthetic. *The British Journal of Criminology, 48*(3), 379–394. doi:10.1093/bjc/azm076

Mills, B. J., & Walker, W. H. (2008). *Memory work, archaeologies of material practices*. Santa Fe, NM: School for Advanced Research Press.

Mitchell, K. J., Becker-Blease, K. A., & Finkelhor, D. (2005). Inventory of problematic internet experiences encountered in clinical practice. *Professional Psychology, Research and Practice, 36*(5), 498–509. doi:10.1037/0735-7028.36.5.498

Mitchell, W. (1995). *City of bits*. Cambridge, MA: MIT Press.

Moeslund, T. B., Hilton, A., & Kruger, V. (2006). A survey of advances in vision-based human motion capture and analysis. *Computer Vision and Image Understanding, 104*(2-3), 90–126. doi:10.1016/j.cviu.2006.08.002

Mohammed, S., & Dumville, B. (2000). Team mental models in a team knowledge framework: Expanding theory and measurement across disciplinary boundaries. *Journal of Organizational Behavior, 22*(2), 89–106. doi:10.1002/job.86

Moholy-Nagy, L. (1967). *Painting photography film*. London: Lund Humphreys. (Original work published 1925)

Montgomery, K. (2000). Youth and digital media: A policy research agenda. *Journal of Adolescent Youth, 27S*, 61–68. PMID:10904209

Moore, L. (2013). *In[bodying] the other: Performing the digital other as a component of self through real-time video performance*. (Unpublished doctoral dissertation). University of Wolverhampton, Wolverhampton, UK.

Moos, D. (1996). *Painting in the age of artificial intelligence*. London, UK: Academy Editions.

Morgan, P. J., & Cleave-Hogg, D. (2002). Comparison between medical students' experience, confidence and competence. *Medical Education, 36*(6), 534–539. doi:10.1046/j.1365-2923.2002.01228.x PMID:12047667

Morgan, P. J., Cleave-Hogg, D., Mcllroy, J., & Devitt, J. H. (2002). Simulation technology: A comparison of experiential and visual learning for undergraduate medical students. *Anesthesiology, 96*(1), 10–16. doi:10.1097/00000542-200201000-00008 PMID:11752995

Morie, J. (2007). Performing in (virtual) spaces: Embodiment and being in virtual environments. *International Journal of Performance Arts and Digital Media, 3*(2&3), 123–138. doi:10.1386/padm.3.2-3.123_1

Mori, M. (1970). The uncanny valley. (K. F. MacDorman & N. Kageki, Trans.). *IEEE Robotics & Automation Magazine, 19*(2), 98–100. doi:10.1109/MRA.2012.2192811

Moritz, W. (2004). *Optical poetry: The life and work of Oskar Fischinger*. London: John Libbey.

Morowitz, H. (2002). The emergence of everything: How the world became complex. New York: Oxford.

Morris, C. W. (1964). *Signification and significance: A study of the relations of signs and values*. Cambridge, MA: MIT Press.

Morse, P. (2007). *IMAGinING Antarctica*. Retrieved from http://johncurtingallery.curtin.edu.au/exhibitions/archive/2007.cfm#Ant

Moser, M. A. (Ed.). (1996). *Immersed in technology: Art and virtual environments*. Cambridge, MA: MIT Press.

Müller, U. (1998). *Klassischer Geschmack und gotische Tugend: Der englische Landsitz Rousham*. Worms, Germany: Wernersche Verlagsgesellschaft.

Mumford, M. D., Baughman, W. A., Supinski, E. P., & Maher, M. A. (1996b). Process-based measures of creative problem-solving skills: II. Information encoding. *Creativity Research Journal, 9*(1), 77–88. doi:10.1207/s15326934crj0901_7

Mumford, M. D., Connelly, S., & Gaddis, B. (2003). How creative leaders think: Experimental findings and cases. *The Leadership Quarterly, 14*(4-5), 411–432. doi:10.1016/S1048-9843(03)00045-6

Mumford, M. D., & Gustafson, S. B. (1988). Creativity syndrome: Integration, application, and innovation. *Psychological Bulletin, 103*(1), 27–43. doi:10.1037/0033-2909.103.1.27

Mumford, M. D., Schultz, R. A., & Doorn, J. R. (2001). Performance in planning: Processes, requirements, and errors. *Review of General Psychology, 5*(3), 213–240. doi:10.1037/1089-2680.5.3.213

Mumford, M. D., Zaccaro, S. J., Harding, F. D., Jacobs, T., & Fleishman, E. A. (2000). Leadership skills for a changing world: Solving complex social problems. *The Leadership Quarterly, 11*(1), 11–35. doi:10.1016/S1048-9843(99)00041-7

Mumford, T. V., Van Iddekinge, C. G., Morgeson, F. P., & Campion, M. A. (2008). The team role test: Development and validation of a team role knowledge situational judgment test. *The Journal of Applied Psychology, 93*(2), 250–267. doi:10.1037/0021-9010.93.2.250 PMID:18361630

Munster, A. (2006). *Materializing new media: Embodiment in information aesthetics*. University Press of New England.

Murch, W. (2000). *Stretching sound to help the mind see*. Retrieved October, 21, 2012, from http://www.filmsound.org/murch/stretching.htm

Murphie, A. (2002). Putting the virtual back into VR. In B. Massumi (Ed.), *A shock to thought: Expression after Deleuze and Guattari* (pp. 188–214). London: Routledge.

Murray, J. (2012). *Inventing the medium: Principles of interaction design as a cultural practice*. Cambridge, MA: MIT Press.

Murray, J. M. (1997). *Hamlet on the holodeck: The future of narrative in cyberspace*. Cambridge, MA: MIT Press.

NAEYC. (1996). *Technology and young children: Ages 3 through 8*. Retrieved from https://www.google.hr/?gws_rd=ssl#q=http:%2F%2Fwww.naeyc.org%2Fresources%2Fposition_statements%2Fpstech98.htm

Nake, F., & Grabowski, S. (2008). The interface as sign and as aesthetic event. In P. Fishwick (Ed.), *Aesthetic computing*. Cambridge, MA: MIT Press.

Narayana, M., & Haverkamp, D. (2007). A Bayesian algorithm for tracking multiple moving objects in outdoor surveillance video. In *Proceedings of CVPR* (pp. 1–8). New York: IEEE Press.

National Association for the Education of Young Children (NAEYC). (1996). Technology and interactive media as tools in early childhood programs serving children from birth through. *Age, 8*.

National Council of Teachers of Mathematics (NCTM). (2000). *Principles and standards for school mathematics*. Reston, VA: NCTM.

National Council of Teachers of Mathematics (NCTM). (2014). *Principles to actions: Ensuring mathematical success for all*. Reston, VA: NCTM.

National Information Society Agency. (2013). *2012 yearbook of information society statistics*. Retrieved from http://eng.nia.or.kr/english/eng_nia.asp/

National Research Council (NRC). (2011). *A framework for K-12 science education*. Washington, DC: The National Academies Press.

Natter, W. (1994). Place, power, situation and spectacle, the city as cinematic space: Modernism and place in Berlin, symphony of a great city. In Place, power, situation and spectacle: A geography of film (pp. 203-228). Lanham, MD: Rowman and Littlefield.

Nayar, P. K. (2010, December25). Wikileaks, the new information cultures and digital parrhesia. *Economic and Political Weekly*, *52*(45), 27–30.

NEA. (2008). *An NEA policy brief*. Washington, DC: NEA Education Policy and Practice Department.

Neckel, G. (1927). *Edda: Die Lieder des Codex Regius*. Heidelberg, Germany: Carl Winters Universitätsbuchhandlung.

Negroponte, N. (1996). *Being digital*. New York, NY: Vintage.

Nehring, W. M., & Lashley, W. R. (2004). Current uses and opinions regarding human patient simulators in nursing education: An international survey. *Nursing Education Perspectives*, *25*(5), 244–248. PMID:15508564

Neirotti, P., Marco, A., Cagliano, A., Mangano, G., & Scorrano, F. (2014). Current trends in Smart City initiatives: Some stylised facts. *Cities (London, England)*, *38*, 25–36. doi:10.1016/j.cities.2013.12.010

Next Generation Science Standards (NGSS) Lead States. (2013). *Next generation science standards: For states, by states*. Washington, DC: The National Academies Press.

Nguyen, N.T., Phung, D.Q., Venkatesh, S., Bui, H. (2005). Learning and detecting activities from movement trajectories using the hierarchical hidden Markov model. In *Proceedings of IEEE Computer Society Conf. on Computer Vision and Pattern Recognition* (vol. 2, pp. 955–960). IEEE.

Nickerson, R. (1999). Enhancing creativity. In R. Sternberg (Ed.), *Handbook of creativity* (pp. 392–430). Cambridge, UK: Cambridge University Press.

Nicolelis, M. (2011). Beyond boundaries, the new neuroscience of connecting brains with machines – And how it will change our lives. New York: Time Books, Henry Holt & Company.

Nieto, M., Ortega, J. D., Cortes, A., & Gaines, S. (2014). Perspective multiscale detection and tracking of persons. *LNCS*, *8326*, 92–103.

Nikolopolou, A. (1993). Play, cognitive development and the social world: Piaget, Vygotsky,and beyond. *Human Development*, *36*(1), 1–2. doi:10.1159/000277285

Nitsche, M. (2004). Spatial structuring, cinematic mediation, and evocative narrative elements in the design of an RT 3D VE: The common tales project. *Digital Creativity*, *15*(1), 52–56. doi:10.1076/digc.15.1.52.28147

Nitsche, M. (2008). *Video games spaces: Image, play and structure in 3D worlds*. Cambridge MA: MIT Press. doi:10.7551/mitpress/9780262141017.001.0001

Noorani, R. (2006). *Rapid prototyping principles and applications*. Hoboken, NJ: John Wiley and Sons.

Norris, C. (1995). Gilles Deleuze. In T. Honderich (Ed.), *The Oxford companion to philosophy* (pp. 182–183). Oxford, UK: Oxford University Press.

Norris, C., Moran, J., & Armstrong, G. (Eds.). (1998). *Surveillance, closed circuit television and social control*. Aldershot, UK: Ashgate.

Northwestern University. (2007, September 27). Music training linked to enhanced verbal skills. *ScienceDaily*. Retrieved February 2, 2015 from www.sciencedaily.com/releases/2007/09/070926123908.htm

O'Brien, C. (2013). How the i-Phone and i-Pad transformed the work of David Hockney. *Los Angeles Times*. Retrieved 27.10.2013 from http://www.latimes.com/business/technology/la-fi-tn-how-the-iphone-and-ipad-transformed-the-art-of-david-hockney-20131024-story.html

O'Mahony, M. (2006). *World art: The essential illustrated history*. London: Flame Tree Publishing.

O'Sullivan, S. (2010). *Deleuze and contemporary art*. Edinburgh, UK: Edinburgh University Press.

Oldfield, F., Barnosky, A. D., Dearing, J., Fischer-Kowalski, M., McNeill, J., Steffen, W., & Zalasiewicz, J. (2014). The anthropocene review: Its significance, implications and the rationale for a new transdisciplinary journal. *The Anthropocene Review*, *1*(1), 3–7. doi:10.1177/2053019613500445

Oldham, G. R., & Cummings, A. (1996). Employee creativity: Personal and contextual factors at work. *Academy of Management Journal, 39*(3), 607–634. doi:10.2307/256657

Oldham, G. R., & Silva, N. D. (2013). The impact of digital technology on the generation and implementation of creative ideas in the workplace. *Computers in Human Behavior, 1*, 1–7.

Orledge, J., Phillips, W. J., Murray, W. B., & Lerant, A. (2012). The use of simulation in healthcare: From systems issues, to team building, to task training, to education and high stakes examinations. *Current Opinion in Critical Care, 18*(4), 326–332. doi:10.1097/MCC.0b013e328353fb49 PMID:22614323

Osburn, H., & Mumford, M. (2006). Creativity and planning: Training interventions to develop creative problem-solving skills. *Creativity Research Journal, 18*(2), 173–190. doi:10.1207/s15326934crj1802_4

Ouroussoff, N. (2010). In Arabian desert, a sustainable city rises. *The New York Times.*

Ovens, A., Hopper, T. F., & Butler, J. I. (2012). *Complexity thinking in physical education: Reframing curriculum, pedagogy and research* (A. Ovens, T. F. Hopper, & J. I. Butler, Eds.). London: Routledge.

Owen, H., Mugford, B., Follows, V., & Plummer, J. L. (2006). Comparison of three simulation-based training methods for management of medical emergencies. *Resuscitation, 71*(2), 204–211. doi:10.1016/j.resuscitation.2006.04.007 PMID:16987587

Page, R. I. (1987). *Runes (reading the past)*. London: British Museum Publications.

Pallasmaa, J. (2005). *The eyes of the skin: Architecture and the senses*. Chichester, UK: John Wiley & Sons.

Pals, N., & Esmeijer, J. (Eds.). (2007). *New millennium/new media: FP6 IST – 004124 – report D 7.9 Evaluation report on RuneCast*. EC. Internal Report. Retrieved from www.ist-nm2.org

Parents Attitudes toward Computer Use by Young Children. (n.d.). Accessed 30.03.2014., from http://jrre.vmhost.psu.edu/wp-content/uploads/2014/02/2-4_1.pdf

Parikka, J. (2012). *What is media archaeology*. Cambridge, UK: Polity Press.

Parnes, S. (1965). The nurture of creative talent. *Music Educators Journal, 51*(32-3), 92-95.

Patton, P. (1997). *Deleuze: A critical reader*. London, UK: Blackwell Publishers Ltd.

Paul, C. (2003). *Digital art*. London: Thames & Hudson Ltd.

Pauwels, L. (Ed.). (2006). *Visual cultures of science*. NH, Lebanon: Dartmouth College Press.

Paz, O. (1979). A draft of shadows. In *A draft of shadows and other poem* (E. Weinberger, Trans.). New York: New Directions Books.

Pearson, M. J. (2011). *The original I Ching: An authentic translation of the Book of Changes*. Rutland, VT: Tuttle Publishing.

Peck, J. (2007). Banal urbanism: Cities and the creativity fix. *Monu, 7*.

Peck, J., Theodore, N., & Brenner, N. (2009). Neoliberal urbanism: Models, moments, mutations. *SAIS Review, 29*(1).

Peckham, M. (2014). *Romantic puzzler Entwined is an understated triumph*. Retrieved 01.07.2014 from http://www.wired.co.uk/news/archive/2014-06/23/entwined-review

Peck, J. (1998). Geographies of governance: TECs and the neoliberalisation of local interests. *Space and Polity, 2*(1), 5–31. doi:10.1080/13562579808721768

Peck, J., & Tickell, A. (2002). Neoliberalizing space. *Antipode, 34*(3), 380–404. doi:10.1111/1467-8330.00247

Pedersen, S., & Macafee, C. (2007). Gender differences in British blogging. *Journal of Computer-Mediated Communication, 12*(4), 1472–1492. doi:10.1111/j.1083-6101.2007.00382.x

Pentikäinen, J. (1987). The shamanistic drum as cognitive map. In R. Gothoni & J. Pentikäinen (Eds.), Mythology and cosmic order (pp. 17-36). Helsinki: Suomalaisen Kirjallisuuden Seura.

Pentikäinen, J. (Ed.). (1996). *Shamanism and northern ecology (religion and society)*. Berlin: Mouton de Gruyter. doi:10.1515/9783110811674

Perkins, J. (2009). The role of Masdar initiative and Masdar Institute of Science and Technology in developing and deploying renewable technologies in emerging economies. *ATDF Journal, 5*(1/2), 10–15.

Perry-Smith, J. E., & Shalley, C. E. (2003). The social side of creativity: A static and dynamic social network perspective. *Academy of Management Review, 28*(1), 89–106.

Petrini, C. (1991). Kaleidoscopic thinking for creativity. *Training & Development, 45*, 27–34.

Petz, B. (2004) *Osnove statističke metode za nematematičare*. Jastrebarsko: Naklada Slap.

Phillips, P. (2012). *The sixth shore details*. Retrieved from http://www.perditaphillips.com/index.php?option=com_content&view=article&id=313:the-sixth-shore-details&catid=17:now-news&Itemid=31

Phillips, K. (2014, September 16). How diversity makes us smarter. *Scientific American*.

Phillips, P. (2009). Clotted life and brittle waters. *Landscapes, 3*(2), 1–20.

Piaget, J., & Inhelder, B. (1973). *Memory and intelligence*. London: Routledge and Kegan Paul.

Pillay, H. (2003). An investigation of cognitive processes engaged in by recreational computer game players: Implications for skills of the future. *Journal of Research on Computing in Education, 34*(3), 336–350.

Pilling, J. (Ed.). (1997). *A reader in animation studies*. John Libbey and Co.

Pink, S. (2007). *Doing visual ethnography* (2nd ed.). Sage publications.

Pink, S., Hubbard, P., O'Neill, M., & Radley, A. (2010). Walking across disciplines: From ethnography to arts practice. *Visual Studies, 25*(1), 1–7. doi:10.1080/14725861003606670

Polanyi, K. (2001). *Great transformation: The political and economic origins of our time*. Boston: Beacon Press.

Polli, A. (2004). *Heat and the heartbeat of the city*. Retrieved from http://www.turbulence.org/Works/heat/index2.html

Polli, A. (2011). *Communicating air: Alternative pathways to environmental knowing through computational ecomedia*. (Doctoral Dissertation). University of Plymouth. Available from British Library EThOS database. (546308). Retrieved from http://ethos.bl.uk/OrderDetails.do?did=1&uin=uk.bl.ethos.546308#sthash.Ga04gfdo.dpuf

Polli, A. (2012, 14 July). *Profile of 90 degrees south by filmmaker Meredith Drum*. Retrieved from http://www.90degreessouth.org/

Polli, A. (Producer). (2010). *Particle falls*. [Video file]. Retrieved from http://vimeo.com/16336508

Porikli, F., Ivanov, Y., & Haga, T. (2008). Robust abandoned object detection using dual foregrounds. *EURASIP Journal on Advances in Signal Processing*, (8): 197875.

Portal o e-learning u AHyCo.uniri.hr! (n.d.). Retrieved from http://ahyco.uniri.hr/portal/Pocetna.aspx

Prager, P. (2009). *Play, creativity and exuberance: Avant-Garde legacies for interactive cinematics*. (Unpublished doctoral dissertation). University of Cambridge, Cambridge, UK.

Prager, P. (2006). Back to the future: Interactivity and associational narrativity at the Bauhaus. *Digital Creativity, 17*(4), 295–304. doi:10.1080/14626260601073195

Prager, P. (2012). Making an art of creativity: The cognitive science of Duchamp and Dada. *Creativity Research Journal, 24*(4), 266–277. doi:10.1080/10400419.2012.726576

Prager, P. (2013). Play and the Avant-Garde: Aren't we all a little Dada? *American Journal of Play, 5*, 239–256.

Prager, P. (2014). Making sense of the modernist muse: Creative cognition and play at the Bauhaus. *American Journal of Play, 7*, 27–49.

Prensky, M. (2001). Digital natives, digital immigrants. *On the Horizon, 9*(5). Retrieved July 16, 2012 from http://www.marcprensky.com/writing/

Preparata, F., & Shamos, M. (1985). *Computational geometry: An introduction.* New York: Springer-Verlag. doi:10.1007/978-1-4612-1098-6

Previšić, V. (2000). Slobodno vrijeme između pedagogijske teorije i odgojne prakse. *Napredak, 4*(141), 403–411.

Prokhovnik, R. (2007). Rationality. In G. Blakeley & V. Bryson (Eds.), *The impact of feminism on political concepts and debates* (pp. 12–24). Manchester, UK: Manchester University Press.

Prophet, J. (2004). Re-addressing practice-based research: Funding and recognition. *Digital Creativity, 15*(1), 2–7. doi:10.1076/digc.15.1.2.28153

Putman, R., & Borko, H. (2000). What do new views of knowledge and thinking have to say about research on teacher learning? *Educational Researcher, 29*(1), 4–15. doi:10.3102/0013189X029001004

Qin, Y., & Simon, H. A. (1990). Laboratory replication of scientific discovery processes. *Cognitive Science, 14*(2), 281–312. doi:10.1207/s15516709cog1402_4

Radetić Paić, M., Ružić Baf, M., &Dragojlović, D. (2010). The role of parents and computer use of pupils perpetrators of criminal acts. *Metodički obzori, 10*(5), 7-20.

Radsch, C., & Sahar, K. (2013). In their own voice: Technologically mediated empowerment and transformation among young Arab women. *Feminist Media Studies, 13*(5), 881–890. doi:10.1080/14680777.2013.838378

Rajchman, J. (2000). *Constructions.* Cambridge, MA: The MIT Press.

Rajchman, J. (2001). *The Deleuze connections.* Cambridge, MA: The MIT Press.

Rami, Y. (2013). *Planning the city of the future in Qatar Lusail integrated transportation system.* Paper presented at QFIS.

Rancière, J. (2008). Jacques Rancière and indisciplinarity. Glasgow, UK: Glasgow School of Art Press.

Ratcliffe, J. H. (2008). *Intelligence-led policing.* Cullompton, UK: Witlan.

Reas, C., & Fry, B. (2007). *Processing: A programming handbook for visual designers and artists.* Cambridge, MA: MIT Press.

Reeve, A. (1998). The panopticisation of shopping: CCTV and leisure competition. In Surveillance, closed circuit television and social control. Aldershot, UK: Ashgate.

Reeves, S. (2011). *Designing interfaces in public settings: Understanding the role of the spectator in human-computer interaction.* Heidelberg, Germany: Springer-Verlag. doi:10.1007/978-0-85729-265-0

Reiche, D. (2010). Renewable energy policies in the gulf countries: A case study of the carbon-neutral "Masdar City" in Abu Dhabi. *Energy Policy, 38*(1), 378–382. doi:10.1016/j.enpol.2009.09.028

Reinhardt, S., Saathoff, G., Buhr, H., Carlson, L. A., Wolf, A., Schwalm, D., & Gwinner, G. et al. (2007). Test of relativistic time dilation with fast optical atomic clocks at different velocities. *Nature Physics, 3*(12), 861–864. doi:10.1038/nphys778

Reiter-Palmon, R. (2009). A dialectic perspective on problem identification and construction. *Industrial and Organizational Psychology: Perspectives on Science and Practice, 2*(3), 349–352. doi:10.1111/j.1754-9434.2009.01157.x

Reiter-Palmon, R., Wigert, B., & de Vreede, T. (2012). Team creativity and innovation: The effect of group composition, social processes, and cognition. In M. D. Mumford (Ed.), *Handbook of organizational creativity.* London, UK: Elsevier. doi:10.1016/B978-0-12-374714-3.00013-6

Renaud, C. (2012). *Creating a digital media curriculum for the high school.* (Unpublished master's thesis). Carthage College, Kenosha, WI.

Resnick, M. (2013, June 25). *Keynote address.* Paper presented at EdMedia World Conference on Media and Technology.

Reyes, E. (2011). Pervasive virtual worlds. In G. Mura (Ed.), *Metaplasticity in virtual worlds: Aesthetics and semantic concepts.* Hershey, PA: IGI Global. doi:10.4018/978-1-60960-077-8.ch004

Reynolds, A. (2002). *Mount fear statistics for crimes with offensive weapon south London 2001-2002.* Retrieved August 29, 2014, from http://www.tradegallery.org/gallery.html#abigailreynolds

Rheingold, H. (1991). *Virtual reality*. New York: Summit Books.

Ricca, B. (2012). Beyond teaching methods: A complexity approach. *Complicity:An International Journal of Complexity and Education, 9*(2), 31–51.

Ricci, S., & Vigevano, F. (1999). The effect of videogame software in video-game epilepsy. *Epilepsia, 40*(4), 31–37. doi:10.1111/j.1528-1157.1999.tb00904.x PMID:10487171

Richtel, M. (2012, May 29). Wasting time is the new digital divide. *New York Times*.

Richter, H. (1965). *Dada: Art and anti-art*. New York: Harry Abrams.

Rideout, V., & Hamel, E. (2006). *The media family: Electronic media in the lives of infants, toddlers, preschoolers, and their parents*. Kaiser Family Foundation. Retrieved from http://www.childrenandnature.org/research/volumes/C42/42/#sthash.LBYsTm0w.dpuf

Rieser, M. (2002). The poetics of interactivity: The uncertainty principle. In M. Rieser & A. Zapp (Eds.), *New screen media: Cinema/art/narrative* (pp. 146–162). London: British Film Institute.

Rieser, M., & Zapp, A. (Eds.). (2002). *New screen media: Cinema/art/narrative*. London: British Film Institute.

Rietzschel, E. F., Nijstad, B. A., & Stroebe, W. (2006). Productivity is not enough: A comparison of interactive and nominal brainstorming groups on idea generation and selection. *Journal of Experimental Social Psychology, 42*(2), 244–251. doi:10.1016/j.jesp.2005.04.005

Rietzschel, E. F., Nijstad, B. A., & Stroebe, W. (2006). Relative accessibility of domain knowledge and creativity: The effects of knowledge activation on the quantity and originality of generated ideas. *Journal of Experimental Social Psychology, 43*(6), 4–14.

Riggins, S. (Ed.). (1994). *The socialness of things: Essays on the socio-semiotics of objects*. Berlin, Germany: Mouton de Gruyter. doi:10.1515/9783110882469

Rijavec, M. (1994). Čuda se ipak događaju- psihologija pozitivnog mišljenja. Zagreb: IEP d.o.o.

Rijavec, M., & Brdar, I. (2001). Pozitivna psihologija. Zagreb: IEP d.o.o.

Rijavec, M., Miljković, D. & Brdar, I. (2008). *Pozitivna psihologija: Znanstveno istraživanje ljudskih snaga i sreće*. Zagreb: IEP d.o.o.

Rizzuto, T., & Reeves, J. (2007). A multi-disciplinary overview of person-related barriers to technology implementation. *Consulting Psychology Journal: Practice and Research, 59*(3), 226–240. doi:10.1037/1065-9293.59.3.226

Roberts, D. F., Foehr, U., & Rideout, V. (2005). *Generation M: Media in the lives of 8 to 18 year olds*. Kaiser Family Foundation.

Roche, S. (2013). *Four puzzle pieces for the spatially enabled smart campus*. Available at http://www.spatial.ucsb.edu/eventfiles/ASESC/docs/Roche-position.pdf

Roe, K., & Muijs, D. (1998). Children and computer games: A profile for the heavy user. *European Journal of Communication, 13*(2), 181–200. doi:10.1177/0267323198013002002

Root, A. (2014). Your business needs to tweet – Here's how to make it worth your while. *Forbes.com*. Retrieved from http://www.forbes.com/sites/theyec/2014/07/02/your-business-needs-to-tweet-heres-how-to-make-it-worth-your-while/

Rosengarten, A. (2000). *Spectrums of possibility: When psychology meets tarot*. St Paul, MN: Paragon House.

Ross, D., & Hood, J. (1998). Closed circuit television (CCTV) - The Easterhouse case study. In L. Montanheiro, B. Haigh, D. Morris, & N. Hrovatin (Eds.), *Public and private sector partnerships: Fostering enterprise* (pp. 497–516). Sheffield Hallam University Press.

Rothenberg, A. (1976). Homospatial thinking in creativity. *Archives of General Psychiatry, 33*(1), 17–26. doi:10.1001/archpsyc.1976.01770010005001 PMID:1247359

Rothenberg, A. (1986). Artistic creation as stimulated by superimposed versus combined-composite visual images. *Journal of Personality and Social Psychology, 50*(2), 370–381. doi:10.1037/0022-3514.50.2.370 PMID:3701584

Rudolf, J. W., Simon, R., Dufresne, M. S., & Raemer, D. B. (2006). There is no such thing as non-judgmental debriefing: A theory and method for debriefing with good judgment. *Simulation in Healthcare*, *1*(1), 49–55. doi:10.1097/01266021-200600110-00006 PMID:19088574

Ruestow, E. G. (1985). Piety and the defence of natural order: Swammerdam on generation. In M. Osler & P. L. Faber (Eds.), *Religion, science and worldview: Essays in honor of Richard S. Westfall* (pp. 217–241). New York: Cambridge University Press.

Runco, M. A. (1991). *Divergent thinking*. Westport, CT: Ablex Publishing.

Runco, M. A., & Jaeger, G. J. (2012). The standard definition of creativity. *Creativity Research Journal*, *24*(1), 92–96. doi:10.1080/10400419.2012.650092

Russett, R., & Starr, C. (1976). *Experimental animation: An illustrated anthology*. New York: Van Nostrand.

Ružić Baf, M. I., & Radetić Paić, M. (2010). The influence of computer games on young people and the use pegi tool. *Život i škola*, 56(24).

Ryan, D. (2001). *Hybrids*. London, UK: Tate Gallery Publishing Ltd.

Ryan, D. (2002). *Talking painting: Dialogues with twelve contemporary abstract painters*. London, UK: Routledge.

Ryan, M.-L. (2001). *Narrative as virtual reality: Immersion and interactivity in literature and electronic media*. Baltimore, MD: Johns Hopkins University Press.

Sabaneev, L., & Pring, S. W. (1934, April). Music and the sound film. *Music & Letters*, *15*(2), 147–152. doi:10.1093/ml/15.2.147

Sager, R. (2009, August 18). Keep off the astroturf. [Electronic version]. *The New York Times*. Retrieved January 22, 2012, from http://www.nytimes.com/2009/08/19/opinion/19sager.html

Salen, K. (2008). Toward an ecology of gaming. In K. Salen (Ed.), *The ecology of games: Connecting youth, games and learning* (pp. 1–17). Cambridge, MA: MIT Press.

Salomon, G., & Perkins, D. N. (1996). Learning in wonderland: What computers really offer education. In S. Kerr (Ed.), Technology and the future of education (pp. 111-130). Chicago: University of Chicago Press.

Salpeter, J. (1999). *How can technology benefit our students?* Technology and Learning Magazine.

Sands, G., & Reese, L. A. (2008). Cultivating the creative class: And what about Nanaimo? *Economic Development Quarterly*, *22*(1), 8–23. doi:10.1177/0891242407309822

Sanford, K., & Hopper, T. (2009). Videogames and complexity theory: Learning through game play. *Loading...*, *3*(4). Retrieved October 31, 2009, from http://journals.sfu.ca/loading/index.php/loading/article/view/62

Sanford, K., & Merkel, L. (2011). Emergent/see: Viewing adolescents' video game. In E. Dunkels, G.-M. Frånberg, & C. Hallgren (Eds.), Interactive media use and youth: Learning, knowledge exchange and behavior (p. 102). Hershey, PA: IGI Global.

Sanford, K., Merkel, L, & Madill, L. (2011). "There's no fixed course": Rhizomatic learning communities in adolescent videogaming. *Loading Journal...*, *5*(8).

Sanford, K., Starr, L., Merkel, L. & Bonsor-Kurki, S. (2015). Serious games: Videogames for good? *E-Learning and Digital Media Journal*, *12*(1). doi:10.1177/2042753014558380

Sanford, K., & Bonsor Kurki, S. (2014). Videogame literacies: Purposeful civic engagement for 21st century youth learning. In K. Sanford, T. Rogers, & M. Kendrick (Eds.), *Everyday youth literacies: Critical perspectives for new times* (pp. 29–45). London: Springer. doi:10.1007/978-981-4451-03-1_3

Sanford, K., & Madill, L. (2007). Understanding the power of new literacies through videogame play and design. *Canadian Journal of Education*, *30*(2), 421–455. doi:10.2307/20466645

Sanford, K., & Madill, L. (2007b). Critical literacy learning through video games: Adolescent boys' perspectives. *E-Learning and Digital Media*, *4*(3), 285–296.

Sanford, K., & Merkel, L. (2012). The literacies of videogaming. In K. James, T. Dobson, & C. Leggo (Eds.), *English in secondary classrooms: Creative and critical advice from Canadian teacher educators*. UBC.

Santrock, J. W. (1997). *Psychology* (5th ed.). Dubuque, IA: Brown & Benchmark Publishers.

Saussure, F. (1977). *Course in general linguistics*. Fontana: Collins.

Saussure, F. (1983). *Course in general linguistics*. (R. Harris, Trans.). London: Duckworth. (Original work published 1916)

Schafer, R. M. (1994). *The soundscape: Our sonic environment and the tuning of the world*. Destiny Books.

Scherer, Y. K., Bruce, S. A., & Runkawatt, V. (2007). A comparison of clinical simulation and case study presentation on nurse practitioner students' knowledge and confidence in managing cardiac event. *International Journal of Nursing Education Scholarship*, *4*(1), 22. doi:10.2202/1548-923X.1502 PMID:18052920

Schlemmer, O. (1961). Theatre (Bhne). In W. Gropius (Ed.), *Theatre of the Bauhaus* (pp. 81–91). Middletown, CT: Wesleyan UP. (Original work published 1925)

Schon, D. A. (1983). *The reflective practitioner: How professionals think in action*. San Francisco, CA: Jossey Bass.

Schroeder, D. C., & Lee, C. (2013). Integrating digital technologies for spatial reasoning: Using Google SketchUp to model the real world. In D. Polly (Ed.), *Common core mathematics standards and implementing digital technologies* (pp. 110–127). Hershey, PA: IGI Global. doi:10.4018/978-1-4666-4086-3.ch008

Schroeder, R. (Ed.). (2002). *The social life of avatars: Presence and interaction in shared virtual environments*. London: Springer. doi:10.1007/978-1-4471-0277-9

Schutte, N. S., Malouff, J. M., Post-Gorden, J. C., & Rodasta, A. L. (1988). Effects of playing videogames on children's aggressive and other behaviors. *Journal of Applied Social Psychology*, *18*(5), 454–460. doi:10.1111/j.1559-1816.1988.tb00028.x

Scott, J., & Porter Armstrong, A. (2013). *Impact of multiplayer online role-playing games upon the psychosocial well-being of adolescents and young adults: Reviewing the evidence* (Vol. 2013). Psychiatry Journal. doi:10.1155/2013/464685

Sculi, G. L. (2010). *Nursing crew resource management*. VA National Center for Patient Safety.

Seaman, B. (2002). Recombinant poetics: Emergent explorations of digital video in virtual space. In M. Rieser & A. Zapp (Eds.), *New screen media: Cinema/art/narrative* (pp. 237–255). London: British Film Institute.

Selin, C. (2007). Expectations and the emergence of nanotechnology. *Science, Technology & Human Values*, *32*(2), 196–220. doi:10.1177/0162243906296918

Sermon, P. (1992). *Telematic dreaming*. An exhibition curated by the Finnish Ministry of Culture in Kajaani, with support from Telecom Finland, in June 1992. Retrieved from http://creativetechnology.salford.ac.uk/paulsermon/dream/

Sermon, P. (1992). *Telematic dreaming*. Performance Installation. Available at: http://creativetechnology.salford.ac.uk/paulsermon/dream/

Sermon, P. (2005). *Unheimlich*. Multi-User Performance Installation. Available at: http://creativetechnology.salford.ac.uk/unheimlich/

Sermon, P., & Gould, C. (2009). *Picnic on the screen*. Interactive Public Video Installation. Available at: http://creativetechnology.salford.ac.uk/paulsermon/picnic/

Shaer, O., & Hornecker, E. (2010). *Tangible user interfaces*. Delft: Now Publishers Inc.

Shaffer, D., Squire, K., Halverson, R., & Gee, J. (2005). Video games and the future of learning. *Phi Delta Kappan*, *87*(2), 104–111. doi:10.1177/003172170508700205

Shanken, E. (1998). The house that jack built: Jack Burnham's concept of "software" as a metaphor for art. *Leonardo Electronic Almanac*, *6*(10). Retrieved July 14, 2014, from http://www.artexetra.com/House.html

Shanken, E. (Ed.). (2009). *Art and electronic media*. London: Phaidon Press.

Sharma, A. (1999). Central dilemmas of managing innovation in large firms. *California Management Review*, *41*(3), 146–164. doi:10.2307/41166001

Shashaani, L. (1997). Gender differences in computer attitudes and use among college students. *Journal of Educational Computing Research Issue*, *16*(1), 37–51. doi:10.2190/Y8U7-AMMA-WQUT-R512

Shearer, J. E. (2013). High-fidelity simulation and safety: An integrative review. *The Journal of Nursing Education*, *52*(1), 39-45. doi: 10.3928/01484834-20121121-01

Sheikh, T., Javed, O., & Kanade, D. (2009). Background subtraction for freely moving cameras. In *Proceedings of IEEE 12th Int.Conference on Computer Vision*. IEEE.

Shelley, M. (2010). *Frankenstein*. London, UK: Harper Collins Classics.

Sherman, W., & Craig, A. (2003). *Understanding virtual reality: Interface, application, and design*. San Francisco, CA: Morgan Kaufmann.

Shibata, M., Yasuda, Y., & Ito, M. (2008). Moving object detection for active camera based on optical flow distortion. In *Proc. of the 17th World Congress the International Federation of Automatic Control* (pp. 720–725). Academic Press.

Shields, R. (2003). *The virtual*. London: Routledge.

Shove, E., Watson, M., Hand, M., & Ingram, J. (2007). *The design of everyday life*. Oxford, UK: Berg.

Shuter, R. (2012). *When Indian women text message: Culture, identity, and emerging interpersonal norms of new media*. Retrieved October 16, 2014, from http://epublications.marquette.edu/cgi/viewcontent.cgi?article=1109&context=comm_fac

Sider, L. F., & Sider, J. (2003). Soundscape. The school of sound lectures 1998-2001. London: Wallflower Press.

Siikala, A.-L. (2002). *Mythic images and shamanism*. Helskinki: Academia Scientiarum Fennica.

Silvern, S. B., & Williamson, P. A. (1987). The effects of video game play on young children's aggression, fantasy, and prosocial behavior. *Journal of Applied Developmental Psychology*, *8*(4), 453–462. doi:10.1016/0193-3973(87)90033-5

Simard, C., & Gammal, D. (2012). *Solutions to recruit technical women*. Retrieved December 1, 2014, from http://anitaborg.org/wp-content/uploads/2014/01/AnitaBorgInstitute_SolutionsToRecruitTechnicalWomen_2012.pdf

Simmel, G. (2006). The adventurer. In J. Cosgrave (Ed.), *The sociology of risk and gambling behaviour* (pp. 215–224). New York: Routledge. (Original work published 1911)

Simondon, G. (1989). *Du mode d'Existence des Objets Techniques*. Paris: Aubier.

Simon, H. (1973). The structure of ill structured problems. *Artificial Intelligence*, *4*(3-4), 181–201. doi:10.1016/0004-3702(73)90011-8

Singh, R., Bhalla, A., Lehl, S. S., & Sachdev, A. (2001). Video game epilepsy. *Neurology India*, *49*(4), 411–412. PMID:11799420

Skalli, L. (2013). Young women and social media against sexual harassment in North Africa. *Journal of North African Studies*, *18*(5), 244–258.

Skilton, P. F., & Dooley, K. J. (2010). The effects of repeat collaboration on creative abrasion. *Academy of Management Journal*, *35*, 118–134.

Smirnoff, A. (2011). *Graphical sound*. Moscow: Theremin Centre. Retrieved on May 3, 2011 from http://asmir.info/graphical_sound.htm

Smith, A. (1982). John Cage the mycologist. In P. Gena & J. Brent (Eds.), *A John Cage reader* (pp. 165–166). New York: Peters.

Smith, C., Rieser, M., & Saul, S. (Eds.). (2010). *Inside out: Sculpture in the digital age*. Leicester, UK: De Montfort University.

Smudge Studio. (2010). *Geologic time viewer*. Retrieved from http://www.smudgestudio.org/smudge/projects/MIT/timeviewer.html

Smudge Studio. (2014a). *For future north*. Retrieved from http://smudgestudio.org/smudge/change.html

Smudge Studio. (2014b). *Pompeii of the north: Heimaey*. Retrieved from http://fopnews.wordpress.com/2014/06/05/heimaey/

Smudge Studio. (2014c). *Turning at the limits of the urban: Tjuvhommen*. Retrieved from http://fopnews.wordpress.com/2014/06/06/thief/

Snyder, S. (2013). *The simple, the complicated, and the complex: Educational reform through the lens of complexity theory* (OECD Education Working Papers, No. 96). Paris: OECD Publishing.

Snyder, L. (2009). *Masdar City: The source of inspiration or uneconomical spending?* Repps Hudson.

Sobchack, V. (1992). *The address of the eye: A phenomenology of film experience*. Princeton University Press.

Sohn, J., Kim, T. J., & Hewings, G. (2004). Intrametropolitan agglomeration, information technology, and polycentric urban development. In R. Cappelo & P. Nijkamp (Eds.), *Contributions to economic analysis*. Elsevier. doi:10.1016/S0573-8555(04)66008-1

Soja, E. W. (1996). *Thirdspace: Journeys to Los Angeles and other real-and-imagined places*. Malden, MA: Blackwell Publishers.

Solarski, C. (2012). *Drawing basics and video game art: Classic to cutting-edge art techniques for winning video game design*. New York: Watson-Guptill.

Solet, D. J., Norvell, J. M., Rutan, G. H., & Frankel, R. M. (2005). Lost in translation: Challenges and opportunities in physician-to-physician communication during patient handoffs. *Academic Medicine, 80*(12), 1094–1099. doi:10.1097/00001888-200512000-00005 PMID:16306279

Somolu, O. (2007). "Telling our own stories": African women blogging for social change. *Gender and Development, 15*(3), 477–490. doi:10.1080/13552070701630640

Sorenson, B., Meyer, B., & Eigenfeldt-Nielsen, S. (Eds.). (2011). *Serious games in education: A global perspective*. Copenhagen: Aarhus University Press.

Sparks, J. A. (1986). *The effect of microcomputers in the home on computer literacy test scores*. Central Missouri State University.

Spera, C., Wentzel, K. R., & Matto, H. C. (2009). Parental aspirations for their children's educational attainment: Relations to ethnicity, parental education, children's academic performance, and parental perceptions of school climate. *Journal of Youth and Adolescence, 38*(8), 1140–1152. doi:10.1007/s10964-008-9314-7 PMID:19636777

Squier, S. M. (2004). *Liminal lives: Imagining the human at the frontiers of biomedicine*. Durham, NC: Duke University Press. doi:10.1215/9780822386285

Squire, K. (2008). Open-ended video games: A model for developing learning for the interactive age. In K. Salen (Ed.), *The ecology of games: Connecting youth, games and learning* (pp. 167–198). Cambridge, MA: MIT Press.

Squire, K. (2008b). Video game literacy: A literacy of expertise. In J. Coiro, M. Knobel, C. Lankshear, & D. Leu (Eds.), *Handbook of research on new literacies* (pp. 635–669). New York: Lawerence Erlbaum Associates.

Stables, K., Benson, C., & de Vries, M. (2011). PATT 25: CRIPT 8: Perspectives on learning in design & technology education. Goldsmiths, University of London.

Steeves, J. B. (2007). *Imagining bodies: Merleau-Ponty's philosophy of imagination*. Pittsburgh, PA: Duquesne University Press.

Steffen, W., Grinevald, J., Crutzen, P., & McNeill, J. (2011). The anthropocene: Conceptual and historical perspectives. *Philosophical Transactions of the Royal Society A: Mathematical, Physical and Engineering Sciences, 369*(1938), 842-867.

Stelarc. (2003) *Exoskeleton*. 2nd Biennale of Contemporary Art in Goteborg Museum of Art, Goteborg, Sweden. Retrieved from http://stelarc.org/video/?catID=20258

Sternberg, R. J., & Lubart, T. I. (1996). Investing in creativity. *The American Psychologist, 51*(7), 677–688. doi:10.1037/0003-066X.51.7.677

Sternberg, R. J., & O'Hara, L. A. (1999). Creativity and intelligence. In R. J. Sternberg (Ed.), *Handbook of creativity* (pp. 251–272). Cambridge, UK: Cambridge University Press.

Sternberg, R. J., O'Hara, L. A., & Lubart, T. I. (1997). Creativity as investment. *California Management Review*, *40*(1), 8–21. doi:10.2307/41165919

Stockburger, A. (2007). Playing the third place: Spatial modalities in contemporary game environments. *International Journal of Performance Arts and Digital Media*, *3*(2&3), 223–236. doi:10.1386/padm.3.2-3.223_1

Stokes, M., & Maltby, R. (Eds.). (1999). *American movie audiences*. London: BFI.

Stokstad, M. (2002). *Art history: Volume two* (2nd ed.). New York: Harry N. Abrams, Inc.

Strindberg, A. (2000). A dream play. In August Strindberg, plays: Two (M. Mayer, Trans.; pp. 175-254). London: Methuen. (Original work published 1902)

Stuckey, H., & Nobel, J. (2010). The connection between art, healing, and public health: A review of current literature. *American Journal of Public Health*, *100*(2), 254–263. doi:10.2105/AJPH.2008.156497 PMID:20019311

Subcommission on Quaternary Stratigraphy. (2014). *Working group on the 'anthropocene'*. Retrieved from http://quaternary.stratigraphy.org/workinggroups/anthropocene/

Sumrell, R., & Varnelis, K. (2007). Love: In Blue monday: Stories of absurd realities and natural philosophies (pp. 134-144). Actar Publishers.

Sutherland, I. (1965). The ultimate display. In *Proceedings IFIP Congress* (pp. 506-508). IFIP.

Sutton, P. (1989). *Dreamings: Art from Aboriginal Australia*. Melbourne: Viking/ Penguin.

Swammerdam, J. (1681). *Ephemeri vita, or, the natural history and anatomy of the ephemeron, a fly that lives but five hours*. London: Henry Faithorne and John Kersey. (Original work published 1645). Retrieved from Ann Arbor, Michigan: University of Michigan, Digital Library Production Service: http://trove.nla.gov.au/version/31186689

Swyngedouw, E., Moulaert, F., & Rodriguez, A. (2002). Neoliberal urbanization in europe: Large-scale urban development projects and the new urban policy. *Antipode*, *34*(3), 542–577. doi:10.1111/1467-8330.00254

Tabor, M. (1989). *Chaos and integrability in nonlinear dynamics: An introduction*. New York: Wiley.

Tacitus, C. (2009). Germania. (H. Mattingly, trans; J. Rives, revised). Oxford, UK: Oxford University Press. (Original work published 96AD)

Tampabay.com. (2012). *Comments policy*. Retrieved January 22, 2012, from http://www.tampabay.com/universal/comment_guidelines.shtml

Tangey, J., & Fischer, K. W. (1995). *Self conscious emotions: The psyhology of shame, guilt, embarassement and pride*. New York: Guilford Press.

Tanner, D. A., Padrick, K. P., Westfall, U. E., & Putzier, D. J. (1987). Diagnostic reasoning strategies of nurses and nursing students. *Nursing Research*, *36*(6), 358–365. doi:10.1097/00006199-198711000-00010 PMID:3671123

Tatalović Vorkapić, S. & Milovanović, S. (2013). Computer use in the preschool age: The attitudes of future preschool teachers. *Education 3-13: International Journal of Primary, Elementary and Early Years Education*, 1-13. 10.1080/03004279.2012.673003

Tátar, M. (1996). Mythology as an areal problem in the Altai-Sayan area. In J. Pentikäinen (Ed.), *Shamanism and northern ecology* (pp. 267–278). Berlin: Mouton de Gruyter. doi:10.1515/9783110811674.267

Tatković, N. & Ružić Baf, M. (2011). Računalo – Komunikacijski izazov djeci predškolske dobi. *27 Informatologia*, *44*(1), 27-30.

Taylor, D. W., Berry, P. C., & Block, C. H. (1958). Does group participation when using brainstorming facilitate or inhibit creative thinking? *Administrative Science Quarterly*, *3*(1), 23–47. doi:10.2307/2390603

Tazawa, Y., Soukalo, A. V., Okada, K., & Takada, G. (1997). Excessive playing of home computer games by children presenting unexplained symptoms. *The Journal of Pediatrics*, *130*(6), 1010–1011. doi:10.1016/S0022-3476(97)70298-1 PMID:9202632

Terzidis, K. (2009). *Algorithms for visual design*. Indianapolis, IN: Wiley Publishing.

Thackeray, R., Neiger, B. L., Hanson, C. L., & McKenzie, J. F. (2008). Enhancing promotional strategies within social marketing programs: Use of web 2.0 social media. *Health Promotion Practice*, 9(4), 338–343. doi:10.1177/1524839908325335 PMID:18936268

Thierauf, R. (1995). *Virtual reality systems for business*. Westport, CT: Quorum.

Thomas, M. (2005). Playing with chance and choice – Orality, narrativity and cinematic media. In B. Bushoff (Ed.), Developing interactive narrative content (pp. 371- 442). Sagas/Sagas.net Reader. Munich: High Text.

Thomas, M. (2008). Digitality and immaterial culture: What did Viking women think? *International Journal of Digital Cultural Heritage and Electronic Tourism*, 1(2), 177–199. doi:10.1504/IJDCET.2008.021406

Thomas, M., Selsjord, M., & Zimmer, R. (2011). Museum or mausoleum? Electronic shock therapy. In M. Lytras, E. Damiani, L. Diaz, & P. Ordonez de Pablos (Eds.), *Digital culture and e-tourism: Technologies, applications and management* (pp. 10–35). Hershey, PA: IGI Global. doi:10.4018/978-1-61520-867-8.ch002

Thomas, P. (2007). Boundaryless nanomorphologies. In *MutaMorphosis: Challenging art and sciences*. Prague, Czech Republic: MutaMorphosis.

Thomas, P. (2009). Midas: A nanotechnological exploration of touch. *Leonardo*, 42(3), 186–192. doi:10.1162/leon.2009.42.3.186

Thompson, R., & Bowen, C. J. (2009). *Grammar of the shot* (2nd ed.). Amsterdam: Focal Press.

Thorburn, D., & Jenkins, H. (2003). *Rethinking media change*. Cambridge, MA: MIT Press.

Thorne, K. (1994). *Black holes and time warps*. Norton & Co.

Tisdall, C., & Bozzola, A. (1978). *Futurism*. London: Thames and Hudson.

Todd, K. (2007). *Chrysalis: Maria Sybilla Merian and the secrets of metamorphosis*. London: I.B. Tauris.

Tolkien, J. R. R. (1954/5). *The lord of the rings*. London: George Allen & Unwin.

Tolstoy, L. (2011). *What is art?* Bristol, UK: Bristol Classical Press. (Original work published 1896)

Toseland, M., & Toseland, S. (2012). *Infographica: The world as you have never seen it before*. London, UK: Quercus Publishing Plc.

Transmediale Archive. (2014). *Amundsen/l-landscape*. Retrieved from http://www.transmediale.de/amundsen-i-landscape-en

Transmediale. (2014). *Transmediale.09 deep north*. Retrieved from http://www.transmediale.de/past/2009

Trilling, B., & Fadel, C. (2009). *21st century skills: Learning for life in our times*. San Francisco, CA: Jossey-Bass.

Tripp, S. D., & Bichelmeyer, B. (1990). Rapid prototyping: An alternative instructional design strategy. *Educational Technology Research and Development*, 38(1), 31–44. doi:10.1007/BF02298246

Trischler, H. (Ed.). (2013). *Anthropocene: Envisioning the future of the age of humans* (Vol. 3). Munich, Germany: Rachel Carson Center for Environment and Society.

Truckenbrod, J. (2008). *Digital ritual and ceremony*. Paper presented at College Art Association Conference, Los Angeles CA.

Truckenbrod, J. (2010). *Video sculpture*. Paper presented at the International Sculpture Conference, London, UK.

Truckenbrod, J. (2011). *Transforming the physicality of emotion*. Paper presented at ISEA Conference, Istanbul, Turkey.

Truckenbrod, J. (2012). *The paradoxical object: Video film sculpture*. London: Black Dog Publishers.

Tschannen, D., & Aebersold, M. (2010). *Second Life: Innovative simulation development-making it REAL!* Meaningful Play.

Tschannen, D., Aebersold, M., Sauter, C., & Funnell, M. M. (2013). Improving nurses' perceptions of competency in diabetes self-management education through the use of simulation and problem-based learning. *Journal of Continuing Education in Nursing*, 44(6), 257–263. doi:10.3928/00220124-20130402-16 PMID:23565600

Tufte, E. (1983). *The visual display of quantitative information*. Cheshire, CT: Graphics Press.

Tufte, E. (1997). *Visual explanations: Images and quantities, evidence and narrative*. Cheshire, CT: Graphics Press.

Turpin, E. (Ed.). (2013). *Architecture in the anthropocene: Encounteres among design, deep time, science and philosophy*. Open Humanities Press, University of Michigan. doi:10.3998/ohp.12527215.0001.001

Turville-Petre, E. O. G. (1976). *Scaldic poetry*. Oxford, UK: Clarendon Press.

United Nations Educational, Scientific and Cultural Organization (UNESCO). (2014). *Dorset and east Devon coast*. Retrieved from http://whc.unesco.org/en/list/1029

Urban Institute. (2011). *Evaluating the use of pulic surveillance cameras for crime control and prevention* (Final Technical Report). Author.

Ursu, M. F., Zsombori, V., Wyver, J., Conrad, L., Kegel, I., & Williams, D. (2009). Interactive documentaries: A golden age. In Computers in entertainment. New York, NY: ACM. Retrieved from http://dl.acm.org/citation.cfm?doid=1594943.1594953 doi:10.1145/1594943.1594953

Ursu, M. F., Kegel, I., Williams, D., Thomas, M., Mayer, H., Zsombori, V., & Wyver, J. et al. (2008). ShapeShifting TV: Interactive screen media narratives. *Multimedia Systems*, *14*(2), 115–132. doi:10.1007/s00530-008-0119-z

Ursu, M. F., Thomas, M., Tuomola, M., Wright, T., Williams, D., & Zsombori, V. (2007). Interactivity and narrativity in screen media. In *Proceedings of the IEEE Symposium on Multimedia Systems* (pp. 227-232). IEEE Computer Society.

US Department of Commerce. (1995). *Falling through the net: A survey of the "have nots" in rural and urban America*. Retrieved from http://www.ntia.doc.gov/ntia-home/fallingthru.html

US Department of Commerce. (1998). *Falling through the net II: New data on the digital divide*. Retrieved from http://www.ntia.doc.gov/report/1998/falling-through-net-ii-new-data-digital-divide

US Department of Commerce. (1999). *Falling through the net: Defining the digital divide*. Retrieved from http://www.ntia.doc.gov/report/1999/falling-through-net-defining-digital-divide

Utjecaj kompjutera na IQ djece. (n.d.). Accessed 12.1.2014, from (http://www.*roda*.hr/article/read/utjecaj-kompjutera-na-iq-djece).

Van Knippenberg, D., & Schippers, M. (2007). Work group diversity. *Annual Review of Psychology*, *58*(1), 515–541. doi:10.1146/annurev.psych.58.110405.085546 PMID:16903805

Van Ness, E. (2005, March 6). Is a cinema studies degree the New M.B.A.? *New York Times*, p. M1.

Van Sickle, K. R., McClusky, D. A., Gallagher, A. G., & Smith, C. D. (2005). Construct validation of the ProMIS simulator using a novel laparoscopic suturing task. *Surgical Endoscopy and Other Interventional Techniques*, *19*(9), 1227–1231. doi:10.1007/s00464-004-8274-6 PMID:16025195

Varela, F. J., Thompson, E., & Rosche, E. (1993). The embodied mind: Cognitive science and human experience. Cambridge, MA: The MIT Press.

Varela, F. J., Thompson, E., & Rosch, E. (1991). *The embodied mind*. Cambridge, MA: The MIT Press.

Velastin, S., Boghossian, B., & Vicencio-Silva, M. (2006). A motion-based image processing system for detecting potentially dangerous situations in underground railway stations. *Trans. Research Part C*, *14*(2), 96–113. doi:10.1016/j.trc.2006.05.006

Verenikina, I., & Belyaeva, A. (1992). *Sensitivity of preadolescents to complex activity in the computer mediated telecommunication environment*. Paper presented at East-West Human, Computer Interaction Conference, St.Petersburg, Russia.

Verenikina, I., Harris, P., & Lysaght, P. (2008). *Child's play: Computer games, theories of play and children's development*. University of Wollongong, Faculty of Education.

Verenikina, I., & Herrington, J. (2006). *Computer play, young children and the development of higher order thinking: exploring the possibilities.* Faculty of Education, University of Wollongong.

Verenikina, I., Herrington, J., & Peterson, R. (2008). *The affordances and limitations of computers for play in early childhood.* University of Wollongong.

Veron, E. (1988). *La sémiosis sociale: Fragments d'une theorie de la discursivité.* París: Presses Universitaires de Vincennes.

Vesna, V. (n.d.). *Nanomandala.* Retrieved from http://nano.arts.ucla.edu/mandala/mandala.php

Vesna, V. (n.d.). *Zero@wavefunction.* Retrieved from http://notime.arts.ucla.edu/zerowave/zerowave.html

Vickery, A. (Presenter), & Hodgson, J. (Producer/ Director) (2014, May). *The story of women and art* [television series]. United Kingdom: BBC2.

Vishwakarma, S., & Agrawal, A. (2013). A survey on activity recognition and behaviour understanding in video surveillance. *The Visual Computer, 29*(10), 983–1009. doi:10.1007/s00371-012-0752-6

Vitebsky, P. (1995). *The shaman.* London: Macmillan.

Vivek, S. D., Beatty, S. E., & Morgan, R. M. (2012). Customer engagement: Exploring customer relationships beyond purchase. *Journal of Marketing Theory and Practice, 20*(2), 127–145. doi:10.2753/MTP1069-6679200201

von Franz, M.-L. (1980). *On divination and synchronicity: The psychology of meaningful chance.* Toronto: Inner City Books.

Voss, P., Collignon, O., Lassonde, M., & Lepore, F. (2010). Adaptation to sensory loss. *Wiley Interdisciplinary Reviews: Cognitive Science, 1*(3), 308–328. doi:10.1002/wcs.13

Vygotsky, L. (1978). *Mind in society.* Cambridge, MA: Harvard University Press.

Vygotsky, L. S. (1977). Play and its role in the mental development of the child. In *Play: Its role in development and evolution.* New York: Basic Books.

W3C. (2014). *World wide web consortium (W3C).* Retrieved July 14, 2014, from http://w3.org

Walker Bynum, C. (2001). *Metamorphosis and identity.* New York: Zone Books.

Wang, Y., & Horvath, I. (2013). Computer-aided multi-scale materials and product design. *Computer Aided Design, 45*(1), 1–3. doi:10.1016/j.cad.2012.07.013

Wardrip-Fruin, N. (2009). *Expressive processing.* Cambridge, MA: MIT Press.

Ward, T., Smith, S., & Finke, R. (1999). Creative cognition. In R. Sternberg (Ed.), *Handbook of creativity* (pp. 189–212). Cambridge, UK: Cambridge University Press.

Ware, C. (2004). *Information visualization: Perception for design.* San Francisco, CA: Morgan Kaufmann.

Warr, A., & O'Neill, E. (2005). Understanding design as a social creative process. In *Proceedings of the 5th Conference on Creativity & Cognition* (pp. 118-127). New York: ACM Press. doi:10.1145/1056224.1056242

Warschauer, M. (1996). *Motivational aspects of using computers for writing and communication.* Retrieved from http://nflrc.hawaii.edu/NetWorks/NW01/NW01.html

Warschauer, M. (1996). Computer assisted language learning: An introduction. In *Multimedia language teaching* (pp. 3–20). Tokyo: Logos International.

Waters, N. (1996). Street surveillance and privacy. *PLPR, 3,* 48.

Waterworth, E., & Waterworth, J. (2010). Mediated presence in the future. In C. C. Bracken & P. D. Skalaski (Eds.), *Immersed in media: Telepresence in everyday life* (pp. 183–196). New York, NY: Routledge.

Wayne, D. B., Didwania, A., Feinglass, J., Fudala, M. J., Barsuk, J. H., & McGaghie, W. C. (2008). Simulation-based education improves quality of care during cardiac arrest team responses at an academic teaching hospital: A case-control study. *Chest, 133*(1), 56–61. doi:10.1378/chest.07-0131 PMID:17573509

Webster, W. R. (2004). The diffusion, regulation and governance of closed-circuit television in the UK. *Surveillance and Society, 2*(2/3), 230-250.

Webster, W. R. (2004). *The policy process and governance in the information age: The case of closed circuit television.* (Unpublished PhD Thesis). Glasgow Caledonian University, Glasgow, UK.

Wells, P. (1998). *Understanding animation.* London: Routledge.

West, M. A., & Altink, W. M. (1996). Innovation at work: Individual, group, organizational, and socio-historical perspectives. *European Journal of Work and Organizational Psychology, 5*(1), 3–11. doi:10.1080/13594329608414834

West, M. A., & Anderson, N. R. (1996). Innovation in top management teams. *The Journal of Applied Psychology, 81*(6), 680–693. doi:10.1037/0021-9010.81.6.680

Wexelblat, A. (1993). *Virtual reality: Applications and explorations.* Waltham, MA: Academic Press.

Wharburton, S. (2009). Second Life in higher education: Assessing the potential for and the barriers to deploying virtual worlds in learning and teaching. *British Journal of Educational Technology, 40*(3), 414–426. doi:10.1111/j.1467-8535.2009.00952.x

Wheatley, M. (1999). *Leadership and the new science: Discovering order in a chaotic world* (2nd ed.). San Francisco, CA: Berrett-Koehler.

Wheatley, M., & Kellner-Rogers, M. (1996). *A simpler way.* San Francisco, CA: Berrett-Koehler.

Wheeler, M. (1964). *Roman art and architecture.* London: Thames and Hudson.

Where Do We Start? (n.d.). Accessed 30.02.2014, from https://www.thinkuknow.co.uk/parents/Primary/Conversation-Starters/)

Whitehead, I. (2010). *Models of sustainability? A comparative analysis of ideal city planning in Saltaire and Masdar City.* Academic Press.

Whitehead, A. (1971). *The concept of nature.* Cambridge, UK: Cambridge University Press. (Original work published 1920)

Whitelaw, M. (2010). *Measuring cup (Sydney, 1859-2009).* Retrieved August 20, 2014, from http://mtchl.net/measuring-cup/

Whitelaw, M. (2004). *Metacreation: Art and artificial life.* London: MIT Press.

Wickers, M. P. (2010). Establishing the climate for a successful debriefing. *Clinical Simulation in Nursing, 6*(3), e83–e86. doi:10.1016/j.ecns.2009.06.003

Wiggins, S. (1990). *Introduction to applied nonlinear dynamical systems and chaos.* New York: Springer-Verlag. doi:10.1007/978-1-4757-4067-7

Wikipedia. (2014a). *List of data structures.* Retrieved July 14, 2014, from https://en.wikipedia.org/wiki/List_of_data_structures

Wikipedia. (2014b). *List of algorithms.* Retrieved July 14, 2014, from https://en.wikipedia.org/wiki/List_of_algorithms

Wilke, S. (2013). Anthropocenic poetics: Ethics and aesthetics in a new geological age. In H. Trischler (Ed.), *Anthropocene: Envisioning the future of the age of humans* (pp. 67–74). Munich, Germany: Rachel Carson Center for Environment and Society.

Willerslev, R. (2007). *Soul hunters: Hunting, animism, and personhood among the Siberian Yukaghirs.* Ewing, NJ: University of California Press. doi:10.1525/california/9780520252165.001.0001

Wilson, M., & van Ruiten, S. (Eds.). (2014). *SHARE handbook for artistic research education.* Retrieved from http://www.sharenetwork.eu/resources/share-handbook

Winograd, T., & Flores, F. (1986). *Understanding computers and cognition: A new foundation for design.* New York: Addison Wesley.

Wittkower, R. (1977). *Sculpture, processes and principles.* London: Penguin.

Woolley, A., & Malone, T. (2011). What makes a team smarter? More women. *Harvard Business Review, 89*(6), 32–33. PMID:21714385

Worden, S. (2014). The earth sciences and creative practice: Exploring boundaries between digital and material culture. In D. Harrison (Ed.), *Digital media and technologies for virtual artistic spaces* (pp. 186–204). Hershey, PA: IGI Global. doi:10.4018/978-1-4666-5125-8.ch062

Works Corporation. (2004). *Japanese games graphics: Behind the scenes of your favourite games*. New York: Harper Collins Design International.

World Health Organization (WHO). (2010). *Framework for action on interprofessional education & collaborative practice*. Geneva: World Health Organization. Retrieved August 30, 2014 from http://www.who.int/hrh/resources/framework_action/en/

World Summit on the Informational Society. (2003). *Declaration of principles: Building the information society: A global challenge in the new millennium*. Retrieved from http://www.itu.int/wsis/docs/geneva/official/dop.html

Wotanis, L., & McMillan, L. (2014). Performing gender on YouTube. *Feminist Media Studies*, *14*(6), 1–17. doi: 10.1080/14680777.2014.882373

Wright, C. R. (1986). *Mass communication: A sociological perspective*. New York: Random House.

Wu, C. H., Cheng, Y., Ip, H. M., & Mcbride-Chang, C. (2005). Age differences in creativity: Task structure and knowledge base. *Creativity Research Journal*, *17*(4), 321–326. doi:10.1207/s15326934crj1704_3

Wurtzler, S. J. (2007). *Electric sounds: Technological change and the rise of corporate mass media*. New York: Columbia University Press.

Yahoo Developer Network. (2014). *Yahoo design pattern library*. Retrieved July 14, 2014, from https://developer.yahoo.com/ypatterns/

Yau, N. (2013). *Data points: Visualization that means something*. Indianapolis, IN: John Wiley & Sons.

Ybarra, M., Diener-West, M., Markow, D., Leaf, P. J., Hamburger, M., & Boxer, P. (2008). Linkages between internet and other media violence with seriously violent behavior by youth. *Pediatrics*, *122*(5), 929–937. doi:10.1542/peds.2007-3377 PMID:18977970

Yelland, N. (2005). The future is now: A review of the literature on the use of computers in early childhood education (1994–2004). *AACE Journal*, *13*(3), 201–232.

Yigitcanlar, T., & Han, J. H. (2010). Ubiquitous eco cities: Telecommunication infrastructure, technology convergence and urban management. *International Journal of Advanced Pervasive and Ubiquitous Computing*, *2*(1), 1–17. doi:10.4018/japuc.2010010101

Yilmaz, A., Javed, O., & Shah, M. (2006). Object tracking: A survey. *ACM Computing Surveys*, *38*(4), 1–45. doi:10.1145/1177352.1177355

Yokokoji, M., & Harwood, G. (2014). *Wrecked*. Retrieved from http://yoha.co.uk/wrecked

Yokoyama, M., & Poggio, T. (2005). A contour-based moving object detection and tracking. In *Proceedings of 2nd Joint IEEE Int. Workshop on Visual Surveillance and Performance Evaluation of Tracking and Surveillance* (pp. 271–276). IEEE. doi:10.1109/VSPETS.2005.1570925

Youngblood, P., Harter, P. M., Srivastava, S., Moffett, S., Heinrichs, W. L., & Dev, P. (2008). Design, development, and evaluation of an online virtual emergency department for training trauma teams. *Simulation in Healthcare*, *3*(3), 146–153. doi:10.1097/SIH.0b013e31817bedf7 PMID:19088658

Young, K. (1996). Psyhology of the computer use. XL.addictive use of the internet: A case that breaks the stereotype. *Psychological Reports*, *79*(3), 899–902. doi:10.2466/pr0.1996.79.3.899 PMID:8969098

Youngs, G. (2008). Public/private: The hidden dimensions of international communication. In K. Sarikakis & L. R. Shade (Eds.), *Feminist interventions in international communication: Mind the gap* (pp. 17–29). Lanham, MD: Rowman & Littlefield.

Zapp, A. (2002). *The imaginary hotel*. Networked Installation. Available at: https://www.digitalartarchive.at/database/general/work/the-imaginary-hotel.html

Zapp, A. (2005). *Human avatars*. Interactive Installation. Available: http://www.art.mmu.ac.uk/profile/azapp/projectdetails/228

Zellweger, C. (2007). *Christoph Zellweger*. Retrieved April 20, 2011, from http://www.christophzellweger.com/

Zhang, Y. W. (July 5, 2011). 网络时代也要好好说话 [Speaking with civility in social media age]. *Beijing Morning Post*. Retrieved January 16, 2014, from http://www.donews.com/net/201107/526203.shtm

Zhang, D., Gatica-Perez, D., Bengio, S., & McCowan, I. (2006). Modeling individual and group actions in meetings with layered hmms. *IEEE Transactions on Multimedia*, *8*(3), 509–520. doi:10.1109/TMM.2006.870735

Zhang, W., & Kramarae, C. (2008). Feminist invitational collaboration in a digital age: Looking over disciplinary and national borders. *Women & Language*, *36*(2), 9–19.

Zhang, W., & Kramarae, C. (2012). Women, big ideas, and social newtworking technologies: Hidden assumptions. In R. Pande, T. van der Weide, & N. Flipsen (Eds.), *Globalization, technology diffusion and gender disparity: Social impacts of ICT* (pp. 70–82). Hershey, PA: IGI Global.

Zhang, W., & Kramarae, C. (2014). "Slutwalk" on connected screens: Multiple framings of a social media discussion. *Journal of Pragmatics*, *73*, 66–81. doi:10.1016/j.pragma.2014.07.008

Zhou, J. (1998). Feedback valence, feedback style, task autonomy, and achievement orientation: Interactive effects on creative performance. *The Journal of Applied Psychology*, *83*(2), 261–276. doi:10.1037/0021-9010.83.2.261

Zhou, J. (2003). When the presence of creative coworkers is related to creativity: Role of supervisor close monitoring, developmental feedback, and creative personality. *The Journal of Applied Psychology*, *88*(3), 413–422. doi:10.1037/0021-9010.88.3.413 PMID:12814291

Ziarek, K. (2011). The limits of life. *Angelaki*, *16*(4), 19–30.

Zielinski, S. (1996). Thinking the border and the boundary. In Electronic culture: Technology and visual representation. Aperture Foundation.

Zielinski, S. (2006). *Deep time of the media: Toward an archaeology of hearing and seeing by technical means*. Cambridge, MA: MIT Press.

Zizek, S. (1992). *Looking awry: An introduction to Jacques Lacan through popular culture*. Cambridge, MA: The MIT Press.

Žižek, S. (1999). Is it possible to traverse the fantasy in cyberspace? In E. Wright & E. Wright (Eds.), *The Žižek reader* (pp. 102–124). Oxford, UK: Blackwell.

Žižek, S. (2006). *Interrogating the real*. London: Continnum.

Žižek, S. (2007). *The indivisible remainder: On Schelling and related matters*. London: Verso.

Žižek, S. (2008a). *The plague of fantasies*. London: Verso.

Žižek, S. (2008b). *The sublime object of ideology*. London: Verso.

Žižek, S. (2009). *The parallax view*. Cambridge, MA: MIT Press.

Žižek, S. (2012). *Organs without bodies: On Deleuze and consequences*. London: Routledge.

About the Contributors

Dew Harrison is Professor of Digital Media Art at the University of Wolverhampton, where she is Chair of the University Professoriate and Director of the CADRE research centre. With a BA in Fine Art, an MSc in Computer Science, an MA in the History and Theory of Contemporary Art, and a PhD from the Planetary Collegium, CAiiA, in Interactive Art, her practice undertakes a critical exploration of Conceptual Art, semantic media, and intuitive interfaces, which bridge the virtual to the real world. She often works collaboratively and considers digital curation as a form of art practice. Her early work in hypermedia articulates the creative thinking of Marcel Duchamp as the initiator of conceptual practice. More recent works concern the application of human-like behaviours to virtual objects and have extended from exploring the ideas of Duchamp to that of the "big idea" of Darwin culminating in the "Shift-Life" hands-on interactive installation commissioned for the Darwin bicentenary 2009. She continues to exhibit internationally and has over 70 publications to date spanning digital art, media art history, new media theory, interactive games, museology, and consciousness studies.

* * *

Michelle Aebersold is a Clinical Assistant Professor and Director of the Clinical Learning Center. Her program of scholarship focuses on the science of learning applied in simulation to align clinician and student practice behaviors with research evidence to improve population health. She has worked extensively with virtual environments, learning technologies and high-fidelity simulation. She was a recent presenter at TEDxUofM-on simulation in nursing education, her talk was titled. "One patient… so many lives!"

Maha Al Merekhi is the Director of Strategic Planning in Qatar Foundation. Ms. Maha studied Economics at Qatar University and she currently pursues her Master's Degree at Hamad Bin Khalifa University, Faculty of Islamic Studies, Public Policy in Islam Program.

François Allard-Huver is interested in questions dealing with transparency policies and communication strategies in European and French Institutions, especially risk assessment authorities like EFSA (European Food Safety Autority) or ANSES (the French Agency for Food, Environmental and Occupational Health & Safety). His dissertation deals with transparency, GMOs and pesticides controversies in the public sphere. He is interested in the question of frankness (parrhesia in Foucaldian theory) in the public sphere, as well as in the digital media strategies of risk assessment authorities and civil society actors.

Garfield Benjamin is a digital artist and cultural theorist working with new conceptions of the relation between consciousness and technology. Having previously studied electroacoustic composition and mixed media digital art with BEAST at the University of Birmingham, Garfield Benjamin has been undertaking a doctoral studentship in the Centre for Art, Design, Research and Experimentation at the University of Wolverhampton, where he has recently submitted a thesis entitled 'The Cyborg Subject: Parallax Realities, Functions of Consciousness and the Void of Subjectivity'. His digital art practice involves interactive works, avatar-mediated spaces and computer animation, incorporating a remediation of cultural artefacts from both the arcane and the ultramodern, fusing alchemy with 'geek' culture and an often harsh, fractal, digital aesthetic. Research interests include the work of Žižek and Deleuze, the philosophy of quantum physics, science fiction, computer games and digital art theory.

Paul Chilsen started in Film and TV in Los Angeles, but left to pursue graduate school at Columbia College Chicago where he made the Student Academy Award-nominated short Gross Ratings. Paul was a Follet Fellow at Columbia and did postgraduate work at UW-Madison. He has directed and written feature films, documentaries, and Emmy Award-winning TV. A filmmaker and published author, he has taught at Columbia, Northwestern and Carthage. Through the Rosebud Institute and Carthage, his focus is defining and using digital media to enhance screen media literacy.

Lily Cushenbery is an Assistant Professor of Management at Stony Brook University. Her research focuses on 1) the process by which leaders overcome failures and 2) the dynamics of innovative teams. Her primary research examines the consequences of leader mistakes and mistake recovery on leader-follower relationships. Her innovation research includes constructs such as team member influence, team climate, and malevolence. Dr. Cushenbery received her PhD in Industrial-Organizational Psychology from Penn State University.

Denise Doyle is an Artist-Researcher, and Senior Lecturer in Digital Media at the University of Wolverhampton, and Adjunct Professor in Virtual Worlds and Digital Practice, Ontario College of Art and Design University (OCAD U), Toronto, Canada with a background in Fine Art Painting and Digital Media. During her PhD research she developed an art laboratory space in the virtual world, Second Life, to investigate creative practice in virtual world spaces. Denise has published widely on the subject of the virtual and the imaginary, the experience of the avatar body in virtual worlds and game spaces, and the use of virtual worlds for creative practice. She sits on two editorial boards: the International Journal of Performance Art and Digital Media (Routledge) and the Journal of Gaming and Virtual Worlds (Intellect). Her research interests include: virtual worlds, art-sci dialogues, interactive film, philosophies of the imagination, practice-based research methods, phenomenological research methods, and digital narratives. She is currently developing a project entitled Astronauts and Avatars exploring bodies in real and virtual space.

Hanaa Elghaish is a researcher. She got a Master of Art in public Policy in Islam and a Diploma in Islamic Studies in Qatar Faculty of Islamic Studies, which is a member of of Hamad Bin Khalifa University in Qatar. Dr. Hanaaâ€™s main research interests are in political/social studies (particularly connections between good governance, Arab societies problems and Islamic values as a framework). She is the author of The Role of Arab Youth Effectiveness in Evolution of Arab Spring (Doha, 2013), and co-editor with Dr.Evren Tok and Rachael Calleja of Arab Development Aid and the New Dynamics of

Multilateralism: Towards better Governance (European Scientific Journal, 2014). Before being a public policy researcher, Dr.Hanaa used to be a dental surgeon; she is graduated in Dental College, Alexandria University, Egypt, where she got a Master degree in dental surgery.

Joshua Fairchild earned his doctorate from Penn State University, where he studied leadership and innovation in the workplace, with an emphasis on the role of teams in the creative process. He has authored or co-authored a number of manuscripts, book chapters, and conference presentations on these topics. His current research centers on how teams navigate the creative process, how individuals appraise novel products, and how technology impacts creativity and innovation.

Nicholas Gilewicz is a doctoral student at the Annenberg School for Communication at the University of Pennsylvania. He researches the history of journalism, how journalists construct the social meaning of their work through journalism products, and how to theorize new frameworks with which to analyze texts and communities produced by digital communication. He holds a master's degree in journalism from Temple University, and a bachelor's degree in the humanities from the University of Chicago.

Ian Gwilt is a Professor in the Art and Design Research Centre at Sheffield Hallam University, England. He has a PhD from the University of New South Wales, Sydney Australia, which examined the theory and practice of mixed-reality art. He also holds an MA in Interactive Multimedia (MAIMM), jointly conferred by the University of Balears (UIB) in Spain, and the Royal College of Art (RCA) London, and a BA Hons in Communication Media (Educational Media Design) from Manchester Metropolitan University. Current areas of research include practice and theory into visual communication design and social innovation, information visualization, augmented reality artifacts and locations, interactive installations, the design of hybrid environments and experiences for museum interaction and other educational contexts including design in the healthcare environment. He is also interested in how we can incorporate visual communication design practices into interdisciplinary research teams and in better defining design research practices. He is a member of council for the Design Research Society. His own practice reflexively uses the visual language of the computer graphical user interface to explore the role that digital technologies have taken in our everyday social, cultural and creative environs. He works across a number of media often combining analogue and digital forms including painting, digital print, video, interactive installation and Rapid Prototype sculptures. He has been making and writing about new media art since the mid 1990s and has exhibited at a number of international new media events and galleries. Originally from the UK, he lived and worked in Australia and New Zealand for a number of years where he began to develop his research/practice around augmented reality and the graphical user interface.

Jung Hoon Han is an Urban Planner and Convenor of Smart Cities Research Cluster (SCRC) in Faculty of the Built Environment at University of New South Wales, Sydney Australia. He began at UNSW in January 2011 after holding lecturing and researching positions at Griffith University (2009-20011) and the Australian Housing and Urban Research Institute at the University of Queensland, Australia (2004-2009). He has led the Smart Cities Research Cluster, one of the five major research clusters in the Faculty of Built Environment, UNSW, which was established in 2009 under the Faculty research strategy to promote a high performance research intensive culture. His research interest focuses on the spatial and temporal changes in urban service, digital technology and infrastructure in Australia. In particular he has investigated the ways in which planners should conceptualise, and respond to, constraints and opportunities in cities. His current research focuses on the dynamic changes in housing market and the spatial politics of urban land use and development in Australia and China. Dr Han's impact and contribution to the field is reflected in his recent publication record, which includes over 70 refereed publications with over 200 citations.

Scott Hawken is an Urban Designer, Landscape Architect and Landscape Archaeologist. His work uses a synergistic approach integrating advanced geospatial technologies with innovative fieldwork methods. Research subjects include the mapping and analysis of Southeast Asian urban settlements in both contemporary and medieval contexts.

Rachel Heinen is currently a psychology student at Creighton University in Omaha, NE, where she researches creativity, teamwork, and leadership in organizations. After graduation, she plans to enroll in a PhD program in I-O psychology.

Tim Hopper is an associate professor in the School of EPHE, Faculty of Education. He received his Masters and PhD from the University of Alberta. Dr. Hopper's scholarly work focuses on teacher education in physical education. His research explores the use of complexity thinking as a theoretical frame. He is currently involved in two externally funded research grants with Dr Kathy Sanford, (1) Electronic-portfolio development in three professional programs, and (2) Youth Civic Engagement: Real Life Learning through Virtual Games Environments.

Sam Hunter is an associate professor of psychology in the Industrial and Organizational Psychology program area at Penn State University. He is the director for the Leadership and Innovation Lab at PSU. Sam received his PhD in Industrial and Organizational Psychology from the University of Oklahoma in 2007. His research interests include leadership, innovation, and managing unique workforce populations such as those on the autism spectrum.

Cheris Kramarae is senior courtesy research associate, Center for the Study of Women in Society, University of Oregon, USA, where she also served as director. She is a former director of women's studies at the University of Illinois, USA, and an international dean at the International Women's University, in Germany. She has taught and collaborated on research with colleagues in England, the Netherlands, Germany, South Africa, China, India, and France. Her current research areas include gender and technology, education, and discourse analysis. She and Dale Spender are editors of the 4 vol. *Routledge International Encyclopedia of Women: Global Women's Issues and Knowledge.*

Carl Lee earned his BA degree in Mathematics from Yale University with conditional certification to teach secondary math, and his MS and PhD degrees in Applied Mathematics from Cornell University. He joined the Department of Mathematics at the University of Kentucky in 1980, where he is now Professor. He is presently a Chellgren Endowed Professor associated with the University of Kentucky Chellgren Center for Undergraduate Excellence. His research interests include polyhedra, discrete geometry, and mathematics education. He has served as a PI or co-PI for a variety of NSF grants, including a Center for Learning and Teaching (ACCLAIM), a Math Science Partnership (AMSP), and a DRK-12 project on Geometry Assessments for Secondary Teachers, and he collaborates in many projects on the teaching and learning of mathematics.

Salvatore A. Leone is currently studying Industrial-Organizational psychology at Creighton University in Omaha, Nebraska. Working with Dr. Joshua Fairchild, I am a part of the Creativity, Teamwork and Leadership research lab within the university psychology department. My research interests are currently focused on leadership emergence and virtual work environments, but also include personality and motivational factors in work settings, and the role incentives play in the modern workplace.

Jason McSparren is a second year PhD. student in the Global Governance and Human Security program at John W. McCormack School of Policy and Global Studies at the University of Massachusetts, Boston. His research interests include the international political economy (IPE) of the Gulf States and natural resource governance in Africa.

Liz Merkel has a Masters in Curriculum and Instruction from the University of Victoria. She worked with Dr. Sanford on numerous projects over four years and continues to implement research into her classroom teaching. She is an elementary school teacher but is currently working at Woosong University in South Korea.

Fatema Mohamed is a teaching assistant in the Department of International Affairs at Qatar University. She has a Master's Degree in Public Policy in Islam, Faculty of Islamic Studies (2014), and a Bachelor of Art Degree in International Affairs, Qatar University (2010).

Margaret Mohr-Schroeder is an Associate Professor of Middle/Secondary Mathematics Education at the University of Kentucky. Since her arrival to UK, Dr. Mohr-Schroeder has been involved in over $13 million in NSF funding, expanding STEM Education through various initiatives including the creation of a STEM Education major, and has been instrumental in garnering internal and external funding to support transdisciplinary teacher preparation. When she is not boating, camping, or using her mathematical and engineering design abilities to remodel her home, she enjoys researching informal learning experiences for preservice teachers and increasing STEM interest in underrepresented populations.

Lorna Moore is a video performance artist and works with real-time video technology. She received her doctorate at the University of Wolverhampton, UK. Her research explores ways to suspend the corporeality of participants' within the digital Other as an In[body] experience – to be in the body of the artwork/subjects in the moment afforded by real-time video technologies. Her practice is concerned with creating inter-corporeal experiences between subjects and the artwork using head mounted display systems and bio-sensing technology. Her work has been exhibited nationally and internationally where she has collaborated with many artists and co-ordinated a number of art festivals. Dr Moore has currently returned from an art residency in Italy.

Alistair Payne is the Head of the School of Fine Art at Glasgow School of Art. Previously he was the Undergraduate Programme Leader in Fine Art and before that MA Fine Art Course Leader and Senior Lecturer in Fine Art (Painting) at The University of Wolverhampton. He has also worked at Manchester Metropolitan University in the Painting Department (2002-2005) and as a Visiting Lecturer at different UK institutions. In 2006 he was awarded a PhD from Chelsea College of Art, he also has a BA Fine Art Degree from The University of Hertfordshire and an MFA from The University of Newcastle upon Tyne.

Elma Polanec, mag.paed., is a preschool teacher in the kindergarden "Little Sparrow", Šenkovec, Croatia. For eleven years, she has been working with preschool children aged from three years till seven years. Also, she currently teaches preschool aged children basic English. In July 2014, she has finished the graduate study Early and preschool education at Faculty of Teacher Education, University of Rijeka. Her research interests are related to the computer games influence on children development.

Phillip Prager is Assistant Professor in Aesthetics at the IT University of Copenhagen, where he teaches practice-based digital art, film studies, media history and play theory. He holds a BA in History from Yale University (2001), and completed an MPhil in Architecture and the Moving Image (2004) and a practice-based PhD in Screen Media and Cultures at the Cambridge University Digital Studio (2009). He then embarked on a postdoctoral fellowship in cognitive aesthetics at the Minerva Foundation, UC-Berkeley (2010). Phillip's work relates scientific research on creative cognition and play behavior to 20th and 21st century art. He is particularly interested in why outdated romantic, psychoanalytic and classical notions of creativity remain prevalent within art and media history even in the 21st century, and how a scientific understanding of creativity challenges the conventional interpretation of avant-garde art. He also works as a consultant and offers creativity workshops for the private sector.

Everardo Reyes (b. 1976, Mexico City) is Associate Professor in Information and Communication Sciences at the University of Paris 13 since 2011, where he is also member of the LabSic research center. Internationally, he is research member of the Software Studies Initiative. He received his PhD degree in 2007 from the University of Paris 8. His research areas combine methods from the cultural and scientific domains to study, analyze, experiment, and develop tools for understanding uses and implications of computation in digital images. He is affiliated to several international associations dealing with cognitive semiotics, digital art, arts and science, and digital humanities.

Kathy Sanford is Professor in the Faculty of Education at the University of Victoria. Her research interests include gender and literacy, alternative literacies, popular culture, and teacher education. She is currently working on research focused on Video Games in relation to youth civic engagement, and literacy learning and E-Portfolios development in three professional programs.

D. Craig Schroeder holds dual BS degrees in Physics and Mathematics from Centre College, a MS and PhD in Mathematics Education and an EdS in Educational Leadership from the University of Kentucky. He began teaching high school in Kentucky in 2002 and served as a middle school mathematics coach for a grant project in Fayette County in 2011-2012. He is presently a middle school mathematics and science teacher at Beaumont Middle School and director of the See Blue™ STEM Camp for middle school students. His interests include using technology effectively in the mathematics and science classroom, developing self-regulated learning, and helping students to explore and apply real-world STEM concepts in informal learning settings.

Marianne Selsjord, creative digital media artist and painter (www.marianne.selsjord.com/) and a passionate gardener, was a conservationist of medieval polychrome sculpture, who taught traditional and modern painting techniques and Autodesk Maya at the Norwegian National Academy of the Arts. Her digital artwork has been shown at 'Ultima' Oslo Contemporary Music Festival; Samuel Dorsky Museum, New York; Federal Reserve System Fine Arts, Washington DC; Henie Onstad Art Centre, Galleri Vanntårnet and Drøbak kunstforening: Varmbade, Norway. She created 3D projections for the dance performance on snow, Mot Himlaleite, Sauda and for Händels Acis and Galatea (Oslo Baroque Opera). Marvellous Transformations (2013/4), comprising a 3D navigable environment, prints on aluminium, video of Kinabalu rainforest and 3D-printed sculptures, plus audio, was her final work. Marianne died of multiple myeloma in Spring 2014.

Maureen Thomas is a dramatist, director, and screenwriter, and has been experimenting with creative digital media, interactivity and the spatial organisation of narrative since 2000, as Senior Creative Research Fellow, Interactive Institute, Sweden; Visiting Artist, Media Lab, Helsinki and Senior Research Associate, Digital Studio, Cambridge (www.expressivespace.org), focusing on performance and engagement in integrated media. She is a Senior Research Fellow (Screen Media and Cultures) at Churchill College, Cambridge. Maureen has a particular interest in Nordic mythology, archetypal drama, the oral composition of sung tales and the arts of chance. As well as London (Southbank Centre) and Cambridge (International Film Festival; MIST), her work has been exhibited in Reykjavík (Rádhús), Copenhagen (Bella Centre), Stockholm (Fylkingen Centre for Music and Intermedia Arts) and Helsinki (Gloria Theatre).

Evren Tok obtained his collaborative Ph.D degree from the School of Public Policy and Administration and Institute of Political Economy at Carleton University, Ottawa/Canada. He previously obtained his MA degree from the Institute of Political Economy at Carleton University. He was a research assistant under the supervision of Hany Besada at the North South Institute. He was designated as a distinguished research associate for the NSI in February 2012. He worked as a sessional instructor in the Department of Political Science and Department of Social Work at Carleton University, Koc University and Okan University, teaching courses on International Development, Political Economy, Public Opinion and Politics of Developing Countries between 2007 and 2012 Since January 2012, he has been affiliated as an Assistant Professor and Program Coordinator at Hamad Bin Khalifa University, Public Policy in Islam Program, Faculty of Islamic Studies, Doha/Qatar.

Joan Truckenbrod is an internationally known new media artist. She first digital artwork was computer drawing created in the mid 1970's using Fortran programming. In 1988, she published the book Computer Imaging that illustrated creating artwork using these devices. She developed computer paintings following this early work, that involved fiber and photography. Currently she is creating video sculptures, juxtaposing handmade objects with video projction. Her recent book The Paradoxical Object: Video Film Sculpture discusses this work together with artists who have inspired her. Professor Truckenbrod is Professor Emeritus at The School of the Art Institute of Chicago, where she taught in the Art and Technology Department.

Dana Tschannen is a Clinical Associate Professor at University of Michigan School of Nursing and Program Lead for the Health Systems, Nursing Leadership and Effectiveness Science Program. My research area has included work environment characteristics (as related to patient outcomes), informatics, interdisciplinary collaboration, patient safety, and educational use of Simulation. I have developed several virtual simulations related to patient safety, conflict management, communication, adverse drug events, and priority-setting, which have been integrated into several quality improvement, academic, and practice initiatives.

Sanja Tatalović Vorkapić, Ph.D., is assistant professor and currently teaches students at Faculty of Teacher Education, University of Rijeka, Croatia in: Developmental psychology, Psychology of early learning and teaching, General psychology, Emotional intelligence, Developmental psychopathology, Methodology of quantitative research, Positive psychology. Her contemporary research interests include biological basis of personality, personality of (pre)school teachers and child personality, contemporary issues from developmental psychopathology and methodology of quantitative research, positive psychology (well-being, optimism, life satisfaction, virtues) and (pre)school teachers' professional development. She has published numerous psychology related articles and has been actively involved within various interdisciplinary research projects.

Angelique Williams (LLB BA) is a graduate lawyer at Lindsay Taylor Lawyers, a firm specialising in local government, planning and environmental law. Prior to this, Angelique worked as a Legal Researcher and sessional staff member in the Planning and Urban Development Program, Faculty of Built Environment, at the University of New South Wales.

Ross Winning was originally trained as a Sculptor and has a long-standing interest in making objects and producing short animated films. Now researches sound and animation and makes kinetic projects that combine real form in conjunction with motion and illusory figurative structures. Sculpture and various art works are located in private and public collections in the UK, Scandinavia and Japan. Interests in sound and music has also led to working as a professional musician for many years. Currently engaged in PhD study at The Animation Academy, LUSAD, Loughborough University. Teaches Animation and Drawing and is currently Departmental Head of Digital Media in the Faculty of Arts at the University of Wolverhampton, UK.

Suzette Worden is an Honorary Professor of RMIT University, Australia. Her current research considers the social implications of technology for design and new media. With a background in design history she has an interest in the materiality of design and continues to supervise doctoral research projects in a part-time role. From 2002-2011 she was Professor of Design at Curtin University, in Perth, Western Australia where previous research included an Australian Research Council Linkage project 'Innovative Solutions for Wool Garment Comfort through Design' (2007-2010). She also published on art/science projects concerned with geology, mineralogy and West Australian mining heritage. She has co-written three books; contributed chapters to seven; presented peer reviewed research papers at many international conferences; and co-curated exhibitions on design.

Wei Zhang is a professor of English linguistics at Peking University, China. She received a PhD from Columbia University. Her research interests include gender studies, language and new media, multilingual and digital literacy. She has published internationally in journals such as Discourse & Society, Women & Language, and English Today. Her recent article "'SlutWalk' on connected screens: Multiple framings of a social media discussion" (co-author with Cheris Kramarae) appears in the *Journal of Pragmatics*.

Index

3D Art 143, 148
3D Digitizer 58
3D Printing 33-34, 46, 55, 59, 244, 311, 388

A

Activism 139, 421, 424, 429
Advocacy Speech 404-405, 410-411
Analytical Maps 225, 246
Animation 42, 83-86, 88, 90, 92-97, 99, 101-106, 109, 116, 122, 127, 244
Antarctica 124, 126, 128-129
Anthropocene 110-116, 118, 122, 124-125, 128-131, 133, 135-136, 139
Anti-social behaviour 433
Arts Practice 1, 4-5
Astroturfing 404-408, 410-412, 414-415
Audio 84, 86, 88-89, 98-99, 109, 128, 149, 152, 156, 168, 171-173, 177, 185, 233, 237, 256, 381, 410
Auto-Ethnophenomenology 22, 32
Automata 92-93, 106, 109
Avant-Garde 85, 141-142, 155-156, 160, 179, 184-185, 192

B

Be[ing] 18-19, 24, 26, 28, 30-32
Big Data 33, 35, 43-45, 112, 135
Biomedical Imaginary 13, 16
Brainstorming 272, 383-386, 402
Brian Massumi 68, 80, 201

C

Chance Operations 152-153, 171, 192
Chiasm 18-20, 25-26, 28, 30, 32
Child Development 326, 371
Cinema 79, 82, 84-86, 91, 93-95, 104-106, 109, 157, 175, 200, 205, 261

Climate Change 110-111, 120, 124, 128-129, 133, 135-136, 454
Clinical Reasoning 267, 269, 274, 277, 283
Closed Circuit Television (CCTV) 430-439, 441-442, 447
CNC Router 59
Cognition 33, 36, 87-88, 103-104, 131, 141, 160, 177, 185, 192, 211, 213, 226, 241, 293, 296, 335, 381
Computer-Aided Design (CAD) 309, 320-321, 378, 383, 387-388, 395, 402
Computer Games 4, 33, 54, 123, 148, 165, 267, 322-333, 335, 337-340, 344-346, 350, 353, 355, 357-358, 361-362, 364, 371
Consciousness 1, 5-6, 19, 26, 29, 148, 154, 172, 184, 201-202, 206-207, 209-216, 218-219, 222-223, 418
Corporeal Self 18-19, 21, 23-27, 29, 31-32
Creative City 449, 451, 460
Creative Practices 1, 181, 200, 217, 220, 244, 418
Croatia 336-337, 356, 362-363, 365
Crowd Dynamics 430
Crowd Funding 389-390, 402
Cyber Activism 424, 429
Cybernetics 203, 207, 219, 222
Cyborg 28, 207, 223

D

Dada 153, 160, 179, 185
Data-Object 36-37, 39-43, 45
David Gunkel 201, 208
Decentralized Control 293, 305
Deep Time 110-111, 115, 119, 122, 124, 130, 135, 139
Deleuze, Gilles 60, 62, 64-66, 68-74, 77-80, 82, 201, 206, 209-212, 214-219, 226-227, 247
Digital Aesthetics 141, 193
Digital Asset 264

Digital Divide 208-209, 223, 251, 262, 264
Digital Humanities 225, 229, 237, 243, 246
Digital Immigrant 264
Digital Media Literacy 249-255, 259-261, 264
Digital Native 264
Digital Other 18-19, 21, 23-27, 29, 31-32
digital parrhesia 404-405, 407-408, 411-415
Digital Ritual and Ceremony 49, 59
Disruption 23, 30, 62, 73, 209, 218, 225, 241, 244, 246
Dynamic Geometry Software 320

E

earth sciences 110-111, 113, 124, 135, 139
Ecomedia 127-128, 132, 140
Educational Pedagogy 268
Effective Communication 256, 268, 271, 283, 378, 380-381, 391, 393
Embodied Imagination 11-12, 16
Emergence 11-13, 23, 29, 66, 71, 181, 213, 219, 237, 290-294, 297, 305, 431, 448
Emergent Imagination 1, 17
Engineering Design 307-310, 313, 319-320
Entrainment 101-103, 109
ePortfolio 255-256, 264
Experimentation 9, 95, 112-113, 118, 160, 180, 182, 225, 241, 246

F

Facebook 50, 254, 256, 378, 388, 390, 392-393, 407, 414, 423-424
Foucault, Michel 227, 404
Freedom of Speech 422-423, 429

G

Games Technologies 149, 184
Gastromancy 85
GCC 449, 452, 460
Gender 21, 331, 335, 337, 344, 353, 358, 418-426, 429
Geology 110-111, 119, 122, 124, 128
Geometry 238, 240, 242-243, 308, 310, 317, 319-321
Google 29, 52-53, 128, 379, 381, 383, 385-386, 391, 394, 411
Governance 115, 133, 407, 448-449, 457, 460
Guattari, Félix 201

H

Hearing 83-85, 87-88, 92, 95, 105, 109, 148, 170, 173, 193, 327
Heim, Michael 203
Human–Computer Interaction 447
Hybridity 45, 60, 82

I

Image Processing 238, 241, 438, 447
Image recognition 435
In[bodi]ment or In[body] 32
Informatic Knowledge 341, 372
Information Design 35, 45, 112
Information Visualisation 34-36, 39, 43, 46, 112, 125, 237, 241
Integrated Media 148, 152
Interaction Design 156, 172, 185, 193, 425
Interactive Sensors 53, 59
Inter-Corporeal 18-20, 29-30, 32
Interdisciplinarity 60-62, 64, 72-74, 76-77, 80, 82
Internet Violence 322-323, 333-334, 336, 338, 340, 344, 356-358, 361-364, 372
Invitational Discussion 417, 429

J

Jacques Lacan 18, 20

L

Lacan 18, 20, 23, 25, 27, 30, 201, 211-214, 219
Learning Framework 283
Liberating Constraints 293, 305
Liminal Space 2, 5, 13, 17, 59, 62, 72

M

Manipulated Video 150
Materializing Code 46
mathematical modeling 308
mathematical practices 310
McLuhan, Marshall 153, 225, 227, 229, 249, 410
Mechanisms 147, 185, 231, 290, 292-297, 305, 325, 333, 352, 393, 448-449, 454, 457, 460
Media Archaeology 229-231, 246
Media Convergence 112, 264
Media Literacy 249-255, 259-262, 264
Metamorphosis 25, 60, 67-68, 76, 82, 166, 168
middle grades 306-307, 309
Mirror Stage 18, 20, 23, 25, 31

Motion Detection 435-438, 447

N

Nanotechnology 111, 115-116, 118, 136
Neoliberalism 450, 460
New Literacies 300, 305

O

Oral Composition 142, 147, 173, 193

P

Painting Techniques 161
Parallax 200, 202, 213-215, 217-220, 223
parental control 338, 353-354, 357-358, 362, 364
Patient Safety 265-266, 268-269, 274, 283
perceptions 19, 31-32, 42, 47, 66, 87, 122, 132, 340, 358
Pervasive Virtual Worlds 224-229, 232-234, 236, 241, 244, 247
Production Blocking 383-386, 402
Proprioception 23, 28, 30-32
Proto-Cinematic 83-84, 94, 109
Psychological Safety 384, 390, 402
Public Relations 407

Q

Qatar 449, 452-454, 460

R

Rapid Prototyping 34, 39-40, 46, 387-388, 402
real-time video 18-20, 23, 29
Remediation 141, 227, 231
Repurposing 152
robotic arms 55, 57
Rosebud Institute 249-250, 252, 255, 257, 259-261

S

Screen Media 183, 249-255, 257, 259-260, 262, 264
Semiotics 11, 228, 237, 408-409, 416
Signal Processing 241, 430-431, 434-438, 447
Simulation 201, 204, 210-211, 216-217, 228, 236, 238, 244, 265-267, 269-277, 283, 285-286, 330, 337

SketchUp 306-311, 313-317, 319-321
Smart CCTV 430, 434-435, 441, 447
Smart City 430, 441, 447-450, 452, 454-455, 457, 460
Social Networking 35, 256, 259, 305, 417-418, 420-423, 425-426, 429
Sockpuppeting 412, 414-415
Sonified 83-84, 97, 99, 101-103, 109
Spatially Organised Narrativity 193
Spatial reasoning 306-308, 310, 319-320
Spatial Visualization 321
Squier, Susan Merrill 1
STEM 62, 87, 306, 310, 319, 422
STEM pipeline 306
Storytelling 94, 141, 144, 147, 152, 155-156, 172
sympathetic attention 141-144, 146-147, 153, 165, 184

T

Tangiality 47, 58-59
Tangible Interface 148, 150, 193
Technological Determinism 409, 416
Techno-Semiotic 404, 408-416
Transdisciplinary 110, 112-115, 128-129, 135, 310
Transformation 49, 51, 60, 65, 73-74, 76, 82, 123, 142, 166, 243, 309-311, 431
Transitional Space 5, 17
Twitter 242, 254, 261, 378, 388, 390, 392-393, 407, 424

U

Urban Crime 433-434, 447
Urban Design 34, 438
Urbanization 448, 450
User-Interface Convention 247

V

video performance 18-22, 24, 29-30
Video Sculpture 50, 54, 59
Virtual Simulations 265, 270, 275-277, 283
VR 200, 202-214, 216-220

W

Willerslev 18, 20, 24-25, 28, 30

Printed in the United States
By Bookmasters